VISUAL QUICKSTART GUIDE

DREAMWEAVER MX

FOR WINDOWS AND MACINTOSH

J. Tarin Towers

 Peachpit Press

Visual QuickStart Guide
Dreamweaver MX for Windows and Macintosh
J. Tarin Towers

Peachpit Press

1249 Eighth Street
Berkeley, CA 94710
510/524-2178
800/283-9444
510/524-2221 (fax)
Find us on the World Wide Web at: http://www.peachpit.com
To report errors, please send a note to errata@peachpit.com
Published by Peachpit Press in association with Macromedia Press
Peachpit Press is a division of Pearson Education

Editors: Cary Norsworthy, Becky Morgan
Production Coordinator: David Van Ness
Copyeditor: Dave Awl
Compositors: Maureen Forys, Kate Kaminski
Indexer: Emily Glossbrenner
Cover Design: The Visual Group, Maureen Forys

ISBN 0-201-84445-1

9 8 7 6 5 4 3
Printed and bound in the United States of America

Dedication

For Katy Towers,
my favorite monster

Special Thanks to:

I'd like to thank everyone who helped me with this book: Cary Norsworthy, my editor and reluctant dictator, for attempting to keep me and the book in line; Dave Awl, for being a magnificent copyeditor and ocelot tender; Karen Whitehouse, who contributed to Chapters 5 and 7 and now knows everything; Eunice Holland, who contributed to Chapters 6, 15, and 17, all while on the Space Shuttle; and Sasha Magee, who contributed to Chapter 16 with a vengeance; Marjorie Baer and Nancy Ruenzel for their diligence and patience; David Van Ness and Maureen Forys, for gluing the electrons onto the pages and producing the excellent relative linking art; David Van Ness, for the initial 1.2 design; Wendy Sharp, Peachpit's Macromedia Press contact; Eric Ott, Scott Unterberg, and the whole Dreamweaver/Kojak team at Macromedia, for helping me get the stuff I needed; Julie Hallstrom, Macromedia's eagle-eyed tech reviewer, particularly for her OS X help; Adrian Chan, Christian Cosas, Amy Franceschini, Derek Powazek, Jamie Zawinski, Dave Eggers, Zhenia Timmerman, Bitch Magazine, and ye olde Cocktail designers, for lending me their art; the good folks behind the scenes at Macromedia, for writing an even better product; and many, many faithful readers who sent in comments, suggestions, compliments, questions, and encouragement.

I'd also like to thank my cheerleading squad, including Katie Degentesh, Kelleigh Trowbridge, Brett Bowman, Richard Marshall, and Kenne MacKillop. And large, fuzzy thank-you's to Brian Matheson, Sean Porter, jwz, Scott Kildall, all my friends who are geeks, and all my friends who aren't.

CONTENTS AT A GLANCE

TABLE OF CONTENTS

Chapter 18: **Customizing Dreamweaver** **607**

Chapter 19: **Managing Your Web Sites** **647**

INTRODUCTION

Figure 1 Here's Dreamweaver MX, including the Document window, where you edit your pages. Below that is the Property inspector. To the right are some of Dreamweaver's panels, including the CSS Styles panel, for designing page typography and other style sheets; the Tag Inspector, which displays a cascading view of all the tags on the page; and the Assets panel, for tracking and reusing objects.

Figure 2 The Site window lets you manage your files locally and on your Web site.

Welcome to the *Dreamweaver MX for Windows and Macintosh: Visual QuickStart Guide!* Dreamweaver (**Figures 1** and **2**) is exciting software: It's simple to use and it's one of the very best WYSIWYG (What You See Is What You Get) Web-page editing tools ever to come down the pike.

Dreamweaver isn't just another visual page-making tool. It does do what all the best editors do: creates tables, edits frames, and switches easily from page view to HTML (code) view.

But Dreamweaver goes way beyond the other editors to allow you to create Dynamic HTML (DHTML) gadgets and pages. Dreamweaver fully supports Cascading Style Sheets (CSS), as well as layers and JavaScript behaviors. And Dreamweaver flexes great site-management muscles, including a built-in, full-fledged FTP client, complete with visual site maps and a link checker.

What's New?

Dreamweaver MX introduces several new features that simplify page production and site management.

If you've used past versions of Dreamweaver, you'll notice the way the software looks has changed quite a bit. The panels are stacked in panel groups over to the side, and the Objects panel is now the Insert toolbar. Dreamweaver's new features include the following:

Panel groups (Chapters 1 and 18, and throughout the book): Dreamweaver's various panels are now organized in a stack to the right of the Document window (Figure 1).

The Standard toolbar (Chapter 3): This toolbar (**Figure 3**) is hidden by default, but you can show it if you like having buttons available for common functions such as saving files and cutting and pasting text and objects.

The Insert toolbar (Chapters 1 and 4, and throughout the book): Once known as the Objects panel, this toolbar (**Figure 4**) offers shortcuts for inserting common objects such as tables and form fields. You can dock or undock this toolbar.

The Site window (Chapters 2 and 19): This file-management tool is docked as a panel in Windows machines and can be expanded and collapsed. It still stands alone on the Macintosh (Figure 2, previous page), and in this book, it will continue to be referred to as the Site window. Also new in the Site window, you can access your desktop files so that you can more easily transfer files into a local site from other folders on your computer. You can now copy, cut, delete, and duplicate files anywhere on your computer using Dreamweaver's Site window.

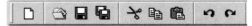

Figure 3 The Standard toolbar (View > Toolbars > Standard) offers buttons for common file and editing functions.

Figure 4 The Insert toolbar, with its many tabs, contains buttons for inserting common Web page objects.

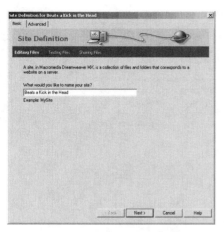

Figure 5 The Site Definition Wizard walks you through the basic process of designating a place for your files called a local site.

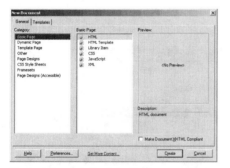

Figure 6 The New File dialog box lets you choose from many different types of both blank files and pre-built designs.

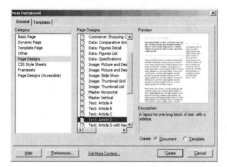

Figure 7 You can get a head start by starting out with one of Dreamweaver's page designs.

The Site Setup Wizard (**Figure 5**; Chapter 2) makes it easier for the beginners to set up a local site on their computers. The term "local site" is really just a synonym for picking which folder all your Web files are going to live in for a particular site. Also new in site setup land are the ability to cloak files from being uploaded; the option to select your default images folder; and the ability to export site definition settings and import them on other computers.

The new New File dialog box (Chapter 3): This dialog box (**Figure 6**) lets you choose from many different file formats. Dreamweaver MX now supports editing TXT, CSS, XML, XTML, XHTML, JavaScript, JSP, ASP, ASP.NET, PHP, and some ColdFusion files in the Document window. In Chapter 3 I also tell you how to choose a default file type and bypass this dialog box.

Page Designs (Chapter 3): The New File dialog box also includes pre-built page designs (**Figure 7**), including CSS pages and framesets. You can also access your own **Dreamweaver template files** (Chapter 18) from the New File dialog box. And speaking of templates, Dreamweaver's new template features include editable tag attributes, nested template designs, repeating template regions, and repeating tables.

WHAT'S NEW?

Improved Style Sheet Management
(Chapter 11): Once again, Dreamweaver has improved style sheet management. It's twice as easy both to link to an external style sheet and to edit styles located in that style sheet. The CSS styles panel now includes an apply mode and an editing mode (**Figure 8**). Also, a new feature called Design Time Style Sheets lets you attach multiple style sheets and choose which ones to display while you're working.

New Code Editing Tools (Chapter 4): Many of Dreamweaver MX's new features are in the realm of editing HTML code. The **Snippets panel** (**Figure 9**) is a repository for saving and reusing useful snatches of code such as footers and JavaScript widgets, and it comes with many time-saving predesigned snippets. The **Tag inspector** (**Figure 10**) is a tree view of all the tags on your page. The **Tag Chooser** (**Figure 11**, next page) lets you explore HTML and write it at the same time. **The Edit Tag command**, also known as the **Tag Editor dialog box** (**Figure 12**, next page), lets you edit your tag attributes with additional information available. **Tag Hints** now show up (**Figure 13**, next page) while you're editing in Code view (we'll learn both how to use these menus and how to turn them off).

WHAT'S NEW?

Figure 8 The CSS Styles panel now includes an edit mode that displays all styles in the current page and in any external style sheets.

Figure 9 The Snippets panel offers gadgets and design shortcuts.

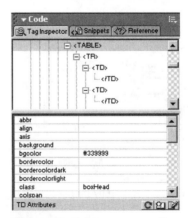

Figure 10 The Tag Inspector panel lets you browse through the HTML tags on your page and edit them as you go.

Figure 11 The Tag Chooser lets you insert nearly any existing HTML tag by choosing it from a list organized by category.

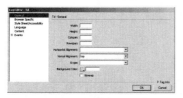

Figure 12 In the Tag Editor, you can apply many different attributes at once to a single tag.

Figure 13 Tag hints menus now appear when you're using Code view.

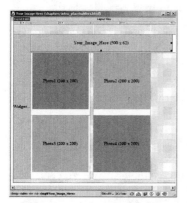

Figure 14 If you're waiting for your art, you can flesh out your layout using image placeholders.

Image Placeholders (Chapter 5): Now you can insert an image placeholder (**Figure 14**), which displays the image's dimensions, so you can fill out your page layouts before you've got all your files—without having to see those yucky "broken image" icons.

File Parameters in the Insert File dialog box (Chapter 7) You can specify parameters for plug-ins and other files while you're inserting them onto your pages.

Added Layer Layout Tools (Chapter 14): Now you can align the edges of your layers and send layers to the back or to the front, as you do with text boxes and objects in page-layout programs.

Newly Supported Form Fields (Chapter 15) include the tags <label>, <fieldset>, and <legend>, for organizing and optimizing your form interfaces. Also new in MX is the Insert Radio Button Group command, which makes it easier to set names and values for radio buttons.

Enhanced Integration with Fireworks and Flash allows you to double-click any image or Flash file in the Assets panel, or click a button on the Property inspector, and edit that object. It also allows you to go back and forth between these programs and Dreamweaver to edit your HTML files along with your media objects.

The Reload Extensions Command (Chapter 18) makes it easier to customize Dreamweaver while the program itself is still running. Also new in Chapter 18 are panel management tips, and instructions on adding the Launcher back to the status bar.

Dynamic Sites: Please see the section *About Dynamic Sites, Application Servers, and Databases,* later in this Introduction.

WHAT'S NEW?

QuickStart Conventions

If you've read any other Visual QuickStart Guide, you know that this book is made up of two main components: numbered lists that take you step by step through the things you want learn, and illustrations that show you what the heck I'm talking about.

I explain what needs to be explained, but I don't pontificate about the acceleration of information technology or wax dramatic about proprietary tags.

✔ Tips

- In every chapter, you'll find tips like these that point out something extra handy.

- Sometimes you can find extra tidbits of info in the figure captions, too.

- Code in the book is set off in `code font`.

- When I refer to the menu bar, it's the main Document window menu bar unless I specify otherwise.

My technology

This book was written and researched on several computers: PCs running Windows XP, NT, and 98; and Macintosh computers running OS 9.1 and OS X. Excepting the first chapter, in which I used the "round" XP Appearance Settings, I used the "oldschool" Windows Classic Style Appearance Settings in the PC screen shots to try to represent what the average Windows user would see when using Dreamweaver.

The functionality of OS 9 and OS X is pretty much the same as far as Dreamweaver MX is concerned, in most instances.

Who Should Use This Book?

No matter what your level of Web experience, you can use Dreamweaver and this book. I'm assuming you've used some sort of page-creation tool before, even if it's just a text editor. You should use this book if you're:

- An absolute beginner who wants to create a site without having to look under the hood.

- Someone who knows that great code is important, but is still learning and wants an editor that will help them write clean code.

- A graphic designer who's used to using document editors like Illustrator, PageMaker, or Photoshop, but who isn't as proficient with HTML.

- An HTML expert who likes to hand code but wants automation of simple tasks.

- Frightened of tables, layers, or CSS.

- Someone who needs to learn Dreamweaver quickly.

What's in this Book

Here's a quick rundown of what I cover in this book.

Getting started

In the first three chapters I introduce you to the Dreamweaver interface, setting up local file management, and creating a basic page. Chapter 2 walks you through setting up a local site, which is the first thing you should do so that all of Dreamweaver's site management, linking, and updating tools will work for you. Chapter 3 presents a walk-through of how to set up a basic page. We'll take our first look at Web typography, links, images and media, and tables in that chapter.

Writing code

Chapter 4 discusses Dreamweaver's code editing tools and learning HTML. If you never want to look at any HTML when you use Dreamweaver, you don't have to; on the other hand, if you want to learn HTML, there's no better way than by creating a page and looking at the code you just made. And if you want to control tiny, nitpicky little things on your page, you need to get comfortable going backstage into Code view and moving things around. In this chapter I explain the wide variety of code-editing tools that Dreamweaver presents, all offering variations on hand coding: the Code inspector, Code view, the Snippets panel, the Tag selector and Tag inspector panel, the Edit Tag command, the Quick Tag editor, and the Tag Chooser.

Links and media

It's simple to insert images, sound files, Flash, and other media using Dreamweaver. Basically, all media on Web pages is inserted using links, and you'll find out about those in here, too. Chapter 6 describes linking in more detail than you thought possible. Chapter 5 includes everything you need to know about inserting images, and Appendix A, on the Web site for this book, describes how to make client-side image maps with the image map editor. Chapter 7 includes multimedia basics, including creating Flash buttons and Flash text; inserting Flash and other plug-ins; and designing image rollovers and navigation bars.

Browser Wars

FYI, this is a sidebar. You'll often find advanced, technical, or interesting additions to the how-to lists in sidebars like these throughout the book.

Netscape Navigator and Microsoft Internet Explorer (IE) have a few display differences that may affect your pages subtly. The best way to design for both browsers is to test your pages on both browsers and to compromise where you see differences. Fonts may appear slightly larger in IE (as pictured in Chapter 11). Margins may appear off in IE (or off in Netscape, if you prefer Explorer's way). Table and layer placement are mostly the same, but they're based on slightly different browser margins, so you need to check your work. And there are some differences in how style sheets are processed, the most common of which are covered in Chapter 11.

While I was writing this book, the Mozilla project released the first shipping version of the open-source Mozilla browser, which may yet democratize the browser experience. Netscape also released the first beta of Netscape 7.

In this book, I show pages in a combination of Netscape 6, Navigator 4, and Internet Explorer 4, 5, and 6. Netscape 6 differs in a few places from Navigator 4.x—mostly by supporting former Internet Explorer-only features. Just as Explorer supported more and more Netscape-only features in each subsequent release, Netscape is picking up some W3C specifications that formerly only Explorer supported. These newly supported attributes appear mainly in style sheets (Chapter 11), layers (Chapter 14), and behaviors (Chapter 16), and I mention, where relevant, what Netscape 4.x does not support and what Netscape 6 does.

Netscape isn't as stable as it could be in terms of displaying tables and layers. The first thing you should try when addressing strange placement problems is the Netscape Resize Fix (Commands > Add Netscape Resize Fix), which is covered in Chapter 12. Netscape 6 is also a stickler for correct code, more than earlier versions of Navigator.

Appendix C on the Web site for this book goes into more detail about browser compatibility issues, including designing for older and text-only browsers and considering the accessibility specifications.

Text and typography

Chapters 8 through 11 talk about text and all the things you can do with it. Text is the meat of most pages, and we'll go into detail about how to format it, how paragraphs and block formatting work, and how to make useful things like lists and headlines. Chapter 10 discusses how to create reusable HTML styles to speed up text formatting. Chapter 11 covers Cascading Style Sheets, which also allow you to reuse your formatting—but CSS formatting is infinitely updateable, across any number of pages.

Page layout

Chapters 12 through 14 are what most folks consider the "intermediate" range in HTML. Chapter 12 is tables, 13 is frames, and 14 is layers. Chapter 12 discusses both the standard and layout views for creating tables. Chapter 13 makes it easy to use a complex layout with frames. And Chapter 14 introduces layers, which are part of dynamic HTML. All these layout tools are much easier to construct in Dreamweaver than by hand coding.

Interactivity

The Web is about interaction, from simple guestbooks to complicated user interfaces that change the way the page looks based on preferences. Chapter 15 introduces forms, the basic way to collect user input on everything from shopping sites to online quizzes. Chapter 16 covers behaviors, in a "buffet style" way of putting together JavaScript actions—choose one from column A and one from column B. Appendix N on the Web site, which previously appeared in this book, discusses Timelines, Dreamweaver's DHTML animation tool.

But Wait, There's More on the Web Site!

The companion Web site for this book contains lots and lots of links to developers' pages, handy shareware tools, and example sites, and because the page is on the Web, you don't have to type in a bunch of URLs. You'll also find online appendixes covering the image map editor, HTML preferences, and browser compatibility.

Visit http://www.peachpit.com/vqs/ dreamweavermx/ and let me know what you think of the book and the Web site by emailing dreamweaver@tarin.com.

WHAT'S IN THIS BOOK

Exploiting Dreamweaver

Dreamweaver comes out of the box ready to go and easy to use, but you can add your own reusable widgets and modify the existing interface without doing any sort of programming. Chapter 17 discusses three ways of automating common tasks in Dreamweaver: libraries, templates, and history. Libraries let you reuse common page elements across an entire site. You can also create versatile templates with read-only design features, and you can update the design of pages based on these templates just by updating the template file. The History panel tracks all your actions while you're editing, so that you can have more control over what you can undo or redo. You can even save or record common, useful actions as commands so that you can reuse them from the Commands menu.

Chapter 18 is all about customizing the Dreamweaver interface. First, I go into basics about customizing the Dreamweaver workspace. And if you miss having the Launcher in the status bar, you can put it back there.

Getting more complex, you can add objects to the Insert toolbar and even create your own categories on it. You can also rearrange and add items to the menus on the Document or Site window. And if you're picky about keyboard shortcuts for your common tasks, you can not only more easily manage those, you can save several different sets of keyboard commands.

Putting It online

Chapter 19 is all about site management with Dreamweaver's Site window, a full-fledged FTP client. You can upload and download files easily. You can also track links across your entire site and have Dreamweaver fix them for you. You can use the Site Map to visually examine and add links. You can also use different checkout names to keep track of who's working on which file.

Some material previously found in this book is now in Appendix O on the Web site. This material includes site reporting and design notes, which allow you to save data about Web pages and media files, such as due dates, template versions, or file status.

HTML is HTML

Like the song, HTML remains the same, whether you construct it on a Mac or PC.

No matter how you produce a Web page, it can transport from computer to computer—there's really no such thing as "Mac HTML" or even "Dreamweaver HTML."

Even better, Dreamweaver's Roundtrip HTML feature ensures that HTML you create outside the program will retain its formatting—although obvious errors, like unclosed tags, will be fixed.

If you like hand coding, Dreamweaver MX comes with HomeSite+, a powerful code-editing tool with lots of time-saving features. You can set up Dreamweaver to work with any HTML editor you like, however. See Appendix D, on the companion Web site for this book, to find out how to set up an external editor and how Dreamweaver will treat your HTML.

Special to Mac Users

I wrote this book, for the most part, on two computers sitting three feet from one another: a PC running Windows XP, and a Macintosh Powerbook running OS 9.2. Most of the screen shots are from the PC version, but wherever there are any observable differences, I include Mac screen shots.

The largest difference between the PC version and the Mac version is in the Site window, so to balance the chapters that focus on that tool, I used mostly the Mac view in Chapter 19 and mostly the PC view in Chapter 2.

The differences between the Mac and Windows versions are minimal, as you can see in **Figures 15** and **16**.

There are some basic platform differences that will cause the screen shots to look slightly different. Windows windows (ha ha) have a menu bar affixed to each and every window; the Mac menu bar is always at the top of the screen, and it changes based on the program that you've got open.

Windows windows close by clicking on the close box on the upper right, whereas on the Mac, close boxes (or buttons, on OS X) are on the upper left.

There is also the occasional menu difference. In Windows, the Site window includes a Site menu bar. On the Mac, those same commands are included under the Site menu, but occasionally they're under the submenu Site > Site Files View or Site > Site Map View. I point these differences out where they occur.

And finally, on Mac OS X, each application has its own menu to the right of the Apple menu and to the left of the File menu (**Figure 17**). The Preferences dialog box on PCs and OS 9 is found by selecting Edit > Preferences, but on OS X, you'll find it by selecting Dreamweaver > Preferences.

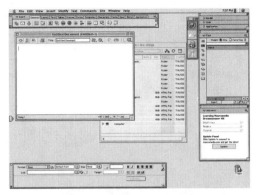

Figure 15 Dreamweaver's Document window and some of its panels, as seen on the Mac.

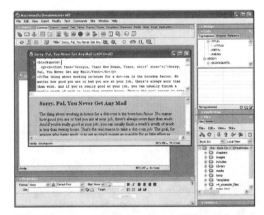

Figure 16 Dreamweaver's Document window and some of its panels, as seen on a PC. Not many differences other than the title bar and menu bar, and the way the tops of the panels look.

Running MX on a Mac

Dreamweaver MX runs on OS 9.1 or later and OS 10.1 or later. If your Mac won't run a current system, you'll need to stick with Dreamweaver 3 or 4. That's not the end of the world; you'll still be able to make great Web sites, but the newer features in MX won't be available to you.

Figure 17 On Mac OS X, there's an Application menu, containing commands such as Preferences and Quit, for each program. Other than that, things work pretty much the same as on either OS 9 or a PC.

Figure 18 The Mac OS X Application menu.

Figure 19 If you're a Windows user, you can right-click on an object to pop up a contextual menu. If you're a Mac user, just click on the object while holding down the Control key. The pop-up menu will appear in a second or two.

Keyboard and button conventions

When I refer to key commands, I put the Windows command first and the Mac command in parentheses, like this: Press Ctrl+L (Command+L). Occasionally, you'll see both commands in parentheses, but the Windows command is always printed first.

Occasionally, buttons will have different names. For instance, in some dialog boxes, the button says Browse in Windows and Choose on the Mac. They're always close enough; I usually indicate differences like so: Browse (Choose).

For Select File dialog boxes, buttons are different on PCs, Mac OS 9, and Mac OS X, and I use the following terminology: Click on OK (Open/Choose).

Mouse conventions

Some Mac mice have more than one button; some don't. For that matter, some folks don't really use mice at all, they have those touchpad and stylus thingies. That said, I do refer to right-clicking a lot. On a Windows machine, when you click the right (rather than the left) mouse button, a contextual pop-up menu appears (**Figure 19**).

Pop-up menus, or context menus, are available on all Mac systems that can run Dreamweaver MX. To make a pop-up menu appear on a Mac, Control+click on the object. Options available from pop-up menus are always available as menu bar options, too, so you'll never miss functionality in Dreamweaver even if you don't right-click.

About Databases, Application Servers, and Dynamic Sites

Macromedia Dreamweaver MX is the result of combining two powerful pieces of software that existed as standalone elements before: Dreamweaver, for creating Web sites, Web pages, and user interfaces; and Dreamweaver UltraDev, for creating and maintaining dynamic Web sites.

First off, let me apologize for the industry and its propagation of confusing jargon—the terms *dynamic Web site* and *Dynamic HTML* are pretty much unrelated and *sound* way too similar, although Dreamweaver MX's capabilities include both.

What is Dynamic HTML?

Dynamic HTML concerns pages that can change after they're loaded, and this can be done in any number of ways, although it's usually done on the *client side*, meaning in the browser window on your computer. This Web page alchemy is accomplished using cascading style sheets (CSS), layers (CSS-P), and JavaScript (including Dreamweaver Behaviors), all of which are covered in this book.

What are dynamic Web sites?

Dynamic Web sites, on the other hand, are Web sites in which the pages are changed, customized, or filled out *before* being loaded by the Web browser, on such sites as search engines, "My" personalized sites, shopping catalogs, and online communities.

All such sites present information using a *front end* or *interface*, which is the Web page that visitors see; and a *back end*, which is called an *application server*. This application server consists of one or more *databases* that store information and the *scripts* which retrieve data from them and add data to them.

The next level: advanced techniques

People get degrees in creating, using, and maintaining databases and the server technologies that go with them. For the most part, these advanced techniques are beyond the scope of *this* book—but knowing that would be the case, I've made sure another book about using Dreamweaver MX would exist to cover the fancy stuff.

If you want to know specific details about constructing and maintaining dynamic sites with an application server, look for *Dreamweaver MX Visual QuickPro Guide* (that's QuickPro, as opposed to QuickStart) for Windows and Macintosh, by myself, J. Tarin Towers, Abie Hadjitarkhani, and Sasha Magee. That'll be out Fall 2002 from Peachpit Press/Macromedia Press.

What is in this book

If you're creating a dynamic site, you will need some of the information in this volume to construct Web pages and user interfaces. This book is designed to help you learn Dreamweaver's features and shortcuts, including its myriad code-editing tools; maintain a site structure both locally and remotely; create both basic and complex layouts using tables, frames, and layers; work with typography, CSS forms, and JavaScript; insert and manage images and media, including Flash; and save time by exploiting, automating, and customizing the program. In other words, everything you need to know to construct those front-end interfaces is in here. Please feel free to peruse the table of contents and the index to decide whether this book belongs on your desk.

APPLICATION SERVERS AND DYNAMIC SITES

What isn't in this book

Because of size limitations, this book does not cover setting up and connecting to a testing server and an application server, although those processes are quite similar to setting up a remote server in Chapter 19.

This book does not cover the Applications panel group, which contains the panels Databases, Bindings, Server Behaviors, and Components.

This book does not cover inserting the server objects in the Insert menu and on the Application tab of the Insert toolbar.

This book does not cover using Optional Template regions, which involve an ability to hand code XML and JavaScript.

Look to the Pro book for information about Web Site Accessibility*, Site Reporting*, Design Notes*, Timelines*, and Tag Libraries. Items with an asterisk are covered in some form on the companion Web site for this book, because they have been included in the past in the *Dreamweaver Visual QuickStart Guide* series. I listened to the feedback from readers of the 4 book, who overwhelmingly said that I included *too much information* in a book meant for beginner-intermediate users.

What if this database stuff scares me?

Dreamweaver MX now includes so many features that it can be hard to tell what you need to know in order to produce a simple Web site.

Chapter 2 in this book helps you organize your files so you can capitalize on Dreamweaver's extremely helpful link management features. And Chapter 3 introduces every feature you'll need to know in order to produce a real Web page.

The rest of the book goes into detail about those features, adding advanced features as the book progresses. If all you want is to put up a Web site for your small business, non-profit organization, university, or family; or your rock band, art portfolio, or interest in Kung-Fu movies; you can use this book. Once you get into the swing of Dreamweaver, you can start toying around with the fancy tricks, but you don't have to get fancy just to have a Web site of your own.

Additionally, if you send me an email at menus@tarin.com, I'll send you a configuration file that you can use to hide all those database features.

And now... on to the book!

APPLICATION SERVERS AND DYNAMIC SITES

GETTING STARTED

Document toolbar   Assets

Insert toolbar Site window/panel

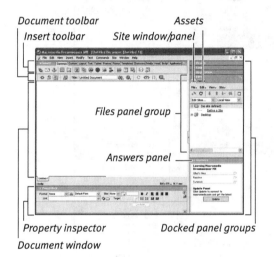

Files panel group

Answers panel

Property inspector   Docked panel groups

Document window

Figure 1.1 Here's the Dreamweaver work environment, complete with the panels you'll see on startup.

When you start Dreamweaver for the first time, you'll see a main window, called the Document window, and several panels (**Figure 1.1**).

You'll use the Document window and its trusty fleet of panels for everything from typography to templates. Dreamweaver can make your work life easier, no matter whether you're creating a simple home page or a large and complex site. If you've used Dreamweaver before, the first difference you'll notice is the column of stacked panels and the new Insert toolbar.

The main components of Dreamweaver that I'll introduce in this chapter are the Site window, the Document window and its various panels, the Document toolbar, the Code inspector, the Insert toolbar, and the Property inspector.

Dreamweaver Tools

Tag inspector panel

Document window

Code panel group

Document toolbar

Code view of
current page

Insert toolbar

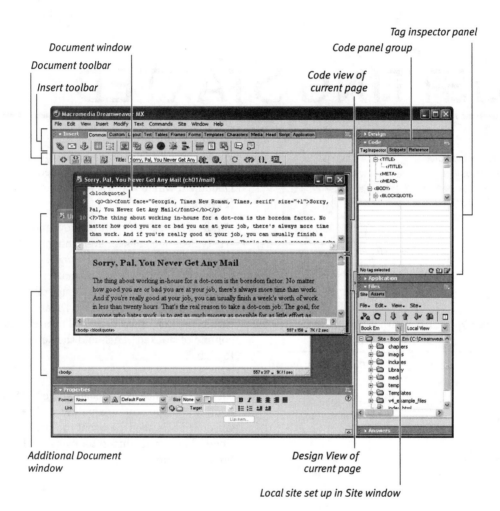

Additional Document
window

Design View of
current page

Local site set up in Site window

Figure 1.2 Here's the Dreamweaver MX environment, with a few changes. I've opened the Code panel group; the Document window is minimized inside the Dreamweaver window; the Document window is in Split view; and I've set up a local site in the Site window to manage my files. On Windows machines, the site window is also a panel.

Figure 1.3 You can open any of Dreamweaver's windows, panels, and inspectors from the Document window's Window menu.

Expander button

Figure 1.4 The Site window allows you to manage local and remote Web sites, including HTML pages and media objects. PC users: Undock the Site window from its position in the Files panel group by clicking the Expander button.

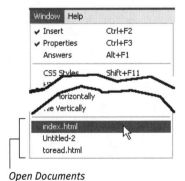

Open Documents

Figure 1.5 When you're working with multiple documents, each will appear in its own Document window. Each of these will be accessible from the Window menu.

The Dreamweaver Environment

Oddly, all those windows that are available from the Window menu aren't necessarily called windows (**Figure 1.3**). These are the panels and inspectors that make up Dreamweaver. Some of them are so useful you'll have them open all the time; others are specialized, and you can put them away when you're not using them.

A *window* is a stand-alone screen element that will show up on the Windows status bar (the Mac doesn't display each window separately in the Finder menu or Dock). The Document window is one example of a window. Another example is the expanded Site window (**Figure 1.4**), which we'll explore in Chapter 2 when we set up a local site, and which we'll use in Chapter 19 to put our files up on the Web.

You can have multiple Document windows open; the filename for each will appear at the bottom of the Window menu (**Figure 1.5**).

continued on next page

✔ Tips for Windows Users

■ You can also choose, on Windows machines, whether to maximize or minimize open Document windows within Dreamweaver MX (see Figures 1.1 and 1.2).

■ When the Document window is maximized within Dreamweaver, you'll see tabs in the Document window status bar listing each open file (**Figure 1.6**).

■ I recommend showing file extensions when working in Dreamweaver. From the menu bar of any Windows folder in Windows Explorer, select Tools > Folder Options. Click the View tab, and deselect the check box Hide Extensions for Known File Types. You'll see file extensions such as .html displayed, as in Figures 1.5 and 1.6.

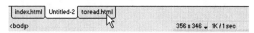

Figure 1.6 On Windows, the current open files are listed in the status bar when the Document window is maximized within Dreamweaver, as in **Figure 1.1**.

Panel group name   Panels

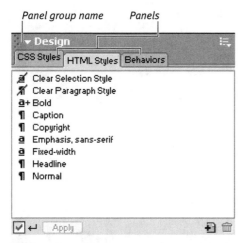

Figure 1.7 A panel group may contain several panels. Here, the Design panel group contains three panels: CSS Styles, HTML Styles, and Behaviors. To open any of these panels I can click on its tab. To open or close a panel group, I can double-click its name.

Figure 1.8 Some very useful panels are hidden on startup and are also submerged in the Others submenu of the Window menu.

Panels and inspectors

The miniature floating windows that you use to edit various elements of your Web pages are called either *inspectors* or *panels.* These are similar to the tools you may have used in other multimedia creation programs, such as Quark, Fireworks, Word, or Flash. You can control your workspace by docking and undocking panel groups.

✔ Tips

■ To view any window, panel, or inspector, select its name from the Window menu, or select its tab on an open panel group (**Figure 1.7**).

■ Keyboard shortcuts for each panel are listed in the Window menu.

 Read the next section, *Arranging Your Workspace*, to find out how to control panel positions and even hide all the panels at once.

■ Upgrading? Some of your favorite panels, such as Frames, Layers, Code inspector, and History, are now listed in the Others submenu of the Window menu (**Figure 1.8**).

Panels vs. Inspectors

In general, an *inspector* (such as the Property inspector, Tag inspector, or Code inspector) changes its appearance and options based on the current selection, whereas a *panel* controls elements, such as styles or library items, that are available on the entire current page or site. Not that it's a huge distinction, but you may wonder why a window is called one thing or the other.

THE DREAMWEAVER ENVIRONMENT

Arranging Your Workspace

Dreamweaver's floating windows are contextual—for example, you don't need to have the Frames panel open unless you're working with frames at the moment. You don't need to keep everything open, only the stuff you're working with.

To expand or collapse a panel group:

◆ Click on the expander arrow in the upper-left corner of the panel group (**Figure 1.9**).

To undock a panel group:

◆ Click on the panel group's gripper bar, and drag it where you like (**Figure 1.10**).

To hide a panel group:

1. If it's docked, select Close Panel Group from the Options menu (**Figure 1.11**).

2. If it's undocked, click on the X in the upper-right corner (on the Mac, the close box is in the upper-left corner).

Gripper bar

Expander arrow   *Options menu button*

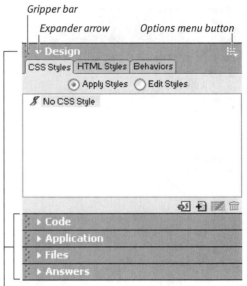

Panel group names

Figure 1.9 Panel groups, all docked together.

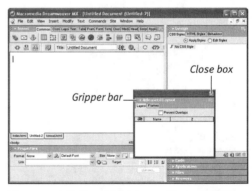

Figure 1.10 I displayed the Advanced Layout panel group by selecting Layers from the Window menu; then I undocked the panel group.

Figure 1.11 Because I'm not going to be doing anything with databases, I'm going to close the Application panel group.

This black line means you can dock here

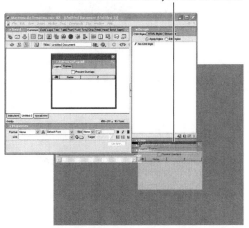

Figure 1.12 Here I'm docking the Advanced Layout panel group we saw in **Figure 1.10** into the stacked panels. It's transparent because I'm dragging it.

Panel group Expander arrow

Panel group slider bar

Figure 1.13 On both Windows and Mac, panel edges are "sticky" and will snap to any adjacent window. On Windows machines, use the slider bar to adjust the amount of space the Document window and panel groups have.

To re-dock a panel group:

◆ **Windows:** Click on the panel group's gripper bar, and drag back to the docked panel groups. When a black line appears in the column of panel groups, that's where you can drop your panel group (**Figure 1.12**).

◆ **Mac:** The panel groups are aesthetically docked and their edges will snap together, but when you drag one away from the bunch, you need to move them around to get it re-docked.

In the course of this book, I use nearly every possible combination of docking and undocking panels, showing and collapsing panels and panel groups, and using minimized and maximized Document windows.

In particular, I undock the Property inspector and the Insert toolbar fairly often to show them right next to selected text and objects.

continued on next page

ARRANGING YOUR WORKSPACE

✔ Panel Tips

- Unless Dreamweaver is maximized to full screen, undocked panels will snap together at any window edges so you can dock a panel to the side of the Document window. Try dragging an open panel to the side of the window, and watch it snap into place. (**Figure 1.13**). Even if Dreamweaver is maximized, you can snap panel edges to the inside edge of a window.

- Dreamweaver will remember where your panels are when you exit. When you reopen Dreamweaver, only the panels you had open will appear, and they'll be where you left them (**Figure 1.14**).

- Macintosh (or DW4 workspace for Windows, see next page): To move the floating panels back to their original, default positions, select Window > Arrange Panels from the Document window menu bar (**Figure 1.15**). You can also do this if you've accidentally dragged a panel off-screen.

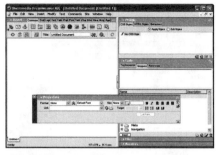

Figure 1.14 Dreamweaver remembers panel positions; if this is where your panels are when you exit the program, this is where they'll be when you open Dreamweaver again the next time.

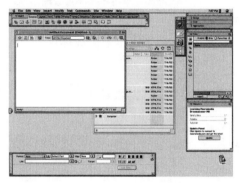

Figure 1.15 To have Dreamweaver clean up your workspace, select Arrange Panels from the Window menu bar.

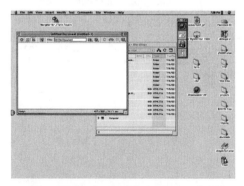

Figure 1.16 To hide all panels for an uncluttered view of your workspace, press F4. Because Dreamweaver remembers where everything was (and which panels were open), you can press F4 again to bring it all back.

Panel group Expander arrow

Panel group slider bar

Figure 1.17 Windows users: Click the Expander arrow on the panel group slider bar to show or hide all panels at once.

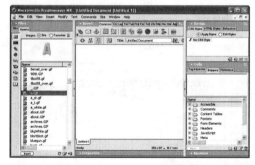

Figure 1.18 Windows users: You can also dock some or all panel groups to the left of the Document window. Mac users, you can drag yours anywhere.

- To hide all panels, press F4, or select Window > Hide Panels from the Document window menu bar (**Figure 1.16**). On Windows, you can also click the Expander arrow on the panel group slider bar to show or hide all panels at once. (**Figure 1.17**).

- You can also dock panels to the left of the Document window (**Figure 1.18**).

ARRANGING YOUR WORKSPACE

Using alternate workspaces (Windows only)

When you first start up Dreamweaver, you'll be confronted with a choice of workspaces (**Figure 1.19**). You can also change this setting in the Preferences dialog box (**Figure 1.20**). After changing your preferences, you need to quit and restart Dreamweaver to change workspaces.

In the Dreamweaver 4-style workspace (**Figure 1.21**), the panel groups are docked in their own window; the Site window always stands alone; the Property inspector is undocked; and the Insert toolbar looks and behaves like the old Objects panel. If you really love the old way, or really hate the new way, you can always switch workspaces and pretend that you're still using the old version. All the new features are included; I use the Dreamweaver MX standard workspace exclusively in this book.

In the HomeSite/Coder Style workspace, panels are docked on the left; the Property inspector is collapsed to start out; and the default editing view is Code view instead of Design view.

When you switch workspaces, the panels will rearrange themselves to the way they appeared on startup the first time you launched the program.

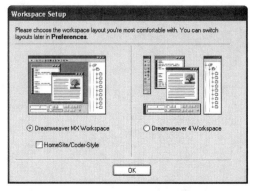

Figure 1.19 You'll see this window on startup; you can also access it from the General panel of the Preferences dialog box.

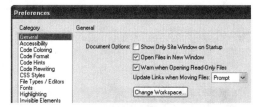

Figure 1.20 A close-up of the General panel of the Preferences dialog box.

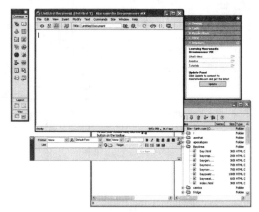

Figure 1.21 In the Dreamweaver 4-style workspace of Dreamweaver MX (Windows machines only), everything floats and the Insert toolbar looks like the Objects panel.

Figure 1.22 You can set up different sites for different projects. Each site has its own set of files in the Site window.

Planning Your Site

Links between pages in your Web site will work best if you set up a local site.

A Web site is just a collection of files and folders on a computer that's connected to the Internet. When these files are on your local computer, they're called a local site. When they're on a Web server, they're called a remote site. If you set up your files locally in the same way as they'll appear online—using the same folder names and keeping things in the same places—everything will be easy to track.

You can keep different projects in different local sites (**Figure 1.22**). Start out with a main folder (also called the *root* folder), and put other folders for that site inside it. I usually create specific folders for images, movies, and sound files, as well as style sheets.

You must set up a local site in order to use the Library, the Assets panel, HTML styles, the Link checker, automatic link updates, and Templates.

The Site window

The Site window (**Figures 1.23** and **1.24**) is Dreamweaver's tool for tracking local and remote site files. When you start creating a site, you should go to Chapter 2, so that you can set up your local site.

The Site window also makes it easy for you to put your files up on the Web, in the remote site. Chapter 19 tells you all you need to know about getting your stuff online.

Most Web page programs don't include their own FTP client. In Dreamweaver, you create, edit, and upload your files to the Web all in the same environment. You can use this tool for file management, too.

Figure 1.23 The Site window lets you work with local and remote files at the same time.

Expander button

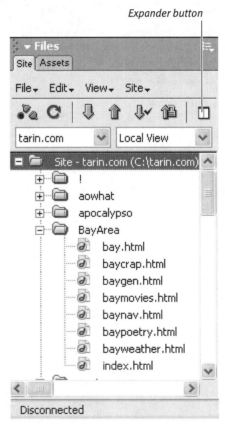

Figure 1.24 On Windows machines, the Site window appears docked as part of the Files panel group unless you expand it to show both the local and remote panels.

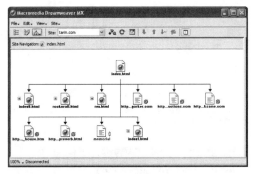

Figure 1.25 The Site Map view of your site shows you where links go in a visual format.

Figure 1.26 You can check all the links between files in your site with the Link Checker, which is part of the Results panel group.

The Site map

The Site map (**Figure 1.25**) is a visual depiction of how your files are interrelated. You can see broken links and draw paths between files.

The Link Checker

The Link Checker (**Figure 1.26**) can look for broken links and can change any link in your site when you move or update a file.

The Document Window

The Document window (shown in detail on the next page in **Figure 1.30**) is the main center of activity in Dreamweaver.

At the top: The *title bar* displays the file-name and the title of the current Web page. All of Dreamweaver's commands are available from the Document window *menu bar*. In a maximized Document window, and on the Mac (**Figure 1.29**), the *Document toolbar,* which offers shortcut menus and different page views, is part of the Document window.

In the middle: The body of the HTML document is displayed in the main viewing area of the Document window. Because Dreamweaver is a WYSIWYG (What You See Is What You Get) HTML tool, the Document window approximates what you'll see in a Web browser window.

At the bottom: The *status bar* indicates three things about the current document:

◆ The *Tag selector* displays all the HTML tags surrounding your current selection.

◆ The *window size indicator* displays the current size of the Document window so you can flip between common window sizes. The numbers will change if you resize the document window; you can select a preset window size by clicking the down arrow to display a pop-up menu (**Figure 1.28**).

◆ The *download stats* area displays the total size, in K (kilobytes), of the current page, and the amount of time it would take to download over a 28.8 Kbps modem.

To hide the Document toolbar:

◆ From the Document window menu bar, select View > Toolbars > Document toolbar.
The toolbar will disappear. (**Figure 1.27**).

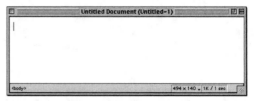

Figure 1.27 Here's the Mac Document window without the Document toolbar.

Figure 1.28 Click the arrow on the window size indicator to select a common, preset window size. This is the Document window minimized within Dreamweaver for PCs.

Title bar

Close box   Document title   Filename

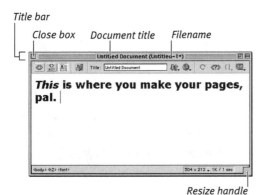

Resize handle

Figure 1.29 Dreamweaver's Document window for the Mac.

✔ Tip

■ You can resize the Document window as you would any other window: by clicking on the lower-right corner and dragging to make the window larger or smaller. I show the Document window in many different sizes throughout this book, depending on the kind of content I'm discussing at the time. As you can see in **Figures 1.29** and **1.30**, the Mac and Windows versions of the Document window are nearly identical.

Menu bar   Close button

Dreamweaver title bar   Maximize/Restore button

Application Control Menu button   Minimize button

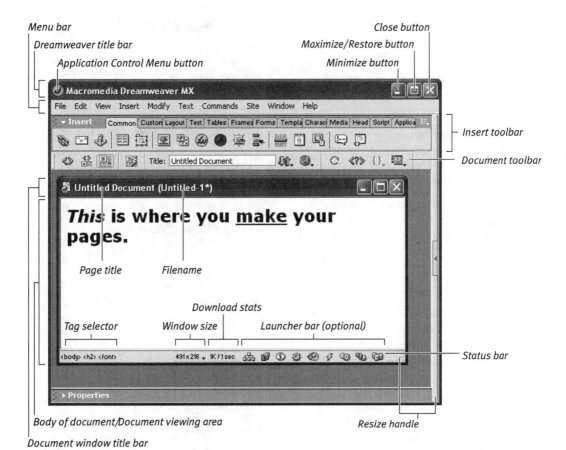

Insert toolbar

Document toolbar

Page title   Filename

Download stats

Tag selector   Window size   Launcher bar (optional)

Status bar

Body of document/Document viewing area   Resize handle

Document window title bar

Figure 1.30 The Document window is where you compose your pages. This is the Windows version of Dreamweaver with the Document window minimized.

THE DOCUMENT WINDOW

15

The Document Toolbar

The Document toolbar (**Figure 1.31**) offers quick access to common tasks.

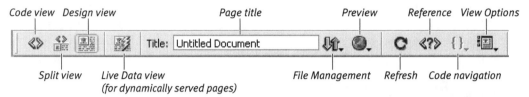

Code view Design view Page title Preview Reference View Options

Split view Live Data view *(for dynamically served pages)* File Management Refresh Code navigation

Figure 1.31 The Document toolbar offers quick access to common tasks.

Switching Views The view options allow you to look at just the WYSIWYG (or Design) view, to see Code and Design views at the same time, or to see just code without opening the Code inspector. See *Looking at Code* on page 25 and Chapter 4 for more.

Page Title Edit the title of your page without opening the Page Properties dialog box. See Chapter 3 for more on page properties.

File Management The File Management menu (**Figure 1.32**) lets you put files on the Web or get the most recent version from your remote site. See Chapter 19.

Preview Preview/Debug in the browser menu (**Figure 1.33**) offers a list of browsers in which to view your page. See Chapter 3.

Refresh The Refresh Design View button updates your page when you're working on the code in Dreamweaver or another editor.

Reference The Reference button pops open the definition of the current tag in the Reference panel. See Chapter 4.

Code Navigation The Code Navigation menu lets you set a breakpoint for debugging JavaScript.

View Options The View Options menu (**Figure 1.34**) offers toggles for turning on borders and other elements, as well as the grid and the ruler. In Code view, this menu offers HTML viewing options (**Figure 1.35**).

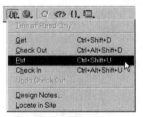

Figure 1.32 The File Management menu lets you upload files directly from the Document window.

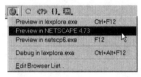

Figure 1.33 You can choose a browser quickly using the Preview menu.

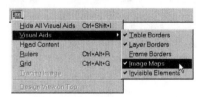

Figure 1.34 The View Options menu lets you turn visual aids off and on, among other things.

Figure 1.35 In Code view or in the Code inspector, the View Options menu offers HTML options.

THE DOCUMENT TOOLBAR

The Insert Toolbar

The Insert toolbar (**Figure 1.36**), formerly known as the Objects panel, offers shortcut buttons for inserting common page elements.

Tabs for object categories

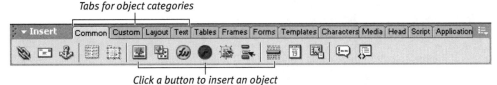

Click a button to insert an object

Figure 1.36 Click on a button in the Insert toolbar to insert the associated object. When you mouse over the buttons on the Insert toolbar in Windows, a tool tip will appear to remind you of what each button does.

In Macromedia documentation, you may also see the Insert toolbar referred to as the Insert bar or the Insert panel. It can be undocked.

To view or hide the Insert toolbar:

◆ From the Document window menu bar, select Window > Insert or press Ctrl+F2 (Command+F2). The Insert toolbar will appear.

The Insert toolbar consists of several categories, divided into tabs such as: Characters, Common, Forms, Frames, Media, and Templates.

To change Insert toolbar categories:

◆ Just click on a tab to display its contents (**Figure 1.37**).

Figure 1.37 Here, I've undocked the Insert toolbar and I'm displaying the Forms tab.

To insert an object:

1. With both the current page and the Insert toolbar in view, click on the icon for the object you wish to insert.

   If Dreamweaver needs more information to insert the object, a dialog box will appear.

2. Fill out the dialog box, if necessary, and then click OK.

   The object will appear in the Document window.

To select and modify an object:

◆ You can select most objects by highlighting them or clicking on them. The Property inspector will display an object's properties once you've selected it.

   For specifics, refer to the chapter in which the type of object in question is discussed.

THE INSERT TOOLBAR

Figure 1.38 Objects available from the Insert menu. Submenus include Interactive Images, Media, Frames, Template Objects, Form Objects, Head Tags, and Special Characters.

Figure 1.39 Special Characters—helps you insert special symbols without memorizing their HTML code.

Figure 1.40 Common objects.

Dreamweaver Objects

All of the objects available from the Insert toolbar are also accessible from the Insert menu (**Figure 1.38**). The handiest submenus in the Insert toolbar are Characters, Common, Layout, Frames, Forms, Media, and Head.

The Characters category (**Figure 1.39**) includes special text symbols such as copyright marks and Euro signs (Chapter 8), as well as the line break and the nonbreaking space (Chapter 9).

Common elements (**Figure 1.40**) include (from left to right):

◆ Links (Chapter 6)

◆ Email Links (Chapter 6)

◆ Named Anchors (Chapter 6)

◆ Tables (Chapter 12)

◆ Layers (Chapter 14)

◆ Images and Image Placeholders (Chapter 5)

◆ Fireworks HTML (Chapter 5)

◆ Flash (Chapter 7)

◆ Rollover Images (Chapters 5 and 16)

◆ Navigation Bars (Chapter 7)

◆ Horizontal Rules (Chapter 9)

◆ Date (Chapter 3)

◆ Tabular Data (Chapter 18)

◆ Comments (Chapter 4)

◆ The Tag Chooser dialog box (Chapter 4)

continued on next page

DREAMWEAVER OBJECTS

Layout elements (**Figure 1.41**) are used in designing tables (Chapter 12). Form elements (**Figure 1.37**) appear on pages that feature interactive forms, which are discussed in Chapter 15. Frame elements (**Figure 1.42**) are actually prefab frames layouts and are described in Chapter 13. Head elements (**Figure 1.43**), which help you insert information about your document for use by search engines and other Web index tools, are discussed on the Web site for this book. Media elements (**Figure 1.44**) (Chapter 7) include some of the Common elements, as well as Flash Buttons, Flash Text, and browser plug-ins.

Figure 1.41 Layout tools.

Figure 1.42 Frame objects.

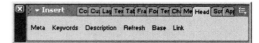

Figure 1.43 Head elements.

Figure 1.44 Media objects.

✔ Tips

- Other categories include Text (Chapters 4, 8, and 9); Tables (a redundant tab for layout, it's covered in Chapters 4 and 12); Forms (Chapter 15); Templates (Chapter 17); and Script (Chapters 16 and 17). The Application tab is used only with dynamically served pages.

- You can create custom objects and even add categories to the Insert toolbar. See Chapter 18 to find out how.

- You can view text in addition to (Figure 1.44) or instead of (Figure 1.43) images on the Insert toolbar. View the Preferences dialog box (Edit > Preferences or on OS X, Dreamweaver > Preferences), and click General. From the Insert Panel drop-down menu, select the option you want, and click OK to apply your changes.

DREAMWEAVER OBJECTS

Undocking the Insert Toolbar Like the Objects Panel

You can undock the Insert toolbar if you'd rather it hover like the Objects panel from previous versions of Dreamweaver. I show the toolbar undocked from time to time in this book—like in this chapter, for instance. Macromedia likes to call this toolbar a panel, or a bar, but I find it easier to think of as a toolbar rather than a palette or a drinking establishment.

To undock the toolbar, just grab the panel's gripper bar and pull it away from its location below the menu bar. You can then resize the panel. You cannot dock it on the side, but you can dock it on the bottom.

In Windows, when the Insert toolbar is undocked, you may see a blank Dreamweaver button in the taskbar. Just ignore it.

Measuring in the Document Window

You can add a ruler and a grid to the Document window to help you with sizing and placing elements.

Using the rulers

The rulers are especially useful for resizing tables, layers, and images.

To view the rulers:

◆ From the Document window menu bar, select View > Rulers > Show. You can also select this from the View Options menu on the toolbar (**Figure 1.45**).

The rulers will appear (**Figure 1.46**).

To change ruler units:

◆ From the Document window menu bar, select View > Rulers > and then choose Pixels, Inches, or Centimeters. The ruler measurements will change.

By default, the rulers' zero points, or starting points for measurements, start at the top left corner. You can change this, if you want, so that it's at the corner of a table or layer.

To change the zero point:

◆ Click on the zero point (**Figure 1.47**), and drag it into the window. When the point is where you want it to be, let go of the mouse button.

Now, when you look at the rulers, the measurements will reflect the new zero point. If you change your mind, you can reset the zero point to its original position (View > Rulers > Reset Origin).

Figure 1.45 Select Rulers from the Options menu.

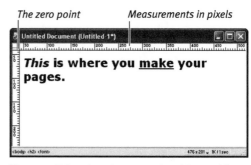

Figure 1.46 View the rulers to see how big your ideas are. Pixels are the default ruler unit.

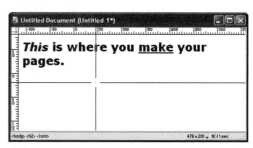

Figure 1.47 Click on the zero point and drag it to a new location to change the ruler origins.

Gridlines lined up at 50 pixels

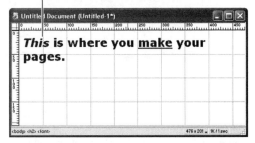

Figure 1.48 To get even more precise measurements, turn on the grid.

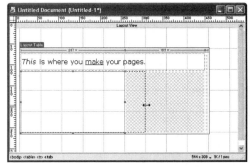

Figure 1.49 When I drag the table border, it snaps to the grid. I can change the grid increments using the Grid Settings dialog box.

Using the grid

The grid proves its usefulness when you're placing elements by dragging them on the page.

To view the grid:

◆ From the Document window menu bar, select View > Grid > Show Grid.

The grid will appear (**Figure 1.48**).

You can make draggable items snap to the grid lines. That means that when you drag a layout cell (Chapter 12) or a layer (Chapter 14), its borders will snap to the grid lines like a weak magnet.

To turn on the "snapping" option:

1. Show the grid, if you haven't.

2. From the Document window menu bar, select View > Grid > Snap To Grid.

Now table borders and layers that you drag in the Document window will snap to the grid (**Figure 1.49**).

MEASURING IN THE DOCUMENT WINDOW

To change grid settings:

1. From the Document window menu bar, select View > Grid > Grid Settings. The Grid Settings dialog box will open (**Figure 1.50**).

2. To change the color of the grid lines, click on the color box, and the color picker will appear. Click on a color to choose it.

3. The Show Grid checkbox turns the grid on. The Snap to Grid option turns on snapping which means the edges of objects will stick to gridlines. You can have snapping, turned on and the grid hidden at the same time.

4. To change the spacing of the grid lines, type a number in the Spacing text box, and choose a unit of measure from the Spacing drop-down menu: Pixels, Inches, or Centimeters.

5. To display dotted rather than solid lines, click the Dots radio button.

6. To view your changes before you return to the Document window, click Apply.

7. To accept the changes, click OK. The Grid Settings dialog box will close, and you'll return to the Document window.

✔ Tip

■ Rulers and grids are most useful for positioning tables and layers, discussed in Chapters 12 and 14. Both elements can provide visual guidelines for sizing and laying out content.

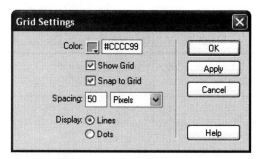

Figure 1.50 Control the grid by changing the Grid settings.

Looking at Code

The Code inspector (formerly the HTML inspector, **Figure 1.51**, next page) shows the HTML code for the current page. You can also view HTML code in Code view (see *The Document Toolbar*, earlier in this chapter). Dreamweaver always adds the code shown in Figure 1.51 to a new page.

To open or close the Code inspector:

◆ From the Document window menu bar, select Window > Others > Code Inspector.

or

Press F10.

In any case, the Code inspector will appear.

Any changes that you make to the code in the Code inspector will appear in the Document window when you click in that window or close the Code inspector, and any changes that you make in the Document window will be automatically updated in the Code inspector.

✔ Tip

■ Click on the View Options menu on the toolbar to turn on Word Wrap or Line Numbers. These options are fully described in Chapter 4.

continued on next page

LOOKING AT CODE

Line numbers

Toolbar (same as Document window)

Panel group name

Options menu button

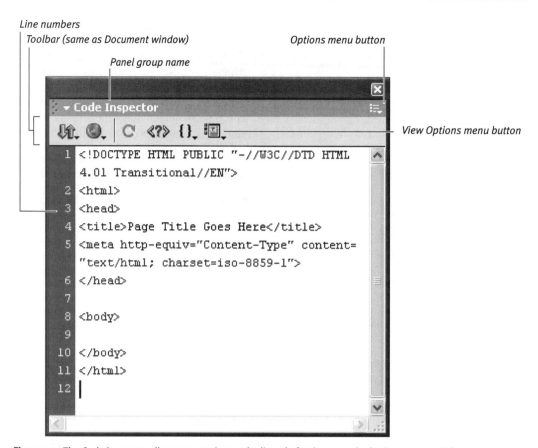

View Options menu button

Figure 1.51 The Code inspector allows you to view and edit code for the pages in the Document window.

About HTML

Chapter 4 presents an introduction to working with HTML. Although you never, ever have to look at the code if you don't want to, you can learn a lot about HTML by working in the Document window and then checking what the code is doing in the Code inspector or the Code view. You'll also be better equipped for fine-tuning your pages, which in some instances can only be done by working directly with the code.

Unlike many Web page apps, Dreamweaver doesn't use made-up HTML tags, nor does it rewrite your painstaking code. (In some cases, Dreamweaver uses proprietary XML or JavaScript, but it uses purely legal HTML.) It does offer tools to help you clean up bad code or fix common errors, and it even synchronizes with other editors.

Chapter 4 discusses these tools, as well as the plethora of code-writing gadgets such as the Snippets panel, the Edit Tag command, the Tag Chooser, and the Quick Tag editor. It also describes how you can set Dreamweaver's preferences for rewriting and formatting your code.

Selecting Objects and Code

Figure 1.52 The Document window and the Code inspector offer parallel selection: Highlight code in one window, and it will also be selected in the other.

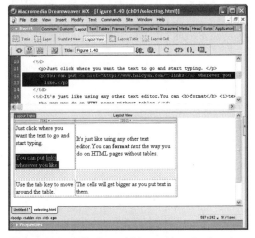

Figure 1.53 In Split view, which combines Design view and Code view, you can select code and objects will be selected in Design view, and vice versa.

Selecting objects in the Document window is similar to selecting them in any other program:

◆ To select a word, double-click on it.

◆ To select a line of text, click to the left of it to highlight the entire line at once, or press Shift+Arrow to select a few characters at a time.

◆ To select an image, click on it.

◆ To select a table, right-click on it (Control+click on the Mac), and from the context menu that appears, choose Table > Select Table.

When an item is selected, you can cut, copy, delete, or paste over it. You can also modify it with the Property inspector.

If you select an item in the Document window and then open the Code inspector or Code view, the item will remain selected in the code, which is really handy for finding things in particular table cells or on pages with a lot of content (**Figure 1.52**).

Similarly, if you select some code in the Code inspector, or Code view in the Document window, the objects that that code represents will appear highlighted in Design view (**Figure 1.53**).

To select code:

1. To select all the code and content that appears between a particular set of tags, first click on a word or image that's formatted by the tag, in either the Code inspector or Document window.

2. Click on the appropriate tag in the tag selector that appears in the Document window's status bar (**Figure 1.54**).

For instance, to select an entire paragraph, you can click on a word within it and then click on the <p> tag on the tag selector. This makes it easier to select any tags, such as links <a>, tables <table>, and the entire body of a page <body>.

✔ Tip

■ You can also select a line of code in the Code inspector or Code view by clicking on one of the line numbers in the left margin.

Code for cell selected

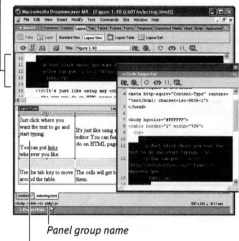

Panel group name

TD tag for cell selected

Figure 1.54 Click on one of the tags in the tag selector in the Document window's status bar to select the tag and everything it encloses. The tag I selected was <td>, a table cell.

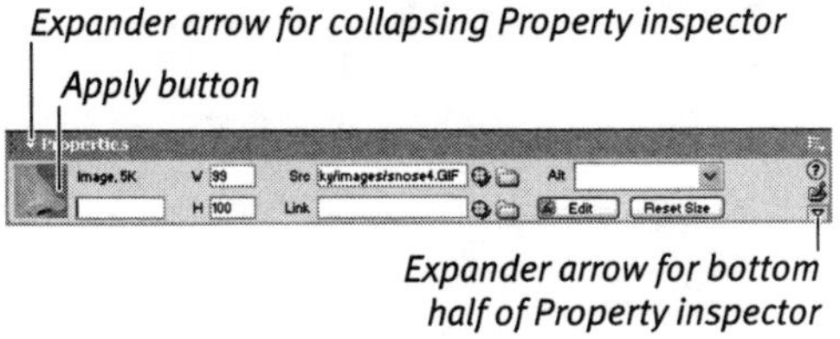

Expander arrow for collapsing Property inspector

Apply button

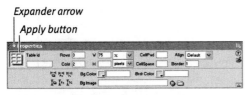

Expander arrow for bottom
half of Property inspector

Figure 1.55 The Property inspector changes appearance depending on what item is selected. This figure shows image properties.

Expander arrow

Apply button

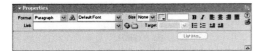

Figure 1.56 Click on the Expander arrow, and the Property inspector will expand to show more options. This figure shows table properties.

Figure 1.57 Text properties are the ones you'll see most often.

✔ Tips

- All Property inspectors except text have an Apply button (Figures 1.55 and 1.56). It's basically a metaphor; you can click anywhere on the Property inspector to apply your changes. This works mainly on the PC. To apply changes on a Mac, you must click within a text box on the Property inspector.

- You can also display the Property inspector by double-clicking on some objects in the Document window.

The Property Inspector

You'll use the Property inspector more than any other panel, because it lets you work with the specific attributes of almost every object you can put on your page. It displays text properties most often, and it changes appearance depending on what object you have selected.

To display the Property inspector:

1. From the Document window menu bar, select Modify > Selection Properties or Window > Properties, or press Ctrl+F3 (Command+F3). The Property inspector will appear (**Figure 1.55**).

2. To display the entire Property inspector, click on the expander arrow in the bottom-right corner of the Property inspector (**Figure 1.56**).

If no object is selected, the Property inspector will display text properties (**Figure 1.57**).

To modify object properties:

1. Select the object you wish to modify.

2. Display the Property inspector, if it isn't already onscreen.

3. Based on your selection, you can: click on formatting buttons, make menu selections from the drop-down menus, type numbers or names in the text boxes, and select check boxes or radio buttons.

4. Some of your choices will be applied immediately; to make sure properties are applied to the selection, click the Apply button (shown in Figures 1.55 and 1.56).

Invisible Elements

Dreamweaver's Document window approximates what you'd see in a Web browser window; it tries to replicate the way a browser would interpret HTML.

One exception to this is invisible elements. These elements would not be visible to a Web browser, but you may have occasion to display them in order to select, edit, or move them.

To view invisible elements:

◆ From the Document window menu bar, select View > Visual Aids > Invisible Elements.

   Any invisible elements on the current page will show up in the form of little icons (**Figure 1.58**).

To change invisible element preferences:

1. From the Document window menu bar, select Edit > Preferences. The Preferences dialog box will appear.

2. In the Category box at the left of the Preferences dialog box, click on Invisible Elements. The Invisible Elements panel of the dialog box will appear (**Figure 1.59**).

3. The Invisible Elements panel of the dialog box displays all the invisible elements that will become visible when you select View > Invisible Elements.

   Each invisible element has a corresponding checkbox. Line breaks are deselected by default.

4. To deselect any element, click on its check box to remove the checkmark.

   To select any element without a checkmark, click on its check box to add one.

5. When you're finished, click OK to close the Preferences dialog box.

Figure 1.58 When you view invisible elements, you may see all kinds of little icons that weren't visible before.

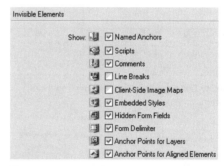

Figure 1.59 You can choose not to view certain invisible elements when you want to see some, but not all, of them. The Invisible Elements panel of the Preferences dialog box is shown in close-up so you can read it.

✔ Tips

■ Figure 1.59 is also a handy reference for what the symbols stand for.

■ Click on an invisible element icon to examine it with the Property inspector.

INVISIBLE ELEMENTS

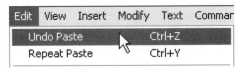

Figure 1.60 From the Edit menu, you can see what your last action was, so you can Repeat it or Undo it.

Figure 1.61 The History panel contains a list of the previous actions you performed during this session of Dreamweaver (until you quit). You can repeat any one of them by selecting it and then clicking Replay.

About History

Dreamweaver stores the actions that you perform in a History file, similar to how a Web browser stores the sites you visit.

Dreamweaver now supports multiple levels of Undo. For example, suppose you accidentally backspace to delete a table, and then you paste an image on the page. A single undo would un-paste the image. A second undo brings back the table.

To undo an action:

◆ Press Ctrl+Z (Command+Z)

   or

   From the Document window menu bar, select Edit > Undo [Action Name] (**Figure 1.60**).

You can also repeat your last action.

To repeat an action:

◆ Press Ctrl+Y (Command+Y)

   or

   From the Document window menu bar, select Edit > Repeat [Action Name] (Figure 1.60).

You can also repeat any action you have performed while Dreamweaver is open.

To use the History panel:

1. From the Document window menu bar, select Window > Others > History. The History panel will appear (**Figure 1.61**).

2. In the History panel is a list of actions you have performed. Click on an action, and then click on Replay to repeat the action.

You can also combine and even save actions. The History panel is described in more detail in Chapter 17.

SETTING UP
A LOCAL SITE

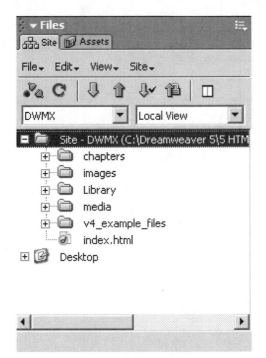

Figure 2.1 The Site window operates as a local site management and site planning tool, as well as an FTP client. This is the local site view. In Chapter 19, I'll discuss the Remote Site view and the Site Map view.

What you probably want to do with this book is jump to the fun parts and start making Web pages. You can skip this chapter and make Web pages willy-nilly, but if you do, you'll miss out on some of the best time-saving tools that Dreamweaver includes.

This chapter describes how to set up Dreamweaver so that it helps you manage a set of pages as a local site. A local site is simply a folder on your computer that contains the collection of pages that are destined to be part of a site on the Internet.

You always set up your pages in a set of folders. These folders must use the same names, and exist in the same order and hierarchy, in both places: on your computer (your local site) and on the Web (your remote site).

Dreamweaver's file management tools (**Figures 2.1** and **2.2**) don't preclude having to check your links, but they do make it easier to administer things, especially if you keep your pages and folders in the same order they'll be on your site.

The Site window and the Assets panel are the tools we'll learn about in this chapter.

If you're not careful, half the battle of creating a Web site will be figuring out where all your files are. If they're scattered all over your hard drive, you need to locate them, check all the links and image locations, upload the files, and then check all the links again.

✔ Tip

- Things you can't use without setting up a local site: HTML styles; the links checker and the automatic links updater; the Site map or the Point to File link tool; the Assets panel, the Library, and Dreamweaver templates; and the FTP functions, among other things.

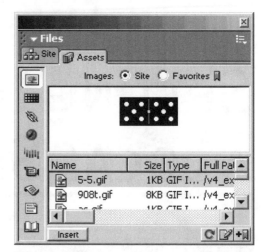

Figure 2.2 The Assets panel helps you keep track of images and other site resources.

About the Site Window

Dreamweaver's Site window (**Figure 2.3**) is both a file-management tool and a full-fledged FTP client that helps you put your site online. On Windows, the Site window is a part of the Files panel group. On the Macintosh (**Figure 2.4**), the Site window is always a stand-alone window, but it functions pretty much the same.

continued on next page

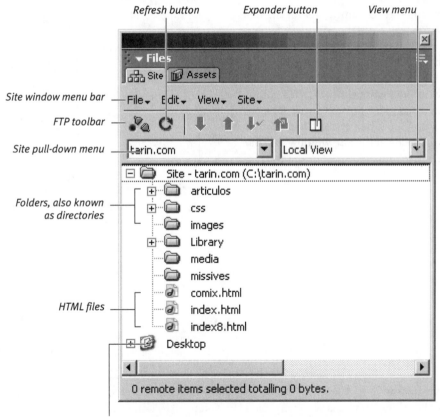

Refresh button   Expander button   View menu

Site window menu bar

FTP toolbar

Site pull-down menu

Folders, also known as directories

HTML files

Desktop link—click to browse your entire local machine

Figure 2.3 The Site window is a combination file-management tool and FTP client.

✔ Tips

■ Click the Expander button (Windows only) to display both areas, local and remote (**Figure 2.5**). On the Macintosh, both areas are always visible.

■ All the column headings are also buttons; click on any one of them to sort the directory contents by that criterion.

■ You can drag the borders between the column buttons to adjust the column width. If the Site window is docked as a panel on the PC, as in Figure 2.1, you won't see these column headings as buttons, or anything else.

■ On the Mac, the Site window will open when you start Dreamweaver for the first time. You can close the window whenever you want, and if you do so before you quit, it will remain closed when you restart the program. I find the Site window easier to work with when it's not maximized to occupy the entire screen. Click the Zoom box, the left-hand box on the right side of the Site window title bar, to zoom in and out.

Figure 2.4 The Site window on the Mac looks like it always has—it's a stand-alone window rather than the panel it is on Windows. As with all Mac windows, the menu bar appears at the top of your screen instead of on the window itself.

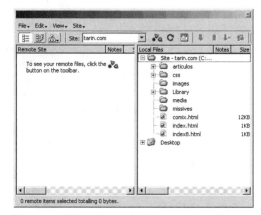

Figure 2.5 Click the Expander button to open both local and remote views.

ABOUT THE SITE WINDOW

What's Where

This short chapter will teach you how to set up a local site—or several. You'll get acquainted with the site window, the assets panel, and all the tools you need to manage your sites locally.

Chapter 19 describes everything you need to know about link management and putting your sites online. Chapter 6 tells you everything else you need to know about links. You'll find more tips on site management on the Web site for this book, including how to use `<head>` tags to your advantage.

The Site Window

In the Site window, you pick a folder, or *directory,* on your computer or local network to hold your a local site.

This folder becomes the *site root folder—* which means that it's at the top of the folder hierarchy for your site and serves as the central folder that holds all other folders and files in your site.

To make this work, you set up this folder to contain all the folders and files that will appear on your Web site—in the same order. That is, if your homage to Grandma will be in a folder on the Web called Family, it should be in the Family folder on your local site, too.

Dreamweaver uses the location of the site root folder to code relative links, including the paths for images. (Relative links, which are described more fully in Chapter 6, are efficient shortcuts to pages within the same Web site.)

Managing files in local and remote sites takes place in the Site window (Figure 2.2).

To view the Site window:

◆ From the Document window menu bar, select Window > Site Files.

or

Press F8.

or

Open the Files panel group and click on the Site tab. Either way, the Site window will appear (**Figure 2.6**).

When you first view the Site window, it will be empty. Before you can begin working with a local site, you must set one up on your computer.

Figure 2.6 Here, I'm showing remote files in the Site window as well as local files. The remote stuff is covered in Chapter 19. First, though, you need to set up a local site to hold all your files so that you can get Dreamweaver to keep track of your links.

It's Not That Hard!

After five years of helping people learn Dreamweaver, I've consistently found that the thing that trips people up more than anything else is the concept of setting up a local site.

It's not supposed to be an ordeal—all you're doing here is choosing a folder that will hold all the files in your site. It's just like choosing a folder that will hold all the recipes or kitten photos on your hard drive.

You can either create a new folder to hold your files or you can select an existing folder. Then, you save your new files into it.

You can also move files from other folders, other disks, or other computers into this folder if you want them to be part of your site.

Do you have a site already and want to set up Dreamweaver to work with it? Super! There's no "import" process—simply tell Dreamweaver which folder your Web site files are in. (Guess what—after the setup that folder *is* your local site!) If you don't have local copies, you may have to download some of them from the Web first. That's all there is to it.

Basic tab (select to use wizard)

*Advanced tab
(if you already know what you're doing)*

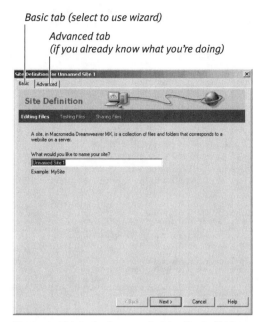

Figure 2.7 This is the first panel of the Site Definition wizard. Type a name for your site, such as FrogsOnline or Basura.com.

Figure 2.8 In the second panel of the wizard, click No.

Setting Up a Local Site

You need to designate a local site to use the site tools, and you must set this up in Dreamweaver even if you've designated this folder in your head, or in another program.

You can base a local site on the contents of an existing Web site, or you can set up a new local site before any version of it exists at all. Before you do either, you need to pick a site root folder (a home folder) for your local site.

Using the wizard

In Dreamweaver MX, we now have a wizard you can use to help you figure out how to set up a local site by answering a few questions at a time. If you're upgrading or if you want to skip the wizard, go ahead to the section *Using the Advanced tab*.

To set up a new local site using the wizard:

1. From the Document window menu bar, select Site > New Site. The Site Definition wizard will appear (**Figure 2.7**).

   If you want to use the wizard, be sure to click the Basic tab if the Advanced tab is on top.

2. Type a name for your site. Dreamweaver suggests "MySite," but I recommend typing something more specific, such as "Family Pages" or "Hot Sauce Store".

3. Click Next. The Editing Files, Part 2 panel will appear (**Figure 2.8**). Dreamweaver will ask you if you want to use its server technology tools. Unless you have all the information you need to set up your site to work with a database, click No. (See the Introduction for details.)

continued on next page

4. Click Next. The Editing Files, Part 3 panel will appear (**Figure 2.9**). In most cases, leave the first option, Edit local copies, selected. If you know you'll be editing files directly on the server, select one of those options. You can change any of these options later by returning to the Site Definition.

5. Now, in the same panel, here's the most important part: Pick the folder you want your files to live in. Click Browse 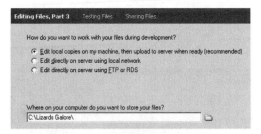 to open the Choose Local Root Folder dialog box (**Figures 2.10, 2.11**). You can:

- Browse through your folders and select an existing folder anywhere on your computer, *or*

- Browse to a likely area, like your desktop, My Documents, or a project folder, and click the Create New Folder button to create a new folder to hold your files. You probably want this folder to live in an area you frequent, such as the Desktop or My Documents.

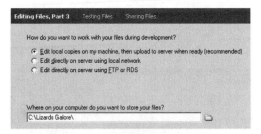

Figure 2.9 In this panel of the wizard, you're most likely going to edit your files locally. (See the Advanced section for details on the other options.) Then you'll choose where your site root folder will be.

New Folder button, if I want to create a new folder for my local site files

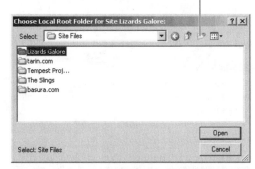

Figure 2.10 Here, I've got a folder on my Desktop called Project Files, and I've just created a folder called Lizards Galore to hold the files for my new site. I need to click on the folder name, then click Open, and then click Select.

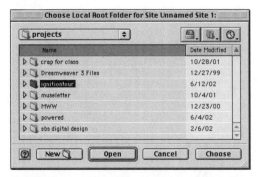

Figure 2.11 On the Mac, things work pretty much the same way. I select the folder I want to use, and then I click Choose.

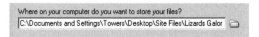

Figure 2.12 Dreamweaver now displays the path of the folder I just chose. It might also look like `C:\Site` or `Macintosh HD: Site`.

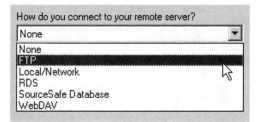

Figure 2.13 We'll stop here for now and set up our remote site information later, in Chapter 19.

How do you connect to your remote server?

| None |
| None |
| FTP |
| Local/Network |
| RDS |
| SourceSafe Database |
| WebDAV |

Figure 2.14 These are your setup choices—choose None so you can come back to this later.

6. When you've got the right folder selected, click on Select (Choose), and there you go. You'll return to the wizard, which will display the *path* (computer address) you just set (**Figure 2.12**).

7. We're almost done for now. Click Next, and the Sharing Files panel of the wizard will appear (**Figure 2.13**). We're going to skip the rest of the steps for now, so you can:
   - Select None from the menu (**Figure 2.14**), *or*
   - Go to Chapter 19 to find out how to set up Remote site information.

8. Click Next again and you'll see a preview of your selections. Then, click Done.

Using the Advanced tab

If you're upgrading, or if you just don't like wizards, follow these instructions to set up your Local Site info.

1. From the Document window menu bar, select Site > New Site.

   The Site Definition dialog box will appear. If it is still in wizard mode, click on the Advanced tab. If Local Info isn't selected in the category box, select it. You'll see The Local Info panel of the dialog box (**Figure 2.15**).

2. Type a name for your site (**Figure 2.16**).

3. Click Browse 📁 next to the Local Root Folder text field. The Choose Local Folder dialog box will appear (as seen in Figures 2.10 and 2.11).

4. You can select an existing folder or create a new one. Click Select (Choose) when you've found or created the folder you want to use as your local site root folder.

5. Other options:

   Leave the Refresh Local File List and Enable Cache checkboxes checked (**Figure 2.17**). Type the full URL for your site, if you know it, in the HTTP Address text box. And if you want to tell Dreamweaver the location of your most-used images folder, such as *images*, select that folder the same way you did in steps 3 and 4.

6. Click OK to close the dialog box.

The remote options in the Site Definition dialog box are explained in Chapter 19, *Managing Your Web Sites*.

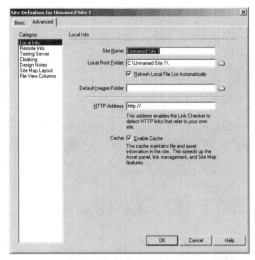

Figure 2.15 The Advanced tab of the Site Definition dialog box lets you set up the same information much faster.

Figure 2.16 Type a descriptive name for your site. You can use spaces and punctuation here if you like, whereas you shouldn't use spaces for Web site folder names.

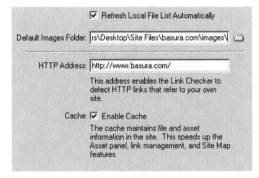

Figure 2.17 These other options help you keep track of your files, links, and images.

Figure 2.18 I have several different local sites set up for different projects in progress.

Figure 2.19 After you click OK in the Site Definition dialog box, this dialog box (or another, similar one) will appear, confirming whether you'd like to create the cache.

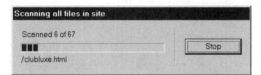

Figure 2.20 While the cache is being created, a dialog box will appear informing you of Dreamweaver's progress.

✔ Tips

- A new local site may or may not have any documents in it when you create it. You can create a local site based on an existing folder that's chock full of docs, or you can create a blank folder and download part or all of an existing site into it.

- Or, you can create a blank folder for a site that doesn't have any docs at all yet—because you're going to create them. I recommend setting up a local site at the point you begin using Dreamweaver, even if you haven't created a single page yet.

- You can create as many local sites as you want. I have different local sites for different parts of my main remote site (**Figure 2.18**).

- Dreamweaver can create an index, called a cache, of your local site, which keeps track of the names and locations of all your files. The cache also remembers when you link one file to another on your local site. You can then update a link site-wide when you move or rename a file (see *To rename a file*, later in this chapter; the process is described in further detail in Chapter 19). To create a local cache in which Dreamweaver stores information about the local site root, relative links, and filenames, simply leave the Enable Cache checkbox checked in the Site Definition dialog box. You must enable the cache to use the Assets panel.

- When you create a site and click on OK in the Site Definition dialog box, a dialog box will tell you that the cache will be created (**Figure 2.19**). Creating the cache will take a few seconds (**Figure 2.20**).

- Remember that everything having to do with a remote site, including how to put your pages on the Web, is discussed in Chapter 19. Chapter 19 also describes how site maps work.

It's All Relative

You may have noticed that Dreamweaver is picky about coding relative paths (a.k.a. relative links or relative URLs). When you insert an image or a link to a local file on an unsaved page in Dreamweaver, a dialog box appears notifying you that the link will use a `file://` path until you save the page. When you do so, Dreamweaver converts these `file://` paths into the same relative paths that will be used online.

When you create a local site in Dreamweaver, it codes site-root relative paths based on the directory structure of the local sites. Take this example: Your local site root is `C:\HTML`. The current page is in `C:\HTML\Bubba`, and your images folder for the project is `C:\HTML\Images\Current`. When you save the page, Dreamweaver will make a relative link like this one:

```
<img src="/Images/Current/Bubba.gif">
```

Using local sites in Dreamweaver is easier than hand-coding relative links.

I designate each project folder on my computer as a separate local site. Then, when I put the files online, the links remain intact.

You can choose to have Dreamweaver update all relative links when you perform a Save As, rename a page, or move a page into a different folder. You set this option in the Preferences dialog box. Press Ctrl+U (Command+U) to view the Preferences dialog box, and click on General from the Category list to bring that panel to the front. From the Update Links drop-down menu, select Prompt, Always, or Never, and then click OK to close the Preferences dialog box. See Chapter 6 for more about relative links.

To speed Dreamweaver in storing and updating the paths for relative links and filenames, make sure the Cache checkbox in the Site Definition dialog box is checked.

Figure 2.21 The information for these local sites was imported into Dreamweaver MX from Dreamweaver 4.

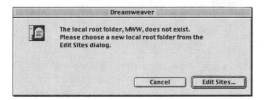

Figure 2.22 I moved one of my site folders before I installed Dreamweaver MX, and now this annoying dialog box keeps showing up. I need to delete or update the folder locations.

Figure 2.23 Update this portion of your site definition, under Local Info, to keep the Site window at bay.

If You're Upgrading

Dreamweaver MX keeps track of local sites from previous versions of Dreamweaver when you upgrade from an older version to version MX. This watchfulness can be either useful or annoying, depending on what happens.

When you first start Dreamweaver MX

Dreamweaver MX will import all local site information from Dreamweaver 4 or UltraDev 4 so you don't have to re-input it—that's great (**Figure 2.21**).

If your sites have moved

If you moved or deleted a site folder for a local site, you'll get this annoying, persistent dialog box (**Figure 2.22**). How do you make it go away? See the next section, *Editing and Deleting Local Sites*, and either remove the site from the list (you can set it up again later) or update the address of the folder so that it reflects the folder's current location.

For example, say my site Polkanoia used to live in the Polka folder on my Desktop. Then, I moved the Polka folder into a different folder called Web Projects. The address of my local site is now Macintosh HD: Web Projects: Polka. I should update this information to reflect the folder's new location—see **Figure 2.23** for where to make the change.

✔ Tip

■ I like to keep my Web site folders in an easy-to-find folder called Projects or Sites or something like that, on the Desktop or at the top level of my hard drive. That way all site files for all my sites are near each other in case I want to share resources or move easily from one site update to the next.

Importing and Exporting Site Information

Dreamweaver can save your site definitions, which consist of the locations of files and site preferences in all panels of the Site Definition dialog box, including remote site info and login information. Once you have this file (**Figure 2.24**), you can share it between several computers or with people collaborating on a site.

To export site info:

1. From the Document window's Site drop-down menu, select Edit Sites. The Edit Sites dialog box will appear (see Figure 2.21).

2. Select the site name you're exporting.

3. Click Export. If you have no remote site info yet, skip to the next step. If you do have remote site info, a dialog box will appear (**Figure 2.25**), asking you whether you want to save your password and login.

4. The Export Site dialog box will appear (**Figure 2.26**), which is just like a Save As dialog box.

   Choose which kind of expert you want and click OK.

5. Type a name for your file, ending in .ste. This is the file extension Dreamweaver uses for the XML files that contain the site definition information.

   Make sure you're saving the site info in a folder where you can find it again.

6. Click Save.

✔ Tip

■ You can also select Site > Export from the Site window menu bar.

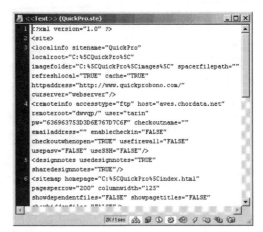

Figure 2.24 This is what the XML file, whose extension is .STE, looks like.

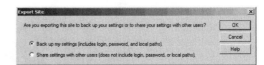

Figure 2.25 This dialog box will appear if you're exporting a site that contains remote site information such as login names and passwords. Choose Share if you don't want to include this information.

Figure 2.26 The Export Site dialog box is just like a Save As dialog box.

Figure 2.27 Importing Site information using this dialog box will add the site definition information, including the name of the site, to your list of sites.

To import site info:

1. From the Document window's Site drop-down menu, select Edit Sites. The Edit Sites dialog box will appear.

2. Click Import. The Import Site dialog box will appear (**Figure 2.27**), which is just like an Open File dialog box.

3. Locate the STE file that contains the site information you want to import.

4. Click Open. The site will appear in the Edit Sites dialog box.

✔ Tip

■ You may want to change certain information after you import site information. Be sure to double-check or correct the location of the local site folder, and be sure to enter your own login information in the Remote Info panel of the Site Definition dialog box.

IMPORTING AND EXPORTING SITE INFORMATION

Editing and Deleting Local Sites

You can edit the information about a local site, or delete one that you're no longer using.

To edit a local site:

1. From the Document window menu bar or the Site panel menu bar, select Site > Edit Sites (**Figure 2.28**).

   or

   In the Site panel, select Edit Sites from the [site name] drop-down menu (**Figure 2.29**).

   Either way, the Edit Sites dialog box will appear. (You can also double-click a site name in this menu to skip to step 3.)

2. In the dialog box, select the name of the site you want to edit (**Figure 2.30**).

3. Click Edit. The Site Definition dialog box will appear.

4. Make any necessary changes to the local site information in the Site Definition dialog box, including updating where the site root folder is if you've moved it (Figure 2.23)

5. When you're done, click OK to return to the Edit Sites dialog box. You can edit more site information or you can click Done to return to the Site panel.

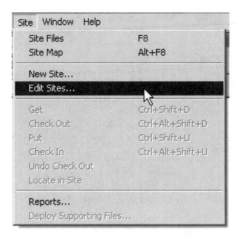

Figure 2.28 Select Edit Sites from the Site window menu bar (or the Document window menu bar).

Figure 2.29 This drop-down menu allows you to switch from local site to local site; it also offers the quickest way to open the Edit Sites dialog box.

Figure 2.30 In the Edit Sites dialog box, select the name of the site you want to edit.

Figure 2.31 Do you really want to delete this site? If so, click Yes. Dreamweaver won't delete any files, but the site will be removed from your list of local sites.

To delete a site:

1. Follow steps 1 and 2, above, to select your site in the Edit Sites dialog box.

2. Click Remove. A dialog box will appear, asking if you really want to do that (**Figure 2.31**). Click Yes.

   Dreamweaver will remove the site from the list, but it will not delete any files or folders from any remote or local site.

✔ Tip

■ If you're working with two sites that have similar settings or login information, click Duplicate in the Edit Sites window to start with a copy of an existing site.

Site Window Tips and Shortcuts

You can perform a lot of common Dreamweaver file tasks with a couple of clicks. The first step in all of these tasks is to open the Site window and view the site you want to work with.

To open a file:

◆ In the Site window, double-click on the file name. The file will open in the Document window (**Figure 2.32**).

To preview a file:

◆ Right-click (Control+click) on the file. From the context-up menu that appears (**Figure 2.33**), choose Preview in Browser > [Name].

The file will open in the selected browser.

To duplicate a file:

1. Right-click (Control+click) on the file. From the context menu that appears, choose Duplicate. A copy of the file will appear, called Copy of [filename.html].

2. Rename the file (see next page).

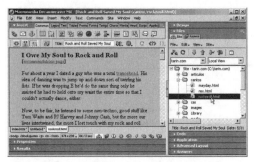

Figure 2.32 Double-click on a file icon in the Site window, and the page will open in the Document window.

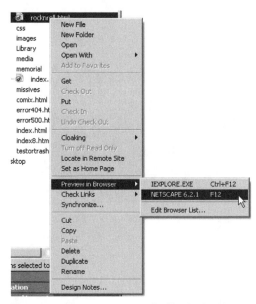

Figure 2.33 The context menu for files in the Site window offers lots of handy shortcuts. Windows users: Just right-click on a file or folder. Mac users: Control+click to pop up the menu.

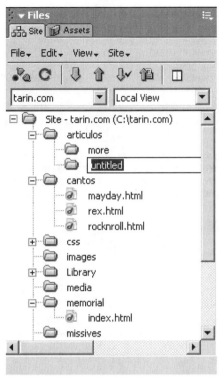

Figure 2.34 I'm creating a new folder in the Site window. I clicked on the folder called `articulos` to create the new folder beneath (and inside) it. Now I just need to type a name for the new folder.

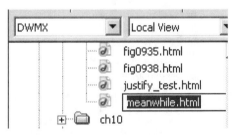

Figure 2.35 When a box appears around the filename, you can type the new one.

To create a new folder:

1. In the Site window, right-click (Control+click) on the folder within which you want the new directory (folder) to appear. For a top-level folder, click on the first folder listed, called Site (Site Name).

2. From the context menu that appears, select New Folder. A new folder will appear.

3. Type a name for the folder, press Enter (Return), and you're done (**Figure 2.34**).

✔ Tip

- To create a new folder, you can also do one of the following:
    - ◆ Click on the folder and press Ctrl+Alt+Shift+N (Command+Option+Shift+N), or
    - ◆ Select File > New Folder from the Site window menu bar (Mac: Site > Site Files View > New Folder).

To delete a file or folder:

1. Right-click (Control+click) on the file or folder you want to delete.

2. From the pop-up menu that appears (Figure 2.33), choose Delete. A dialog box will appear to confirm your choice; click OK to delete the file.

To rename a file or folder:

1. Click on the file name and hold down for a couple seconds. When a box appears around the file or folder name, you can type a new one (**Figures 2.34** and **2.35**).

continued on next page

2. Type the new filename and press Enter (Return).

A dialog box will appear while Dreamweaver scans for links to this file. If it finds any affected files, the Update Files dialog box will appear, asking if you want to update links in that set of files (**Figure 2.36**).

You may instead get a dialog box that asks you whether you wish to scan for files (**Figure 2.37**). If this dialog box appears, click Scan to look for affected pages.

3. Click Update, and Dreamweaver will change links in any files that link to the page you renamed.

✔ Tips

- There are also menu options for each of these shortcuts. Open, Preview, Check Target Browsers, Delete, New Folder, and many other options are available under the File menu on the Site window menu bar, or on the context menu when you right-click or Control+click a file. On the Macintosh, the menu command for some options is Site > Site Files View > [...].

- New in Dreamweaver MX: Your local computer is included in the Site window's list of local files so you can browse the files and copy or move them (**Figure 2.38**). See the next section, *Moving Files,* for details, and you can move or copy files from other places on your hard drive into your local site folder.

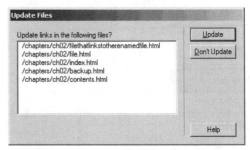

Figure 2.36 Once Dreamweaver knows about your links, either through a cache or by scanning the site, the Update Files dialog box will appear, and it will tell you which pages link to the renamed or moved page.

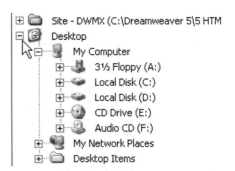

Figure 2.37 If you haven't created a cache for your site, this dialog box will appear and ask you whether you wish to scan for links to a renamed or moved file.

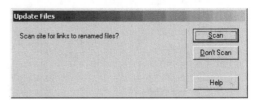

Figure 2.38 Besides the files in your local site, Dreamweaver allows you to access any file on your computer using the Site window. You can open files that aren't in your local site and work on them; you can move files into your local site; you can make copies of files in your local site and them move them into other folders on your computer, and so on.

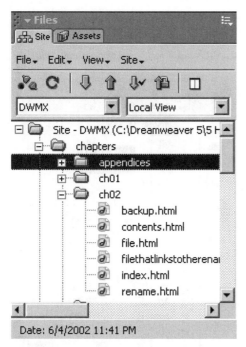

Date: 6/4/2002 11:41 PM

Figure 2.39 Folders with hidden contents have a plus sign to the left of them. Folders with their contents displayed have the files indented under them. To open or close a folder, double-click on it. The Mac uses blue arrows instead of plus signs.

Expander button

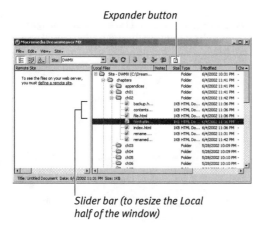

Slider bar (to resize the Local half of the window)

Figure 2.40 I've expanded the Site window and now I can see additional file information for each file.

Moving Files

You can also use the Site window like a file manager to move files around.

To move files from folder to folder:

1. View the file(s) you want to move by double-clicking the folder that contains them. To select multiple files, hold down Ctrl (Command) while clicking. To select contiguous files, hold down Shift while clicking.

2. Click on the selected file(s) or folder(s), hold down the mouse button, and drag them to a new location.

See steps 2 and 3 under *To rename a file or folder* at the top of the previous page to find out about updating links to renamed or moved files.

To toggle between local sites:

◆ In the Site window, select the name of the site you want to display from the Site drop-down menu. The Site window will display the files and folders of the site you selected.

✔ Tips

■ Folders on local and remote sites that contain files will be indicated by a symbol next to the folder. To display the contents of the folder, double-click on the folder icon (**Figure 2.39**), or click on the symbol, which is a + sign if you are using Windows, or an arrow symbol on the Mac.

■ Windows only: If you undock the Site window by clicking on the Expander button (**Figure 2.40**), you can see more file information, such as file type, file size, last date modified, and so on. You cannot, however, use the Document window with the Site window expanded. (On the Mac, the window stands alone at all times.)

Managing Assets

The Assets panel keeps track of several kinds of media, allowing you to find and preview any image or movie in your site, no matter what folder it's in.

About the Assets panel

You must create a local site and enable the site cache in order for the Assets panel to display anything (**Figure 2.41**). Dreamweaver keeps track of Assets as a separate set for each site.

To view the Assets panel:

◆ From the Document window menu bar, select Window > Assets.

or

Press F11.

In any case, the Assets panel will appear.

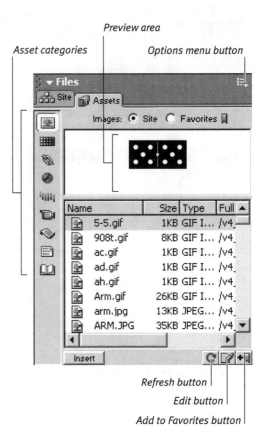

Preview area

Asset categories

Options menu button

Refresh button

Edit button

Add to Favorites button

Figure 2.41 The Assets panel keeps track of images, movies, URLs, color swatches, and other files in your local site.

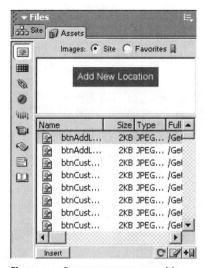

Figure 2.42 Dreamweaver comes with a folder called Samples that includes some images. If you're bereft of images and you want to play around with assets, you can use these files to figure out the Assets panel.

To view the Assets for a different local site:

◆ From the Document window menu bar, select Site > Open Site > [Site Name].

The Site window will appear, displaying files for that local site. When you return to the Document window or open the Assets panel, the panel will display assets in the site you just opened (**Figure 2.42**).

✔ Tip

■ If you don't have many files but you want to play with the Assets panel now, create a new site with Dreamweaver's sample files. The default address is C:\Program Files\Macromedia\Dreamweaver MX\Samples or Macintosh HD: Applications: Macromedia Dreamweaver MX: Samples.

Kinds of Assets

The Assets panel keeps track of the following types of files.

Images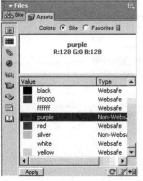

Any JPEG, GIF, or PNG image files stored in your local site.

Colors

All colors, including background, link, and text colors, used in local site pages (**Figure 2.43**).

Figure 2.43 All colors in your local site are stored as swatches in the Assets panel, whether they're Web safe or not, and whether they're hex codes or alpha-numeric names.

URLs

All external, or absolute, URLs used on HTML pages. These include `http://` and `https://` URLs, as well as `mailto:` addresses and Gopher, FTP, and `file://` paths (**Figure 2.44**).

Flash

Any Flash movies, Flash buttons, and Flash text objects in your local site (**Figure 2.45**). Flash movies should be saved as `.SWF` files; `.FLA` files are source files and aren't displayed.

Figure 2.44 All absolute URLs in your local site are stored in the Assets panel, including FTP and mail to links.

Shockwave

Any Shockwave movies, games, and the like stored in your local site.

Movies

Any QuickTime or MPEG movie files stored in your local site.

Scripts

External, not inline, JavaScript or VBScript files that are stored locally as independent files.

Figure 2.45 The Assets panel keeps track of all your Flash movies, buttons, and text objects.

Templates and Library items

These are special, reusable HTML files in Dreamweaver and are described in Chapter 18.

Figure 2.46 If your Assets panel is empty, Dreamweaver may need to refresh its memory about your site.

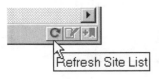

Figure 2.47 Click on the Refresh button to make Dreamweaver re-read the site cache.

Figure **2.48** This dialog box will appear for just a second if you click on Refresh, or for a little longer if you have to rebuild the site cache.

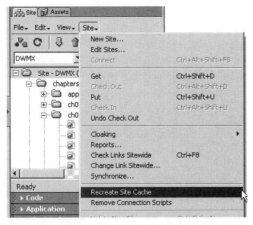

Figure 2.49 Rebuild the site cache if Dreamweaver can't find your assets

How Assets Work

When you create a local site, Dreamweaver tracks all its files and builds a *site cache*, or index, of these files. Dreamweaver keeps track of the relative links between files in your local site, as well as minding the locations of all the items described on the previous page.

If the Assets panel is empty:

◆ On the Assets panel (**Figure 2.46**), click the Refresh button (**Figure 2.47**).
Dreamweaver will reread the site cache (**Figure 2.48**) and index your assets. In a moment or two, the Assets panel will display your assets (assuming you have some).

Keep in mind that if you don't have any Flash objects, for example, then the Assets panel can't display them.

If you add or delete an asset and the panel doesn't change:

1. Open the Site window (Window > Site Files).

2. From the Site window menu bar, select Site > Recreate Site Cache (**Figure 2.49**) or select the same command from the Asset panel's Options menu.

   or

   Hold down the Ctrl (Command) key while clicking on the Assets panel's Refresh button.

Dreamweaver will rebuild the site cache (see Figure 2.48), which may take some time on large sites. (It has to index all those links.)

✔ Tip

■ Sometimes when I switch from site to site the Assets panel won't refresh—it shows assets from the last site I had open—and I have to quit and restart Dreamweaver to use the panel properly.

Using the Assets Panel

The Assets panel displays vital statistics about assets, including previews. For more about previewing, see the next section, *Previewing and Inserting Assets*.

To view assets:

◆ To view a category, click on its button on the Assets panel (**Figure 2.50**).

◆ To view site files (all assets for a category), click on the Site radio button (**Figure 2.51**). To view Favorites (see *Using Favorites and Nicknames*, later in this chapter), click the Favorites radio button. The Favorites list will be empty until you add items to it.

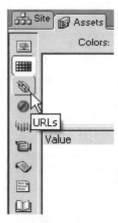

Figure 2.50 Click on a category button in the Assets panel to view that kind of asset.

Figure 2.51 Click the Site radio button to view all the assets in your site, or Favorites to view only those files you've designated as such.

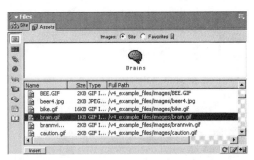

Figure 2.52 You can sort images by file type, size, and name. You can also sort them by path, as I did with this image, which also sorts by the folder the image is in.

Value		Type
▨ #996666		Websafe
▨ #9966ff		Websafe
▨ #339966		Websafe
▨ #000000		Websafe
▨ #ffffff		Websafe
▨ #cc3333		Websafe
▨ #00ff33		Websafe

Figure 2.53 Here, I've sorted colors into Web-safe and non-Websafe. Within each group, or all together if you click the Value column heading, they'll be arranged by value. That often means that similar colors are grouped together. Named colors are also grouped together. Finally, I'm clicking and dragging the column between the category borders.

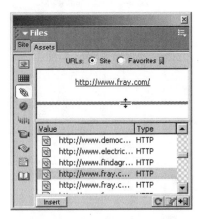

Figure 2.54 I've sorted links by protocol type. I've also shortened the preview area; you can enlarge it if you're dealing with images or movies.

To sort assets:

1. View the category you want to sort.

2. Click on one of the column headings to sort by that heading (**Figure 2.52**).

For example, you can sort images by ile type to separate GIFs from JPEGs; you can sort colors by the Type column (**Figure 2.53**); and you can sort links into HTTP, mailto, and FTP (**Figure 2.54**).

✔ Tips

■ You can drag the borders between column headings to resize the columns if you want to make a particular column more readable (Figure 2.53). You can resize the Assets panel, too, as I have in Figure 2.52.

■ To resize the preview area, drag the border between it and the Assets list box (**Figure 2.54**). See the next page for more about previews.

Previewing and Inserting Assets

The Assets panel lets you preview items before inserting them.

To preview an asset:

◆ Select the asset in the Assets panel.

   ◆ If the asset is an image, a preview will appear (**Figure 2.55**).

   ◆ If the asset is a color, the tone will appear in the list box, and the preview area will display the Hex and RGB codes for the color (**Figure 2.56**).

   ◆ If the asset is a URL, the preview area will display the full path (**Figure 2.57**).

   ◆ If the asset is a Flash, Shockwave, or other movie, a placeholder will appear in the preview area (**Figure 2.58**). Click the green Play arrow to play the movie. You may need to mouse over some objects for them to play. Click the red Stop button to stop the movie once you've played it.

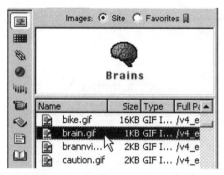

Figure 2.55 A preview of the image will appear.

Figure 2.56 The hex and RGB codes for the color will appear, and you'll see the color in use as text. See Chapter 3 for more on color codes.

Figure 2.57 The preview area shows the full URL.

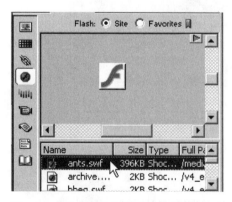

Figure 2.58 If your Flash object is made by Dreamweaver (Flash text or Flash button), it'll appear as in **Figure 2.45**. Otherwise, you'll get a placeholder and a Play button.

Insertion point
(where image would land if you clicked
on the Insert button)

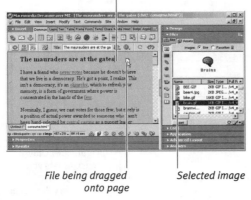

File being dragged   Selected image
onto page

Figure 2.59 Here, I'm dragging the image onto the page.

To insert an asset:

1. Select the asset in the Assets panel.

2. How you insert an asset depends on what you want to do and what kind of asset it is.

◆ If the asset is an image, movie, or script, you can drag it into the Document window (**Figure 2.59**), or click the Insert button at the bottom of the panel to drop it onto your page at the insertion point.

◆ If the asset is a link or color, select some text in the Document window. Then select the asset and click the Apply button at the bottom of the panel.

◆ If the asset is a link and you drag it into the Document window, the full path will be displayed, and you can edit this text.

◆ If the asset is a color and you drag it into the Document window, the next text you type will appear in that color.

Using Favorites and Nicknames

If you have 4,000 images in your site, having a list of all those files might be more unwieldy than just using the Site window to find things. However, you can create a list of Favorites for each category (excepting Library items and Templates) so you can track your most-used assets separately.

To add an asset to Favorites:

1. Select the asset in the Assets panel.

2. Click the Add to Favorites button (**Figure 2.60**). A dialog box may appear telling you that you have to view Favorites in order to see them (um, okay).

   The asset will be added to your list of Favorites (**Figure 2.61**).

To view Favorites:

1. In the Assets panel, click on the category you want to manage.

2. Click the Favorites radio button (**Figure 2.62**).

   The Favorites list will appear (Figure 2.61).

To create a folder for Favorites:

1. Select a Favorites category (see above).

2. On the Assets panel, click the New Favorites Folder button (**Figure 2.63**).

3. In the space that appears, type a name for the folder (**Figure 2.64**) and press Enter (Return).

4. Now you can select Favorite assets and drag them into the folder (**Figure 2.65**). To select several assets, hold down Ctrl (Command) while you click, or Shift for consecutive items.

Figure 2.60 Click the Add to Favorites button.

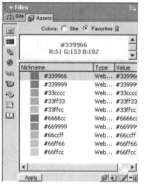

Figure 2.61 Only those assets you designate as Favorites will appear in the Favorites list.

Figure 2.62 Click the Favorites radio button.

Figure 2.63 Click the New Favorites Folder button.

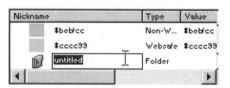

Figure 2.64 Type a name for the new folder.

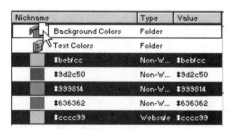

Figure 2.65 Select assets and drag them into the folder. Hold down Ctrl (Command) or Shift to select nonadjacent or consecutive assets, respectively.

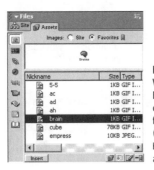

Figure 2.66 When you view Favorites for images or movies, the full filename is truncated (for example, brain.gif appears as brain).

Figure 2.67 Click the Remove From Favorites button.

Figure 2.68 Here, I've got four folders —including one subfolder—holding all my favorite colors. You can move the order of folders and subfolders by dragging them around in the Assets panel.

Figure 2.69 From the pop-up menu that appears, select Edit Nickname.

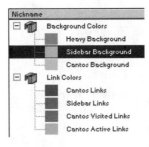

Figure 2.70 I've nicknamed all my colors so I know what's what.

To remove a Favorite:

1. View Favorites for a category in the Assets panel, as described on the last page (**Figure 2.66**)

2. Select the item to remove.

3. Click the Remove From Favorites button (**Figure 2.67**).

The asset will be removed from the Favorites list, but it will still appear in the Site list. If you remove an entire Favorites folder, you will remove all the assets within it from the list.

Nicknaming assets

You can create nicknames for frequently used assets in addition to putting them in the Favorites list—but you can nickname them only after you add them to Favorites.

To nickname a Favorite:

1. View Favorites for a category in the Assets panel, as described on the last page (**Figure 2.68**).

2. Select the Favorite you want to nickname.

3. Right-click (Control+click) the Favorite and, from the pop-up menu that appears (**Figure 2.69**), select Edit Nickname.

4. When the box appears around the name, type a nickname and press Enter (Return).

This won't change the filename—the nickname is used only in the Favorites list (**Figure 2.70**).

✔ Tip

■ For colors and URLs, a descriptive name may better serve memory when trying to choose between three shades of blue or three similar links. For images, media and scripts, you may find nicknames handy for buttons or form handlers that may have filenames like m_button_default_home.gif or NN_serve.js.

USING FAVORITES AND NICKNAMES

Editing and Sharing Assets

You can edit assets directly from the Assets panel. You can also share assets between sites.

Editing assets

Editing images and movies in the Assets panel consists of opening them in an external editor. To find out how to set up an external editor, see *Image Editor Integration* in Chapter 5.

To edit an image or movie:

1. Select the asset in the Assets panel.

2. Click the Edit button (**Figure 2.71**).

3. The asset will open in the external editor. Be sure to save your changes. If the new asset doesn't reload in the Document window, select View > Refresh Design View, or press F5.

To edit a color or URL:

1. Add the asset to your Favorites, as described in *Using Favorites and Nicknames*. You can edit only colors and URLs that are stored as Favorites.

2. Select the Favorites radio button, and select the asset.

3. If the asset is a URL, click Edit, and the Edit URL dialog box will appear (**Figure 2.72**). You can then edit both the URL path and the nickname for the asset. (If you drag a URL from the Assets panel into the Document window, and if you gave that URL a nickname, the nickname will appear as the text for the link. Otherwise the link itself will appear as the text.)

   If the asset is a color, click Edit, and the color picker will appear (**Figure 2.73**). You can choose a new color. For more on using the color picker, see Chapter 3.

Figure 2.71 Click the Edit button. The asset will open in an editor, unless it's a color or URL.

Figure 2.72 Edit a URL's path or nickname (default text) using the Edit URL dialog box.

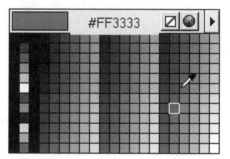

Figure 2.73 You can change any color in your Favorites. For example, if you have a color nicknamed Body Text and you change the color you use for your pages, change the color associated with the nickname.

Creating New Colors

Any time you use a color on your site, it will be added to the Assets panel. If you want to create a color *before* you use it, you can. (For instance, if you're given a list of site colors by the designer.)

Click within the Favorites folder, if you have one. (If not, see *Using Favorites and Nicknames* in this chapter for help setting one up.) Then, click the Options menu button and select New Color. The color picker will appear. Select your color, and it'll appear in the Favorites folder, where you can nickname it.

Figure 2.74 Right-click (Control+click) on an asset, or click on the Options menu button, and select Copy To Site > [Site Name].

Figure 2.75 I copied `brain.gif` from one site into another, and it copied all the surrounding folders as well. I'm free to move the image and delete the extra folders, of course.

Figure 2.76 Right-click (Control+click) on an asset, or click on the Options menu button, and select Locate in Site.

Figure 2.77 Dreamweaver found my image, right where I'd left it.

Sharing assets

If you have an asset you want to use in more than one site, you must place it in both sites.

To copy an asset to a different site:

1. Select the asset in the Assets panel.

2. Click the Options menu button, and in the menu that appears (**Figure 2.74**), select Copy to Site > [Site Name].

3. The asset will be copied to the Favorites list for its category in the other site, and a dialog box will appear listing the copied assets.

    Colors and URLs will be stored in Favorites. If the asset is an image, script, or movie, the file itself will be copied.

After you copy an asset file, you may be curious to know where Dreamweaver put it (**Figure 2.75**). It generally creates a copy of the folder or folders from the first site into the second site. For example, if the file `poppy.gif` is stored in `flowers/images/poppy.gif`, the folder `flowers`, as well as the folder `images`, will be copied in addition to the file.

To locate an asset in a site:

1. Open the site that contains the asset .

2. Right-click (Control+click) on the Asset, and when the context menu appears (**Figure 2.76**), select Locate in Site. You cannot locate a URL or color within a site; see *Find and Replace* in Chapter 8.

    The Files panel group will display the Site panel (or on the Mac, the Site window will appear, if it isn't open already), and the asset will be selected (**Figure 2.77**). You can feel free to move the asset and to delete any extra folders Dreamweaver created. When Dreamweaver updates the site cache, it'll find the asset again.

BASIC WEB PAGES

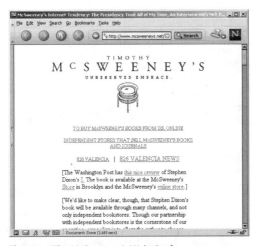

Figure 3.1 The McSweeney's Web site (www.mcsweeneys.net) uses mostly text, but it still looks snappy.

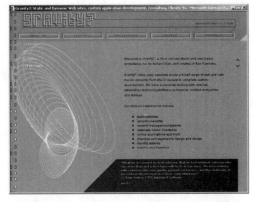

Figure 3.2 Gravity7 (www.gravity.com) is the home of designer Adrian Chan.

In the first chapter, we got acquainted with the Dreamweaver interface. In the second chapter, we learned how to set up a local site to keep track of all our files. This chapter describes how to use the Document window to create and save Web pages (**Figures 3.1** and **3.2**).

To start with, I'll walk you through creating a simple Web page that uses tables, links, images, and text. We'll also learn how to adjust the properties of a page, including the title and the page background.

In this chapter, we'll learn how to:

◆ Open a page

◆ Create a new page

◆ Add content to a page

◆ Set the page title

◆ Adjust the page properties

◆ Save your work

◆ Save a copy of your page

◆ Preview the page in a browser

◆ Print the page from the browser

◆ Close the file

This chapter also describes how to select and use colors in Dreamweaver. I'll refer to this material throughout the book.

Creating New Files

Creating and opening files in Dreamweaver is about the same as in any other program, but with a few more options.

The new Standard toolbar

Dreamweaver MX now includes a Standard toolbar you can use to perform simple functions.

To display the Standard toolbar:

◆ From the menu bar, select View > Toolbars > Standard (**Figure 3.3**). The Standard toolbar will appear (**Figure 3.4**).

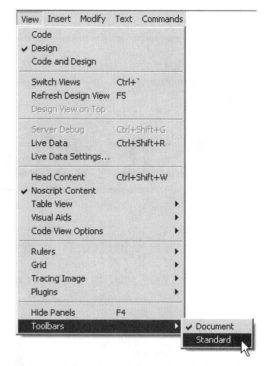

Figure 3.3 Select View > Toolbars > Standard from the menu bar.

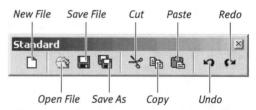

Figure 3.4 The Standard toolbar lets you perform common file and editing functions.

Category list: Basic Page

Page Type: HTML

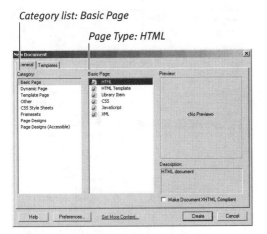

Figure 3.5 The New File dialog box presents a daunting array of choices. For a basic page, select Basic Page, HTML.

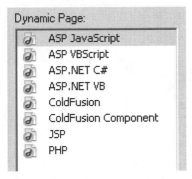

Figure 3.6 These other page types are used with databases, dynamic content, CGI scripts, and other server-side technologies.

Creating new files

When you start Dreamweaver, a new, blank page will appear in the Document window. You can create a new file at any time.

To create a new file:

1. From the Document window menu bar, select File > New, or press Ctrl+N (Command+N). The New Document dialog box will appear (**Figure 3.5**).

2. To create a regular HTML file, click on Basic Page in the General category list and HTML in the Basic Page list.

3. Click Create. A new, blank document will appear.

What are all those other file types?

Besides HTML, you can create and edit many other types of files in Dreamweaver (**Figure 3.6**). If you're not working with a database, you'll probably stick to HTML. If you need to create another type of file, such as ASP, you can edit the page as you would any other. If you're working on a dynamic site, consult your database team to find out what other settings to use.

Getting a Head Start

If you're very new to page design, or if you've laid out pages using other kinds of environments, you may want to start with a page that's not entirely blank. You may want to get a head start on learning Dreamweaver's features by starting with some basic layouts. Or you may be fresh out of layout ideas and may glean some inspiration by starting with a basic page.

To start a page based on a built-in design:

1. From the menu bar, select File > New. The New Document dialog box will appear.

2. In the Category list, select Page Designs (**Figure 3.7**). A list of page layouts will appear (**Figure 3.8**).

3. Click on the name of the design to display an abbreviated preview of the page.

4. When you find something you want to check out, click Create. The page will appear, with image placeholders and dummy text, in a new, unsaved Document window (**Figure 3.9**).

✔ Tips

- Many of these layouts include links, placeholders for images, and tables—the basics of these elements are discussed later in this chapter, and the details are covered in Chapters 6, 5, and 12, respectively.

- To find out about using built-in frameset pages, see Chapter 13. To find out about using built-in CSS style sheets, see Chapter 11.

- These built-in files could be thought of as templates, but in the world of Dreamweaver, a template is a file type ending in .dwt used to create other files. To find out how to use these and the Templates tab of the New Document dialog box, see Chapter 17.

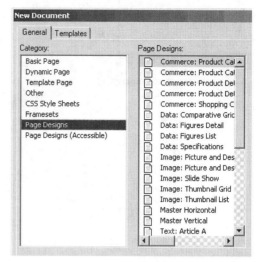

Figure 3.7 Click on Page Designs in the Category list. Page Designs (Accessible) use page designs restricted to certain tags; see Appendix C on the Web site for this book.

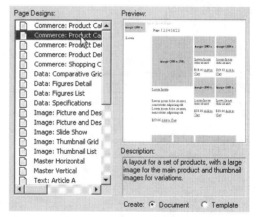

Figure 3.8 When you select the name of a page design, a small preview will appear to the right.

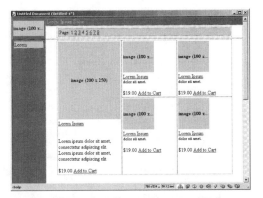

Figure 3.9 Your page will appear in a new, blank Document window—make any changes you want, play around, make a solid page design, whatever you like—but don't forget to save your page.

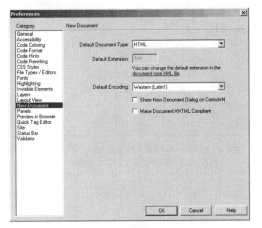

Figure 3.10 Select New Document from the Category list in the Preferences dialog box.

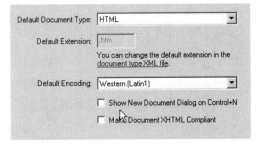

Figure 3.11 Deselect this check box to prevent the New Document dialog box from showing up when you use the Ctrl+N (Command+N) shortcut to create a new file.

Turning off the New Document Dialog Box

If you're planning on creating the same kind of file every time, that new New Document dialog box (Figure 3.5; it's new in Dreamweaver MX) may be more of an annoyance than a helpful feature.

To turn off the New Document dialog box:

1. From the menu bar, select Edit > Preferences (On Mac OS X, select Preferences from the Dreamweaver menu.) The Preferences dialog box will appear.

2. Select New Document from the Category list (**Figure 3.10**). The dialog box will show new file preferences (**Figure 3.11**).

3. Select your default document type from the list—HTML, unless you have another mandate.

4. Uncheck the Show New Document Dialog on Control+N/Command+N check box.

5. Click OK.

Now, when you press Ctrl+N (Command+N), you'll just get a new blank file of the type you selected.

✔ Tip

■ You can still open the New Document dialog by selecting File > New from the menu bar.

Opening Files

If you have previously created HTML files that you want to update, you can open them with Dreamweaver. Dreamweaver won't change your code, but it may alert you of errors such as redundant or unclosed tags (see Chapter 4).

When you open a file in Dreamweaver, it will appear in a new Document window.

To open a file:

1. From the Document window menu bar, select File > Open. The Open dialog box will appear (**Figures 3.12** and **3.13**).

2. Browse through the files and folders on your computer, and select a file you want to open.

   By default, the Open File dialog box lists files categorized as All Documents—not only .htm and .html, but .xml, .asp, .css, and so on).

   You may narrow your selection. If the file extension is not `.htm` or `.html` (you're opening a `.cgi` or `.asp` file, for instance), you may select a specific file type from the Files of Type list box. (On the Mac, select the file type, or All Documents from the Show drop-down menu. See Figure 3.13.)

3. Click Open. The file will appear in a new Document window.

✔ Tips

- You can open the last four files you viewed with Dreamweaver by selecting them from the File menu (**Figure 3.14**).

- By default, Dreamweaver will look in the last open folder from the current, open local site. See Chapter 2 for more on using local sites to keep track of files.

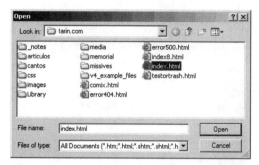

Figure 3.12 Use the Open dialog box to select a file on your computer to open in the Document window. By default, the Open dialog box first looks in the last folder that you opened within the current local site.

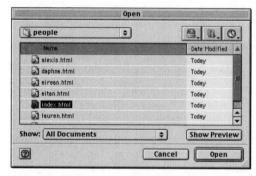

Figure 3.13 The Open dialog box looks a little different on the Mac, but it works the same way.

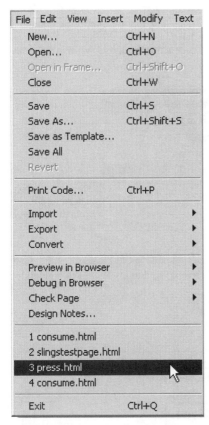

Figure 3.14 Open the last four files that you've edited in Dreamweaver by selecting their names from the File menu.

Paragraph break

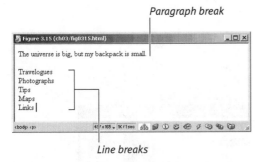

Line breaks

Figure 3.15 Type or paste whatever text you like in the Document window. After the first line, I pressed Enter (Return) to create a paragraph break; the breaks between the next five lines are line breaks (Shift+Enter).

Creating Content

When you open Dreamweaver, the Document window creates a new, blank page. You can start from this *tabula rasa* to create your own Web page.

To place text:

1. Just start typing!

2. Press Enter (Return) to make a paragraph break, or press Shift+Enter (Shift+Return) to make a line break (**Figure 3.15**).

You can also copy text from another program and paste it into the Document window.

CREATING CONTENT

To create a heading:

1. Select the text you want to make into a heading by clicking within that paragraph (**Figure 3.16**).

2. From the Property inspector's Format drop-down menu, select a heading from 1 (largest) to 7 (smallest) (**Figure 3.17**).

   The heading will become bold and its size will change (**Figure 3.18**).

To make text bold or italic:

1. Select the text you want to modify.

2. Click on the Bold or Italic button on the Property inspector.

   The text will change appearance (**Figure 3.19**).

✔ Tips

■ Dreamweaver offers common commands, such as copy, cut, paste, and undo, in the Edit menu (**Figure 3.20**) and on the Standard toolbar (seen in Figure 3.4).

■ For more about formatting text in Dreamweaver, see Chapter 8, *Fonts and Characters,* and Chapter 9, *Paragraphs and Block Formatting.*

■ By default, Dreamweaver MX uses the <strong> tag for bold text and the <em> tag for italic text. See *Using Text Styles,* in Chapter 8 for more on the difference between these tags. You can also change your preference in the General panel of the Preferences dialog box.

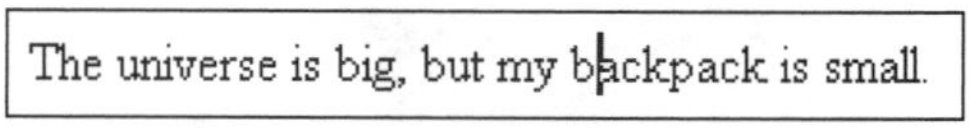

The universe is big, but my backpack is small.

Figure 3.16 Click within the line you want to make into a heading.

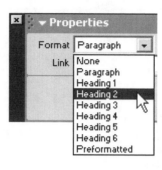

Figure 3.17 Select a heading size from the Property inspector.

The universe is big, but my backpack is small.

Travelogues
Photographs
Tips
Maps
Links

Figure 3.18 Now my text has become a heading, and I've selected some lines to make bold.

Travelogues
Photographs
Tips
Maps
Links

Figure 3.19 I've made the selected text bold.

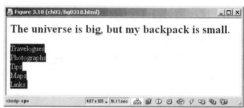

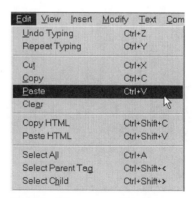

Figure 3.20 You can use Dreamweaver as a text editor, too. The Edit menu offers common commands.

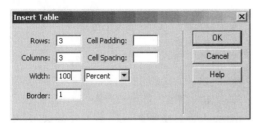

Figure 3.21 These are the settings I've selected for the Insert Table dialog box to create the table shown in **Figure 3.22**.

Figure 3.22 A basic table. To use it as a page layout, set its width to 100 percent.

Laying out a page with tables

On my example page, I'm going to insert a table. Tables are covered in more detail in Chapter 12. Once you insert a table, you can insert, paste, or drag content into its cells.

To insert a table:

1. From the Document window menu bar, select Insert > Table. The Insert Table dialog box will appear (**Figure 3.21**).

2. Type the number of columns and rows you want to appear in your table. For our example, I'm going to use three columns and two rows.

3. Specify the width of your table by typing a number in the Width text box, and selecting either pixels or percent from the drop-down menu. To use the table as a page layout, I'm going to specify the width as 100 percent (of the browser window).

4. Click OK. The Insert Table dialog box will close, and the table will appear on your page (**Figure 3.22**).

To change the layout:

1. Mouse over a border between two cells or around the outside of the table, and the pointer will turn into a double-headed arrow you can use to drag the borders.

2. To change the height of the table (**Figure 3.23**), drag the bottom border.

   To change the height of the two horizontal rows, drag the border (**Figure 3.24**).

3. To change the width of the columns, drag their borders (**Figure 3.25**). You can readjust them at any time.

✔ Tip

■ You can draw complex table layouts using Layout view (Chapter 12) or by drawing layers and converting to tables (Chapter 14).

Figure 3.23 You can set a table height by dragging the bottom border down. The table will also expand if you place content into it.

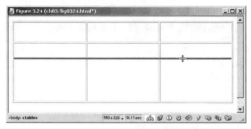

Figure 3.24 You can drag the border between rows to create a smaller top row. See **Figure 3.26** to see what I've done with this.

Figure 3.25 You can drag the border between columns before or after you put content in them.

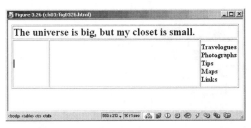

Figure 3.26 Here's my page in progress. I've combined the cells in the top row (see Chapter 12), and I'm going to place an image in the left-hand cell.

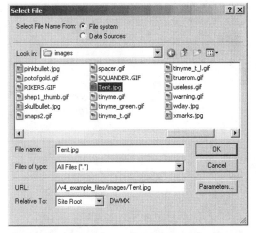

Figure 3.27 Insert an image into your page by selecting its image file in the Select Image Source dialog box. This is the Windows version; the Mac view is shown in **Figure 3.41**.

Figure 3.28 After I inserted the image, the table resized to accommodate it. I can resize either the image, the table, or both.

Adding images and media

Images and media files are not embedded in a page; rather, the Web page contains inline links and spacing information so the browser knows where to go get the files and how to display them. In Dreamweaver, you simply place the file where you want it to go on the page, and it writes the linking code.

To place an image:

1. Click to place the insertion point where you want the image to appear. I'm going to click within a table cell (**Figure 3.26**).

2. From the Document window menu bar, select Insert > Image. The Select Image Source dialog box will appear (**Figure 3.27**).

   Browse through the files and folders on your computer and select the image file. The image pathname will appear in the URL text box.

3. Click OK (Choose). The Select Image Source dialog box will close, and the image will appear on the page (**Figure 3.28**).

To find out more about images and image properties, see Chapter 5, *Working with Images*. Inserting media objects is very similar, and I cover that subject in Chapter 7.

To make a link:

1. Highlight the object (text or image) that you want to make into a link (**Figure 3.29**).

2. In the Link text box on the Property inspector, click Browse , and select a file from your local site.

   or

   Type or paste the URL of an Internet link and press Enter (Return).

   Either way, the object will become linked. (**Figure 3.30**).

For more about links, see Chapter 6, *Working with Links*.

Figure 3.29 Highlight the text you want to make into a link.

Figure 3.30 Type the link in the Property inspector's Link text box, or click on Browse to choose a file. Either way, the text will become linked and the link will be displayed in the Property inspector. The tag for a link is *<a>*.

Data Sources?

So my file is a piece of data, and my hard drive or my Web server is a data source, right?

Nope. A data source, as an option on the Select File dialog box, is a database application server such as a Microsoft Active Server or a ColdFusion server. For regular old Web sites with regular old Web servers, select a file from your local site and then upload all required files to your Web server.

If you're a database guru or you have one in your backyard, you must set up your app server to work with Dreamweaver, and then you can select Data Sources and call a file to be sent down from your app server. See the Introduction for more about dynamic sites.

Figure 3.31 Type your page title in the Title text box.

N Tips for Time Travelers – Netscape 6

Figure 3.32 The title you choose for your Web page will be displayed in the Web browser's title bar.

Text from Other Sources

When you paste text from another program, such as an email or word-processing program, it may lose all its formatting, including paragraph breaks. (If you paste text copied from a Web browser or HTML mail program, it should retain its paragraph formatting.)

One way to prevent loss of formatting is to use a word-processing program to save the text as HTML, and then open the file in Dreamweaver. Many word processors, including AppleWorks, Microsoft Word, Nisus Writer, and Corel WordPerfect, include HTML conversion extensions (try File > Save as HTML, or consult the program's help files).

Although these programs write atrocious HTML in some cases, they're just fine for coding paragraph and line breaks.

Another good shortcut is Microsoft Excel's Save as HTML feature, which saves spreadsheets as not-too-terrible HTML tables.

No matter what other program you use to create an HTML file, you can easily clean up the big boo-boos by selecting Commands > Clean Up HTML (or Clean Up Word HTML for MS Word files) and selecting which common mistakes you want to correct. Chapter 4 describes Roundtrip HTML in more detail.

Page Properties

Page properties are elements that apply to an entire page, rather than a single object on the page. Visual properties include the page's title, a background color or image, and the text and link colors. Other page properties include the document encoding and the site folders, if any.

To change the page title:

1. In the Document toolbar, click within the Title text box.

2. Type a new title and press Enter (Return) (**Figure 3.31**).

Choose a good title for your page, something more descriptive than "My Home Page." Many search engines use the words in the page title to index pages.

✔ Tips

- The page title is stored in the `<title>` tag within the document's `<head>` tag.

- Unlike some other page creation tools, Dreamweaver doesn't prompt you to give your pages a title—in fact, it titles all your pages "Untitled Document" until you change the Page Properties.

- The title you give your page will be displayed in the Web browser's title bar (**Figure 3.32**).

Other page properties

Other page properties are stored in the Page Properties dialog box.

To view page properties:

◆ From the Document window menu bar, select Modify > Page Properties or press Ctrl+J (Command+J). The Page Properties dialog box will appear (**Figure 3.33**).

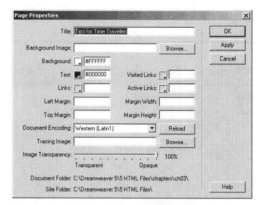

Figure 3.33 The Page Properties dialog box allows you to set options that apply to an entire page.

About Document Encoding

If you're composing Web pages in a language that uses a non-Western (non-Latin) alphabet, you probably browse the Web using Document encoding for that language. Web pages in alphabets such as Chinese, Cyrillic, Finnish, Greek, Japanese, Korean, and some Eastern European languages use special text encoding to display fonts that can interpret and display the characters that language uses.

To set the encoding for your page so that Web browsers can load the proper set of fonts, select your language from the Document Encoding drop-down menu in the Page Properties dialog box.

To find out how to change the encoding for the entire program, see Chapter 4.

Figure 3.34 Set margins larger or smaller than 10 pixels, which is the default margin width.

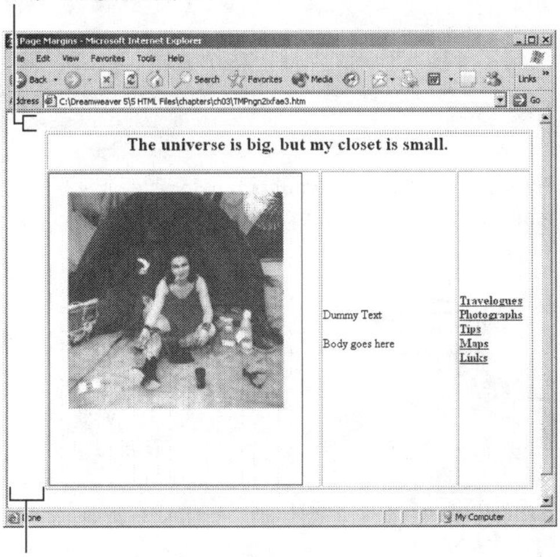

Top margin: 25 px

Figure 3.35 Here's my page with its margin settings. Compare to the default margins in **Figure 3.28**.

Left margin: 50 px

About page margins

Page margins are a relatively recent innovation. They appear as part of the **<body>** tag. Internet Explorer uses the "Left Margin" and "Top Margin" settings, whereas Netscape uses the "Margin Width" and "Margin Height" settings. For best results, set the margins for both browsers.

To set page margins:

1. View page properties, as in the previous list.

2. Set the top margin and left margin as shown, for both browsers (**Figure 3.34**).

3. To check how your settings appear in a specific browser, preview the page in that browser (**Figure 3.35**). See the section *Previewing in a Browser*, later in this chapter.

Modifying the Page Color and Background

Dreamweaver MX will display the background color of your page as plain white and the text color as black, but if you want to make sure your page actually has a white background in the browser window, you must set it as such. You can also choose a different background color, or use a background image instead. (Previous versions of Dreamweaver always included default settings for text and link colors, but Dreamweaver MX does not.)

Background and text colors

You can conceivably use any color as the background color. Keep in mind that you may need to change the text colors as well, so that the text will show up readably (**Figure 3.36**).

To set the background and text colors:

1. Open the Page Properties dialog box by pressing Ctrl+J (Command+J).

2. In the Background text box, type the hex code for the color you wish to use.

   or

   Click on the Background color box. The color picker will appear (**Figure 3.37**). Click on a color with the eyedropper to select it; the color can be any color in the picker or on your desktop (**Figure 3.38**).

   The other color options are described later in this chapter, in the section *Colors and Web Pages*.

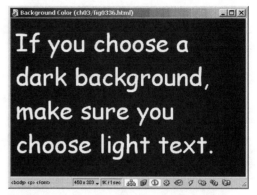

Figure 3.36 Make sure your text color is visible and readable on your background color.

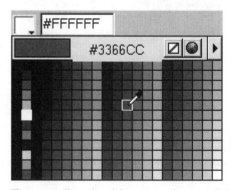

Figure 3.37 The color picker opens when you click on any color button within a dialog box or on the Property inspector.

Visible desktop
(all colors are potential selections)

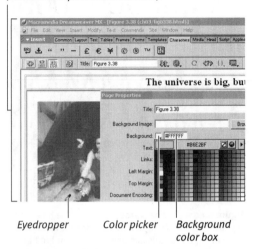

Eyedropper   Color picker   Background
color box

Figure 3.38 Here, I'm selecting a color from my photograph to serve as the background color. Any color I click on with the eyedropper, anywhere on my desktop, can serve as a color choice.

Figure 3.39 Here's my page, with a background color chosen from the photograph on it. I've also changed the link colors.

3. Repeat step 2 for the Text color and the Link colors, if you wish.

4. In any case, when the code for each color appears in its text box, click on Apply to preview the color on your page; or click on OK to apply the colors and close the dialog box (**Figure 3.39**).

✔ Tips

- More details about how link colors work are available in Chapter 6.

- You can find out how to make selected text a different color in Chapters 8 and 11.

Setting a background image

Most browsers created after Netscape Navigator 2 support background images. A background image can consist of one large image, but more frequently, it's a smaller image that the browser window tiles so that it repeats in a contiguous pattern across and down the browser window (**Figure 3.40**).

✔ Tip

■ Take care when using background images. You may have seen pages where the background took primacy over the content, rendering the text unreadable and the other images gratuitous. You may even have thought these looked cool, but I doubt you read them for long. Be subtle, or use table backgrounds to provide blank space for your text (see Chapter 12).

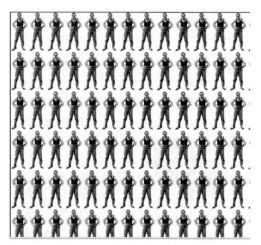

Figure 3.40 A tiled background image. The tiny image repeats from left to right and then down the page. Keep in mind that this is a demo—you wouldn't be able to read text set over a background image with this much contrast and with such a figurative figure. See **Figure 3.42**.

Converting Other Color Numbers into Hex

Colors in HTML are signified by a six-digit code called a hex code. Colors are also definable by a three-number sequence of hue, saturation, and value, or by another three-number sequence: the red-green-blue, or RGB, ratio. There are boxes for these numbers in the Color dialog box (see **Figures 3.43** and **3.63**).

You can get the RGB sequence of a particular color from an image editor, like Photoshop or Paint Shop Pro, and then duplicate the color by typing the correct numbers into the right boxes in the Color dialog box. Then, of course, you should jot down that hex code for further reference. (You can copy RGB numbers into an image editor, too, if you have reason to duplicate a background color in an image.)

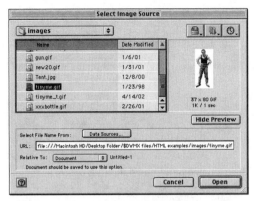

Figure 3.41 The Select Image Source dialog box, like an Open dialog box, lets you browse through your computer's files to select an image. The Image Preview at the right displays the image's dimensions, file size, and download time. Click on Show Preview to view it or Hide Preview to hide it. This is the Mac version; the Windows view was shown in **Figure 3.27**.

Figure 3.42 Here, I've added a subtle background image to my page. I've also modified the central table cell so it uses a solid background color, to ensure readability. See Chapter 12 for details.

To set a background image:

1. Open the Page Properties dialog box by selecting Modify > Page Properties from the Document window menu bar.

2. Click the Browse (Choose) button next to the Background Image field. The Select Image Source dialog box will appear (**Figure 3.41**). This is similar to the Open dialog box.

3. Browse through the files and folders on your computer until you find the GIF or JPEG image that you want to use. Click on the file icon so that the image's pathname appears in the URL text box.

4. Click Select (Open) to close this dialog box and return to the Page Properties dialog box, where the image pathname appears in the Background Image text box.

5. Click OK to close the Page Properties dialog box and return to the Document window, where your background image will appear (**Figure 3.42**).

✔ Tip

■ You can set both a background image and a background color. The image will override the color in most cases, and the color will show up in browsers that support background colors but not background images.

  To find out about tracing images, see Chapter 14. To find out about setting backgrounds for tables, see Chapter 12.

Saving Your Work

If you're creating more than just an afternoon's entertainment, you'll want to save the work you do to the Web pages you make.

To save the current page:

1. From the Document window menu bar, select File > Save, or press Ctrl+S (Command+S). The Save As dialog box will appear (**Figures 3.43** and **3.44**).

2. Make sure you select the correct folder in which you want to store the file. Dreamweaver will automatically prompt you to save the folder within your currently open local site, if you've defined one (see Chapter 2), but do double-check the folder you're saving in so you can find your file again.

3. Type a name for your file in the File name text box. The name should not include any spaces, but you can use underscores (as in main_page.html).

4. Click Save. The dialog box will close, and you'll return to the Document window.

✔ Tips

- You can also click the Save button on the Standard toolbar (**Figure 3.45**).

- You'll see an asterisk in the title bar (**Figure 3.46**) if your page has been changed since you last saved it.

To save all open files:

1. From the Document window menu bar, select File > Save All.

2. All the named files that have been changed since the last time you saved will be saved now.

3. A Save As dialog box will appear for any open files that have not been named and saved. Save any files you need to save.

Figure 3.43 Type a filename for your Web page in the File name text box, then click on Save to save it. Dreamweaver MX will prompt you to save your file within the currently open local site.

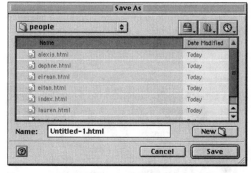

Figure 3.44 The Mac view of the Save As dialog box.

Figure 3.45 Click the Save button on the Standard toolbar.

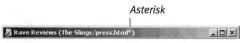

Figure 3.46 The asterisk after the file name in the title bar indicates I've made changes since I last saved the page.

Dial the Right Extension

By default, PCs will save HTML files with the .htm extension, and Macs will save them with the .html extension. If you want to use a different extension, you need to change a setting in one of Dreamweaver's configuration files. (In previous versions of Dreamweaver, you could do this in the Preferences dialog box—now you need to open a file, which isn't hard, but is less convenient.)

To change the default extension for HTML files, open the XML file that defines the document types. You can open this in Dreamweaver or in a text editor. The file's location is as follows:

Windows: C:\Program Files\Macromedia\Dreamweaver MX\Configuration\DocumentTypes\MMDocumentTypes.xml

Mac: Macintosh HD:Applications: Macromedia Dreamweaver MX: Configuration: DocumentTypes: MMDocumentTypes.xml

Near the top of the file, you'll see the following code:

```
<documenttype id="HTML" internaltype="HTML" winfileextension=
"htm,html,shtml,shtm,stm,lasso,xhtml" macfileextension="html,htm,shtml,
shtm,lasso,xhtml" file="Default.html" writebyteordermark="false">
```

Where it says winfileextension and macfileextension, the first item listed is the default file type. To change Windows, list .htm first instead of .html first, so it would look like this:

```
winfileextension="html,htm,shtml,shtm,stm,lasso,xhtml"
```

Save the file, and quit and restart Dreamweaver. You may get some error messages about file types; just click OK and double-check the result in the Preferences dialog box.

To set a default extension other than .htm or .html, just change the preferences. From the Document window menu bar, select Edit > Preferences, and select the New Document category. From the Default Document Type menu bar, select your document type, whether it's ASP.NET, PHP, or ActionScript. The Default Extension text box will show the extension Dreamweaver will add when saving the file. To change this, follow the instructions for changing the default extension for HTML, above.

You'll need to specify any exceptions to this extension by typing the full filename, such as dork.html, when you save a file.

The two most common extensions are .html and .htm. Why use one over the other? I prefer .html. The extension .htm is a throwback to when many PCs (as opposed to Macs or Unix machines) could only read eight-letter filenames with three-letter extensions. Now that that's no longer true, I prefer to standardize with .html.

Saving a Copy of a File

If you want to use a page as a template for another, similar page, you can save a copy of the page with a different filename. Guidelines for using Dreamweaver templates and creating custom templates are in Chapter 17.

To save a copy of a page:

1. Open the page in the Document window, if it's not there already.

2. From the Document window menu bar, select File > Save As. The Save As dialog box will appear (**Figure 3.47**).

3. Type a new filename for the new page in the File name text box.

4. Click on Save. The Save As dialog box will close and return you to the Document window.

The Document window will now display the copy of the file, as indicated by the filename in the Document window's title bar.

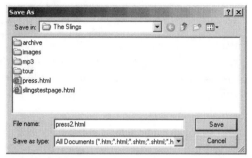

Figure 3.47 You use the same Save As dialog box to save a copy of a file as you do to save it in the first place. In this figure, we're saving the file press.html as press2.html, so we'll have two versions of the same file.

Dreamweaver Templates vs. Copying Files

You may be used to creating a Web page and then saving copies of it over and over in order to create many pages based on the design of the first.

Dreamweaver has a built-in template feature, described in Chapter 17. Dream Templates, as they're called, have their pros and cons. In those templates, you need to designate areas of the page that can be changed. Everything else on the page is fixed, and only those marked areas are editable. These regions may also be used in conjunction with XML.

This is a great idea for locking pages and giving basic data entry work to temps or interns (or marketing). On the other hand, sometimes it's just easier to do it the old-fashioned way and skip the fancy stuff.

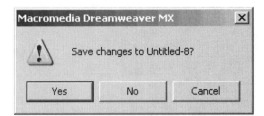

Figure 3.48 To close a file (such as a template, for example) without saving the changes, click on No when this dialog box appears.

To close a page:

◆ Click on the close box, or select File > Close from the Document window's menu bar.

Occasionally, you may open a page, make a few changes, and realize that something has gone horribly wrong. Or you may be fooling around with a document you have no intention of saving. In those instances, you can close without saving the changes.

To close without saving:

1. From the Document window menu bar, select File > Close. A dialog box will appear asking you if you want to save your changes (**Figure 3.48**).

2. Click No. The dialog box and the page will close.

Previewing in a Browser

Although Dreamweaver is pretty much WYSI-WYG, there are some tags it doesn't support. Also, Dreamweaver's representation of HTML is like a cross between how Explorer and Netscape display pages. To find out how your page looks in a particular browser, you need to actually use that browser to view your page.

To view your page in a browser:

1. With the page you want to preview open in the Document window or the Code inspector, select File > Preview in Browser > [Browser Name] from the menu bar (**Figure 3.49**); or from the Preview menu on the toolbar (**Figure 3.50**); or press F12.

   ◆ If the browser isn't open yet, Dreamweaver will launch it and load the current page (**Figure 3.51**).

   ◆ If the browser is already open, Dreamweaver will load the current page into a new window (Explorer, Netscape 6) or into the last-used window (Navigator).

2. To make changes, return to the Document window by using the Taskbar (the Applications menu on the Mac).

✔ Tips

■ Dreamweaver creates a temp file that it uses as the browser preview file. Pressing Reload or Refresh in the browser window may not show the most current version of the file. Instead, you'll need to repeat the steps for previewing.

■ For more details on previewing, and to find out how to edit the browser preview list, refer to the book's Web site.

■ You can also open a saved file on your hard drive in the browser window. Choose File > Open Page from the browser's menu bar.

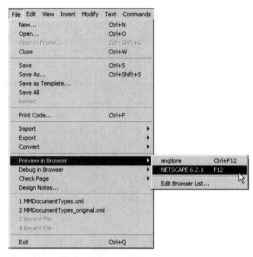

Figure 3.49 Select File > Preview in Browser and then select a browser. Find out how to add browsers to your list on the Web site for this book.

Figure 3.50 Select a browser from the Preview menu.

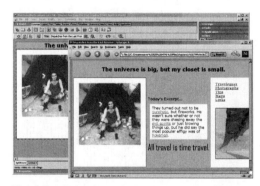

Figure 3.51 Preview your page, at any stage of its progress, in a browser so you can see what it really looks like. In the Document window, visual aids such as table borders are still visible, whereas they are invisible in the browser (unless you specified a border).

Figure 3.52 Navigator 4's Print Preview feature lets you see what you're getting before you send it to the printer. Good thing, because white text won't print on white paper (this page has a dark background when viewed in the browser, which you can choose not to print). You can change printing options in your browser. See the sidebar below.

Printing from the Browser Window

Dreamweaver's Document window does not include a Print command. You can, however, print a file after you preview it in the browser window.

To print a file:

1. Preview the file in the browser window as described in the previous section.

2. From the Web browser's menu bar, select File > Print. The Print dialog box will appear.

3. Verify the number of copies, the destination printer, and the pages to print in the Print dialog box.

4. Click OK. The browser will send the document to the printer.

You can return to Dreamweaver by pressing Alt+Tab or by using the Windows Taskbar (the Applications menu on a Mac, or the Dock in OS X).

Fancy-Schmancy Printing Options

Both Netscape Navigator and Microsoft Internet Explorer offer some convenient printing options. Navigator's Page Setup dialog box (File > Page Setup) offers options for printing backgrounds, black text (instead of printing a background in order to show text), and headers. (On the Mac, open the Page Setup dialog box and select Browser from the Options drop-down menu.) The Print dialog box in Netscape 6 and Internet Explorer (File > Print) lets you choose frame printing options. In Explorer, you can also print a table of all the links on a given page, or print each page linked from that page. And if you have a copy of Netscape Navigator 4.x, (Windows only) you can use the File > Print Preview command (**Figure 3.52**).

Colors and Web Pages

In Web pages, each color you can use is represented by a hexadecimal code, a six-digit number that represents a particular color.

There are many different color selections you can make for your Web pages, including background color, text color, link color, active link color, and visited link color. You can also choose colors for text selections, image borders, table backgrounds, table borders, frame borders, layers, and more.

This isn't even counting any colors that appear in images you add to your pages.

In general, it's a good idea to keep a fixed color scheme in mind while planning your pages. It's an even better idea to plan text and background colors with readability in mind; if you clash yellow text with an orange background, it may look striking, but no one will stick around to read a page that gives them a headache.

System Color button

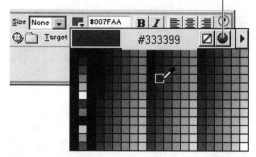

Figure 3.53 Click any Color button, such as the Background color box in the Page Properties dialog box, or the text color button on the Property inspector, and the color picker will appear—then just click on a color to select it. That includes colors not only in the picker but anywhere on your desktop.

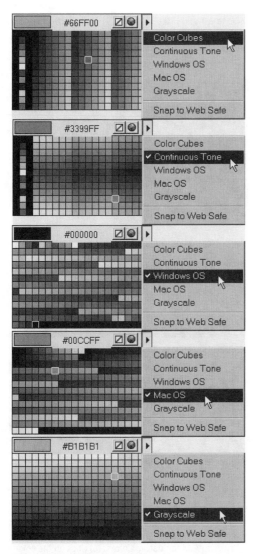

Figure 3.54 Different views of the color picker: Color Cubes, Continuous Tone, Windows OS, Mac OS, Grayscale. Obviously, these all look grayscale in a black-and-white book. Color Cubes and Continuous Tone are Web safe palettes; see the sidebar *Browser-Safe Colors* for more.

Choosing Color

You can choose from millions of colors or only Websafe ones using the System color picker, which you can get to by clicking on the Color Wheel button on the color picker (**Figure 3.53**). Mac and Windows versions of the dialog box are quite different; we'll look at both in detail. Additionally, you can click on the menu button to array the colors in different patterns (**Figure 3.54**). The first two are Websafe; the latter three aren't. See the sidebar *Browser-Safe Colors*, later in this chapter, for more.

Colors and Windows

Windows users have a single, difficult dialog box to deal with, whereas Mac users get seven different user-friendly options for choosing color. Sorry, folks, that's the way it is.

To use the System color picker (Windows):

1. Open the color picker (**Figure 3.55**) by clicking on any color button.

2. On the color picker, click on the Color wheel button. The Color dialog box will appear (**Figure 3.56**).

3. You can choose one of the preselected colors by clicking on it, or you can select a slot for a custom color by first clicking on one of the Custom Colors boxes at the left of the dialog box.

4. Click on a hue (color) in the large colors box, and then click on a shade (lighter or darker) in the narrow panel to the right of that. The combination of your clicks will be displayed in the Color|Solid box.

5. To select this color, click the Add to Custom Colors button. Your color will appear in the box you selected in step 3.

6. Click OK to close the Color dialog box. The hex code for the color you chose will appear in the Color text box.

✔ Tip

■ You can also type the name of a color, such as red or silver, in a color text box.

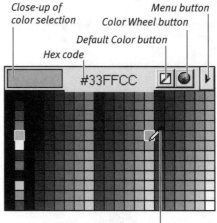

Figure 3.55 Click on the Color Wheel button on the color picker to open the System color picker.

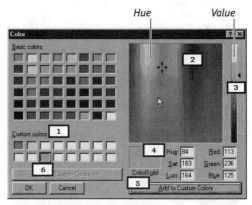

Figure 3.56 The Color dialog box. (1) Select a predefined color, or select an empty Custom Colors box. (2) Select a hue and (3) a shade. (4) click on the Color|Solid box and (5) click on Add to Custom Colors. (6) Click on the color if it isn't selected, and then click OK.

Color-Pickin' Tips

◆ When you open the color picker (Figure 3.55), the mouse pointer turns into an eyedropper that you can use to select a color inside or outside the color picker.

◆ If you have the color picker open and decide that you'd rather not change the color just now, click on the Default Color button to return the color value to default, or press Esc to close with no change.

◆ Read the sidebar called *Browser-Safe Colors*, later in this chapter, to find out more.

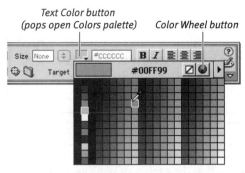

Text Color button
(pops open Colors palette)   *Color Wheel button*

Figure 3.57 Click on the Color Wheel button on the color picker to open the Color dialog box.

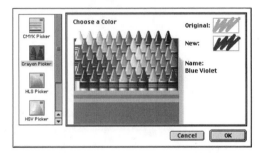

Figure 3.58 The Crayon picker, in the Color dialog box for the Mac. Click on a crayon to choose a color.

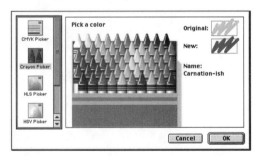

Figure 3.59 If you choose a non-Websafe color when using the Crayon Picker, the name will end in -ish.

Colors for the Mac

The standard System color picker for the Mac looks somewhat different. It offers several different tools for selecting colors: CMYK Picker, Crayon Picker, HLS Picker, HSV Picker, HTML Picker, and RGB Picker. You can use any of these tools by clicking on it in the list box at the left of the dialog box.

You open the Mac Color dialog box the same way you do the Windows one: On the color picker, click on the Color Wheel button (**Figure 3.57**).

Using the Crayon Picker

The easiest color picker to use is the Crayon Picker (**Figure 3.58**). You can choose from preselected colors, all Websafe.

To use the Crayon Picker:

◆ Click on a crayon in the box. The color that you choose will appear in the New color swatch, and its cutesy name will appear in the Name area.

✔ Tip

■ The crayons are all Websafe colors. If you select a non-Websafe color with another picker, a name such as "Carnation-ish" will appear (**Figure 3.59**), indicating an inexact match to the closest Websafe color.

Color-Pickin' Tips

◆ When you open the color picker (**Figure 3.55**), the mouse pointer turns into an eyedropper that you can use to select a color inside or outside the color picker.

◆ If you have the color picker open and decide that you'd rather not change the color just now, click on the Default Color button to return the color value to default, or press Esc to close with no change.

◆ Read the sidebar called *Browser-Safe Colors*, later in this chapter, to find out more.

The HTML Picker

You can select a color in any picker and make it a Websafe color with the HTML Picker.

To use the HTML Picker:

1. When you click on the HTML Picker button, the HTML Picker will appear (**Figure 3.60**) and convert any prior color selection into a Websafe color.

2. To change colors within the Websafe continuum, click on the Hex pairs (00, 33, and so on) on the R, G, or B color sliders. (RGB stands for red, green, and blue.) The hex code will appear in the HTML text box.

✔ Tip

■   To select a non-Websafe color, deselect the Snap to Web color check box, and use the sliders to select whatever color you like.

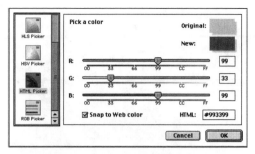

Figure 3.60 The HTML Picker, in the Color dialog box for the Mac. These colors are Web safe unless you turn off the Snap to Web color check box.

Browser-Safe Colors

You may have heard something about browser-safe color schemes. There are 216 colors that both Netscape and Microsoft browsers on both Windows and Macintosh platforms use, and these colors are called browser safe. It's true that nowadays True-Color and High-Color monitors can better match a color palette, and it's also true that today's better video cards can store more than 256 colors in memory. However, Macintosh and Windows still veer apart in their treatment of color palettes. (For a technical discussion of how color palettes work, and the difference between 8-bit, High and True color treatment, see the links page on the Web site for this book.)

At any rate, browser-safe or Websafe colors are colors that most closely match, instead of producing a near match or dithering, when presented on different computer screens. The colors in the browser-safe area all contain pairs of the following numbers in their hex code: 00, 33, 66, 99, CC, or FF. Windows colors are generally slightly darker, whereas Macintosh colors are more accurate and are described as lighter and brighter. If you have access to both Windows and Macintosh computers near each other (try putting a laptop next to a monitor from the other platform), open the same Web page on both machines, and you might be surprised by the differences in many colors.

The color picker that you'll see when you click on any color selection button (**Figure 3.57**), in a dialog box or in the Property inspector, is comprised of these browser-safe colors, some of which repeat in the palette's 252 squares. If you're planning your page around browser-safe colors, the color picker is a good place to start.

Additionally, you'll notice that the pointer for the color picker is an eyedropper rather than a regular pointer. You can use the eyedropper to select any color that you can see on your desktop, including colors in images.

From the options menu on the color picker, you can toggle on and off the Snap to Web Safe option. If you choose a non-Websafe color such as one within a photograph or within one of the non-Websafe panels, Dreamweaver will convert it to a Websafe color if this option is on. That means if you need an exact match, you should turn this snapping off.

About HSV, RGB, and CYMK

The standard color picker that's similar to the Windows Color dialog box is the HSV Picker (**Figure 3.61**). HSV stands for hue, saturation, and value. For those of you unversed in color theory, a hue is a specific named color, such as blue or red; the saturation is the difference between a given tone and the nearest gray; and the value is the relative lightness (tint) or darkness (shade) of the color.

To use the HSV Picker:

1. Click on a color in the color wheel. Your selection will be displayed in the New color box. That sets the hue and saturation.

2. Adjust the slider bar to make the color lighter (towards 100) or darker (towards 0). That's the value.

3. You can fine-tune any of the values by typing a number in its text box.

The HSL Picker (**Figure 3.62**) works the same way; the letters stand for hue, saturation, and lightness. The HSL Picker is not available in OS X.

RGB and CMYK are two ways of measuring color by its components. RGB is used commonly for digital images, whereas CMYK is used for four-color printing. RGB is red-green-blue; those are the primary components of white in visible light, like on a computer screen (as opposed to paint, where we think of the primaries as red, blue, and yellow). The CMYK scale is cyan, magenta, yellow, and black; these are the primary colors for ink, and most color graphics are printed using layers of these colors.

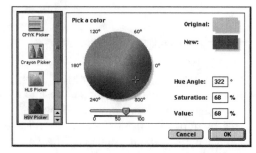

Figure 3.61 The HSV (Hue Saturation Value) Picker, in the Color dialog box for the Mac.

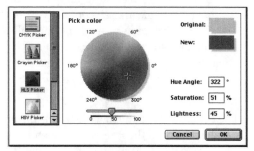

Figure 3.62 The HSL Picker (Hue, Saturation Lightness), in the Color dialog box for the Mac, is quite similar to the HSV picker.

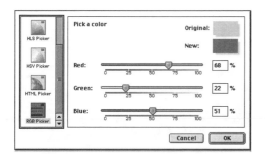

Figure 3.63 The RGB Picker (again in the Mac Color dialog box) uses the Red-Green-Blue values of visible light.

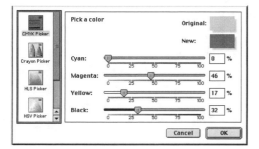

Figure 3.64 The CMYK (Cyan, Magenta, Yellow, and Black) Picker resembles the RGB picker; both are Mac color tools. Printers' inks use these four colors.

In both RGB (**Figure 3.63**) and CMYK (**Figure 3.64**), all colors can be represented by how much of each primary color they contain. You'll mostly want to use these pickers if you have the color values already—from Photoshop or Fireworks, for example. On the Macintosh, these values will be in percentage values rather than numerals.

In any case, you can type values in a color's text box or use the sliders to increase or decrease the amount of each primary color.

✔ Endnote

- That's all the basics. We've made and saved a Web page, and we've learned everything you need to know about Web color. Now we'll go through each set of features and tools in Dreamweaver one at a time.

EDITING CODE

Figure 4.1 When you create a page in Design view, you can drag and drop, insert and edit, without having to know a thing about HTML.

Quick Tag editor

Tag selector

Figure 4.2 Tools like Split view, which shows Design and Code views, and the Quick Tag editor, which hones in on specific tags, can expedite any hand coding.

HTML is the primary language of the Web. A few years ago, you couldn't create any pages without knowing how to write simple HTML code. With Dreamweaver, you can work in the Document window (**Figure 4.1**) to create page layouts and content without ever having to learn the actual code behind your creations. If you're interested in seeing what Dreamweaver does while you're inserting objects or if you like to hand code, you'll find abundant tools to help you do—or learn—the job quickly and well (**Figure 4.2**).

Although no one is going to *make* you learn HTML, knowing what goes on behind the curtain will make you a lot less afraid of the Wizard of Oz. You can fine-tune details and move elements around with much more precision if you become comfortable working with HTML.

The letters *HTML* stand for HyperText Markup Language. *Hypertext* is oldschool speak for "pages that have words that link to things." Now, of course, images and multimedia files can also act as links, and the list of things on the other end of the link has expanded to include any and all digital files.

What, then, is a *markup language*? If you've ever seen proofreader's marks (**Figure 4.3**), that's the basic idea. Each mark indicates what the text should look like in final production.

101

About HTML

HTML evolved from a language called SGML (Standard Generalized Markup Language). In ye olden days of digital book and CD-ROM production, an editor used little pieces of SGML code called *tags* to mark, say, where the italics in a sentence started and stopped. Microsoft Word uses similar tags in its language RTF (Rich Text Format) to indicate the formatting the user creates with buttons and menus.

A tag generally has two parts: an opening and a closing (**Figure 4.4**). The stuff in between any pair of tags is what the tags modify, whether that's text, images, or other tags. Tags generally operate in pairs, like quotation marks and parentheses do, and they can be overlapped, or nested, just like multiple sets of quotation marks (**Figure 4.5**).

For instance, you may have a sentence with a link in it. All the text, including the link, may be included in a paragraph tag. The paragraph may be in a table cell, which is in a table row, which is in a table (**Figure 4.6**). The table, and everything else on the page, is included in the basic tag structure of a page, which tells the Web browser that this is a bona fide Web page and where to go from there.

The browser reads all the tags on a page and then draws the page, filling in the contents and shaping the text based on what the tags have to say.

HTML is an easy language to learn because the tags it uses are self-explanatory for the most part (see **Table 4.1**). P is for paragraph, B is for bold, I is for italic, IMG means image, and so on. Not all the tags are that transparent, but if you follow along using Dreamweaver's code tools as you modify your page, you can pick up quite a bit. For instance, every time you select anything, the Tag selector on the bottom of the document window shows you what tags surround your selection (see Figure 4.2 and the section *Working with Code*).

Figure 4.3 Marking up a page with HTML is just like marking up a page by hand with proofreader's marks.

Opening tag

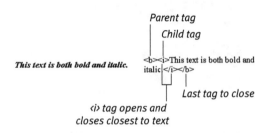

<b>This text is enclosed between an opening and closing tag.</b>

Closing tag

Figure 4.4 This text is enclosed by the two halves of a tag. The tag in this case is the <b> tag, which marks text as bold.

Parent tag

Child tag

This text is both bold and italic.   <b><i>This text is both bold and italic</i></b>

Last tag to close

<i> tag opens and closes closest to text

Figure 4.5 Notice that the tags envelop the text in order. The opening <i> tag is closest to the text, as is the closing </i> tag. The <b> tag envelops the <i> tag in the same way, and is called the parent tag for that reason.

First tag to open (parent tag)   *Modified text*

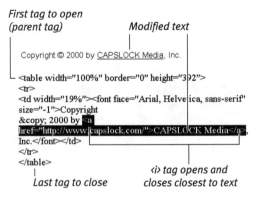

Figure 4.6 The highlighted tag is the <a> tag, which makes a link. The <a> tag includes an attribute, href, which means that it's a Web link, and a value (in quotation marks), which is the address of the Web site.

Head contents

Page contents start with body tag

Figure 4.7 Viewing the source of a Web page reveals the code behind it. From your browser's menu bar, select View > Page Source (or its equivalent command). To save the page for use in Dreamweaver, from the page source's menu bar, select File > Save As.

Figure 4.8 The Reference panel allows you to select a tag or attribute and then find out more about how it works.

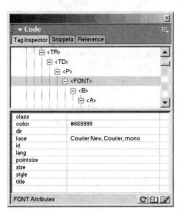

Figure 4.9 The Tag inspector panel allows you to home in on every possible attribute for a tag that's in use.

Learning HTML

The best way to learn about Web pages is to view the source code of pages on the Web that you like. You can save the page and open it in Dreamweaver to learn more. From your browser's menu bar, select View > Source, and you'll get a text window that shows you what's going on behind the scenes (**Figure 4.7**).

A handy tool called the Reference panel (**Figure 4.8**) allows you to select a tag and then read about what it does. See *Using the Code Reference*, later in this chapter.

New in Dreamweaver MX are two code-editing tools, called the Snippets panel and the Tag Inspector (**Figure 4.9**). There's also an improved tag-editing menu you can access by right-clicking (Control+clicking) on any piece of code.

In most chapters of this book, I discuss specific tags and attributes and how they work (**Tables 4.1** and **4.2**). In order to feel comfortable working directly with the code, you need to stop thinking of HTML as a programming language. It's really not. It's more of an electronic shorthand for Post-It notes and highlighter pens.

In this chapter, I'll continue to introduce the basic principles of HTML. You'll find out how to edit pages in the Code inspector or Code view (**Figure 4.10**), as well as in the Quick Tag editor. You'll be able to format the HTML code to your taste using the Options menu. You'll also find out how to clean up HTML mistakes made by software or humans.

Appendix D on the Web site for this book offers copious details about HTML preferences and about using external HTML editors in conjunction with Dreamweaver.

Table 4.1 introduces some common tags we'll be seeing over the course of the book. **Table 4.2** shows you what an attribute is—it's like an adverb that modifies the action of the tag.

Table 4.1

Common HTML tags

Tag	Name	Use	Always Closed?
<HTML>	HTML	Document	Y
<HEAD>	Head	Document	Y
<TITLE>	Page Title	Document	Y
<BODY>*	Body	Document	Y
<H1>, <H2>...<H7>	Headings	Text Block	Y
<P>	Paragraph	Text Block	N
<BLOCKQUOTE>	Blockquote	Text Block	Y
<CENTER>	Center	Text Block	Y
<PRE>	Preformatted Text	Text Block	Y
 	Line Break	Text	Never
<I>	Italic	Text	Y
<B>	Bold	Text	Y
<TT>	Teletype	Text	Y
<FONT>*	Font	Text	Y
<UL>	Bulleted List	List	Y
<OL>	Numbered List	List	Y
<LI>	List Item	List	N
<DL>	Definition List	List	Y
<DD>, <DT>	Definition Items	List	Y
<A>*	Anchor	Links	Y
<IMG>*	Image	Image Paths	N
<TABLE>*	Table	Table	Y
<TR>	Table Row	Table	Y
<TD>	Table Cell	Table	Y
<FORM>*	Form	Form	Y
<INPUT>*	Form Field	Form	N
<SELECT>*	Form Menu	Form	Y

*Indicates tags that usually take attributes

Figure 4.10 The table and its contents from **Figure 4.6** are shown here in the context of the code for an entire page. The first tag on a Web page is <html> and the closing tag is </html>. All visible contents are enclosed within the <body> tag. The <head> tag, not visible in the browser but required at the top of every Web page, contains defining information for the page, such as the language it's in and the title of the page.

Table 4.2

Tags That Take Attributes, with Examples

Tag	Example
<A>	<A href="http://www.nasa.gov"> Mars-2, Earth-0</a>
<BODY>	<BODY bgcolor="#FFFFFF" link="#FF3300" vlink="#CC99CC" alink="#0000FF">Your entire visible page goes here.</BODY>
<IMG>	<IMG src="/images/doggie.gif">
<FONT>	<FONT face="Courier, Courier New" COLOR="red" SIZE="+2">This text will appear in Courier, in red, and two sizes larger than normal text.</FONT>
<TABLE>	<TABLE width="100%" border="1"align="center" cell-padding="10"cellspacing="5"><TR><TD> There must be rows and cells within opening and closing table tags.</TR></TD></TABLE>

Roundtrip HTML

Dreamweaver was designed for use by both codephobes and codephiles. If you never want to see a line of code in your life, you don't have to.

On the other hand, if you know how to tweak HTML to make it work for you, you've probably experienced the frustration of opening a page in a WYSIWYG editor and having it munged to bits by the purportedly helpful code engine of a program like FrontPage. Dreamweaver writes valid code in the first place, and it uses no proprietary tags other than the JavaScript it writes (see Chapter 16). On the other hand, if you want to use mildly illegal code (such as wrapping a single <font> tag around an entire page instead of each paragraph), Dreamweaver can be coaxed into letting that slide.

Dreamweaver will not change the case of any of your tags or attributes, and it does not remove proprietary tags. (Improperly wrapped tags will be marked, but not changed.) Some made-up tags may be valid XML template markup created for a database application (see Chapters 17 and 18). If you write improper HTML in Dreamweaver, however, or if you open a file created in another program, Dreamweaver will mark tags that are unclosed, missing quotation marks, or badly overlapped. Error highlighting may be on automatically in Design view; you can turn it on in Code view by selecting Highlight Invalid HTML from the Options menu (**Figure 4.11**). Click on the yellow mark in either window to read a brief description of the error in the Property inspector. Dreamweaver MX works a bit differently—not all errors are marked in Design view as they have been in previous versions. And unfortunately, Dreamweaver MX missed my extra bold tag here—see *Cleaning Up HTML* for how to catch *all* your boo-boos.

Dreamweaver does have corrective features, which you can modify or turn on (see *Cleaning Up HTML*, later in this chapter). And you can use Dreamweaver simultaneously with an external editor. This group of features together makes up what Macromedia calls Roundtrip HTML. More tips for Roundtrip HTML are included on the book's Web site, in Appendix B. Making Dreamweaver work with external editors is covered in Appendix D, also on the Web site.

Unclosed or extra <center> tag   Extra closing <b> tag (not marked by Dreamweaver)

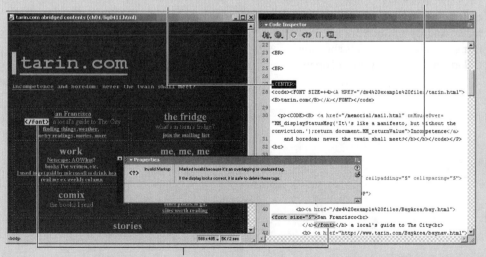

Improperly overlapped <font> and <a> tags

Figure 4.11 If you forget to close a tag, or if you overlap two tags improperly, Dreamweaver will mark the bad tags in yellow in both the Code inspector and the Document window, with descriptions available from the Property inspector.

Working with Code

The Code inspector (**Figure 4.12**) (formerly the HTML inspector) lets you both view and edit the HTML code for a page. The Code inspector displays the code that tells the page how to come together in a Web browser or in the Document window.

To view the Code inspector:

◆ From the Document window menu bar, select Window > Others > Code Inspector.

or

Press F10.

✔ Tips

■ Unfortunate, but true, the Code inspector has been demoted in Dreamweaver MX into the "Others" submenu of the Window menu. Macromedia doesn't believe that people use it as much as they use Code view, but those of us who use laptops or like to look at our code and design side by side (**Figure 4.11**) instead of squished up into one window know better.

■ Dreamweaver's new context-sensitive code editing tools that appear on the Insert toolbar do not work in the Code inspector if Design view is showing, only if Code view or Split view are open.

Line Numbers   *Shortcut menu button for Find and Replace features*

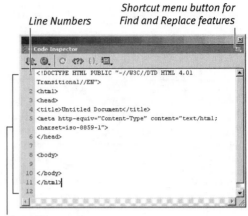

Text editing space

Figure 4.12 The Code inspector is one view of Dreamweaver's built-in HTML code editors.

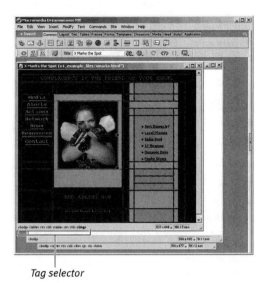

Tag selector

Figure 4.13 When Document windows are minimized within Dreamweaver, the Tag selector appears in the status bar for each window.

Tag selector

Figure 4.14 When the Document window is maximized within Dreamweaver, the Tag selector appears below the file tabs.

<body> <table> <tr> <td> <table> <tr> <td> **<img>**

Figure 4.15 The Tag selector displays the tags surrounding whatever you've clicked on last. Click on any of these tags to select it and modify it. The currently selected tag—img, in this case— is highlighted with boldface type.

About the Tag selector

In any view in the Document window, the tag selector shows the tags wrapped around the current selection, all the way up to <body> (which envelops *all* tags on the visible page). In the Windows version, the Tag selector is in a slightly different place depending on whether your individual Document window is minimized (in which case the Tag selector appears in the status bar of each window; **Figure 4.13**) or maximized (in which case the Tag selector for the currently displayed window appears under the Document tabs; **Figure 4.14**).

Either way, the Tag selector lets you select any tag surrounding the current object (**Figure 4.15**).

About Code View and Split View

Code view and Split view let you view the HTML code for your page directly in the Document window. Code view has the same features and functions as the Code inspector, including line numbers and word wrap. (Ditto for Split view, and with smaller screen real estate.)

The regular Document window WYSIWYG view is called Design view. To view just the code, click on the Code View button (**Figure 4.16**). To view the Code and the Design views in a frames-like split window, click on the Split view button (**Figure 4.17**), which Dreamweaver wordily calls the Show Code and Design Views button.

✔ Tips

- Toggle between Code and Design views by pressing Ctrl+` (Command+` on the Mac). (Buh? That's the accent mark, the one on the same key as the ~, below the Esc key on most keyboards.)

- You can also change views by selecting Code, Design, or Code and Design from the View menu (**Figure 4.18**).

Show Code View button

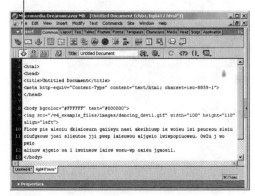

Figure 4.16 To view HTML code in the Document window, click on the Show Code View button on the Document toolbar.

Show Code and Design views button

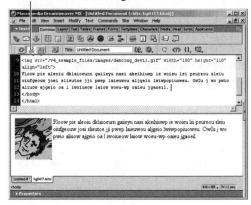

Figure 4.17 To view both Code and Design views— what I call Split view—in the Document window, click on the Show Code and Design Views button on the Document toolbar.

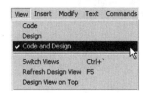

Figure 4.18 The View menu offers the same choices for viewing the page or the code in the Document window. You can also keep the Design view on top of other windows.

Figure 4.19 When I select text in the Document window, the Code window in Split view also highlights the selection. This works the same way if you have the Code inspector open. (If you had Split view and the Code inspector open, you'd be selecting in three places at once!)

About selections

As I described in Chapter 1, any selections you make in the Document window will also be made in the Code inspector (**Figure 4.19**), and vice versa. This of course applies to Code view as well.

Code Options

The Document toolbar and the Code inspector toolbar both include a View Options menu (**Figure 4.20**). The Code view options include Word Wrap, for viewing long lines of code; Line Numbers, for quickly locating a line of code; Highlight Invalid HTML, which marks up bad syntax; Syntax Coloring, for marking types of tags with different colors; and Auto Indent, for formatting chunks of code with indenting. Let's look at each option in turn.

About Word Wrap

In the Code inspector, you can turn on Word Wrap so that the text wraps to the window width. This is soft wrapping—no line breaks are inserted. You can toggle wrapping on and off by selecting Word Wrap from the View Options menu. Unwrapped code is shown in **Figure 4.21**, and Word Wrap is turned on in **Figure 4.22**. For more on wrapping preferences, see *Setting HTML Preferences*, later in this chapter.

About line numbers

When you turn on line numbering, each line of code is numbered in the Code inspector. A line of code may wrap over into an unnumbered line (Figure 4.22). Line numbers can be useful for discussing pages with your colleagues, as in, "Hey, Steph, the table I'm having trouble with starts on line 47." Line numbers—sans wrapping—should be the same in Dreamweaver as in line editors such as vi.

✔ Tip

■ To select an entire line of code, wrapped or unwrapped, click on its line number. Line 15 is selected in **Figure 4.22**.

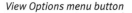
View Options menu button

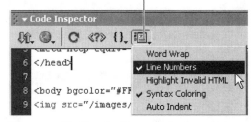

Figure 4.20 The View Options menu for formatting HTML appears on the Code inspector toolbar (shown) and the Document toolbar (see **Figure 4.21**).

View Options menu button

Wrap option unchecked

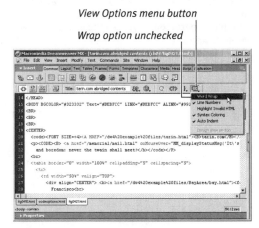

Figure 4.21 I unchecked the Wrap option. Even in Code view, really, really wide, long lines of code scroll offscreen horizontally. Word wrapping is applied to this page in **Figure 4.22**.

Figure 4.22 When text is wrapped, long lines of code, such as lines 15, 21, 23, and 27 here, may wrap over onto unnumbered lines.

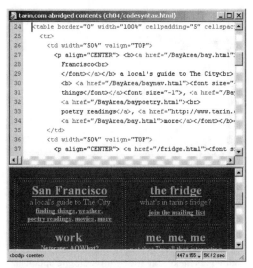

Figure 4.23 Although it's hard to see in black and white, the tags for table elements, tag attributes such as URLs, link tags, and other tags are all marked with different colors in Code view.

Figure 4.24 The tags within this table are indented so that you can find table rows <tr> and table cells <td> easily.

About Syntax Coloring

You can turn on Syntax Coloring so that specific tags are instantly marked by particular colors as soon as you insert an object or type some code (**Figure 4.23**). These colors appear only in Dreamweaver—they won't show up in a browser or text editor. You must turn on Syntax Coloring in the Code inspector's View Options menu in order for Dreamweaver's Reference feature to work properly (see *Using the Code Reference*, later in this chapter). You can toggle coloring on and off by selecting Syntax Coloring from the View Options menu. To pick the colors for a tag or family of tags, see *Setting HTML Preferences*, later in this chapter.

About Auto Indent

As you add code in Dreamweaver, either by creating in the Document window or by hand-coding in Code view, Dreamweaver can automatically indent blocks of code. For example, you probably want your code for the rows and cells in a table to appear indented so that you can spot them easily when checking out the code (**Figure 4.24**). You can toggle auto-indenting on and off by selecting Auto Indent from the View Options menu.

✔ Tip

- To set the space per indent, see *Setting HTML Preferences,* later in this chapter.

Using the Code Reference

Dreamweaver offers tag-by-tag help in the form of a context-sensitive Reference panel. If you want to know what a tag does, you can select it and open the Reference to read a description and some basic rules.

The text in the Reference panel comes from O'Reilly textbooks, which are reliable and well-written.

To use the Reference while working:

1. You must turn on Syntax Coloring in order for the Reference to recognize a tag. In Document window Code view or in the Code inspector, select Syntax Coloring from the View Options menu (**Figure 4.25**).

2. Click within your document (any view) on a tag or modified object that you want to learn more about.

3. Click the Reference button 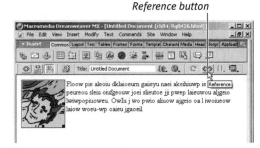 (**Figure 4.26**). The Reference panel will appear (**Figure 4.27**), displaying information about the tag you selected.

To browse the Reference:

1. In the Reference panel, select a topic from the Book drop-down menu. Standard Web topics are HTML, CSS, JavaScript, and Accessibility; dynamic site topics include ASP, JPS, CFML, and SiteSpring.

2. Select an HTML tag, CSS attribute, or JavaScript object from the drop-down menu on the left.

3. To read about additional attributes of HTML tags or JavaScript objects, select an attribute from the Description drop-down menu.

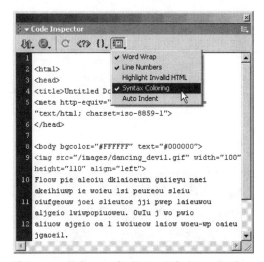

Figure 4.25 Make sure the Syntax Coloring option in the View Options menu is turned on so that the Code Reference's context-sensitive feature will work.

Reference button

Figure 4.26 Select an object or a tag, and then click on the Reference button to read about the associated code.

✔ Tip

■ You can right-click (Control+click) on any tag and select Reference from the context menu that appears. This material is also available in the Edit Tag dialog box. See *Using the Edit Tag Dialog Box* for details.

The Code Reference, Up Close and Personal

Tag description

Browser version compatibility

Tag name

Closing tag required?

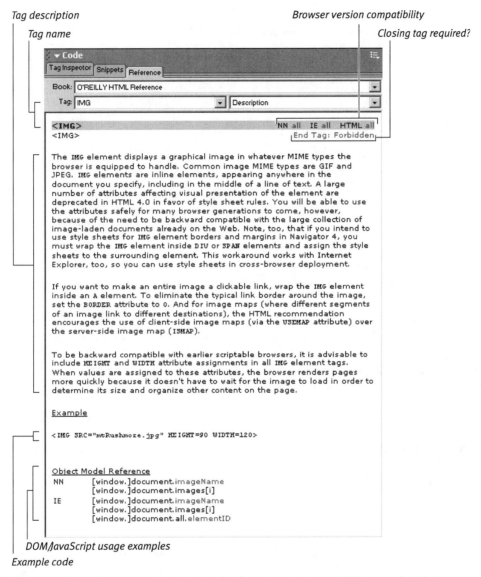

DOM/JavaScript usage examples

Example code

Figure 4.27 The Reference panel provides handy information about most HTML tags and attributes.

Using the Quick Tag Editor

Describing how to use the Quick Tag editor is much harder than actually using it. The QT editor, as I'll call it, allows you to insert or edit HTML code one chunk at a time in the Document window, without even having to open the Code inspector or Code view.

It's true that there are instances when you may find it easier to simply type the code you want in the Code inspector. But if you're learning HTML as you go, the QT editor offers shortcuts and safeguards that virtually guarantee clean code, even if you've never written a line of HTML.

✔ Tip

■ For information on using the Tag Hints menu with the QT Editor or when hand-coding, see *About the Hints Menus,* later in this chapter.

The QT editor (**Figure 4.28**) offers several different modes in which you can fine-tune your HTML. Which mode you work in depends on what item(s) you select (text, tag, object, and so on) before you open the editor.

No matter what selection you make, though, you open the QT editor in one of two ways.

To open the QT editor:

◆ Click on the QT editor button on the Property inspector (**Figure 4.29**).
or
Press Ctrl+T (Command+T).

You'll see a typing area, and the words Edit Tag, Insert HTML, or Wrap Tag. Those are the names of the edit modes.

Figure 4.28 The Quick Tag editor. Pretty unassuming looking, yes?

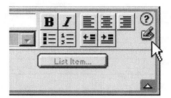

Figure 4.29 Click on the Quick Tag editor button on the Property inspector to pop open the editor. You may not see this button if your insertion point is in Code view rather than Design view—make your selection in Design view.

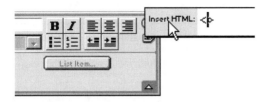

Figure 4.30 Click on the gray selection handle to drag the editor away from the Property inspector.

To close the QT editor:

◆ Simply press Enter (Return).

To move the QT editor:

1. Click on its selection handle; that's the gray part of the editor (**Figure 4.30**).

2. Drag it wherever you like (**Figure 4.31**).

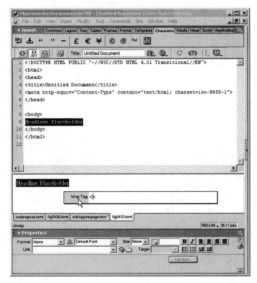

Figure 4.31 You can drag the editor wherever you like.

Working in Wrap Tag mode

Wrap Tag mode (**Figure 4.32**) allows you to select an object or some text and then insert opening and closing tags around it (**Figure 4.33**). For instance, if you select some unformatted text and then wrap the <p> tag in the QT editor, the <p> tag will open at the beginning of your selection and close at the end of it, and your text will be in paragraph format.

✔ Tips

■ You need type only the opening tag, not the closing. Dreamweaver will add the closing tag for you.

■ After you type your tag, press Enter (Return) to wrap it around your selection.

■ In Wrap Tag mode, you can enter only one tag at a time.

■ The editor opens in Wrap Tag mode if you select text or an object rather than an HTML tag.

Figure 4.32 The Quick Tag editor in Wrap Tag mode. Use this mode to insert a tag around some text or another object. Here, I'm going to wrap the <h3> tag around my selection.

Figure 4.33 Now the <h3> tag is wrapped around the text I selected in **Figure 4.31**.

Insert HTML: `<table><tr><td><h3><i>Things we'll take into space when we go</td></tr>`

Figure 4.34 The Quick Tag editor in Insert HTML mode. Use this mode to insert more than one tag, or some code that doesn't directly modify text or an object on your page. Be careful if you paste code into this editor—the default <> that the editor starts out with can accidentally get wrapped around your code. And finally, you don't need to close all your tags—Dreamweaver will close the ones that need closing. I did close the TD and TR.

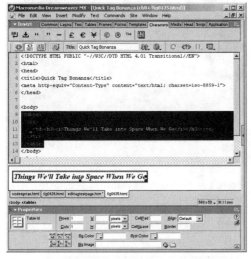

Figure 4.35 The code I wrote in **Figure 4.34** is on my page. Note in the Code view area that I have autoindent turned on and that Dreamweaver nicely closed my tags and indented my table code.

Figure 4.36 If you write invalid code, Dreamweaver will either warn you with this dialog box or, more likely, fix common mistakes and highlight miswrapped tags. This dialog box appeared when I tried to insert code in the middle of the <body> tag.

Working in Insert HTML mode

Insert HTML mode (**Figure 4.34**) allows you to insert as much HTML as you want at the insertion point. You can insert multiple tags if you like.

✔ Tips

■ Insert HTML mode is the default Quick Tag editor mode if you haven't selected a specific object or tag.. Your code will be popped in at the insertion point (**Figure 4.35**).

■ If you insert only an opening tag with Insert HTML mode, the closing tags will be inserted for you if they're required. You can move them afterward, if you like.

■ If you insert invalid HTML, Dreamweaver will do one of the following: close your tags; mark improperly wrapped tags; change incorrect closing tags into the correct tag; omit extra closing tags; or display a dialog box letting you know you inserted invalid code (**Figure 4.36**). Dreamweaver will not change non-standard tags; you can insert <lunch> with impunity if you're using it for XML.

Working in Edit Tag mode

To edit an existing tag, you'll use Edit Tag mode (**Figure 4.37**). You can change the tag itself; or add, delete, or change its attributes.

✔ Tips

■ The best way to select an entire tag, or one of several tags that wrap around the same text, is by clicking on it in the tag selector in the lower-left corner of the Document window (**Figure 4.38**). You can also right-click (Control+click) on a tag there for more options (**Figure 4.39**)—if you select Edit Tag from this menu, the Quick Tag editor will open in Edit Tag mode, as in **Figure 4.37**.

Figure 4.37 The Quick Tag editor in Edit Tag mode. Use this mode to edit existing code.

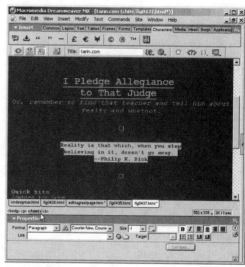

Figure 4.38 Click on a tag in the Tag selector to highlight the entire tag and its contents. This is the best way to select a tag when several tags are wrapped around the same text.

Figure 4.39 Right-click (Control+click) on a tag in the Tag selector to pop up a menu of editing options.

Figure 4.40 I selected just part of the text that's surrounded by a <font> tag.

Figure 4.41 When I open the QT editor, it will appear in Wrap Tag mode, because I didn't select an entire tag. When I switch to Edit Tag mode (pictured) by pressing Ctrl+T (Command+T), the editor will select the entire tag's worth of text.

Figure 4.42 Press Tab to hop to the next attribute or values. (Changes are also applied when you press Tab.) If you pause while editing, the tag hints menu will appear.

■ If you select the contents of a tag, but not an entire tag, the QT editor will second-guess you and select the whole thing (**Figures 4.40** and **4.41**)

■ You can edit the tag itself, or any attribute of the tag. To scroll through the attributes of the tag, press Tab (**Figure 4.42**); to move backward, press Shift+Tab.

✔ More QT Editor Tips

■ When you open the QT Editor, a tag hints menu will appear. You can use this menu or ignore it. Additionally, the menu will reappear if you pause while typing or selecting an attribute (Figure 4.42) or if you type a space after a tag name or attribute. See *About the Hints Menu*, later in this chapter.

■ If you Tab or Shift+Tab after you've edited an attribute, your changes will be applied to the tag immediately. You can pause changes until you close the QT editor. To set this and other preferences, see Appendix D on the Web site for this book.

■ If the QT editor does not open in your preferred mode, press Ctrl+T (Command+T) again, until the QT editor shows the mode you desire.

More Code-Editing Tools

We've already looked at how code selection works in Dreamweaver in its different views: Code view, Split view, Design view, and the Code inspector. We've also taken a tour of the Quick Tag editor, which lets you edit code in Design view.

Dreamweaver includes many other specialized tools for editing your code. These include:

* Context-sensitive code-editing tools, including the Insert toolbar and the Edit Tag dialog box

* Hand-coding autocomplete features, including tag completion and the hints menu

* Three new code-management panels: the Tag Inspector panel, the Snippets panel, and the Tag Chooser dialog box

Using context-sensitive code-editing tools

Dreamweaver tries to guess what you're up to and give you a helping hand. While you're typing code, it closes tags, pops up hint menus, and provides a context menu every time you right-click (Control+click) on a tag in Code view (**Figure 4.43**) or the Tag selector (Figure 4.39). These features may be helpful or annoying—when the latter is true, I'll tell you what to turn off.

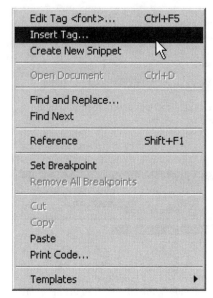

Figure 4.43 Right-click (Control+click) on a tag in Code or Split view to view this context menu.

Code View-only buttons

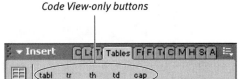

Figure 4.44 These tags on the Table tab of the Insert toolbar become visible when you click within Code view or Split view. Click a button to insert the tag; select some text or code first to wrap the tag around the text. See Chapter 12 for more about tables.

Code View-only buttons

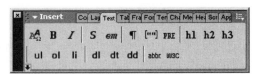

Figure 4.45 These tags on the Frames tab of the Insert toolbar become visible when you open the tab in Code view. Click a button to insert the tag; select some text or code first to wrap the tag around the text. See Chapter 12 for more about tables.

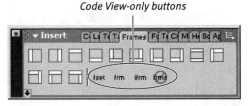

Figure 4.46 These buttons on the Text tab of the Insert toolbar are always visible. Unlike the Property inspector, these buttons don't indicate what formatting is already applied to the text. See Chapter 8 for text formatting and Chapter 9 for paragraphs, lists and other text blocks.

Coding with the Insert toolbar

Of course, every button you click on the Insert toolbar inserts code on your page, but two tabs, Tables (**Figure 4.44**) and Frames (**Figure 4.45**), include buttons that become functional only when you open Code view (but not the Code inspector, unfortunately). For these and the other tabs (such as Text; **Figure 4.46**), you can:

◆ Click a button to insert both the opening and closing tags for your selection.

or

◆ Select some text and then click on a button to wrap the opening and closing tag around your selection.

Using the Edit Tag Dialog Box

The Edit Tag dialog box (which Macromedia also calls the Tag Editor dialog box) provides a handy place to examine and set every possible attribute for a tag, all at once.

To use the Edit Tag dialog box:

1. In Code view, Split view, or the Code inspector, right-click (Control+click) on any tag opener, and from the context menu that appears, select Edit Tag \<tag name>.

    The Edit Tag dialog box will appear (**Figure 4.47**).

2. The General panel of the Edit Tag dialog box includes all common attributes of the tag. This panel differs depending on what tag you're editing (**Figure 4.48**). Make any changes you like to the attributes of the tag.

    See below for more about the other sections of the dialog box.

    Tags that take no attributes, such as \<strong>, omit the General panel inside the dialog box.

3. When you're done editing the tag, click OK to close the dialog box and return to the Document window. You may have to click within the Document window or select View > Refresh Design View from the menu bar in order to see your changes applied.

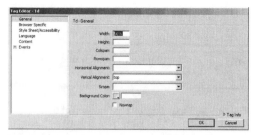

Figure 4.47 The Edit Tag dialog box for the TD tag.

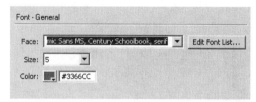

Figure 4.48 The attributes of the FONT tag in the Edit Tag dialog box.

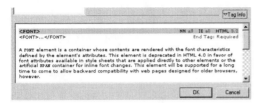

Figure 4.49 Tag info for the FONT tag.

More Edit Tag options

Tag Info Click the expander arrow at the bottom of the Edit Tag dialog box to display information from Dreamweaver's Code Reference (see *Using the Reference Panel*, earlier in this chapter).

Browser Specific Select this option on the left side of the Edit Tag dialog box to view information about how browsers vary in their treatment of attributes for a tag, you can easily check browser versions and apply proprietary attributes (**Figure 4.49**).

continued on next page

USING THE EDIT TAG DIALOG BOX

Style Sheet/Accessibility The least user-friendly of the Edit Tag components offers you space to apply CSS styles and Accessibility attributes (**Figure 4.50**). (When applying CSS styles using this dialog box, type the name of the class or ID in the appropriate text box; see Chapter 11.) The Style attribute, new to CSS-2 as of May 2002, allows you to type shorthand for CSS style and apply it directly to a tag instead of applying a style class. Accessibility attributes allow you to add titles for indexing to nearly any attribute, and additional parameters for elements such as tables and frames. (For more on accessibility, see Appendix C on the Web site for this book).

USING THE EDIT TAG DIALOG BOX

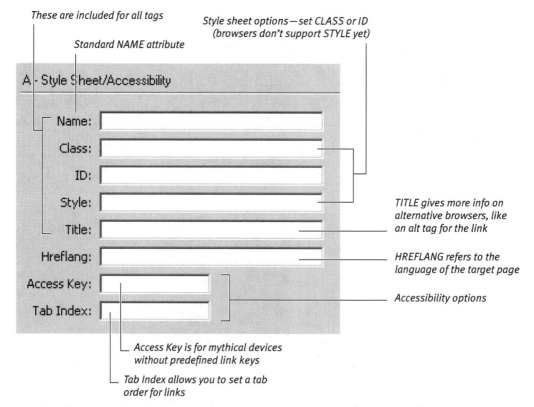

These are included for all tags

Standard NAME attribute

Style sheet options—set CLASS or ID (browsers don't support STYLE yet)

A - Style Sheet/Accessibility

Name:

Class:

ID:

Style:

Title:

Hreflang:

Access Key:

Tab Index:

TITLE gives more info on alternative browsers, like an alt tag for the link

HREFLANG refers to the language of the target page

Accessibility options

Access Key is for mythical devices without predefined link keys

Tab Index allows you to set a tab order for links

Figure 4.50 The A tag has the most text boxes in the Style Sheet/Accessibility area of the dialog box.

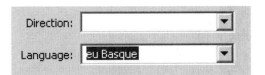

Figure 4.51 The language attribute can be set for any tag, although its usefulness depends on the tag and whether a device will use the information. The direction attribute can be set for right-to-left languages such as Arabic or Hebrew.

Figure 4.52 The content area of the Edit Tag dialog box for tags such as P, shown, lets you view and edit any and all text and code within that tag.

Language (**Figure 4.51**) allows you to set the lang="nn" attribute. This attribute's theoretical uses include indexing by specific language search engines and displaying characters available only in the set language. This attribute's relevance depends on whether you have found a use for it. Applying it to specific tags is at this point discretionary— see the Web site for this book for links to more information.

Content (**Figure 4.52**) For block and block-type elements such as P, DIV, SPAN, TD, CODE, and PRE, you can view and edit the content of the tag, which may include child tags. For H tags, the content is shown in the Header text box on the General panel of the dialog box.

Hand Coding in Dreamweaver

Dreamweaver serves as a full-fledged code editor for all sorts of files: HTML, CSS, XML, XTML, JSP, ASP, ASP.NET, and so on.

When you type code in Dreamweaver, two features track what you type and make suggestions: Tag completion (autocompletion) and Tag hints.

Tag completion

On a blank page or test page, open Code view or the Code inspector and type a left angle bracket: <

The Tag Hints menu will appear (**Figure 4.53**), listing pretty much every dadblasted tag there is. You can select a tag from the menu, but it might be more expedient to keep typing the letter P:

<p

The menu will scroll to the P listings, where your choices are P, PARAM, and PRE (**Figure 4.54**).

Select a tag, if you wish, or complete the tag:

<p>

Dreamweaver will automatically close your tag:

<p></p> (**Figure 4.55**)

Now, when I hand code, I prefer to type my content and *then* close the tag, but here Dreamweaver is performing a public service by making sure that tag gets closed. If you start typing now, your content will appear between the <p></p> tags.

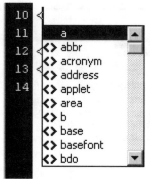

Figure 4.53 Type an opening angle bracket, or less-than sign, and the Tag Hints menu will appear.

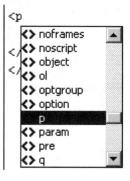

Figure 4.54 I typed the letter p inside the bracket, and the menu scrolled to the p's.

Figure 4.55 I finished typing the <p> tag and Dreamweaver supplied the closing </p> tag.

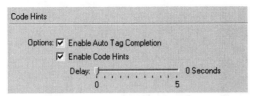

Figure 4.56 Deselect the Enable Auto Tag Completion check box if you don't want closing tags to be supplied for you.

Turning off autocomplete

Is this autocomplete stuff bothering you? Open the Preferences dialog box (Edit > Preferences; on Mac OS X, choose Dreamweaver > Preferences) and select Code Hints from the Category list. Now, deselect the Enable Auto Tag Completion check box (**Figure 4.56**). You can also choose which Hints menus, if any, you want to pop up when you're typing code. See the next section, *About the Hints Menus*.

About the Hints Menus

The Tag Hints menu will appear when you type code just about anyplace in Dreamweaver: Code and Split views, the Code inspector, the Quick Tag editor. It's a regular old drop-down menu. To select a tag, scroll through the menu using the scrollbars or arrow keys, or type a few letters of the tag, and the menu will scroll down alphabetically. For example, type cen, and the menu will scroll to center.

To enter a selection, press Enter (Return), or double-click the entry. Or just keep typing to bypass the menu.

While you're typing, the hints menu will stay until you complete a tag, or if you pause while typing in the QT editor, it may reappear (**Figure 4.57**).

When you type a space after a tag opener, the Hints menu will appear again, suggesting common attributes for that tag (**Figure 4.58**).

If you select the name of an attribute, available standard values for that attribute will appear. For example, the tag <td> (table cell) offers several attributes, including align. If you select the align attribute, the Hints menu will offer left, center, and right as available values (**Figure 4.59**). On the other hand, another attribute of the <td> tag is bgcolor. If you select that attribute, every code for every color will not appear. You'll have to type the hex code yourself, or save your changes and then select the color using the Property inspector.

To make the Hints menu go away, click the QT editor, press Esc, or just keep typing. If the Hints menu doesn't appear when you want it to, I'm afraid you'll have to close the QT editor and try it again, or just type the tag or attribute.

To turn menus on or off, use the Tag Hints panel of the Preferences dialog box (**Figure 4.60**). For full details, see Appendix D on the book's Web site.

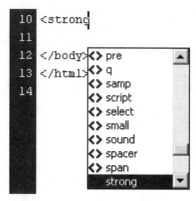

Figure 4.57 Even though I've typed most of my tag, the Hints menu stays open just in case I need it.

Figure 4.58 Type a space after a tag, and a Hints menu of attributes will appear.

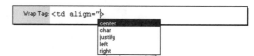

Figure 4.59 Choose an attribute, and type " and, when possible, a menu of common values will appear.

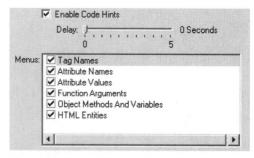

Figure 4.60 You can add delay time before the menu appears and choose which menus to use in the Code Hints panel of the Preferences dialog box.

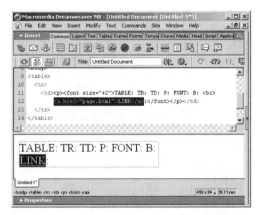

Figure 4.61 You can see in the tag selector that there are seven tags surrounding my link (including the BODY tag).

‹p› tag selected

‹p› tag selected

Figure 4.62 If I click within my link and repeatedly press Ctrl+[, I can scroll through all the parent tags. I pressed the command twice to select the paragraph tag.

Selecting Parent and Child Tags

You can toggle from a tag you've selected with the QT editor to its immediate surrounding tag, called the parent tag (**Figure 4.61**), or to the immediate tag it envelops, called the child tag. This works whether you're working in the QT editor or just in the Document window, but you can't switch tags with the Edit Tag dialog box open. This command has changed in MX.

To select the parent tag:

◆ Press Ctrl+[; on the Mac, it's Command+[.

   or

   From the menu bar, select Edit > Select Parent Tag (**Figure 4.62**).

To select the child tag:

◆ Press Ctrl+]; for Mac, it's Command+Shift+].
This command works only in Design view.

or

From the menu bar, select Edit > Select
Child (**Figure 4.63**). If there is no child
tag inside the selected tag, the tag will
simply remain selected.

Removing a tag

You can also delete tags from within the
Document window. Dreamweaver watches
your back and won't let you remove some
tags; for instance, the **<body>** tag is required.

To remove a tag:

1. Click on the object or text affected by the
offending tag.

2. Right-click (Control+click) on the tag in
the tag selector in the lower-left corner
of the Document window (**Figure 4.64**).

3. From the pop-up menu that appears,
select Remove Tag. The tag will be
deleted (**Figure 4.65**).

⟨font⟩ tag selected

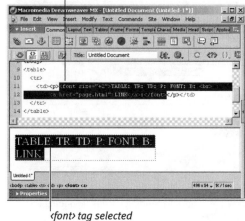

⟨font⟩ tag selected

Figure 4.63 With the ⟨p⟩ tag selected, I pressed Ctrl+],
and the child tag (the ⟨font⟩ tag) was selected. This
can come in very handy when trying to select links,
list items, and blockquotes, as well as text
modifications and table components.

Figure 4.64 Right-click (Control+click) on the tag in
the tag selector, and select Remove Tag from the
menu that appears.

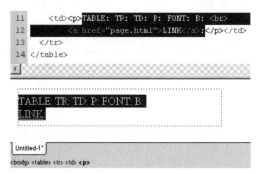

Figure 4.65 The ⟨font⟩ tag that I right-clicked on
in **Figure 4.64** was removed.

SELECTING PARENT AND CHILD TAGS

Figure 4.66 Right-click (Control+click) within some code in the Document window or Code inspector and select Insert Tag.

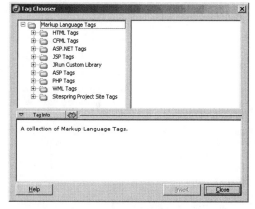

Figure 4.67 The Tag Chooser dialog box offers a choice of several mark-up languages.

The Insert Tag Command and the Tag Chooser

If you want to peruse information about tags as you insert them, particularly if you're setting out to learn HTML or another supported language, you may find the Tag Chooser useful. The one unique feature of the Tag Chooser is the way it categorizes tags. It also lets you take your time looking at different tags, as opposed to the Hints menu or the Edit Tag dialog box.

To use the Tag Chooser:

1. In Code view or the Code inspector, Right-click (Control+click) on the point within your page where you want to insert the new tag. (You can move it later.)

2. From the context menu that appears, select Insert Tag (**Figure 4.66**). The Tag Chooser will appear.

3. The Tag Chooser includes tags for HTML as well as several dynamic languages (**Figure 4.67**). Double-click the folder for HTML or for another language.

continued on next page

INSERT TAG COMMAND AND THE TAG CHOOSER

4. Within each folder, the tags are organized by type. You can view the whole list or the further divisions of General, Browser Specific, Deprecated, and Obsolete. Browse until you find a tag you want (**Figure 4.68**).

5. To view information about the tag, click Tag Info. To view further information, such as definitions of each attribute, click the <?> button, and the tag will open in the Reference panel.

6. To insert the tag (it will appear at the insertion point, where you just clicked), click on Insert.

If the tag is listed with brackets, such as , it will be inserted.

If the tag is listed without brackets, the Edit Tag dialog box will appear and offer you the chance to add attributes and in some cases, content, before inserting the tag.

✔ Tips

■ For more about the tools connected with the Tag Chooser, see *Using the Reference Panel* and *Using the Edit Tag Dialog Box*.

■ I find this tool a bit redundant, but it's a good starting point if you're learning HTML, WML, or ASP.NET in particular.

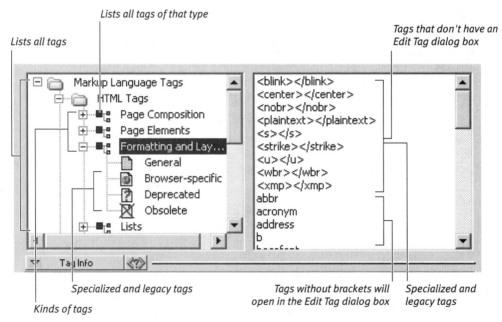

Lists all tags of that type

Lists all tags

Tags that don't have an Edit Tag dialog box

Specialized and legacy tags

Kinds of tags

Tags without brackets will open in the Edit Tag dialog box

Specialized and legacy tags

Figure 4.68 Use the Tag Chooser to browse through tags by category, and further by whether they're considered proprietary (Browser-Specific), on their way out (Deprecated) or Obsolete. Click on Tag Info to find out more.

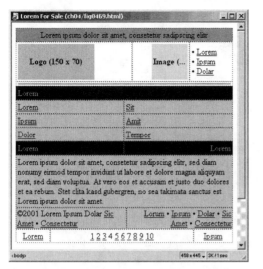

Figure 4.69 This mockup page is made entirely of code blocks from the Snippets panel: a header, a few items from the Content Tables folder, and a footer.

The Snippets Panel

The Snippets panel is a stockpile of reuseable code such as table designs, headers, footers, and form fields. Some are nifty JavaScript tools, such as the Random Number Generator. Some are common design elements such as headers and footers. And if you're short on design ideas or you just want to put a whole page design together quickly, you can use design element snippets (**Figure 4.69**) wholesale and just change the text and the links.

Snippets vs. the Library

This panel is similar to Dreamweaver's Library feature (Chapter 17), with a few major differences. Both tools stockpile snatches of code, but the Library includes only items you create yourself and assign to the Library, whereas the Snippets panel comes fully stocked with prebuilt code to which you can add your own. When you update a Library item, all pages that use it are updated; snippets are not linked to the Snippets panel and no automatic update is included.

Library items, generally speaking, cannot be edited on individual pages that use them. Snippets not only can be edited once you put them on your page, but in most cases you need to edit them before they're at all useful.

Also, remember that other tools exist for similar reasons: Links and colors are already stored in the Assets panel (Chapter 2); entire prebuilt page designs are available from the New Document dialog box (Chapter 2); and you can create updateable templates, which are similar to library items, and also stored in the Assets panel (Chapter 17).

To view the Snippets panel:

◆ From the menu bar, select Window > Snippets, or press Shift+F9.

or

◆ On the Code panel group, click on the Snippets tab.

The Snippets panel will appear (**Figure 4.70**), displaying folders containing named chunks of code.

Kinds of snippets

Snippets are either Wrap-type or Block-type. Block-type snippets get dumped on your page wholesale. Wrap-type snippets (**Figure 4.71**) allow you to insert an opening and closing snippet around selected text. These are a variation on the idea of inserting an opening and closing tag (**Figure 4.72**).

Figure 4.70
The Snippets panel contains blocks of code organized by design element.

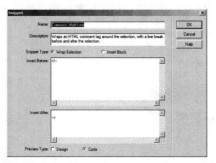

Figure 4.71 A simple example of a wrapping snippet is an opening and closing comment tag.

Figure 4.72 This snippet, which I added myself, makes the selected text, in this case a single letter, take on the specified formatting. The tags open before the selection and close after the selection.

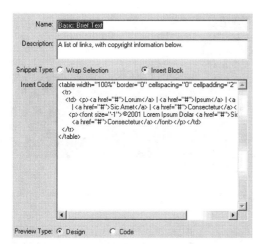

Figure 4.73 Here, I'm editing the Snippet called Basic: Brief Text from the Footers folder. Clever designer, if you like this footer you can replace the dummy text and links with your actual footer content, and rename the footer Real Footer or something.

Figure 4.74 Some snippets preview just Design view.

```
// * Dependencies *
// this function requires the following sn:
// JavaScript/Randomizers/randomNumber
// JavaScript/conversions/base_conversion/(
```

Figure 4.75 Some snippets preview just the code.

To insert a snippet:

1. Locate a snippet that looks interesting.

2. Double-click it or drag it onto the page.

After it's on your page, make any changes you like to the content, the links, the colors, and so on, until the snippet's a useful part of your page.

To edit a snippet that's already in the Snippets panel:

1. In the Snippets panel, select the name of the snippet you want to edit.

2. Click on the Edit Snippet button 🖉 . The Snippet dialog box will appear (**Figure 4.73**).

3. Edit the name and description of the snippet, if you like.

4. Click on the Wrap Selection or Insert Block radio button to change the type of snippet.

5. Edit the code—or paste some of your own code—in the Insert Code text box (or the Insert Before and Insert After text boxes, for Wrap-type snippets).

   If it's a Wrap-type snippet, the Before section will appear before any selected text and the After section will appear after it:

   <BEFORE>selection<AFTER>

6. If you want the snippet to preview in the panel as if it were in Design view (**Figure 4.74**), select the Design radio button. To instead preview code (**Figure 4.75**), select Code.

7. Click OK to close the dialog box and save your changes.

THE SNIPPETS PANEL

135

To add your own snippet to the panel:

1. Select the code or objects on your page that you want to make into a snippet (**Figure 4.76**); or if you want to type it from scratch, don't select anything.

2. Click on the Add Snippet button ![button], or right-click (Control+click) on the text and select Create New Snippet from the context menu of the Snippets panel.

   The Snippet dialog box will appear.

   If you selected some code or objects in step 1, it will appear in the Insert Code or Insert Before text box here (**Figure 4.77**).

3. Follow steps 3-7 above, and be sure to include a name and close all your tags.

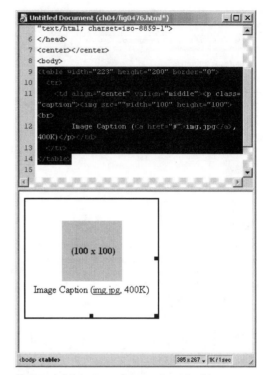

Figure 4.76 Select your future snippet in either Design or Code view.

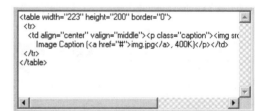

Figure 4.77 The stuff I selected in step 1 appears in the Snippets dialog box.

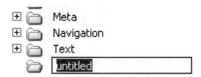

Figure 4.78 Type a name for your new folder.

Figure 4.79 I moved my new folder into the Text folder.

Figure 4.80 You can rename any snippet or folder.

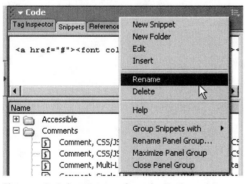

Figure 4.81 Select Rename from the Options menu.

To rearrange snippets in the panel:

◆ To create a new folder, click on the New Snippet Folder button 🗀 and type a name for the folder (**Figure 4.78**).

◆ To move any snippet or folder from one folder to another, just click and drag it to a new location (**Figure 4.79**).

◆ To rename a snippet, click and hold on the name until a text box appears, and type a new name (**Figure 4.80**). Or, select Rename from the Options menu (**Figure 4.81**) and type a new name.

◆ To delete a snippet, select it and click on the Delete button 🗑 on the Snippets panel. A dialog box will ask you to confirm the deletion.

The Tag Inspector Panel

New in Dreamweaver MX, the Tag Inspector panel (**Figure 4.82**) provides a tree view of every single tag on your page. You can both view and edit the tags on your page using this panel.

To view the Tag inspector panel:

◆ From the menu bar, select Window > Tag Inspector, or press F9.

or

On the Code panel group, click on the Tag Inspector tab.

The Tag inspector panel will appear, listing all the tags in your document in tree view.

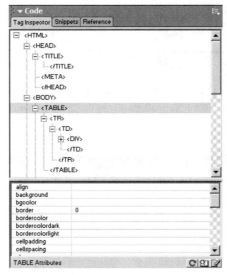

Figure 4.82 The Tag inspector panel lists all the tags and none of the text.

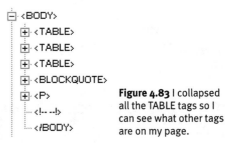

Figure 4.83 I collapsed all the TABLE tags so I can see what other tags are on my page.

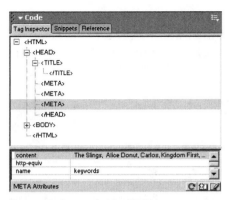

Figure 4.84 I expanded the HEAD tag to examine its contents.

abbr	
align	
axis	
background	
bgcolor	#000000
bordercolor	
bordercolordark	
bordercolorlight	
class	
colspan	2
dir	
headers	
height	
id	
lang	
nowrap	
rowspan	13
scope	
style	
title	
valign	top
width	

Figure 4.85 All possible attributes are listed for a selected tag in its property sheet—this is the one for TD.

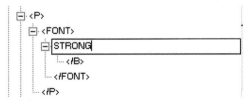

Figure 4.86 To change a tag or an attribute, double-click on it and type something new in its place.

To navigate through your tags:

◆ To expand or collapse a tag, showing or hiding both its closing tag and any tags that appear within it, click on the expander (+ or -) next to it. For example, you can collapse an entire TABLE tag for a more concise view of the rest of your page (**Figure 4.83**); or you could expand the HEAD tag to see what META elements it contains (**Figure 4.84**).

◆ The area below the tag tree is called the property sheet. Click on any tag, whether it's expanded or collapsed, and all its possible attributes will be listed (**Figure 4.85**). Any attributes for which you have already specified values will show that information.

To add or change tags and attributes:

◆ To change a tag, double-click on it, type a new tag in its place (**Figure 4.86**), and press Enter (Return). For example, to change B to STRONG, double-click on a B tag and type STRONG. Brackets will be added.

◆ To add a value for an attribute, click to the right of the attribute and type a new value or, where a menu appears, select one.

Inserting Comments

Comments are invisible notes you want to leave for yourself in the code—they won't show up in the browser window, but anyone can see these comments in the source code. You might want to add a reminder of when you created the file, when you last updated it, or who made the last revision.

You can also use comments to demarcate sections of a document, such as where a table begins and ends, or what part of the document constitutes the footer and copyright notice.

Comments look like this:

```
<!-- You can't see me -->
```

To add a comment:

1. In either Code or Design View in the Document window, click to place the insertion point in the area where you want the comment to appear.

2. From the Document window menu bar, select Insert > Text Objects > Comment.

   or

   On the Common tab of the Insert toolbar, click on the Comment button (**Figure 4.87**).

3. If you're working in Design view or the Code inspector, the Comment dialog box will appear (**Figure 4.88**). If you're working in Code view, you'll get opening and closing comment tags: `<!--   -->`

4. Type the text you want to include in the comment in the Comment text box.

5. Click OK to close the dialog box.

If you have invisible element viewing turned on (View > Invisible Elements), you'll see the comment icon: .

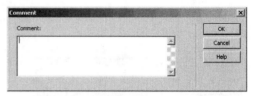

Figure 4.87 On the Common tab of the Insert toolbar, click on the Comment button.

Figure 4.88 Leave a message for yourself or for future producers of the page by using the Comment dialog box. Dreamweaver enters the special opening and closing comment brackets for you.

Figure 4.89 The comment appears in the Code inspector, but not in the Document window.

Figure 4.90 You can view or edit your comment in the Property inspector by clicking on the Comment icon in the Document window.

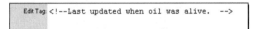

Figure 4.91 You can view or edit your comment in the QT editor by clicking on the Comment icon and pressing Ctrl+T (Command+T).

In any case, you can look at the comment in the Code inspector (**Figure 4.89**) or Code view.

✔ Tips

■ You can view or edit the comments later on by selecting the Comment icon and viewing the Property inspector (**Figure 4.90**) or the Quick Tag editor (**Figure 4.91**).

■ To add comments to a file without storing them in the file itself and making them public, see *Using Design Notes* in Appendix O on the Web site for this book. You can also add comments to non-HTML files this way.

Setting HTML Preferences

If you work somewhere that has a house HTML style guide, it's probably specific about things like indenting (or not), tag case (upper or lower), and how text is wrapped. In production groups, the interaction of individual coders' pages with the entire site and with vi and CVS (two tools used in Unix environments) has a lot to do with these standards. Even if you work for yourself, setting up house rules for consistency is a good idea.

✔ Tip

■ More HTML preferences (including Code Color preferences, Quick Tag editor preferences, and External Editor preferences) are discussed in Appendix D on the Web site for this book. HTML Cleanup preferences are discussed later in this chapter.

To change Code Format preferences:

1. From the Document window menu bar, select Edit > Preferences. The Preferences dialog box will appear.

2. In the Category box at the left of the dialog box, click on Code Format. That panel of the dialog box will appear (**Figures 4.92** and **4.93**).

3. To turn off indenting altogether, uncheck the Indent checkbox.

4. To use Spaces or Tabs for indent, select that option from the Use drop-down menu.

   For more on indenting, see the sidebar, *HTML Code Format Details*, later in this chapter.

5. You can have Dreamweaver automatically wrap text in the Code inspector by checking the Automatic Wrapping check box.

   For more on wrapping, see the sidebar.

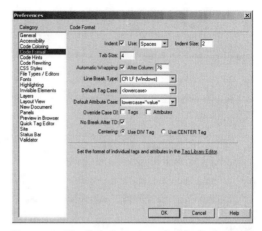

Figure 4.92 The Code Format panel of the Preferences dialog box lets you get nitpicky about how your code is constructed.

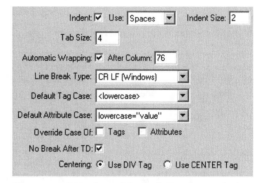

Figure 4.93 A close-up of the Code Format panel of the Preferences dialog box.

6. To set the format for line breaks, select Windows, Macintosh, or Unix from the Line Breaks drop-down menu.

For more on line breaks, see the sidebar.

7. To set the default case for tags and attributes, select lowercase or UPPERCASE from the Default Tag Case and Default Attribute Case drop-down menus. For more on tag case, see the sidebar.

8. You can have Dreamweaver conform to your case options even when you type your tags and attributes in a different case than the one you specified. To have Dreamweaver override your typing for your preference, check the Tags check box or the Attributes check box in the Override Case Of area of the dialog box. You then need to Apply Source Formatting; see the Tips below.

9. No Break After TD means that not every table cell is required to stick to its own line of code. See the sidebar.

10. To set the default tag for centering text, click the Use `DIV` Tag or Use `CENTER` Tag radio button. To go oldschool, use `CENTER`. The `DIV` tag is a block-like tag that's similar to the P tag. These tags are described in detail in Chapters 6 and 14. One note: My preferences are currently set to DIV, but paragraphs whose alignment I set in the Property inspector now commonsensically use the align attribute of the P tag, as in `<p ALIGN="center">`.

11. When you're all set, click OK to save your changes and close the Preferences dialog box.

✔ Tips

■ When you change your Code Format preferences, the changes will be applied to all pages you create in Dreamweaver from here on out, but they won't be applied retroactively to pages you've already created.

■ To format a page using your new preferences, open the page and select Commands > Apply Source Formatting from the menu bar. Your tag case, indents, and so on, will be applied to the page.

■ Previous versions of Dreamweaver allowed you to set separate indent preferences for tables and frames, but in MX, it's either on or off.

HTML Code Format Details

Good code is nitpicky, right? This sidebar describes some of the nitpickier details and rationales for code formatting. Use this sidebar in conjunction with the steps in the preceding sections.

- **Indenting:** By default, Dreamweaver indents certain elements of HTML—the rows and cells in a table, for example. Not indenting may save some download time on very large pages.

  To set an indent size (the default is two spaces or two tabs), type a number in the Indent text box. To set the tab size, because tabs in HTML *are* spaces, type a number in the Tab text box.

- **Wrapping:** To use hard wrapping, check the Automatic Wrapping checkbox. This breaks the line with an actual hard linebreak character after the specified column width is reached. To turn off autowrapping, uncheck this option. (This wrapping is saved in the file and is different from the soft Word Wrap feature you can apply to individual pages by using the Options menu in the Code inspector or Code view.)

  The default column width for text-based programs like vi and Telnet is usually 76 or 80 columns (a column in this context is the number of monospace characters across a window). To set a different width, type it in the After Column text box.

- **Line Breaks:** Line breaks are done differently on different platforms. Because line breaks are actually characters, a line-break character may show up in Unix, for example, if a Mac or Windows line break is inserted.

  If you work with an external editor that uses a specific type of line break, set Mac for Simple Text and Windows for Notepad.

  When using Dreamweaver's FTP client in ASCII mode (used for text files by default), Dreamweaver MX will override your preferences and will set breaks based on your current platform when downloading, and it sets breaks as the Windows entity CR LF when uploading.

  If you work with pages that will be checked in to a document management system like CVS, be sure to check with your house style guide or an engineer to verify your choices here.

- **No Break After TD** means table cells are not required to occupy a unique line of code. Dreamweaver will generally produce each <td> on its own line, but if you want not to require this, go ahead. Your source formatting will allow the following:
  `<td> </td><td> </td>`

- **Tag Case:** Some folks are especially picky about whether tags and attributes are written in UPPERCASE or lowercase.

  To set the case for attributes (the case can be the same or different from tag case), select lowercase or UPPERCASE from the Case for Attributes drop-down menu.

  (Attribute values are always lowercase or case sensitive, as in `<td ALIGN="center">` or `<img SRC="Pansy.gif">`.)

  You can have Dreamweaver override the tag and attribute case for documents that were typed with some of each, produced in other applications, or created before you edited preferences.

  To change the HTML case of older documents opened in Dreamweaver, check the Tags and/or Attributes checkbox in the Override Case Of line. To apply the new case, select Commands > Apply Source Formatting from the menu bar.

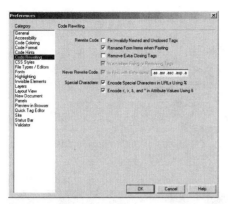

Figure 4.94 The Code Rewriting panel of the Preferences dialog box. Now in Dreamweaver MX the code-fixing is *off* by default.

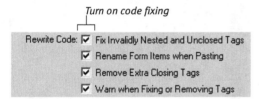

Figure 4.95 Check these boxes if you want your errors to be fixed and if you want to see the prompt in **Figure 4.96**.

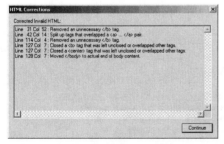

Figure 4.96 When you open a file with errors in it, you can get a prompt like this one that tells you what's being fixed. This is the file that I trashed for **Figure 4.11**.

✔ Tip

■ For more about the other attributes, see Appendix D on the Web site for this book.

Cleaning Up HTML

For the most part, Dreamweaver writes passable, clean code. If you modify the code, Dreamweaver usually avoids changing it back. On the other hand, some applications (most notably Microsoft products) write hideous code that begs intervention from the UN.

Dreamweaver offers several handy shortcuts for cleaning up gnarly code. You may have handwritten code half-smashed on No-Doz and Jolt cola, or an intern may have demonstrated his or her lack of brilliance all over your site, or you may formerly have used a lackluster editor.

Dreamweaver even makes some common errors that are easily fixed. There are three ways to clean up your code: opening a file, using the Clean Up HTML command, and using the Clean Up Word HTML command.

Cleaning up when opening a file

Dreamweaver can make certain revisions to a page when it's first opened—in Dreamweaver MX, these preferences are not on automatically, so if you're a beginning coder or dealing with older pages, you should turn these on.

To modify the auto-cleanup prefs:

1. From the Document window menu bar, select Edit > Preferences. The Preferences dialog box will appear.

2. In the Category list, select Code Rewriting. That panel will appear (**Figure 4.94-95**).

3. To allow Dreamweaver to Fix Invalidly Nested and Unclosed Tags and Remove Extra Closing Tags, check those boxes.

3. To see a prompt (**Figure 4.96**) when Dreamweaver modifies a page, check the Warn When Fixing or Removing Tags check box.

Performing additional clean-up

Aside from Dreamweaver's automatic cleanup functions, you can have it perform more specific code-massaging at any point.

To clean up HTML code:

1. From the Document window menu bar, select Commands > Clean Up HTML. The Clean Up HTML dialog box will appear (**Figure 4.97**).

2. Dreamweaver lets you remove the following boo-boos (**Figure 4.98**):

   ◆ Empty Tags (Lines 8 and 9)

   ◆ Redundant Nested Tags (Line 11)

   ◆ Non-Dreamweaver HTML Comments (regular comments not inserted by the program; Line 13)

   ◆ Dreamweaver HTML Comments (This option removes comments Dreamweaver inserts with scripts and the like).

   ◆ Specific Tags (any specified tag; Line 15). You must type the tag in the text box. Type tags without brackets, and separate multiple tags with commas. For example: blink, u, tt).

   Check the box beside the garbage you want to be removed (Figure 4.97).

3. Even Dreamweaver is sometimes guilty of redundancy when coding <font> tags (**Figure 4.99**). To combine redundant font tags, check the Combine Nested <font> Tags When Possible check box.

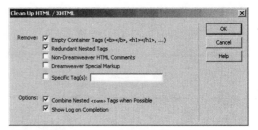

Figure 4.97 Choose which elements to clean up in the Clean Up HTML dialog box.

Figure 4.98 This "page" is really just a catalog of errors to be fixed.

Figure 4.99 The three <font> tags on line 9 can easily be combined into a single <font> tag using the Clean Up HTML command.

CLEANING UP HTML

Figure 4.100 After cleaning up the stuff in Figure **4.98**, this dialog box shows what was done.

4. To see for yourself the errors Dreamweaver catches, check the Show Log on Completion check box.

5. Ready? Click OK. Dreamweaver will scan the page for the selected errors, and if you chose to display a log, it will return a list of what it fixed (**Figure 4.100**).

Nesting Instincts

Valid, by-the-spec HTML asks that <font> tags be nested inside <p> tags. This means that each paragraph contains its own font formatting. This can take up quite a bit of room and add download time to very large pages.

If you want to cheat on this, which the browsers allow, then turn off the Fix Invalidly Nested and Unclosed Tags option. Then, you can use a single <font> tag to modify as many blocks of text as you desire.

Of course, if you really want to save time and not worry about font tags, use CSS to format your text instead (see Chapter 11).

Cleaning up Word HTML

Many text documents, for better or worse, are prepared in Microsoft Word at one stage or another in the production process. Word (95-2000 and 2002/XP/X) offers a timesaving Save As HTML feature that puts in paragraphs, line breaks, links, and most text formatting. But it does it so badly!

Fortunately, the errors Word makes when converting pages to HTML are *consistently* bad. The Dreamweaver team figured out the error patterns and wrote a widget to fix most of them.

To clean up Word HTML:

1. In the Document window, open the page you saved as HTML using Word.

2. From the Document window menu bar, select Commands > Clean Up Word HTML.

   Dreamweaver will read the document info to determine which version of Word was responsible for the damage. If it can't detect this information, a warning will appear (**Figure 4.101**). Your document may not have been prepared in Word; you might want to run through it with the other Clean Up HTML dialog box, as well.

   In any case, the Clean Up Word HTML dialog box will appear (**Figures 4.102**, **4.103**, and **4.104**), perhaps after you click on OK to dismiss the dialog.

3. If Dreamweaver detects the version of Word used to save the HTML, it will appear in the Clean Up HTML From drop-down menu. If not, select your version. (For Word 95, select Word 97/98; for Word XP or Word X, select 2000/2002). You may get a warning that the version is different from what Dreamweaver detected.

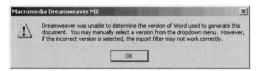

Figure 4.101 This dialog box will appear if you use Clean Up Word HTML to fix a file that wasn't created in Word, or that was created with an ancient version.

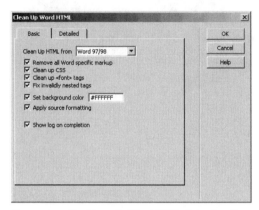

Figure 4.102 The Clean Up Word HTML dialog box for Word 97/98.

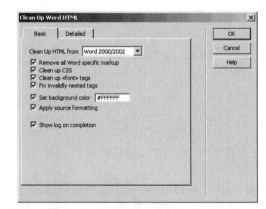

Figure 4.103 The Clean Up Word HTML dialog box for Word 2000/2002. (Word XP and Word X are also known as Word 2002.)

CLEANING UP HTML

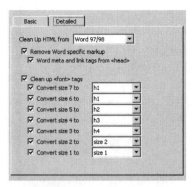

Figure 4.104 The Detailed panel of the Clean Up Word HTML dialog box for Word 97/98.

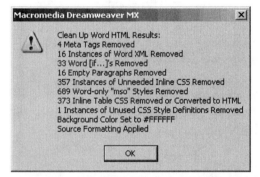

Figure 4.105 This dialog box is a log of the changes that were made using the Clean Up Word HTML command. That's a lot of crap!

4. The following options are available for fixing. For more details about Word-specific markup, see the sidebar, *Detailed Word Markup*.

   ◆ Remove Word-specific markup (tags that aren't standard HTML tags)

   ◆ Clean Up CSS (fixes modifications made using Cascading Style Sheets)

   ◆ Clean Up <font> tags (consolidates redundant text formatting)

   ◆ Fix Invalidly Nested Tags (rearranges tags nested in nonstandard order)

   ◆ Set Background Color. (Type the hex code in the text box; #FFFFFF is white. If you don't know the hex code, skip this one and apply the background color later.)

   ◆ Apply Source Formatting. (Makes modifications to the indenting, line breaks, and case selections. See *Setting HTML Preferences*, earlier in this chapter.)

5. To see a dialog box describing the fixes Dreamweaver made, make sure the Show Log on Completion check box is marked.

6. Ready? Click OK. Dreamweaver will make the selected revisions and display a log if you asked it to do so (**Figure 4.105**).

Detailed Word Markup

Word makes some singular, usually unnecessary additions to standard HTML code when you save a Word file as HTML. If any of this proprietary code is something you want to address on your own, you can ask Dreamweaver not to remove it.

In the Clean Up HTML dialog box, click on the Detailed tab. That panel will come to the front (**Figures 4.104** and **4.106**).

In all versions of Word, the program applies its own `<meta>` and `<link>` tags in the head of the document. If these are useless to you, check the Word Meta and Link Tags from `<head>` checkbox (**Figure 4.107**).

◆ **Word 97/98:** Word 97 and 98 make peculiar choices when it comes to font sizes. To convert Word's font size choices to your own, click the check box for the font size, and then select a heading size or font size from the associated drop-down menu. For example, a wise choice would be to assign size 3 text to the default size in Dreamweaver. If you want to keep Word's size assignment, select Don't Change.

◆ **Word 2000/2002:** Word is getting ahead of itself in using XML, or in other words, it includes proprietary code for perfectly vanilla HTML functions. It also makes a few more boo-boos.

To remove XML from the opening `<html>` document tag, check that box.

To remove other Word HTML markup (in the form of proprietary tags), check the Word XML Markup checkbox.

To remove pseudo-code, check the `<![if …]><![endif]>` Conditional Tags and Their Contents checkbox.

To remove both empty paragraphs and extra margins, check that box.

Word writes CSS code that's both great and awful. Any Word paragraph styles will be saved as CSS styles and applied; that's fine. But Word applied 1,983 lines of style definitions to a relatively uncomplicated page I saved in XP, making the document weigh in at 88K without any images. To clean up CSS, it's best to leave all the check boxes checked, and even then you may want to strip out more styles using the CSS Styles panel.

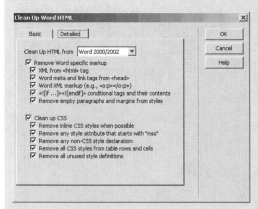

Figure 4.106 The Detailed panel of the Clean Up Word HTML dialog box for Word 2000/2002.

Figure 4.107 Word inserted these META and XML tags; the two META NAME tags will be removed, as will all the extraneous XML markup. You may find these tags useful for importing documents; if so, uncheck the XML check box.

WORKING WITH IMAGES

Figure 5.1 The splash page for Christian Cosas's personal home page uses a simple image against a plain background. Both the image and the text link point to the site's table of contents, shown in **Figure 5.2**.

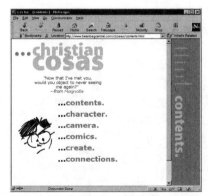

Figure 5.2 The site includes linked images—the words are all image files. With 11 images on the page including the background, the whole page weighs in at only 27K.

Most basic Web pages are composed of a combination of text, links, and images. Used to be, if you found an image online, you had to download it, get offline, and then open the image in a viewing program. That all seems like ancient history these days.

Now that images are easy to use, some Web pages use them at the expense of their visitors' taste and time. **Figures 5.1** and **5.2** show Christian Cosas's site, which makes excellent use of images.

How do you use images well? By making them an integral part of the design of the page, and not by adding them willy-nilly. We've all seen pages with dancing chili peppers sitting beside headlines for no apparent reason—not so good.

In this chapter, we'll find out how to place an image, how to resize it, and how to add a border. We'll discuss image file formats and image alignment, as well as how to make images work with slow connections. And we'll find out about integrating external editors—including Fireworks—with Dreamweaver, so that you can easily edit images while you're making pages.

✔ Tips

- To find out about using background images, refer to Chapter 3.

- For instructions on making an image map, see Appendix A on the Web site.

151

Placing an Image

There are several ways to place images onto Web pages using Dreamweaver.

To place an image:

1. With the desired page open in the Document window, click at the place on the page where you'd like the image to appear.

2. From the menu bar, select Insert > Image (**Figure 5.3**).

   or

   Click on the Image button in the Common tab of the Insert toolbar (**Figure 5.4**).

   or

   Press Ctrl+Alt+I (Command+Option+I).

   Regardless of the method, the Select Image Source dialog box will appear (**Figures 5.5** and **5.6**).

3. If you know the location of the image on the Web or on your computer, type it in the URL text box.

   or

   Browse through the files and folders on your computer until you find the image file. Click on the image file's icon or file name, so that its name appears in the File name text box.

4. Click OK (Open/Choose) to close the Select Image Source dialog box. The image will appear at the insertion point in the Document window.

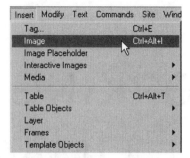

Figure 5.3 Select Insert > Image from the menu bar.

Figure 5.4 Click the Image button in the Common tab on the Insert toolbar.

Figure 5.5 The Select Image Source dialog box is similar to the familiar Open dialog box. If you click on a filename, a preview of the image is displayed.

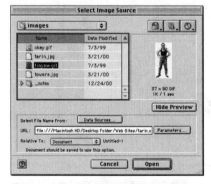

Figure 5.6 The Select Image Source dialog box on the Mac. Click the Show/Hide Preview button to show or hide the image preview.

PLACING AN IMAGE

Definitions

A *splash page* (**Figure 5.1**) is what you call an opening screen that leads in to the rest of a site. Not essential, the splash page should be simple, load quickly, and show you what the point of a site is. A *home page*, on the other hand (**Figure 5.2**), generally serves as a table of contents for the main sections of a site.

SVG, CML, ETC

In the near future you'll probably be hearing more about SVG, which stands for scalable vector graphics. (CML is the Chemical Markup Language, which scientists have used to create 3-D molecular models that you can view with a regular browser.) These images actually consist of a few vector graphics, similar to PNGs or Flash, in combination with specific XML applications that allow the images to be manipulated in the browser window.

Using a combination of image files and XML documents, developers can create 3-D graphic applications that use much less computer overhead than VRML of old.

Currently these can be produced by programs such as Adobe Illustrator using the SVG Export plug-in, and viewed by current browsers using a plug-in for the MIME type "`image/svg+xml`".More information can be found in the Links section on this book's Web site.

✔ Tips

■ If you haven't yet saved your page, a dialog box will appear telling you about file pathnames. Click OK to close this dialog box. Ideally, you should select images from your local site, or you can copy them there. (When you place an image that isn't in your site, a dialog box may appear asking if you want to move that image file into a folder in your site. You can say OK and save a copy there or you can move the file itself on your own to save disk space.) If you haven't yet set up a local site, see Chapter 2. Pathnames are described further in Chapter 6.

■ As with everything else on a Web page, the page starts at the upper-left corner of the window. For more control over page layout, use tables (Chapter 12) or layers (Chapter 14).

PLACING AN IMAGE

Inserting Images with the Assets Panel

Dreamweaver offers a handy tool for managing images and other media objects, called the Assets panel (**Figure 5.7**). I introduced you to the Assets panel in Chapter 2, which is where you'll find a full description of how this time-saving tool works, including how to catalog Favorites. Right now, I'll show you how to insert a simple image with the Assets panel.

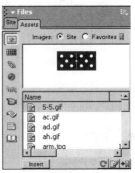

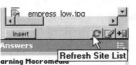

Figure 5.7 The Assets panel can catalog all the images in your local site, no matter what folder they're in. Each local site will display different assets.

✔ Tip

■ In order for the Assets panel to catalog your images, you must create a local site with a site cache. This is discussed in Chapter 2.

Figure 5.8 To update the list of images in your site, click the Refresh button.

To place an image asset:

1. Open the local site in which your images are located by selecting the name of the site from the Site panel menu bar.

2. Open the Assets panel by selecting Window > Assets from the menu bar (or press F11). The Assets panel will appear (Figure 5.7).

Figure 5.9 Click on the name of any image listed in the Assets panel to see a preview of the image.

3. Click the Images button at the left ⊞ to display your images. You may need to refresh the view of the images cataloged in your site by clicking the Refresh button (**Figure 5.8**).

4. To view a preview of any image in the Assets panel, click on its name. A preview will appear (**Figure 5.9**).

5. To place a selected image, simply drag it onto the page (**Figure 5.10**), from either the list box or the image preview panel. You can also click the Insert button to place the selected image.

Select image

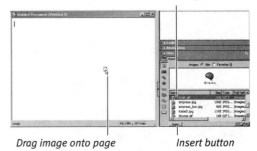

Drag image onto page   *Insert button*

Figure 5.10 Click the Insert button to insert the selected image, or simply drag it onto the page where you want it to appear.

Figure 5.11 When you select an image, boxes called handles will appear in the lower-right corner of the image.

Figure 5.12 The Property inspector, displaying properties for the currently selected image. Note that the Property icon is a tiny thumbnail of the selected image.

Figure 5.13 When multiple images are selected, they appear highlighted in gray, and handles are not visible.

Selecting an Image

When you insert an image using Dreamweaver, it will remain selected, but you'll need to select an image any time you want to work with it.

When you select an image with Dreamweaver, boxes called *handles* will appear in the lower-right corner of the image (**Figure 5.11**), which you can use to resize the image. Also, a preview of the image will appear in the Property inspector (**Figure 5.12**). This image preview acts as the Apply button on Windows machines.

To select/deselect an image:

◆ To select an image, just click on it.

◆ To deselect an image, click in any other part of the Document window.

◆ To select multiple images, hold down the Shift key while you click on each image (**Figure 5.13**), or drag the cursor over multiple images.

✔ Tips

■ When an image is selected, you can copy, cut, delete, or paste over it, just as you do with text in a word processor. All of these commands are available from the Edit menu or the Standard toolbar.

■ Double-click on an image to make the Select Image Source dialog box appear.

■ Double-click on an image in the Assets panel to launch an image editor.

■ If you want to replace one image with a different image, drag the Src Point to File icon 🌐 in the Property inspector to a different image file in the Site window. See Chapters 6 and 19 for more about linking in the Site window.

The Property Inspector

As with most objects in Dreamweaver, the Property inspector (**Figure 5.14**) displays properties specific to images when an image is selected.

To use the Property inspector:

1. Display the Property inspector, if it isn't already visible, by selecting Modify > Selection Properties from the menu bar.

2. Select the image whose properties you'd like to investigate. The Property inspector will display properties for that image, with a thumbnail of the image appearing as the Property icon.

3. To display all the image properties that the inspector has to offer, click on the expander arrow in the bottom-right corner of the inspector (**Figure 5.15**).

✔ Tip

- You can also display the Property inspector by double-clicking the image. If the Select Image Source dialog box appears, click on Cancel.

Expander arrow

Figure 5.14 When an image is selected, the Property inspector will display the image properties. A thumbnail of the image will appear as the Property icon.

Figure 5.15 Click on the Expander arrow in the bottom-right corner of the Property inspector (look at the pointer in **Figure 5.14**) to display the full set of Image properties.

What *Not* to Do

Images can add information to a page, or you can use a Web page as a vehicle to display important images such as artwork, product illustrations, or portraits. Images can also be put to good use for buttons and logos (as in Figures 5.1 and 5.2, where the links and titles are all images rather than HTML text). On the other hand, images aren't essential to good page design, and extraneous images can make a page downright impossible to look at. **Figure 5.16** shows a page that uses images capably to add information to the page. The page in **Figure 5.17** could do without any of the images on it.

Figure 5.16 The Web site for Maximag.com uses images for buttons and logos, and the page has a solid design. Note how the image buttons are all the same size and use the same basic look as the titles.

Figure 5.17 Avoid graphics with no obvious purpose, informational, aesthetic, or otherwise. Note the extraneous bullets, the gangs of horizontal rules, the icons whose backgrounds clash with the page background, the mismatched navigation buttons, and the icky "under construction" signs.

Image Formats

Most Web browsers display two image formats: CompuServe GIF (known as simply GIF) and JPEG (also called JPG). Dreamweaver also supports a relatively new image format called PNG. (PNG has been around for over five years, but regardless of its wonderful properties, most people continue to use GIFs for graphics.)

If you've got digitized images that you want to use in your pages, but they're in a format other than GIF, JPEG, or PNG, you need to use an image-editing program to convert them to the proper format before you can put them on your page. (Generally, you can do this by selecting File > Save As or File > Export from the image editor's menu bar.)

JPEG & GIF: What's the diff?

The JPEG format (**Figure 5.18**) was designed for digitized color photographs. JPEGs can support millions of colors, and they're best used when that's what you need. JPEGs are what's called a "lossy" format: the more you compress them, the more information they lose (in the sense of pixels or colors, which can lead to decreases in the sharpness of the image).

The GIF format (**Figure 5.19**) was invented by CompuServe so that folks on their online service could exchange graphics quickly and easily. GIFs support up to 256 colors (any 256, not a predetermined set). GIFs are the best choice for images with large areas of flat color, most nonphotographic images, and some black-and-white or grayscale photographs, as well as many black-and-white graphics.

✔ Tip

- Animated GIFs in the GIF89a format will display in Dreamweaver, although the animation won't play in the Document window. To watch the animation, preview the page with the graphic on it in your Web browser. For information about creating animated GIFs, see the book's Web site.

Figure 5.18 This image illustrates the best use of the JPEG format. It's a color photograph with lots of different colors, varying levels of contrast, and high-resolution details.

Figure 5.19 The images in this little collage are all GIFs. They have in common a limited palette, large areas that are the same color, and very little fine detail. The lower-right image is an animated GIF.

How Do You Say CHEEZ?

Like a lot of computer lingo, there's some question as to the pronunciation of image file names. Although no one says gee-eye-eff, people can't agree on whether it's pronounced *gif*, like gift, or *Jif*, like the peanut butter. (I personally prefer the gif(t) pronunciation.) The other terms are easier. JPEG is pronounced *jay-peg*, like a hyphenated name. And PNG is pronounced *ping*, as in pong.

Property icon

Figure 5.20 Name your image by typing a name in the image text box and clicking the Property icon.

Figure 5.21 Right-click (Control+click on the Mac) to pop up a menu of options for editing and working with image files.

PNG Pong

PNG is a seven-year-old image format developed by some designers who were frustrated by the limitations of the GIF format and the lossiness of JPEG. Additionally, the GIF format is owned by CompuServe, who requires software that produces GIFs to license the GIF patent.

The PNG development group would like PNG eventually to replace the GIF as a patent-free, lossless image format with dozens of new features. But right now, despite its versatility and grace, people still seem to be using primarily GIFs and JPEGs, although all current browsers that can display images can display PNGs. Versions of Netscape or IE later than 4 can display the PNG format. Additionally, users of Navigator 2 or later can download a plug-in to enable PNG viewing. You can find out all about PNG at http://www.libpng.org/.

Image Properties

Once the image is on the page, there are several properties you can adjust. These include appearance properties (dimensions and border), layout properties (alignment, Vspace, and Hspace), and page loading properties (Alt tags and low source).

You can also provide a name for any of your images. This name doesn't show up on screen, but it can be useful if you're planning on working directly with the code, and it's essential for using images in JavaScript or VBscript code.

To name an image:

1. Select the image by clicking on it.

2. In the Property inspector, type a name for your image (all lowercase, no spaces or funky characters) in the Image text box (**Figure 5.20**).

3. Press Enter (Return) or click the Property icon.
   The image will now be named in the code.

✔ Tip

■ When you right-click (Control+click) on an image in Dreamweaver, a context menu appears that offers many options for working with the selected image (**Figure 5.21**). You can adjust different image properties, including the Low Source image and the Alt Tag (under *Page Loading Properties,* later in this chapter). You can also edit the image tag, open the image with an editor, set Design Notes for the image (see Chapter 19), or work with an attached Template (see Chapter 17).

Appearance Properties

In Dreamweaver, the default is to display images without any border, but you can add a border if you'd like.

To add an image border:

1. Select the image to which you'd like to add a border (**Figure 5.22**). The Property inspector will display the image properties.

2. If necessary, expand the Property inspector by clicking on the Expander arrow in the lower-right corner.

3. In the Property inspector, type a number in pixels in the Border text box (**Figure 5.23**).

4. Press Enter (Return). The border will be displayed around the image in the Document window (**Figure 5.24**).

The default border color is black, unless you link the image, in which case the image border will take on the link color (see Chapter 6). You can also drag to select an image and then use the <FONT> tag to set a border color. See Chapter 8 to find out about font colors.

✔ Tip

■ To guarantee that your image has no borders, set the border to 0.

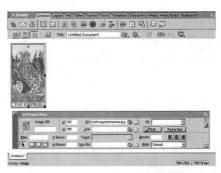

Figure 5.22 Select the image to display image properties in the Property inspector.

Figure 5.23 Type a number, in pixels, in the Border text box.

Figure 5.24 The border will appear around the image. From the left, I used no border, a 5-pixel border, a 10-pixel border, and a 50-pixel border.

Transparent GIFs

All GIFs are rectangular, but some are more rectangular than others. You can use an image editing program to create a GIF89 or GIF89a, which support transparency and interlacing (see the sidebar *Image Size*, later in this chapter). Everything that's a certain color (or colors) in the image will disappear. The trick to making this work to your advantage on a Web page is making the transparency color the same color as your page's background (or vice versa). For obvious reasons, the easiest colors to match are white and black. (To find out how to match the page's background color to an image's RGB color, see Chapter 3.)

Figure 5.25 Type the new measurement in the W or H text box.

Figure 5.26 When the original image dimensions have been changed, the new measurements are displayed in boldface.

Figure 5.27 After I changed the width, the image appeared as shown.

Setting image dimensions

When you first place an image with Dreamweaver, it will have the original dimensions it was given when it was created. It's easy to reassign a new height and width to an image to make it fit into the layout of your page.

To change image dimensions:

1. Select the image you'd like to resize.

The Property inspector will display the Image dimensions in pixels in the W(idth) and H(eight) text boxes.

2. In either text box, type a new measurement in pixels (**Figure 5.25**).

3. Press Enter (Return).

The Property inspector will display your measurements in boldface in the text box (**Figure 5.26**).

The Document window will display the image in its new measurement(s) (**Figure 5.27**).

continued on next page

Drag to Resize

You can drag to resize an image using the three selection handles shown in Figure 5.22, and Dreamweaver will enter the new H and W values in the Property inspector. To constrain the image to its original scale, hold down the Shift key while you drag.

Otherwise, if you type the numbers in the box in the Property inspector, the proportions of the image won't be constrained, and you may end up with a funny-looking image like the one in Figure 5.27. You can turn on the Grid (see Chapter 1) if you want to drag images to fit certain dimensions in pixels, inches, or centimeters.

APPEARANCE PROPERTIES

✔ Tips

- To return the image to its original dimensions using the Property inspector, click on the text box label (the letter W or H), or click the Reset Size button.

- If the browser knows the image dimensions when it loads the page, the page will finish loading faster, because the browser will pre-draw a space of the right size for the image.

- Changing an image's dimensions with Dreamweaver does not change the file size of the image.

- Shrinking an image usually doesn't affect the resolution, but enlarging it may make it look grainy. To enlarge an image, use your image editor rather than relying on dimension settings. The same holds for making large images smaller.

- Although Dreamweaver may re-render the image beautifully, the user's browser may not, and image quality could suffer.

- In previous versions of Dreamweaver, you could specify image dimensions in other units, such as points or inches, and Dreamweaver would convert the measurement to pixels. Although the current documentation still says you can do this, you can't. You'll get instead an error message that says "2in is not a valid value."

- You can specify image widths in percent, as in 100%.

Image Size

When you look at image properties in the Property inspector, one thing you'll see is the image's size. This is a handy shortcut—otherwise, you'd have to use your operating system's file management system to see the file size of the image.

Why do you want to know the file size of your images? Because the smaller your image is—in kilobytes (K), not screen size—the faster it will load. Nothing kills interest in a Web site faster than a horrendous download time, and each image on your page increases that time, so it's wise to keep image size low.

You can see the total file size for your entire page, as well as an estimate of how long it will take to load, in the document window status bar.

What can you do to make images load faster?

- Compress, compress, compress. Most image programs these days have a feature called either Export or Save For Web that includes features that allow you to reduce the number of colors in your image, thus cutting its file size, without losing much visible information from the image. To use this feature in Fireworks (any version), select File > Export Preview from the menu bar, and play around with the options until the displayed file size is as small as you can stand.

- Always specify the dimensions of your image. Browsers will read this information and draw a space for the image, so that the rest of the page can load while it's waiting for the image data to come through.

- Provide a low-res version of high-resolution and other fat images. (See *To use a low-source image*, later in this chapter.)

- Use fewer colors. There are few good reasons to use millions of colors in run-of-the-mill graphics.

- Use GIFs for everything but color photographs and extremely high-color graphics.

- Provide thumbnails. If you're putting art or photographs on the Web, and you really need to use million-color JPEGs, put each large image on a separate page, and provide links to them through tiny, linked thumbnail images (image linking is described in Chapter 6).

- Use interlaced GIFs. This image format will load in chunks. Once all the chunks are loaded, the image will come together.

- Use Progressive JPEGs. Although JPEGs lose information as they're compressed smaller and smaller, you should be able to get by with slightly lower quality and slightly fewer colors, and again, for fabulous photographs, you can offer high-quality images as an option linked from your main page.

Layout Properties

Image alignment is slightly more complicated than text alignment. There are 10 options for image alignment; those options are detailed in the sidebar on this page and demonstrated in **Figures 5.28** through **5.30**.

To adjust image alignment:

1. Select the image whose alignment you want to adjust.

2. In the Property inspector, click the Alignment drop-down menu and select one of the alignment options displayed in Figures 5.28 through 5.30.

   As soon as you select an option, the image will move. Some options visibly differ from others only when combined with other objects.

✔ Tip

■ To center an image on the page, select the image and select Text > Align > Center from the menu bar.

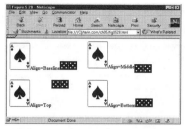

Figure 5.28 Each alignment option was applied to the domino graphic (not the ace). Depending on the option, the domino is either aligned with the largest object in the same paragraph (the ace) or with the text.

Figure 5.29 These options are similar to the ones in **Figure 5.28**. See the sidebar *Notes on Alignment Options* for how these minute distinctions work.

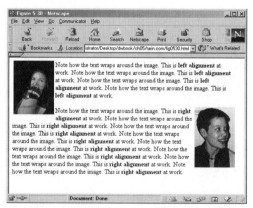

Figure 5.30 Here are the most useful alignment options: Left and Right. Note how the text wraps around the image in both cases; the left alignment applies to the second chunk of text that wraps around the right-aligned image, as well. Left and Right alignment always keep the image at the specified margin of the page (or the table cell).

LAYOUT PROPERTIES

Notes on Alignment Options

- The Default alignment in your browser is usually the same as *Baseline*.

- The Baseline option aligns the bottom of the image with the baseline of the text or the nearest object. A text baseline is the imaginary line the text sits on.

- The Bottom option aligns the image's bottom with the bottom of the largest nearby object, and Top aligns the top of the image with the top of the object.

- Middle aligns the middle of the image with the text baseline.

- Text Top aligns the image's top with the tallest character in the nearest line of text.

- Absolute Bottom aligns the bottom of the image with the lowest descender in the nearest line of text (the letter g in **Figure 5.29**).

- Absolute Middle aligns the middle of the image with the middle of the text.

- The Left and Right options align the image with the respective margin, wrapping the nearby text so that the image stays at the margin.

Adding space around an image

An image can bump right up against text or other images, as seen in **Figure 5.31**. (By default, Dreamweaver places a space between each image.) If you want your image to have some breathing room, you can put some invisible space around the image. Vspace is vertical space, above and below the image. Hspace is horizontal space, to the left and right of the image.

To adjust Vspace & Hspace:

1. Click on the image to which you want to add some space.

2. In the Property inspector, type a number, in pixels, in the Vspace or Hspace text box (**Figure 5.32**).

3. Press Enter (Return) or click the Apply button. You'll see the rectangle of highlighting around the image increase in size when you drag to select it (**Figure 5.33**).

Most likely, you'll want to experiment with the amount of Vspace and Hspace you need on your pages. In **Figure 5.34**, the image at the center has 10 pixels of Vspace and Hspace surrounding it.

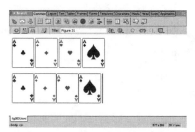

Figure 5.31 By default, Dreamweaver places a space between each image placed in a row. In the second row of images, I removed the spaces to place the images even closer together.

Figure 5.32 In the Vspace and/or Hspace text box, type the amount of space, in pixels, that you want to surround your image.

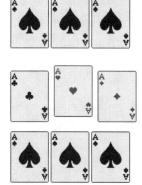

Figure 5.33 I added 10 pixels of both Vspace and Hspace to the image on the right. I dragged to highlight both the image and the space around it.

Figure 5.34 The center image, the ace of hearts, has 10 pixels of Vspace and Hspace surrounding it. Notice how the Vspace affects the entire paragraph (or row): The images above and below it are the same distance from the entire row, even though only one of the images has Vspace added to it.

Figure 5.35
Type the alternate text description in the Alt text box.

Figure 5.36 In the browser window at the left, IE has auto-image loading turned off. Instead of the broken image icon, the user sees the text description, and can decide whether to load the image. At the right are two windows from Lynx, the most popular text-only browser. The upper window shows the page without an Alt tag—all you see is [INLINE] to indicate an image. The other Lynx window displays the Alt tag.

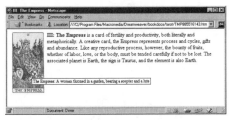

Figure 5.37 Alt tags come in handy even when browsing with images; when you mouse over the image in Navigator 4 for Windows, you can read the Alt tag. (Mac browsers don't necessarily show tool tips; newer versions usually offer them as a preference.)

Page Loading Properties

Not everyone who surfs the Web does so with image capabilities. Some users who have graphical browsers turn off image auto-loading, whereas others browse with a text-only browser. Visually impaired users may use text-to-speech browsers that read the page to them; and finally, mobile users may access the Web on a tiny, text-only screen, or by having their phone service read the page aloud. The only way these users will know the content of your images is if you provide a text alternative, called an Alt tag (even though it's just an attribute of the img tag).

To use an image Alt tag:

1. Select the image for which you want to provide an Alt tag.

2. In the Property inspector, type a description in the Alt text box (**Figure 5.35**).

3. Press Enter (Return).

Users who view your page without image-viewing capability will be able to read the text description to find out whether they want to view or download the image (**Figure 5.36**).

continued on next page

✔ Tips

- Users of many graphical browsers will see the Alt text displayed as a tool tip when they mouse over the image (**Figure 5.37**).

- Unlike a regular HTML entity, the Alt tag can be in plain English with capital and lowercase letters, spaces, and punctuation; and it can be much longer than the tiny box on the Property inspector implies.

- To create an empty Alt tag, for images that present no content, select <empty> from the Alt drop-down menu, or include the attribute `alt=""` in the <img> tag. Images without the Alt attribute are often flagged "Image" by text devices, but images with empty Alt tags are skipped and assumed to contain things like spacers, blocks of color, or bullets.

Beyond the Alt Tag

If you're using an image map (see Appendix A), a button bar, or some other navigational tool that relies on images as links, make sure you supply a text equivalent so that users who aren't loading images can still browse your site. Appendix C on the Web site discusses making a plain-text version of your site, and other ways to accommodate users who don't or can't see images when browsing the Web.

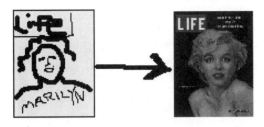

Figure 5.38 The image on the right, which is the image I want to use on my page, is a 21K full-color JPEG. The image on the left, which took me about 10 seconds to make in a paint program, is a 1K black-and-white GIF. The low-source image will load immediately while the browser downloads the larger image. That way, no one has to feel like they're waiting.

Figure 5.39 Another way to use the low source image is to create a simple animated GIF that blinks on and off and says "Loading...". I once thought that this was a scripted icon that actually knew whether the image was loading or not, but it's just a very clever use of the low-source image.

Figure 5.40 Type the location of the image in the Low Src text box; click on the Browse icon to open the Select Image Source dialog box; or drag the Point to File icon to an image in the Sites window.

If your image is larger than 30K, it will take more than a few seconds to load. One option to take the pain out of waiting is to provide a low-source, or low-res, image that will load more quickly. It will be replaced by the regular image once it finishes loading. **Figures 5.38** and **5.39** demonstrate this effect.

To use a low-source image:

1. Use your image editor to create a smaller, faster-loading image, such as a black-and-white or grayscale version of the image.

2. Select the large image for which you created the low-source version in step 1.

3. In the Property inspector's Low Source text box (**Figure 5.40**), type the location of the image, and press Enter (Return).

   or

   Click the Browse icon, and use the Select Image Source dialog box to browse through the files and folders on your computer. When you locate the image, click on its name, and then click OK (Open/Choose) to close the dialog box and return to the Dreamweaver window.

Your selection will not be visible in the Document window. You can try the effect if you preview the page in your browser, although it will be much faster on your desktop than downloading the image from the Internet.

✔ Tips

- When you upload your page to the Web server, be sure to send both versions of the image with the page.

- You can drag the Low Src Point to File icon to the low-source image in the Site window. See Chapter 2 for details.

- For an image from Fireworks, the Low Src option might not appear. Right-click (Control+click) on the image and select Low Source from the menu.

Image Editor Integration

If you want to edit an image while you're working with it, it's a snap. Dreamweaver has full image-editor integration, and you can set Dreamweaver to work with your favorite editor, whether it's Fireworks, Paint Shop Pro, or Photoshop. When you click on Edit, the image will open in the editor, and then when you return to Dreamweaver, your saved changes will reload automatically.

✔ Tip

- If you have installed Fireworks MX, Dreamweaver MX should already be set up to work with its sister program.

To select an image editor:

1. Open the Preferences dialog box by pressing Ctrl+U (Command+U).

2. Click File Types/Editors to show that panel (**Figure 5.41**).

3. In the Extensions list box, select an image extension (.gif, .png, or .jpg, which is listed as .jpg .jpe .jpeg).

4. Click the + button above the Editors list box. The Select External Editor dialog box will appear (**Figure 5.42**).

5. Locate the program file for the image editor (on Windows, it will end in .exe).

6. Click Open to select the program file.

7. Repeat steps 3 through 6 to select more than one image editor.

8. Click OK to save your changes and close the Preferences dialog box.

Step 4: Click + button to add an editor
Click − button to remove an editor

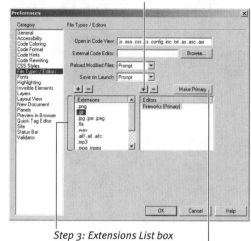

Step 3: Extensions List box

Click Make Primary button to choose the main editor

Figure 5.41 You can set your preferences to work with any image editor so that you can modify images while you're placing them on your pages using Dreamweaver.

Figure 5.42 Using this dialog box—it's just like an Open dialog box—select the program file for your image editor.

IMAGE EDITOR INTEGRATION

More Image Editing Hints

When you want to edit an image, just select it in the Document window and then click Edit in the expanded Property inspector (**Figure 5.43**). The image will be updated when you return to Dreamweaver.

You can choose more than one image editor to work with. For example, you might use Fireworks for most things, but you might also want to use DeBabelizer or GIF Converter to work on specific attributes, like optimization or animation.

If you choose more than one editor, you can make one the primary editor by selecting its name in the Editors list box and clicking Make Primary. The Primary program will open when you click the Edit button on the Property inspector.

If you have specified several different image editors, you can right-click (Control+click) on the image and then from the menu that appears, select Edit With > [Editor Name].

Figure 5.43 Click the Edit button to open the selected image in your editor of choice.

Inserting an Image Placeholder

In some circumstances you may want to insert a placeholder of the proper dimensions in your page design without inserting the actual image. (I've saved this page for last so I didn't have to spend the whole chapter saying "your image or your image placeholder...")

For many different reasons, you may not actually have all your images when you design your page. The files may be coming from a different department, or you yourself might not be done creating them. Dreamweaver MX now offers a simple way to hold a place for an image.

To insert an image placeholder:

1. From the menu bar, select Insert > Image Placeholder. The Image Placeholder dialog box will appear (**Figure 5.44**).

2. To name your image (which you'll do if it's going to be used with rollovers or other scripts), type a name in the Name text box.

3. To set dimensions for the image, type a number in the Width and Height text boxes.

4. To set a color for the placeholder, click the Color button and select a color with the eyedropper.

5. To set the Alt text, type a description in the Alternate Text text box.

   Click OK to insert your placeholder. Dreamweaver will display it in the color you chose, if any, with its dimensions (**Figure 5.45**). Treat this placeholder like an image—cut it, paste it, move it around, drag to resize it.

✔ Tips

- To replace this placeholder with an actual image, double-click it to open the Select File dialog box.

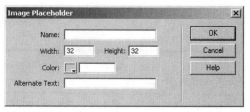

Figure 5.44 With the Image Placeholder dialog box, you can insert a stand-in that will let you flesh out your design even if you don't have all your images yet.

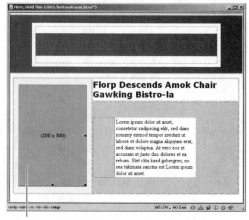

Image placeholder

Figure 5.45 The image placeholder will appear in the Document window with its dimensions proudly displayed. If you name the image placeholder, its name will appear as well.

Figure 5.46 You can set any image properties for your future image—even the source, if you know where your image will live once you have the file in your site. Once you do so, the image placeholder will appear with the famous Broken Image Graphic.

- The Property inspector for image placeholders (**Figure 5.46**) is just like the one for an image, but it includes a Create button (instead of Edit) that can launch Fireworks or your default image editor.

WORKING WITH LINKS

Figure 6.1 This page uses images, a background image, tables, and style sheets, but the real content is in the links. Even if I added background music, Shockwave files, frames, and a flaming logo, the links would still be the meat here.

Figure 6.2 This is the same page as shown in **Figure 6.1,** with all the extras removed. The content remains the same—you can get there from here with nothing but links.

A *hyperlink*, or simply a *link*, is a pointer from one page or file to another. The page that contains the link is called the *referring page*, and the destination of the click is called the *target* of the link. One could easily argue that links, more than fancy typographical or image capabilities, differentiate the Web (**Figures 6.1** and **6.2**) from any of its electronic file-transfer predecessors, including FTP, gopher, and Archie. Although the bells and whistles of the showier pages are what impress the easily impressed and cause the software market to churn out more plug-ins, the fact is that the most important element in the Hypertext Transfer Protocol—that *http* at the beginning of Web URLs—is the word hypertext.

With regular old HTML, you can link your pages to other documents within your own site or anywhere in the world. I say "documents" because you can link to images, multimedia files, and downloadable programs, as well as other Web pages.

In this chapter you'll find out how to make a link, how relative links work, and how to make an email link. You'll be able to link images as well as text. You'll find out how to use the Site window to point to the page you want to link to. And you'll find out about using named anchors to link to specific locations on a page.

Kinds of Links

Before you start putting links on your Web pages, you should be aware of the different kinds of pathnames you can use to link to another document on the Internet (**Figure 6.3**). There are four different kinds of links you can use:

♦ **Absolute pathnames**
(`http://www.tarin.com/BayArea/baynav.html`) point, in most instances, to a location on the Internet outside the site where the current page is located. In the pathname `http://www.tarin.com/BayArea/baynav.html`, the document `baynav.html` is located within the `BayArea/` directory, which is within the root site `www.tarin.com/`.

♦ **Document-relative pathnames**
(`home.html`, `../baynav.html`) point from the current page to another document within the same site, using dots and slashes to tell the browser when it needs to look in another directory to find the page. You can link from one document to another without using the full URL, and Dreamweaver will keep track of what those dots and slashes mean—and it can also make sure your links are correct when you update your site, as long as you make your changes in Dreamweaver.

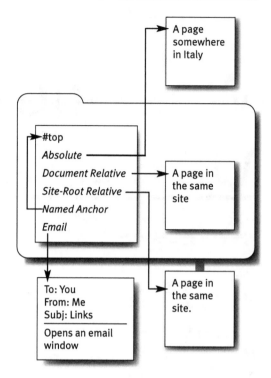

Figure 6.3 For the visual thinkers in the house, a representation of where links go.

A Basic Link

The HTML code for a link looks like this:`<A HREF="file.html">linked text</A>`The A stands for anchor, the original name for links. HREF means Hypertext Reference.

◆ **Site-root-relative pathnames** (/bay-nav.html) also point from the current document to another document that's within the same site. Instead of using dots and slashes to indicate moving from folder to folder, the Web browser starts at the home or root directory and looks for the page from there. If you're constructing a large site in which pages might be moved around outside of Dreamweaver, site-root relative links will still be correct even if the page is moved.

◆ **Named anchors** link to a point within a page; either from point to point on a single page, or from one page to a specific location on another page. See *Linking to a Section of a Page*, later in this chapter.

KINDS OF LINKS

Pick Your Links Carefully

Why use relative links? Why not just include the entire http://ramalamading-dong every time? There are a few basic reasons: One, because Dreamweaver can keep track of your relative links for you and make sure they're correct. Two, because you save time, space, and file size—and minimize the chance of errors—by not spelling out the entire address every time. This includes the browser having to figure out where on the Internet the file is, which it doesn't have to do when the links are relative. Three, if you keep a copy of your Web site in more than one location or if you relocate it to a different domain or server, you want the links to be correct whether the visitor is looking at your page on www.dingdong.com or www.bopshebop.org, and with relative links, you don't need to re-code each page.

More About Relative Links

Everyone knows that a Web address looks like this:

`http://www.site.com/page.html`

On the other hand, if you're linking to pages within the same site, you don't need to include the entire, absolute URL in your link. If you use a relative link, the browser will look for the page within the same site. Then, your link might look like this in the code:

`page.html` **or** `/page.html`

Which is which? The first example is a *document-relative link* from one page to another page in the same folder (**Figure 6.4**). You can also use document-relative links to link pages in different folders together.

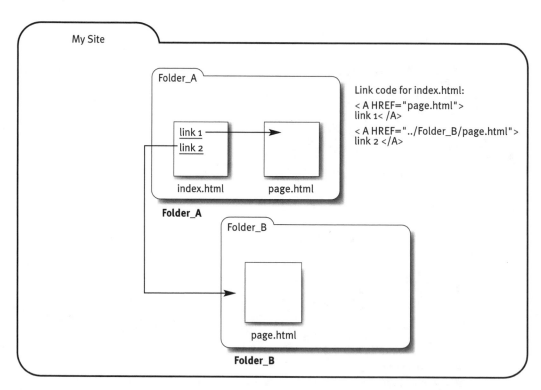

Figure 6.4 Document-relative links can be (A) between pages in the same folder or (B) between pages in different folders within the same site.

The second example is *a site-root relative link* from a page anywhere in the site to a page that's in the main folder of a site (**Figure 6.5**). You can also use site-root relative links to link to pages or images anywhere in your site.

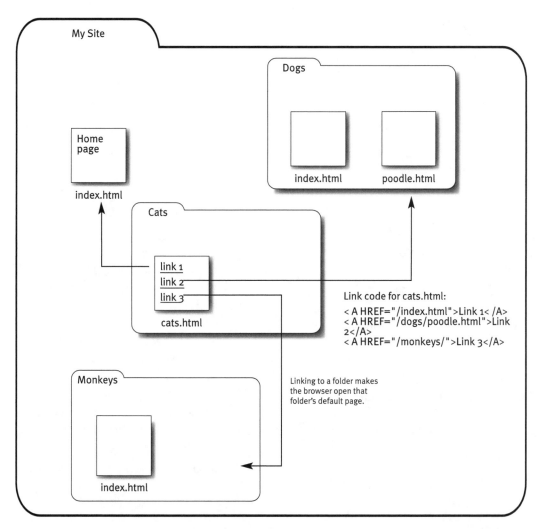

Figure 6.5 Site-root relative links can be (A) between any page and the home page; (B) between any page and a page in a different folder; or (B) between a page and a folder.

In either case, Dreamweaver will do the coding for you—all you have to do is specify which kind of link to use (**Figure 6.6**). Still confused? Here are some pointers:

◆ If the whole concept stumps you, stick with document-relative links.

◆ To link to pages in the same folder, always use document-relative links.

◆ If you're making a large site in which pages might move around a lot, use site-root relative links.

◆ When using media files or images, use site-root relative links.

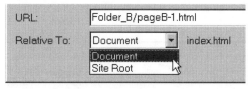

Figure 6.6 In the Select File dialog box, choose whether you want the link to be Site-root or Document relative. See **Figures 6.11** and **6.12** to see the entire dialog box.

✔ Tips

■ If your links are working, don't worry so much about what kind to use as keeping the kind you use pretty consistent. I like to use document relative links for files in the same folder and site-root relative links for everything else.

■ When you link to just a folder or just a domain, the Web browser fetches the default page. Linking to "/monkeys/" or "http://basura.com/" loads the default page in the browser.

■ The default page in a folder on a Web server is usually index.html or default.html. Check with your service provider to see which you should use.

Removing Links

To unlink, delink, or remove a link, highlight the text or image that's currently linked. Then, in the Property inspector, highlight the URL in the Link text box, and delete it. Press Enter (Return), and poof! No more link.

You can also select the link and, from the menu bar, select Modify > Remove link.

In both cases, be aware that Dreamweaver will remove the entire <a> tag—so if you're trying to remove the link from just part of the text, you'll have to reapply it again to the rest.

You can also open the HTML Code inspector or work in Code view and manually move the beginning <a> tag, the closing </a> tag, or both, to change where the link stops and starts.

◆ When you want to make a navigation bar without having to change the links on every different page, use site-root relative links (**Figure 6.7**). This is particularly useful for Library items (see Chapter 17).

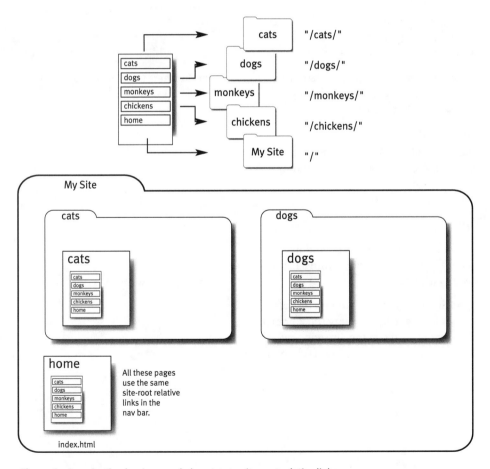

Figure 6.7 A navigation bar is a good place to use site-root relative links.

Making Links

Making links with Dreamweaver is easier than eating pie. You don't even have to remember any keystrokes or use any dialog boxes—just use the ever-handy Property inspector to put your links in there.

To link to a page on the Internet using a full URL, follow these steps. To link to a page within your site, see the next page.

To make a text link:

1. With your page open in the Document window, highlight the text you want to make into a link (**Figure 6.8**).

2. If necessary, display the Property inspector by selecting Modify > Selection Properties from the menu bar.

3. In the Link text box, type (or paste) the location of the document to which you want to link (**Figure 6.9**).

4. Press Enter (Return).

   Your text will now be linked, indicated in your document window by underlining and a change of color for the text you selected (**Figure 6.10**).

✔ Tips

■ The Link text box is also a drop-down menu. Click on it to choose from a list of recently used links.

■ In the Site window, you can link to a file on your local site by dragging the Point to File icon onto a file in the Site window. See *Pointing to a File*, later in this chapter.

Link text box   Browse button

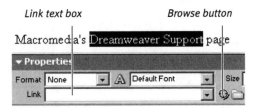

Figure 6.8 Highlight the text you want to make into a link.

Figure 6.9 In the Property inspector's Link text box, type or paste the URL of the document you're linking to.

Figure 6.10 Press Enter (Return), and the text you selected will become a link.

MAKING LINKS

Figure 6.11 The Select File dialog box functions like the Open dialog boxes you're used to by now.

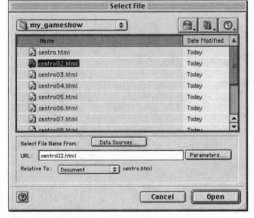

Figure 6.12 The Select File dialog box on the Macintosh.

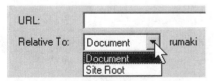

Figure 6.13 From the pull-down menu, select either Document, to make the link relative to the current page, or Site Root, to make the link relative to a central location on your Web site.

Making Relative Links

To have Dreamweaver manage relative links, or links between pages in your site, you must create a local site on your hard drive (explained in Chapter 2).

You can select a page in your local site by selecting a file or by pointing to it.

To select a local file to link to:

1. Save the page you're working on by selecting File > Save from the menu bar. If this is the first time you're saving the page, the Save As dialog box will appear. Make sure you're saving the file in the correct directory (folder), and type a file-name in the File name text box. Click on Save to close the Save As dialog box and save the file.

2. Select the text you want to make into a link (as shown back in Figure 6.8).

3. In the Property inspector, click on the Browse button.

   The Select File dialog box appears (Figures 6.11 and 6.12).

4. From the Relative To pull-down menu, select either Document or Site Root (**Figure 6.13**). If you're not sure which to choose, choose Document.

5. Browse through the files and folders on your computer until you locate the document to which you want to link. Click on the file's icon so that its name shows up in the File name text box. The URL text box will display the link path (**Figure 6.14**).

6. Click OK to choose the file.

The Select File dialog box will close, returning you to the Document window. You'll see your link underlined and the path displayed in the Property inspector.

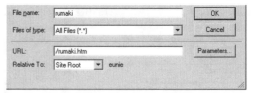

Figure 6.14 When you're all done, you should see a filename in the File name text box and the path to that file in the URL text box.

✔ Tip

■ If you're linking to a page in the same folder as the one you're working on, you can simply type the filename in the Property inspector's Link text box; for example, `contents.html`.

Different Links for Different Things

Except in those cases where you're using a relative link to a document in the same site as the referring page, you always need to specify the protocol type for the link. Even though some browsers can locate sites that lack the http:// when you physically type a URL such as `www.whatever.duh` into the browser's location field, browsers will not recognize any links you click on without a protocol type being specified. When you use relative links, however, you leave off the `http://` and the browser looks for the file in the current site.

Besides http, there are several other kinds of protocols you may use; mailto and ftp are the two most common after http.

`ftp://`   File Transfer Protocol

`mailto:` An Internet email address; launches a mail composition window in some browsers

`gopher://`   Gopher hypertext index

`shttp://`   Secure Hypertext Transfer Protocol, used by secure commerce servers supporting the protocol

`news:`   A Usenet or other network news resource group or discussion group; often launches a newsgroup browser

`telnet:`   Remote access to a Telnet server; often launches a Telnet client

`wais://`   Wide Area Internet Search

In general, if the protocol type is left off a coded URL, the browser will look for a local file rather than an Internet URL.

Image Links

You can make an image into a link, too. Buttons and navigation arrows are obvious examples, but you can make any image point to anything on the Web.

To make an image link:

1. With your page open in the Document window, select the image you want to make into a link by clicking on it (**Figure 6.15**).

2. If necessary, display the Property inspector (Window > Properties).

continued on next page

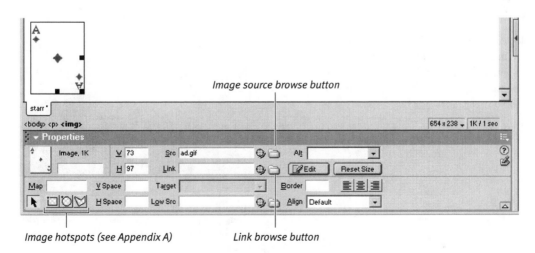

Image source browse button

Image hotspots (see Appendix A)   *Link browse button*

Figure 6.15 Select the image you want to make into a link.

3. In the Link text box, type (or paste) the location of the document to which you want to link (**Figure 6.16**).

Press Enter (Return), or click the Apply button.

or

Click the Link browse button and select the local file to which you want to link. See *Making Relative Links* if you need help with the details.

Make sure you click the Link browse button, instead of the similar button next to the Image Src text box above it, which will ask you to choose an image.

Your image will be linked, and you can add a link border to it (**Figure 6.17**).

To add a border:

1. Select the image by clicking on it.

2. In the expanded Property inspector, type a number in the Border text box (**Figure 6.18**). Try numbers such as 1, 2, and 5.

3. Press Enter (Return), or click the Apply button, and the border will appear (**Figure 6.19**).

✔ Tip

■ Another kind of image link is the image map—that's what those hotspots in Figure 6.15 are for. See Appendix A on the Web site for this book to find out how to make an image map.

Figure 6.16 Type or paste the URL into the Property inspector, or click on the Browse button to choose a file.

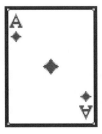

Figure 6.17 After you specify the link in your Property inspector, you can add a border to your image, if you like.

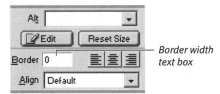

Border width text box

Figure 6.18 To add a border to the image's link, specify a border width of 1 or higher in the Property inspector. Otherwise, specify a border of 0—if you don't, a linked image will have a border of 1 in most browsers. The border color will be the same as the standard link color.

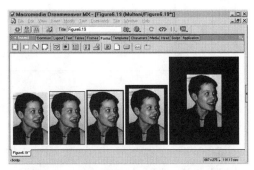

Figure 6.19 Here, the image has, from the left, no border; a 1-pixel border; a 3-pixel border; and a 10-pixel border. The last image has a 50-pixel border.

IMAGE LINKS

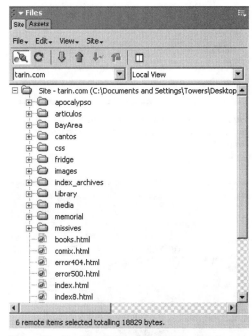

Figure 6.20 The Site window displays the files in your local site. You can create a relative link from a page in your site to any other file in your site.

Figure 6.21 Expand folders as necessary until you find the file you want to link to.

Pointing to a File

Dreamweaver's Site window is a tool for managing your files on both your computer and your remote Web server. The remote stuff is covered in Chapter 19. In terms of linking, though, there's an extremely handy visual tool you can use to make links by drawing a line from your page to the file you want to link to.

If you haven't yet set up a local site, please do so following the instructions in Chapter 2.

To point to a file in the Site window:

1. Save the page you're working on.

2. Open the Site window by selecting Window > Site from the menu bar (**Figure 6.20**).

3. Figure out where the file you want to link to is located, expanding folders as necessary (**Figure 6.21**).

continued on next page

4. Select the text or image you want to make into a link.

5. On the Property inspector, click on the Point to File icon (**Figure 6.22**), and hold down the mouse button while you drag the arrow to the file in the Site window (**Figure 6.23**).

Your link will become underlined, and the path of the link will appear in the Property inspector's Link text box.

✔ Tips

■ When you drag the icon onto a folder, that folder will expand.

■ On the Mac, when you drag the Point to file icon into the Site window, the Site window floats to the top so you can select your link. Of course, to make this easier, you can size your Document and Site windows so that both are visible.

■ You can also change the source of an image or media file by dragging the Point to File icon to a different image or media file in the Site window.

■ If you don't select anything to serve as the link before you drag the icon over, the title of the page or its file name will appear on your page as the link text.

Point to File icon

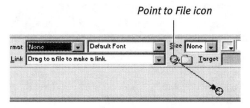

Figure 6.22 After you select the object you want to make into a link, click on the Point to File icon on the Property inspector.

Figure 6.23 Drag the icon onto the file you want to link to. The Site window will automatically float to the top if it's under another window.

POINTING TO A FILE

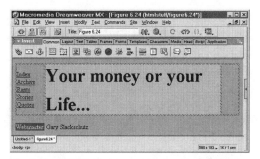

Figure 6.24 Highlight the text you want to become an email link.

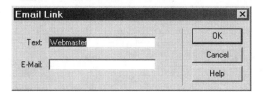

Figure 6.25 Use the Email Link text box to enter your text and your email address.

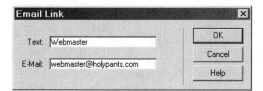

Figure 6.26 Include the full address in the format name@domain.suffix. Do not include the "mailto" protocol or any HTML.

Linking to an Email Address

If you want your fans to be able to contact you, the simplest way is to provide a link to your email address. Email links look like this:

```
<A HREF="mailto:dreamweaver@tarin.com">
send mail</A>
```

You can insert them using a dialog box or the Property inspector.

To insert an email link (auto):

1. Highlight the text you want to make into an email link, or just click the insertion point at the place where you want the link to appear (**Figure 6.24**).

2. From the menu bar, select Insert > Email Link.

   or

   On the Common tab of the Insert toolbar, click on the Email Link button 🖃 . The Email Link dialog box will appear (**Figure 6.25**).

   If you highlighted text to serve as a link in step 1, that text will appear in the Text text box. You may edit it or leave it as is, or you can type new text.

3. Type the full email address in the Email text box (**Figure 6.26**).

4. Click on OK to close the Email Link dialog box and insert your email link.

To make an email link (manual):

1. Highlight the text or image you want to make into an email link (**Figure 6.27**).

2. In the Property inspector Link text box, type mailto:address@domain.com, substituting the proper, full email address for *address@domain.com* (**Figure 6.28**).

3. Press Enter (Return).

   Your text or image will be linked (**Figure 6.29**).

✔ Tips

■ When your visitor clicks on an email link in the browser window, the browser will generally pop open a mail window. You may also want to provide the address in plain text so that people using different software can get the email address easily.

■ Keep in mind that spam sniffers, the robots that go around collecting email addresses, do so by reading mailto: links. You may want to use an alternate email address, or create one on your domain that can filter out the spam. Or you may opt to print your email address on your page without using a mailto: link at all.

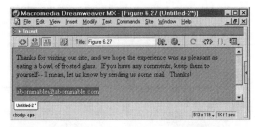

Figure 6.27 Highlight the text you want to turn into an email link.

Figure 6.28 Type the full address in the Property inspector, and type mailto: in front of it, without a space.

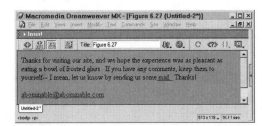

Figure 6.29 Email links look just like any other links: They're underlined and link-colored. I also used italics here. Note that I linked both the word "mail" and the email address, as well as spelling it out for people without mail programs hooked up to their Web browsers.

Always Underlined?

To turn off link underlining on your page or part of your page; and to add the nifty hover effects supported by newer browsers, you use CSS, or cascading style sheets. Chapter 11 tells all, including specific instructions on turning off underlines and managing link colors when modifying the *a* tag.

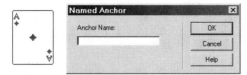

Figure 6.30 Name your anchor with the Named Anchor dialog box. I'd rather name an anchor at this location "aced" than "ace_of_diamonds," because it's easier to spell, type, and remember.

Linking to a Section of a Page

When you link to a specific location on a Web page, it's referred to as using a *named anchor*. A named anchor consists of two parts: a *named entity* at the point on an HTML page where you want your visitor to land, and a *link* to that anchor. Whereas regular old links point to an entire document, named anchors link to a *place on* a document. Very long documents should be broken into separate pages, but there can be cases where you want a clickable table of contents (or something similar) that will direct visitors to an area of a page instead of the top of it. You can also place a link to take users from the bottom of a page to the top (see **Figure 6.36**).

First, you need to name the part of the page you want to link to. You can name a piece of text, an image, or a headline, for instance.

To name a spot on the page:

1. Open the document in which you want to insert a named anchor, or destination, and click to place the insertion point at the place where you want it, or highlight an entity to name (such as a piece of text or an image).

2. From the menu bar, select Insert > Named Anchor.
   The Named Anchor dialog box will appear (Figure 6.30).

3. Type a name for your anchor in the Anchor Name text box. This name should be a single lowercase word or number, for simplicity's sake; don't use spaces.

continued on page xx

What's in a URL?

Your typical Web URL might look like this: `http://www.peachpit.com/`, but then again, it might look like this:

`http://www.macromedia.com/support/dreamweaver/whatsnew/`

or like this:

`http://husky.northern-hs.ga.k12.md.us/`

What's all that stuff mean, anyway?

The `http:` is the name of the protocol, which in the case of a Web site is the Hypertext Transfer Protocol. (See the sidebar *Different Links for Different Things*, earlier in this chapter, for a description of each kind.)

The slashes (and those are forward slashes, not backslashes) indicate something else.

Everything between the first two slashes and the next slash is called the *domain name*.

The www, or whatever is the first "word" in a URL following the slashes, is the name of the Web server. Most folks these days use www because it's easy to remember. Yahoo uses server names such as `maps.yahoo.com` and `mail.yahoo.com` to make it easy for users to visit a particular service.

The ending, such as `.com` or `.gov` is called the *top-level domain*, which is administrated by InterNIC.

In the three-part URLs you see most often, such as `www.peachpit.com`, or `thomas.loc.gov`, the word between the `www.` and the `.com` is commonly called the domain name; it is referred to as the *second level domain* by administrators and the InterNIC. It's the part you buy, if you want to register, say, `macromedia.com`.

In the third example above, there is a several-level hierarchy to the domain name. If you read the URL from back to front, the `.us` is the US domain used by state governments and such. The `.md` is the Maryland sub-domain; the `.k12` is the educational sub-domain of Maryland; and the `.ga` is the county subdomain of the educational system. The `.northern-hs` is the individual high school, and `husky` is the name of the Web server itself.

In the second example, the domain name itself is uncomplicated, and the rest of the URL, `support/dreamweaver/whatsnew/`, indicates three levels of directories within the Web server—which after all is just a computer like any other. Think of it like subfolders on your computer: `C:\Program Files\Macromedia\Dreamweaver`, for instance.

If the URL ends in a filename, as in `http://www.tarin.com/fridge.html`, that means that the `fridge.html` is the document itself that you're requesting. If the URL ends in a slash, it means that you're getting the *default file* for that directory. In most cases, `http://www.dhtmlzone.com/index.html` and `http://www.dhtmlzone.com/` are the same file.

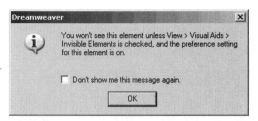

Figure 6.31 This dialog box appears when you insert an invisible element with invisible element viewing turned off.

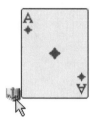

Figure 6.32 The little blip next to the image is the Anchor icon (it has a little anchor on it). You can view or hide these invisible element icons as needed by selecting View > Visual Aids > Invisible Elements from the menu bar.

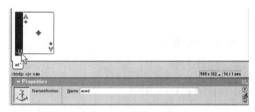

Figure 6.33 Click on an invisible element icon, and the Property inspector will display information about it.

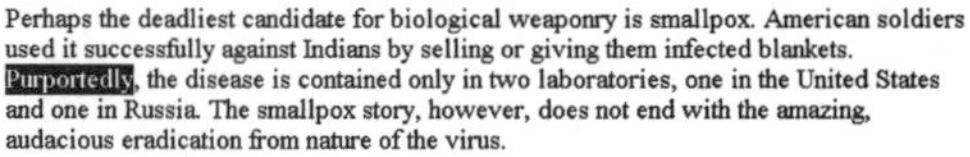

Perhaps the deadliest candidate for biological weaponry is smallpox. American soldiers used it successfully against Indians by selling or giving them infected blankets. Purportedly, the disease is contained only in two laboratories, one in the United States and one in Russia. The smallpox story, however, does not end with the amazing, audacious eradication from nature of the virus.

Figure 6.34 Select the text or image you want to link to the named anchor.

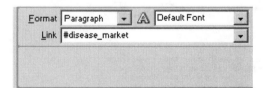

Figure 6.35 Type the name of the anchor in the Link text box, preceded by the # sign.

4. Click OK to close the Named Anchor dialog box and return to the Document window.

A dialog box may appear (**Figure 6.31**) that tells you what I'm about to tell you right now: You won't see any visible evidence of your anchor unless invisible element viewing is turned on. (View > Visual Aids > Invisible Elements).

To view invisible elements:

◆ From the menu bar, select View > Visual Aids > Invisible Elements.

Any invisible elements on your pages will appear, in the form of icons (**Figure 6.32**). To figure out what an invisible element is or does, click on its icon, and the Property inspector will display properties for that element (**Figure 6.33**).

To link to a named anchor:

1. In the Document window, select the text or image you want to use as a link (**Figure 6.34**).

2. In the Property inspector, type the pound sign (#) in the Link text box.

3. With no space between the pound sign and the name of the anchor, type the anchor name in the Link text box. For instance, if your anchor name is top, you'd type #top in the Link text box (**Figure 6.35**).

4. Press Enter (Return), and your text or image will become linked to the named anchor.

continued on next page

✔ Tips

- The page in **Figure 6.36** includes a table of contents at the top of the page. Even though the document is broken up into separate files, each link points to a specific part of each page (right above the section head). A link to the table of contents is included at the end of each section.

- To link to an anchor on the same page, the Link text box only needs to include the # and the name of the link, as in #fred.

- To link to an anchor on a page in the same directory, the link would be something like people.html#fred.

- To link to an anchor on a page elsewhere on the Web, the link would be something like http://www.homer.com/donut.htm#mmm.

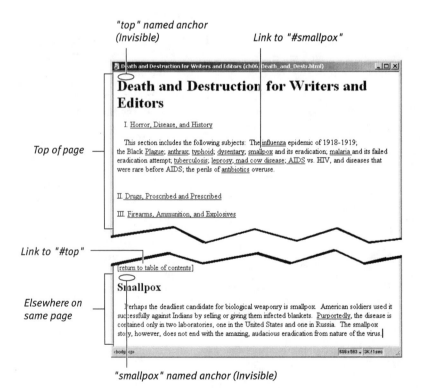

Figure 6.36 This page is an example of a document that uses named anchors.

Figure 6.37 I used a target=_blank setting to make a link in the first browser window (**Figure 6.38**, back) open in a second browser window. Use this setting sparingly; it can get annoying if over-applied.

Figure 6.38 When you use the target=_blank attribute, clicking on a link on one page spawns a new browser window that then loads the link.

Aiming Targets

There are two kinds of targets that you might want to use in non-frames pages.

◆ target=_blank makes the link open in a new, blank browser window.

◆ target=_top makes the link replace the content of the current window. By default, your linked pages will open this way.

The other kinds of targets apply only to frames. If you're making a page that you plan on using in a frames-based site, refer to Chapter 13, which also includes instructions on how to set a base target for an entire page.

Opening Links in a New Window

A linked page opens by default in the same browser window as the previous page. If you want your link to open in a separate window, then you have to assign it a *target*, which is an attribute of the anchor tag that tells the browser in what space it should open the link in question.

The main use of targets is in frames-based sites, which use targets to determine in which frame to open a link. This aspect of targets is thoroughly explained in Chapter 13. However, you may want links to external sites to open in a separate browser window to keep your own page open and your visitors on your site.

To set a target for a new window:

1. Create a link as explained in Making Links, earlier in this chapter.

2. If necessary, expand the Property inspector by clicking the expander arrow in the lower-right corner.

3. From the Target pull-down menu, choose _blank (**Figure 6.37**).

   Choosing _blank will make a brand-new browser window open and load the target of the link (**Figure 6.38**).

   If you choose _top, the link will open in the same window as the current page. (This target is more useful for frames and isn't needed to make links behave, but it's useful if you set a base target, as described in Chapter 13.)

✔ Tip

■ Some HTML editors automatically insert the target="" attribute into the code. This is harmless; it simply reiterates that the link will open in the default or base target location. You can also remove this code with impunity in the Code inspector.

Changing Link Colors

Link colors are part of what's known as page properties—the set of options that are applied to an entire page, rather than to an object on that page. The other page properties are covered in Chapter 3.

To change a page's link colors:

1. With the page open in the Document window, select Modify > Page Properties from the menu bar. The Page Properties dialog box will appear (**Figure 6.39**).

2. The text boxes marked Links, Visited Links, and Active Links control those colors for the current page. (See the sidebar *Link, Alink, and Vlink* for details about those options.) Type (or paste) the hex code for the desired color in the appropriate text box.

   or

   Click the color box beside the appropriate text box. The color picker will appear (**Figure 6.40**). Click a color to select it.

   or

   For details on choosing a color from your desktop or on using the Color dialog box for the PC (**Figure 6.41**) or the Mac, see Chapter 3.

3. After you choose a color, the hex code for that color will appear in the Page Properties dialog box. Click OK to close the dialog box and return to the Dreamweaver window, or keep the dialog box open and modify the other link color options.

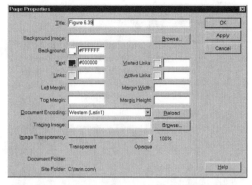

Figure 6.39 You can modify Link, Alink, and Vlink colors with the Page Properties dialog box.

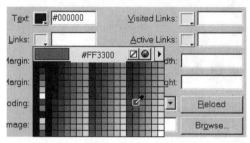

Figure 6.40 Click on the color box, and when the color picker appears, click on a color to select it.

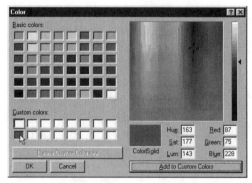

Figure 6.41 For tips on using this dialog box and the equivalent Color dialog box for the Mac, see Chapter 3.

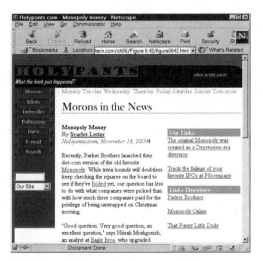

Figure 6.42 This page illustrates good link usage—there are links in the body of the story as well as in the navigation areas, and punctuation is excluded from the link underlining.

Figure 6.43 At the bottom of the same page in **Figure 6.42**, text equivalents of all the button links are provided.

◆ Come up with house rules about link length and structure, and stick to them.

◆ Use readable link colors. Make sure the text is visible on top of any background colors or images you use.

Smart Linking Strategies

Links exist so visitors will click on them. Although there's no single right way to make a link, keep these tips in mind so that your links will make people want to click (**Figures 6.42** and **6.43**).

◆ Link on a meaningful word or phrase that gives the user some idea of where they're headed.

   Right: Visit our renewable energy resource page to find out more.

   Wrong: Click here to find out more about renewable energy.

◆ When you link to something other than an HTML page, such as a sound or multi-media file, warn the user what's coming, and how big the file is.

   Right: Combustion (AU File, 153K)

   Wrong: My Friend Larry (This is wrong if it points to a 500K MIDI file with no warning.)

◆ If you're linking words within a sentence, stop the link before the punctuation, and don't underline spaces unnecessarily.

   Right: I grew up in Texas, Michigan, and Sri Lanka.

   Wrong: The best red wines come from France, Italy, Germany, and California, in that order.

◆ Making links into non sequiturs (such as the word cheese pointing to a Kung Fu movie site) can work well for irreverent sites but isn't as effective when you want someone to visit a particular page on purpose.

◆ If you rely on images (particularly button bars or image maps) as navigational tools, be sure to provide text equivalents of the same links.

Common Top-Level Domains

.com	Commercial entity		.in	India
.edu	Educational entity		.it	Italy
.gov	U.S. Government		.jp	Japan
.mil	U.S. Military		.kr	South Korea
.net	Network provider		.mx	Mexico
.org	Nonprofit organization		.my	Malaysia
.au	Australia		.nl	Netherlands
.ca	Canada		.no	Norway
.ch	Switzerland		.nz	New Zealand
.cn	China		.se	Sweden
.de	Germany		.sg	Singapore
.dk	Denmark		.tw	Taiwan
.es	Spain		.uk	United Kingdom
.fi	Finland		.us	United States
.fr	France		.za	South Africa
.ie	Ireland			

Link, Alink, and Vlink

There are three kinds of Link colors: Link, Alink (Active Link), and Vlink (Visited Link). The link color is what users see when they haven't yet visited the target of the link. The Alink color is what they see while they're in the act of clicking on a link, and the Vlink color is the color the link assumes when the user has already visited the target page. (The last several days, weeks, or months of visits are recorded in the browser's History file, which is how the browser knows which links to assign the Vlink color.) If you don't choose colors for these options, the browser default colors will be used instead. In most cases, make sure that you have two different colors for Link and Vlink, so that users can tell what parts of your site they've already visited.

INSERTING & PLAYING MEDIA

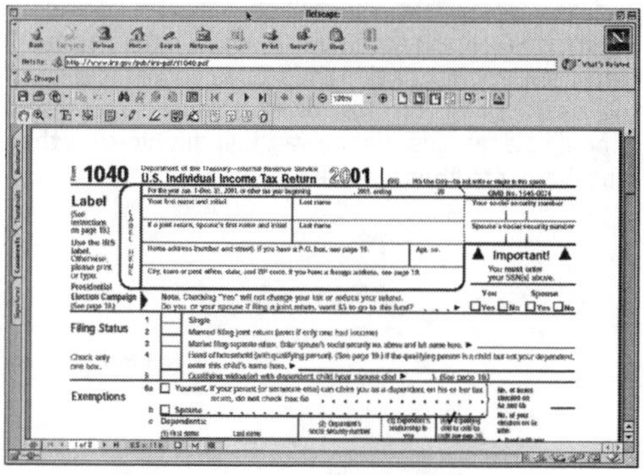

Figure 7.1 All sorts of documents can be accessed over the Web, such as this Adobe Acrobat tax form from the IRS.

Figure 7.2 Plug-ins such as Shockwave turned the Web into a multimedia experience. This is the famously disturbing Ant City, from the fiends at www.bossmonster.com.

A little light history: Before Mosaic, the first graphic Web browser, any file that wasn't text or HTML had to be downloaded and saved to open later with a separate application. All media, including images, were "save and play"—you couldn't view anything inline, and no one had so much as thought of streaming media.

With Netscape Navigator 1.1, you could automatically launch a helper application to play a downloaded file, and audio and Adobe Acrobat started becoming part of the life of the Web (**Figure 7.1**).

Navigator 2 went a step further and forever changed the face of the Web. Plug-ins could play or view darned near any type of file you could think of. At that point, not only could you view Shockwave movies inline (**Figure 7.2**), but music could also be embedded invisibly into Web pages. Java, VRML, and other rich media soon followed.

These days, new plugins proliferate, and many Web browsers automatically detect which plug-in you need and help you install it. The version 6 browsers use plug-ins to play sound files, and they can usually play Flash files inline with no further installations required.

Dreamweaver makes it easy to insert the code for these multimedia objects onto your pages.

In fact, inserting most media objects is just like inserting an image. (See Chapter 5 if you haven't yet worked with images.) Just like when you insert an image, what you're really doing is inserting the URL for the media object. When you do that, a placeholder for the object appears in the document window. After that, you can apply additional properties, including dimensions, Vspace and Hspace, and page-loading helpers (Alt tags and low-res images).

In this chapter, we'll take a look at how to make images interactive using rollovers and navigation bars. Then, we'll explore how to link to media, using sound files as our example. We'll move on to browser plug-ins, including Shockwave and Flash. In Dreamweaver, you can even create simple Flash text objects and buttons without leaving the Document window. We'll also address the basics of putting Java and ActiveX on your pages.

✔ Tips

- You can insert any of these objects using either the Common or the Media tab on the Insert toolbar (Window > Insert) and you can modify them using the Property inspector (Window > Properties or Modify > Selection Properties). I'm just refreshing your memory, in case you'd forgotten.

- With the Assets panel, you can keep track of not only images (see *Inserting Images with the Assets Panel* in Chapter 5), but Flash, Shockwave, and other movies in your local site. To find out more about working with Assets, see Chapter 2.

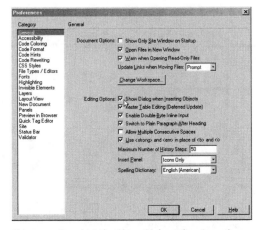

Figure 7.3 Deselect the Show Dialog When Inserting Objects check box to skip the step of choosing a file in the Insert dialog box. Dreamweaver will instead insert a media placeholder right away. Just double-click the placeholder to choose a file.

- You can insert a placeholder for most media instead of choosing a file right away—which is handy if you're creating the page before the file is ready. From the menu bar, select Edit > Preferences. (On Mac OS X, choose Dreamweaver Preferences.) In the General panel of the Preferences dialog box (**Figure 7.3**), deselect the Show Dialog when Inserting Objects check box. Then click OK to close the dialog box and save your changes.

- You can set up external editors for working with media objects in Dreamweaver. See *Image Editor Integration,* in Chapter 5, and follow the instructions for the proper file type (instead of image files, select a different file type).

Figure 7.4 One common use of image rollovers is a set of buttons that "light up" when they're moused over. Dreamweaver's Insert toolbar and Assets panel use image rollovers to make buttons appear "pushed in" or "lit up."

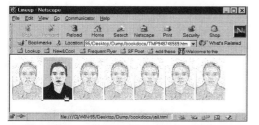

Figure 7.5 You can use any sort of images in a rollover, as long as the pre-roll and the post-roll images are the same size. (Those aren't technical terms.)

Image Rollovers

Image rollovers let you seemingly stack two images on top of one another so that when you perform an action in the browser such as mousing over an image, another image appears. This is how button "highlighting" (**Figure 7.4**) and other, similar image tricks happen.

In technical terms, an image rollover is a JavaScript action that lets you swap the source of one image with another image file, so that when a user event happens, the browser loads the second image (**Figure 7.5**). To find out more about how JavaScript and Dreamweaver Behaviors work, see Chapter 16.

In Dreamweaver, a simple image rollover makes three things happen on your page: First, the images preload when the Web page loads, so that the rollovers are ready to go; second, when the user mouses over the specified image, a different image file is displayed; and finally, when the user mouses away from the image, the original image is restored.

The two images need to be the same size, or the second image will be smooshed into the first one's shape.

For the best results, you must save your page before you begin.

To set up a rollover image:

1. Click on the Rollover Image button on the Common tabs of the Insert toolbar ▣ .

   or

   From the menu bar, select Insert > Interactive Images > Rollover Image. The Insert Rollover Image dialog box will appear (**Figure 7.6**).

2. Select the source of the Original Image and the Rollover Image by typing the file-names in the respective text boxes, or by clicking Browse to use dialog boxes to select local images.

3. You can edit the image name in the Image Name text box. Use a memorable, all-lowercase name.

4. Type the text you want to appear as a tool tip into the Alternate Text text box. Whatever you type there will show up as tool tips in Windows browsers and cur-rent Mac browsers, and will be used by other devices to describe the image or button.

5. Will your image link to another Web page? If so, type the URL in the When Clicked, Go To URL text box. Or click on Browse to select a page from your local site.

6. Click OK to close the Insert Image Rollover dialog box and return to the Document window.

7. Preview your page in a JavaScript-capable browser to test the rollover effect.

✔ Tips

- The Preload Images option will be checked by default—leave it checked. There's no good reason *not* to preload images, because it eliminates wait time that would otherwise be caused by having to download the replacement image only when it's requested.

- For more about links, see Chapter 6. For more about how rollovers work, see Chapter 16.

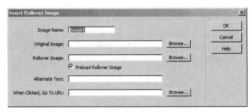

Figure 7.6 The Rollover Image dialog box lets you swap one image for another without even learning behaviors.

Holy Rollovers

In Dreamweaver 1.0, you needed to create three JavaScript Behaviors in order to make a successful image rollover. Now all it takes is a single dialog box. That's great.

To find out how to make more complicated image rollovers, see Chapter 16. You can use Behaviors to have user events other than mouseovers (such as clicks or key-presses) make the images change source; you can have an event for one image trig-ger a source change for a different image or multiple images; you can make it so that mousing out doesn't require the source to swap back; or you can have the mouseout cause an entirely different image to appear.

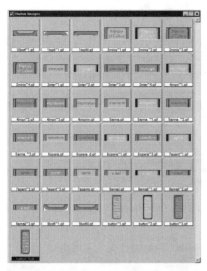

Figure 7.7 This is my collection of future button images, displayed in an image catalog program.

Figure 7.8 These are all the button images, displayed as navbars.

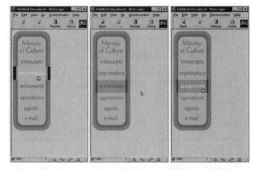

Figure 7.9 The three browser windows depict the three button states: Over, Down, Over While Down.

Using Navigation Bars

If you want to create a navigation bar (also called *navbar* or *button bar*) to guide people through your site, Dreamweaver can simplify the process. Otherwise, you'd have to write a complex rollover for each button in the navigation bar. Using Dreamweaver, you just fill in the blanks.

A button can have as many as four looks in a Dreamweaver navigation bar: Up, or initial; Over, or "lit up" (when the user mouses over the button); Down, or "pushed in" (when the user clicks on the button); and Over While Down (when the user mouses over the button while it's "pushed in"). You need have only one set of images to create a navigation bar, but you must create a separate image file for each state of each button on the bar. **Figures 7.7** and **7.8** show the four sets of images that will be used as buttons in the four different states. **Figure 7.9** shows the buttons in action.

✔ Tips

■ This chapter assumes you're starting from scratch with a batch of images, but you can expedite things if you use Macromedia Fireworks to create your buttons. You can use the Button Editor to export the buttons, along with prewritten HTML and JavaScript. Then you can edit the pages in Dreamweaver. In the Export or Export Preview dialog box of Fireworks MX, select HTML and Images from the Files of Type drop-down menu; and Export HTML File from the HTML drop-down menu. In older versions of Fireworks, select Dreamweaver from the HTML Style drop-down menu.

■ See Chapter 16 for tips on editing navbars by using Behaviors.

To make sure your links work properly, all your images should be stored in your local site (see Chapter 2), and the page should be saved before you begin.

To insert a navigation bar:

1. On the Common tab of the Insert toolbar, click on the Insert Navigation Bar button ▦ .

   or

   From the menu bar, select Insert > Interactive Images > Navigation Bar.

   Either way, the Insert Navigation Bar dialog box will appear (**Figure 7.10**).

2. In the Up Image text box, type the filename of the image you wish to use; or, click on Browse, and use the Select Image Source dialog box (**Figures 7.11** and **7.12**) to select the image from a folder in your local site.

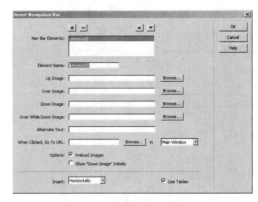

Figure 7.10 The Insert Navigation Bar dialog box.

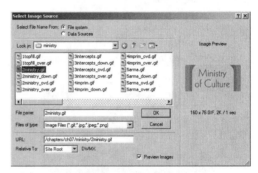

Figure 7.11 The Select Image Source dialog box. With the preview turned on, you can make sure your button states look as they're supposed to.

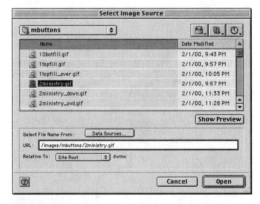

Figure 7.12 The Select Image Source dialog box for the Mac. Click Show Preview to see a thumbnail of the selected image.

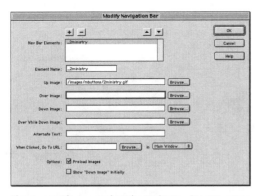

Figure 7.13 After you select the Up image, Dreamweaver inserts the button name in the Name text box.

Figure 7.14 On this navigation bar, the Ministry of Culture page will load with the Ministry button already selected, or down.

Figure 7.15 Navigation bars can be horizontal, too.

3. After you select the first image, Dreamweaver will insert a name for the button in the Element Name text box (**Figure 7.13**). You may edit this name if you wish.

4. Repeat step 2 for any additional states for your button: Up, Down, and Over While Down.

5. If this button should be in the down state when the page loads (**Figure 7.14**), check the Show "Down Image" Initially check box. An asterisk will appear by the name of the selected over-while-down image.

Usage example: You're putting a button bar on the Archive page; one of your buttons says "Archive," and you want the button to be pushed in when the user visits this page. You'd then change this option by showing the appropriate buttons pushed in to highlight each section.

6. Whatever you type in the Alternate Text text box will be used by nongraphical devices to describe the sound, and will show up as a tool tip in newer browsers.

7. In the When Clicked, Go To URL text box, type the URL for your link; or, if the link is a page on your site, click Browse and use the Select HTML file dialog box to select the page and set the local path.

8. To insert another button, click the + button. Then follow steps 1 through 7 to specify images and links.

9. The navigation bar can display across the page or down the page. Select Vertically (Figure 7.14) or Horizontally (**Figure 7.15**) from the Insert drop-down menu.

continued on next page

10. To use tables to make your navigation bar stay in shape, select that check box. You can edit this table later; see Chapter 12.

11. To rearrange the order of the buttons, select a button name and then use the up and down arrow buttons to move the button through the list.

12. If you're not using dynamically served images, leave the Preload Images check box checked, so that the Web browser can fetch all the images for all the button states while the page is loading (instead of having to go get them when the user mouses over them).

13. When you're finished, click OK to close the Insert Navigation Bar dialog box and return to the Document window. Your navigation bar will be displayed (**Figure 7.16**).

14. After the navbar is on your page, you must preview it in a browser to test it (**Figure 7.17**). From the menu bar, select File > Preview in Browser > [Browser Name], or Press F12.

✔ Tips

■ See Chapter 3 for more about previewing.

■ To find out how to modify the table Dreamweaver inserts with your navbar, see Chapter 12; in particular, the sidebar *Getting Nitpicky About Widths* may help.

■ To find out about adding the navbar to the Library so you can reuse it, see Chapter 17.

■ Make sure, when you put this page on the Web, that you upload all the images along with the page (see *About Dependent Files,* in Chapter 19). I'd recommend uploading a test page with the navbar on it, so you can check all the image locations, before you try to use it on a live page.

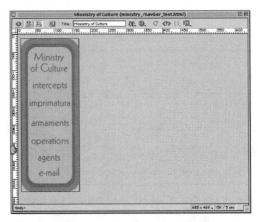

Figure 7.16 The navigation bar appears in the Document window. You can see the table border, barely, around the buttons.

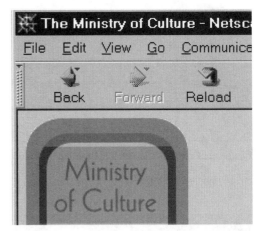

Figure 7.17 Previewing the page in a browser lets you test all the rollover effects.

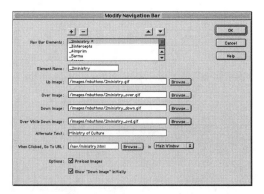

Figure 7.18 Modifying a navigation bar uses practically the same dialog box as the one for adding it.

To modify your navbar:

1. From the menu bar, select Modify > Navigation Bar. The Modify Navigation Bar dialog box will appear (**Figure 7.18**).

2. Make any necessary changes as described in the preceding section.

   For example, you may need to add or change a URL; you might want to select a different image to start in the Down position (as in Figure 7.14, but imagine the entire site, with a different down image for each topic page); or you may want to rearrange the order in which your images appear.

3. When you're done, click OK to close the Modify Navigation Bar dialog box and insert your updated navigation bar.

✔ Tips

- You can create more complex rollovers for your navbar with Behaviors, as described in Chapter 16.

- Also using Behaviors, you can have different actions cause different button states to appear. See the sidebar *Set Navbar Image* in Chapter 16.

USING NAVIGATION BARS

Using Sound Files

Sound files come in more flavors than ice cream (see the sidebar, *Sound File Types*, later in this chapter). Not all browsers support all sound files, but any browser that supports plug-ins or ActiveX (Navigator or Explorer versions 2 or later) should be able to play most sound files. Navigator 3 or later's pre-installed LiveAudio plug-in plays nearly every common sound file type.

There are two ways to add a sound file to your page. One way is to link to the sound file, so that the user downloads and plays it when clicking on the link. The other way is to embed the sound file so that it begins to load when the page loads, and a plug-in will play it automatically.

A sound link is like any other link. See Chapter 6 for more about how links work.

To link to a sound file:

1. In the Document window, select the text or image that you want to make into the link.

2. In the Property inspector, type the path-name for the sound file in the Link text box and press Enter (Return) (**Figure 7.19**).

   or

   Click the Browse button 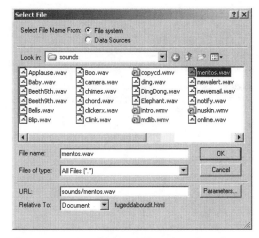, and use the Select File dialog box to choose a sound file from your computer (**Figure 7.20**). Be sure to select All Files (*.*) from the Files of type drop-down menu.

   You can now add sound file settings directly from the Select dialog box by clicking on Parameters. See *Sound File Parameters* and *Extra Parameters* for how to fill out the Parameters dialog box.

Figure 7.19 Type the location of the sound file in the Property inspector's Link text box.

Figure 7.20 Select the sound file in the Select File dialog box.

Figure 7.21 WinAmp is one kind of helper app that plays sound files.

3. The selection will be linked to the sound file.

When users click on the link, they'll download the sound file. One of three things will then happen:

◆ An external program, or "Helper App," will launch to play the sound file (**Figure 7.21**);

or

◆ The browser will play it using its own capabilities or those of a plug-in;

or

◆ If the browser doesn't support or recognize the file type, an error will occur. Sometimes a dialog box will open that says "Unrecognized file type," and sometimes the browser will open the file as if it were text.

The Sound of Downloads

When linking to sound files, it's a good idea to let your users know what they're in for. Unless the sound is very small, it's good practice to indicate the file type and file size of sound files so that users know whether to download them. A user might be at the office or the library and not want to play a sound file right now; or a visitor might be using a mobile device or other tool, wherein either the device can't play the file or the user might choose to skip it for now. And further, some older Mac browsers don't support .WAV files, and some older PC browsers don't support .AIFF files. And of course any user on a dialup modem wants advance notice before they start downloading a 100K+ sound file.

A line like this near the link should do the trick:

They Killed Kenny! (10K .WAV)

or even better:

They Killed Kenny! (10K .WAV, 9K .AIFF)

Embedding sound files

Embedding a sound file is similar to linking to an image. You can add the <embed> tag by inserting the sound file as plug-in content, or you can add the code by hand.

To embed a sound file:

1. Open the document you want to attach the sound file to in the Document window.

2. Click to place the insertion point at the place in the document where you want the sound controller to appear. For invisible sound files, you can place the file anywhere, although at the top or bottom of the document is usually more convenient.

3. View the HTML source for the page in the Code inspector by selecting Window > Others > Code Inspector from the menu bar (or by pressing F10). You can also work in Code view, if you prefer. See Chapter 4.

4. For a sound file with no controls showing, type the following line of code:

   ```
   <embed src="sounds/yoursound.wav"
   -autostart="TRUE" hidden="TRUE">
   </embed>
   ```

   ...where sounds/yoursound.wav is the pathname of the sound file. The Code inspector will offer you tag choices as you type, and even lets you browse for sound files in the same Select File dialog box you can use for linking to sound files.

5. Save your changes to the page (**Figures 7.22** and **7.23**).

6. Preview the page in a browser to make sure it works.

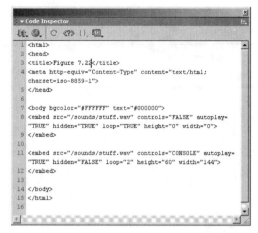

Figure 7.22 The code for a standard, non-visible Netscape controller (top), and for a standard visible controller.

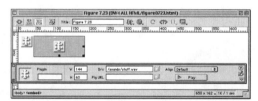

Figure 7.23 This is the same page we saw in **Figure 7.22**. Note that the hidden controller is marked with a standard placeholder, and the visible one is given the specified dimensions. If you forget to adjust dimensions, controllers will show up all squished up into a 32x32 square.

Explorer's <bgsound> Tag

Versions of Internet Explorer before 4.0 do not support embedded sound files. You generally don't have to worry about browsers that old, but you may want to know about a proprietary tag called <bgsound> that Explorer can use. (All versions of Netscape ignore this tag.) It used to be that you could use both the <embed> and <bgsound> tags on the same page and the sound would play only once; in Explorer 6, the browser will play both tags if they're both there, so you're probably better off using one or the other; or you can use the <bgsound> tag in conjunction with an embed tag that does not automatically play the sound; if the user doesn't hear the bgsound they can press Play on the controller.

A <bgsound> tag goes in the body of the document and looks like this:

```
<bgsound src="sounds/mysound.wav"
loop="infinite" autoplay="true"
volume=0>
```

The loop parameter can be either infinite or a number. Volume can be 0 (full) to −10,000 (lowest). There are no user controls to display with the <bgsound> tag, as it by definition plays sounds in the background.

✔ Tips

■ You can embed a sound file with or without the use of the plug-in dialog box. Because Dreamweaver's Insert > Media > Plugin feature doesn't include all the stuff you need for embedding sounds in a page, I'm going to discuss embedded sound and plug-ins as if they were two different entities.

■ A little bug: If you use the embed tag or the Insert Plugin command, and then click the Browse button, Dreamweaver sometimes defaults to showing only Shockwave for Director files in the Select File dialog box. Select All Types from the Files of Type drop-down menu and select the file you want to use.

■ On another footnote, Macromedia spells it Plugin but Netscape, which invented the browser plug-in, spells it Plug-in. So if you have reason to use the word, pick a spelling and stick with it.

■ You can also link to or embed movie files as well as sound files, or you can insert them as plug-ins.

■ You can keep track of movies (such as RealVideo or QuickTime files) using the Assets panel.

Sound File Parameters

If you want your visitors to enjoy your embedded sound, they'll need to have the correct plug-in on their computer, which is no sweat if they're using a browser that supports such things. If you want to use a dialog box to insert these parameters (rather than typing them into the code), see *Extra Parameters*, later in this chapter.

Keep in mind that depending on what browser your visitors use to play sound files, they may have different controllers—don't depend on the look of a particular controller when designing your page.

Here's the skinny on some of the different parameters you can employ with sound files that use the <embed> tag. First, I'll list the official HTML specs for this tag; then I'll list some proprietary parameters that work with popular sound plug-ins.

◆ **src=""** (required)

The source of the file.

◆ **type=["MimeType"]**

Use for listing the mime type of a plug-in. You don't need to specify the mime type of popular plug-ins the browser will recognize; when it spots a .wav, it recognizes it as a Windows Audio file. If you're serving a sound file dynamically, however, you should specify the type.

◆ **name=""**

Name the embedded file if you want to call it from a script. If you use the **name** value, you must also include the **master-sound** attribute (no value).

◆ **hidden (no attribute)**

Hides the controller. In past versions of Netscape, hidden took the **true|false** attribute, but current versions use **hidden** alone to hide controls, and a setting of **hidden=false** acts like **hidden=true**. The **hidden** setting overrides **height** and **width**.

◆ **height** and **width** (Required for visible controllers.)

Determines the height and width of the controller. For console: height=60 width=144. For smallconsole: height=15 width=144. See the next page for details about console types.

When you adjust the height and width of an embedded controller, its placeholder changes shape in the Document window.

◆ **align="LEFT|RIGHT|TOP|BOTTOM"**

Defines alignment for visible controllers.

◆ **HSPACE="n" VSPACE="n"**

Sets space around visible controllers.

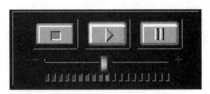

Figure 7.24 A standard Netscape LiveAudio sound controller, embedded in a page.

Figure 7.25 A QuickTime controller in Explorer. Explorer 6 obeys the `width` parameter and saves space for the `height` parameter, but older versions tend to use a standard size controller and ignore dimensions.

Optional parameters

The following parameters are commonly used by sound players such as Windows Media Player and QuickTime. If you're aiming for a particular plug-in, check its documentation to see what parameters they recommend including.

◆ `autostart=true|false` or `autoplay=true|false`

Determines whether the sound begins playing as soon as it loads.

◆ `controls=console|smallconsole| true|false`

Used by some plug-ins to determine whether to show controls, or what style.

◆ `loop=true|false|n`

Determines whether the sound will loop continuously. A setting of loop=3 would make the file loop three times.

◆ `volume=0%–100%`

Percent of system volume used.

A standard audio controller (**Figures 7.24** and **7.25**) would have the following settings:

```
<embed src="sounds/yoursound.wav"
height="60" width="144"
controls="CONSOLE" autostart="FALSE"
loop="FALSE"></embed>
```

continued on next page

✔ Tips

- If the source for the sound file isn't correct, the console will not show up in Navigator.

- Quotation marks are not essential for anything but SRC, but proper HTML prefers them.

- It's a good idea to include on the page the URLs of the plug-in and your favorite browser.

- Netscape used to play lots and lots of sound files inline automatically, but in Netscape 6 you need a plug-in for practically everything.

Common Sound File Types

`.AIFF`: Macintosh Audio format.

`.AU`: Sun Audio format.

`.DCR`: Shockwave audio (also used for Shockwave movies). Requires Shockwave plug-in.

`.LA, .LAM, .LMA`: Netscape streaming audio. Handled automatically by Netscape 4 and higher.

`.MID, .MIDI`: MIDI electronic music format. Requires plug-in in Netscape 2.0 and 6.

`.MOD, .RMF`: Beatnik audio format. Requires Beatnik plug-in. (Note: once Beatnik is installed, it will also handle `.AIFF`, `.AU`, `.MID`, and `.WAV` by default.)

`.MOV`: QuickTime audio (also used for QuickTime movies). Requires QuickTime plug-in.

`.MPG, .MP3`: MPEG, or MP3 files, which provide CD-quality sound. Requires an audio plug-in such as RealPlayer or QuickTime or a helper app such as WinAmp.

`.RAM, .RPM`: RealAudio (also used for RealVideo). Requires RealAudio or RealPlayer plug-in.

`.WAV`: Windows Audio. Requires plug-in in Netscape 6.

Noembed

If you want to provide a description of a sound or other plug-in for browsers without plug-in capability, use the noembed tag:

`<noembed>`

```
This page contains content available
only with the DorkBlast plug-in and
a plug-in capable browser.
```

`</noembed>`

Figure 7.26 Browse for the plug-in files on your computer. Remember that you're looking for the media file to be played, not the plug-in component (DLL) that plays it.

Playing Plug-ins in Dreamweaver

Dreamweaver supports some plug-ins; you can play them inline in the Document window. You must have the plug-in installed in Netscape to be able to play the plug-in.

On the Property inspector for a selected plug-in, there's a Play button with a green arrow. Press this button to play the selected object. The button will turn into a red Stop button, the use of which you can guess.

Alternatively, you can select View > Plug-ins > Play (and Stop), or View > Plug-ins > Play All (or Stop All) for multiple plug-ins.

Your mileage may vary. A couple notes: Don't do this with ActiveX. The Play button's there, but Macromedia doesn't recommend doing so. I have also had problems getting Dreamweaver to play even a simple .WAV file. The support for playing Flash and Shockwave files has improved, though, and you can easily play Flash.

Netscape Plug-ins

Netscape plug-ins work in Netscape 2 or later and in Internet Explorer version 5 or later. Many plug-ins can be set either to run inline or to launch a helper app. They can also be set to play different qualities of content depending on the computer or modem speed. The RealPlayer is a good example of both of these traits.

There are some ActiveX equivalents to Netscape plug-ins; see *ActiveX,* later in this chapter, and the documentation for the specific plug-in.

To insert a Netscape plug-in:

1. In the Document window, click to place the insertion point at the place on the page where you want the plug-in to appear.

2. From the menu bar, select Insert > Media > Plugin.

   or

   Click the Plugin button on the Media tab of the Insert toolbar 🔧.

3. Either way, the Select File dialog box will appear (**Figure 7.26**). When you locate the file, click OK (Choose).

4. The dialog box will close and a plug-in placeholder will appear in the Document window 🔧.

✔ Tip

■ You can use the Behavior called Check Plug-in to determine whether a visitor has a particular plug-in installed. See Chapter 16 for more details.

After you insert the placeholder, you can set additional properties for the plug-in. Note that most of these properties are quite similar to the image properties discussed in Chapter 5. See the sidebar *Plug-in Properties* for details.

To set plug-in properties:

1. Select the plug-in placeholder in the Document window. The Property inspector will display plug-in properties (**Figure 7.27**).

2. Change any properties in the Property inspector, and press Enter (Return).

3. To set extra parameters, click the Parameters button. (See *Extra Parameters*, later in this chapter.)

✔ Tips

■ In previous versions of Dreamweaver, you had to select the appropriate file type or All Types from the Files of Type drop-down menu. Now Dreamweaver displays files of All Types by default.

■ Most properties for other media types are quite similar to the properties for plug-ins. Additional properties for items such as Java, Shockwave, Flash, and ActiveX are discussed in *Additional Media Properties*, Appendix G on the Web site for this book.

Figure 7.27 The Property inspector, displaying plug-in properties.

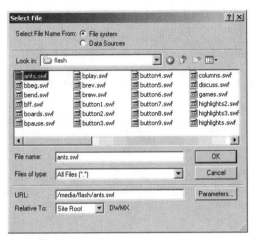

Figure 7.28 Choose a .DCR, .DIR, or .DXR file (Shockwave) or a .SWF, .SPL, or .SWT (Shockwave Flash Template) file from your computer.

Shockwave and Flash

Shockwave and Flash Player are Netscape plug-ins, but you get more up-front ability to set their attributes by using the Insert > Media > Shockwave and Insert > Media > Flash tools. Director, Flash, and Dreamweaver are developed by Macromedia, after all, and integration of the three is one of Dreamweaver's big selling points.

To insert a Shockwave or Flash file:

1. In the Document window, click to place the insertion point at the place on the page where you want the Shockwave or Flash movie to appear.

2. From the menu bar, select Insert > Media > Shockwave or Insert > Media > Flash.

or

Click on the Shockwave or Flash button on the Media tab of the Insert toolbar.

3. The Select Shockwave or Select Flash dialog box will appear (**Figure 7.28**). Locate the file on your computer. Click OK (Open) when you find the file.

The dialog box will close and a placeholder will appear in the Document window: . If the file includes preset dimensions, such as 500x500px, the placeholder will take up that amount of space.

continued on next page

✔ Tips

- You can set additional properties for Flash (**Figure 7.29**) and Shockwave (**Figure 7.30**). They're quite similar to the plug-in properties discussed earlier in this chapter; for additional details, see Appendix G on the book's Web site.

- Behaviors for detecting whether a browser has Shockwave or Flash installed and for inserting Shockwave or Flash controls are discussed in Chapter 16.

Figure 7.29 The Property inspector, displaying Flash properties. Note that Flash has a few extra attributes.

Figure 7.30 The Property inspector, displaying Shockwave for Director properties.

Using Aftershock and Flash HTML with Dreamweaver

Aftershock is an old HTML tool used with Director and Flash to create HTML files using Shockwave. The current versions of Flash and Shockwave include their own HTML engines. You can open files created with any of these programs and edit them in Dreamweaver. You can also select the relevant HTML and paste it into other Dreamweaver documents.

If you want to edit files that have been inserted into Dreamweaver HTML documents, select the Flash or Shockwave object, view the Property inspector and click on Edit. Edit the file and click the Done button. For more on using Dreamweaver with external editors, see the earlier Tip in *Using Navigation Bars*.

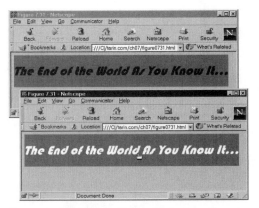

Figure 7.31 A Flash text object in Navigator, with and without the rollover.

Figure 7.32 A bank of Flash buttons. In the StarSpinner button style, the rollover effect makes the star get bigger and spin around.

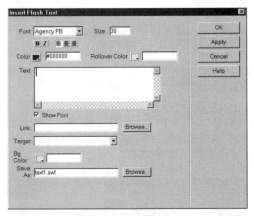

Figure 7.33 Create your Flash Text elements using the Insert Flash Text dialog box.

Creating Flash Objects in Dreamweaver

Macromedia Flash is a versatile form of multimedia that uses incredibly compressed vector graphics to present interactive images and movies. The program, however, can be complicated to learn, and if you want to get your site up in a hurry, you might need to contract out the fancy stuff. For the simple Flash object, however, Dreamweaver MX offers an easy-to-use tool for creating basic Flash text objects and buttons.

Both Flash text (**Figure 7.31**) and Flash buttons (**Figure 7.32**) can feature rollovers and can link to other pages. Keep in mind, however, that the user must have a Flash-capable browser to see your buttons or text at all. Current versions of Netscape and Explorer come ready to play Flash movies.

About Flash text

Flash text objects are the fastest, easiest way to create a text image in the font you want, with an automatic rollover effect. You can't put a border around a Flash object.

To insert Flash text:

1. Save your page. You can't insert Flash text on an unsaved page.

2. From the menu bar, select Insert > Interactive Images > Flash Text.

   or

   On the Media tab of the Insert toolbar, click the Flash Text button 🄰 .

   Either way, the Insert Flash Text dialog box appears (**Figure 7.33**).

continued on next page

3. To select the folder the Flash file will be stored in, click Browse. The Select File dialog box appears. Browse until you find the right folder. (Be sure to name your Flash file something memorable, not just text1, text2, and so on.)

If you don't choose a folder before saving your Flash Text file, the file will be stored in the same folder as the current page. Dreamweaver requires that you use Document-relative rather than Site-root relative paths when *placing* these objects, but after you place them you can click the Browse button in the Property inspector to set the relative path to Site Root. See Chapter 6 for more on relative links.

4. Type the text you want to use in the Text text box.

You can modify the way the text will appear in several ways (**Figures 7.34 and 7.35**):

Choose a font from the Font drop-down menu. To preview the font face in the Text text box, leave the Show Font checkbox checked.

Type the font size in the Size text box.

To make the text bold or italic, select the text and click the B or I button. Unfortunately, you can't select just part of the text; it must *all* be bold or italic.

To set the alignment of the text within the rectangle, click on the left, right, or center alignment button.

To choose a color for the text, you can type a hex code or click on the Color button and use the eyedropper to choose a color. For more on using colors, see Chapter 3.

If you want the text color to change when the user mouses over the button, choose a rollover color that's different from the text color (**Figure 7.36**).

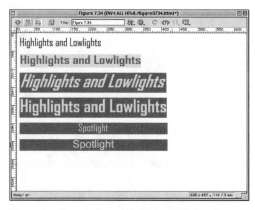

Figure 7.34 I created several similar Flash Text items. The second image is the same size as the first, with Bold text and different colors. The middle two images use a large font size. The bottom two images show alignment—but I couldn't find any appreciable difference in the alignment settings.

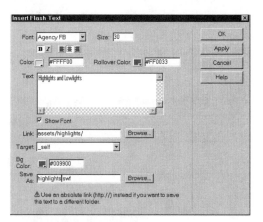

Figure 7.35 These are the settings I used for the fourth item in **Figure 7.34**.

Figure 7.36 The text changes color when the user mouses over it.

Figure 7.37 I made changes to my text in the dialog box and clicked Apply to preview them before I returned to the Document window.

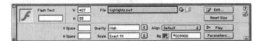

Figure 7.38 You can change the background color, the dimensions, the alignment, and the Vspace and Hspace of your Flash text object in the Property inspector.

To set a background color other than white, choose a background color using the Bg Color button. In Figure 7.31, I used a different background color than the page's background; in Figure 7.36, they're the same.

If the text should link to another page, type the link in the Link text box, or click Browse and choose a file from your local site.

5. If your site uses frames and you need to set a target for the link, select it from the Target text box (see *Targeting Links* in Chapter 13). You can also set other targets based on pop-up windows in your site (see *Pop-up Browser Window* in Chapter 16).

6. To preview the way your text looks, click Apply. (This saves any changes made up to that point.) You can make changes before you continue (**Figure 7.37**).

7. Click OK to close the dialog box and save your changes.

✔ Tips

■ You can use any font you like for the text without having to worry about the user's font set (see Chapter 8). The font is stored in the Flash file rather than on the page.

■ To edit your Flash text, double-click on it, and the Insert Flash Text dialog box will reappear.

■ You can change the background color of your Flash text in the Property inspector (**Figure 7.38**).

■ To preview the rollover effect, click the Play button on the Property inspector, and mouse over your Flash Text object.

continued on next page

- To change the way the Flash text fits within the borders of the object, you can change the Scale in the Property inspector (**Figures 7.39** and **7.40**). Default (Show All) makes all the text fit in the box without distorting the font. Exact fit stretches the text to fit the dimensions of the box. No border may make the text run outside the box.

- You can set alignment and Vspace and Hspace in the Property inspector as you would for an image. See Chapter 5.

Figure 7.39 You have three scaling options for your Flash text.

Figure 7.40 The first image on this page has not been resized. The second three images have been resized, and, from top to bottom, their Scaling attributes are Show All, Exact Fit (which stretches the text), and No Border (which scales the text out of the box). The bottom two images are scaled to 100 percent of the window, and again are scaled as Show All and Exact Fit.

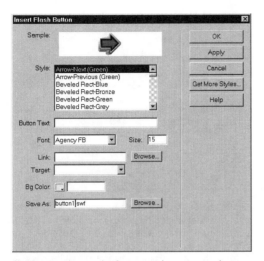

Figure 7.41 Choose the format and create your button in the Insert Flash Button dialog box.

Figure 7.42 Some of the buttons are text-free arrows and Play buttons. These buttons are the "Control" series.

Figure 7.43 You can choose from a variety of looks for text buttons. Of course, you'll probably want your buttons to say different things, and you'll probably want a set of them to look the same.

Figure 7.44 You've got a limited amount of space on a button, even if you enlarge it.

Figure 7.45 The top button is fine at size 12, but the bottom one's text is too big with a point size of 16.

Using Flash buttons

Flash buttons, like Flash text, are small files that can include text and links as well as rollover effects. Flash buttons are templates that offer preset styles and visual effects.

To create a Flash button:

1. Save your page first.

2. From the menu bar, select Insert > Interactive Images > Flash Button.

   or

   On the Media tab of the Insert toolbar, click the Flash Button button 🔲.

   Either way, the Insert Flash Button dialog box will appear (**Figure 7.41**).

3. Browse through the list of available looks for your button. You can choose from various kinds of arrows and the like (**Figure 7.42**), or you can choose a button that has room for text (**Figure 7.43**).

4. To select the folder the Flash file will be stored in, click on Browse. The Select File dialog box will appear. Browse until you find the right folder. (Be sure to name your Flash file something memorable.)

   If you don't choose a folder before saving your Flash Button file, it will be stored in the same folder as the current page.

5. If you chose a button that has text, type the text in the Button Text text box. You may have to find out by trial and error whether your text is too long to fit on the button (**Figure 7.44**).

6. Choose a Font Face from the Font drop-down menu.

   The Font Size is often non-negotiable; if you enlarge the font, the words on the button may get cut off (**Figure 7.45**).

continued on next page

CREATING FLASH OBJECTS IN DREAMWEAVER

7. Set the background color for your button; you can click the eyedropper on the background color of the page to choose that color (**Figure 7.46**).

8. Type the link for the button in the Link text box, or click on Browse and choose a file from your local site.

9. If your site uses frames or additional windows, and you need to set a target for the link, select it from the Target text box.

10. To preview the way your button looks, click Apply. You can make changes before you continue.

11. Click OK to close the dialog box and save your changes.

✔ Tips

■ To edit your Flash text or Flash button, double-click on it, and the Insert Flash Text (or Button) dialog box will reappear.

■ To preview the rollover effects in the Document window, select the Flash object. In the Property inspector, click Play (**Figure 7.47**). Now, when you mouse over the button, you'll see the rollover in play. When you're done, click Stop.

■ You can resize the Flash object as you would an image by selecting it and dragging its handles (**Figure 7.48**). The resizing will be done to scale; the text will grow to fit the new dimensions, but that doesn't mean that too-large text will fit on a button. See the tips under Flash Text for more on scaling.

■ You can get additional button templates from Macromedia Exchange by clicking on Get More Styles in the Insert Flash Button dialog box. Your browser will open and take you to the Exchange, where you can download new button templates created by other users.

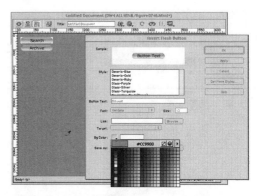

Figure 7.46 In the first visible button here, I didn't choose a background color, so it defaulted to white, which looks bad. On the second one, I chose the background color of the page. Click the Background Color button, and click the eyedropper on the page background to choose that color.

Figure 7.47 Select the button you want to test, and click Play in the Property inspector. This works with Flash text, too.

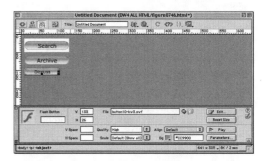

Figure 7.48 You can resize a button by dragging its handles or by typing new dimensions in the H and W text boxes on the Property inspector. To reset the size, click on Reset Size on the Property inspector.

Duplicating Your Efforts

When you create a Flash button, you probably want to create a whole set of buttons that look and act the same. Each button will say something different, presumably, and will link to a different page.

Instead of going through the motions of selecting a button type and a background color and so on over and over, you can save your changes in a new file and then insert the new files onto your page.

1. Create a Flash button that has all the attributes you want to reuse.

2. Double-click on the button to display the Insert Flash Button dialog box.

3. Important: Type a new filename for the button in the Save As text box.

4. Make appropriate changes in the Button Text text box and the Link text box.

5. Click OK to save your changes in the new file.

Now, your new button will be displayed, but the old one will have disappeared. Don't worry. Go ahead and follow the steps above for each button in your set, taking care to provide a new filename for each one.

To insert your new buttons, open the Flash category of the Assets panel (Window > Assets) or the appropriate folder in the Site window, and drag each button in turn into its place on the page. To stack a group of buttons vertically in a table cell or elsewhere, press Shift+Enter (Shift+Return) after each button to insert a line break.

CREATING FLASH OBJECTS IN DREAMWEAVER

Java Applets

Java is an object-oriented programming language based on C++ and developed by Sun Microsystems. The goal of Java is to be as cross-platform as possible. Currently, most Java applets (little applications) are run inline inside a Web browser, although stand-alone programs—and even operating systems—have been written for Java.

Java applets run on Netscape 2 or later for PCs, Netscape 2.2 or later for the Mac, and Internet Explorer 3 or later for either platform. It must be said here that Microsoft wishes Java didn't exist, and that to use Java without crashing, Mac users should use IE 5.1 instead of 5.0.

To insert a Java applet:

1. In the Document window, click to place the insertion point at the place on the page where you want the Java applet to appear.

2. From the menu bar, select Insert > Media > Applet.

   or

   Click the Applet button on the Media tab of the Insert toolbar 👆 .

   Either way, the Select Java Applet File dialog box will appear (**Figure 7.49**).

3. Locate the applet on your computer. When you locate the source file, click Open.

4. When the pathname of the applet appears in the File name text box, click OK. The dialog box will close and a placeholder will appear in the window 🖼️ .

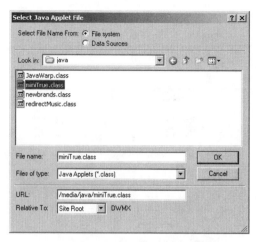

Figure 7.49 Select the class file from your computer. The file will probably have the .CLASS extension.

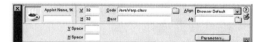

Figure 7.50 The Property inspector, displaying Applet properties.

✔ Tips

- Some applets will run on your computer; others must be on a Web server, depending on how many additional classes they require to run.

- You can set additional properties for Java applets (**Figure 7.50**). Many of them are similar to plug-in properties; for additional details, see Appendix G on the book's Web site.

ActiveX

Now that Internet Explorer supports plug-ins, not that many people are using ActiveX for the same purpose, although some database applications that run on Microsoft servers still use ActiveX applets (called *controls*) on active pages in the ASP and ASP.NET formats.

ActiveX is a software architecture developed by Microsoft and introduced with IE3 as its answer to the Java language—answering the cry for cross-platform portability with a proprietary code system. An ActiveX control can act like a plug-in and invisibly play multimedia content, or it can act like Java or JavaScript and serve as a miniature program that runs inside the Internet Explorer Web browser.

Netscape 6 supports ActiveX but it's recommended that you test your controls in Netscape before launching them on your live site. There is a plug-in for Netscape 4 that plays some ActiveX controls, but support is not built into the program and the plug-in should not be counted on to work. Dreamweaver tries to be as cross-platform as possible about this; you can insert an ActiveX control and specify the Netscape plug-in equivalent, if any, and Dreamweaver will write code for both programs simultaneously.

To insert an ActiveX control:

1. In the Document window, click to place the insertion point at the place on the page where you want the ActiveX control to appear.

continued on next page

ACTIVEX

2. From the menu bar, select Insert > Media > ActiveX.

or

Click the ActiveX button on the Media tab of the Insert toolbar  .

Either way, an ActiveX placeholder will appear in the Document window at the insertion point .

3. Click on the placeholder to display ActiveX attributes in the Property inspector (**Figure 7.51**). Fill in the Class ID and other required properties (refer to the documentation for the control if you need help).

Figure 7.51 The Property inspector, displaying ActiveX properties.

✔ Tips

■ You can use JavaScript to have the browser go to one URL if the browser is ActiveX-capable and to a different URL if it's not. See the section in Chapter 16 called *Check Plug-in*, and use the ActiveX checkbox.

■ Macromedia recommends that you refer to the documentation for the ActiveX control to determine the requisite IDs and parameters needed.

■ You can set additional properties for ActiveX controls. Many of them are similar to plug-in properties; for additional details about ActiveX properties, see Appendix G on the companion Web site for this book.

■ Frequently used Class IDs are stored in the Property inspector, which also lists Shockwave, Flash, and Real for you. To delete one permanently, such as if you write your own Flash ID and want not to use the default one by mistake, select the ID type and then click the Minus (–) button on the Property inspector for ActiveX.

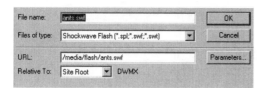

Figure 7.52 Click the Parameters button to apply parameters while you're inserting a file.

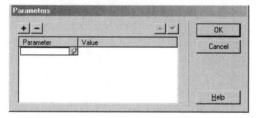

Figure 7.53 Add any extra attributes for your multimedia files in the Parameters dialog box.

Extra Parameters

Some multimedia objects require other parameters for optimal performance. These parameters may be indicated in the documentation for the language or program you're using. Of course, if it's an applet or object you wrote yourself, you'll know all about it already. (See the sections on sound for details about embedded sound parameters.)

To set additional object parameters:

1. In the Document window, select the placeholder for the object. The Property inspector will display the object's properties.

2. On the Property inspector, click on the Parameters button.

   or

   On any Insert File dialog box shown in this chapter, click the Parameters button (**Figure 7.52**).

   Either way, the Parameters dialog box will appear (**Figure 7.53**).

3. Click the Plus (+) button. The Parameter text field becomes available.

4. Type the name of the parameter in the Parameter text field (such as loop).

5. Press the Tab key. The Value text field becomes available.

6. Type the value of the parameter in the Value text field (such as TRUE).

continued on next page

EXTRA PARAMETERS

7. Repeat steps 3 through 6 for any additional parameters.

8. When you're all set, click on OK to close the dialog box, and return to the Document window.

Figure 7.54 shows parameters for an embedded sound file.

✔ Tip

■ What's that lightning bolt? That's used exclusively with a testing server to set up these parameters to play from an object on an application server. Ignore it if you're not using a testing server.

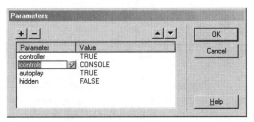

Figure 7.54 These are the parameters for an embedded sound file. I sometimes find it more expedient to type the parameters in the HTML inspector and then proof them in the Parameters dialog box.

Reordering and Removing Parameters

You can change the operation order of parameters by clicking on the name of the parameter in question and clicking the up or down arrow buttons to move the parameter through the list. You can also delete a parameter:

1. Follow steps 1 and 2 in the list on this page to open the Parameters dialog box.

2. Click on the name of the parameter you want to delete.

3. Click the – (Minus) button. The parameter will be deleted.

FONTS AND CHARACTERS

Figure 8.1 You can use different sizes, colors, and text styles on a single Web page, or even in a single paragraph.

Text comes in all shapes, sizes, and colors— or at least it can on Web pages (**Figure 8.1**). In this chapter, we'll go over the most basic ways of working with text, including cutting and pasting. Then, we'll find out how to accomplish rudimentary typographical changes: font size, font face, and font color. We'll also look at various text styles, from bold and italic to code fonts.

We'll also find out how to insert special characters like accented letters and copyright marks.

And we'll see how you can use Dreamweaver's word-processing tools, such as find-and-replace and spell check, to keep your Web pages clean and shiny.

Basically, this chapter covers changes that you can make on the character level—that is, to individual words or groups of words. There's a lot more you can do with text, of course—see the sidebar on this page.

What's Where

This chapter covers font sizes, font faces, text styles, font colors, special characters, finding and replacing text, and spell checking.

Chapter 9 covers all the basics of laying out blocks of text: paragraphs versus line breaks, headings, preformatted text, numbered lists, bulleted lists, definition lists, paragraph alignment, divisions, indent and outdent, nonbreaking spaces, and horizontal rules. Chapter 9 also includes HTML comments.

Chapter 10 deals with saving formatting as an HTML Style, and Chapter 11 will teach you all about CSS Styles, or Cascading Style Sheets.

Placing Text

There are several ways to put text on your pages with Dreamweaver (**Figure 8.2**).

To put text on your page:

◆ Just start typing in the Document window!

or

Select some text from another program or window, copy the text to the clipboard (usually by pressing Ctrl+C (Command+ C)), return to the Dreamweaver window, and paste it there by pressing Ctrl+V (Command+V).

or

Convert a text file or word-processed document to HTML, and then open it with Dreamweaver.

Once you have text on your Web page, you can treat it like you do in any other text editor. You can highlight the text and then copy, cut, delete, or paste over it. Use these commands:

◆ Copy: Ctrl+C (Command+C)

◆ Cut: Ctrl+X (Command+X)

◆ Paste: Ctrl+V (Command+V)

◆ Clear: Delete/Backspace

✔ Tips

■ If you copy text from another source and paste it into the Document window, it may not retain any formatting you've given it—including paragraph breaks. See Chapter 9 for information on using preformatted text.

■ You can copy and paste formatted text. To copy the text with its HTML formatting, select Edit > Copy HTML. To paste the formatted text in the Document window, select Edit > Paste. To paste the HTML code itself, select Edit > Paste HTML.

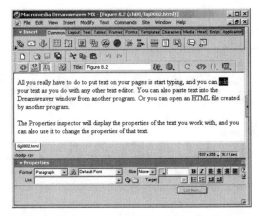

Figure 8.2 You can use the Dreamweaver Document window to type and edit text as you do with any other text editor.

Mom, What's Deprecated?

CSS is making obsolete a lot of the physical font manipulations people have been using for a while—most of the stuff in this chapter. The <font> tag, for instance, is purportedly going to die quietly—a process called *deprecation* (meaning the tags are being phased out of the HTML standard).

But it won't be a quick or easy death. Tons of people still use Navigator and Explorer 3 and 4; they still look at pages that use the <font> tag. And people who use versions of Navigator earlier than 4, and Explorer earlier than 3, can't see all the wonderful things that style sheets can do. The audience that uses older browsers may be shrinking, but it's not gone.

If you want to design for a wide audience, you need to be able to use these deprecated tags, and be able to get along without them. Although the deprecated tags may eventually be phased out, they won't die until no one on earth is surfing with an out-of-date browser: not a likely prospect, unless the earth loses all electrical power tomorrow.

Figure 8.3 This is the same page viewed in two different base font sizes—that is, the size of the font as chosen in the browser window, here as Medium and Small in Internet Explorer.

Language Encoding

Not everyone makes Web pages in the English language, and Dreamweaver addresses that. Western encoding is what most European languages use, and you can also set the encoding as Japanese, Traditional Chinese, Simplified Chinese, Korean, Central European, Cyrillic, Greek, Icelandic for the Mac, or any other non-Western encoding set you have installed. To do this, open the Preferences dialog box by pressing Ctrl+U (Command+U), and then click on Fonts to bring that panel to the front of the dialog box. Choose your language group from the Font Settings list box, and click on the language to choose a font group. In order to use non-Western encoding, you need to have the appropriate fonts installed; Asian languages in particular require a system that supports double-byte encoding.

You can also set encoding for a single page in the Page Properties dialog box (Modify > Page Properties).

Changing Font Size

There are several ways to indicate font size in HTML. Using style sheets (see Chapter 11), you can set a font size in points, like you do in word-processing and page-layout programs.

Without style sheets, however, you set font sizes relative to a base size. This base size is not something you can fix exactly, because every user has the option of customizing the default font size in their browser program to whatever size they choose. The font sizes that you set will be relative to this default font size, which is usually 12 or 14 points.

There are two separate scales you can use to determine size: the "absolute" scale (1–7), which is still relative to the user's preferences; and the relative-to-base-font scale (-3 to +4). Some folks also prefer using the very relative, but rather outdated `<big>` and `<small>` tags.

In **Figure 8.3**, you can see that the user's font size preferences in the browser window can make the same page appear different; that's why all sizes are relative. Open any page in a current browser, and select View > Text Size and then toggle the size up and down to see how your page will look to different users. Some folks like to view pages with a base of 10 points to fit more text; some choose 14 points to make it easier on the eyes.

Absolute font sizes

Absolute font sizes are based on the default text size of 3, which in most browsers is about 12 points. When you set an absolute size, you're not setting a point size, but rather telling the Web browser to display bigger fonts (size 4–7, which would be 14–24 points, based on a 12-point default) or smaller fonts (size 1–2, which would be 9–10 points).

Keep in mind, too, that the various browsers, platforms, and screen resolutions display point sizes relative to how they draw fonts in the first place.

To use the absolute scale:

1. Select the text that you want to resize.

2. From the Document window menu bar, choose Text > Size > and then choose a number between 1 and 7 (**Figure 8.4**).

   or

   In the Property inspector, click on the Size drop-down menu, and choose a number between 1 and 7 (**Figure 8.5**). You can also simply type the number in the Size text box.

In any case, the size of your text will change (**Figure 8.6**).

✔ Tips

■ If you choose size 3, you likely won't see any change in size, because size 3 is the default font size unless you specify otherwise.

■ If you change font size and then change your mind, select the offending text, and then select Default from the Text > Size menu.

■ When changing font size, you can click within the text and select an existing `<font>` tag in the tag selector to ensure that you apply the formatting to the entire tag.

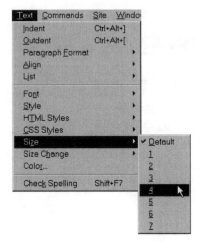

Figure 8.4 To adjust text size on the absolute scale, select Text > Size > N (where N is the absolute text size you want) from the Document window menu bar.

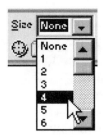

Figure 8.5 You can also choose a text size from the Property inspector's Size drop-down menu.

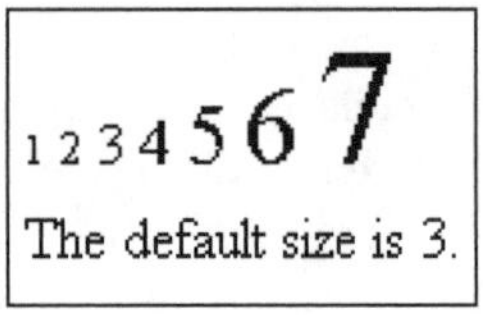

Figure 8.6 The absolute scale of text starts with size 1 as the smallest available size and moves up to a maximum font size of 7.

■ To change the size of all the text on a page, select Edit > Select All Ctrl+A/Command+A) from the Document window menu bar. Then follow the steps described earlier. Or, you can change the base font size, as described in *Setting a Base Font Size*, later in this chapter.

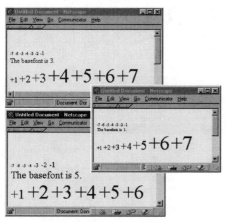

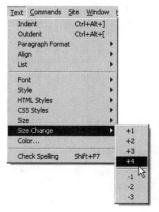

Figure 8.7 In these three examples, the base font size is 3, 1, and 5 (moving clockwise). Notice how none of the examples exceeds the maximum absolute size of 7 or the minimum absolute size of 1 (see Figure 8.6).

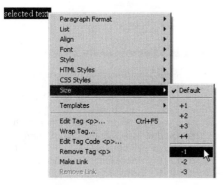

Figure 8.8 To increase relative font size, select Text > Size Change > N (where N is the absolute text size you want).

Figure 8.9 The context menu for selected text includes a great big text size menu. Just right-click the text (Control+click on the Mac).

Relative font sizes

Relative font sizes let you add or subtract from the user's font size to make the text, no matter what, appear larger or smaller. The sizes are in relation to a base font size of 3, unless you change that size, as described in the next section. The effects of relative font sizes are displayed in **Figure 8.7**. Relative font sizes are the best choice if you want your page to look basically the same to everyone—that is, if you want all your sizes to be on the same scale.

To use relative font sizes:

Select the text you want to resize.

◆ To choose from a menu of common relative sizes, select Text > Size Change from the menu bar, and then choose a number from +1 to +4 or -1 to -3 (**Figure 8.8**).

◆ To either increase or decrease size, select a number from the Size drop-down menu on the Property inspector (see Figure 8.5).

◆ To see a menu of all font sizes, select the text and then right-click (Control+click) on it, and then from the pop-up menu, select Size (**Figure 8.9**).

You'll see the size change immediately, but if you set a base font size, it won't show up properly until you preview the page in a browser.

✔ Tips

■ You can also type a font size, whether it's absolute or relative, in the Property inspector or the Quick Tag editor.

■ The Property inspector's Size drop-down menu doubles as a text box.

■ As there are only seven gradations of font size in total, the actual deportment of the font will vary depending on the base font size. In other words, if your base font size is 5, and you increase it by +4, the size still won't get any bigger than 7 (Figure 8.7).

233

Setting a base font size

You can set a base font size other than 3 for your page, in which case all differing font sizes will be set relative to this new size.

To set the base font size:

1. Open the Code inspector for your page by selecting Window > Others > Code Inspector from the Document window menu bar (or by pressing F10).

2. At the top of the document, locate the <body> tag.

3. Directly after the <body> tag, but before any other text, type the following line of code:

   <basefont size="n">

   where *n* is a number between 1 and 7. Your code would look something like this:

   <body>

   <basefont size="4">

   although there may be other stuff inside the <body> tag (**Figure 8.10**).

4. Press Ctrl+S (Command+S) to save the changes to the code.

5. Close the Code inspector by pressing F10.

Because Dreamweaver doesn't directly support the <basefont> tag, you won't see any size changes in the Dreamweaver window. However, any size changes you make will be based on the base font number you specified, rather than on the default base font size of 3. (You didn't go to all that trouble to set a base font of 3, did you?) You'll see the change to the base font size when you preview the page in your Web browser (File > Preview in Browser), as shown in **Figure 8.11**. See Chapter 3 for details on previewing.

Figure 8.10 Here's the code for a page using the <basefont> tag. You can see the <body> tag at line 7, and the inserted <basefont> tag at line 8.

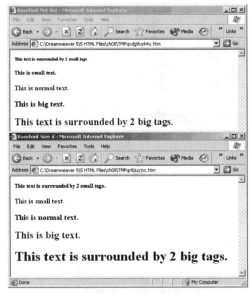

Figure 8.11 The page on the top is a page with no base font setting (which means a base font setting of 3). The page on the bottom is the same document with the <basefont> code added. Note that the "normal" sized text is a size bigger because I set the base font size to 4. Resetting the base font size works with the numerical sizes I discuss in this chapter as well.

Figure 8.12 In many browsers, the `<strong>` tag displays as bold and the `<em>` tag displays as italic. In Lynx, a text-only browser, all four tags are given the same emphasis. Other browsers, such as text-to-speech browsers or cell phone browsers, may interpret the `<strong>` and `<em>` tags differently.

Using Text Styles

You're probably used to using text styles, such as **bold**, *italic*, and underline, in your word-processing program or page-layout tool. You can use these styles in HTML, too, to add emphasis or visual contrast to pieces of text.

There are two kinds of styles in HTML: physical and logical. Physical styles tell the text exactly how to look, whereas logical styles suggest an attribute and let the browser decide how to interpret it. For example, `<b>` (bold) is a physical style. On the other hand, `<strong>` (strong emphasis) is a logical style. Although most graphical browsers display the `<strong>` tag as bold text, other software may treat it differently. Text-to-speech browsers, for instance, may read `<strong>` text with verbal emphasis.

Figure 8.12 contrasts the bold and strong tags, as well as the italic and emphasis tags.

✔ Tips

- Text styles are not the same as style sheets. Text styles are specific tags that affect how text is interpreted on screen. They have not been deprecated along with the `<font>` tag, because there's more call to make them available to single words and not groups of layout elements. (See the sidebar, *Mom, What's Deprecated,* earlier in this chapter.) Style sheets, as explained in Chapter 11, offer even more text attributes than regular text styles, but not all browsers have style-sheet-processing capabilities.

- Text styles as discussed in this section are also different from HTML styles, discussed in Chapter 10. HTML styles and CSS both allow you to create a set of attributes and combine a text style, such as bold, with another text attribute, such as color or font face. HTML styles, however, use the `<font>` tag rather than style sheets, and they can't be automatically updated.

Physical Text Styles

The most common physical text styles in most documents are bold and italic. See the next page for how Dreamweaver codes these styles. You can also underline text (see Tips, below).

To make text bold:

1. In the Document window, select the text you'd like to make bold (**Figure 8.13**).

2. In the Property inspector, click the Bold button **B** . The text will become bold (**Figure 8.14**).

To italicize text:

1. In the Document window, select the text you'd like to make italic (**Figure 8.15**).

2. In the Property inspector, click the Italic button *I* . The text will become italic (**Figure 8.16**).

To underline text:

1. In the Document window, select the text you'd like to appear underlined (**Figure 8.17**).

2. From the Document window menu bar, choose Text > Style > Underline. The text will become underlined (**Figure 8.18**).

✔ Tips

■ If you prefer menu commands to the Property inspector, you can choose Bold and Italic from the Text > Style menu instead.

■ The key commands for bold and italic are Ctrl+B (Command+B) and Ctrl+I (Command+I), respectively.

■ To remove a text style, reapply it by repeating the key command, reselecting the menu command, or clicking again on the style button.

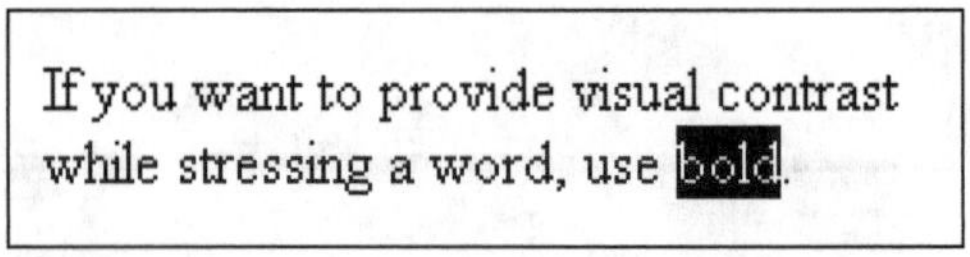

Figure 8.13 Select the word you want to make boldface.

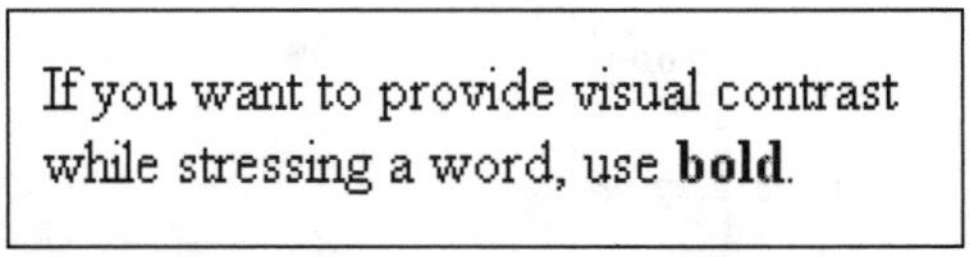

Figure 8.14 Your selection is now bold. I like using boldface to make links stand out.

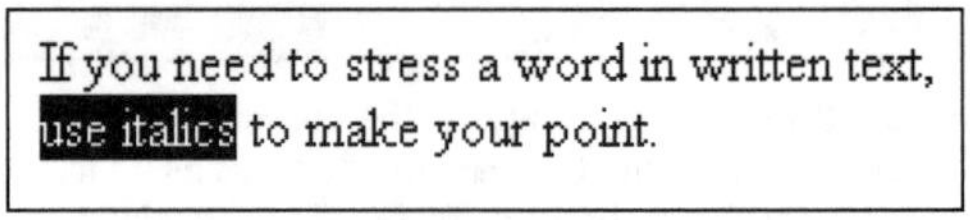

Figure 8.15 Select the word you want to make italic.

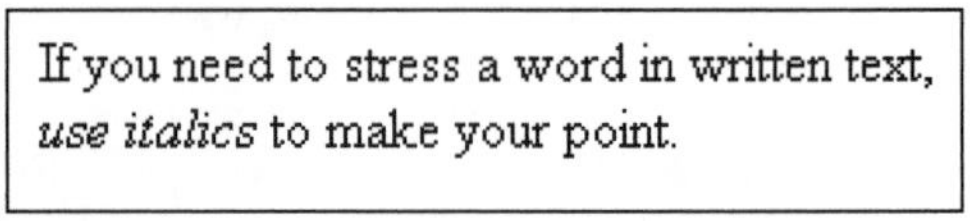

Figure 8.16 Your selection is now italic. Use it the same way you would in any written communication—to provide emphasis without disrupting the flow of the text.

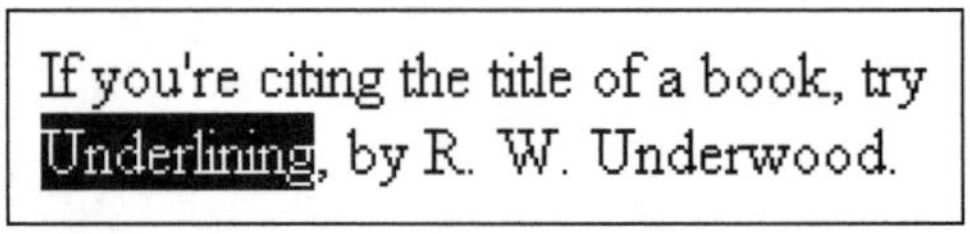

Figure 8.17 Select the word you want to underline.

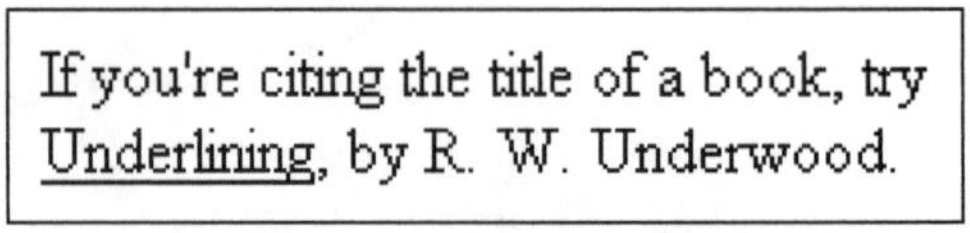

Figure 8.18 Your selection is now underlined. Use it sparingly so that people don't think you're linking to something.

More Physical Text Styles

Physical text styles (other than the ones on the previous page) are demonstrated in **Table 8.1**. Strikethrough and teletype are supported by Dreamweaver, and you can apply them by using the Text > Style menu. You may want to use teletype for things like blocks of code that will appear on your page.

Bold and Italic vs. Strong and Emphasis

After all that about physical text styles like bold and italic, I need to mention that Dreamweaver MX now by default codes italic text not with the `<i>` tag but with the `<em>` tag, meaning emphasis; and it codes bold text not with the `<b>` tag, but with the `<strong>` tag, meaning strong emphasis. This is what's called an accessibility feature, so that different kinds of devices such as text-to-speech readers will produce an equivalent presentation, such as tone of voice, in place of typographical emphasis.

In regular visual Web browsers the logical tags, `<strong>` and `<em>`, look the same as their physical equivalents, `<b>` and `<i>`.

You can switch back to using `<b>` and `<i>` in Dreamweaver's preferences. From the menu bar, select Edit > Preferences (Mac OS X: Dreamweaver > Preferences), and in the General category, deselect the last check box, Use `<strong>` and `<em>` in place of `<b>` and `<i>`.

If you want to use one tag or the other selectively, you must first change your preferences as I just described. Then, view the Text tab of the Insert toolbar. There you can choose from the physical, `<b>` and `<i>`, and the logical `<strong>` and `<em>`, by selecting your text and clicking the appropriate button.

Note: Although it appears that you could choose between the four tags on the Text tab anyway, that's not the case. Until you change your preferences, clicking on the `<b>` and `<i>` buttons will actually produce the code for `<strong>` and `<em>`—even though the buttons appear to present you with a choice.

Read the sidebar *Using the Text Tab* for more about using that tool.

Table 8.1

Physical Text Styles		
STYLE	**APPEARANCE**	**CODE EXAMPLE**
Strikethrough	~~strikes out text~~	`<strike>strikes out text</strike>`
Superscript	E=MC^2	`E=MC<sup>2</sup>`
Subscript	H$_2$o	`H<sub>2</sub>O`
Typewriter or teletype	old fashioned monospace font	`<tt>old fashioned monospace font</tt>`

Using the Text Tab

The Text tab on the Insert toolbar replicates many of the text formatting options you can apply using the Property inspector. The behavior of block formatting tags such as <p>, <pre>, <blockquote>, and the various headings and list items are discussed in Chapter 9, while styles such as <b>, <em>, <acronym>, and <abbreviation> are discussed in *Logical Text Styles* and *Physical Text Styles* in this chapter. (Be sure to see the previous section, *Bold and Italic vs. Strong and Emphasis* for details about using those buttons.

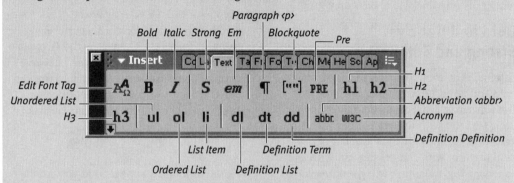

In one way, applying a tag works the same with the Text tab as it does with the Property inspector: You select some text, a word or a few lines, and click the button to apply the formatting. Or, you click the button before typing, and the formatting will be applied to the next text that you type.

The difference between the Property inspector and the Text tab is that the Property inspector displays, with highlighted buttons and menu choices, what formatting is already applied to the text you've selected or clicked within. The Text tab buttons don't change; they just apply the tags to the selection. Since the Property inspector is more user-friendly, that's the method I chose to describe in the lists in this chapter and Chapter 9.

I further discuss working with text at the tag level in Chapter 4, particularly in a section called *Contextual Code Writing Tools*.

Logical Text Styles		
Style Name and Appearance	Tag	Uses
Emphasis	`<em>`	indicates importance
Strong	`<strong>`	indicates strong importance
Code	`<code>`	programming code and scientific equations
Variable	`<var>`	in tutorials, marks placeholders for user-defined text; also mathematical
Sample	`<samp>`	samples of code output
Keyboard	`<kbd>`	in tutorials, indicates text the user should input
Citation	`<cite>`	a citation or reference to a work used as a source
Definition	`<dfn>`	marks the first use of a keyword in educational texts
~~Deleted~~	`<del>`	indicates text that, in this draft, has been marked for deletion
<u>Inserted</u>	`<ins>`	indicates text that, in this draft, has been added by the current editor or producer

Figure 8.19 This figure illustrates how the logical text styles supported by Dreamweaver are displayed in most browsers. There are many other such styles; these are merely some of the most common. To mark up text with any of these styles, select your text and then choose Text > Style > N (where N is the style you wish to use) from the Dreamweaver menu bar.

Logical Text Styles

The logical styles that Dreamweaver includes in its Style menu are shown in **Figure 8.19** as displayed by most browsers. If you have a special concern as to how they're used in a specific browser, such as an email program or a hand-held device, you'll need to load the page into that browser.

To use a logical style:

1. In the Document window, select the text for which you'd like to change the style.

2. From the Document window menu bar, select Text > Style and then choose an item from the list. The text will change appearance to reflect your choice.

✔ Tips

■ To use a style that Dreamweaver doesn't support, apply the style to the code. See Chapter 4 if you need help with HTML.

■ Why use these styles? You may find use in text-to-speech or text-only browser for **strong** and em. Code is like teletype—good for monospace blocks of text. The others may come in handy for use in conjunction with CSS (apply these tags and then redefine them, or use them when the <i> or <b> tags have styles attached), with databases, or with XML.

■ To find out more about the intended purpose of these and other obscure tags, Select Help > Reference and look up the tag to find usage, examples, and attributes.

Using Font Faces

You can set the typeface, or font, for any text on your page. Unless you specify a font face, any text on your pages will appear in the user's browser window in their browser's default font face (**Figure 8.20**). Most users probably have Times New Roman (Times) as their default proportional font, although some may have changed it.

When specifying font faces on a Web page (**Figure 8.21**), keep in mind that not every user has every font installed—far from it. Additionally, fonts that come from the same typeface family can be named several different things (such as Arial, Helvetica, and Univers), or the same font may be named

different things on different platforms (Times New Roman on Windows is nearly the same as Times and New York on the Mac).

To get around trying to guess who has what font, you can use one of Dreamweaver's pre-set combinations, which include fonts nearly everyone owns. You can also create your own *font group* or *font combination* that offers the Web browser several choices. The browser will check to see if the first suggested font is installed, and then the second, and so on. If none of the recommended display fonts are available, the text will be displayed in the user's default browser font—not the end of the world.

Old Style and Old Style Light

Some text styles are hardly used anymore, and you might wonder what they were ever used for in the first place. You'll find many of these tags if you browse through the list in the Tag Chooser or the Reference panel (both are described in Chapter 4).

When the computer scientists at CERN invented the protocols now known as the Web, the Internet was used largely by scientists working for the government or universities. The Web Tim Berners-Lee envisioned was an updateable library of papers, theories, data findings, and discussion. That helps explain why tags such as <acronym>, <citation>, <code>, <keyboard>, <sample>, and <variable> appeared in the definition of the HTML language, now under the care of the W3C (World Wide Web Consortium). These tags were invented with the supposition that they could be searched on or otherwise indexed to help people or databases find information.

Some of the more common tags are illustrated in **Figure 8.19**. The <acronym> tag does not change the appearance of text, but the code looks like this:

```
The <acronym title="World Wide Web Consortium">W3C</acronym> is located in
Switzerland.
```

As with many of these tags, the <acronym> tag is used rarely; it's included in the Tag menu, but not in the menu bar. It would be convenient for indexers if all uses of acronyms carried the tag with the title attribute defined; however, its use isn't widespread enough to be practical. Of course, there's probably a research lab somewhere that loves it for in-house cataloguing. If you're out there, let me know.

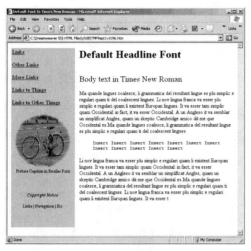

Figure 8.20 On this page, I haven't set the font face for any of the text, so most of it appears in Times New Roman, a very readable font that everyone has installed. The insert is in the `<tt>` tag, one of the text styles we saw earlier, so it appears in Courier, a monospace font.

Figure 8.21 I've added some variety here using Arial and Verdana, two of the font groups that Dreamweaver includes as available selections.

✔ Tips

- Dreamweaver's preset font combinations consist of system fonts that are found on nearly every computer sold in the last five years. If you want users to be able to see a special font if they have it installed, be sure to back up that font with a similar-looking, more-common font.

- For logos and other collateral that absolutely, positively needs to be in the right font face, you'll have to use images. You can also create Flash text objects right in Dreamweaver and use whatever fonts you have installed in those pieces of text. Everything you need to know about inserting images is in Chapter 5; Flash and Flash text are described in Chapter 7.

- When changing font face, you can click within the text and select an existing `<font>` tag in the tag selector to ensure that you apply the formatting to the entire tag and that you don't add any additional, redundant `<font>` tags. So, if you've applied a size, you should apply the face settings to the same tag.

- If Dreamweaver does create redundant `<font>` tags, use the clean-up feature to combine them. Select Commands > Clean up HTML from the document window menu bar. See Chapter 4 for more details on cleaning up your code.

Setting a Font Face

Dreamweaver comes with several common font face groups specified (**Figure 8.22**). If you want to add one to the list, see the next section. In either case, you'll follow these instructions for setting selected text in a new font face.

To set the face for selected text:

1. With the document open in the browser window, highlight the text for which you wish to change the font.

2. In the Property inspector, choose a font face group from the Font Face drop-down menu (**Figure 8.23**).

   or

   From the Document window menu bar, choose Text > Font and then choose a font group from the list (**Figure 8.24**).

The selected text will change to the first installed font face on the list.

Arial, Helvetica, sans serif

Times New Roman, Times, serif

Courier New, Courier, mono

Georgia, Times New Roman, Times, serif

Verdana, Arial, Helvetica, sans serif

Figure 8.22 These are the preset font combinations available in Dreamweaver. You can include any number of fonts in a font combination; the browser will try each one in turn, from left to right. Serif, Sans Serif, and Mono are not fonts but types of fonts. See the sidebar *I Shot the Serif*, later in this chapter.

Paragraph Format menu   *Font Size menu*

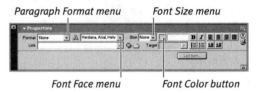

Font Face menu   *Font Color button*

Figure 8.23 The Property inspector allows you to set the font face for text, among other things.

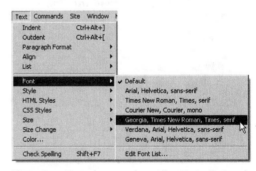

Figure 8.24 From the menu bar, select Text > Font and then choose a font combination.

Base Font Face

You can set the base font for a page, too, by adding the FACE attribute to the `<basefont>` tag. Follow the instructions in the section *Setting a Base Font Size*, and to the base font tag, add the attribute FACE ="Name", where "Name" is the name of the font you want to specify. Your code will look something like this:

```
<basefont size="4" FACE="Arial">
```

Older versions of Explorer and some "third-party" browsers don't support this attribute; the worst that can happen is that the page's font face will still be the browser default.

I Shot the Serif

Serifs are those curly things some fonts use at the ends of strokes in letters. They have their origins in ancient times when stonecutters had to make a terminating stroke in a letter in order to remove the chisel from the stone.

A sans serif font, then, is a font without any serifs. As illustrated in **Figure 8.22**, sans serif fonts look different than serif fonts.

Mono refers to a monospace, or a fixed-width font. In a fixed-width font, each letter occupies the same amount of space. Email and Telnet programs use these.

A proportional font is designed so that each character takes up only as much space as it needs. Letter combinations such as fi and th are fitted together.

Proportional fonts are used for body text on most Web pages, whereas fixed-width fonts are used for the text typed into forms and for several text styles, such as teletype, code, and citation. Preformatted text (Chapter 9) also uses a fixed-width font.

Courier New (Courier), used in **Figure 8.22**, is the most popular fixed-width font. Some browsers, however, allow their users to change their proportional and fixed-width fonts so that the choices don't necessarily correspond to their character.

✔ Tips

- To remove any font face specifications, select the text for which you've changed the font face, and then change the font face settings to Default Font, using either the Text > Font menu or the Property inspector.

- To set the face for an entire page, select all the text (Edit > Select All) and then choose a font group from the list. You can then change selections within that page to a different font, if you like.

- To change the font face for a tag such as <code> or <kbd>, the font tag must appear *inside* that tag. Either select the text inside that tag in Code view, or apply the style tag after applying the font. Either way, your code should look something like this:

```
<kbd><font face="Georgia, Times New
Roman, Times, serif">selection
</font></kbd>
```

The Font Tag Editor

You can click on the Font Tag Editor button ![A] on the Text tab of the Insert toolbar to open a dialog box that lets you edit attributes such as size, face, and color all at once. Using the Tag Editor dialog boxes to edit code is more thoroughly covered in Chapter 4.

Creating a Font Group

Dreamweaver offers several preset font combinations, shown in Figure 8.22. You can also define your own font combinations and add them to the list of available fonts.

To create a font group:

1. From the Document window menu bar, select Text > Font > Edit Font List.

   or

   In the Property inspector, choose Edit Font List from the Font Face drop-down menu (**Figure 8.25**).

   In either case, the Edit Font List dialog box will appear (**Figure 8.26**).

2. Dreamweaver's existing font combinations will appear in the Font List text box. All system fonts installed on your computer will appear in the Available Fonts list box.

3. Locate your first-choice font in the Available Fonts list box and click it.

4. Click the Left Arrow button, and the font's name will appear in the Chosen Fonts list box (**Figure 8.27**).

5. Repeat steps 3 and 4 for all the font faces you want to appear in this particular font combination. You may want to add additional choices that resemble your font in case the user doesn't have it available.

6. To add the name of a font you don't own, type it in the text box below the Available Fonts list box. For example, you may have Bookman on your Mac, but if you want to make Bookman Old Style your second choice and you don't have it, you need to type it here.

Figure 8.25 Choose a font combination from the Property inspector's Font Face drop-down menu.

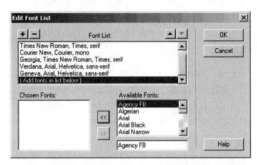

Figure 8.26 The Edit Font List dialog box lets you define font combinations using any font on your computer.

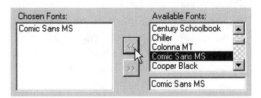

Figure 8.27 Choose the font from the Available Fonts list box, then click the Left Arrow button to move it to the Chosen Fonts list box.

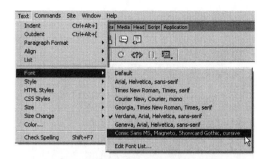

Figure 8.28 I've added a font combination to the Font Face drop-down menu. You can select Edit Font List from the same menu to add more fonts.

Figure 8.29 Here's a demo of my new font combination applied to text—users will only see one of these fonts, depending on what fonts are on their computers.

7. To remove a font you chose, click the Right Arrow button.

8. When you've chosen the right combination of fonts, click the + button to add the font combination to the Font List list box.

9. When you're all done, click OK to close the dialog box and return to the Document window. Your new font combination will be available in the Text > Font menu and in the Property inspector's Font Face drop-down list (**Figure 8.28**).

Now you can apply your new font combination (**Figure 8.29**). Read the previous section if you need to remember how.

✔ Tips

- There's no preview available in the Font List dialog box, and Dreamweaver doesn't allow you to display an individual font without adding it to the Font List. Therefore, it's advisable to view your font faces in another program (such as Word or PageMaker) so that you know what you're getting.

- You can change the order in which the font combinations appear in the list. Open the Edit Font List dialog box, and in the Font List list box, click on a font combination you'd like to move up or down in the list of fonts. Then click the Up or Down Arrow buttons. When you're done, click OK to close the Font List dialog box.

- Note for upgraders: Any font combinations already defined in Dreamweaver 4 will be imported into your preferences in Dreamweaver MX, so you don't have to add them to the font list again.

Changing Font Color

You learned how to set the text color for an entire page in Chapter 3. You can also set a different font color for specific pieces of text.

To change font color:

1. Select the text you want the color change to affect.

2. In the Property inspector, click the Color button beside the Color text box. The Color picker will appear (**Figure 8.30**). Click on a color to select it.

   or

   See Chapter 3 for details on using hex codes, the Colors dialog box, and the eyedropper for more color choices.

No matter the method you use, the color of the text will change to reflect your choice and a hex code will appear in the Color box on the Property inspector.

✔ Tips

■ To remove a font color, select the text in question and then delete the hex code from the Font Color text box in the Property inspector.

■ If you want to apply a font color to a link without changing the link color of the entire page, you must put the <font> tag *inside* the <a> tag for the link. The easiest way to do this is to use Code view or the Code inspector to select all the text inside the tag; then apply the color as usual. Your code should look something like this:

```
<a href="link.html"><font
color="FFCCCC">selected text
</font></a>
```

■ More details about setting link colors for an entire page appear in Chapter 6.

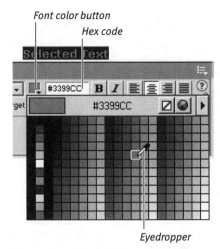

Font color button
Hex code
Eyedropper

Figure 8.30 Click the font color button, and then select a color by clicking a color choice in the color picker. Note how the pointer becomes an eyedropper.

Color Theory

When choosing the colors for your Web page, keep in mind readability first. Make sure your text has enough contrast with the background. You should also limit your palette and coordinate your colors. If the logo and buttons for your site are bright, primary hues, use similarly vibrant colors, if not the same colors, for headlines and selected links. If you're using subdued colors, stick to a subdued palette.

The Assets Panel stores all the colors that appear in your site, in link and font colors; in page backgrounds; and in backgrounds for tables, table elements, layers, and the like. That way, you can reuse your colors without having to remember which red you were using or having to cut and paste Hex codes.

Hex codes are defined in Chapter 3; in short, it's sufficient to say they have six (hex) digits and they use the hexadecimal, or 16-digit method, of counting (which is why they use letters and numbers).

Chapter 3 also talks about Web-safe colors.

CHANGING FONT COLOR

Special Characters

HTML is a language based on plain English text (also called ASCII), in which the characters you see on your keyboard are also the standard characters in the language. There are many other characters, however, that you may need to use on your pages. Special codes, called escape sequences, are used to reproduce these characters. The code for a copyright mark looks like this:

©

Dreamweaver lets you insert these special characters using a dialog box similar to Keycaps on the Mac or to Word's Insert Symbol feature.

Those Wacky Characters

A few characters that aren't included in Dreamweaver's set of characters are the ampersand and the left and right angle brackets (greater-than and less-than signs). They require special codes because they are essential characters in HTML code that don't normally get printed in body text. Dreamweaver doesn't include these tags in its list of special characters because you can type them directly in the Document window. Dreamweaver recognizes what you want and supplies the code for them in the background. If you're curious, those codes are:

&	&amp;
<	&lt;
>	&gt;

Another good tip about characters: the code for an accented e, or é, is é —self explanatory, it means "an e with an acute accent." You can work from here: A capital e with an acute accent is É, and an i with an acute accent is í. Same goes for ñ, ü, and ò. (Try them and see.)

On the Web site for this book, I've included links to pages that list *all* the special character codes.

Using the History panel described in Chapter 18, you can repeat a character without having to use the menu or dialog box. Also discussed in Chapter 18 are the Library and the Snippets panel, which are a good places to store updateable pieces of your site that get repeated from page to page, such as copyright notices or commonly used words with accents in them.

To insert a special character:

1. In the Document window, click within the text at the point where you want the special character to appear.

2. From the Document window menu bar, select Insert > Special Characters.

   If the character you want appears in the menu (**Figure 8.31**), select it. The character will appear in the Document window.

   or

   If the character you want doesn't appear in the menu, select Other. The Insert Other Character dialog box will appear (**Figure 8.32**).

3. When you see the character you want to use, click it, and its escape sequence will appear in the Insert text box. You can also type a word in this text box and insert the word with its character ("piñata," for example).

4. Click OK to close the Insert Other Character dialog box and place the character on your page.

To insert special characters using the Insert toolbar:

1. Click the Characters tab to display special characters (**Figure 8.33**).

3. To insert a character, just click it, or drag it onto the page. For more options, click the "Other" button ⊞ and see steps 3 and 4 in the previous list of instructions.

✔ Tip

- To make the buttons easier to read, I set my Insert toolbar to display both Icons and Text. You can do this in the General panel of the Preferences dialog box (Edit > Preferences, or on Mac OS X, Dreamweaver > Preferences).

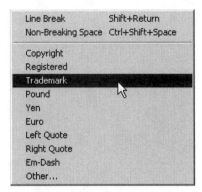

Figure 8.31 These are the characters available from the Insert > Special Characters menu.

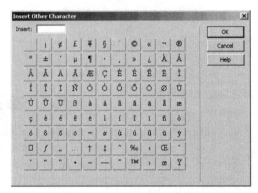

Figure 8.32 To insert a character other than the ones in the menu, choose Other from the Insert > Special Characters menu, and this dialog box will appear.

Figure 8.33 Using the Special Characters panel of the Insert toolbar, you can add a special character to your text with a single click. The panel is undocked here.

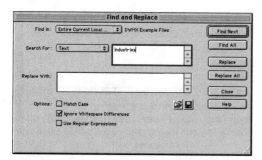

Figure 8.34 Type the text you want to find in the Search For text box.

Find and Replace

Dreamweaver can search your document and locate a particular piece of text. It can also replace one text string (a bunch of characters, whether they're code or words) with another.

To find a piece of text in the current page:

1. With the current page open in the Document window, choose Edit > Find and Replace from the menu bar, or press Ctrl+F (Command+F). The Find and Replace dialog box will appear (**Figure 8.34**).

   For details on searching more than one page at a time or searching code, see the sidebar *Seek and Ye Shall Find*, later in this chapter.

2. Make sure Text is selected in the Search For drop-down menu.

3. Type what you're looking for in the text box. This can be a whole word, a phrase, or part of a word.

4. To look for a particular case pattern (upper or lower), place a check mark in the Match Case checkbox.

5. To look for text and ignore spacing differences (e.g., to find both "tophat" and "top hat"), place a check mark in the Ignore Whitespace Differences checkbox.

6. Click Find Next. If Dreamweaver finds what you're looking for, it will highlight the text or code in question on the current page (in either Code or Standard view, although you may have to move the Find dialog box to see it).

7. Click Close to close the Find dialog box, or Find Next to find the next instance.

✔ Tips

- If Dreamweaver can't find the text in question, a dialog box will appear telling you it didn't find the search item.

- To find the same item again (even after you open a different page), select Edit > Find Next from the Document window menu bar, or press F3.

- You can also use the Find command in the Code inspector. Right-click (Control+click) on some space in the Code inspector to get the command from a context menu.

- Click Find All in the Find and Replace dialog box, and the Search tab of the Results panel will appear. When the search is complete, a list box will show all instances of your query (**Figure 8.35**)—double-click on an entry to open the page and highlight the instance (**Figure 8.36**), or click the Play arrow ▷ to search again.

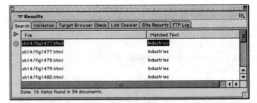

Figure 8.35 I chose Current Site from the Find In drop-down menu and then clicked Find All. The Search tab of the Results panel appeared, listing every instance of my search string.

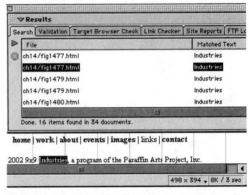

Figure 8.36 I can double-click any entry in the Results dialog box to open that page and highlight the text.

Figure 8.37 Find source code after typing it in the box.

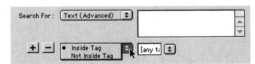

Figure 8.38 Search for text inside or outside of any specific tag or any tag at all.

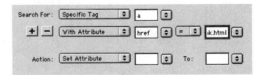

Figure 8.39 Find any tag, any attribute, and any variable that you specify.

Seek and Ye Shall Find

Dreamweaver includes some exhaustive search features for the current page, a local directory, or an entire local site. You can also use regular expressions and load or save searches.

To search an entire local site, a page from that site must be open. (See Chapter 2 for more about setting up a local site.) Choose **Entire Local Site** from the Find In menu to search the folders that make up your site. To search within a few files in your site, select **Selected Files in Site**, open the Site window, and hold down Ctrl or Command while clicking. Then go back to the Find dialog box.

To search a local directory, select **Folder** from the Find In menu. Type the name of the directory in the text box, or click the folder icon to browse and choose a folder. You can also choose what type of text to find by choosing one of these options from the Search For drop-down menu:

◆ **Text** Regular old text.

◆ **Source Code** HTML, XML, and other tags and attributes, ignoring text not in tags (**Figure 8.37**).

◆ **Text (Advanced)** Defines a search for text within or outside tags (**Figure 8.38**). Additional menus include one that lets you choose Inside Tag or Not Inside Tag, and a menu to choose tags. Select [any tag] from the menu to search for, say, the "bgcolor" attribute inside any tag. Click + to add additional search options for attributes.

◆ **Specific Tag** Lets you search for a certain tag or an attribute or value within a tag (**Figure 8.39**). To search for a specific tag, select it from the menu, or select [any tag] to search for an attribute such as "border" within any tag. To narrow your search to an attribute, type it in the With Attribute text box or select it from the menu. Then, specify a value, such as a hex code or a font face, or select [any value] from the menu. You can also set the = menu to equals, does not equal (!=), or < or >.

You can add as many variables as you want or subtract them using the + and - buttons. And when you're performing a replace operation, you can use the menus and text boxes in the Action area to specify what your value should be replaced with. For example, you could replace all instances of `"tr bgcolor="FFFFFF"` in selected files with `"tr bgcolor="FFCCCC"`.

◆ **Regular Expressions** Special text descriptors that let you refine a search. To enable regular expressions, click that checkbox. To find out more about Regular Expressions, see this book's Web site.

You can save a search query by clicking the Disk icon. To load it later, click the Folder icon and choose the file.

FIND AND REPLACE

To replace one piece of text with another:

1. From the Document window menu bar, select Edit > Find and Replace, or press Ctrl+H (Command+H). The Find and Replace dialog box will appear (**Figure 8.40**).

2. Type the text you want to destroy in the Search For text box.

3. Type the text you want to replace it with in the Replace With text box.

4. If you want to restrict the search to a specific case pattern (upper or lower), place a check mark in the Match Case checkbox.

5. To look for text and ignore spacing differences (e.g., to find both "tophat" and "top hat"), place a check mark in the Ignore Whitespace Differences checkbox.

6. To supervise the search, click Find Next, and when Dreamweaver finds an instance of the Find text string (the words or tags in the Find text box), it will highlight it in the document window. Then, you can click Replace to supplant it with the text in the Replace text box.

   or

   To have Dreamweaver automatically replace all Find What text with the Replace With text, click Replace All. A dialog box will appear telling you how many replacements were made.

7. When you're all done, click Close to return to the Document window.

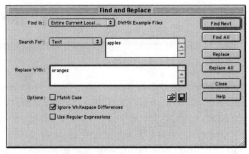

Figure 8.40 Type the text you want to find in the Search For text box, and the text you want to replace it with in the Replace With text box.

✔ Tip

■ Keep in mind that automatically replacing all instances of text can create problems. Imagine replacing all instances of "cat" with "dog" and ending up with a site full of words like "dogegory" and "Aldograz." Or replacing all misspelled instances of "stationery" with "stationary" may change some words that were meant to stay put.

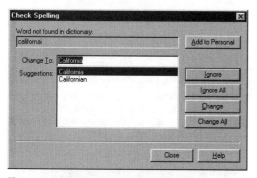

Figure 8.41 The Check Spelling dialog box allows you to ignore the unrecognized word, add it to your personal dictionary, or change it, either by typing it into the Change To text box or by choosing a word from the Suggestions list box.

Checking Your Spelling

One nice thing about using a WYSIWYG editor to do HTML is that you can check the spelling on your pages without the spell checker constantly stopping to ask you about tags or URLs. You can check the spelling of an individual selection or an entire page.

To check the spelling of a page:

1. With the page in question open in the Document window, click to place the insertion point at the beginning of the page (or the place at which you'd like to begin the spell check). You can also select a single word you're unsure about.

2. From the Document window menu bar, select Text > Check Spelling, or press Shift+F7. The Check Spelling dialog box will appear (**Figure 8.41**).

3. When Dreamweaver finds the first questionable word, that word will appear in the Word Not Found in Dictionary text box. You have several options here:

   ◆ If the word is spelled correctly, click Ignore.

   ◆ If the word is spelled correctly, and you think it might appear more than once on your page, click Ignore All.

   ◆ If the word is misspelled, and the correct spelling appears in the Suggestions list box, click on the correct word, and then click Change.

   ◆ If you think the word may be misspelled more than once, click on the correct word in the Suggestions list box, and then click Change All.

   ◆ You can also manually correct the word by typing the correction in the Change To text box and then clicking Change.

   Make this choice for each word the spell check questions.

continued on next page

4. When the spell check reaches the end of the page, Dreamweaver may ask you if you want to check the beginning of the document (**Figure 8.42**). It's usually a good idea to click Yes.

5. When the spell check is complete (including cases where there are no spelling errors), a dialog box will appear telling you so (**Figure 8.43**). Click OK to close this dialog box and return to the Document window.

✔ Tips

■ If a word is spelled correctly but is not in the dictionary, such as unusual proper names (Ronkowski or Gravity7), slang, abbreviations, or lingo, you can add it to the custom dictionary. Click the Add to Personal button in the Check Spelling dialog box. The word will be added to your personal dictionary, and future spell checks will not question this word. Keep in mind, though, that you may also have to add variations on the word, such as plurals (gorrillafishes) or possessives (Dorkface's).

■ To spell check a single word or phrase, highlight the text in question, and then start the spell check as described in Step 1. If you want to skip the rest of the page, when the dialog box appears asking you if you want to check the rest of the document (shown in Figure 8.42), click No, and the spell check will go away.

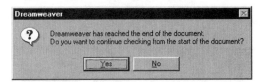

Figure 8.42 If you're checking the spelling of a single word or sentence, click No. If you started the spell check partway through the document and you want to check the whole document, click Yes.

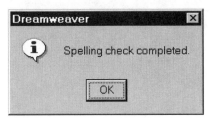

Figure 8.43 When the spell check is complete, you'll be told how many errors were found. Unfortunately, this includes words you ignored or just added to your personal dictionary.

PARAGRAPHS AND BLOCK FORMATTING

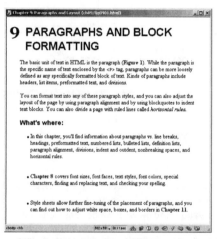

Figure 9.1 I formatted an HTML version of this page in Dreamweaver by applying paragraph breaks, two kinds of headings, blockquotes, and a bulleted list. If I had wanted to replicate the layout of this page (including columns), I would have used tables.

The basic unit of text is the paragraph, although in HTML the paragraph is a specific tag. Paragraphs in HTML are blocks of text enclosed by the **<p>** tag (**Figure 9.1**), but paragraphs can also be more loosely defined as any specifically formatted block of text. Paragraph types include headers, list items, preformatted text, and divisions.

You can format text into any of these paragraph styles, and you can adjust the layout of the page by using paragraph alignment and by using blockquotes to indent text blocks. You can also divide a page with ruled lines called *horizontal rules*.

What's Where

In this chapter, you'll find information about paragraphs versus line breaks, headings, preformatted text, numbered lists, bulleted lists, definition lists, paragraph alignment, divisions, indents and outdents, nonbreaking spaces, and horizontal rules.

Chapter 8 covers font sizes, font faces, text styles, font colors, special characters, finding and replacing text, and checking your spelling.

Style sheets allow further fine-tuning of the placement of paragraphs; you can find out how to adjust white space, boxes, and borders in Chapter 11.

Paragraphs vs. Line Breaks

Your elementary school English teacher probably told you that a paragraph contains a minimum of three sentences, and that longer paragraphs include a topic sentence. In HTML, the paragraph is simply a unit of text enclosed by <p> tags, and each paragraph is automatically separated from other paragraphs by a blank line. **Figure 9.2** shows a page that consists of four paragraphs.

To make a paragraph:

1. In the Document window, type the text that will constitute the first paragraph. The text will wrap automatically.

2. At the end of the paragraph, press Enter (Return).

The line will be broken, and a line of blank space will be inserted between the paragraph and the insertion point (**Figure 9.3**).

To apply paragraph formatting to existing text:

1. Click within the block of text to which you want to apply paragraph tags.

   or

   Select several blocks of text by highlighting them.

2. In the Property inspector, select Paragraph from the Format drop-down menu (**Figure 9.4**).

The paragraph tag will be applied to the text. See the upcoming section, *About Paragraph Tags*, to find out more about this.

✔ Tips

- Click within a block of text that needs to be formatted as a paragraph and press Ctrl+Shift+P (Command+Shift+P) to apply <p> formatting.

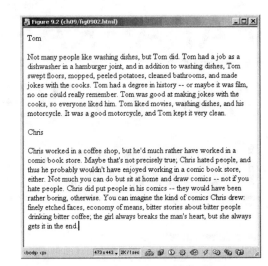

Figure 9.2 There are four paragraphs on this page: The single-word lines are paragraphs, too.

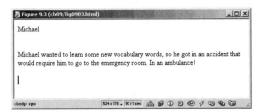

Figure 9.3 The text will wrap in the Document window—and in the browser window, as well—until you insert a paragraph break. When you press Enter (Return), the insertion point will skip a line of blank space and then start a new paragraph. Technically, there are three paragraphs on this page.

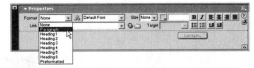

Figure 9.4 To easily surround text with paragraph tags, select the text and then choose Paragraph from the Property inspector's Format drop-down menu.

- You can also place the insertion point within an existing block of text and press Enter (Return) to break the text into two paragraphs.

Figure 9.5 The only way to break a line without adding white space, as you would in a poem, is to use a line break rather than a paragraph break. Press Shift+Enter (Shift+Return).

Figure 9.6 You can keep breaking lines until the cows come home. All these lines exist within the same paragraph, or <p> and </p> tags.

Insert Line Break button

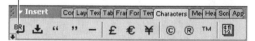

Figure 9.7 Click the Insert Line Break button to insert a line break at the insertion point; or, drag the button onto the page.

More Formatting Tools

The text tab on the Insert toolbar includes more formatting tools for adding list items, formatting preformatted text and block-quotes, and adding <p> and <hn> tags to selected text. Basically, you select some text and click on a button on the Insert toolbar, and the opening and closing tags for that paragraph format are wrapped around your selection. See the sidebar *Using the Text Tab* in Chapter 8. Using tag tools on the Insert toolbar is also covered in *Contextual Code Writing Tools* in Chapter 4.

Breaking Lines Without Adding a Blank Line

If you want to break the line without inserting a line of blank space, you can use a line break.

To make a line break:

1. In the Document window, type the text in the first paragraph. The text will wrap automatically.

2. At the end of the line you want to break, press Shift+Enter (Shift+Return).

The line will break, and the insertion point will begin at the next line (**Figures 9.5** and **9.6**).

✔ Tips

■ You can also insert a line break using the Characters tab of the Insert toolbar (**Figure 9.7**). You can then click the Insert Line Break button 🔳 or drag the button to the page.

■ You can achieve the same effect by selecting Insert > Special Characters > Line Break from the menu bar.

■ Line break tags don't use a closing </br> tag. As such, they can (and often should) exist within other tags. The code for Figure 9.5 looks like this:

```
<p>Light goes so fast,<br>
  it doesn't even notice. </p>
```

■ Ever get funny *leading* (line spacing) in the last line of a paragraph, so that the last line is spaced an extra half-line down? If so, insert a space after the period and before the closing </p> tag. Dunno why, but it works that way.

■ What about paragraph spacing? FrontPage lets you add spacing . This is actually not an HTML attribute but a property of CSS, which is covered in Chapter 11.

About Paragraph Tags

The tag for a paragraph is <p>. In the old days of hand-coding HTML, people often didn't close paragraphs with a </p> tag—technically, the <p> tag doesn't need a closing tag. However, the most recent HTML specifications prefer that you surround a paragraph with <p> and </p> tags, as Dreamweaver does.

Until the introduction of style sheets, this wasn't an issue anyone worried about; however, style sheets allow you to change the properties of an enclosed tag, and defining the <p> tag's properties only does any good if you close your paragraphs with the </p> tag.

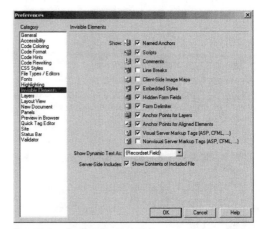

Figure 9.8 The Invisible Elements panel of the Preferences dialog box allows you to select which objects have visible markers when you view invisible elements.

Figure 9.9 Check the Line Breaks check box to turn line-break viewing on and off.

What's My Line Break?

The tag for a line break is <br>. The <br> tag is one of a few tags that doesn't need to be closed. You close your paragraphs with the </p> tag

Line breaks are invisible on screen. By default, they aren't even visible with invisible-element viewing turned on (View > Invisible Elements). To view <br> tags as invisible entities, you'll need to change your preferences.

1. From the menu bar, select Edit > Preferences. The Preferences dialog box will appear.

2. In the Category list box, click on Invisible Elements. That panel of the dialog box will become visible (**Figure 9.8**).

3. Check the box next to Line Breaks (**Figure 9.9**).

4. Click OK to update your preferences and close the dialog box.

Now line breaks will show up in the Document window with placeholders . You'll be able to select them to view their properties or edit them in Edit Tag Mode using the Quick Tag editor. For detailed information about line break properties, see Appendix I on the Web site for this book.

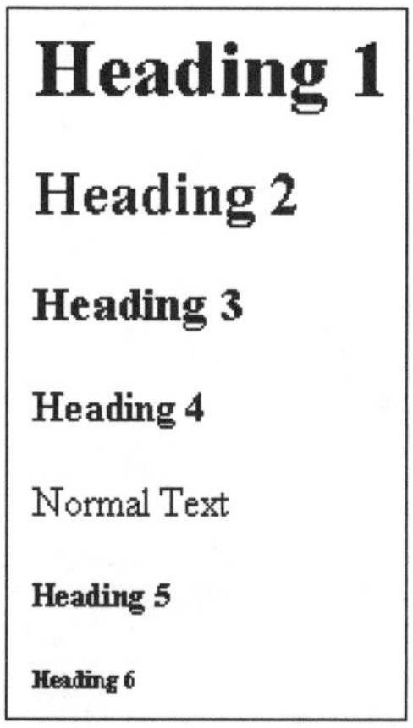

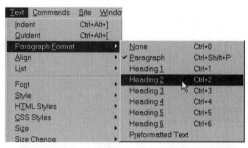

Figure 9.10 There are six levels of headings, from 1 (largest) to 6 (smallest). Heading 4 is the same size as the default font size.

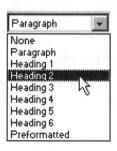

Figure 9.11 Choose a heading size, from 1 to 6, from the Text > Paragraph Format menu.

Figure 9.12 You can also set headings using the Property inspector's Format drop-down menu.

Figure 9.13 There are two text blocks on this page; the first is in Heading 2 format, and the second is in Paragraph format.

Creating Headings

Think of headings (also called headers) as being the same as headlines in a newspaper. They're generally larger than the body text of an article and bold. A heading is a block-type tag; that is, a line of white space precedes and follows a heading, just like other kinds of paragraphs.

There are six sizes, or levels, of headings (**Figure 9.10**). Heading 1 is the largest, and Heading 6 is often smaller than default body text.

To format a heading:

1. Click within the line or block of text you want to make into a heading.

2. From the menu bar, select Text > Paragraph Format > and from the menu that appears (**Figure 9.11**), select a heading (size 1–6).

   or

   On the Property inspector, select a heading (size 1–6) from the Format drop-down menu (**Figure 9.12**).

The text will become a heading: That is, there will likely be a size change; the text will become bold; and a blank line will be inserted after the heading (**Figure 9.13**).

✔ Tip

■ In this book, I use <hn> to represent any of the heading tags, which are <h1>, <h2>, and so on up to <h6>. The n stands for the heading size.

Using Preformatted Text

In general, when you paste text into the Document window, it doesn't retain any of its formatting. This includes line breaks, paragraph breaks, spacing, tabs, text-formatted tables, and the like.

If you have formatted text in another program and you wish it to retain its shape, you can insert it into the page's HTML as preformatted text. None of the other conventions of HTML will govern this text; for instance, in HTML, only one typed space will be displayed, even if you type 50 in a row. In preformatted text, any shaping of the text done with spaces or line breaks will be preserved.

Figure 9.14 shows a piece of ASCII art preserved with preformatted text, and **Figure 9.15** shows the same characters without the preformatted text format applied.

It's generally easier to set up the preformatted style before you paste in the text.

To place preformatted text:

1. In the Document window, click to place the insertion point where you want the preformatted text to begin.

2. From the menu bar, select Text > Paragraph Format > Preformatted Text.

   or

   On the Property inspector, select Preformatted Text from the Format drop-down menu (**Figure 9.16**).

3. Now you can paste in the text from the other program and it will retain that program's formatting.

✔ Tip

- You can also apply the preformatted style to text already on a page, or type the work directly into Dreamweaver.

Figure 9.14 Someone worked very hard formatting this map of the United States in a text editor. (Pictures made with plain text are called *ASCII art*.)

Figure 9.15 If you don't preserve the preformatted text, the picture looks like a jumble of characters. This is true not just for ASCII art but for any text that's been formatted using spaces or tabs.

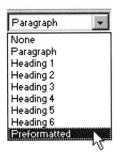

Figure 9.16 Select Preformatted from the Property inspector's Format drop-down menu.

Div and Span

There are two other kinds of text blocks that you might run across: <div> and <span>. The <div> tag stands for division, and it's used to mark blocks of text that span more than one paragraph. You can't end the division within a paragraph, because the </div> closing tag automatically breaks the paragraph. The <span> tag, on the other hand, can be used to mark up an area of text within a single block of text, such as within a paragraph or blockquote.

These two tags are mostly used in conjunction with style sheets, but I'm pointing them out here because of their properties of breaking paragraphs (or not). In the sidebar called *Terms of Alignment* (later in this chapter), we'll look more closely at the alignment properties of the <div> and <span> tags.

Preformatted Face

By default, the font used in preformatted text is the default monospace font, generally Courier or Courier New. The reason for this, as explained in Chapter 8, is that each character in a monospace font is the same width, which means that you can more easily control formatting of ASCII art, poetry, equations, or other formatting that uses page space as part of its content (**Figure 9.17**).

You can change the font face, however, in addition to designating it as preformatted. Follow the steps in Chapter 8, in *Changing Font Face,* to change the face of the preformatted text. Or you can refer to Chapter 11 to find out how to change the attributes of the <PRE> tag.

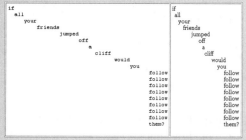

Figure 9.17 If you apply a non-monospace font to preformatted text, you'll get a different effect, because each character (including spaces) is not the same width.

Formatting Lists

Dreamweaver directly supports two kinds of lists: *numbered lists*, also called *ordered lists*; and *bulleted lists*, also called *unordered lists*. An additional kind of list, called a *definition list*, is partially supported by Dreamweaver.

Numbered lists

The tag for a numbered list is <ol>. Each list item uses the <li> tag.

To make a numbered list:

1. In the Dreamweaver window, type (or paste) the items you'd like to make into a numbered list, *omitting any numbers* (**Figure 9.18**).

2. Select the list items.

3. From the menu bar, select Text > List > Ordered List.

   or

   On the Property inspector, click on the Ordered List button.

The list will become numbered (**Figure 9.19**).

To add an item to a numbered list:

1. To add an item to the end of a list, click to place the insertion point at the end of the last numbered line, and press Enter (Return). A new number will appear at the end of the list.

2. To add an item to the middle of the list, click to place the insertion point at the end of one of the lines, and press Enter (Return). A new number will appear in the middle of the list (**Figure 9.20**).

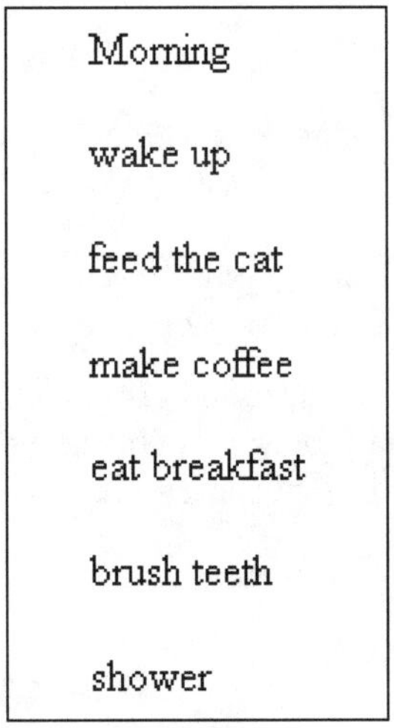

Figure 9.18 Type the items you want to make into a list.

Figure 9.19 After the Ordered List style is applied, the list items will be numbered and indented from the left margin. A paragraph break is automatically applied before and after the list.

Figure 9.20 If you add or remove items from the list, it will automatically renumber itself.

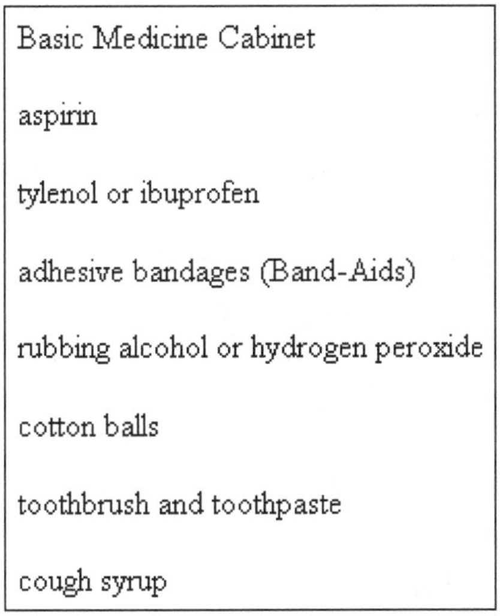

Basic Medicine Cabinet

aspirin

tylenol or ibuprofen

adhesive bandages (Band-Aids)

rubbing alcohol or hydrogen peroxide

cotton balls

toothbrush and toothpaste

cough syrup

Figure 9.21 Type the items you want to appear in the list, one to a line.

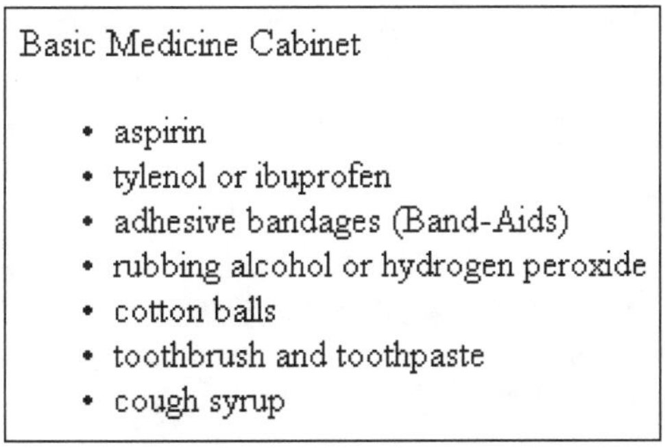

Basic Medicine Cabinet

- aspirin
- tylenol or ibuprofen
- adhesive bandages (Band-Aids)
- rubbing alcohol or hydrogen peroxide
- cotton balls
- toothbrush and toothpaste
- cough syrup

Figure 9.22 After you select the Unordered List format, the list items will be single-spaced and indented, and bullets will be added.

Additional List Properties

Some additional list properties are available in Dreamweaver. See Appendix E on the Web site for this book for details on how to use them.

To remove an item from a numbered list:

1. Select the item to be removed, and press Backspace (Delete). The text will disappear.

2. Press Backspace (Delete) again, and the numbered line will be removed.

The list will renumber itself to reflect any additions or subtractions from the list.

Bulleted lists

An unordered list is also called a bulleted list. As you might imagine, the list is outlined with bullets instead of numbers. The tag for a bulleted list is `<ul>`. Each list item uses the `<li>` tag.

To make a bulleted list:

1. In the Dreamweaver window, type (or paste) the items you'd like to make into a bulleted list, *omitting any asterisks or other bullet placeholders* (**Figure 9.21**).

2. Select the list items.

3. From the menu bar, select Text > List > Unordered List.

or

On the Property inspector, click on the Unordered List button ▤ .

The list will become bulleted, single-spaced, and indented (**Figure 9.22**).

To add or remove items from the list, follow the instructions under *To add an item to a numbered list* and *To remove an item from a numbered list*.

continues on next page

FORMATTING LISTS

✔ Tips

- To convert a list back to paragraph style, reapply the style (select it from the menu bar or deselect the list button on the Property inspector).

- If some extraneous text before or after the list gets added to the list, select the offending line of text and click on the corresponding list button to deselect it.

- You can also select Text > List > None From the menu bar to clear list attributes from selected text.

- Lists can only be bulleted or numbered, not both (thank goodness). To convert a list from bulleted to numbered (or vice versa), select the list and then apply the other list format.

- By default, a paragraph break will be inserted both before and after the list. Press Enter (Return) to end the list.

- The items in the list will be single-spaced by default. To add a line of blank space between the list items, press Shift+Enter (Shift+Return) after each list item.

- Netscape 6 (**Figure 9.24**) uses diamonds instead of round bullets.

- If you indent a second bulleted list within the first, the sub-bullets will appear with an extra indent, and the bullets themselves will be drawn as hollow circles (**Figure 9.25**). To do this, open the Code inspector and surround your list items with a second set of <ul> and </ul> tags, like so:

```
<UL>
<LI>Zoo</LI>
<UL>
<LI>Monkey House</LI>
<LI>Snake Pit</LI>
</UL></UL>
```

- Other list options are available using style sheets; see Chapter 11.

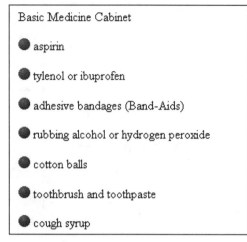

Figure 9.23 You can use tiny images on each line instead of making a bulleted list.

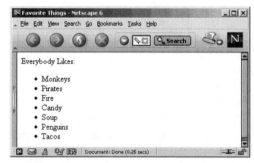

Figure 9.24 Netscape 6 uses diamonds instead of round bullets.

Images as Bullets

You may have seen a page that appears to use small images as bullets (**Figure 9.23**). This does not, in fact, use the bulleted list code. Each image is placed on a line (you can copy and paste them with Dreamweaver), and then the lines can be optionally indented. (See *Indenting Text*, later in this chapter.) You can also create image bullets using CSS. See Chapter 11.

FORMATTING LISTS

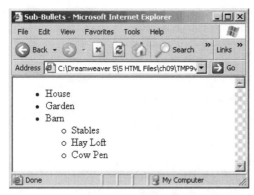

Figure 9.25 When you nest one bulleted list within another, the second list uses hollow bullets and gets an extra level of indent. This is Explorer 5; if you compare these bullets with Dreamweaver's, Explorer's are a little larger and a little heavier on the spacing.

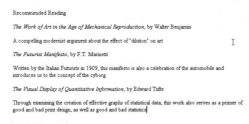

Figure 9.26 Type the terms and definitions, one to a line, in the Document window.

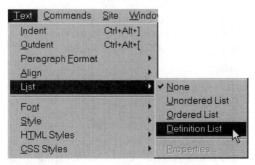

Figure 9.27 From the Document window menu bar, select Text > List > Definition List.

Definition lists

A third kind of list, called a definition list <dl>, is also partially supported by Dreamweaver—that is, you can apply a definition list to a block of text, but to fine-tune the list you'll need to work in Code view. In a definition list, there are two kinds of list items: a definition term <dt>, and a definition <dd>.

As you'd find in a glossary, the definition is indented under the definition term. The items in a definition list don't have to be definitions; you can use the definition list style anywhere you want this sort of formatting.

To make a definition list:

1. Type the definition terms and the definitions in the Document window **(Figure 9.26)**. Press Enter (Return) after each term and definition, and omit any indentations.

2. Select the list items. From the menu bar, select Text > List > Definition List **(Figure 9.27)**.

continues on next page

The list will be formatted so that every other item is a term and a definition (**Figure 9.28**).

✔ Tips

- If you're having trouble getting Dreamweaver to format the list properly, try selecting the text for each definition or term in the Code inspector. Make sure you select all opening and closing tags (including <p> and </p> tags).

- If you want to format the definition list yourself, surround each definition term with <dt> and </dt>, and every definition with <dd> and </dd>.

- You can include more than one definition per definition term, but you must add the proper tags yourself.

- You can cheat on indents by creating a definition list with just <dt> tags. This is an alternative way to indent blocks of text, because each is indented only from the left margin, not from both margins (as opposed to blockquotes).

Recommended Reading

The Work of Art in the Age of Mechanical Reproduction, by Walter Benjamin
 A compelling modernist argument about the effect of 'dilution' on art
The Futurist Manifesto, by F.T. Marinetti
 Written by the Italian Futurists in 1909, this manifesto is also a celebration of the automobile and introduces us to the concept of the cyborg
The Visual Display of Quantitative Information, by Edward Tufte
 Through examining the creation of effective graphs of statistical data, this work also serves as a primer of good and bad print design, as well as good and bad statistics

Figure 9.28 The list will be formatted so that every other item is a term or a definition. You can add extra formatting and line breaks later.

Adding Definitions and Terms

You can easily add an extra definition beneath a term, or a term without a definition, to a definition list in progress. Type your line of text and then, on the Text tab of the Insert toolbar, click on <dt> or <dd>. Work within the code to be sure the tags don't overlap.

Terms of Alignment

Dreamweaver uses the align attribute to align your text, and applies this attribute to either the <p> or <div> tag, depending on what tag surrounds your text. The code looks like this:

```
<p align="right">text</p>
```

The <center></center> tag can also be used. This is a text block; that means that it breaks the line like a paragraph.

Headers are aligned by using the align attribute within the <H*n*> tag. For instance: <H2 align=center>.

In general, alignment works on an entire text block, regardless of the tag. There is one cheat you can use, though: To align part of a paragraph or division, you can use the <span> tag to surround a few lines of text within a <p> or <div>:

```
<span align=right> one line<br></span>
```

Also, see Appendix I on the Web site, about using break properties to align or wrap text.

Figure 9.29 You can align text to the left margin, the center of the page, or the right margin. This can be the margin of the page or the margin of a table, layer, or frame.

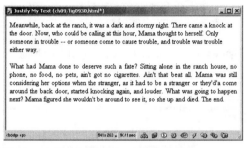

Figure 9.30 The first paragraph here has no alignment, and the second has been justified—that means more space is added between words so that the lines more closely meet the right margin.

Aligning Paragraphs

As is the case with word-processing programs, you can align part or all of a page of text with the left margin, the right margin, or the center of the page (**Figure 9.29**). New in Dreamweaver MX, you can also justify paragraphs (**Figure 9.30**).

To change the alignment of text:

1. Select the text for which you want to change the alignment. This can be a single paragraph, a heading, a list, or an entire page.

2. From the menu bar, select Text > Align > and then Left, Right, Center, or Justify.

or

On the Property inspector, click on the Left, Right, Center, or Justify alignment button 🖹🖹🖹🖹.

The text will become aligned according to the option you selected.

✔ Tips

■ *Justified* text means text that is aligned to come close to *both* margins, in which case space is usually added between words in order to make the text stretch to fit. Some people say that justified text is easier to read than so-called *rag-right* text, which is why nearly all books with long paragraphs justify text. On the Web, I don't think it makes as much of a difference because people tend to read in small chunks rather than for several pages at a time.

■ When you're working with images, or with tables, there are more than these alignment options available. Refer to Chapter 5 or to Chapter 12 for more on other alignment options.

Indenting Text

There are no tabs in regular HTML; the kind of five-space paragraph indent used in standard printed paragraphs is replaced on Web pages (and in this book) by the paragraph break, in which each paragraph is set off by a line of white space.

You can, however, indent an entire block of text. One way to accomplish this is by using definition lists (see *Formatting Lists,* earlier in this chapter). Or use the <blockquote> tag, which is what Dreamweaver does.

To indent a block of text:

1. In the Dreamweaver window, click within the paragraph you wish to indent; to select more than one paragraph, highlight the text you want to indent (**Figure 9.31**).

2. From the menu bar, select Text > Indent.

or

In the Property inspector, click on the Indent button.

Either way, the text will become indented (**Figure 9.32**).

✔ Tips

■ You can repeat step 2 for multiple indent levels (**Figure 9.33**).

■ The <blockquote> tag indents text from both margins; to indent text from one margin only, use a definition list (see *Formatting Lists,* earlier in this chapter).

■ You can also create an artificial indent by using nonbreaking spaces (see *The Nonbreaking Space,* later in this chapter).

■ Tables, especially with cell padding and cell spacing, are another way to create wider margins. See Chapter 12.

■ Paragraph indents and page margins are available by using style sheets (see Chapter 11); and by using frames (see Chapter 13).

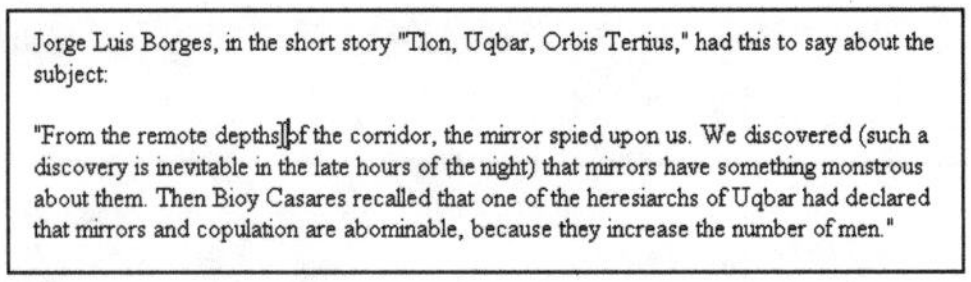

Figure 9.31 Click within the paragraph you want to indent.

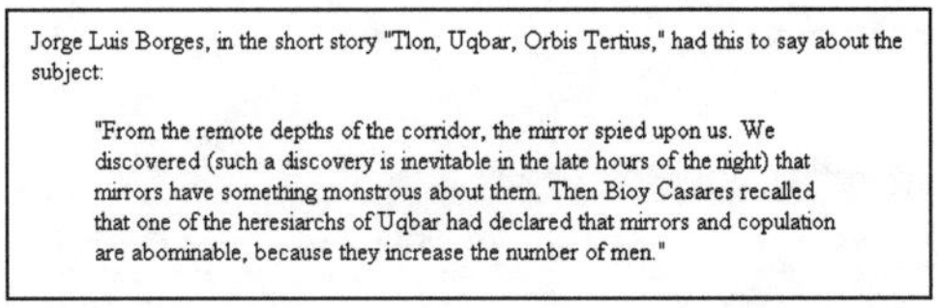

Figure 9.32 Dreamweaver indents text by applying the <blockquote> tag.

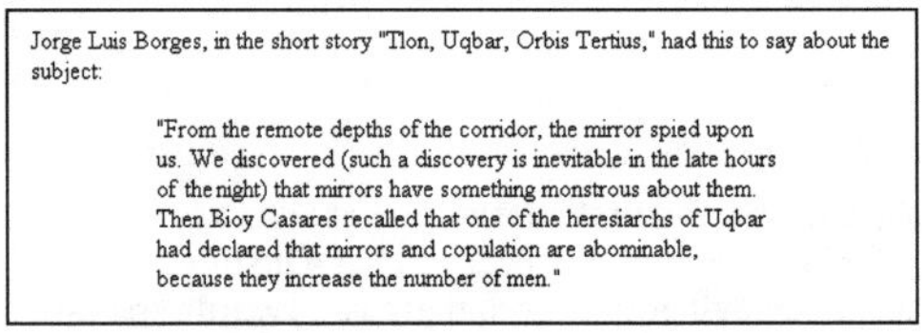

Figure 9.33 You can indent the paragraph more than one level; by doing so here, it becomes more apparent that blockquotes are indented from both margins.

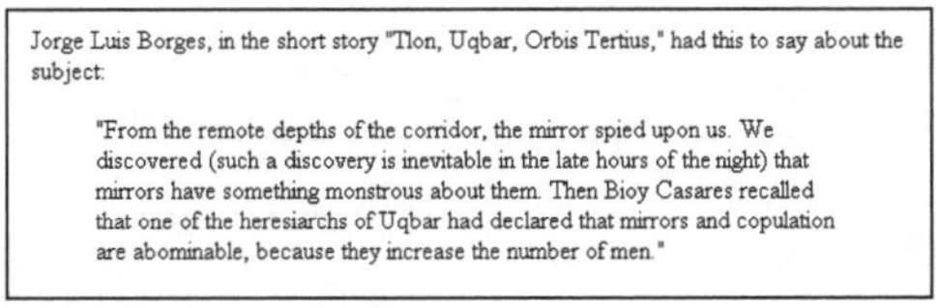

Jorge Luis Borges, in the short story "Tlön, Uqbar, Orbis Tertius," had this to say about the subject:

"From the remote depths of the corridor, the mirror spied upon us. We discovered (such a discovery is inevitable in the late hours of the night) that mirrors have something monstrous about them. Then Bioy Casares recalled that one of the heresiarchs of Uqbar had declared that mirrors and copulation are abominable, because they increase the number of men."

Figure 9.34 You can remove a level of indent by clicking on the Outdent button. This often works for removing list formatting, too.

Removing indents

If you change your mind, you can remove one or more indent levels. Dreamweaver calls this "outdenting," and it's also known as "unindenting."

To remove a level of indentation:

1. In the Dreamweaver window, click within the paragraph from which you wish to remove a level of indent; to select more than one paragraph, highlight the text.

2. From the menu bar, select Text > Outdent.

   or

   On the Property inspector, click on the Outdent button 　.

Either way, one level of indent will be removed (**Figure 9.34**).

✔ Tip

■ You can repeat step 2 until the text is back at the margin, if you like.

Outdenting?

Here's a completely useless sidebar. The word *indent* derives from the Latin in- (in) + dent (tooth), meaning to bite into (in Middle English, the word *endenten* meant "to notch"). The text, then, bites its way into the page. Because you can't "unchew" something, this explains why "outdenting" isn't a conventional layout term.

I heard from a reader in Italy who suggested an alternate interpretation. He said to think of the indent as the tooth itself, in which case the outdent would be a space or gap between the teeth.

The Nonbreaking Space

In HTML code, although spaces count as characters, they're shady ones. Only one simple spacebar-typed space will display in an HTML browser, even if you type 50 of them in a row. (Similarly, typed line breaks in HTML that don't include a **
** tag or other line-breaking code don't break lines in the Web browser. You can use spaces, tabs, and returns to format HTML code without it showing up in the Document window or the Web browser.)

The   entity

An entity called the nonbreaking space exists for use where a plain old space won't get the job done. This entity, printed ** ** in the code, is part of a family of special characters that you can't type easily with ASCII text; each character is represented by a *control code* or *escape sequence*. Of course, you can easily insert these spaces using Dreamweaver. The use of other special characters is described in Chapter 8.

Invisible placeholders

Dreamweaver automatically puts nonbreaking spaces in the code where it guesses you might need them. For instance, when you need more than one line of blank space, you can press Enter (Return) repeatedly, and Dreamweaver inserts multiple paragraph breaks. Because paragraphs won't appear without any text in them, the nonbreaking space is used as a placeholder to fill the paragraph. Note that you also can't type empty, multiple **<p>** tags to create multiple paragraph breaks. Same goes for table cells—a completely empty table cell won't get drawn by a Web browser, but one with an ** ** in it will.

Figure 9.35 shows a page and its code; although most of the page appears to be blank, it requires some behind-the-scenes code to work. **Figure 9.36** shows a closeup of that code.

Figure 9.35 As this page indicates, the nonbreaking space is a useful placeholder. See **Figure 9.36** for a closeup of the code.

```
8   <table width="100" border="1">
9     <tr>
10      <td> </td>
11      <td> </td>
12    </tr>
13    <tr>
14      <td> </td>
15      <td> </td>
16    </tr>
17  </table>
18  <p>A little and thus far empty table</p>
19  <p> </p>
20  <p> </p>
21  <p>Some blank space after the table</p>
22  <p> </p>
23  <p> </p>
24  <p>       An
     indent, and some blank space between
25     lines of text</p>
```

Figure 9.36 Here's the code—the nonbreaking space is serving as a placeholder for otherwise-empty paragraphs and table cells, as well as a placeholder for old-style paragraph indents on line 24.

Figure 9.37 Insert a nonbreaking space or a line break from the Characters panel.

✔ Tip

■ I talked more about special characters, such as accented letters and copyright marks, in Chapter 8.

To insert a nonbreaking space:

1. Click to place the insertion point where you want the nonbreaking space.

2. From the menu bar, select Insert > Special Characters > Nonbreaking Space.

   or

   On the Insert toolbar, view the Characters tab (**Figure 9.37**).

   Then, click on the Insert Nonbreaking Space button ⬇.

Either way, the Nonbreaking Space will "appear," albeit invisibly, on the page.

✔ Tips

■ You can repeat the above steps to insert a string of five nonbreaking spaces to create an artificial indent. You can then save that five-space string of text in the Snippets panel or the Library, if you like. (See Chapter 17, *Automating Dreamweaver*).

■ A keyboard shortcut for inserting a non-breaking space: Shift+Ctrl+spacebar (Shift+Command+spacebar).

Coding a Nonbreaking Space

If you're comfortable working directly with the code, you may want to insert a nonbreaking space exactly where you want it: between the <p> and </p> tags, or in a table cell, for example. To do so, follow these steps:

1. View the Code inspector by selecting Window > Others > Code Inspector from the menu bar. (You can also work in Code view by clicking that button on the Document toolbar.)

2. Click within the code where you want to add the space, and type the following characters:

3. When you close the Code inspector, Dreamweaver will automatically convert the escape sequence into its visual equivalent, an ordinary-looking space.

If you take a look at the code, you'll see that the   sequence is still where you put it.

THE NONBREAKING SPACE

Inserting Ruled Lines

A *horizontal rule* is a line that runs across the page horizontally and provides an explicit rather than implied division between parts of a document (**Figure 9.38**). The tag is <hr>. Some people swear by them; others think they're the ugliest tag in HTML, but I'm going to show you how to make one, regardless.

To insert a horizontal rule:

1. Click to place the insertion point where you want the ruled line to appear.

2. From the menu bar, select Insert > Horizontal Rule.

A ruled line will appear that is the width of the page, with a paragraph break before and after it.

To change the rule:

1. Select the horizontal rule and, if the Property inspector is hidden, double-click the line to display Horizontal Rule properties (**Figure 9.39**).

2. To adjust the width, first choose the unit of measure from the W drop-down menu (either pixels or percent of window size). Then, type a number in the W text box (**Figure 9.40**).

3. To adjust the height, type a number (in pixels) in the H text box.

4. To adjust the alignment, choose Left, Center, or Right from the Align drop-down menu (**Figure 9.41**).

5. To remove the 3-D shading (also called beveling), deselect the Shading checkbox.

Your changes will be applied when you click elsewhere on the Property inspector.

✔ Tip

■ You can also insert a horizontal rule by viewing the Common panel of the Insert toolbar, and clicking on the Insert Horizontal Rule button 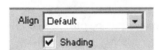 .

Insert Horizontal Rule button

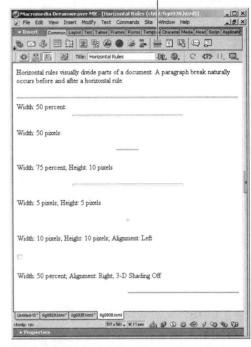

Figure 9.38 Horizontal rules can come in many different shapes and sizes; the first horizontal rule in this figure has the default attributes of 100 percent width, center alignment, and 3-D shading.

Figure 9.39 You can change the appearance of a horizontal rule with the Property inspector.

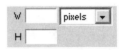

Figure 9.40 You can adjust the width in pixels or percentage of the window, and you can specify a height in pixels.

Figure 9.41 You can change a horizontal rule's alignment and turn shading on or off.

CREATING HTML STYLES

HTML Styles vs. CSS

The main difference between HTML styles and cascading style sheets (CSS) is that with CSS (discussed in Chapter 11), if you change a style, all instances of that style will be changed as well. For example, if you create a style called A-Head, one of its attributes may be the color blue. In CSS, if you change its color to red, all uses of the A-Head style will turn red automatically. There is no automatic update in HTML styles.

When you change an HTML style and want your changes to be applied to prior uses of the style, you'll need to reapply the modified style to those portions of your text.

Why then, does Dreamweaver provide HTML styles instead of relying on CSS? Because some people don't want to learn CSS; because CSS is not available to all browsers; because it acts differently in different browsers; and because Dreamweaver is for editing Web pages, not just style sheets. As long as people continue to use the old HTML text standards, why not make using them easier?

When you're formatting text, it can get a little tedious applying the same formatting over and over again. Dreamweaver helps by allowing you to save sets of formatting, such as `Bold +Arial +Heading 3 +Red`, as a named HTML style.

HTML styles are similar to styles in Microsoft Word or QuarkXPress. They're a collection of text attributes that you can save and use again and again. HTML styles are also similar to cascading style sheets, or CSS (see sidebar).

First, we're going to take a look at the HTML Styles panel and learn the difference between paragraph and selection styles. Then, we're going to learn how to create new styles and modify existing ones. Finally, we'll be able to apply HTML styles with a single click.

We'll be able to remove styles from text and delete styles altogether, too.

The HTML Styles panel

Dreamweaver's tool for creating and applying HTML styles is the HTML Styles panel.

To view the HTML Styles panel:

◆ From the menu bar, select Window > HTML Styles.

or

Press Ctrl+F11 (Command+F11).

The HTML Styles panel will appear (**Figure 10.1**), as a part of the Design panel group.

✔ Tips

■ HTML Styles are saved in the Library folder of each local site. You must create a local site before you can save a style; go back to Chapter 2 if you haven't set one up yet.

■ The HTML Styles panel for a new site starts out blank, with no styles in it (Figure 10.1). In previous versions of Dreamweaver, it came pre-loaded with sample styles.

■ If you're upgrading from a previous version of Dreamweaver, any HTML styles you created for a specific local site will show up in the HTML Styles panel when that local site is open (**Figure 10.2**). In other words, to see and use the styles for the local site "Hot Dog," select the name of the site from the Site window toolbar, or from the Document window menu bar Site > Open Site > Hot Dog (Mac only), and styles saved in that site will appear in the HTML Styles panel.

■ If you're working with more than one local site, make sure you open the correct site before saving HTML styles.

■ To copy HTML styles from one site to another, or to share styles between computers, see the last section of this chapter, *Sharing the Styles File.*

Figure 10.1 The HTML Styles panel lets you name and save a set of text formatting so that you can easily apply the formatting repeatedly.

Styles from site tarin.com appear in HTML styles panel   *Choose the correct site from this menu*

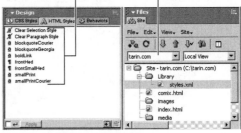

Figure 10.2 When I open a site in the Site window that already includes the `styles.xml` file, the styles in that file appear in the HTML Styles panel.

0 *corpHed_A*
2 *bodyText*
3 *highlightRedBold*
4 *emphasis*
5 *boldLink*
6 *smallPrint*
7 *photoCaptionGray*

Figure 10.3 A page that features paragraph styles and character styles.

Additive styles ——
Character style ——
Paragraph style ——

Figure 10.4 Paragraph styles are marked with a paragraph symbol, and character or selection styles are marked with the letter a. A plus sign (+) indicates that the style is additive and that it will not remove other formatting from the selection.

Kinds of HTML styles

HTML styles can format entire text blocks (paragraph styles), or they can format just selections (character or selection styles). **Figures 10.3** and **10.4** show both kinds of styles.

Additionally, HTML styles can either remove any previous text formatting (such as colors and font faces), or they can add additional formatting to your selection (such as adding a color to a piece of text formatted as a headline). Additive styles are marked in the HTML Styles panel by a plus sign (+) (Figure 10.4).

Creating New Styles

There are several ways to create your own HTML style. One way is to select some text you have formatted as you like, and then save that formatting as a style. Another way is to create a style from scratch using the Define HTML style dialog box. And to create two similar styles, you can make a copy of an existing style, and then make changes to the copy.

To save formatting as a style:

1. In the Document window, open a page that includes text formatting you want to reuse.

   or

   Make some changes to a paragraph or a selected piece of text using the Property inspector. For example, in **Figure 10.5**, I clicked within the first paragraph and applied the Heading 2 format and centered it; then I applied the Georgia font face, and changed the font color to maroon.

2. Click within your text selection or paragraph, and then click on the New Style button ![btn] on the bottom of the HTML Styles panel (**Figure 10.6**).

   The Define HTML Style dialog box will appear (**Figure 10.7**).

Figure 10.5 I modified this paragraph to have the formatting you see. Now I want to save the attributes as a style so I can apply them again and again.

Figure 10.6 Click on the New Style button on the bottom of the HTML Styles panel.

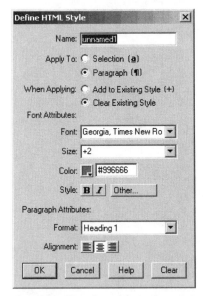

Figure 10.7 All my formatting appears in the Define HTML Style dialog box.

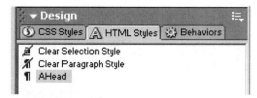

Figure 10.8 Now my new style, which I named AHead, appears in the HTML Styles panel.

3. The Define HTML Style dialog box will show the formatting applied to your text. For example, if you made the text blue, the Color button will be blue.

Type a memorable style name (such as Caption or BlueHed) in the Name text box.

4. Click the radio button for Selection or Paragraph, depending on whether you want to create a character or a paragraph style.

When you apply a paragraph style, you can also apply paragraph formatting. Select an option such as Paragraph or a Heading size from the format drop-down menu, or select None to allow the style to be applied to more than one type of text block.

5. The name of your style will appear in the HTML Styles panel (**Figure 10.8**). Now you can apply it to other pieces of text.

Building a style from scratch

In the previous section, we saw our selected text displayed in the Define HTML Style dialog box. To create a style from scratch, you choose the attributes you want directly in the dialog box rather than formatting your text beforehand with the Property inspector. If you want to make sure no formatting appears in the dialog box before you begin, click on some blank space or some unformatted text.

To create an HTML style from scratch:

1. On the HTML Styles panel, click the New Style button 📲 .

   or

   Click the Options menu button and, from the menu that appears, select New (**Figure 10.9**). Either way, the Define HTML Style dialog box will appear. **Figure 10.10** shows the dialog box along with the steps I used to create a new style.

2. Type a name for your new style in the Name text box. Try to name it something memorable; Blue Centered Arial is more descriptive than Style 4.

3. To create a paragraph style, click the Paragraph radio button. To create a character or selection style, click the Selection radio button.

4. To create a style that supercedes any existing text formatting, click the Clear Existing Style radio button. To create a style that adds its attributes to existing formatting, click Add to Existing Style.

5. Select any attributes you like for the style. For help with Font attributes, see Chapter 8. For help with Paragraph attributes, see Chapter 9.

6. When you're finished, click OK to save your changes and close the Define HTML Style dialog box.

Your new style will appear in the HTML Styles panel.

Options menu button

New Style button

Figure 10.9 Click the menu button, and select New from the menu; or click on the New Style button.

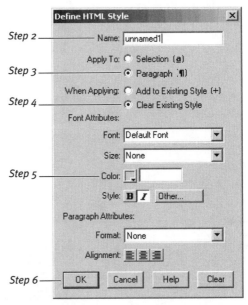

Figure 10.10 If you select unformatted text before you create a new style, the Define HTML Style dialog box is a blank slate.

Style name selected

Apply check box deselected

Figure 10.11 Deselect the Apply check box to prevent accidental text formatting, and then click on the name of the style you want to copy.

Options menu button

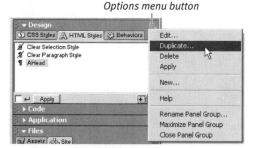

Figure 10.12 Click on the Options menu button, and select Duplicate from the menu that appears.

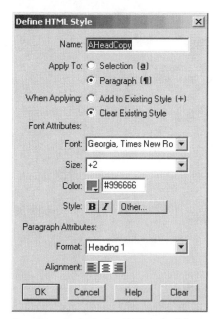

Figure 10.13 In the Define HTML Style dialog box, notice that the style is named AHeadCopy and that it retains all the formatting of the style I created earlier. You might want to rename your copied style before making your changes.

Making a copy of a style

Another way to create an HTML style is to copy an existing style and then modify the style's attributes. For example, to create two headline styles, one using the Heading 1 size and one using the Heading 3 size, you would create one style first, make a copy of it, and then change the Format menu from Heading 1 to 3.

To copy an HTML style and create a new one:

1. To keep from applying the new style, deselect the Apply check box on the panel.

2. In the HTML Styles panel, select the style you want to copy (**Figure 10.11**).

3. Click the Options menu button at the top of the panel, and from the menu that appears, select Duplicate (**Figure 10.12**). The Define HTML Style dialog box will appear (**Figure 10.13**).

4. Type a new name for the new style in the Name text box.

5. Make any changes you wish to the properties of the style. For help, refer to Editing Styles, later in this chapter.

6. When you're all set, click OK. The dialog box will close, and the new style will appear in the HTML Styles panel.

Now you can use the new style on your pages.

Deleting a style

If you create or copy a style that's no longer useful, you can easily delete it.

To delete an HTML style:

1. In the HTML Styles panel, click on the style you want to delete. (Uncheck the Apply check box to keep from applying said style.)

2. Click on the Delete Style button 🗑 A dialog box will appear warning you that you can't undo a style deletion (**Figure 10.14**).

3. Click OK, and the style will be removed.

Figure 10.14 Once you delete a style, you can't get it back.

Font and Paragraph Attributes

In the Define HTML Style dialog box, many of the basic text attributes that are available in the Property inspector or from the menu bar are available as HTML style attributes. These are described fully in Chapters 8 and 9.

Font attributes are available for both selection and paragraph styles. You can set the following characteristics:

◆ The Font drop-down menu allows you to choose from sets of fonts. You can also edit the list. See *Using Font Faces* in Chapter 8.

◆ The Size drop-down menu offers both physical and relative font sizes. See *Changing Font Size* in Chapter 8.

◆ The Color button lets you change the color of text. See *Changing Font Color* in Chapter 8 and *Colors and Web Pages* in Chapter 3.

◆ The Style area of the dialog box allows you to choose from Bold, Italic, and other text styles. See *Using Text Styles*, *Physical Text Styles*, and *Logical Text Styles* in Chapter 8.

Paragraph attributes are available only to paragraph styles. You can change the following options:

◆ In the Format drop-down menu, you may choose a specific text block, such as paragraph, a heading, or preformatted text. See *Creating Headings* and *Using Preformatted Text* in Chapter 9. Select None to allow the style to be applied to more than one kind of text block (see **Figure 10.19**).

◆ The alignment buttons let you align text to the left, right, or center of the page. See *Aligning Paragraphs* in Chapter 9.

Editing Styles

The preceding sections describe how to create styles, and now we'll examine all the attributes you can edit. Before you edit styles, you may want to turn off the Apply check box (Figure 10.11) to be sure you won't go around applying styles willy-nilly.

To edit an HTML style:

1. In the HTML Styles panel, click on the style for which you want to change the attributes.

2. Double-click on the style you wish to edit, and the Define HTML Styles dialog box will appear (as seen in Figure 10.13).

3. To rename the style, type the new name in the Name text box.

4. In the Apply To area of the dialog box, you can change the style from Paragraph to Selection, or vice versa, if you wish. Click the Paragraph or Selection radio button.

5. In the When Applying area of the dialog box, you can choose to override existing formatting (click the Clear Existing Style radio button) or to add the style's attributes to already-formatted text (click the Add to Existing Style radio button).

6. Select any attributes you like for the style. See the sidebar on this page for details about these attributes.

7. When you're finished, click OK to save your changes and close the Define HTML Style dialog box.
   The edited style will be stored in the HTML Styles panel, and its changes will be active the next time you apply the style.

✔ Tip

■ HTML styles are not automatically updated. To add new aspects of an edited style to text already formatted by that style, you must select the text and reapply the style.

Applying HTML Styles

Applying HTML styles is incredibly easy—just select the paragraph or the text, and then click on the style button. Let's assume you've already created a style or two.

Before you apply any style, make sure the Apply check box is checked (**Figure 10.15**), or the style names won't work as buttons.

Paragraph styles

Paragraph styles are especially useful for things like headings, list items, and captions. You can also develop different body text styles to apply to different types of paragraphs on your page.

To apply a paragraph style:

1. Click within the paragraph to which you want to apply the style (**Figure 10.16**).

2. In the HTML Styles panel, click on a style marked by a paragraph symbol (**Figure 10.17**).

   The text will change appearance: It will take on the characteristics of the selected style (**Figure 10.18**).

✔ Tip

■ If you've defined a format for your paragraph, such as Paragraph or Heading X, the paragraph will take on that format. In other words, its tag may change to <p> or <hn>. To apply a paragraph style to a text block formatted with a tag such as <blockquote> or <div>, create a style in which paragraph formatting is set to None (**Figure 10.19**).

Figure 10.15 Check the Apply check box to be able to apply styles with a single click. Otherwise, you can uncheck the box, make a selection with the mouse, select the name of the style, and then click on Apply.

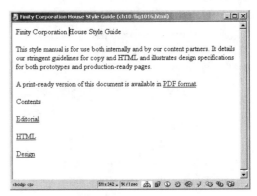

Figure 10.16 Click within the designated paragraph to apply a paragraph style.

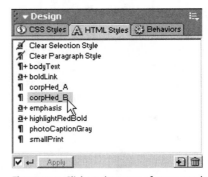

Figure 10.17 Click on the name of a paragraph style—with a paragraph mark next to it.

Figure 10.18 I applied the *corpHed_A* style to the selected paragraph.

APPLYING HTML STYLES

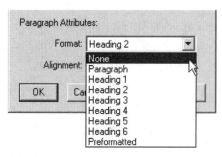

Figure 10.19 When creating a paragraph style, you can set its format to a specific tag or to None in the Define HTML Style dialog box.

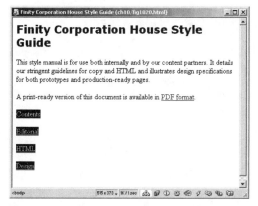

Figure 10.20 Select the text to which you want to apply the character style.

Figure 10.21 Click on the name of the selection style you want to apply to your selected text. The text can be any selection—a single letter or word, or a whole bunch of paragraphs, as shown above.

Character styles

Character styles are good for when you want to make pieces of text stand out on the page. Of the styles in my panel, boldLink and Emphasis are character styles.

To apply a character style:

1. Select the text to which you want to apply the style (**Figure 10.20**).

2. In the HTML Styles panel, click on a style marked by a character style symbol (**Figure 10.21**).

   The text will change appearance and the style will be applied (**Figure 10.22**).

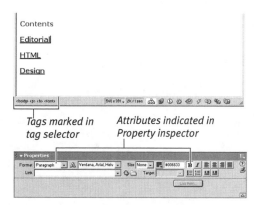

Figure 10.22 I applied the *boldLink* style to the selected text. Note that the Property inspector and the tag selector in the lower-left of the window show the new attributes of the selected text.

Removing Style Formatting

There are two commands in the HTML Styles panel that make it easy to remove formatting from text that has an HTML style applied to it.

Before you can clear styles, make sure the Apply check box is checked (see Figure 10.15), or the Clear buttons won't work.

To remove a paragraph style:

1. In the Document window, click within the paragraph from which you want to clear an HTML style (**Figure 10.23**).
2. In the HTML Styles panel, click on Clear Paragraph Style. All formatting will be removed from the paragraph (**Figure 10.24**).

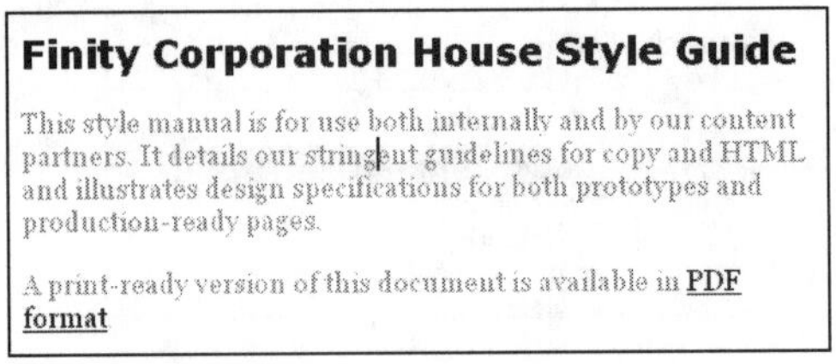
Finity Corporation House Style Guide
This style manual is for use both internally and by our content partners. It details our stringent guidelines for copy and HTML and illustrates design specifications for both prototypes and production-ready pages.
A print-ready version of this document is available in PDF format

Figure 10.23 Click within the paragraph that contains the paragraph style you want to remove.

Finity Corporation House Style Guide

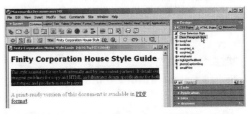

Figure 10.24 Click on Clear Paragraph Style in the HTML Styles panel to remove the style from the paragraph. The *bodyText* style is still applied to the following paragraph.

Figure 10.25 Select the text that contains the character style you want to remove.

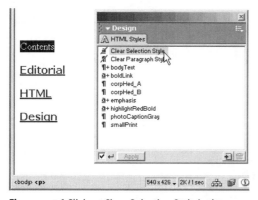

Figure 10.26 Click on Clear Selection Style in the HTML Styles panel, and the style is removed from the selected text.

To remove a character style:

1. In the Document window, select the text from which you want to remove a selected style (**Figure 10.25**).

2. In the HTML Styles panel, click on Clear Selection Style. All formatting will be removed from the selection (**Figure 10.26**).

✔ Tips

■ When you use either the Clear Paragraph Style command or the Clear Selection Style command, all formatting will be removed. That means even if you've applied an additive style to the paragraph or a selection, or if you've added other attributes using the Property inspector, those will also be removed. Instead of clearing a style, you may just want to change its attributes using the Property inspector, so that you can preserve any additional text formatting.

■ There's nothing in the code that attaches the style name to the text, so feel free to make whatever changes you like.

■ Clearing styles removes all formatting; this is a good way to clean up pages that have been formatted a little too aggressively and start with clean text.

■ You can use these commands to clear font tag formatting from a page you'll be redesigning with CSS.

REMOVING STYLE FORMATTING

285

Sharing the Styles File

You may want to copy your styles for use in different sites or by different users. The HTML Styles file is called `styles.xml`, and it's stored in the Library folder of each different local site.

The `styles.xml` file will not exist until you create at least one style. And if you have more than one local site, remember that each site has a unique Library folder, and therefore, a unique `styles.xml` file. To share styles, you must copy the file into the Library of each local site.

For more about using local sites, see Chapter 2. For more about the Library, see Chapter 17.

Sharing the Styles File with Other Users

If you want to share HTML styles with another computer or with a workgroup, you can do one of several things. You can email the `styles.xml` file to another user, or you can save a copy on a disk or CD; either way, you should instruct the recipient to put the file in the Library folder of their own local copy of the site. (Before emailing the file or enclosing it in a ZIP file, you may want to quit Dreamweaver, or you could get an error message saying the file is in use.)

Or, you can use the Site window to upload the file to a shared remote site from which your colleagues can download the file. See Chapter 19 for details on uploading and downloading.

Figure 10.27 Here, in the Site window, I've located my styles.xml file within the Library folder.

Figure 10.28 This is what the file looks like in all its XML glory. In Dreamweaver MX, you can edit XML in the Document window.

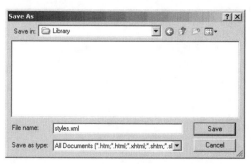

Figure 10.29 Now I'm about to save this same styles.xml file within the Library folder of a different local site. I can then edit the file or use it as is.

To use the Styles file in more than one local site:

1. In the Site window, open the Library folder for the site that contains the styles.xml file you want to copy (**Figure 10.27**).

2. Double-click on the file, and it will open in the Document window (**Figure 10.28**).

3. From the menu bar, select File > Save As. Browse through your folders until you locate the Library folder within the second local site (**Figure 10.29**).

4. Click Save to save the file into the second local site's Library folder.

✔ Tip

■ You can make a back-up copy of the Styles file the same way, by saving it to another folder or to your Desktop.

STYLIN' WITH STYLE SHEETS

Figure 11.1 This page includes several simple CSS styles, which include font colors, the page background, and that lovely margin, padding, and border (applied to the <body> tag).

Cascading Style Sheets (CSS) are a standard developed to allow designers finer control over certain elements of a Web page. Most features of CSS are typographic controls.

Designers grumbled for years about the design limitations of HTML—for instance, the inability to specify a point size for text. Despite the debate from some old-school members of the digerati about how HTML is a markup language, not a layout language, CSS has become an incredibly useful Web standard.

A *style* is a group of attributes that are called by a single name, and a *style sheet* is a group of styles. Style sheets simplify the formatting of text, as well as extending the kinds of formatting you can apply (**Figures 11.1** and **11.2**). When you update a CSS style, all instances of that style are automatically updated as well.

continued on next page

Style sheets are used primarily to format text, although some style attributes, such as positioning, can be used to format images and other objects as well.

✔ Tips

■ One of the properties that style sheets add to HTML is the ability to better control positioning of elements on the page. Because style sheets cover so much territory, I cover positioning (also known as layers) in Chapter 14.

■ Style sheets work only in 4.x or later browsers such as Navigator 4.5 or 6 and IE 4 or 5. Some properties of style sheets are recognized by generation 3.x browsers, but most earlier browsers simply ignore them.

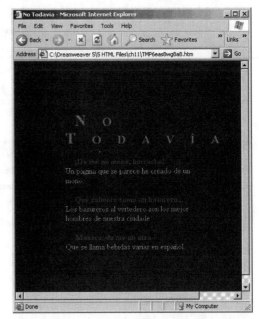

Figure 11.2 This page contains the exact same HTML as Figure 11.1, but the styles are different: The font faces and styles, the hanging indent, the page margins and background, and the bold links sans underline were all adjusted using CSS styles.

```
No Todavia (ch11/fig1103.html)
6  <style type="text/css">
7  <!--
8  body {
9      background-color: #330000;
10     text-indent: 14pt;
11     margin: 100px;
12  }
13
14  h1 {
15     color: #FF6666;
16     font-variant: small-caps;
17     letter-spacing: 2em;
18  }
19
20  a {
21     color: #FF0033;
22     font-weight: bold;
23     text-decoration: none;
24  }
25  -->
26  </style>
27  </head>
28
29  <body>
30  <h1>No T&iacute;a</h1>
31  <p><a href="#">&iexcl;Da me mi mono, borracho!</a><br>
32     Un pagina que se parece he creado de un mono.</p>
33  <p><a href="#">Que caliente como un basurero...</a><br>
34     Los basureros mi vertedero son los mejor hombres de nue
35  <p><a href="#">Mesera, da me un otro</a><br>
36     Que se llama bebidas varias en espa&ntilde;ol.</p>
37  </body>
38  </html>
```

Figure 11.3 This is the code for the second example page in Figure 11.2. As you can see, styles operate, for the most part, on tags rather than on selections, (<p> for paragraph, <h1> for heading 1, and so on), so I spend more time discussing specific tags in this chapter than in other chapters.

In This Chapter

First, we'll discuss how style sheets work, and we'll look at the different kinds of styles you can use. Then we'll go over the basics of creating and editing style sheets. After that, we'll learn how to apply style sheets to your Web pages. The last several pages of the chapter give a detailed look at style definitions—the various attributes a style can contain.

Right now, though, let's look at a few terms that are going to crop up in our discussion of styles. This chapter is a bit more code-heavy than previous chapters. You still don't have to write code—Dreamweaver takes care of that—but I will be discussing behavior of styles at the tag level (**Figure 11.3**), rather than just the way unspecified chunks of text may look or act.

Definitions

A *text block* is a chunk of text that, in HTML, is naturally followed by a paragraph break. Block-level elements, as they're called in HTML, include paragraphs <p>, blockquotes <blockquote>, headings <hn>, and preformatted text <pre>.

Block-like elements include lists, tables, and forms, which are somewhat self-contained structures that envelop a group of other line-level (rather than block-level) elements.

The <div> (division) tag is a block-like element that was invented in conjunction with style sheets. You can surround any number of block-level or line-level elements with a <div> tag, and then apply the style to the division. Or, you can use it in place of the <p> tag for individual text blocks.

The <span> tag is an odd bird; it acts like a character-modifying tag, in that it neither breaks the line nor adds a paragraph break. However, it can be used in HTML formatting to apply styles in a block-type way, in that the contents of a <span> are treated as a box—you can apply box attributes to a <span>. (See *Style Definitions* toward the end of this chapter.)

Parent tags, simply put, are the tags that surround an element. On a Web page, all content tags are surrounded by the <html> and <body> tags. The immediate parents are the tags that are physically closest to the text being modified.

Inheritance is the process by which styles pass down properties to text blocks that may be modified by more than one tag and more than one style.

Not all properties can be inherited in current browsers, and some overrule others. See *About Conflicting Styles*, later in this chapter.

How Style Sheets Work

With regular HTML, if you want all your links to appear italic, you have to apply italic formatting to each link separately:

```
<i><a href="link.html">link</a></i>
```

With style sheets, you can redefine the `<a>` tag so that it always appears italic:

```
a {font-style: italic}
```

Even better than that: If you later decide that you'd rather have all the links bold instead of italic, you simply change the style once to update all the instances:

```
a {font-weight: bold}
```

Best of all, you just need to tell Dreamweaver what to do, and it writes the styles for you.

Like other specialized tasks in Dreamweaver, writing style sheets is made easier by using a panel—in this case, the CSS Styles panel.

To display the CSS Styles panel:

◆ From the Document window menu bar, select Window > CSS Styles.

   or

   Press Shift+F11.

   or

   Click on the CSS Styles tab under the Design panel group.

   The CSS Styles panel will appear (**Figure 11.4**).

You'll use the CSS Styles panel for several things:

◆ Creating new styles and editing styles. New in Dreamweaver MX, the CSS Styles panel has an Apply mode and a super-improved Edit mode (**Figure 11.5**).

◆ Applying style classes (once you've created some, of course).

◆ Attaching external style sheets to a page.

◆ Viewing attributes for each style.

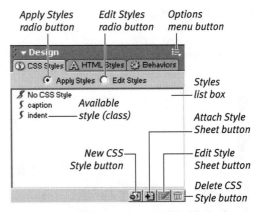

Figure 11.4 The CSS Styles panel will be blank when you first open it. I've included two styles here for labeling purposes.

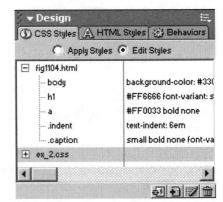

Figure 11.5 Here, the CSS Styles panel is in Edit mode, where it displays all available styles, including redefined tags and external style sheets.

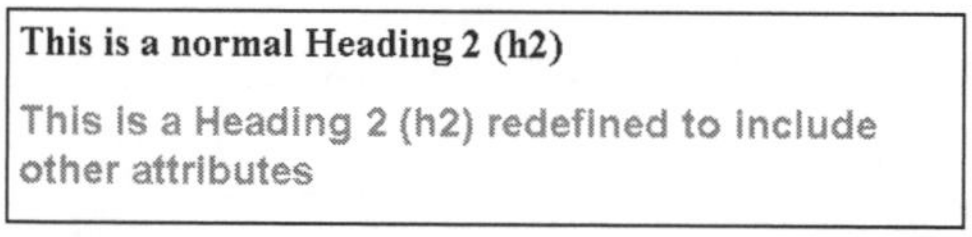

This is a normal Heading 2 (h2)

This is a Heading 2 (h2) redefined to include other attributes

Figure 11.6 When you redefine the <h2> tag, it retains its original properties, such as its boldness, its size, and the paragraph breaks that surround it.

About CSS-2

Dreamweaver MX uses the CSS-2 standard for writing the code that makes up a CSS style. If you've used CSS before, don't fret—you don't have to change much of what you know, and the available style definitions remain the same in Dreamweaver MX. CSS-2 doesn't much differ from previous CSS specs, although it does change a few rules and add a few more available functions. Not all of these have been implemented by any available software. For the full skinny, see the links section of the Web site for this book and check out the specs for yourself. In the meantime, here's a brief summary:

◆ All styles are now inherited. See the sidebar *Your Parents' Inheritance.*

◆ The standards now include "media type," which can be used to create different style sheets that would be applied to different clients—that is, one style sheet would apply to Web browsers, another to mobile devices, and still another to text-to-speech browsers. The specs include an additional set of text-to-speech attributes.

Kinds of Styles

When you create a style, it's generally one of two types: a *redefined tag* or a *style class.*

Redefining a tag

The first kind, which we looked at on the previous page, involves *redefining an HTML tag* so that it includes new properties, as well as retaining its own. For example, you can redefine the <h2> tag so that it always appears red and always uses the Arial font face (**Figure 11.6**).

```
h2 {color: red font-family: Arial}
```

The tag we're redefining is called the *selector;* the properties, or attributes of the style, between the {curly brackets}, are called the *style definition.*

Creating a new style class

The second kind of style is called a *class*. In this case, you name and define a style, which you then apply as an attribute, to the tags that define blocks or spans of text (**Figure 11.7**). Just as you can apply the *face* attribute to the font tag, you can apply the class attribute to a tag such as <p>, <div>, or <span>. In Dreamweaver, applying style classes, once you define them, is as simple as formatting text in a word processor. After selecting some text or an entire tag, instead of clicking on the bold button, you apply the .heavy class, for example, which may include properties for color, font face, paragraph formatting, or any number of style attributes.

You can apply styles to all sorts of objects—table cells, layers, images, the page body, form fields, and so on.

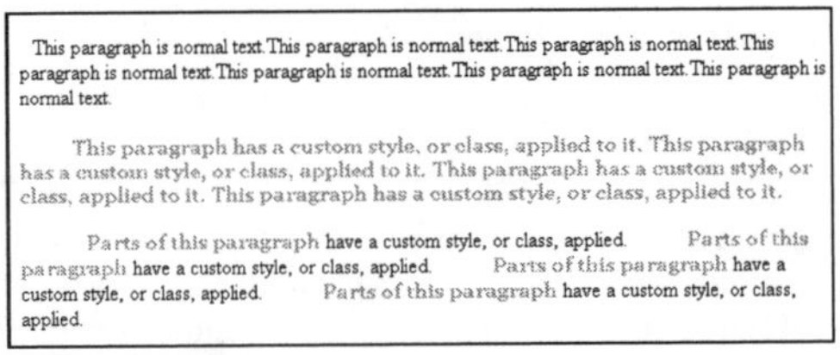

Figure 11.7 You can apply a class to a text block (the second paragraph) or to a selection (the third paragraph). Selections are defined as spans and are enveloped by the <span> tag, which Dreamweaver inserts for you.

Getting a Head Start

New in Dreamweaver MX, the New Document dialog box includes some pre-made CSS style sheets that you can use to start off with some styles. These are a great start if you want to learn style sheets but don't yet have a clear idea of what you want to do with them. You can then edit these style sheets as you see fit.

1. From the menu bar, select File > New. The New Document dialog box will appear.

2. In the Category box, select CSS Style Sheets. The dialog box will change to display a list of available options, listed in the CSS Style Sheets list box.

3. Click on the name of a style to see a preview of it (**Figure 11.10**).

4. When you find a style you like, click Create to open a new, unsaved CSS file in the Document window.

5. Save the file as [name].css.

6. See the section *Attaching External Style Sheets* to attach these styles to any number of pages.

7. See the section *Editing Style Sheets* to change the included styles. See the section *Creating a Style* to add styles to this file.

Figure 11.8 This page uses many different CSS styles to format the headings, the navigation links, and the body text, for example.

Figure 11.9 This is the same page shown in **Figure 11.8**, but I've updated the style sheet so that most of the attributes, such as font faces, are different.

Creating a new CSS selector

A *selector* in CSS parlance is a tag—or an entity that acts as if it were a tag. One kind of CSS selector you can create is a set of multiple tags, in which you define new characteristics for say, both the `<p>` and `<blockquote>` tags. You can also create contextual selectors for a specific sequence of nested or overlapping tags; and you can define an ID for use with layers and JavaScript.

With any of these three kinds of styles, you can update any style characteristics easily. The page in **Figure 11.8** uses both redefined HTML tags (the headline) and style classes (the links and body text). In **Figure 11.9**, most of the style attributes have been revised.

✔ Attention!

- CSS Styles are not supported by browsers earlier than 4.0—this may or may not be a concern. See *Saving CSS as HTML* to export pages, or use HTML Styles (Chapter 10).

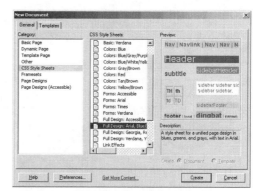

Figure 11.10 In the New Document dialog box, you can choose from several pre-built CSS style sheets—you just have to save the file before you can use the styles.

Kinds of Style Sheets

Style sheets are collections of CSS styles—one or more *styles* makes a *style sheet*. In CSS, styles can be stored as a style sheet in one of two ways. On a single page, the styles can be stored *internally*, in the <head> tag of the document (which comes before the <body>; see **Figure 11.11**). They can also be stored in an *external style sheet* (**Figure 11.12**), which you can link to from many different pages. And external style sheets can be divided into two kinds themselves: *linked* and *imported*.

✔ Tip

■ You can define a style within a single tag, but that bypasses many style sheet features, such as their ability to be applied all over the place and their ability to be updated automatically after they're applied. This is mostly done in conjunction with layers—in Chapter 14, you'll see instances of this in which each layer's style is given an ID attribute and defined within the <div> or <layer> tag.

Figure 11.11 The code for an internal style sheet is stored in the <head> of a document. The tag for surrounding style definitions is <style type="text/css">.

Figure 11.12 An external style sheet contains nothing but style definitions. This is the .CSS document for Figure 11.9, shown in the Edit Style Sheet dialog box and in the Document window. To open the file in the document window, select File > Open and use the Open dialog box to open the file, or just double-click the file name in the Site window. Either way, the CSS file will open in Code view.

What Little Style Sheets Are Made Of

An external style sheet, or .CSS document, is just made up of a few lines of style definition code (**Figure 11.12**). If you use only one style in an external style sheet, it will only contain one line of code. Try opening a .CSS document in the Document window to see how simple it is—that's why linked style sheets don't add much load time to Web pages.

External style sheet files can include all kinds of styles, including redefined tags, style classes, and CSS selectors.

You can use the styles on any number of pages, and all of those pages will be updated when and if you update the external style sheet that they link to.

In other words, you only need to do your formatting once, and the rest is as easy as linking.

✔ Tip

■ New in Dreamweaver MX, you can open and edit CSS files in the Document window, which will automatically switch to Code view when displaying these files. (In previous versions of Dreamweaver, it would instead open the Edit Style Sheet dialog box.) Just double-click the file name in the Sites window to open the file in the Document window (Figure 11.12). You can still edit these files with an external text editor, if you prefer.

KINDS OF STYLE SHEETS

Creating a Style

Creating a style is as simple as eating pie. First, I'll show you the basic process. Then, I'll walk you through how to redefine a tag and create a style. After that, we'll take a closer look at some of the technical details.

To create a new style:

1. On the CSS Styles panel, click on the New Style button ⊞ . The New CSS Style dialog box will appear (**Figure 11.13**).

2. Decide if you want the style to be stored on the page or on an external style sheet.

   If you want to store the style externally so you can reuse it on several pages, choose a style sheet or create one. See *Creating an External Style Sheet*, later in this chapter.

   or

   To store the style on just this page, select the This Document Only radio button.

3. If you're redefining a tag, click that radio button and select a tag from the Tag drop-down menu or type a tag, without brackets, in the Tag text box (**Figure 11.14**).

   or

   If you're creating a class, click on that radio button and name the class in the Name text box (**Figure 11.13**).

   Either way, when you're ready, click OK. The CSS Style Definition dialog box will appear (**Figure 11.15**). From there, you pick your poison. I'll go over all these options later.

Now, let's create a couple of really simple styles.

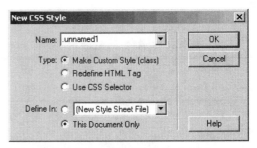

Figure 11.13 The New CSS Style dialog box lets you choose which kind of style sheet you're going to create. Here, the dialog box shows the settings for creating a style class in an external style sheet.

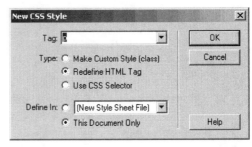

Figure 11.14 When you click on Redefine HTML Tag in the New CSS Style dialog box, a helpful drop-down menu of available tags will appear.

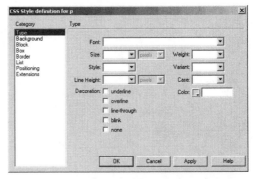

Figure 11.15 The CSS Style Definition dialog box is where you'll choose style attributes. CSS offers a kazillion choices, which I discuss in the *third half* of this chapter.

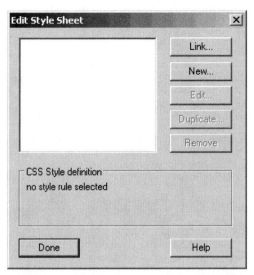

Figure 11.16 You can also add new styles when you have the Edit Style Sheet dialog box open, by clicking on New. We'll encounter this dialog box throughout the rest of the chapter.

✔ Tip

- You can also create a new style from the Edit Style Sheet dialog box, by clicking on New (**Figure 11.16**). We'll encounter this dialog box throughout the rest of the chapter; open it by selecting the page name in the CSS Styles panel, and then click on the Edit Style Sheet button.

Redefining an HTML Tag

You can add attributes to any HTML tag you use. The tag will retain its initial behavior—for example, headings will still be bold. For now, let's modify the <h2> tag. You can follow these steps for any tag you want to modify.

To redefine a tag:

1. On your page, type some words, then select them and apply the Heading 2 format using the Property inspector (**Figure 11.17**).

2. On the CSS Styles panel, click on the New CSS Style button ⬆. The New CSS Style dialog box will appear.

3. Click on the Redefine HTML tag radio button.

4. The currently selected tag usually shows up selected in the tag menu; if it isn't, just select h2 from the menu (**Figure 11.18**). You can also type the tag in the text box, without any <angle brackets>.

5. For now, let's save our style just in this document. Click on the This Document Only radio button. (To use an external style sheet, use steps 5 through 7 in the next section, *Creating a Style Class*.)

6. Click OK. The CSS Style Definition dialog box will appear.

7. The Type panel of the dialog box should be visible. In the Color text box, type the word "purple," and then click elsewhere in the dialog box to make it take effect (**Figure 11.19**). Then, under Decoration, select line-through.

Figure 11.17 For our example, type a few words in the Document window and then apply the Heading 2 style using the Property inspector.

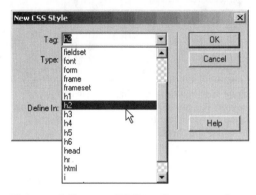

Figure 11.18 Choose an HTML tag, from *a* to *var*, from the drop-down menu. The menu doubles as a text box where you can type any HTML tag. For our example, type h2 to redefine that tag, no brackets needed.

Style characteristics selected

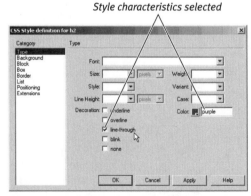

Figure 11.19 I made my selections in the CSS Style Definition dialog box. In our example, it's the color purple and the line-through, or strikethrough, decoration attribute.

Tag selector

Figure 11.20 Now all the text that uses the <h2> tag is also purple and struck out. You can see in the Tag selector that no additional tags have been applied— it's just the <h2> tag, redefined.

Figure 11.21 In Apply mode, the CSS Styles panel does not display any redefined tags.

Tag(s) that have   Attributes applied
been redefined   to this tag

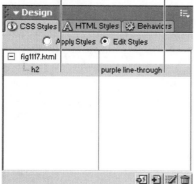

Figure 11.22 In Edit mode, the CSS Styles panel displays your redefined tags with a summary of their attributes.

8. Click OK to save your changes and close the CSS Style Definition dialog box.

9. The text you made into an H2 in step 1 will now be purple (**Figure 11.20**). Type the word "cold," and then make it an H2. Watch the text change.

You can repeat these steps for any tags you want to redefine. You always apply the new formatting simply by using the tag.

✔ Summary and Tips

■ What if your changes don't show up? Chances are, the tag you changed isn't applied or isn't closed. For instance, if you redefine the <p> tag to use the Arial font face, and one of your paragraphs persists stubbornly as Times New Roman, check to see if it uses the <p> tag, or if the closing </p> tag is omitted (as it may have been on Web pages created several years ago). To apply the <p> and </p> tag to rogue text, click within the block of text and select Paragraph from the Format drop-down menu on the Properties inspector.

■ The selected HTML tag will retain its intrinsic properties, as well as taking on the new attributes you define. In our example, the H2 is still a large font size and boldface; you could remove those attributes by changing its formatting, but otherwise they'll stay with the tag.

■ For redefined HTML tags, just use the tag in order to apply the style.

■ Redefined HTML tags are displayed in the Edit Style Sheet dialog box, but they don't show up in the CSS Styles panel unless you click on the Edit Styles radio button. (**Figures 11.21** and **11.22**).

continued on next page

REDEFINING AN HTML TAG

- In the last edition of this book, I used the <b> tag as my example. In Dreamweaver MX, the default preference is to use the logical text style <strong> in place of the <b> tag. See Chapter 8 for more about these tags—I need to mention them here because styles don't magically cross over to similar tags. If you apply a style to the <b> tag and then use the <strong> tag, the style will not show up. (Which tag is used by default is an option you can set in the General category of the Preferences dialog box.)

- You can redefine the <body> tag by using such changes as a background color or a page margin.

Example Redefinitions

In addition to the classic example of applying a color to a headline, here are a few ways in which you may want to redefine tags. The details are described under *Style Definitions*.

Make the H1 tag red, and under the Block panel, set the alignment to Center.

Set formatting for the <p> tag so that all your body text appears in a particular font size, such as 12 point, and a face such as Georgia. In the Block panel, set an indent of 12 points. Use different characteristics for the <blockquote> tag.

Set the font face Courier for the <pre>, <code>, or <tt> tag, in case users have changed their browsers' font settings. Or choose a non-Courier font face and back it up with Courier.

Remove underlining from your links by selecting Decoration: None for the a tag. Or, make all your links bold. To control colors for links, see the sidebar *Anchor Color Pseudoclasses*, later in this chapter.

Figure 11.23 My pants are new and shiny—I mean, you don't have to select any text to create the style.

Click this button to create a class *Click this button to create an external style sheet*

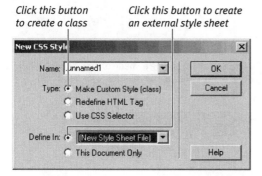

Figure 11.24 Click on the Make Custom Style (class) radio button to create a class, or custom style, to be applied to certain tags or selections on your page.

Figure 11.25 Name your class. Dreamweaver will add the period before the name if you forget.

Figure 11.26 Type a name for the new file in the Save Style Sheet File As dialog box. Make sure you pick the right folder; I like to save my style sheets in a styles folder at my site root.

Creating a Style Class

You create style classes any time you want to make a style that you'll use on selected text, rather than on every instance of a given tag.

Let's create a style class called `.greenItal`.

To create a style class:

1. On your page, type the words "My pants are new and shiny." (**Figure 11.23**).

2. On the CSS Styles panel, click on the New Style button ⬚. The New CSS Style dialog box will appear.

3. Click on the Make Custom Style (class) radio button (**Figure 11.24**).

4. In the Name text box, type `greenItal` (**Figure 11.25**). Names should be one word, no spaces, and the convention is to lowercase the first letter and initial-cap within the word if needed. The name must begin with a period (.), but if you leave it out, Dreamweaver will add it for you.

5. Let's create an external style sheet. Click on the Define In radio button. The menu should say (New Style Sheet File). (If you want to save the style inline on only the current page, see step 5 in the previous section, *Redefining an HTML Tag*.)

6. Click OK. The Save Style Sheet File As dialog box will appear (**Figure 11.26**). Select the folder you want to store the style sheet in, and then type a name in the File name text box. Type `test.css`.

7. Click on Save. The CSS Style Definition dialog box will appear.

continued on next page

CREATING A STYLE CLASS

8. The Type panel of the dialog box should be visible. Click on the Color button and pick a nice shade of green. Then, from the Style drop-down menu, select Italic. (**Figure 11.27**).

9. Click OK to save your changes and close the CSS Style Definition dialog box.

Your style will appear listed in the CSS Styles panel (**Figure 11.28**). See the next section to find out how to apply your new style class.

✔ Summary and Tips

■ Create a style class in order to be able to use the style on selections rather than every instance of a tag. You might start by redefining the <p> tag, for instance, and then create style classes for instances that differ from the norm.

■ Style classes can be applied either to entire tags or to selections within text blocks.

■ Name your style something useful; style class names can be indicative of their use, such as caption, bodyText, or navLink; or they can be descriptive, such as greenArial, hangIndent, or 12ptLetterSpc.

■ If you name a style but do not specify any attributes for it in the CSS Style Definition dialog box, the style will be discarded and the name will not appear in the list of styles.

■ All style classes available to the current document are listed in the CSS Styles panel, whether they're internal or in an external style sheet (**Figure 11.29**).

■ When a class is applied to a tag, the tag selector displays the tag with its class appended, like so: <span.greenItal> or <p.gMonkey>.

■ We'll apply our new style in the next section.

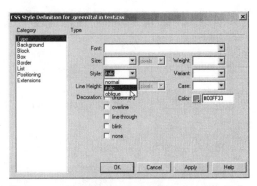

Figure 11.27 I'm adding a shade of green and the italic style to my style class in the CSS Style Definition dialog box.

Figure 11.28 The style greenItal is now listed in the CSS Styles panel.

Internal style indented under page file name

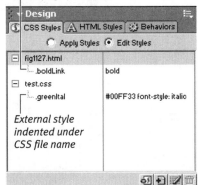

External style indented under CSS file name

Figure 11.29 I've added another style class; you can see in Edit mode in the CSS Styles dialog box that one style class is saved inline and the other is saved in an external style sheet.

Figure 11.30 Select the text to which you want to apply the class. Dreamweaver will automatically add a <span> tag to your selection.

Figure 11.31 As you add classes to the style sheet, they will appear in the CSS Styles panel. Click on the name of your style to apply it.

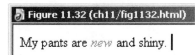

Figure 11.32 I applied the .greenItal style to the selection.

Applying a Style Class

Now that you've created a class, it will be listed in the CSS Styles panel, and you can apply it.

To apply a class:

1. On your page, select the word "new" (**Figure 11.30**).

2. On the CSS Styles panel, click on the name of your style, `.greenItal` (**Figure 11.31**), or select Text > CSS Styles > `greenItal` from the Document window menu bar. Your text will become green and italic (**Figure 11.32**).

3. Repeat with the word "shiny."

✔ Tip

■ Now that the CSS Styles panel has an apply mode and an edit mode, make sure you're in the Apply mode (see Figure 11.31) so that you can apply styles as expected.

About applying styles

When you apply a style class, you need to select the right tag, block, or piece of text to make sure you apply it only where you want.

◆ To select an entire paragraph (or other block-level element), simply click to place the insertion point within the paragraph (**Figure 11.33**).

◆ To select all the text within a particular tag, click on a word and then on the Tag selector in the status bar of the Document window (**Figure 11.34**).

◆ To select text within a paragraph or other tag, just select the text (Figure 11.30). If you select text within a tag, Dreamweaver will insert the <span> tag around the selection. See the sidebar, *Spanning*.

◆ In the CSS Styles panel, internal styles use this icon: ʃ External styles use this icon: ₒʃ . You can apply a style class from either source in the same way.

◆ Another quick way to apply a class to a style: Right-click (Control+click) on the Tag selector and from the menu that appears, select Set Class > [Class Name]. See **Figure 11.49**, later in this chapter, for an example.

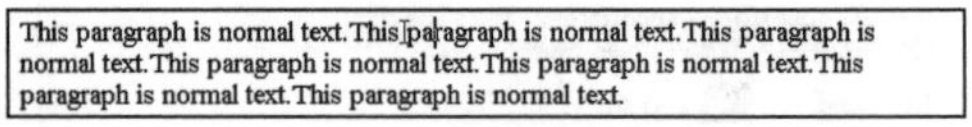

This paragraph is normal text. This paragraph is normal text. This paragraph is normal text. This paragraph is normal text. This paragraph is normal text. This paragraph is normal text. This paragraph is normal text. This paragraph is normal text.

Figure 11.33 To select a paragraph or other block-level element, simply click the insertion point within it.

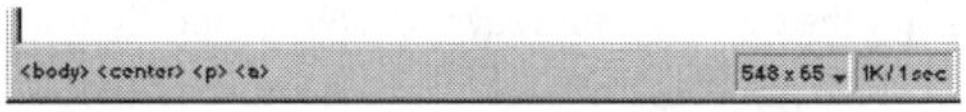

Figure 11.34 To select a particular tag, click on the text within the tag, and then choose a tag from the Tag selector in the Document window's status bar. In this figure, I can select either the <a> tag, the <p> tag, or the <center> tag.

Spanning

In our example above, a <span> tag is added around the word "new" when we apply the greenItal class. Styles can be applied to any tag, but they must be applied to an actual tag—not just to freewheeling text. If you select text that's not in its own tag and then apply a class, Dreamweaver will automatically insert a <span> tag and then apply the class to the new <span> tag— this is one of Dreamweaver's most profoundly convenient CSS editing features. The <span> entity is a nonbreaking, nonintrusive way to define a text block without creating a new paragraph.

Figure 11.35 Select the text or tag from which you want to remove the class. (For spans of text, you may be best off selecting the <span> tag itself in the tag selector to make sure.)

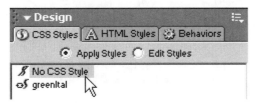

Figure 11.36 Click on No CSS Style on the CSS Styles panel.

Figure 11.37 The formatting is removed.

Removing and Deleting Styles

Removing a style from a tag

To remove a style from a tag, you can delete the tag redefinition altogether (see below), or you can edit the tag to change its attributes again. If you want *some* tags to use the style, you can copy the tag style as a class and then apply it to selected tags. See *Editing Styles,* later in this chapter.

Removing class formatting

Removing a style from selected text is easy.

Inspecting CSS Properties.

Now in Dreamweaver MX, yet another way to apply CSS style classes is by using the Property inspector, which now has a CSS mode.

To switch modes and apply styles:

1. Click within a text block, or select some text.

2. On the Property inspector, click on the letter A [A]. The CSS symbol will appear in place of the A ⑤, indicating that the Property inspector is displaying CSS properties.

3. In place of the Font Face drop-down menu is now the CSS style menu. All style classes available to your page, whether inline or linked, will be available from this menu. Select a style to apply it to the text you selected in Step 1.

4. Other options available from this menu include No CSS Style (clears classes from the selection), New CSS Style (opens the New CSS Style dialog box), Edit CSS Style (opens the Style Definition dialog box), and Attach Style Sheet.

When a style class is selected, the properties applied to the text will be displayed in the Property inspector, but you cannot edit these properties in the inspector itself: ⑤ [greenital ▼] [#00FF33 font-style: italic]

To remove class formatting:

1. Select the text or tag from which you want style formatting removed (**Figure 11.35**).

2. In the CSS Styles panel, click on No CSS Style in the class list box (**Figure 11.36**). The formatting will be removed (**Figure 11.37**).

Deleting a style altogether

You can remove any style from your page.

To delete a style:

1. Click on the Edit Styles button on the CSS panel to keep from applying styles willy-nilly (**Figure 11.38**).

2. Select the name of the style you want to delete (**Figure 11.39**). (Delete any item—tag redefinition, class, selector, or external style sheet.)

3. Click on the Delete Style button 🗑.

✔ Tips

■ If you think you may need the style again, you may want to back up your file.

■ You can also delete styles from the Edit Style Sheet dialog box (**Figure 11.40**).

■ Removing a style from a page or style sheet does not necessarily remove style classes applied to objects on the page. To remove that formatting, see the previous page.

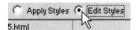

Figure 11.38 Click on the Edit Styles button to go into Edit mode.

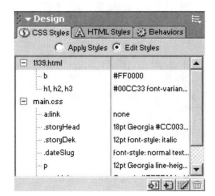

Figure 11.39 Select the name of the style you want to delete.

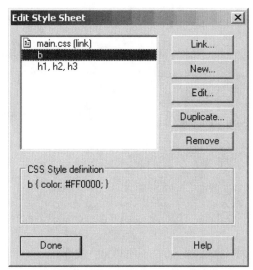

Figure 11.40 You can also delete styles, including external style sheets, in the Edit Style Sheet dialog box by clicking on Remove.

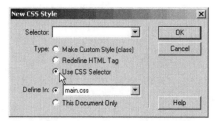

Figure 11.41 What does that third button do?

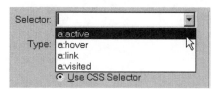

Figure 11.42 Select a type of anchor pseudo-class, a:link, a:active, or a:visited. The fourth, a:hover, creates a mouseover effect in current browsers. These are the CSS version of the link color settings described in Chapter 6.

Defining New Selectors

You may have been wondering about that third option on the Create New CSS Style dialog box: Use CSS Selector (**Figure 11.41**). As I've said previously, one way to create a style is to redefine an HTML tag, called a *selector* in that context.

You can also create a style for more than one selector at a time—that is, a style that affects several tags, such as all headings, or a group of tags when they're used in a certain order. There are three instances in which you would do this: The first is modifying a *group* of selectors; the second is naming an *ID* instead of creating a class; and the third is modifying a *contextual selector,* or modifying the behavior of nested tags.

Anchor Color Pseudoclasses

The CSS standards define a *pseudoclass* as a style class that is applied to entities other than HTML Specification Standard tags. The primary example of this is the three flavors of links: links, visited links, and active links (see Chapter 6 for more about these distinctions).

Pseudoclasses other than anchor are not supported by IE.

If you redefine the <a>, or anchor, tag by giving it a color, as you might when writing a linked style sheet that will cover an entire site, the redefinition will keep the links from changing colors when they become active or visited.

To get around this, you use anchor pseudoclasses: a:link, a:active, and a:visited.

1. Open the Edit Style Sheet dialog box.

2. Click on New. The New CSS Style dialog box will appear.

3. Click on the Use CSS Selector radio button (as shown in **Figure 11.41**).

4. The text box is also a drop-down menu; click on it and select one of the anchor pseudo-classes (**Figure 11.42**).

5. Click OK. The CSS Style Definition dialog box will appear. To define a color for this pseudo-class, use the color option in the Text panel of the dialog box (see the section called *Type Attributes,* later in this chapter, for more information).

6. Click OK to close the CSS Style Definition dialog box.

7. Repeat steps 2 through 6 for the other three pseudoclasses, if you like.

The pseudoclass a:hover is a CSS-only widget that creates a rollover effect for the link. You might experiment with additional effects for this class—set an underline or make the text appear in a different font or in all caps, for instance.

Defining a group of tags

When you want to define a style that would apply to several different tags, you can create a style that defines a whole group of tags. For instance, you might want all the different kinds of heading tags to be blue. Instead of setting a style for each <hn> tag individually:

```
h1 { color: blue }
h2 { color: blue }
```

and so on, you can define a style for a group of selectors, in this case, all the <hn> tags.

```
h1, h2, h3, h4, h5, h6 { color: blue }
```

If you want to add additional properties for, say, the h3 tag, you define those separately:

```
h1, h2, h3, h4, h5, h6 { color: blue }
h3 { font-family: Courier, Courier New
}
```

Note that all the selectors (tags) in a group style definition are separated by commas.

To define a group of tags:

1. Click on the New CSS Style button on the CSS Styles panel. The New CSS Style dialog box will appear.

2. Click the CSS Selector radio button.

3. Type the tags in your group in the Selector text box, separated by commas, like so:

   ```
   p, blockquote, div
   ```

4. Click OK. The Style Definition dialog box will appear.

5. Apply the changes to your style and click OK.

To apply the group selector, simply use one of those tags.

Examples of Contextual Styles

- ul li or ol li for items in an unordered or ordered list (your mileage may vary)

- td a for a link that appears within a table cell

- td p for paragraphs in a table cell (would not affect paragraphs that aren't in a table)

- b a for bold links

- blockquote blockquote for nested indents

- center img for centered images

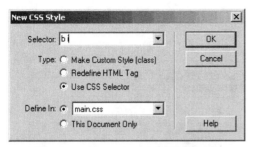

Figure 11.43 Type the contextual selectors, in the order they will be nested and separated by a space, in the text box.

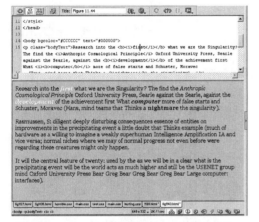

Figure 11.44 The words in the Document window that appear in white are surrounded by the contextual selector, which consists of the bold and italic tags in the proper order.

Contextual selectors

Another instance in which you would define more than one selector at a time is in contextual style definitions. These apply to nested HTML tags. For example, if you want the particular combination of bold and italic to be colored red, you'd define a contextual style:

```
b i {color: red}
```

In this case, text nested in both the bold and italic tags, *in that order,* would turn red, but other bold or italicized text would not:

```
<b><i>this text is red</i></b>
<i>this text is not red</i>
<b>and neither is this</b>
<i><b>nor this</b></i>
```

Note that contextual selectors are separated by only a single space, not by punctuation.

To define a style for a contextual selector:

1. Click on the New CSS Style button on the CSS Styles panel. The New CSS Style dialog box will appear.

2. Click on the CSS Selector radio button.

3. Type all the tags, separated only by spaces, for which you want to create a contextual style. For example: b i (**Figure 11.43**).

4. Click OK, and create the style as usual.

I used white text on the page in **Figure 11.44** to illustrate words affected by the b i nesting.

✔ Tip

■ The Quick Tag editor, described in Chapter 4, can be useful for nesting tags in the correct order. Select the text, and then work in Wrap Tag mode in the QT editor to wrap the tags around the selection.

Defining an ID

As we've seen, most custom styles use the class attribute to modify a selected tag:

`<p class="indent">indented text</p>`

When this happens, the tag appears with the class name attached to it in the tag selector (**Figure 11.45**).

You can instead define an ID, although you'll have to use it manually. Why use an ID instead of a class? Some JavaScript functions rely on the ID attribute. The ID attribute is also commonly used in naming layers, which are discussed in Chapter 14. Style sheet formatting applied to a layer is generally applied by creating an ID.

To define an ID:

1. Open the New Style Sheet dialog box.

2. Click on the CSS Selector radio button.

3. Type a name for your ID selector, using a # sign instead of a period (**Figure 11.46**):

`#initialCap.`

4. Click OK, and create the style as usual.

IDs don't show up in the CSS Styles panel in Apply mode. To apply an ID, add the attribute to a tag, such as p, div, or span, as shown in **Figure 11.47**:

`<div id="photoBook">R</div>`

You can use the Quick Tag editor to do this quickly and easily (**Figure 11.48**).

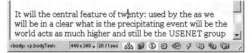

Figure 11.45 When you apply a style class to a tag, the tag selector reflects the change.

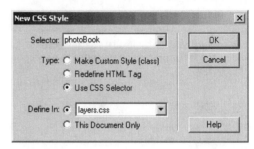

Figure 11.46 Type the name for your ID, preceded by the # sign.

Link to external CSS file that contains ID

ID applied to DIV tag

Attributes such as color applied in Document window

External CSS file

ID name

CSS attributes of ID

Figure 11.47 To apply an ID, add the attribute to a tag. Here I added my new ID attribute to an existing <div> tag. This means I can use the same border and color characteristics for layers on several different pages.

DEFINING NEW SELECTORS

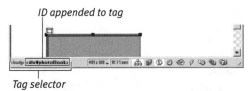

Figure 11.48 You can use the Quick Tag editor to quickly add an ID to a tag. See Chapter 4.

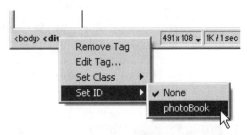

Figure 11.49 To set an ID or a class for a specific tag, right-click (Control+click) on the Tag in the tag selector to pop up this menu.

ID appended to tag

Tag selector

Figure 11.50 Now we see the ID displayed appended to the tag in the tag selector. You'll notice this again in Chapter 14 when we use <div> tags to make layers.

✔ Tips

■ You can also apply an ID or a class by right-clicking the tag name in the Tag selector (**Figure 11.49**).

■ IDs do show up in the Edit Style Sheet dialog box so that you can edit them.

■ When you define an ID for a tag, the Tag selector shows the tag with its ID appended to it (**Figure 11.50**).

■ Some good uses for IDs and layers: If you want a similar layer to appear on each of several pages, create an ID for the layer in an external CSS style sheet. This ID does not have to contain positioning coordinates: It could be a set of characteristics like color, border, margins, and padding. You can use a layer with a unique ID only once per page. After it's on your page, Dreamweaver will add positioning and size attributes.

DEFINING NEW SELECTORS

Using External Style Sheets

If you want to create a style sheet that can be used on more than one page, then you should create or export an external style sheet.

We went over the basics for creating a linked style sheet in *Creating a Style Class*.

If you already have external style sheets you want to link to, skip ahead to *Attaching an External Style Sheet*.

To create an external style sheet while creating its first style:

1. On the CSS Styles panel, click on the New Style button. The New CSS Style dialog box will appear (**Figure 11.51**).

2. Click the appropriate radio button and then select a tag to redefine, or name your class.

3. Select the Define In radio button and select (New Style Sheet File) from the menu.

4. Click OK. The Save Style Sheet File As dialog box will appear (**Figure 11.52**).

5. Select the appropriate folder, and then type a name for your style sheet file, ending in .css, in the File name text box.

6. You can make the link to the style sheet Document or Site-Root relative. If you're saving all your style sheets in a central location, choose Site Root. For more on these options, see Chapter 6.

7. Click Save. The CSS Style Definition dialog box will appear. Select at least one attribute for the style, and click OK to save it.

Now you've got a new external style sheet. To add more styles to it, see *Editing Style Sheets*.

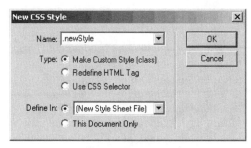

Figure 11.51 Click on Define In (New Style Sheet File) to create a new external style sheet.

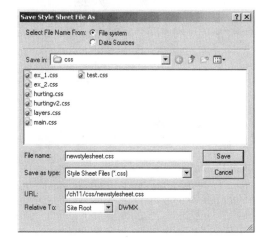

Figure 11.52 Save your style sheet file just as you would any other.

Figure 11.53 The Define In drop-down menu now lists the new style sheet. You can add new styles directly to any style sheet attached to your page.

✔ Tip

■ The next time you add a new style to your page, the name of your style sheet will be listed in the Define In drop-down menu (**Figure 11.53**), and you'll be able to add more styles to it. The menu displays only those style sheets already attached to the current page; to attach additional style sheets, read on.

Uploading Style Sheets

You need to upload external style sheets to your remote Web site in order for them to work (see Chapter 19 for instructions). I like to keep my style sheets in a central folder, similar to the /images folder or the /Library folder, so I always know where they are and I can link to one from any page in my site.

Be sure to check the link URL when you upload the page to your Web site. It's in the code and looks something like this:

```
<link rel="stylesheet"
href="/styles/master.css">
```

For imported styles, the code will look something like this:

```
@import "import.css"
```

Attaching an Existing External Style Sheet

Attaching an existing style sheet to a page is very simple. After you have an external style sheet, you can attach it to any number of pages in your site.

To attach an external style sheet:

1. In the Document window, open the page to which you want to link the style sheet, or save the page you're working on.

2. Click on the Attach Style Sheet button on the CSS Styles panel ⬚. The Link External Style Sheet dialog box will appear (**Figure 11.54**).

3. Choose a linking method:
   - ◆ To use the new file as a linked style sheet, click on Link.
   - ◆ To import the styles onto the pages, click on Import.

4. Click on Browse (Choose) to select the folder your style sheets are stored in. The Select Style Sheet File dialog box will appear (**Figure 11.55**).
   - ◆ To attach an existing style sheet, select the file and click OK.
   - ◆ To create a new style sheet, type a filename for your new file, ending in .css, in the File/URL text box. A dialog box will ask you if you want to create the file—click Yes.

Your style sheet will be attached to the page. Any redefined tags Dreamweaver can display will appear on your page, and any style classes in it will be listed in the CSS Styles panel.

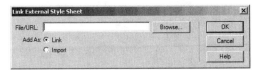

Figure 11.54 In the Link External Style Sheet dialog box, click on Browse to locate the style sheet or create a new one. Or, just type the pathname for your new style sheet, and Dreamweaver will link to the file or create a new one in the location you specify.

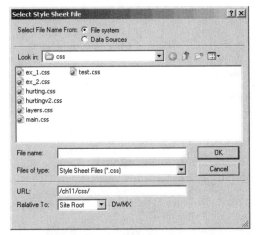

Figure 11.55 In the Select Style Sheet File dialog box, choose the style sheet you want to use, or type the name of a new style sheet to create.

✔ Tip

■ The kinks aren't yet worked out of style sheet importing in any current browser, so linking to the style sheet is recommended rather than importing it. The exception: When linking from one CSS file to another, you *must* import the second CSS file—and the Link option will appear grayed out.

Adding Styles to an External Style Sheet

The methods we've explored so far have you creating an external style sheet and then saving it with one or zero styles in it. You can add as many styles to this style sheet as you want.

To add styles to an external style sheet:

1. Start off with a page open that already links to your style sheet, or save the current page and link to the style sheet in question.

2. Click on the New CSS Style button on the CSS Styles panel.

3. In the New CSS Styles dialog box, click on the Define In radio button, and select the name of the style sheet from the list (you can link to more than one style sheet per page).

4. Create your style as usual.

Exporting Internal Styles into an External Style Sheet

If you've created styles on a single page, and you want to use them again on other pages, you can export the styles to an external style sheet and then link to it. (Previously, you had to use a text editor and cut and paste everything.)

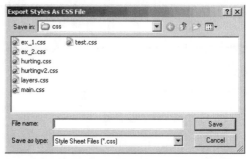

Figure 11.56 It's easy to save internal styles as a new style sheet. Just type the file name.

To export internal styles:

1. Open the page that includes the styles you want to export.

2. From the Document window menu bar, select File > Export > CSS Styles. The Export Styles as CSS File dialog box will appear (**Figure 11.56**).

3. Select the folder you want to save the style sheet in, and then type a name for the file, ending in .css, in the File name text box.

4. Click on Save. Now you can attach the style sheet to a different page.

Cutting and Pasting Styles

You can also cut and paste the styles from a document into a CSS file, and you can copy styles from one CSS file to another.

Internal styles are in the <head> of the document, and they look like this:

```
<style type="text/css">
<!--
.hh {
    font-size: 10px;
}
-->
</style>
```

The bold text is the style itself. When pasting styles into the head of a document, make sure that you add the <style> tags, if they're missing. And be sure that style definitions themselves appear between the <!--comment markers --> and that they include the closing } (curly bracket) for each.

In contrast, when pasting styles into a CSS document, include *only* the style definitions and none of the other text or tags.

About Design Time Style Sheets

You may find yourself creating different versions of the same page for different purposes in such situations as presenting different mockups of a site design, creating a redesign, or repurposing material for different sites. Or you may want to create a site that's used one way by one set of browsers and another way by another set.

In any case, you can attach multiple style sheets to your page, and new in Dreamweaver MX, you can choose which style sheets to display while you're working and which to attach after you're done designing.

Two examples: If you're designing a page that will have its text imported dynamically, you may not want to actually apply the styles to the page. And if for insertable items that will go on larger pages, such as snippets, server-side includes, and library items, you may want to design the item with visible formatting. After the item is inserted onto the page, it will of course be formatted by the page's own style sheets.

1. Save the page you're working on.

2. On the CSS Styles panel, click the Options menu button and select Design Time Style Sheets. The Design Time Style Sheets dialog box will appear.

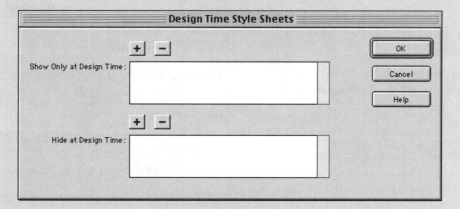

3. To attach a style sheet you want visible while you're designing, but that won't be attached to the page later, click on the + button at Show Only At Design Time. The Select File dialog box will appear—choose your CSS file and click OK.

4. To specify a style sheet you want hidden while you're designing, but that will be attached to the page later, click on the + button at Hide At Design Time. The Select File dialog box will appear—choose your CSS file and click OK.

5. Click OK to save your changes.

Saving a Page with CSS Formatting as Plain HTML

After you create a page with CSS, you may decide to create a plainer version of it for your technologically deficient visitors.

1. Open the page with CSS in the Document window (**Figure 11.57**).

2. From the Document window menu bar, select File > Convert > 3.0 Browser Compatible. The Convert to 3.0 Browser Compatible dialog box will appear (**Figure 11.58**).

3. In the dialog box, click on the CSS Styles to HTML Markup radio button.

4. Click OK. Dreamweaver will open the converted page in a new, untitled window.

5. Make any modifications you want, then save the page.

Figure 11.59 shows the converted page. It lost the indents, but the font formatting is mostly the same.

✔ Tips

- Create the page with CSS first, and clear that page of all HTML text formatting before you begin.

- You can clear text formatting with the HTML Styles panel: Select the entire page, and then click on the Clear Character Styles button.

- To find out about converting from layers to tables and vice versa, see Chapter 14.

- To create a script that serves a CSS or non-CSS version of the page based on the browser version, see *Checking Browser Version,* in Chapter 16.

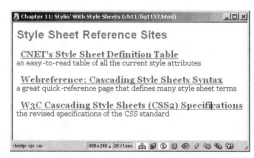

Figure 11.57 Here's a page on which I redefined the H1, p, and a tags.

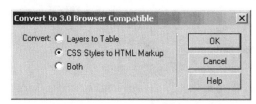

Figure 11.58 Choose CSS Styles to HTML Markup in the Convert to 3.0 Browser Compatible dialog box.

New page is not saved.

Figure 11.59 After backwards conversion, the text formatting looks like this.

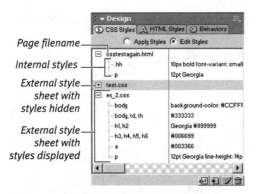

Page filename

Internal styles

External style sheet with styles hidden

External style sheet with styles displayed

Figure 11.60 Click on the Edit Styles radio button, and all styles and style sheets will be displayed. A summary of each style's attributes appears to the right of its name to remind you what the style already contains. Double-click on the name of the style that you want to edit.

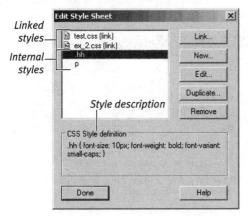

Linked styles

Internal styles

Style description

Figure 11.61 The Edit Style Sheet dialog box displays the names of styles and style sheets for a page. You can also link to style sheets from here.

Editing Styles

Editing styles is now much easier in Dreamweaver MX—everything you need is available in the CSS Styles panel. When you edit a style, all instances of it will be updated on the pages that use it. Whether you change from brown to green, right-aligned to justified, Arial to Courier, or scrap a style entirely, your changes will be automatic. Remember to upload your edited pages and style sheet.

To edit a style:

1. On the CSS styles panel, click on the Edit Styles radio button (**Figure 11.60**). All styles in your page, whether classes, redefined tags, or selectors, and whether they're in an external style sheet or internal, will appear listed, including a brief summary of their attributes.

   External style sheets will have a + button next to them. You can display or hide all the styles below a style sheet by clicking the +. When you make a change to an external style sheet, all pages linked to that style sheet will also be changed.

2. Double-click the name of the style you wish to edit.

   or

   To open the Edit Style Sheet dialog box (**Figure 11.61**), select the name of your page or an external style sheet in the CSS Styles panel and then click the Edit Style sheet button ✏️ .

   Either way, the CSS Style Definition dialog box will appear, and you can add, change, and delete attributes.

3. When you're done, click on OK to close the CSS Style Definition dialog box. Your edited style will appear in the CSS Styles panel.

Copying a Style Sheet to Edit

You may want to create two styles that are very similar. You can make a copy of a style and then edit it. You can duplicate tag and selector styles as themselves or as classes, or vice versa.

To make a copy of a style:

1. From the menu bar, select Text > CSS Styles > Edit Style to open the Edit Style Sheet dialog box.

2. Click on the name of the style in the list box (**Figure 11.62**).

3. Click on Duplicate. The Duplicate Style dialog box will appear (**Figure 11.63**); this is pretty much the same as the New CSS Style dialog box.

4. You must rename the style before you can duplicate it:

   ◆ To save the duplicate style as a class, click on the Make Custom Style (Class) radio button, and type a name for the style in the text box.

   ◆ To apply the duplicate style to a different HTML tag, click on the Redefine HTML Tag radio button, and select a tag from the drop-down menu (or type a tag without the <brackets> in the text box).

   ◆ To apply the duplicate style to a set of tags, type the tags, either a pseudo-class, an ID, or a contextual set (such as b i) in the text box.

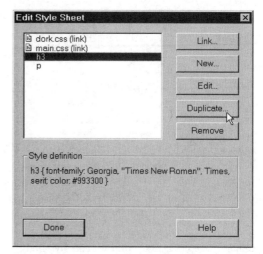

Figure 11.62 In the Edit Style Sheet dialog box, you can duplicate a style so that you can apply it to a different entity. You can delete a style from here, too.

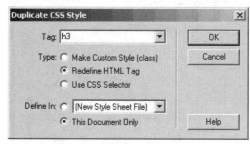

Figure 11.63 The Duplicate CSS Style dialog box is pretty much the same as the New CSS Style dialog box.

EDITING STYLES

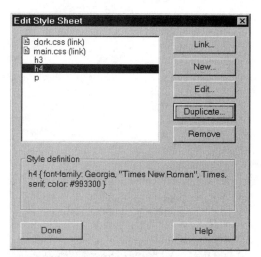

Figure 11.64 Now the style I duplicated (h3 as h4) appears in the Edit Style Sheet dialog box. If you duplicate a style into an external style sheet, you need to double-click the name of the style sheet and view its own Edit Style Sheet dialog box before you can edit the new, duplicated style.

5. Click OK. The Duplicate CSS Style Sheet dialog box will close, and you'll return to the Edit Style Sheet dialog box, where you'll see the name of your new style selected in the list box (**Figure 11.64**).

Now you can edit your new style, if you wish, by clicking on the Edit button.

✔ Tip

- You can't duplicate external style sheets this way—instead, open them in the Document window and do a Save As to make a copy.

About Conflicting Styles

What happens when you apply two conflicting styles to the same text?

Suppose you have defined the paragraph style with the following properties:

```
p { font-family: "Courier New",
Courier, mono; font-size: 14pt}
```

And then, suppose your link style is as follows:

```
a { font-family: Arial, Helvetica,
sans-serif;}
```

Who would win? That's where the cascading in Cascading Style Sheets comes in. First off, any non-conflicting attributes are applied. When a conflict arrives, rules of proximity apply.

Styles, like tags, are nested around elements. The style that's closest, physically, to the text that it modifies has precedence over the other styles that might effect it. Additionally, a class will override any tag modifications (see sidebar, this page), and internal styles override linked ones.

Your Parents' Inheritance

Tags that surround a piece of text are called parents. Parent tags also have parent tags, the whole way up through the <body> and <html> tags that surround all the content in a document. The cascading rule applies to these nested tags, but what about nested styles? In other words, what happens when you have a style sheet that has a linked style sheet as well as style sheets located on that page?

In CSS-2, all properties can be inherited, or passed down, but current browsers still use the old inheritance rules. For example, the attribute text-decoration: none, which keeps links from being underlined, was not inheritable before. That means you had to apply it directly to the <a> tag, not just to a paragraph with a link in it. CSS-2 allows that that attribute should be inherited, but both Netscape 6 and IE6 follow the old rules and don't let the property inherit.

Again, the closer the style is, the more influence it has. Classes overrule tag redefinitions. Modifications made to particular pieces of text win out over modifications made to an entire document (called global styles); global styles win out over imported styles; and imported styles win out over linked styles.

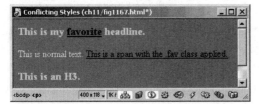

Figure 11.65 This is what the example code below looks like in the Document window.

Figure 11.66 The various styles alone and mixed.

Figure 11.67 Here's the code for Figure **11.66**.

So in this example, the <a> tag would have precedence:

```
<p>All of this text is in the same
paragraph, but this <a
href="piece.html">piece</a> is also
linked.</p>
```

In the following example, no matter what style modifications have been made to the <body> and <h3> selectors, the <span> tag will dominate them in the hierarchy for the word "favorite." (See **Figures 11.65** through **11.67**)

```
<head><style type="text/css">
<!-- body { color: white;
background-color: gray}
h3 {color: yellow}
.fav {color: black; text-decoration:
underline}
-->
</style></head>
<body>
<h3>This is my <span class="fav">
favorite</span> headline</h3>
</body>
```

Style Definitions

Now, at last, we come to the section of the chapter where I describe the style attributes you can use in your custom styles. There are eight different categories of custom styles in Dreamweaver, each of which contains several different single attributes you can apply to a block of text. The categories are:

* **Type** attributes (**Figure 11.68**), which refer to font formatting, such as font face, font size and color, and weight and style.

* **Background** attributes (**Figure 11.69**), such as background color and image, which can be applied either to a text block or to the <body> tag to control an entire page.

* **Block** attributes (**Figure 11.70**), which control the spacing and shape of text. Alignment and indent are block attributes.

* **Box** attributes, which are applied to the box that surrounds a block element, and can also be applied to <span> selections. Box attributes include padding and margin controls to shape the space.

* **Border** attributes, which are a subset of box attributes. Border attributes can make the usually invisible box around a style box visible with borders and colors.

* **List** attributes, which affect the formatting of ordered and unordered lists, including the appearance of the numbers or bullets.

* **Positioning** controls, which allow you to determine the location of elements on the page. (Because there are so many, and because this chapter is quite long enough already, I discuss positioning in the next chapter.)

* **Extensions** to style sheets, which are generally unsupported by current browsers, although some visual effects are supported by IE 4 and 5 and by Netscape 6.

Name of style being defined

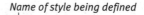

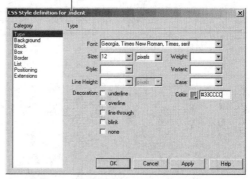

Figure 11.68 All the attributes you could ever want, eight categories high.

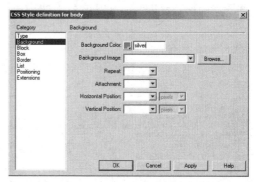

Figure 11.69 If you change text colors using style sheets, you can also modify the page background. That way, users with 3.0 or earlier, non-CSS browsers will see one complete color scheme, and 4.0 or later browsers will display another.

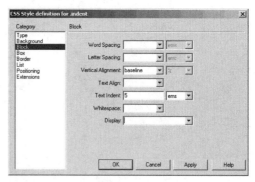

Figure 11.70 Block attributes allow for more typographic control, such as indents and line wrapping (white space).

Units

The following units are used to define various spatial relationships in style sheets:

pixels (px) are the little dots that make up the picture on your computer monitor. **inches (in), centimeters (cm),** and **millimeters (mm)** are the same as their real-world equivalents.

picas and **points** are typographical measurements from the days of hand-set type. There are six picas in an inch, 12 points in a pica, and 72 points in an inch. (That's why many font sizes are based on the number 12.)

ems and **exs** are also handset-type measurements. An em, as in the letter m, is a square piece of type. The width of an em is one pica in a monospace font; in digital terms, this width may vary slightly from font to font and should be treated as a relative measurement. An ex, on the other hand, is the height of the letter x, which is shorthand for "average height of the lowercase alphabet in this font without any ascenders or descenders."

percent (%), in the case of style sheets, refers to percentage of the parent tag. If the only parent tag is the <body> tag, then % will apply to the width of the screen. If the parent tag is a table cell, then the style block will occupy x% of that cell. If the parent unit is a text block such as a paragraph or <span>, things might get funky. Experiment with percentages to see what happens.

When using the CSS Style Definition dialog box:

◆ It's easy to open the CSS Style Definition dialog box. When creating a new style, the dialog box opens after you choose the kind of style you're making, in the New CSS Style dialog box, and click OK.

Or, in the CSS Styles panel, double-click the name of any style class, or when in Edit Styles mode, any class, redefined tag, or other entity.

◆ To move from one panel of the dialog box to another, click on the category's name in the list box on the left side of the dialog box.

◆ Select items from pull-down menus, check check boxes, and type number values.

◆ Some pull-down menus double as text boxes.

◆ To select units for an attribute, first select a value from the drop-down menu, then type a number (you can change it later) over the word value in the text box, and then choose a unit from the units pull-down menu.

◆ Leave blank or unchanged any items that aren't needed.

◆ To see how your styles will look in a certain browser, you should define the style, save the page, and then preview the page in the browser in question.

STYLE DEFINITIONS

Type Attributes

Type attributes are probably the styles you're going to use most often, and they include those previously defined by the <font> tag (slowly being deprecated). The Type panel of the CSS Style Definition dialog box is shown in **Figures 11.71** and **72**.

Type attributes include:

Font chooses a font face or a font family.

✔ Tip

■ You can add fonts to the list; select Edit Font List and refer to *Changing Font Face* in Chapter 8.

Size (**Figure 11.73**) sets a font size for the text. You can choose from a number of different units to set the size for the text.

The size attribute offers point sizes ranging from 9 (smallest) to 36 (largest), which roughly correspond to the 1–7 font size scale in basic HTML.

If point sizes don't do it for you, you can set a size in a number of other units, including pixels (px), inches (in), centimeters (cm), millimeters (mm), picas, ems, and exs.

Additionally, you can set relative sizes ranging from "largest" to "xx-small."

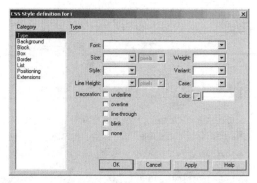

Figure 11.71 The Type panel of the CSS Style Definition dialog box.

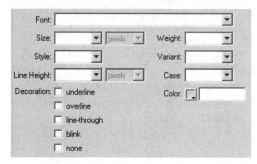

Figure 11.72 A close-up of the Type panel.

Figure 11.73 The whole family of font sizes.

Key to Icons Used in This Chapter

* Dreamweaver does not display attributes with an asterisk (*).

☞ Pointer items discuss how different browsers may treat an attribute.

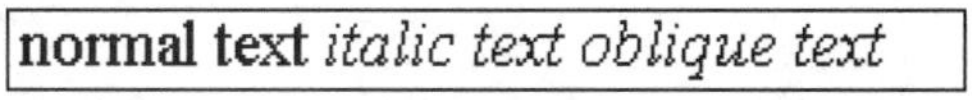

normal text *italic text oblique text*

Figure 11.74 Font styles in Internet Explorer: Normal, Italic, and Oblique.

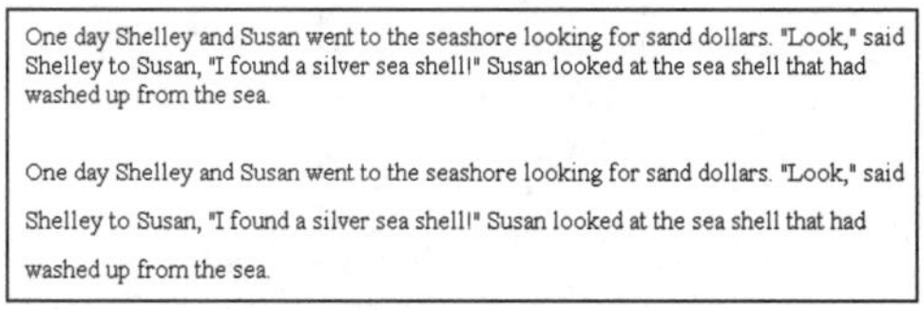

One day Shelley and Susan went to the seashore looking for sand dollars. "Look," said Shelley to Susan, "I found a silver sea shell!" Susan looked at the sea shell that had washed up from the sea.

One day Shelley and Susan went to the seashore looking for sand dollars. "Look," said

Shelley to Susan, "I found a silver sea shell!" Susan looked at the sea shell that had

washed up from the sea.

Figure 11.75 Line height as interpreted by Navigator 4.5. The top paragraph has no line height set. The second paragraph has a line height of 24 points (to a font size of 14 points).

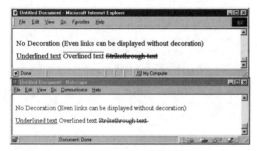

Figure 11.76 Text decoration, as displayed by Internet Explorer (above) and Netscape Navigator 4.5 (below). Note that Navigator 4.5 does not display overline; Netscape 6 does.

Style, meaning text style, lets you set text as Normal, Italic, or Oblique (**Figure 11.74**).

☞ Normal, or "upright," italic, and oblique are three font styles; oblique means "slanted." Netscape follows the rule for font selection literally here: It looks for a font with "oblique" properties in the selected font family, and if it doesn't find one, it uses a normal font, whereas Explorer will display oblique text as italic.

Line Height, a typographical setting not available in regular HTML, determines the height of each line in the text block (**Figure 11.75**). If the font size is 12 points, and the line height is 16 points, you'll have a good bit of extra space between each line. (Normal line height provides an offset of approximately two points.)

☞ Browsers may interpret "normal" line height however they choose. Line height settings may cause problems with IE3.

Decoration (**Figure 11.76**) can apply underlining, overlining*, strikethrough (line-through), or blinking* to the text.

✔ Tip

■ Because the default for regular text is no decoration, and the default for linked text is underlining, you can remove the default underlining from links by creating a style class or by redefining the <a> tag. In either case, you'd select None from the Decoration category and applying it to the *<a>* tag. (Text decoration is not inherited in CSS-1, which is the standard current browsers use, so if you apply it simply as a paragraph style or body style, links will still appear underlined.)

Weight (Figure 11.77) is the same as boldness, the tag for which is usually **<b>** or **<strong>**. You can apply a relative weight (lighter, normal, bold, bolder), or a numerical weight from 100–900. The weight of normal text is generally 400, whereas boldface text has a weight of about 700.

☞ The only font **Variant*** (**Figure 11.78**) currently supported by Dreamweaver is SMALL CAPS. Explorer 5 and Netscape 6 both display small caps. Dreamweaver displays small caps as uppercase.

Case (Figure 11.78) allows you to apply all-lowercase, all-uppercase, or title case (The First Letter In Each Word) to a text block. This would come in especially handy for setting headers or captions. Dreamweaver MX now displays case properly, as do both version 6 browsers.

Color, of course, acts the same as **<font color=n>**.

✔ Tip

■ To find out all about color theory and methods, see *Colors and Web Pages* and *Modifying the Page Background* in Chapter 3.

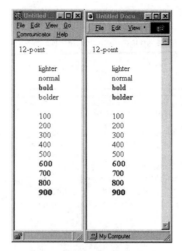

Figure 11.77 Weight variations, at 12 points. Neither browser does anything with lighter weights, and Navigator 4.x also handles "bolder" unpredictably. You can see the typographical differences between Navigator and Explorer here; Netscape 6 acts the same as 4.x regarding font-weight.

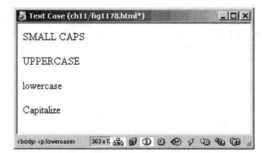

Figure 11.78 Here's Explorer 6 showing the text variant Small Caps and the text cases Uppercase, Lowercase, and Capitalize. Netscape 4.5-present also displays case properly. Use this for an unusual rollover effect on *a*:hover.

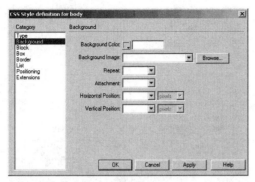

Figure 11.79 You can define properties of a background color or image for either a text block or the page body using the Background panel of the CSS Style Definition dialog box.

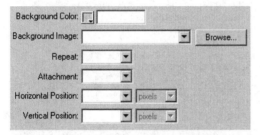

Figure 11.80 A close-up of the Background panel.

Background Attributes

Background attributes allow you to place a background color or image behind a text block. They will be superimposed over any other background color or image on the page. The Background panel of the CSS Style Definition dialog box is shown in **Figures 11.79** and **11.80**.

✔ Tips

- To set the background color or image for a page, see *Modifying the Page Background* in Chapter 3.

- To set the background color or image for a table, see *Coloring Tables* in Chapter 12.

- To use style sheets to apply a background color or image to an entire page, apply the style to the <body> tag.

Background attributes include:

☞ Background color and background image. These can be applied to an entire page or to a text block (**Figure 11.81**). If both are used, the text block background will be superimposed over the page background (**Figure 11.82**).

The rest of the attributes all apply to a background image.

Repeat (Figure 11.83). This determines whether the background image is tiled, and if so, how. If the image is displayed in an element that is smaller than the image dimensions, the image will be cropped to fit the element's dimensions.

No-repeat prevents the image from tiling.

Repeat tiles the image as it would be tiled in a page background image: from left to right in columns proceeding down the page.

Repeat-x displays a horizontal "band" of images; the image is tiled in one row across the page.

Repeat-y displays a vertical "band" of images; the image is tiled in one column down the page.

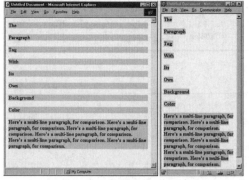

Figure 11.81 I redefined the paragraph tag to have its own background color. Explorer 5 (on the left) makes paragraphs occupy 100 percent of the parent tag (the page body, in this case) by default, and colors in the entire width. Navigator 4.5 (on the right) colors in only the part of the paragraph that contains content. Netscape 6 now displays backgrounds for paragraphs like Explorer does.

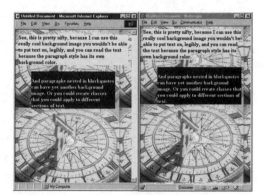

Figure 11.82 If you use a background color (first paragraph) or background image (second paragraph) for a text block, it will be superimposed over the page background. Note how the blockquote style (second paragraph) is rectangular in both Explorer (left) and Navigator (right).

Repeat-y (vertical)   *Repeat-x (horizontal)*

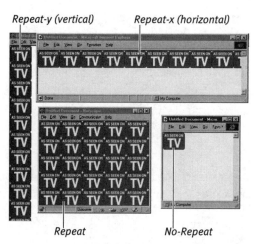

Repeat   *No-Repeat*

Figure 11.83 The four flavors of background repeat.

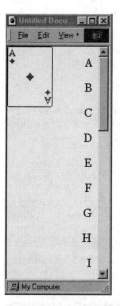 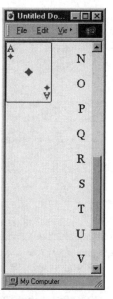

Figure 11.84 A demonstration of the fixed attachment background attribute (also called a watermark) in version 6 browsers. The image of the ace is set to not repeat. (Use with the repeat option no-repeat.) Normally, a tiny background image like this one would scroll off the screen. With fixed attachment set, the ace stays in place while you scroll through the text at right.

Attachment*. This means the relative attachment of the background image to the page, in particular for full-page background images. Normally, when you scroll through a page, the background image moves, and so does the content—this is both default and scroll. The fixed attachment attribute fixes the background image in place, so that when you scroll through a page, the content "moves," and the background image "stands still" (**Figure 11.84**).

☞ Currently, IE4-IE6 and Netscape 6 support the fixed option. Navigator 4.5 treats fixed as scroll.

Horizontal position and vertical position. These mark the position of the background image, relative to the element. If you want a small background image centered on the page or in a table or table cell, set both settings to Center. You can also set a pixel value from the left and top of the page. See Chapter 14 for more about positioning.

Block Attributes

Block attributes apply typographical constraints to the alignment and spacing of words and characters within the selected element. The Block panel of the CSS Style Definition dialog box is shown in **Figures 11.85** and **11.86**.

Block attributes include:

Word spacing*. This is used to adjust the space between words, and **Letter spacing** is used to adjust the space between characters.

Units available for using word and letter spacing include "normal" (no units), pixels, inches (in), centimeters (cm), millimeters (mm), picas, ems, and exs.

☞ 4.x doesn't support letter spacing, but IE and Netscape 6 do (**Figure 11.87**).

☞ The only browser that currently supports word spacing is Netscape 6 (**Figure 11.88**).

☞ You can specify either positive or negative values, although not all browsers will support the latter.

☞ If property alignment is set to justify, this will most likely overrule word spacing, whereas letter spacing will override justification.

☞ The "normal" settings for word and letter spacing are left up to the individual browser.

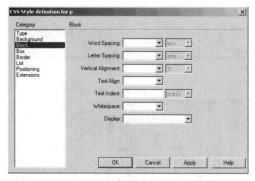

Figure 11.85 The Block attributes panel of the CSS Style Definition dialog box.

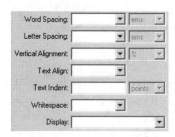

Figure 11.86 A close-up of the Block attributes panel.

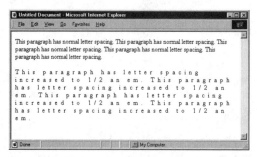

Figure 11.87 Explorer 6 and Navigator 6 both process letter spacing.

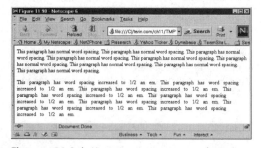

Figure 11.88 Only Netscape 6 supports word spacing.

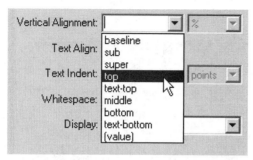

Figure 11.89 Vertical alignment attributes include subscript and superscript, as well as options similar to those used for images.

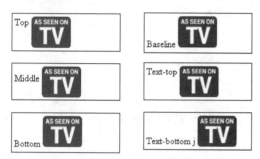

Figure 11.90 Vertical alignment options for text aligned with floating images.

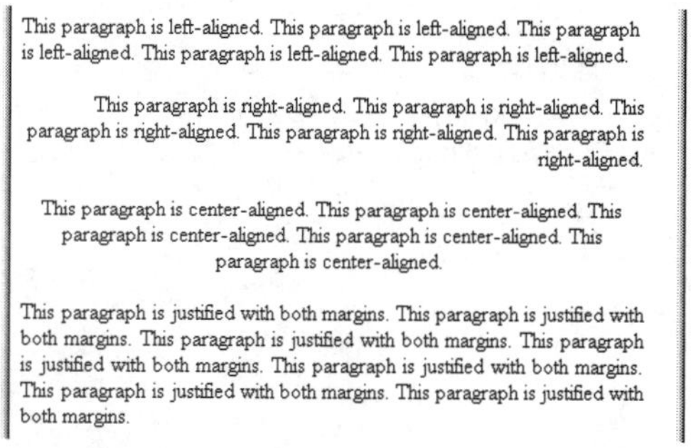

This paragraph is left-aligned. This paragraph is left-aligned. This paragraph is left-aligned. This paragraph is left-aligned. This paragraph is left-aligned.

This paragraph is right-aligned. This paragraph is right-aligned. This paragraph is right-aligned. This paragraph is right-aligned. This paragraph is right-aligned.

This paragraph is center-aligned. This paragraph is center-aligned. This paragraph is center-aligned. This paragraph is center-aligned. This paragraph is center-aligned.

This paragraph is justified with both margins. This paragraph is justified with both margins. This paragraph is justified with both margins. This paragraph is justified with both margins. This paragraph is justified with both margins. This paragraph is justified with both margins.

Figure 11.91 Text block alignment options, from top to bottom, are left, right, center, and justify. Note that the margin gutter is greater on the right than on the left; Navigator is leaving room for a scrollbar. (Explorer displays vertical scrollbars whether they're needed or not.)

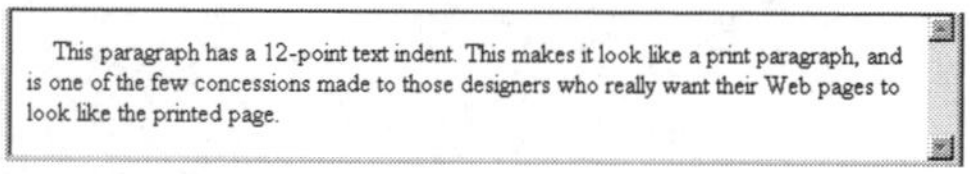

This paragraph has a 12-point text indent. This makes it look like a print paragraph, and is one of the few concessions made to those designers who really want their Web pages to look like the printed page.

Figure 11.92 A paragraph with a 12-point indent.

Vertical alignment*. This (**Figures 11.89** and **11.90**) controls the vertical position of the selection. You may use these attributes most often to align text and images within a table cell (Chapter 12) or a layer (Chapter 14).

Superscript (super) text. This is smaller text raised above the baseline text, as in $E=mc^2$. **Subscript (sub)** text dips below the baseline, as in H_2SO_4.

The other vertical alignment options are used with text and images in combination (Figure 11.90), or with two images aligned within a parent layer.

The baseline. This is the imaginary line that text sits on. (Descenders, as in the letters j and g, dip below the baseline, whereas ascenders, as in the letters l and d, rise above lowercase text.) Baseline alignment makes text vertically align to the baseline of nearby text, or the bottom of an image align to the text baseline.

Top, **middle**, and **bottom** are self-explanatory.

Text-top and **text-bottom.** These align an object with the tallest ascender in the text or the lowest descender in the text, respectively.

Text align. This sets alignment for the text within the margins of the page or the block unit. As in regular HTML, alignment options are left, right, and center, with the additional justify option (**Figure 11.91**).

Text indent*. This applies a tab-like indent to the first line of a block-type element (**Figure 11.92**).

*Dreamweaver displays indents unpredictably. Units available for using indents include "normal" (no units), pixels, inches (in), centimeters (cm), millimeters (mm), picas, ems, and exs.

☞ You can use negative values to create a hanging indent, but not all browsers will support this.

continued on next page

BLOCK ATTRIBUTES

✔ Tip

■ Indents are not inherited, which means that line breaks used within paragraphs can cause unpredictable indent behavior. You might experiment with applying a class with indent properties to spans within paragraphs, which is what I did to get the indents in **Figure 11.93**. Current browsers still obey the old inheritance rules.

Display. This is new in CSS-2 and is not implemented in current browsers. This property has the following attributes (**Figure 11.94**):

block: creates a text block; *inline:* creates a non-breaking, or block-like entity; *list-item:* creates a block with a sub-block that acts like a list item; *marker:* used only after a pseudo-element, cannot float, uses line height, and can use padding and borders, but not margins (see CSS-2 spec); *none:* generates no boxes; *run-in* and *compact* are contextual and can be floating or inline; *table-types* cause the block to act like a table element.

Whitespace*. This controls the use of spacing within the selection. *Normal* ignores extra spaces and text-based breaks; *Pre* treats the text as if it were enclosed in `<pre>` tags, conserving the use of spaces and text-based breaks; *Nowrap*, similar to the `nowrap` setting for table cells, allows the line to break only when a `<br>` tag is used. This last setting is useful particularly for layers and block elements with dimensions smaller than 100 percent of the page.

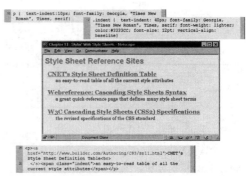

Figure 11.93 The indent property is not inherited, so tags within the block element—the `<p>` in this case—won't be indented unless you apply separate `<span>` formatting.

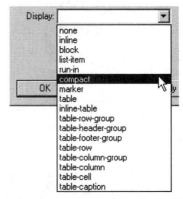

Figure 11.94 The display attributes are not currently available to browsers.

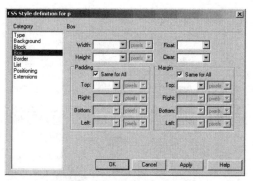

Figure 11.95 The Box attributes panel of the CSS Style Definition dialog box allows you to define the dimensions of the imaginary box that surrounds text blocks.

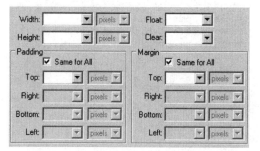

Figure 11.96 A close-up of the Box attributes panel.

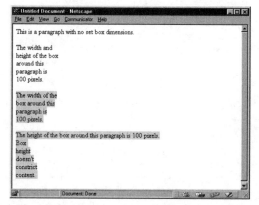

Figure 11.97 The box attributes of these paragraphs, from top to bottom: None, 100x100 pixels, 100 pixels across, and 100 pixels high. Horizontal measurements will break a line, but vertical measurements will not crop content. I used a background color on the bottom two paragraphs so you could see the dimensions more clearly.

Box Attributes

You can imagine all style modifications to HTML elements as being rectangular, or box-shaped. Box attributes, then, are styles applied to the (generally invisible) box that surrounds a block (or span) of text. The Box panel of the CSS Style Definition dialog box is shown in **Figures 11.95** and **11.96**.

Box attributes include the following:

Height* and **Width*** of the box can be expressed in a number of units, including pixels, inches (in), centimeters (cm), millimeters (mm), picas, ems, and exs, and percentage of the parent unit (%). To use the default dimensions of the box, leave these spaces blank, or choose Auto. Dreamweaver handles box dimensions correctly only for images and layers.

Box width will break a line, but box height will not crop the content of the box to fit within the box (**Figure 11.97**).

Navigator respects box dimensions, but Explorer does not. Navigator 4.5 only displays boxes as true rectangles if borders are applied (see next section).

Float* places the entity at the left or right margin, effectively separating it from the regular flow of the page. Other elements will wrap around floating elements. Dreamweaver displays floating images correctly, but not all elements.

The **Clear*** setting determines the relationship of floating elements to the selected entity. A clear setting of Both keeps objects from occupying the margins on either side of a selected entity. A clear setting of None allows floating entities to occupy either margin. Settings of Left or Right protect the respective margin. Settings of Both protect both margins, and None dismisses margins. Dreamweaver only displays this attribute correctly when it is applied to images.

continued on next page

BOX ATTRIBUTES

Padding* is similar to cell padding used in tables. Padding is blank space between an object and its margin or visible border. To use the same padding for left, right, top and bottom, check the Same for All check box. Uncheck it to vary the padding.

Padding is set as a unit value in pixels, inches (in), centimeters (cm), millimeters (mm), picas, ems, and exs, and percentage of the parent unit (%).

✔ Tips

- Dreamweaver MX can display padding correctly for some elements.

- To set percentage values for any attribute other than height, you need to type the % directly into the code.

- Padding is only visible when you use a visible border (see the next section, *Border Attributes*).

- You can specify padding for the top, bottom, left, and right independently.

Margin* (**Figure 11.98**) is the location of the border around the box (whether or not that border is visible). To use the same margins for left, right, top and bottom, check the Same for All check box. Uncheck it to vary the margins.

Margins are set as either auto, or as a number of units, including pixels, inches (in), centimeters (cm), millimeters (mm), picas, ems, and exs, and percentage of the parent element (%). Dreamweaver displays margins properly only when they are applied to block elements.

✔ Tips

- Setting top and bottom margins is a nice alternative to line spacing; you can subtly increase the spacing between paragraphs.

- You can set margins for the top, bottom, left, and right independently.

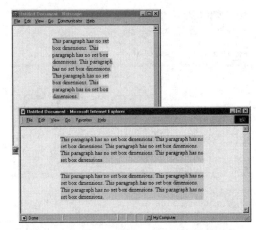

Figure 11.98 In this example, I added the following margins to the <p> tag: 100 pixels on the left and right, and 25 pixels at the top. I showed two different window sizes here (Netscape is at the top) to show how window size affects left and right margins.

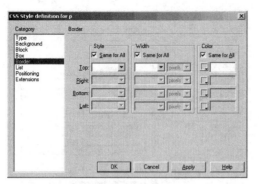

Figure 11.99 Border attributes allow you to make the border around the box visible.

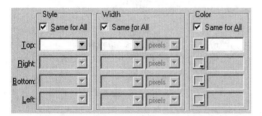

Figure 11.100 A close-up of the border attributes.

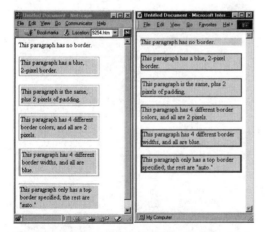

Figure 11.101 Border settings on Netscape (L) and IE5 (R). I set a box width of 200 pixels, which Navigator requires and IE ignores. Border colors are treated differently by the two browsers.

Border Attributes

Border attributes are a subset of box attributes, but in the interests of space and neatness, Dreamweaver displays them in their own panel in the CSS Style Definition dialog box (**Figures 11.99** and **11.100**).

*Border elements are displayed inconsistently by Dreamweaver in the Document window. A border the same width around a layer, for example, may show up as different widths in the right and bottom margins.

Borders are composed of four entities: the **top**, **right**, **bottom**, and **left**.

You can set a **width** and a **color** for each entity (**Figure 11.101**); to set the same attribute for all sides, leave the Same for All checkbox checked. In addition to setting a value for border width, you can set a relative value such as thin, medium, or thick. The auto setting will display the browser's default border width (generally a pixel or two).

☞ Navigator 4.x will display different border widths, but not different border colors. In fact, it may handle them pretty strangely.

☞ Navigator 4.x will only display box borders if a box width is specified (you can specify 100 percent). Explorer ignores box widths.

☞ Navigator and Explorer deal with color combinations differently.

You can also choose from a number of **border styles** (**Figure 11.102**). You *must* set a border style (solid is a good choice) in order for borders to show up at all. Navigator 6 displays all border styles correctly.

✔ Tips

- Padding, a box property, starts doing its thing once you set visible borders.

- You can try interesting beveled effects by specifying borders for two of the four sides of the box and leaving the other two sides blank.

List Attributes

List attributes are applied to ordered (numbered) and unordered (bulleted) lists. The List panel of the CSS Style Definition dialog box is shown in **Figure 11.103** and **11.104**.

* Dreamweaver does not display all list attributes in the Document window.

The **Types*** of list attributes that apply to Ordered Lists (**Figure 11.105**) are decimals (1., 2., etc.) lower-roman (i., ii., etc.), upper-roman (I, II, etc.), lower-alpha (a., b., etc.), and upper-alpha (A., B., etc.).

For unordered lists, the **Types*** of bullets available include discs, circles, and squares (**Figure 11.106**).

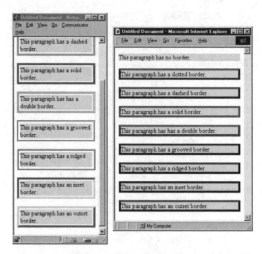

Figure 11.102 Border styles, displayed by Netscape (L) and IE (R). Neither browser displays all border styles as described: "dotted" and "dashed" don't look like their names.

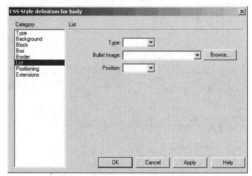

Figure 11.103 The List panel of the CSS Style Definition dialog box lets you define the format of ordered (numbered) or unordered (bulleted) lists.

Figure 11.104 A closeup of the List panel.

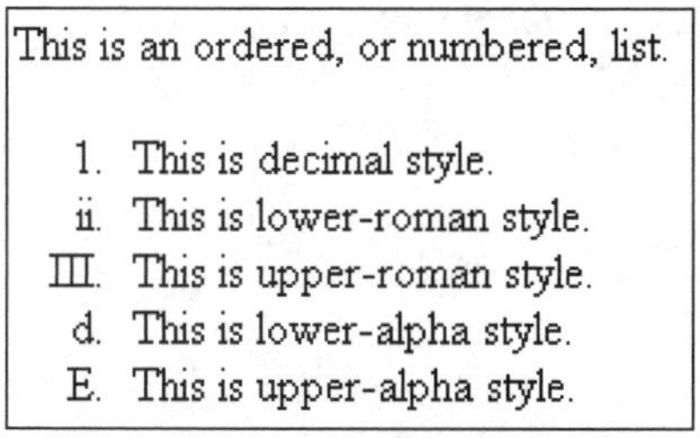
This is an ordered, or numbered, list.

1. This is decimal style.
ii. This is lower-roman style.
III. This is upper-roman style.
d. This is lower-alpha style.
E. This is upper-alpha style.

Figure 11.105 An ordered list, formatted with the five different types of ordered list styles.

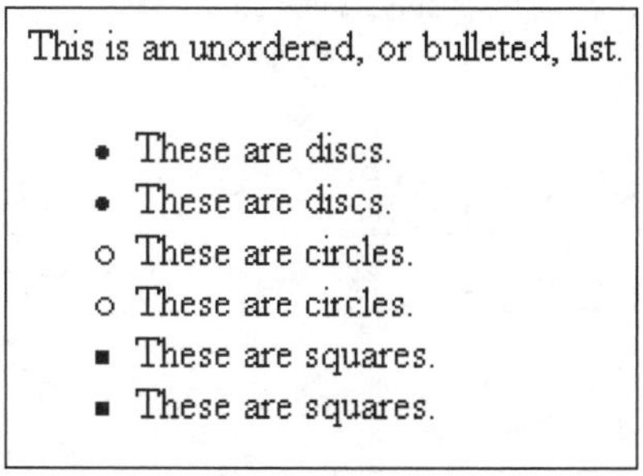
This is an unordered, or bulleted, list.

- These are discs.
- These are discs.
- These are circles.
- These are circles.
- These are squares.
- These are squares.

Figure 11.106 An unordered list, formatted with the three different types of unordered list styles.

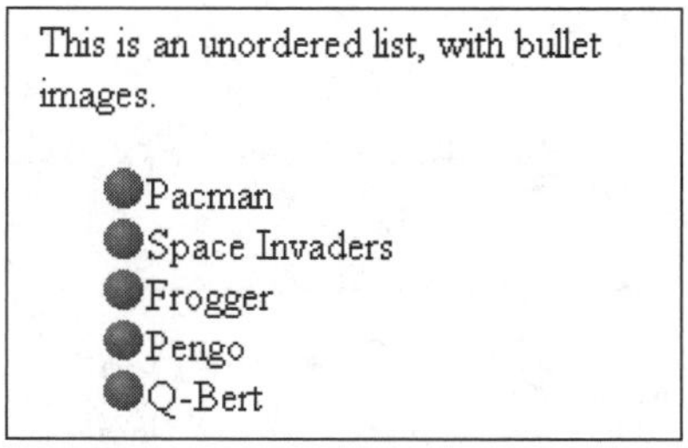
This is an unordered list, with bullet images.

- Pacman
- Space Invaders
- Frogger
- Pengo
- Q-Bert

Figure 11.107 An unordered list, using bullet images.

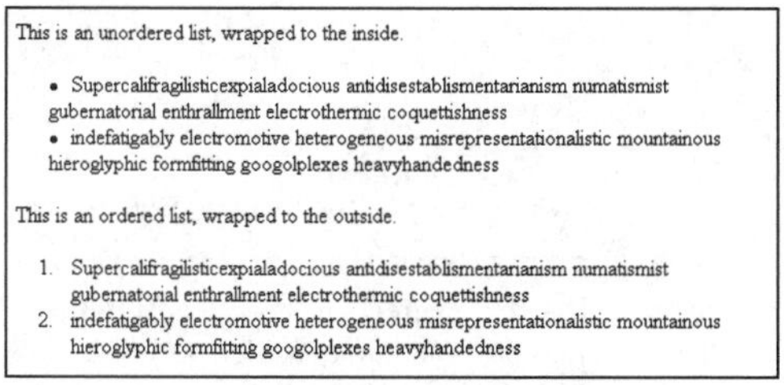
This is an unordered list, wrapped to the inside.

- Supercalifragilisticexpialadocious antidisestablismentarianism numatismist gubernatorial enthrallment electrothermic coquettishness
- indefatigably electromotive heterogeneous misrepresentationalistic mountainous hieroglyphic formfitting googolplexes heavyhandedness

This is an ordered list, wrapped to the outside.

1. Supercalifragilisticexpialadocious antidisestablismentarianism numatismist gubernatorial enthrallment electrothermic coquettishness
2. indefatigably electromotive heterogeneous misrepresentationalistic mountainous hieroglyphic formfitting googolplexes heavyhandedness

Figure 11.108 The first list is wrapped to the inside, and the second list is wrapped to the outside.

You can also apply a **Bullet Image*** (**Figure 11.107**) to unordered lists, for which you supply an image URL.

☞ Navigator 4.x does not display bullet images.

The **Position*** of the list items applies to what the text will do when it wraps. Inside will indent all the text to the bullet point, whereas outside will wrap the text to the margin (**Figure 11.108**).

☞ Navigator 4.x does not display inside wrapping.

✔ Tip

- The next set of elements, Positioning, are layer attributes described in Chapter 14.

Extensions

The attributes in the Extensions panel of the CSS Style Definition dialog box (**Figures 11.109** and **11.110**) are not supported by most browsers.

The **Page Break** extension is a proposed style attribute that is not currently supported by any browser. This extension will allow you to recommend a page break before or after a given text block that would break the page when printing the document.

The **Cursor** extension is supported by IE 4 and 5. When the user mouses over a style callout, the cursor (pointer) changes into an icon other than the pointer.

The **Visual Effects Filters** are theoretically supported by IE 4 and 5 and some by Netscape 6. I had extremely mixed results using these filters, and I suggest you experiment with them rather than count on them. To apply a visual effects filter, choose it from the drop-down menu (**Figure 11.111**). You need to replace any question marks with values. I'm guessing that you use hex codes for colors; the units for the other values are anyone's guess, as these are not covered by the W3C guidelines.

As with all things, in style sheets and in general Web design, experimentation is the key.

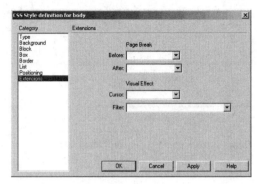

Figure 11.109 The Extensions panel offers extensions to the W3C style sheet specifications.

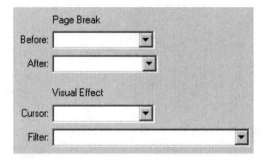

Figure 11.110 A close-up.

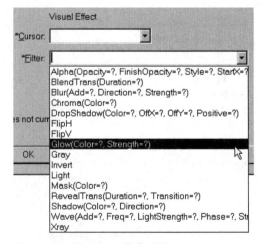

Figure 11.111 The visual effects filters are proprietary, unsupported gimmicks that may work in Internet Explorer or Netscape 6. Test drive them.

SETTING UP TABLES

Club Luxe February Schedule		
Date & Time	Band Name	Booking Contact
02/12 9 p.m.	Inspired	Karen
02/13 10 p.m.	Long Walk Home	Karen
02/14 8:30 p.m.	Poetry Night	Leonard
02/16 10 p.m.	The Hangnails	LuAnn
02/17 9 p.m.	Little Lost Dog	Karen
02/18 9 p.m.	Bonewart	LuAnn
02/20 TBA	Rumpled Stilt Walker	Karen
02/21 8:30 p.m.	Poetry Night	Leonard
02/23 9 p.m.	Cardboard Milk Truck	LuAnn
02/25 10 p.m.	Alonzo & the Rats	Karen
02/26 9 p.m.	Lesson Plan	Karen
02/27 10 p.m.	Karaoke From Mars	Karen
02/28 9 p.m.	Poetry Night	Leonard

Figure 12.1 HTML tables can be used to create all kinds of data tables.

Figure 12.2 With a little imagination, you can use tables to replicate nearly any layout you can make with page layout programs such as Quark or PageMaker.

Before table functionality was added to HTML, all images and text aligned on the left side of a Web page, with no other choice offered. Originally, tables were used to present columns and rows of data, such as scientific reports or night-club schedules (**Figure 12.1**), but clever designers quickly realized that tables could also be adapted to increase design options and give designers more control over layouts and spacing (**Figure 12.2**). You can create complex table layouts for entire-page designs.

Each individual cubbyhole, called a cell, holds discrete information that doesn't ooze over into the other boxes. As you can see in **Figure 12.3** on the next page, tables are divided into rows and columns.

Hand-coding a table is tiresome at best. In fact, simplifying the creation of complex tables is one of the most appealing reasons to use a WYSIWYG Web page creation tool at all. Dreamweaver writes admirable table code. It offers an additional table drawing environment called *Layout view,* in which you actually draw tables and table cells on a page, exactly where you want them to go. The program then fills in columns and rows to hold the layout together. Once you have this basic design, you can add, resize, and move the elements on the page.

Setting Up Tables

Creating a table is a three-part process, although the second and third steps often take place simultaneously.

To create a table:

1. Insert a table into your page.

2. Once your table exists in a basic form, you can modify the properties of the table and its cells. You can change the size, the layout, the spacing, the color scheme, and so on.

3. After your table is complete, or even while you're still niggling with the layout, you can insert content, such as text and images, into the table.

✔ Tips

- It helps to draw a sketch of your page before you get started (**Figure 12.4**) and then add or subtract elements as you proceed.

- You can do any of these things in Standard view or Layout view (**Figure 12.5**). Some additional actions, such as combining or splitting cells, you can do only in Standard view. Others, such as creating autostretch columns, you can do only in Layout view. I'm going to use both views in this chapter, as I do when I'm working on my own pages.

- Although virtually every current Web browser handles tables correctly, a few older browsers, and some nongraphic browsers, don't. See Appendix A on the Web site for tips on working with different kinds of browsers.

- You can also draw complex layouts using layers and then have Dreamweaver convert the page into tables. From the menu bar, select Modify > Convert > Layers to Tables. See Chapter 14 for more on layers.

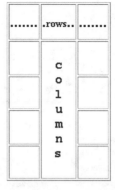

Figure 12.3 This table consists of three columns and five rows. The center column consists of only two cells, the larger of which was created by merging together four cells.

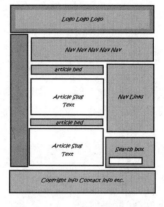

Figure 12.4 Draw a sketch of your table before you begin. You can use pencil and paper or a paint program.

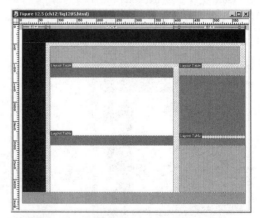

Figure 12.5 This is the finalized table layout based on the rough sketch in **Figure 12.4**. I drew the cells in Layout mode; you can see I have four tables and several cells contained within one page-sized table.

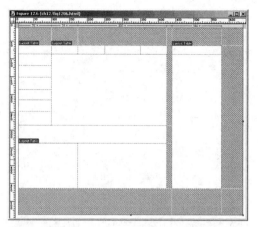

Figure 12.6 In Layout view, each individual table has a tab marking it; you must draw a cell in a specific spot in order to place content within it. The white areas are useable cells and the gray areas are undefined areas used to space out the rest of the table.

Figure 12.7 Click the Layout View button. The other button returns you to Standard view.

About Layout Tables

Dreamweaver uses an innovative tool for drawing page layouts. You draw boxes on your page, and Dreamweaver fills in the HTML for the rest of the page design. These layouts use tables, which Dreamweaver calls *layout tables* when you create or edit them in Layout view.

Layout view and Standard view

To work with layout tables, Dreamweaver uses a different editing paradigm, called Layout view (**Figure 12.6**). You draw cells on the page the same way you draw text boxes in Quark or image slices in Fireworks.

To turn on Layout view:

◆ On the Layout tab of the Insert toolbar, click on the Layout View button (**Figure 12.7**).

   or

   From the menu bar, select View > Table View > Layout View.

Dreamweaver will show the page in Layout view. If there are no tables on your page, the Document window will look the same. If there are tables on your page, they'll appear with tabs like the ones in **Figure 12.6**.

continued on next page

✔ Tips

- Layout tables do not use different tags than regular tables; however, they do employ *spacer gifs*, which are invisible, one-pixel images used to force the spacing of tables. See *About Spacer Gifs*, later in this chapter.

- The first time you select Layout view, a dialog box will appear (**Figure 12.8**) explaining what Layout view is. To make this thing go away forever, click the Don't show me this message again check box.

- You can't insert a table the usual way (Insert > Table) in Layout view, and you can't draw a layout cell or layout table in Standard view. To tell which view you're in, look at the Layout tab or the Table View menu .

- To hide the tabs, select View > Table View > Show Layout Table Tabs.

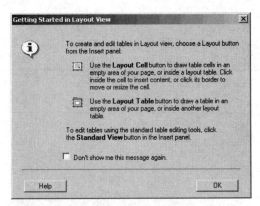

Figure 12.8 The purpose of this dialog box is to introduce you to Layout view. Check the box to make it go away.

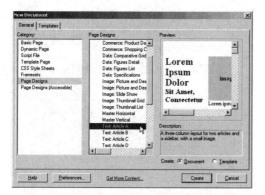

Figure 12.9 You can start with a prebuilt design from Dreamweaver's File > New dialog box.

Getting Help Starting Your Table

Dreamweaver MX contains some pre-built HTML pages that contain tables; you can use one of these designs as the basis for your page, or you can resize the table and insert it into a page already in progress.

To use a prebuilt template:

1. From the menu bar, select File > New. The New Document dialog box will appear.

2. From the Category list at the left, select either Page Designs or Page Designs (Accessible). (The latter uses code meant for a wide variety of browser types, as discussed in Appendix A on the Web site.)

    A list of available designs will appear in the Page Designs list box.

3. Select the name of a page design, and a cropped preview of the page will appear in the preview area (**Figure 12.9**).

4. Find something that looks promising? Click on Create, and the page will appear in a new, unsaved Document window.

continued on next page

GETTING HELP STARTING YOUR TABLE

Not all the available page designs use tables; some handy page layouts include "Text: Article A-D" (**Figures 12.10** and **12.11**); Image: Picture and Description; and Image: Thumbnail Grid. Master Horizontal and Master Vertical include the basis for inserting toolbars or other navigation schemes onto a page with tables.

Once you've started with one of these table designs, you can edit it using the features described in this chapter by adding and removing columns and rows; merging and splitting cells; inserting other tables within your table; and by changing alignment and background options.

These designs use dummy text and placeholder images to recreate simple, common page or element designs. You can do whatever you want with the designs, putting text or images wherever you like.

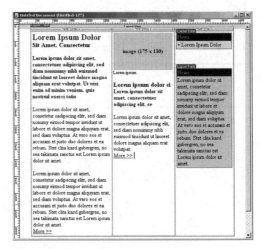

Figure 12.10 Here's the design called Text: Article D, seen in Layout view.

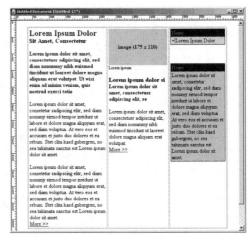

Figure 12.11 Here's the same design, seen in Standard view.

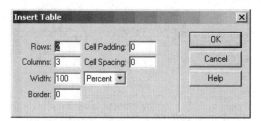

Figure 12.12 Set the initial size of your table in the Insert Table dialog box.

Figure 12.13 Here, I'm setting the table width to 100 percent of the browser window.

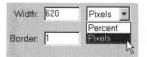

Figure 12.14 I'm setting the table width to an exact pixel width.

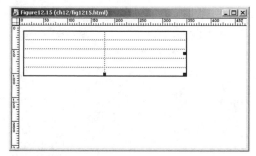

Figure 12.15 I inserted a new table with five rows and two columns. It takes up 75 percent of the window.

✔ Tips

■ Even if you specify an exact width in pixels, your table may resize itself—it will stretch to fit the content you put in it. If you set a percentage width, the table will resize based on the width of the user's browser window.

■ You can always go back later to add additional rows or columns or to make other adjustments to your table specifications. See *Adding Columns and Rows in Standard View*, later in this chapter.

Inserting a Table in Standard View

When you insert a table in this mode, you first choose a starting width and decide how many columns and rows you want to begin with.

To insert a table (Standard view):

1. Click to place the insertion point where you'd like the table to appear. This can be on a blank page or inside an existing table cell.

2. From the menu bar, select Insert > Table.
   or
   Click on the Table button 🔳 on one of three different tabs on the Insert toolbar: either the Common tab, the Layout tab, or the Tables tab (whoa—now *that's* redundancy!).
   Either way, the Insert Table dialog box will appear (**Figure 12.12**).

3. Type the number of rows you want in your table in the Rows text box.

4. Type the number of columns you want in your table in the Columns text box.

5. Choose a width for your table in either Pixels or Percent.
   To set the table width to a percentage of the page width, select Percent from the Width drop-down menu and type a number in the Width text box (**Figure 12.13**).
   or
   To set an exact width, select Pixels from the Width drop-down menu and type a number in the text box (**Figure 12.14**).
   I'll discuss the other table options later in this chapter.

6. Click OK to close the Insert Table dialog box. Your new table will appear (**Figure 12.15**).

Drawing a Layout

When you work with layout tables, keep the sketch of your page in mind (**Figure 12.4**).

There are two ways to go about drawing layouts: You can draw a layout cell first, or you can draw a layout table first and add cells to it.

Drawing a layout cell

First, we're going to draw a layout cell and watch Dreamweaver populate the rest of the table to complete a full-page layout.

To draw a layout cell:

1. Make sure you're working in Layout view.

2. On the Layout tab of the Insert toolbar, click the Draw Layout Cell button (**Figure 12.16**). The pointer will turn into crosshairs.

3. In the Document window, draw a rectangle that's big enough to hold your content (**Figure 12.17**).

When you let go of the mouse button, your cell will appear, and Dreamweaver will also draw more cells to complete a table. Cells can't float in space; they live in tables (**Figure 12.18**).

Drawing a layout table

You can also draw a layout table on the page and then populate it with cells.

To draw a layout table:

1. On the Layout tab of the Insert toolbar, click the Draw Layout Table button (Figure 12.16). The pointer will turn into crosshairs.

2. In the Document window, draw a rectangle on your page where you want a table to go (**Figure 12.19**).

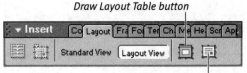

Draw Layout Table button

Draw Layout Cell button

Figure 12.16 Click the Draw Layout Cell or Draw Layout Table button on the Layout tab of the Insert toolbar.

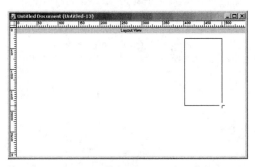

Figure 12.17 Draw a cell that's a container for content in your overall page design.

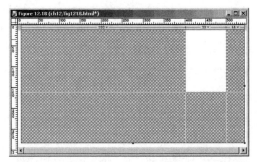

Figure 12.18 When you draw a layout cell, Dreamweaver fills in the content to make a full-page table layout.

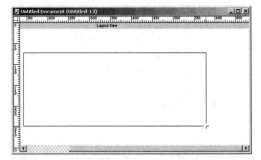

Figure 12.19 Draw a table on your page. If your table doesn't start at the left margin, it will be placed, like a layout cell, within a larger table that spans the entire page.

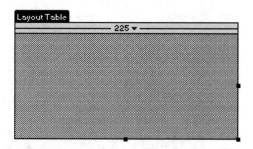

Figure 12.20 When you draw a blank layout table, it starts its life without any layout cells.

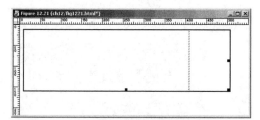

Figure 12.21 The page layout shown in **Figure 12.18** in Layout view doesn't actually exist as such in reality, also known as Standard view. You need to finish drawing any cells that you want to hold content and let Dreamweaver fill in the placeholders for layout areas without text or images.

Placeholder cells (grayed out)   *Column and row borders*

New layout cell

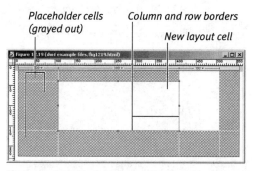

Figure 12.22 I added a layout cell to the table. Note the borders that mark the other, unfilled cells that hold the table together.

When you let go of the mouse button, your table will appear—with nary a cell to be seen (**Figure 12.20**). You need to add them. As with cells (Figure 12.18), if your table does not begin at the upper left of the page, it will be embedded in a table that does so.

Adding cells to a layout table

Whether you start by drawing a layout cell or a layout table, you need to add cells to it to hold content. **Figure 12.21** shows how the table I drew in Figure 12.18 looks in Standard view—in reality, there are only two cells I can populate with content, until I draw more cells.

✔ Tip

■ You cannot overlap layout cells.

To add a cell to a layout:

1. Start in Layout view with a table created by drawing a layout cell or a layout table.

2. On the Layout tab of the Insert toolbar, click the Draw Layout Cell button. The pointer will turn into crosshairs.

3. Within the boundaries of the table, draw a rectangular container for your content. Dreamweaver will create the cell and show column and row borders (**Figure 12.22**).

DRAWING A LAYOUT

Drawing a table inside a table

You can nest a table within a table just by drawing it there (**Figure 12.23**).

Drawing a table around cells

You may want to draw a table around a set of contiguous cells. Click Draw Layout Table, and drag the cursor around the cells (**Figure 12.24**). You can even extend the table past the cells you included (**Figure 12.25**).

Drawing a sequence of cells

If you hold down the Ctrl (Command) button while you draw, you can keep drawing cells instead of having to click the button each time. The cursor will snap to any column or row borders so you can match heights and widths easily.

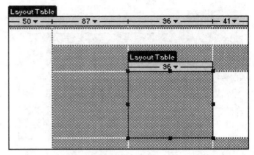

Figure 12.23 Nest a table within a table by drawing it on some blank space inside the larger table.

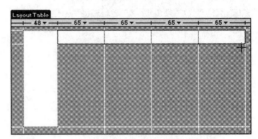

Figure 12.24 Click on Draw Layout Table, and then drag the cursor around the cells to enclose them in a table.

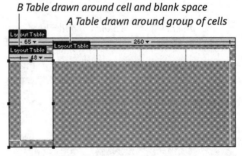

Figure 12.25 You can draw a table to enclose just a group of cells (A) or a cell and some blank space (B).

Wherefore the Tables Tab?

So if there's already a Layout tab on the Insert toolbar that offers you buttons for inserting a table and working in either Layout view or Standard view, why is there a Tables tab?

I'm not entirely sure myself, because you can *also* insert a table from the Common tab. The only feature on the Tables tab that isn't duplicated elsewhere are the context-sensitive table code buttons for inserting code for a table (the inexplicably named **tabl**), table row (**tr**), table header (**th**), table cell (**td**), and table caption (**cap**). These buttons become active when you view your page in Split view or Code view.

You can insert an opening and closing tag by clicking these buttons, or you can select some text and wrap a tag around your selection. More on using tools like this is covered in Chapter 4, especially in the section *Context Sensitive Code Editing Tools*.

Name That Table

If you're planning on working with table code directly, it may help to know which table you're working on, particularly if you've inserted a table within a table. You can name your table, in which case the table code will say something like:

```
<table name="main">
```

To name your table, first select it. Then, while in Standard view, in the Property inspector, type a name in the Table ID text box , and press Enter (Return). The table name will be inserted into the code. You can also use this name if the table will be affected by a script or by CSS.

Selecting Elements

To modify a table cell, column, or row, or a table itself, you need to select it.

To select a table in either view:

1. Click within the table.

2. Click the `<table>` tag in the tag selector (**Figure 12.26**).

   or

   Click on the table's outside edge.

   Either way, your table will be selected (**Figure 12.27**) and you can copy, cut, drag, or delete it.

To select a table in Standard view:

◆ From the menu bar, select Modify > Table > Select Table. (This works in Layout view, too.)

   or

   Right-click (Control+click) on the table, and from the context menu that appears, select Table > Select Table.

To select in Layout view:

1. Click within the table or cell.

2. Click on the item's outside edge or the table's tab (**Figure 12.28**).

   Handles will appear around a selected layout table or layout cell, as we saw in **Figure 12.25**.

To select a column or row:

◆ In Standard view, hold down the mouse button and drag up to select a column or across to select a row (**Figure 12.29**).

   or

   When you mouse over the top or left table border, the cursor will turn into a black arrow (**Figure 12.30**). Then, you just click to select the entire column or row.

Figure 12.26 When you click within a table, these tags appear in the tag selector. Click on a tag to select it. The tags are <table>, <tr> for table row, and <td> for table data, a.k.a. cell. Table columns do not have their own tags.

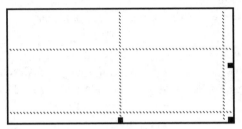

Figure 12.27 The entire table will be selected. In Standard view, a dark outline will appear around the table and resize handles will appear in the lower-right corner of the table.

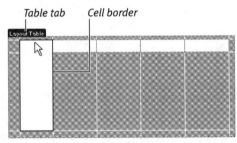

Figure 12.28 To select an item in Layout view, click on a folder's tab or the outside edge of any cell or table.

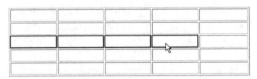

Figure 12.29 Click and drag to select all or part of a row. You can drag vertically to select a column.

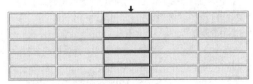

Figure 12.30 When the cursor becomes a black arrow, click to select a column or row.

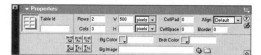

Figure 12.31 When the table is selected, the Property inspector will display Table properties. This is in Standard view.

Figure 12.32 Here's the Property inspector showing Table Properties in Layout view.

Property icon (formerly Apply button)
Selected object's name (cell)

Figure 12.33 The Property inspector, displaying Table Cell properties in Standard view. The Property inspector also displays text properties in its upper half when displaying cell, column, and row attributes. You can identify the Property inspectors for each view by the appearance of the icon and the displayed name of the selected object.

Figure 12.34 The Property inspector, displaying Table Cell properties in Layout view. Where the options are the same, oddly, they're arranged quite differently. Layout view also includes the Autostretch option.

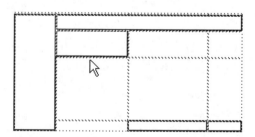

Figure 12.35 Hold down the Ctrl (Command) or Shift key to select multiple cells in Standard view. Then, you can modify a property such as background color or add a CSS style to all the selected cells.

✔ Tips

■ **Figures 12.31** to **12.34** show the Property inspector for tables and cells in both views.

■ In Layout view, table borders are green, and cell borders are blue. Click the border and then look at the Property inspector and the tag inspector to verify you have selected the appropriate tag and object.

■ Occasionally, when you click on the `<td>` tag in the tag selector in Layout view, the Property inspector will instead bring up `<table>` properties. Click on the edge of the cell to select it.

■ Hold down the Shift key while clicking to select or deselect multiple cells in Standard view. Hold down the Ctrl (Command) key and you can even select noncontiguous cells (**Figure 12.35**).

■ You can toggle off table borders in Standard view while you're working by selecting View > Visual Aids > Table Borders. Then, you'll need to rely on the tag selector to select a table or cell surrounding your content.

continued on next page

SELECTING ELEMENTS

- To delete a table in either view, select it and press Delete. The table contents will also be deleted, unless you move the contents into another container or onto another page before you delete the table.

- When Dreamweaver creates cells (any cell in Standard Mode or layout cells in Layout Mode), it includes a character called a nonbreaking space, which looks like this: . Many browsers will not draw space for tables that include no content; this invisible character is a marker for the cell. (In some cases, an invisible image is used; see *About Spacer Gifs*, later on.)

- After you select a column or row in Standard view, you can delete it by pressing Delete. You can also click within an area of the table and select Modify > Table > Delete Row (or Delete Column).

SELECTING ELEMENTS

Figure 12.36 Select the table by clicking on its tag in the tag selector.

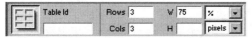

Figure 12.37 Type a new number in the Rows and Cols text boxes. Press Enter (Return) to add the new items.

Adding a Single Cell to a Table

If you want to add a row with only one cell in it to your page, you can edit the code. The blank space in the row will not be able to hold content unless you add more cells or increase the column span of the existing cell.

1. From the menu bar, select Window > Others > Code Inspector. The Code inspector will appear.

2. To add a cell at the end of a table, locate the closing table tag, `</table>`, and type the following line of code just before it: `<tr><td> </td></tr>`.

This adds a new row `<tr>` with only one cell in it `<td>` (**Figure 12.38**, on next page). Cells are not displayed unless they have something in them. The ` ` entity adds invisible content to the cell so it will show up as a layout element. To increase the column span of the pictured cell, you'd add this code to the `<td>` tag:

`colspan="2"`

That would make the cell span two columns.

Adding Columns and Rows in Standard View

You can add more columns or rows to your table. Later in this chapter, we'll resize columns and rows and split and merge cells in a table.

Adding cells to a table

There are several ways to add cells to a table. One quick way to change the dimensions of your table is by using the Property inspector.

To change the number of columns or rows:

1. Select the entire table by clicking on its outside border or by clicking within it and selecting `<table>` in the tag selector (**Figure 12.36**). The Property inspector will display table properties.

2. Type a new number of columns in the Cols text box, and a new number of rows in the Rows text box. (**Figure 12.37**).

   Your table will change size as it adds or deletes columns and rows from its layout.

✔ Tip

■ If the cursor is in the last cell in the table, pressing Tab will add another row.

To delete a row or column:

1. Click to place the insertion point within the row or column you want to delete.

2. From the menu bar, select Modify > Table > Delete Row (or Delete Column).

   The row (or column) and all its contents will disappear.

Adding columns and rows

You can also easily insert a column or row in Standard view using the Modify menu.

To add columns or rows:

1. Click in a cell adjacent to where you want to add a column or row.

2. From the menu bar, select Modify > Table > Insert Rows or Columns and the dialog box shown in **Figure 12.39** will appear.

3. Click the Rows radio button to add rows, or the Columns radio button to add columns.

4. In the Number of Rows (or Columns) text box, type the number of rows (or columns) you want to add.

5. Select the position of the new elements:
   ◆ Rows: Click on the Above the Selection or the Below the Selection radio button.
   ◆ Columns: To add them to the left of the selected cell, click on the Before current Column radio button. To add them to the right of the selected cell, click on the After current Column radio button.

6. Click OK to close the dialog box and add the new rows or columns to your table.

To add a single row:

1. Click in a table cell below where you want the new row to appear (**Figure 12.40**).

2. From the menu bar, select Modify > Table > Insert Row, or press Ctrl+M (Command+M). The new row will appear above the insertion point (**Figure 12.41**).

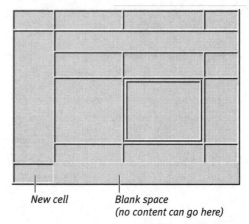

New cell   Blank space
(no content can go here)

Figure 12.38 A single cell was added to this table. Note the blank space in the rest of the row. To put cells in that space, a <TD> tag would be added for each cell in the rest of the row.

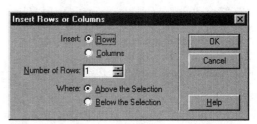

Figure 12.39 Use the Insert Rows or Columns dialog box to add columns and rows where you want them.

Angela	Barbara
Ethel	Florence

Figure 12.40 Click in the cell below where you want the new row to appear, or to the right of where you want the new column to appear.

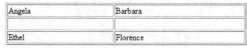

Figure 12.41 The new row will appear above the cell you selected.

Figure 12.42 Right-click (Control+click) on the table, and choose Table > Insert Column from the pop-up menu. You can also add a single row above the insertion point this way.

Angela		Barbara
Ethel		Florence

Figure 12.43 A new column will appear to the left of the column you selected.

To add a single column:

1. Right-click (Control+click) in the column directly to the left of where you want the new column to appear (as in **Figure 12.40**).

2. From the context menu, select Table > Insert Column (**Figure 12.42**).

   A new column will appear to the left of the column you selected (**Figure 12.43**).

ADDING COLUMNS AND ROWS IN STANDARD VIEW

Resizing Table Elements

You can set the size of a table, a column, or a row. When you add or remove elements from a table, it often resizes, and you may also wish to make adjustments then.

You may have set a width for your table when you created it, or by dragging a table edge, but you can adjust the width of the table at any time. Table widths are set either in pixels or percent of screen width.

To set the table width (either view):

1. Select the table.

2. In the Property inspector:

   ◆ For Standard view, select either Pixels or Percent (%)from the W (Width) drop-down menu (**Figure 12.44**).

   ◆ For Layout view, select the Fixed radio button to set a pixel width, or Autostretch to set the width to 100 percent of the screen.

3. Type a number in the W (Width) text box (the Fixed text box, in Layout view) and press Enter (Return).

To resize a table by dragging (either view):

1. Select the table. Selection handles will appear around the table (**Figure 12.45**).

2. Drag the table to resize it (**Figure 12.46**). In Layout view, Dreamweaver will fill in space between the cells and the table; you can then resize the cells, if you want.

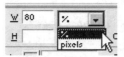
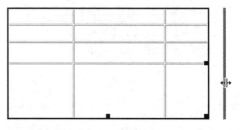

Figure 12.44 Type the width of the table in the W (Width) text box.

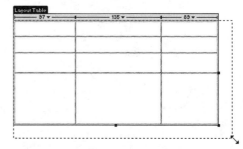

Figure 12.45 Grabbing a table by its selection handles in Standard view.

Figure 12.46 Resizing a layout table in Layout view by dragging. To make a table smaller, you may first need to clear heights and widths or resize cells.

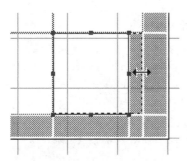

Figure 12.47 You can resize a cell by dragging it over unfilled space in the table. To enlarge one cell, you may first need to reduce the size of adjacent cells.

Figure 12.48 You can set exact height and width for columns, rows, and cells, as well as tables.

✔ Tips

- You can also resize cells by dragging in Layout Mode (**Figure 12.47**).

- To make a table smaller, you may need to clear row heights or column widths. See the sidebar *Getting Nitpicky About Widths*, later in this chapter.

- You can also set an exact height or width for a column, row, or cell by selecting the column or row in Standard view, or the cell <td> in either view, and typing values in the Property inspector (**Figure 12.48**).

- You can use Dreamweaver's grid and rulers for exact measurements when resizing your table and its cells (**Figure 12.47**). To turn on the grid, select View > Grid > Show Grid from the menu bar. For more about the grid and rulers, see Chapter 1.

You Ought to Be in Pixels

If you set a column's width in pixels, the text you type or paste into the cells in that column will wrap to fit in the column. However, if you place an image wider than the column in one of those cells, the column will still expand to fit the image.

Also, keep in mind that cell height settings, in either percentages or pixels, don't always respond as you planned. Avoid setting cell heights, and if they get set when you drag their borders, you can clear them. (See *About Height Settings* and *Getting Nitpicky About Widths* later in this chapter.)

Mom & Pop's Row & Column Span

Selecting cells and then merging them or splitting them is the easiest way to change column span or row span; this is described in the upcoming section *Merging and Splitting Cells*. However, if you want to do it the old-fashioned way using old-fashioned terminology, you're welcome to. Note that you cannot split a single-span cell this way.

In the code, a cell generally occupies one column and one row, but if you combine two or more cells into one, it can span any number of columns using the `colspan` and `rowspan` attributes:

```
<td colspan="2" rowspan="2"> </td>
```

To increase (or decrease) row span:

1. Click to place the insertion point in the upper of the two cells you want to combine (or in the cell you want to split).

2. From the menu bar, select Modify > Table > Increase Row Span (Decrease Row Span). The table cell will combine with the cell directly below it (split from the table cell it was previously combined with).

To increase (or decrease) column span:

1. Click to place the insertion point in the leftmost of the two cells you want to combine (or in the cell you want to split).

2. From the menu bar, select Modify > Table > Increase Column Span (Decrease Column Span). The table cell will combine with the cell directly to the right of it (split from the table cell it was previously combined with).

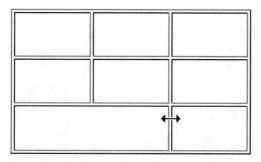

Figure 12.49 Mouse over the table border and the pointer will turn into a double-headed arrow.

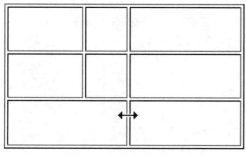

Figure 12.50 Use the double-headed arrow to drag the border to a new location.

Dragging Columns and Rows in Standard View

You can adjust column width or row height by simply clicking and dragging.

To drag column and row borders:

1. When you move the mouse over a border between cells, the pointer will turn into a double-headed arrow (**Figure 12.49**).

2. Click on the border and drag it to a new location (**Figure 12.50**). This will set the height or width of the rows or columns involved.

✔ Tips

■ Although you *can* set row height, a row's height will expand to fit the content. You may want to set row height for rows that will contain a graphic or a media object with a height you want to fit exactly.

■ If a row height is set too high by dragging a row to fit, try selecting the table to resize the row. If that doesn't do it, see *Getting Nitpicky About Widths* for information about resetting row heights.

■ As with column and row dimensions, cell heights and widths are not an exact science; the size of the content and the quirks of the browser will vary your mileage. Using Layout view to draw the table and Standard view to set the details works well for me.

Dragging Columns and Rows in Standard View

Moving a Layout Element

You can use the grid (View > Grid > Show Grid) to help you place things. See Chapter 1 for details on adjusting the grid.

You cannot overlap any containers—cells can't overlap with each other, or with tables, or vice versa. Before your table is hyperpopulated, though, you can move a cell or table anywhere you like. You can move a nested table within a table, but you can't place a table just anywhere on the page without using a layout table.

To move a container:

1. Select the layout cell or layout table by clicking on its outside edge so that handles appear (**Figures 12.51** and **12.52**).

2. Click and hold and drag the container to a new location in the table (**Figure 12.53**).

   or

   Use the arrow keys to move the container one pixel at a time. Hold down the Shift key while using the arrow keys to move the container 10 pixels at a time.

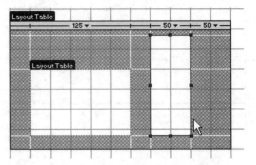

Figure 12.51 Select a layout cell so you can move it within the table.

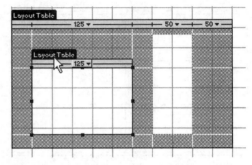

Figure 12.52 Select a nested layout table to move it within the parent table.

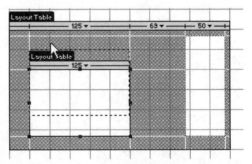

Figure 12.53 In this figure, I've moved the layout cell to the right and I'm in the process of moving the nested layout table up. When you drag a layout element, it will snap to the grid if snapping is turned on.

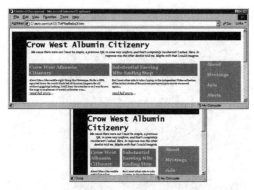

Figure 12.54 Here you see two browser windows both displaying the table at 100 percent width. The center column—which holds another two-column table—is set to autostretch.

Fixed-width set in pixels

Autostretch set   *Two conflicting widths*

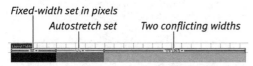

Figure 12.55 Column headers above the top cell in each table indicate the widths.

Stupid No-Wrap Tricks

Text in table cells usually wraps to fit the width of the cell. There is a setting that forces a cell to expand to the width of the text, regardless of the width of the cell itself.

To set the no-wrap option, click within the cell (either view), or the column or row (Standard view), and then select the No Wrap checkbox on the Property inspector.

To break a line in non-wrapped text, press Enter (Return) to start a new paragraph, or Shift+Enter (Shift+Return) for a line break. If you change the cell's contents so there is extra blank space in the unused cell, you can clear column widths to close up empty space. See *Getting Nitpicky About Widths*, later in this chapter.

About Width Settings in Layout View

Width settings in tables are generally expressed in pixels or in percent of the window size. In Layout view, you can also set the width of a table or column to autostretch; that is, the table will always fill the browser window, no matter what size the window is (**Figure 12.54**). Autostretch columns are spaced proportionally to preserve your design.

Reading width settings

The width of each column in a selected table appears as the column header (**Figure 12.55**).

◆ If it's a pixel width, you'll see a whole number.

◆ If it's an autostretch width, you'll see a wavy line.

◆ If the content of the column is wider than the column's fixed width, you'll see two numbers in the column header.

Applying width settings

It's likely that in your table you'll want to set some columns to exact widths and some to autostretch (**Figures 12.56** and **12.57**). You need to have some columns with fixed widths in order for other columns to be able to guess their widths.

The columns whose widths you fix exactly may be a narrow, table-of-contents type of column, a column that holds images of a particular width, or a column used as a margin between columns of content. I tend to make the widest column or columns on my page, such as a column of body text, the ones that I set to autostretch.

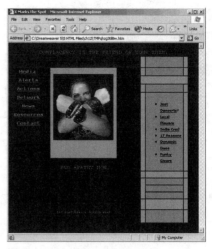

Figure 12.57 Here, the browser window shows you a much narrower view of the same table, and the column stretched (or rather, shrank) successfully.

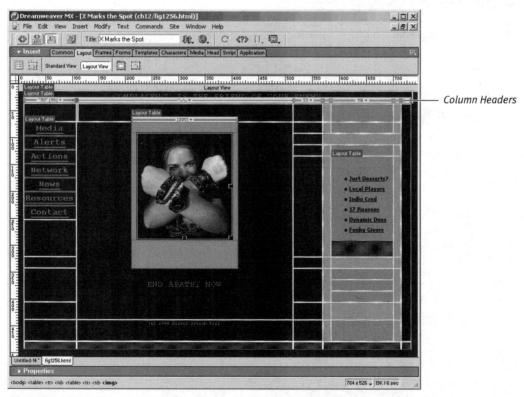

Column Headers

Figure 12.56 In this table, I set the largest column to autostretch. I don't want the navigation columns to expand, but the large one can do so without spoiling the look.

Figure 12.58 If your column has expanded to fit the content in it, you may want to reset the width to reflect reality.

Figure 12.59 Click on the column header of the most flexible cell in your layout, and select Make Column Autostretch from the menu.

Figure 12.60 The first time you use autostretch, Dreamweaver will ask you to choose or create a spacer image.

Making widths consistent

If you see two numbers in a column heading, it means that the width that's currently displayed in the Document window, or the width of the content in the cell, conflicts with the width setting in the code for the table.

To make widths consistent:

1. Click on the column heading.

2. From the menu that appears, select Make Cell Widths Consistent (**Figure 12.58**).

Now, only the actual column width will be specified.

Using Autostretch

Autostretch is a Layout view feature that makes a table stretch or collapse according to the user's browser-window width. When you set an entire table to autostretch, Dreamweaver will select columns in your table to relative widths in order to accomplish this. You can choose which columns to make stretchable.

To set autostretch for a column in Layout view:

1. Click the tab of the layout table that contains your column. The column headings will appear.

2. Select the column you want to set to autostretch, and click the column header button. From the menu that appears, select Make Column Autostretch (**Figure 12.59**).

   If you haven't selected a spacer, you'll be asked to do so in the Choose Spacer Image dialog box (**Figure 12.60**).

To select a spacer gif:

- The Choose Spacer Image dialog box will appear if you haven't yet chosen a spacer. You're offered three choices:
  - To create a spacer gif, choose Create a spacer image file. The Save Spacer Image File As dialog box will appear. Choose the folder (such as /images), and type a filename for the image, then click Save. From here on, reuse this image by following the next choice.
  - To use a spacer that's already in your site, choose Use an existing spacer image. The Select Spacer Image File dialog box will appear. Select your image, and click OK (Choose).
  - To avoid spacers altogether, choose Don't use spacer image for autostretch tables. Your mileage may vary—the autostretch properties will be based on fixed and percentage widths, and the table may not shrink to accommodate small browser windows.

About Spacer Gifs

A spacer image is a 1-pixel by 1-pixel transparent gif that is resized in order to stretch the width of a column. For example, to make a column stay 100 pixels wide, whether or not it includes content—and no matter how wide the browser window is—the image dimensions are set to 100 x 1.

If a column includes no content, neither a spacer nor a nonbreaking space, it basically won't exist as a layout element.

In order for autostretch to work, you may need spacer gifs to make the fixed-width columns stay fixed. Yes, it's cheating—but it works, so it's okay. You can reuse the same spacer gif each time you need one.

To find out how to reset the spacer you use, see *Spacer Preferences*, later in this chapter.

Figure 12.61 Select Make Column Fixed Width from the column header menu.

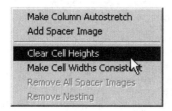

Figure 12.62 Select Clear Cell Heights from the column header menu.

Setting exact widths

If it's important that a column have an exact width (for instance, if it contains a navigational or layout element that's *purrfect*), then you should set that column's width.

To set an exact width in layout mode:

1. Click the tab of the layout table that contains your column. The column headings will appear.

2. At the top of the column for which you want to set the width, click the column header button.

3. From the menu that appears, select Make Column Fixed Width (**Figure 12.61**). Dreamweaver will set the width of the column to the content that appears in it. The number in pixels will appear in the column header.

You can also set a width by dragging; or you can use the Property inspector. Select the table or cell, and in the Property inspector's Fixed text box, type a number in pixels.

About height settings

Dreamweaver sets table and row heights in layout tables to fill out the page, based on the size of the Document window when you first draw the table. After you fill the table with content, you may want to clear these settings.

To clear row heights:

1. Click on the column header so that the menu appears (**Figure 12.62**).

2. From the menu, select Clear Cell Heights.

Rows without content may shrink.

Getting Nitpicky About Widths

You can clear row heights and column widths to reflect new content in your table. Cells without content may shrink if you clear these values.

1. Select the table in either view.

2. From the menu bar, select Modify > Table > Clear Cell Heights (or Clear Cell Widths).

or

In the Property inspector (**Figure 12.63**), click the Clear Row Heights button or the Clear Column Widths button (Standard view).

You can also convert all widths expressed in pixels to percents, or vice-versa. Afterwards, you can use the column headings in Layout view to reset some values, if you want.

To convert from percentages to pixels:

1. Select the table in either view.

2. In the Property inspector, click the appropriate button (**Figure 12.63**).

or

From the menu bar, select Modify > Table > Convert Widths to Pixels (or Percent).

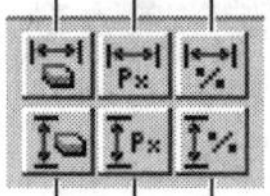

Clear Column Width button
  Convert Widths to Pixels button
    Convert Widths to Percent button

      Convert Heights to Percent button
    Convert Heights to Pixels button
  Clear Row Heights button

Figure 12.63 In either view, you can use the Property inspector to clear row heights. In Standard view (pictured), you can also clear column widths and convert the units of your widths.

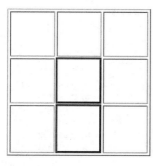

Figure 12.64 Select the cells you want to combine. You can select an entire column or row, if you wish.

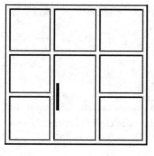

Figure 12.65 Cells in two rows merge to create one large cell that spans two rows.

Merging and Splitting Cells

In Standard view, you can combine two adjacent cells into a single, larger cell. You can also split a cell into one or more other cells.

To merge cells:

1. In Standard view, select two or more cells you want to combine (**Figure 12.64**).

2. On the Property inspector, click the Merge Cells button ☐ .
The cells will be combined (**Figure 12.65**).

✔ Tips

■ You can merge an entire column or row into one cell.

■ If you change your mind, you can split the cell using the Split Cell button ☐ .

To split a cell:

1. In Standard view, click within the cell you wish to split (**Figure 12.66**).

2. From the menu bar, select Modify > Table > Split Cell.
   The Split Cell dialog box will appear (**Figure 12.67**).

3. Choose whether to split the cell into rows or columns by clicking the appropriate radio button.

4. Type a Number of Rows (or Columns) in the text box.

5. Click OK to close the dialog box and add the cells to the table (**Figure 12.68**).

✔ Tip

■ What you're doing here is changing the number of rows or columns a cell spans—see the sidebar *Mom & Pop's Row & Column Span* for more technical details.

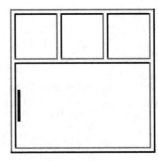

Figure 12.66 Select the cell you want to split. It may already span more than one row or it may be a single, unadulterated cell.

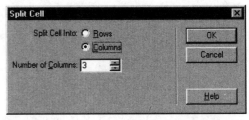

Figure 12.67 In the Split Cell dialog box, specify how many columns or rows to split the cell into.

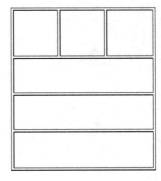

Figure 12.68 The cell divides into three rows.

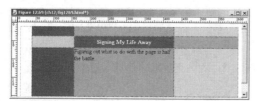

Figure 12.69 You can type and format text in a table just as you would on a blank page. See the upcoming sections on alignment and spacing for more about formatting table content.

Figure 12.70 Each image made its row taller after I inserted it, and the five-dollar bill stretched its column—and the adjacent one became smaller, since I'm using autostretch. See the previous sections on table and cell widths to control the dimensions of your cells and columns.

Figure 12.71 In Standard view, tick the Header check box in the Property inspector.

Number of Days in Each Month	
January	31
February	28 (29)
March	31
April	30
May	31
June	30
July	31
August	31
September	30
October	31
November	30
December	31

Figure 12.72 The text in the new table header cell becomes bold and centered in the cell.

Adding Content to a Table

Now that you've got your table right where you want it, you need to put stuff in it.

To add text to your table, just click in the cell where you want your text to go, and start typing and formatting (**Figure 12.69**). The table and its cells may expand to accommodate the content (**Figure 12.70**).

✔ Tips

■ You can move from cell to cell in a table by pressing the Tab key. Shift+Tab moves the cursor backwards.

■ You can drag images and text into table cells from elsewhere on the page. Highlight the text or image, and then click on it and drag it into its new home.

■ You can create a table within a table in both Standard and Layout views.

Table header cells

You can format a table header cell to mark the purpose of your table. The tag is <th>.

To use a header cell:

1. In Standard view, click within the cell, row, or column that you'd like to format as a header cell.

2. In the Property inspector (**Figure 12.71**), select the Header check box.

 The text in the selected cell will be centered and boldfaced. (**Figure 12.72**).

✔ Tip

■ The appearance of table header cells may vary slightly from browser to browser, but the concept is the same: They stand out from the rest of the table.

Aligning Tables and Content

You can set the alignment for a table on a page or within another table, just as if it were text.

To set table alignment:

1. Select the table in Standard view.

2. In the Property inspector, click on the Align drop-down menu, and select Default, Left, Center, or Right (**Figure 12.73**).

   Your table will change alignment (hopefully for the forces of good) (**Figure 12.74**).

Content alignment

In addition to table spacing, you can adjust how the content in your table's cells is aligned:

◆ In both horizontal and vertical alignment, choosing Default sets the alignment to the browser's default—usually left (horizontal) and middle (vertical). Therefore, you won't need to set alignment specifications for left or middle unless you're "changing it back."

◆ Cell alignment properties override column specs, and columns override row specs.

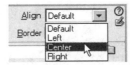

Figure 12.73 Use the Align drop-down menu in the Property inspector to choose the alignment setting.

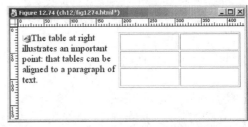

Figure 12.74 A right-aligned table, complete with placeholder icon.

Terms of Alignment

If you align a table to the right, a small placeholder icon will appear in the left margin to mark the beginning of the table on the page. This icon may disappear if you change the alignment back to left. You can place the insertion point near this icon to put text to the left of the table, as seen in **Figure 12.74**.

Choosing the Default setting will make the table follow the default browser settings.

ALIGNING TABLES AND CONTENT

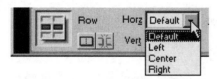

Figure 12.75 Horizontal alignment (Horz) options include Default, Left, Center, and Right.

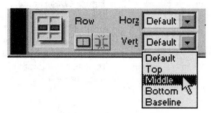

Figure 12.76 Vertical alignment options (Vert) include Default, Top, Middle, Bottom, and Baseline.

	H=Left, V=Top	
H=Default, V=Default		H=Center, V=Middle
	H=Right, V=Top	
H=Right, V=Bottom		H=Right, V=Middle
H=Default, V=Baseline	H=Center, V=Baseline	H=Right, V=Baseline

Figure 12.77 This table runs the gamut of content alignment options. The position of the Baseline vertical alignment is based on the imaginary lines that the characters rest on, and it generally follows the baseline of the bordering cells.

To change content alignment:

1. Select the column, row, or cell for which you want to specify the content alignment.

   In Layout view, take care that you've selected a cell instead of a table. You may have to click the edge of the cell again; check the Property inspector to see what you've selected.

2. Click the Horz drop-down menu, and select an alignment option: Default, Left, Center, or Right (**Figure 12.75).**

3. Click the Vert drop-down menu and select an option: Default, Top, Middle, Bottom, or Baseline (**Figure 12.76**).

   Your changes will be apparent when you place content in that area of the table (**Figure 12.77**).

ALIGNING TABLES AND CONTENT

Adjusting Table Spacing

When you're using a table as a page layout tool, it's important to be able to control the space between elements in a table. We've already talked about table borders, which in part control the space between the table and the rest of the page.

Cell spacing is the amount of space between cells—sort of like table borders, but between the cells in a table rather than around the outside of the table. *Cell padding* is the amount of space between the walls of the cells and the content within them.

To adjust cell spacing (either view):

1. Select the table.

2. In the CellSpace text box, type a number (in pixels) (**Figure 12.78**).

   Your changes will be visible in the width of the table's borders (**Figure 12.79**).

To adjust cell padding (either view):

1. Select the table to display table properties in the Property inspector.

2. In the CellPad text box, type a number (in pixels).

   You'll notice a difference in the spacing between the content (or the cursor) and the borders (**Figure 12.80**).

✔ Tips

■ You can make these changes only to tables, not to individual cells. In Layout view, you can draw a layout table around one cell or a group of cells, and then adjust spacing properties for the new table.

■ Cell spacing changes may not be immediately apparent on tables with borders set to 0.

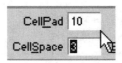

Figure 12.78 Type values for cell padding and cell spacing in the Property inspector.

Figure 12.79 I made the cell spacing 10 pixels wide. If I make the border width 0, the cell spacing will remain the same but appear less dramatic.

Figure 12.80 This is the same table shown in **Figure 12.79**, but I added 10 pixels of cell padding. Notice the space between the characters and the walls of the cells.

Using Vspace and Hspace

You can surround a table with extra space called Vspace and Hspace (above and below the table and to the left and right of the table, respectively), just as you can with images. Macromedia removed this feature from both the Property inspector and the WYSIWYG in Dreamweaver as of version 4 because it doesn't work gracefully with Layout view.

To add Vspace or Hspace around a table, add it to the opening table tag, using the Code inspector or the Quick Tag editor:

```
<table vspace="4" hspace="10">
```

Preview the page in a browser to see what your changes look like.

Figure 12.81 I gave my table a border width of 10. Borders larger than 1 pixel affect only the outside edge of the table, whereas border widths of zero render all borders invisible.

Month	Birthstone
January	Garnet
February	Amethyst
March	Aquamarine
April	Diamond
May	Emerald
June	Pearl
July	Ruby
August	Peridot
September	Sapphire
October	Opal
November	Yellow Topaz
December	Blue Topaz

Figure 12.82 Dreamweaver displays a table with a border width of zero with light, dashed lines in the Document window.

Month	Birthstone
January	Garnet
February	Amethyst
March	Aquamarine
April	Diamond
May	Emerald
June	Pearl
July	Ruby
August	Peridot
September	Sapphire
October	Opal
November	Yellow Topaz
December	Blue Topaz

Figure 12.83 This is the same table we saw in **Figure 12.82**, as viewed in the browser window. The borders are invisible if their width is zero. You can also see your table without dashed lines by toggling off the table borders. From the Document window menu bar, select View > Visual Aids > Table Borders to uncheck that option.

- You can also set a border color for a table. Select the table and use the color picker, as described in the next section.

- You can toggle off the dashed lines for a quick preview. With table borders set to 0, select View > Visual Aids > Table Borders from the menu bar and they'll disappear.

Working with Table Borders

By default, when you insert a table in Standard view, a 1-pixel line, called a border, delineates the edges of the cells and the table. In Layout view, borders are set to 0 by default and marked with the blue and green lines we've come to know and love. In either view, you can easily change the width and visibility of this border. (See the previous section on cell padding and cell spacing for more about table spacing.)

To adjust border size:

1. Select the table.

2. In the Border text box, type a number and press Enter (Return).

   You'll see your border adjustments immediately (**Figure 12.81**); if you set the border width to 0, you'll see a light, dashed line in Standard view (**Figure 12.82**). No worries: it won't show up in your browser (**Figure 12.83**).

✔ Tips

- You can change the border width to whatever you want, including 0.

- Setting the border width to 0 is also known as turning off table borders.

- And what if you actually *want* that dashed border to appear? Or what if you want your tables to look like layout tables? The only solution I can think of is to take a screen shot of your Dreamweaver workspace, crop it to show only the table, and save the image as a GIF to insert on your Web page. You'll have to use an image map if you want different areas to link to different pages.

Coloring Tables

You can give a table a background color or background image that differs from the background of the overall page. You can also use different backgrounds in rows, columns, or individual table cells, as well as on borders.

To set a table background color:

1. Select the table, cell, column, or row (in either view) for which you want to change the background color (**Figure 12.84**).

2. On the Property inspector, locate the Bgcolor text box for your selection (rather than for text; **Figure 12.85**). Then:

   ◆ Type or paste a hex value for the background color in the Bgcolor text box.

   or

   ◆ Click the gray Color selector button to pop up the color picker (**Figur**e **12.86**), and select a color.

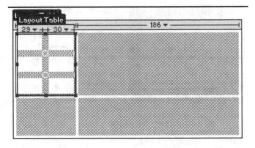

Figure 12.84 Select the table or other element for which you want to set the background.

Cell background color box

Text color box

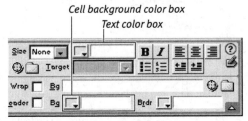

Figure 12.85 Find the Bg button on the Property inspector. If you've selected a cell, column, or row, there will also be a color box for text properties; it's easy to get them confused.

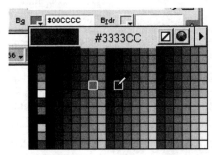

Figure 12.86 Click the color box to pop up the color picker, and then choose a color by clicking it.

COLORING TABLES

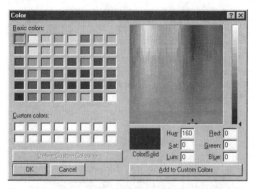

Figure 12.87 The Color dialog box offers additional color selection options. The Color dialog box for the Macintosh is substantively different, as discussed in Chapter 3.

Figure 12.88 I colored one column in this table. Notice that the table, the page, and the column use three different colors.

or

◆ On the color picker, click the System Color button 🔘 to open up the Color dialog box (**Figure 12.87**). For more on using the Color dialog box, see Chapter 3.

When you're finished making your selection, click OK to close the Color dialog box, if required. The color change should be apparent immediately.

✔ Tips

■ You can also follow these steps for a single cell, a selection of cells, a column (**Figure 12.88**), or a row.

■ To close the palette without choosing a color, press the Esc key (Windows only), or click the Default Color button ⬜ . Chapter 3 includes more color tips and instructions for using the dialog boxes.

Saving Excel Spreadsheets and Word Tables as HTML Tables

You can't paste formatted spreadsheet data from Microsoft programs into Dreamweaver as you can into FrontPage. (You can copy the data and paste it, but it doesn't retain the cell data.) You can still convert your Excel spreadsheets into tables. Dreamweaver's features can also help. For Word, see *Cleaning Up Word HTML* in Chapter 4. For Excel, see *Inserting and Exporting Tabular Data*, on the Web site for this book. For basic advice on converting tables into HTML, read on.

Excel (versions 95-2000 and XP) includes a utility for saving spreadsheets as HTML. In Excel 95, choose Tools > Internet Assistant Wizard from the menu. For Excel 97-2000, the command is File > Save as HTML. Both of these programs use Wizards to guide you. In Excel XP, the command is File > Save As Web Page.

You can also save Microsoft Word table data as HTML. In Word 95 and Word XP, you select File > Save As from the menu bar, and choose HTML (*.htm) as the file type. In Word 97-2000, the command is File > Save as HTML.

Once you have one of these Office-created documents saved, you can open it in Dreamweaver and edit the page or cut and paste the table onto an existing page.

Setting a Background Image

You can set a background image for an entire table, a table cell, a column, or a row.

To use a table background image:

1. In Standard view in the Document window, select the table or table element you want to supply with a background image.

2. In the Property inspector, type the pathname of the image you want to use in the Bg Image text box (**Figure 12.89**).

   or

   Click the Browse button to open the Select Image Source dialog box and select the image from your local machine.

   or

   If you're using a local site, drag the Point to File icon onto the image file in the Sites window.

   Either way, the image path will appear in the Bg Image text box, and the image will load in the table in the Document window

Figure 12.90 shows a table that uses a background image.

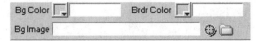

Figure 12.89 Type the pathname of the background image in the Bg Image text box on the Property inspector, or click the Browse or Point to File buttons to use those options.

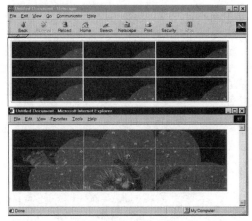

Figure 12.90 I used a table background image in this table. Navigator 4 (top) tiles the image in each cell, whereas IE 5 (bottom) uses this large image as a background for the entire table. Were the image smaller, it would tile behind the table. Netscape 6 now acts like Explorer and tiles the image over the entire table, not in each cell.

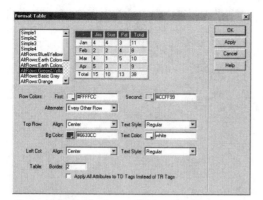

Figure 12.91 Use the Format Table dialog box to choose from predetermined color schemes. Any color choices you make for columns or individual cells will override these default schemes.

■ A convenient shortcut for coloring tables is the Format Table dialog box (**Figure 12.91**), which allows you to choose from predetermined background color schemes. To use the dialog box, select the table in Standard view, and then select Commands > Format Table from the menu bar. You can set border width, content alignment, and text options for rows and columns, too. **Figure 12.92** shows a table formatted this way.

Figure 12.92 This data table was formatted using the Format Table dialog box.

Sorting Table Contents

Typing stuff into a table can be a pain in the butt if you need the contents to be in order. In Microsoft Word and Microsoft Excel, you can type the stuff in any order you like and then sort table contents alphabetically or numerically. In Dreamweaver, you can do it, too. No, really!

To sort table contents:

1. In Standard view, click within the table you want to sort.

2. From the menu bar, select Commands > Sort Table. The Sort Table dialog box will appear (**Figure 12.93**).

3. From the Sort By drop-down menu, select the column (by number) to sort by first.

4. From the Order drop-down menu, select Alphabetically or Numerically.

5. From the next drop-down menu, select Ascending (A–Z, 1–9) or Descending (Z–A, 9–1).

6. To sort by a secondary column next, repeat steps 3 through 5 for the Then By section of the dialog box.

7. To include the first row in your sort, check the Sort Includes First Row check box. To include table headers and footers in your sort, select the check boxes for THEAD and TFOOT rows.

8. To have any row formatting travel with the sort, check the Keep TR Attributes With Sorted Row check box.

9. Click OK to close the Sort Table dialog box. The table will be sorted according to the criteria you specified.

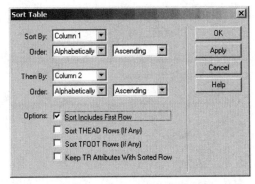

Figure 12.93 Use the Sort Table dialog box to specify criteria by which to sort the contents of a table.

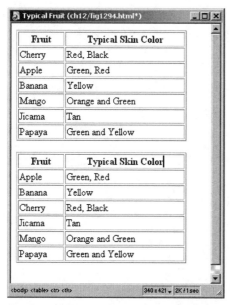

Figure 12.94 This table demonstrates Dreamweaver's Sort Table command—The first column was alphabetized, and the second column traveled along with the first, preserving the associations (Banana is still Yellow).

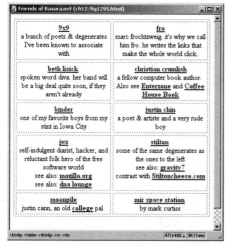

Figure 12.94 The process demonstrated in **Figure 12.95** can work against you, too—here, I wanted both columns to be alphabetized, but even though I selected "Then Sort by Column 2", Dreamweaver sorted my table by entire rows. If I want to sort each column separately, I open this page in Microsoft Word, sort each column (Table > Sort), and clean up the page in Dreamweaver.

✔ Tips

■ This sort keeps rows together. If you've lined up two columns of data and each should be alphabetized, you should perform your sorting either manually or in a program such as Microsoft Word, in which you can sort each column. **Figure 12.94** shows how Dreamweaver sorts rows. **Figure 12.95** shows an abortive attempt to sort both columns at once.

■ You cannot sort a table that includes any merged cells. If you want a merged row like the top row in **Figure 12.92**, perform the sort and then merge the cells.

■ You cannot sort a table that uses one of the following tags: TBODY, THEAD, COLGROUP, TFOOT. Your table must consist only of TR, TH, and TD tags. TBODY and its compatriots are used when hand-coding a table to apply formatting to part of a table, such as several rows. Other Web page programs, such as FrontPage, may apply these tags without your knowing it; you must remove them to use the Sort Table command.

FRAMING PAGES

Figure 13.1 Each frame in a frames-based page, such as Hotwired's Cocktail, is a distinct document with its own content—including different link and background colors and background images. When you click a link in one frame (here, the left frame has a table of contents), the targeted page appears in another window.

Web pages that use frames are versatile because they allow you to keep parts of your Web site—such as a logo or navigation bar—stationary, while allowing other parts of the same page, in the same window, to change their content. Using frames, you don't have to place the same elements onto every Web page that you build, and the viewer won't have to reload them each time in the browser. A frames-based page is divided into several windows within windows, like the panes in an old-fashioned window (**Figure 13.1**). Frames pages can also blur obvious borders (**Figure 13.2**, on next page).

Although a frames-based page acts like a single Web page, each frame contains a unique document that can include completely distinct contents, its own colors and page properties, and independent scrollbars.

The glue that holds these documents together is called *the frameset definition document,* or the *frameset page*. This *frameset* is a set of frames, and the frameset page is what defines them as a set. The frameset page is what the Web browser opens, and the page tells the Web browser where to look for each document, what it's called, and what the layout of the whole thing looks like.

Frames and Navigation

You can use frames to create some nifty layouts. Because each frame is a discrete HTML document, it can contain any HTML element except another `<frameset>` tag—although we'll find out how to embed frames within frames in the section called *Nested Framesets*.

As I mentioned earlier, frames are best used when you want part of your page, such as a toolbar or a table of contents, to be visible the entire time the page is in the window—regardless of what kind of scrolling or clicking your visitors do.

Each frame in a frameset is an individual HTML document. In the background, the frameset page acts as mission control, holding together all the documents. Each frame on the page has a default document anchored to it so that when you first load the frameset, each page will have content in it already. Some of those frames might remain stationary, while when you click on a link, other frames may replace their default pages with new content. **Figure 13.3** presents a diagram of the frame structure. You can see the code for a frameset page in **Figure 13.4**—the frameset page is holding together the twelve frames pictured.

Figure 13.2 Designer Derek Powazek uses unusual frames layouts such as this one in his storytelling site The Fray (www.fray.com). The picture on the left stays visible while you scroll through the story on the right. On this page, frame borders are turned off.

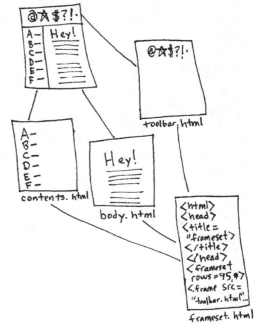

Figure 13.3 An infinite number of pages can be associated with a frames page via links so that your main design remains, while any number of pages can open in different frames within your main page.

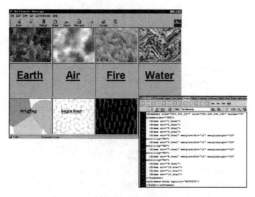

Figure 13.4 A frames-based page is held together behind the scenes by a frameset page, which keeps track of what belongs where. This page has twelve individual frames. The code is for the frameset page that holds these frames together; see Coding Frames, later in this chapter, for details about frame tags.

✔ Tips

- The frameset page is called that because it includes the `<frameset>` tag, which defines the layout of the frames-based page, the location and names of the initial pages that occupy each frame, and details about the appearance and actions of the frames.

- For advanced users: if you want some help hand-coding frameset code in the Dreamweaver environment, open Code view or Split view in the Document window, and context-sensitive code-editing tools will appear on the Insert toolbar (**Figure 13.4**). (For some reason, this feature is not available in the Code inspector unless Code view is open.) Code-editing is described more fully in Chapter 4; suffice it to say that these buttons on the Frames tab of the Insert toolbar let you click to insert `<frameset>`, `<frame>`, `<iframe>` and `<noframes>` tags:

  fset   frm   ifrm   frms

Setting Up a Frames Page

Dreamweaver will automatically create a frameset document for you when you divide a page into more than one frame.

To create frames by splitting the page:

1. Open a blank Document window, if one isn't already available.

2. From the Document Window menu bar, select Modify > Frameset > (see **Figure 13.5**).

From there, choose one of the following options:

- Split Frame Left (**Figure 13.6**)

- Split Frame Right (**Figure 13.6**)

- Split Frame Up (**Figure 13.7**)

- Split Frame Down (**Figure 13.7**)

The window will split to display two frames.

You'll see new borders around each of the frames, as well as around the entire page. The frame border outlines each frame. When you first split the frame, the frame border along the outside of the page appears dashed (**Figure 13.7**), indicating that the entire frameset page is selected.

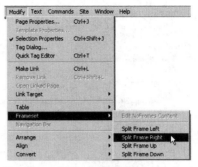

Figure 13.5 Choose Modify > Frameset from the Document window menu bar.

Figure 13.6 The Split Frame Left and Split Frame Right commands both split the current frame in half with a vertical frame border.

Figure 13.7 The Split Frame Up and Split Frame Down commands both split the current frame in half with a horizontal frame border.

Wherefore Untitled Frame 6?

Occasionally, you'll close a document on which you've created no frames, and Dreamweaver will ask you if you want to save an untitled frameset page. Why? Who knows. Just go ahead and click on No, you don't want to save the changes. You won't be losing any data.

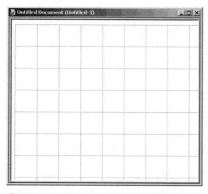

Figure 13.8 The heavy outline that appears should resemble the frame borders you've seen on pages around the Web.

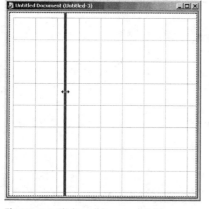

Figure 13.9 Click and drag an outside border, and you can create a new frame by splitting the original page.

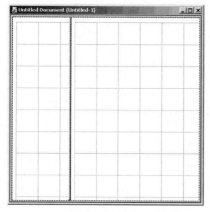

Figure 13.10 Let go of the mouse button when the frame border is where you want. Ta-da! You now have two frames.

Creating Frames by Dragging

You can also create a frame border by viewing the default frame border around the page and then dragging the border to create multiple frames. Again, an unsaved frameset page will be created automatically when you perform these steps.

To create a frame by dragging:

1. Open a new Document window, if you need one, by pressing Ctrl+N (Command+N).

   In the New Document dialog box, if it appears, select a plain, blank HTML document and click on Create.

2. From the Document window menu bar, select View > Visual Aids > Frame Borders. A heavy outline will appear around the blank space in the window (**Figure 13.8**).

3. Mouse over one of the outside borders, and the mouse pointer will turn into a double-headed arrow.

4. Drag it to a new location (**Figure 13.9**), and release the mouse button when you've positioned the border where you choose (**Figure 13.10**).

You now have two frames in the window.

continued on next page

CREATING FRAMES BY DRAGGING

✔ Tips

- If you mouse over one of the corners of the page, the mouse pointer will turn into a four-headed arrow (**Figure 13.11**), or a grabbing hand on the Mac. You can drag the corner into the page and release the mouse button to create four new frames at once.

- To split existing frame borders, hold down the Alt (Option) key while dragging a border or a corner border. (**Figure 13.12**).

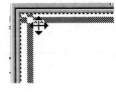

Figure 13.11 If you grab the corner of the page, the pointer will turn into a four-headed arrow, or a grabbing hand on the Mac. Drag the cursor to the middle of the page and let go to create four frames at once.

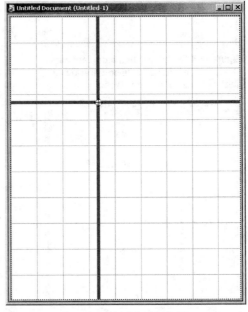

Figure 13.12 Here, I grabbed the top-left corner border, and I'm splitting the page into four frames.

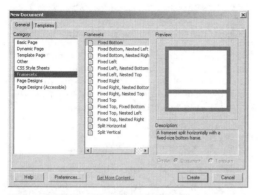

Figure 13.13 Select File > New from the Document window menu bar, and select the Frameset category to display a list of built-in layouts you can use, with previews of what those pages look like.

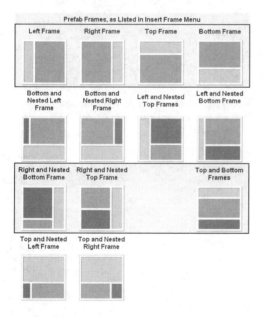

Figure 13.14 The heading over each layout is its name on the Frames tab of the Insert toolbar. The names in the Insert > Frames menu are slightly abbreviated, as shown in the list on the next page.

Quick and Dirty Frames

Dreamweaver MX features three methods for creating frames layouts based on prefab designs: the New Document dialog box; the menu command Insert > Frames; and the Frames tab on the Insert toolbar. All allow you to choose a basic layout without having to split frames or nest framesets (see *Nested Framesets*, later in this chapter).

If you create a frames page using one of these methods and want to skip ahead, be sure to read *Targeting Links* to control where links open.

To use a built-in template file:

1. From the Document window menu bar, select File > New. The New Document Dialog box will appear.

2. In the Category list box, select Framesets. The panel will change to display a new list of choices (**Figure 13.13**).

3. Select a frameset page description—these options are described in the next two sections and pictured in a slightly different order in **Figure 13.14**.

4. Click on Create. A new document window will display the frames layout you chose.

To use the Insert Frames menu or the Frames tab on the Insert toolbar:

1. Create a new, blank page.

2. **Button method:** On the Insert toolbar, click on the Frames tab. In **Figure 13.15**, I've undocked and resized the Insert toolbar so I can show all the options.

   Each button is a tiny preview of what the layout will look like. If you mouse over the objects displayed, a Tool tip will describe each option, each of which is a wordier version of those in the Insert menu (**Figure 13.16**). The Insert menu and the Insert toolbar display the frame choices in a slightly different order.

   Click on any button to create that layout, or drag the button into an existing frame to split a single frame in the manner pictured.

   or

   Menu method: From the Document window menu bar, select Insert > Frames (**Figure 13.16**), and then choose one of the following options, as mocked up in **Figure 13.14**:

   ◆ Left
   ◆ Right
   ◆ Top
   ◆ Bottom
   ◆ Bottom Nested Left
   ◆ Bottom Nested Right
   ◆ Left Nested Top*
   ◆ Left Nested Bottom*
   ◆ Right Nested Bottom*
   ◆ Right Nested Top*
   ◆ Top and Bottom*
   ◆ Top Nested Left
   ◆ Top Nested Right

   The Document window will create the frameset design you selected (**Figure 13.17**). Items with an asterisk appear in a different order on the Insert toolbar.

Figure 13.15 Click on the Frames button on the Insert toolbar to display prefab frames layouts. Here, I've undocked the toolbar and resized it. When you mouse over the Frames buttons on the Insert toolbar, a tool tip will give you a description of that frameset.

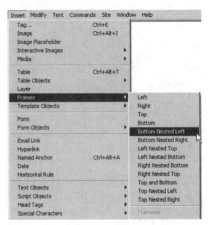

Figure 13.16 Select Insert > Frames from the Document window menu bar, and then choose a layout option.

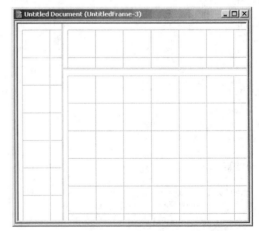

Figure 13.17 I selected Left Top from the Insert > Frames menu, and the layout appeared in the Document window. Note that the frame borders are not heavy; this is how Dreamweaver displays borders that have been turned off (or set to zero width)—in this case, in the preset attributes of the layout.

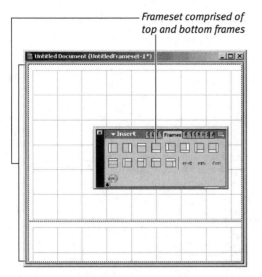

Frameset comprised of top and bottom frames

Figure 13.18 First, I created a frameset with two frames by clicking on "Bottom Frame."

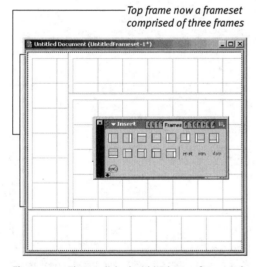

Top frame now a frameset comprised of three frames

Figure 13.19 Then, I clicked within the top frame and applied the "Left and Nested Top Frame" to the selected, top frame, and that frame became a frameset divided into three individual frames.

✔ Tips

- Frames pages created using the New Document dialog box, the Insert > Frames menu, or Insert toolbar shortcuts do not use visible frame borders, and they may have preset resize and scrollbar settings. (See *Frameset Options,* later in this chapter, to change these settings). The frames on these pages are also prenamed; see *Naming Frames* for more about using frame names.

- When you apply any prebuilt layouts that contain more than two frames, you are dividing a frame into an additional frameset, also known as a *nested frameset.* Also, if you click within an existing frame and then select one of the preset frames layouts (**Figure 13.18**), the frame you selected will itself be divided into that frames layout, which will also involve nesting (**Figure 13.19**).

About Nested Framesets

As described previously, a frameset controls many attributes of a frames-based page, such as scrollbars, border visibility, and margins.

On pages with more than one frameset, you'll need to select the proper frameset, or perhaps each of several framesets, in order to modify the parts of the page that you want.

When you split a frame in two, or apply a prefab layout that includes a nested frameset, Dreamweaver adds the extra frameset code.

How can you tell whether your page includes a nested frameset? In framesets with no nested framesets inside them, all frame borders go from one edge of the browser or document window to the other (**Figure 13.20**). Any frame with borders that don't go from one edge of the page to the other is part of a nested frameset.

The original frameset is called the *parent,* and a nested frameset is the *child*. Children may inherit some properties of the parent, such as visible borders.

A single frameset is shown in **Figures 13.20** and **13.21**. In **Figures 13.22** and **13.23**, the right-hand frame has become a second frameset that includes two frames. The page in **Figure 13.19** actually includes three framesets: the top and bottom seen in **Figure 13.18** are one frameset; then the top frame is divided into a right and left frame; then the left, top frame is split into two more frames.

✔ Tip

- The main reason you need to be aware of nested framesets is so that you can select and modify them separately. I bet you're glad you don't have to hand-code this stuff. To set those properties, see *Frame Page Options*, later in this chapter.

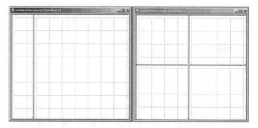

Figure 13.20 On the left, we have a page that contains one frameset made up of two frames. The right-hand window contains one frameset and four frames.

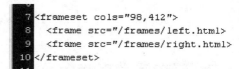

```
 7 <frameset cols="98,412">
 8    <frame src="/frames/left.html>
 9    <frame src="/frames/right.html>
10 </frameset>
11
```

Figure 13.21 Here, I'm viewing the code for the left-hand frameset from Figure 13.20, which includes the locations of the documents within it. Two frames, one frameset.

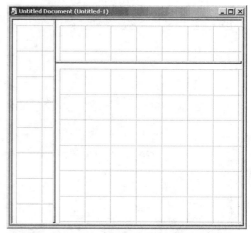

Figure 13.22 I split the right-hand frame in two; in order for one frame to contain two more frames (whose borders don't go across the whole frame, in contrast to the right-hand example in Figure 13.20), the original frameset must be subdivided to include a new frameset.

```
 6
 7 <frameset cols="98,412">
 8   <frame src="/frames/left.html>
 9   <frame src="/frames/right.html>
10   <frameset rows="144,144">
11     <frame src="/UntitledFrame-3">
12     <frame src="/UntitledFrame-4">
13   </frameset>
14 </frameset>
```

Figure 13.23 Now, in the Code inspector, you can see a new frameset tag nested within the original right-hand frame tag. Now, there are three frames and two framesets. (The frame tag appears four times, but the frame currently occupied by "right.html" will be replaced by the frameset below it.)

Selecting nested framesets

To select frames and framesets, you'll use the Frames panel. See the following section, *Selecting Frames and Framesets*, for details on how to tell if you've selected the right frameset.

Selecting Frames and Framesets

In order to modify a frame or a frameset, as you'll be doing throughout the rest of this chapter, you'll need to select the element in question using the Frames panel. To view the Frames panel, select Window > Others > Frames from the Document window menu bar, or press Shift+F2. The Frames panel will appear (**Figure 13.24**) under the Advanced Layout panel group.

To select a frame:

◆ Hold down the Alt (Shift+Option) key and click within the frame in the Document window.

   or

   In the Frames panel, click within the frame you want to select (**Figure 13.24**).

In either case, a dashed line will appear in the Document window around the frame you selected, and the inspector will display frame properties (**Figure 13.25**).

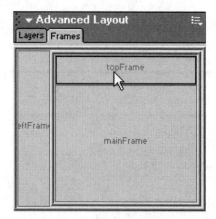

Figure 13.24 The Frames panel. When you select a frame, a heavy line appears around the frame in the Frames panel, and a dashed line appears around it in the Document window.

Figure 13.25 When you select a frame, the Property inspector displays Frame properties for the frame you selected.

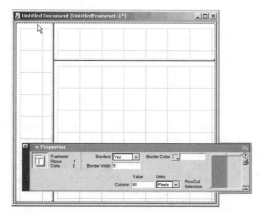

Figure 13.26 I clicked on the outside frame border to select the parent frameset. As you can see in the Property inspector, the frameset contains two columns, but they aren't drawn proportionally as they are in the Frames panel.

Figure 13.27 Here, I've selected the nested frameset, as you can see by the dark black border.

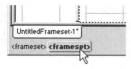

Figure 13.28 In the Tag selector, select either the parent or the child frameset (the latter is selected here).

To select a frameset:

◆ Click on a frame border in the Document window (**Figure 13.26**); or, in the Frames panel, click on the heavier border around the outside edge of the frameset. If your layout includes more than one frameset, click on the outside border to select the parent, or an inner border to select a child. See the last section, *Nested Framesets*.

Either way, the Property inspector will display frameset properties; a dashed line will appear around those frames in the Document window; and a heavy, black line will appear around the frameset in the Frames panel (**Figure 13.27**).

✔ Tip

■ You can also select a nested frameset by clicking on a frameset tag in the Tag selector or the Tag Inspector panel (**Figure 13.28**). Also, hold down the Alt key while using arrow keys to select adjacent and nested frames and framesets.

Modifying the Frame Page Layout

You have limitless options when it comes to laying out pages with frames. Whether you started with a blank page or with a prefab Dreamweaver layout, you can add frames by splitting a frame into two or more frames within a nested frameset, and you can adjust the proportions of the frames on the page by dragging the frame borders to new locations on the page. You'll probably do some experimenting before you achieve the layout you want.

To add frames by splitting a frame:

1. In the Document window, click within the frame you want to split.

2. From the Document window menu bar, select Modify > Frameset > (as shown earlier in **Figure 13.5**), and then choose one of the following options: Split Frame Left, Split Frame Right, Split Frame Up, or Split Frame Down. This will split a frame into a nested frameset consisting of two frames.

Splitting left vs. right, or up vs. down may look exactly the same unless there is already content in the frame. For example, **Figure 13.29** shows the same window, first split left, and then split right.

To add frames by dragging:

◆ To split a frame by dragging a border, as we did earlier in this chapter, hold down the Alt (Option) key while you click and drag the frame border (**Figure 13.30**), or drag a frame border from the edge of the frameset. This will add a frame to the frameset.

To reposition frame borders:

◆ Mouse over the border between two frames, and the pointer will turn into a double-headed arrow (**Figure 13.31**). Click on the border, and drag it to a new location. When the border appears where you want it to, release the mouse button.

Figure 13.29 These two frames pages are pretty much the same. In the one on the left, the top frame was split left, whereas in the right-hand window, the same frame was split right. Which option you choose depends on where you want any pre-existing content in the frame to land.

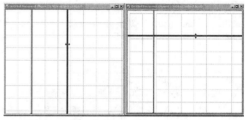

Figure 13.30 If you hold down the Alt (Option) key while clicking on a frame border as I'm doing on the right here, or if you drag an outside border as I'm doing on the right by pulling the top border down, you will divide the existing frameset into additional frames.

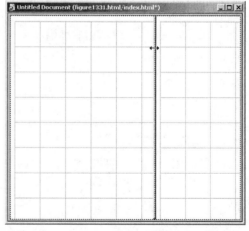

Figure 13.31 When you mouse over a border between frames, the pointer becomes a double-headed arrow that you can use to drag and reposition the border.

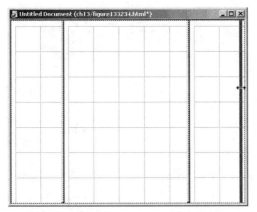

Figure 13.32 Click on the border of the unwanted frame, and drag it off the page. You'll get rid of both the frame and the border.

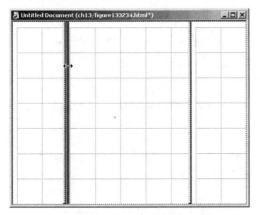

Figure 13.33 You can also drag a frame border into another frame border to get rid of it.

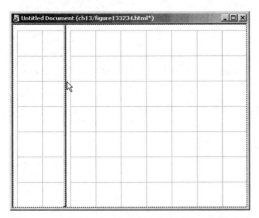

Figure 13.34 Either way, you'll be free of the unwanted frame.

Deleting a Frame

You can keep splitting frames until you achieve the layout you want, but if you create a few frames too many, getting rid of them is easy.

To delete a frame:

◆ Click on the frame border, and drag it off the page (**Figure 13.32**).

   or

   Click on the frame border, and drag it until it meets another border (**Figure 13.33**).

   Let go of the mouse button. The frame will disappear (**Figure 13.34**).

Moving Content Between Frames

Before you delete that frame, you can drag its content into another frame on the page. This works for all sorts of objects, including text, images, multi-media objects, and form fields. Click on the object to select it, or highlight the text you wish to move. Click and hold down the mouse button while you drag the object to a new frame. When the stuff is where you want it, let go of the mouse button, and it will reappear in the new location.

Setting Exact and Relative Sizes for Frames

You can set the position of a frame border, as we've just seen, by dragging it into a new place on the page. If you want to set a more exact position, you'll set row height and column width.

When you split a frame or drag a frame border, Dreamweaver takes the information about the position of the frame border and translates it into a height or width amount for each frame, in either pixels or as a percent of the available space—either the Document window or the parent frameset.

The width of a frame is called the column width. The height of a frame is called the row height. You can adjust these settings using the Property inspector.

The page in **Figure 13.35** is comprised of two framesets (you can tell the bottom frame is a frameset because its vertical border doesn't span the entire window). The first, or parent frameset is made up of two rows. The top frame, or row, is 112 pixels high. The bottom row is set relative to that height; it will take up the rest of the browser window, however small or large (**Figure 13.36**).

In the same figures, the child frameset, which occupies the bottom row, is made up of two columns. The left column occupies 25 percent of the available space—in this case, it's both 25 percent of the parent frame and 25 percent of the window. The right column, then, can be set to either 75 percent or to *relative* (which means that it fills out the available space in the frame or window).

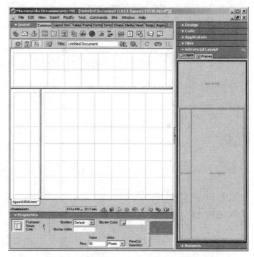

Figure 13.35 The frameset is made up of two rows (across the window), and a nested frameset that has two columns (the lower frame is divided in two, vertically). In this figure, the Property inspector is displaying Frameset properties for the child (nested) frameset.

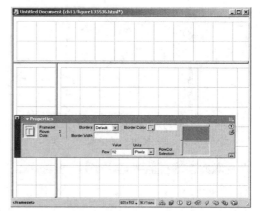

Figure 13.36 Here, you see the same frameset, in a resized (larger) window. Notice how the top frame retains the same, exact size (112 pixels) whereas the bottom frames retain their proportional settings. The left frame still occupies 25 percent of the window.

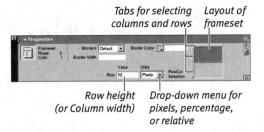

Tabs for selecting   Layout of
columns and rows   frameset

Row height   Drop-down menu for
(or Column width)   pixels, percentage,
or relative

Figure 13.37 The Property inspector displays frameset options when you click on a frame border in the Document window.

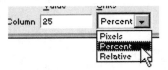

Figure 13.38 Click on a tab in the frameset preview of the Property inspector to adjust settings for that column or row.

Figure 13.39 Select either Pixels, Percent, or Relative as the units for the height or width measurement.

✔ Tips

■ Because the dimensions of any column or row affect the dimensions of the entire frameset, row height and column width are frameset properties, rather than frame properties.

■ It makes sense to set the height and width for one column or row in particular, and to set all other heights and widths as relative to that area of the page.

■ You must set a height or width for each frame in a document in order to guarantee that pixel or percentage widths will be followed when a visitor resizes the window.

To adjust row height and column width:

1. Select the frameset by clicking on a frame border. Frameset properties will appear in the Property inspector (**Figure 13.37**).

2. If the Property inspector isn't fully expanded, click on the Expander arrow in the bottom-right corner of the inspector.

3. Select the column or row whose area you wish to define by clicking on the associated tab, above the column or to the left of the row, in the Property inspector (**Figure 13.38**).

4. Type a value for the column or row in the associated text box and select one of the following units from the drop-down menu (**Figure 13.39**):

   ◆ *Pixels* sets an exact height or width. When the frameset is loaded in the browser, pixel measurements are followed exactly.

   ◆ *Percent* refers to a percentage of window (or frameset) size.

   ◆ *Relative* means that the height or width will be flexible in the frameset, compared to other elements that were given specific pixel or percent measurements.

continues on next page

5. Click in the Document window to apply the height or width changes to the frameset.

6. Repeat these steps for the remainder of the elements in the frameset, or for additional framesets (**Figure 13.40**).

✔ Tips

■ When a browser is loading a frameset page, it draws the layout in the following order:

◆ *Pixel* measurements are given their space allotment first.

◆ Columns or rows with *Percentage* measurements are drawn next.

◆ Frames with *Relative* settings are drawn to fill the rest of the available space.

■ Percentage widths can be used for all measurements, as in 40 and 60 for two frames.

■ Pixel widths must be used in combination with relative widths. When the browser window is resized, at least one frame will act like it's sized relative if you try to set all widths as exact pixel widths.

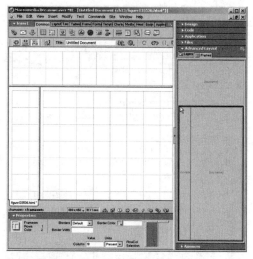

Figure 13.40 On this page, I first selected the parent, or whole-page, frameset and set the top row to 114 pixels and the bottom row to relative. Next, I selected the nested frameset and set the left-hand column to 25 percent and the right-hand column to relative. Always set the most-exact measurements you need first.

Relativity Theory

In my experience, browsers prefer that frames documents be linked to one another using *document-relative* links rather than *site-root relative* links. If you use site-root relative links, you may run across a problem when previewing your pages, whereas that doesn't happen if you set your links as document-relative to the frameset page. Internet Explorer in particular likes frames pages to use document-relative links.

As you can see in **Figure 13.42**, when you select a file to use in a frame, you can use the drop-down menu at the bottom of the Select HTML File dialog box to choose that the files be Relative To the Document or to the Site Root. Choose Document, and Dreamweaver will automatically choose the Frameset page as the relative one.

After you save a page, you can check to see if it has a document relative relationship by attaching it to a frame, as described in *Setting Content Pages*, earlier in this chapter, and then making sure that the Relative To drop-down menu says Document instead of Site Root. For more about how these two types of links are different, see Chapter 6.

Figure 13.41 When the Property inspector displays frame properties, you can set the location for the default frame document in the SRC text box.

Figure 13.42 Use the Select HTML File dialog box to choose a file to load in the frame. Be sure to select Document from the Relative To drop-down menu.

Frames page source is a remote file on the Internet

Frames page stored locally is displayed within frame

Figure 13.43 Here I've loaded pages into the top and left frames, and I've chosen an Internet URL for the center frame. If you're connected to the Internet when you preview this page in your browser, the browser should load the remote file in the frame.

Setting Content Pages

There are two ways you can go about putting content into those pretty, blank frames. One way is to open an existing page in one of the frames of the frameset; the other way is to create your new page right now in one of the frames in the Dreamweaver Document window.

In either case, to determine what your frames page will display when it's loaded into a Web browser, you'll attach a URL to each of the frames in the set. If you want to save your frameset first, skip ahead to *Saving Frameset Pages*.

To attach a page to a frame:

1. Select the frame you want to put some content in. The Property inspector will display the properties of that frame (**Figure 13.41**).

2. The SRC text box currently displays the pathname of the blank, untitled, unsaved page that's in it now. You can:

   ◆ Type (or paste) a location of an existing page—on the Web or on your computer—into the text box; or

   ◆ Click on the Property inspector's Browse button to open up the Select HTML File dialog box (**Figure 13.42**); *or*

   ◆ From the Document window menu bar, select File > Open in Frame to display the Select HTML File dialog box.

If you use one of the two latter options, locate the file on your computer, and then click OK (Open/Choose) to attach the file to the frame you selected.

If the file you selected is on your local machine, it will appear in the frame within the Document window (**Figure 13.43**, left-hand frame).

If you type a full Internet URL in the Frame Properties SRC text box, the Document window will display the "Remote File" message (**Figure 13.43**, right-hand frame).

Creating Content within a Frame

Creating and editing content within one of the frames in a frameset is the same as doing so in a full Document window, only with less screen real estate.

On frames pages you can put text, images, multimedia objects, and tables—anything that you can use on a non-frames page.

Setting the background color for a frame is just like setting the background color for a stand-alone page. Each frame, remember, is a single HTML document, or page, and each page in the frameset has its own page properties. Figure **13.44** shows a frames page in which every frame has a different background.

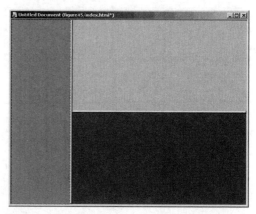

Figure 13.44 This page has three frames, each of which uses a different background color. Back in Figure 13.4, eight of the 12 frames used different background images.

To set a frame background:

1. Display the page properties for the frame in one of two ways:

   Right-click (Control+click) within the frame and select Page Properties from the pop-up menu.

   or

   From the Document window menu bar, select Modify > Page Properties.

   Either way, the Page Properties dialog box will appear.

2. From here, you can adjust page properties for that frame, including background color, background image, page margins, text colors, and link colors.

For more on working with Page Properties, see Chapter 3.

✔ Tip

- Of course, you can create a page in Dreamweaver, save it, and then attach it to a frameset (as described in the preceding section), but if you're creating simple content, you can work easily in the frameset.

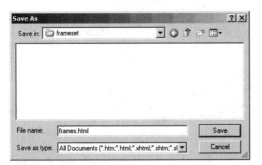

Figure 13.45 This Save As dialog box is no different from any other one in Dreamweaver. Some other Web page programs, such as Microsoft FrontPage, have distinct Save As dialog boxes for the different parts of a frameset.

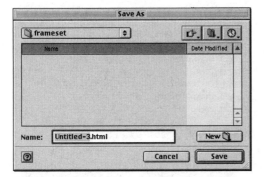

Figure 13.46 The Save As dialog box on the Mac. Be sure you're saving the pages in the folder you want them to live in. If you want your frameset to appear as the default page in a directory, name the frameset document index.html, or whatever your house convention is for a default page.

Saving Your Work

Because frames pages are made up of multiple documents, saving them is a multi-step process. If you just press Ctrl+S (Command+S), you might not be quite sure of which page you're saving, because Dreamweaver's Save As dialog box doesn't offer any distinguishing marks. You can, however, perform the Save All command to save all open pages and the frameset itself. In this case, the Document window indicates which frame you're saving.

You need to save each frame separately because they are distinct documents, and they may also differ from additional content pages that may populate them later.

You can skip these steps for any previously completed pages you attached to the frameset, as described in *Setting Content Pages*, earlier in this chapter.

To save your new frames and frameset:

1. These steps assume you haven't saved any frames yet. Additional instructions follow for saving individual documents.

From the menu bar, select File > Save All. The Save As dialog box will appear (**Figures 13.45** and **13.46**).

continued on next page

Saving All Your Work at Once

After you've saved all the pages in your frameset once, you can periodically save all of them at the same time.

From the Document window menu bar, select File > Save All. Changes to any frames currently open in any Dreamweaver window will be saved. A Save As dialog box will appear for any previously unsaved documents that you have open in Dreamweaver.

Another File menu option, Save Frame As, lets you copy your frames pages to reuse the style and layout. You can also save a frame page as a template; see Chapter 17.

Make sure that the Save In list box displays the folder you want to save the files in; otherwise, browse through the folders on your computer and select one. You'll most likely want to save all the pages for a frameset in their own folder.

2. Type a file name for the frameset file such as `index.html` or `index.htm` in the File Name text box—or another file name if you use a different convention or want a different URL.

3. Click on Save. Another Save As dialog box will appear, and behind it, the Document window will highlight the frame you're about to save (**Figure 13.47**).

4. Type a meaningful filename in the File Name text box. You'll want to be able to distinguish one frame file from another when dealing with these documents later, so choose a name such as `left.html` or `main_body.html` rather than `frame1.html`.

5. Choose Document from the Relative drop-down menu unless you're sure about your Site-Root Relative links.

6. Click on Save, and repeat steps 3-5 for each frame in your frameset.

Frame I'm about to save is selected (with a dashed line) in the Document window

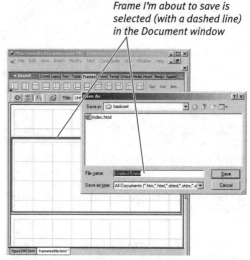

Figure 13.47 The current page is selected in the Document window. I'll name it something like middleframe.html. The URL for this page will end up being something like http://www.yoursite.com/frameset/frames.html. If you want your frameset to appear as the default page in a directory, name the frameset document index.html, or whatever your house convention is for a default page.

✔ Tips

- If you create work within a frame in the Document window, you can save your page, and Dreamweaver will automatically set the location of that page as the default page for that frame.

- To save an individual frame at any point in your work, click within that frame and then select File > Save Frame from the Document window menu bar.

- When you post your site on the Web or open it in the browser window, it's the frameset document that you will be using as the URL.

- To save a frameset without saving all your pages at once, click on a frame border (you must do this in Dreamweaver MX before you can save a frameset) and then select File > Save Frameset from the menu bar.

- To make a copy of a frameset, select File > Save Frameset As from the menu bar.

- It's helpful to save all the files in a frameset in the same folder in order to keep those files together. That way, not only will you be able to locate the files easily and distinguish them from your other projects, you'll have them tidily in their own folder when you get ready to upload them all to the Web.

- Of course, if you also place frameset files in their own directory on your Web site, you should use document-relative filenames, which work in all browsers.

Titling the Frameset Page

Because the frameset page is the one with the URL you'll point to, and because it's the page in charge, you need to give it a page title.

1. Select the parent frameset by clicking on the outermost frame border in the Document window or in the Frames panel. You can double-check that you've selected the frameset rather than an individual frame by looking for its file-name or the words "Untitled Frameset" in the title bar.

2. Type the title in the Document tool-bar's Title text box and press Enter (Return).

You can also set the page title for the frameset page in the Page Properties dialog box. If your other pages will be indexed or viewed without frames, you can specify titles for them, too, but when you preview your frameset in a browser, it's the frameset's title you'll see in the browser window title bar.

Frame Page Options

There are several options you can set for the frames in your page, including options for scrollbars and borders, whether the frames can be resized, and margin settings for each frame.

Using scrollbar settings

You can set scrollbar options for each frame on a page, as you can see in **Figure 13.48**.

To set scrollbar options:

1. Select the frame whose scrollbar settings you want to change.

2. In the Property inspector, choose a scrollbar option from the Scroll drop-down menu (**Figure 13.49**):

   ◆ **Yes** (the frame will always have scrollbars, whether they're needed or not)

   ◆ **No** (the frame will never have scrollbars, whether they're needed or not)

   ◆ **Auto** (the frame will display scrollbars when they are needed)

   ◆ **Default** (uses browser default settings, which are usually Auto)

Note that these scrollbar settings affect both horizontal and vertical scrollbars. The Yes and No settings should be used with discretion.

Generally, when a frames page is loaded into a browser window, the user can resize the frames to personal taste or viewing convenience. If you want some or all of the frames in your page not to be resized, you can set the No Resize option.

To use the No Resize option:

1. Select the frame whose size you want to control. The Property inspector will display settings for that frame.

2. Place a check mark in the No Resize checkbox.

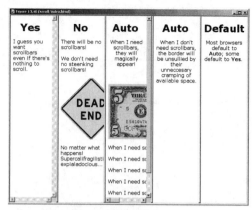

Figure 13.48 Scrollbar options demonstrated here are, from left to right, Yes, No, Auto (with scrollbars), Auto (without scrollbars), and Default. Obviously, Auto makes the most sense most of the time.

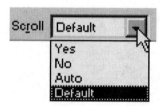

Figure 13.49 Choose one of the scrollbar options from the drop-down menu on the Property inspector.

✔ Tips

■ Obviously, all frames adjacent to frames with the No Resize option selected will not be able to be resized on that border. In Figure 13.48, it sure would be nice to be able to resize some of those frames.

■ If you turn off borders, as described on the next page, the user will not be able to resize any frames that do not display a visible frame border.

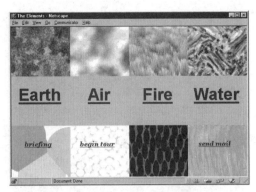

Figure 13.50 Here's the page we saw in Figure 13.4 with its border width set to zero. You can also turn off borders by selecting an entire frameset and then choosing No from the Borders drop-down menu on the Properties inspector. To return to the look in Figure 13.4, turn borders on and set the width to 5.

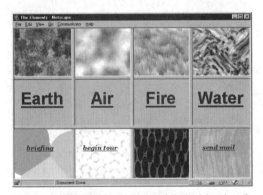

Figure 13.51 Same thing, with a rather thick border of 10. Play around with it; the most interesting effects are between 0 and 10. You can experiment with using different widths for nested framesets or different settings for frames within different framesets.

Frameset		Borders	No ▼
Rows:	2		
Cols:	1	Border Width	5

Figure 13.52 Frameset properties allow you to set width and visibility of borders. You can also set Yes, No, and Auto for a single frame.

Using frame borders

You can turn visible frame borders off or on for any frames page, and you can set the width of all the borders on a page. You can set these options for a frameset or a single frame.

Figures 13.50 and **13.51** show the same page, with frame borders turned off in **Figure 13.50**, and a border width of 10 in **Figure 13.51**.

To turn borders off or on and set widths:

1. Select the frameset or the single frame to which you want to apply border settings. The Property inspector will display options for the frameset (**Figure 13.52**) or the frame.

2. From the Property inspector's Borders drop-down menu, choose one of the following options:
   ◆ **Yes** (displays all frame borders)
   ◆ **No** (hides all frame borders)
   ◆ **Default** (uses browser default settings, usually displaying borders)

3. To change the border width, select the entire frameset and type a number, in pixels, in the Property inspector's Border Width text box.

✔ Tips

■ If adjacent frames or nested framesets have different border settings, No often overrides Yes. You must preview your page in a browser to see which borders will actually appear.

■ The default border width is 5.

■ You can display or hide borders while you're working in Dreamweaver, regardless of what your final browser settings are. Just select View > Visual Aids > Frame Borders to toggle the borders on and off.

■ Border width affects the spacing between the frames on a page whether or not the borders themselves are displayed. In other words, you can set a frame border of 10 and also turn off borders.

Coloring frame borders

You can set a border color as long as you don't turn off frame borders or set their width to zero.

To choose a border color:

1. Select the frameset, and the frameset properties will appear in the Property inspector.

2. Choose a border color by clicking on the Border Color button Border Color to display the color picker, and then clicking on a color. See Chapter 3 for ways to choose colors.

The color you selected will be displayed on the frame borders (**Figure 13.53**); the appearance will differ depending on border width.

✔ Tip

■ You can set border colors for individual frames, which will override any border color settings you made for the entire frameset, although your mileage may vary (**Figure 13.54**).

Figure 13.53 This frameset has colored borders and a border width of 3.

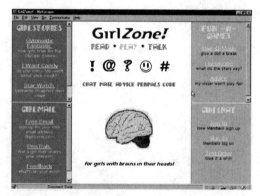

Figure 13.54 I changed the border color setting only for the top-left frame, and all the borders were affected except the border between the middle and right frames.

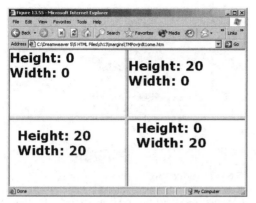

Figure 13.55 Each of these four frames has different margin settings. Experiment with different settings for pages that use images or different sizes of text.

Setting Margins

You can set page margins for any frame—that is, you can adjust the amount of space between your content and the frame borders. You can set two border values for each frame in a set: Margin Width (left and right margins) and Margin Height (top and bottom margins).

To set margins:

1. In the Frames panel, select the frame for which you'd like to set margins.

2. In the Property inspector, type a number (in pixels) in the Margin Width and/or Margin Height text boxes.

3. Press Enter (Return) to make your changes take effect.

Figure 13.55 demonstrates various margin settings. See Chapter 11 to use style sheets to set other kinds of margins.

Specialized Targets

In addition to targeting links to open in a specific frame, you can set targets that will control which window the pages will appear in.

◆ `target=_blank` makes the link open in a new, blank browser window. Putting external links in a new window is a good way to keep people from leaving your site.

◆ `target=_top` makes the link replace the content of the current window.

◆ `target=_parent` makes the link open in the parent frame, in cases where you're using nested framesets.

◆ `target=_self` makes the link open in the same frame as the link.

Targeting Links

Now you have a frames page that looks exactly like you want it to, and you have a default document attached to all the frames in your page. Before you can call your page finished, you need to set targets for the links in your pages (**Figures 13.56** and **13.57**).

When you click on a link in a regular Web page, it generally opens in the same window as the last document you were viewing. In a frames page, however, in which several documents occupy the same window, you don't always want the result of the user's next click—the target page—to appear in the same frame as the link they clicked on. A target tells the link in which frame it should open.

You can set targets so that when you click on a link in a frame, the link opens either in a particular frame in the frameset, or in a specialized target option such as a new window.

◆ If you don't declare any targets for a particular frame, the target page will open in the same frame as the link.

◆ You can set targets so that clicking on a link in one frame opens the page in another frame. Or, you can use one of the special targets (see the sidebar on the previous page) to control where a document opens.

◆ You can set a default, or base target, for all your frames; then you only need to set individual targets for links that differ from the frame's default target.

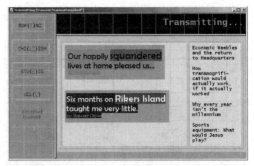

Figure 13.56 This page has an obvious navigation scheme: Click on one of the links in the left frame, and it should appear in the large frame at right. This is only possible using targets.

Figure 13.57 Two versions of the page in Figure 13.56. On the left, the targets haven't been set, and the navigation links open in the narrow frame at left. On the right, the left-hand frame was given a default target so the links would open properly in the right-hand frame.

Figure 13.58 Name each frame by selecting it and then typing a meaningful word in the Frame Name text box.

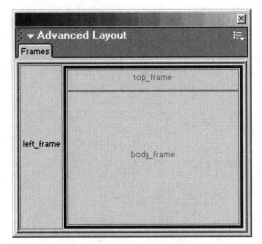

Figure 13.59 After you've named your frames, the Frames panel will display the name of each frame.

✔ Tips

■ After you name your frames, their names will appear in the Property inspector's Target drop-down menu. In the upcoming section, *Setting Individual Targets,* you'll choose a target from that menu.

■ As is the case with most HTML entities, no spaces are allowed in frame names. Underscores are okay, but hyphens are not. Try to restrict yourself to lowercase letters and numbers.

■ Another great Dreamweaver advantage: You don't have to remember, memorize, write down, or tattoo the names of your frames on your forehead; just refer to the Frames panel and select the target from the drop-down menu on the Property inspector.

Naming frames

Before you can set targets, you need to name each frame. A frame name is different from a filename (such as `page.html`) or a page title (such as "Blargh Resources"). The frameset page needs to know both the filename and the frame name of each page in order to be able to load the pages in the proper position and order.

If you used one of Dreamweaver's preset frames layouts, your frames may already have names you can use; you can change them or use the defaults.

✔ Tip

■ The frame name is different from the page title, which, in cases of frames pages, may be unnecessary for all but the frameset page. The page title, as you'll recall, appears in the title bar of the Web browser; it's the frameset page's title that shows up when the frameset page is loaded. See the sidebar *Titling the Frameset Page,* earlier in this chapter.

To name a frame:

1. Select the frame you want to name by clicking on it in the Frames panel. Frame properties will appear in the Property inspector.

2. Type a meaningful name in the Frame Name text box (**Figure 13.58**). You should be able to distinguish one frame from another by their names; for example, `upper_left`, `main`, or `toolbar`.

3. Press Enter (Return), and the name will appear in the Frames panel.

4. Repeat these steps for all the frames in the window.

When you're finished, the Frames panel will display all frame names (**Figure 13.59**).

Setting Targets

Once you name your frames, you can set a target for an entire frame or for individual links.

Setting a base target for a frame

By default, the target for each link in a frame is the frame itself. To set a different default target, also known as a base target, you need to specify the name of the target in the code. If you know that you'll want every link in your frame to open in a particular target frame, this could save you a lot of time, so you don't have to set each target individually.

To set a base target:

1. Click in the frame for which you'd like to set a base target. This is the frame that contains the links you need to direct into another frame.

2. Open the Code inspector for that frame by pressing F10, or by selecting Window > Others > Code Inspector from the Document window menu bar.

3. Locate the `<head>` tag, near the top of the Code inspector. It should look something like this: ⟶

```
<head>
<title>Untitled Document</title>
<meta http-equiv="Content-Type"
content="text/html; charset=
iso8859-1">
</head>
```

4. Within the `<head>` tag, but after the `<title>` tag, type the following line of code:

   `<base target="name">`

   where "name" is replaced by the name of the frame you want to make the default target, or one of the special targeting instructions, such as "_top" (quotation marks included).

   Do not use a closing `</base>` tag; if Dreamweaver adds one, delete it.

5. Your code should now look something like this: ⟶

6. Press Ctrl+S (Command+S) to save the changes to your code. You can close the Code inspector, if you like.

```
<head>
<title>Untitled Document</title>
<base target="main_frame">
<meta http-equiv="Content-Type"
content="text/html; charset=
iso8859-1">
</head>
```

Figure 13.60 Select the desired target from the Target drop-down menu.

Figure 13.61 Here's what you'll see when you first visit numbers.html: two frames introducing you to the site.

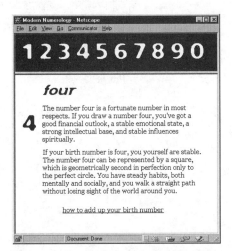

Figure 13.62 Click on one of the numbers in the top frame, and a new page opens in the bottom frame. The top frame has a base target of body, which is the name of the bottom frame.

Although behind-the-scenes changes like this one won't show up visibly in the Dreamweaver window, you can preview your frames pages in the browser window and test them to make sure they work.

Setting individual targets

When you want to set a target for a link that differs from the default, or base target, use the Property inspector to select a target for the link.

To target individual links:

1. Select the text or image that you want to target. The Property inspector will display properties for that object.

2. If there's not a link specified for that object as yet, type or paste the URL, or browse for the link in the Link text box.

3. From the Target drop-down menu on the Property inspector (**Figure 13.60**), select a target. This can be either the name of one of the other frames on the page, or one of the special targets discussed in *Specialized Targets*, earlier in this chapter.

   or

   From the Document window menu bar, select Modify > Link Target > and then select a frame name, a specialized target, or Default target, to select your default setting (if you set a base target, that's how you reselect it for a given link).

You're all set.

Figures 13.61 and **13.62** demonstrate a simple, common use of targeting: Click on a link in the top frame, and it opens in the bottom frame.

Testing Your Targets

It's vitally important, more so than with almost any other kind of Web page, that you test every link on your frames-based pages. You need to make sure that the links open where you think you told them to open. Targets can be tricky—they don't need to be difficult, but they absolutely must be done correctly if you don't want to drive your visitors away for good. **Figure 13.63** shows the evil recursive frame problem: A link to the entire frameset was accidentally targeted to open in one of the frames.

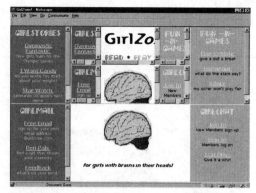

Figure 13.63 A misplaced target can be ugly, at best. Here, we see a recursive frameset—a link to the entire frameset was accidentally targeted to open in the top, center frame.

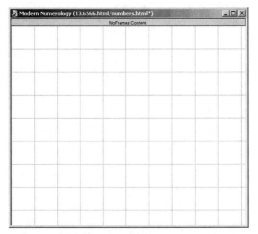

Figure 13.64 From the Document window menu bar, select Modify > Frameset > Edit No Frames Content, and the Document window will display the blank no-frames page.

Figure 13.65 With very little effort, I created a no-frames page that includes all the same links as the frameset page. To appease very old browsers, I also avoided frills like tables, background images, and image maps. See Appendix C on the book's Web site for more details.

Creating No-Frames Content

Not everyone who visits your site will have a frames-capable browser. Although most people are using some version or other of Netscape Navigator or Internet Explorer, not everyone is. See Appendix C on the Web site for the details. The point is that if you don't offer your non-frames visitors something, they won't see anything at all.

At the very least, you need to leave a message that says something like, "This site requires a frames-capable browser, such as Netscape Navigator 2 or later, or Internet Explorer 3 or later." Providing links to a site where they can download this software is also a good idea.

But even that is shortchanging your guests, in a way. Without much work at all, you can give them a fully functional page that will connect them with much of the same information.

To create a no-frames page from scratch:

1. To view the no-frames page, from the Document window menu bar, select Modify > Frameset > Edit No Frames Content. The Document window will display the blank no-frames page (**Figure 13.64**).

2. You can edit this page, including page properties such as background color, the same way you would when creating a page from scratch.

   or

   Select the contents of an existing page, and copy and paste into the no-frames page.

Figure 13.65 shows the no-frames page we created as the alternative to the frames-based page shown in **Figures 13.61** and **13.62**.

To return to the frames view, just select Modify > Frameset > Edit No Frames Content again.

To use existing code in a no-frames page:

1. Open the Code inspector or Code view to see the HTML for the page you want to use as your no-frames content.

2. Select all the code between (and including) the <body> and </body> tags, and copy it to the clipboard (Ctrl+C/ Command+C).

3. In the Document window, display the (thus far, blank) no-frames page by selecting Modify > Frameset > Edit No Frames Content from the menu bar.

4. View the code for this page—which is really just part of the frameset document. The empty no-frames code should look like this:

```
<noframes>
<body bgcolor="#FFFFFF">
</body></noframes>
```

5. Select everything between the <noframes> and </noframes> tags, and delete it.

6. Paste in the HTML from the code you copied in step 2. You should get something like this:

```
<noframes>
<body bgcolor="#000000">
This is all the neat content that's
on my frames page, including <A
HREF="links.html">links</A> and
everything!
</body>
</noframes>
```

7. Save the changes to your HTML, and close the Code inspector or return to Design view. The page you pasted in will show up as the No Frames Content in the Document window.

8. To return to business as usual, select Modify > Frameset > Edit No Frames Content again.

No-Frames Tips

Check to make sure that:

◆ You don't include any <html> or </html> tags within the <noframes> tags.

◆ You include one, and only one set of <body> and </body> tags between the <noframes> tags.

When you preview no-frames content in your regular browser, it won't show up. Why? Because your regular browser is probably frames-capable, and it will load the frames-based page instead—they are the same document, after all.

See Appendix C, on the Web site, for information about getting and using a non-frames browser for previewing your documents. Or, paste the same code into a blank document, and preview that page to test it.

LAYERS AND POSITIONING

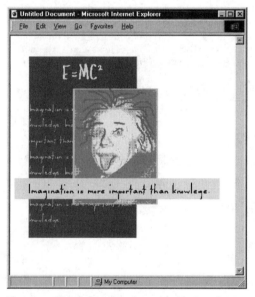

Figure 14.1 This little collage is made with three layers, positioned so that they overlap in the browser window. Can't do that with tables!

Layers enable you to control the exact position of your elements on a Web page. A layer is basically a container for HTML content, delineated by the **<div>** or **<span>** tag, that you can position anywhere on a page. Unlike table cells, you can make layers overlap, or stack on top of one another. You can also use separate layers to make objects appear, disappear, or even move across your page.

Layers are called layers because they can be positioned in three dimensions. You can set an absolute or relative location for a layer along the page's X and Y axes. The third dimension is called the Z-index, which allows layers to overlap one another (**Figure 14.1**).

Designers really love layers for their versatility: They make Web pages more dynamic. For example, you can hide layers (through visibility), or even parts of layers (with the Z-index or with clipping areas) when a page initially loads. Then you can write a script that will cause the hidden areas to appear after a certain amount of time or when a certain user event happens (see Chapter 16 and Appendix N for information on Behaviors and Timelines, respectively).

continued on next page

You can also use layers in a manner similar to tables to control the layout of your page (**Figure 14.2**)—the added benefit being that you can then show, hide, or swap layers after the page has loaded.

✔ Tip

■ Browsers prior to IE or Netscape 4.0 will display the content of a layer. However, they ignore most layer properties, including positioning. See Appendix C on the Web site to find out how to accommodate older browsers.

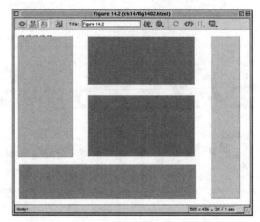

Figure 14.2 Here's a starting layout with five layers drawn on the page. As I fill the page with content, I can create several layers for each piece of the layout. Then I can swap any of these layers with a layer of the same size, rather than having to link to a new page.

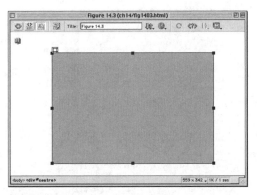

Figure 14.3 This layer is positioned 100 pixels from the left side of the window, and 50 pixels from the top of the window.

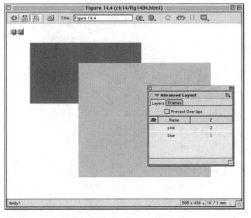

Figure 14.4 The larger layer is positioned over top of the smaller one. That's because the layer on top has a bigger Z-index.

Layers and Animation

Dynamic HTML means that you can make layers change or move after the page is finished loading. Timelines, discussed in Appendix N on the Web site for this book, are used to animate layers over time. The Show Layer Behavior and the Drag Layer Behavior both allow layers to change when the user performs an action. I describe both these behaviors in Chapter 16.

CSS Positioning

Layers are part of the world of Cascading Style Sheets and Dynamic HTML. Cascading Style Sheets Positioning, or CSS-P, allows the most specific positioning in HTML to date. Earlier methods, using tables, frames, and frame margins, don't approach the specificity you can reach with CSS-P. Layout tables (see Chapter 12) give you some of the design flexibility, but they don't let you overlap elements, or animate parts of your page with timelines and behaviors.

You can apply CSS Positioning to a block of text, a block-type element, an image, or a layer. There are two ways to apply positioning: One is to create a style class and apply it to the selections or text blocks you want to position on the page (at which point the object becomes a layer, for all practical purposes). The other is to create a layer in the Document window that you can modify independently of creating a style.

X and Y coordinates

A layer or other positioned element is positioned using X and Y coordinates. X and Y correspond to Left and Top. This can be the left and top of the page itself or of another parent container, such as another layer or a text block (**Figure 14.3**).

The Z-index

The third property of a layer aside from positioning on the X and Y axes is the *Z-index,* or stacking order. This property is used when there are two or more layers on a page that overlap, and it indicates the order in which the layers stack on top of one another (**Figure 14.4**). The higher a layer's Z-index, the closer it is to the top of the stack.

Absolute vs. Relative Positioning

The position of an element in an HTML document can be either absolute, relative, or static. Layers, by definition, use absolute positioning.

Normal positioning is called *static,* and causes the element to be positioned within the normal flow of text. Specifying coordinates for static positioning does you no good, as they will be ignored (**Figure 14.5**).

Relative positioning means that a layer or other element is given a position relative to the top-left corner of the parent container. However, the relative element is included in the flow of the page, and is also inline—it does not automatically cause any line breaks (**Figure 14.6**). To activate inline properties, a `<span>` tag should be used instead of a `<div>` tag (**Figure 14.7**).

An element such as a layer that is positioned *absolutely* is completely outside the flow of the document. The regular flow of the material on the page neither contains the layer, nor is it interrupted by the layer (**Figure 14.8**). Instead, a layer's position is determined by coordinates, which you can set by drawing.

Figure 14.5 In static positioning, the layer is simply treated as a text block and thrown into the normal flow of text.

Figure 14.6 Relative positioning places the layer according to the specified X and Y coordinates, but it still affects the flow of text. The `<div>` tag causes a paragraph break after the layer.

Figure 14.8 The layer is back to being a `<div>` now, and it's positioned absolutely. That means that the regular text flow once again starts at the top of the page, and the layer simply overlaps it.

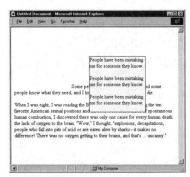

Figure 14.7 This code is exactly the same as in **Figure 14.6** except it uses a `<span>` instead of a `<div>` tag.

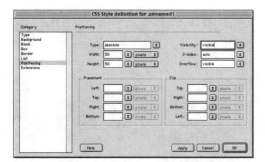

Figure 14.9 The Positioning panel of the CSS Style Definition dialog box. I describe everything else to do with styles in Chapter 11; positioning is discussed in this chapter in terms of layers.

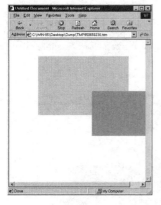

Figure 14.10 Two simple, rectangular layers. One is stacked on top of the other.

Figure 14.11 Each of these images is in a layer, and both images are transparent, so that each appears to float on the page.

Positioning Properties

Positioning properties can be applied to any object, but when you set these properties, the behavior of the object becomes similar to layer behavior. Dreamweaver then treats it as a layer, although the browsers may respond differently to positioned elements that are not enclosed in <div> or <span> tags.

To apply positioning to objects other than layers, create and apply a style, as described in Chapter 11, using the Positioning properties in the CSS Style Definition dialog box (**Figure 14.9**). In general, it's easier to create layers individually using the steps detailed in this chapter. Once you have the hang of both layers and style sheets, you can create a style that you can use to create batches of layers.

The following properties are discussed more fully throughout this chapter in terms of layers.

Type lets you designate the positioning as *absolute, relative,* or *static.*

Visibility determines whether the element will be visible when the page loads. You can declare an element as visible or hidden, or you can allow it to inherit its properties from the parent element. Using behaviors (Chapter 16), you can make a layer's visibility change over time or when the user performs an action.

Z-Index (**Figure 14.10**) determines the stacking order of overlapping elements; the Z-index is the third coordinate, combined with X and Y, that determines the location of the layer on the page in three dimensions. The higher the number, the higher priority the element is given (a layer with a Z-index of 3 will be stacked on top of elements with a Z-index of 1 and 2).

If the layers have no background colors, and the images within the layers use transparency, you can stack layers so that images appear to overlap one another (**Figure 14.11**).

Overflow determines the behavior of the layer when the content exceeds the borders of the layer. You can designate the out-of-bounds content as visible or hidden; or the layer can be given scrollbars to make the rest of the content accessible (generally, auto also provides scrollbars) (**Figure 14.12**).

✔ Tip

■ Overflow treatment is not displayed properly in Dreamweaver or supported by Navigator 4.x, but it is supported by Netscape 6. In Navigator 4, overflow content is visible, even if another option is set.

Placement (Figures 14.10 and 14.11) of a layer is determined by its distance from the *Left* and *Top* of the parent unit. The *Width* and *Height* measurements are related to placement in that they determine the position of the lower-right corner of the layer.

Clip refers to the clipping area of the layer: the area of the layer in which content shows through (**Figure 14.13**). You could give a layer an area of 200 pixels by 200 pixels, and then allow only a 100x100 pixel area to show through. You set a clipping area as a rectangular area comprised of four measurements (Top, Right, Bottom, and Left).

✔ Tips

■ Other attributes that might be construed as having something to do with positioning include Block attributes, which control paragraph placement; Text Align, which you can use to control spacing within a layer; Line Height, which is a Text attribute; the Position List attribute, which relates to indents; and most Box attributes, particularly Float, Clear, Margins, and Padding. You can also use Border attributes to place borders around a layer. All of these attributes are covered in Chapter 11.

Figure 14.12 Internet Explorer and Netscape 6 can provide scrollbars for content that exceeds the dimensions of the layer. You can also designate this content as visible or hidden.

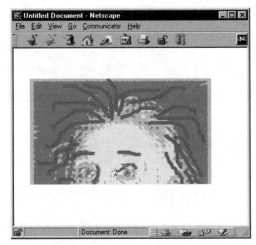

Figure 14.13 The clipping region allows you to define which areas of the layer are visible or hidden when the page loads. In this instance, only the top half of the image is being displayed on load.

■ The clipping area is unrelated to overflow. Overflow is simply related to the layer's dimensions, regardless of whether a clipping region is defined.

POSITIONING PROPERTIES

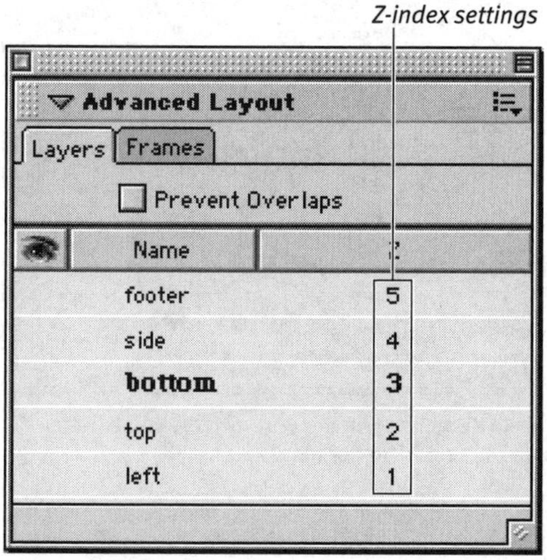

Z-index settings

Figure 14.14 The Layers panel lists all the layers on the current page. The layer name displayed in bold is the one currently selected.

About the Layers Panel

The Layers panel (**Figure 14.14**) lists all the layers on the current page. When you create a new layer, a generic name, such as Layer1, will appear in the Layers panel.

To view the Layers panel:

◆ From the menu bar, select Window > Others > Layers.

or

Press F2.

Either way, the Layers panel will appear as a part of the Advanced Layout panel group.

ABOUT THE LAYERS PANEL

About the Grid

The grid displays an incremental series of boxes that look like graph paper. You can use grid lines to guide you in positioning or resizing layers.

To view the grid:

◆ From the menu bar, select View > Grid > Show Grid.

The grid will appear (**Figure 14.15**).

About the rulers

The rulers can be displayed along the top and left of the Document window to guide you in positioning and resizing layers.

To view the rulers:

◆ From the menu bar, select View > Rulers > Show.

The rulers will appear (**Figure 14.16**).

✔ Tip

■ I discuss changing the preferences, snap-to settings, and units of the grid and rulers in *Customizing the Document Window* in Chapter 1.

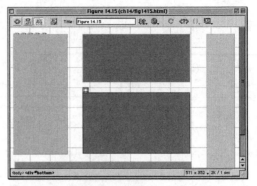

Figure 14.15 Viewing the grid can give you a better idea of the position of things.

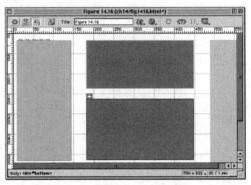

Figure 14.16 View the rulers, with or without the grid, when you want to measure exactly where things are.

Draw Layer button on Insert toolbar

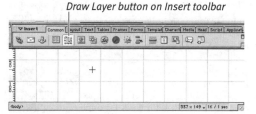

Figure 14.17 After you click on the Draw Layer button, the pointer will turn into crosshairs you can use to draw the layer.

Layer marker

Figure 14.18 After you draw a layer, it appears exactly where you positioned it. A layer marker also appears in the window, indicating the layer's location in the code.

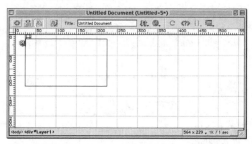

Figure 14.19 When you place a layer using the Insert menu, a default layer appears. You can change the properties of this layer after placing it.

Creating Layers

Before you can dig your fingers into all the nifty layer features, you need to put a layer on the page. You insert a layer by drawing it on the page.

To draw a layer:

1. On either the Common or the Layout panel of the Insert toolbar, click on the Draw Layer button: 🔲. The cursor will appear as crosshairs in the Document window (**Figure 14.17**).

2. Click the cursor at the point where you want the top-left corner of the layer to begin, and drag the cursor to where you want the bottom-right corner to be.

3. Let go of the mouse button, and a layer will appear in the Document window (**Figure 14.18**).

Along with the layer, a layer marker will appear that shows where the layer's code appears within the code of the page 🔲.

✔ Tips

■ If the layer markers aren't visible, view them by selecting View > Visual Aids > Invisible Elements. You can toggle the markers on and off this way.

■ You can also use the command Insert > Layer to insert a default layer on your page. This layer looks like the one in **Figure 14.19**. You can modify the layer's size and location after placing it.

■ You can modify the default layer properties. See *Layer Preferences*, near the end of this chapter.

■ If you've been using Layout view to draw tables, switch back to Standard view; you can't draw layers while in Layout view.

■ To stop drawing a layer and cancel out, press Esc.

CREATING LAYERS

Selecting Layers

In order to delete, move, or resize a layer, you need to select it. Clicking within a layer does not select a layer, but you can do so in several ways.

To select a layer:

1. Click on or within the layer.

2. Click on the layer's selection handle at the top-left corner of the layer (**Figure 14.20**).

    or

    Click on the name of the layer in the Layers panel.

    or

    Click on the layer's border.

    or

    Click on the layer's marker in the Document window.

    or

    Click on the layer's tag (<span>, <div>, <layer>, or <ilayer>) in the tag selector at the left of the Document window's status bar (Figure 14.20).

Eight points, called handles, will appear on the edges of the layer (**Figure 14.21**), and the name of the layer will become selected in the Layers panel. And, of course, our good old friend the Property inspector will display Layer properties (**Figure 14.22**).

Deleting a layer

When a layer is selected, you can edit it, or you can delete it if you choose.

To delete a layer:

1. Select the layer.

2. Press the Delete or Backspace key.

The layer will go away.

Layer marker
Layer selection handle
Name of layer in the Layers panel

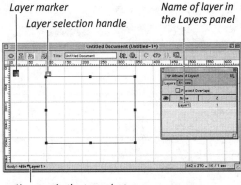

<div> *tag in the tag selector*

Figure 14.20 To select a layer, you can click on the layer's selection handle; the layer marker in the Document window; the <div> or <span> tag in the tag selector; or the layer's name in the Layers panel.

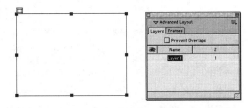

Figure 14.21 When a layer is selected, eight handles will appear around the borders of the layer, and its name will appear highlighted in the Layers panel.

Figure 14.22 The Property inspector, displaying Layer properties.

Figure 14.23 Type a new name for your layer in the Property inspector's Layer ID text box.

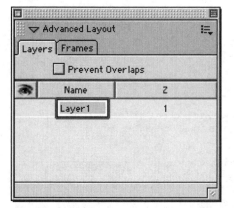

Figure 14.24 Type a new name for your layer in the Layers panel.

Figure 14.25 If you're working with pages that use Netscape's proprietary `<layer>` tag, the Property inspector will display properties for that tag, even though you can't insert it in Dreamweaver MX unless you hand-code it.

Renaming a Layer

Layer names are used by the browser and by any scripts that treat the layer as a script object. By default, Dreamweaver names each successive layer "Layer1," "Layer2," and so on.

You may want to give your layers more meaningful names so that you can easily decipher them from the list in the Layers panel.

To rename a layer:

1. Select the layer.

2. In the Property inspector, select the old layer name and delete it (**Figure 14.23**).

    or

    In the Layers panel, click on the name of the layer and hold down the mouse button (Windows) or double-click on the layer name (Macintosh). The row holding the name of the layer will become highlighted, and the name of the layer will appear in a text box.

3. Type the new name of the layer in the text box (**Figure 14.24**).

The layer will be renamed.

About Layer Tags

There are four possible tags that can be used in creating layers. The `<div>` and `<span>` tags create what is called a CSS layer; absolute positioning is only available to the `<div>` tag.

Additionally, some designers use Netscape's proprietary layers tags, `<layer>` and `<ilayer>`. In past incarnations of Dreamweaver, you could choose these tags from the Property inspector's Layer tag drop-down menu. See the Appendix P on the Web site for more about these tags.

All you need to know about them for our purposes is that when you open a page that uses these tags, you can still select the layer by clicking on its handle, and the properties of the layer will still appear in the Property inspector (**Figure 14.25**). Note: the Property inspector may still erroneously display the layer's tag as DIV in the tag drop-down menu..

Moving Layers

The location of a layer on the page is measured by the distance from the top-left corner of the page (or the parent layer) to the top-left corner of the layer itself. You can change the location of a layer at any point—before or after you put content in it.

To change the layer's location by dragging:

1. Select the layer.

2. Click on the layer's selection handle (**Figure 14.26**) and drag it to its new location (**Figure 14.27**).

   or

   Use the arrow keys to move the layer in one-pixel increments.

✔ Tip

■ To move the layer using the grid's snapping increment, select the layer and hold down the Shift key while using the arrow keys to move the layer.

Layer selection handle

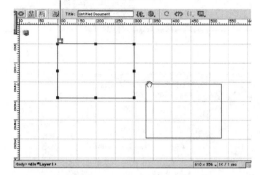

Figure 14.26 Click on the layer's selection handle and drag it to a new location.

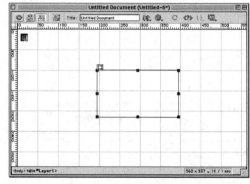

Figure 14.27 The layer is now in its new location.

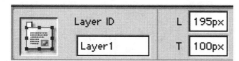

Figure 14.28 Type the X and Y (Left and Top) coordinates in the Property inspector's L and T text boxes.

To change a layer's location using exact measurements:

1. Select the layer.

2. In the Property inspector, type the distance of the layer from the left margin in the L (Left) text box, and the distance of the layer from the top margin in the T (Top) text box (**Figure 14.28**).

3. Press Enter (Return), or click on the Apply button (Apply does not work on Mac OS X).

The layer will change position on the page.

✔ Tip

- The default units for positioning are pixels, but you can use cm, in, and other units. See the sidebar *Units,* in Chapter 11.

Aligning Your Layers

New in Dreamweaver MX: You can align the edges and the sizes of any two or more layers. This is a great boon, because otherwise you have to select each layer and then check its dimensions with the Property inspector to make sure they're the same. Because we're drawing layers by hand, it's dang-nigh impossible to get them lined up and sized right by eyeballing it.

Select the first layer, and then select additional layers by holding down the Shift key while you click to select them.

To make your layers the same height or width, select Modify > Align > Make Same Width *or* Make Same Height.

To make your layers edges line up vertically or horizontally, from the menu bar, select Modify > Align > [Left, Right, Top, or Bottom].

I lined up the layers in **Figure 14.2** by using both of these commands. For example, after you line up the top of two layers, you can then use the Make Same Height command to stretch a layer so the bottoms are lined up, too. I recommend doing these steps both at the beginning layout stage and at the final cleanup stage of designing your page. After you place content, you may need to perform these steps to get the details right.

Note: The layers will align to or resize to the *last* layer selected. This layer will also have black selection handles, while the other selected layers will have white handles.

MOVING LAYERS

Resizing Layers

You can change the height and width of a layer at any time, before or after you add content to the layer. You can resize a layer by clicking and dragging, by using the keyboard, or by typing exact measurements in the Property inspector.

To resize a layer by dragging:

1. Select the layer. The handles will appear.

2. To change both the height and width of the layer, click on one of the corner handles and drag it (**Figure 14.29**).

3. To change only one of the dimensions, click on one of the side handles and drag it (**Figure 14.30**).

When you let go of the mouse button, the layer will be resized.

To resize a layer using the keyboard:

1. Select the layer.

2. To resize by eyeballing it, press Ctrl+arrow (Option+arrow) to move the left or bottom edge a couple pixels at a time.

3. To resize using the grid's snapping increment, press Shift+Ctrl+arrow (Shift+Option+arrow).

✔ Tip

- To find out how to change the grid settings, refer to *Measuring in the Document Window* in Chapter 1.

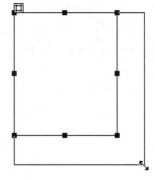

Figure 14.29 Click on the corner handle and drag it to resize two sides of a layer at once.

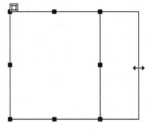

Figure 14.30 Click on a side handle and drag it to move one side of a layer.

Figure 14.31 You can type new dimensions for your layer in the W(idth) and H(eight) text boxes in the Property inspector.

To resize a layer using exact measurements:

1. View the Property inspector, if you haven't already.

2. Select the layer.

3. In the Property inspector, type the width of the layer in the W (Width) text box, and the height of the layer in the H (Height) text box (**Figure 14.31**).

4. Press Enter (Return), or click on the Apply button (Apply does not work on Mac OS X).

✔ Tip

■ If you resize a layer with content already inside it, such as an image or a piece of text, you cannot make the layer visibly smaller than the content it contains. You can still resize the layer's measurements (as displayed by the Property inspector), but the layer will expand, or rather, not shrink, to fit the content. See *The Clipping Area* and *Content Overflow* to find out how to manage content size.

Overlapping and Nesting

One neato thing about layers is that you can overlap two layers, and you can also create a layer that's positioned relative to another (called *nesting*).

To overlap two or more layers:

◆ All you need to do is move two layers so that they overlap, or create a layer that shares window area with another layer (**Figure 14.32**). Make sure the Prevent Overlaps checkbox is unchecked before you try overlapping.

Nesting layers

You can nest layers, which may or may not also overlap. Nested layers are placed on the page in relative position to the top left corner of another layer rather than the top left corner of the page.

To nest a layer within a layer:

1. Create the first layer.

2. If you want the layers to overlap, make sure the Prevent Overlaps checkbox is unchecked on the Layers panel.

3. To nest two layers, you can:

   Draw a layer anywhere on the page (inside the first, overlapping the first, or anywhere else on the page) while holding down the Ctrl (Option) key to make sure the second layer is positioned relative to the first (**Figure 14.33**).

   Or, see the next page to nest two existing layers.

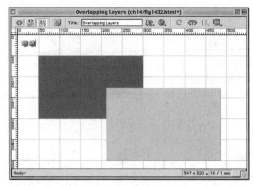

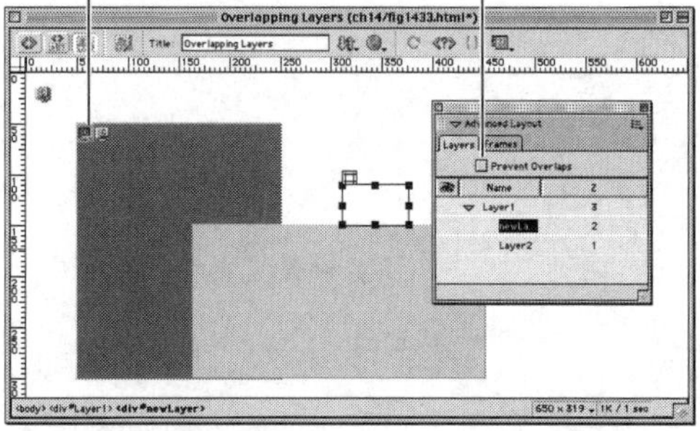

Figure 14.32 Two overlapping layers.

Prevent Overlaps checkbox unchecked

Layer markers of nested layers

Figure 14.33 I drew one layer nested with the other—that means that if I move the parent layer, the nested layer will move, too. Nested means positioned in relation to the parent. In this case, two of the nested layers overlap, and the third nested layer does not. Note how the layer markers appear inside the parent layer

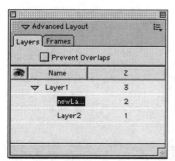

Figure 14.34
The Layers panel displays nested layers indented beneath their parent layer.

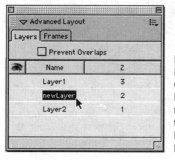

Figure 14.35 Hold down the Ctrl (Command) key and click on the name of the to-be-nested layer in the Layers panel.

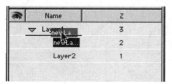

Figure 14.36 Drag the layer onto its parent layer's name.

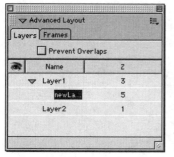

Figure 14.37 Let go of the child layer, and it will become nested, and its name will be indented under its parent.

In the Layers panel, nested layers are indented beneath the name of the *parent* layer—that is, the layer that contains them (**Figure 14.34**).

✔ Tip

- To prevent layers from overlapping or nesting at all, check the Prevent Overlaps checkbox on the Layers panel. If you have already overlapped some layers when you check this option, and you want to un-overlap them, you'll need to do it manually, by dragging.

To nest two existing layers:

1. In the Layers panel, click on the name of the layer you wish to nest inside another layer (the child layer). A layer icon will appear (**Figure 14.35**).

2. Hold down the Ctrl (Command) key and drag the name of the layer on top of the name of the parent layer. A box will appear around the name of the new parent (**Figure 14.36**).

3. Let go of the mouse button. The name of the child layer you dragged will appear indented beneath the name of the new parent (**Figure 14.37**).

You may decide that you don't want one layer to be nested inside the other.

To un-nest a layer:

◆ Click on the layer's name (**Figure 14.38**) and drag it so that it's no longer indented beneath the parent layer's name.

✔ Tips

■ When you nest or un-nest a layer, its position may change (in other words, it may move; see **Figure 14.39**), because nested layers' positions (on the X-Y axis) are based on the parent layer's position. Just drag it back to where you want it.

■ In the Layers panel, you can collapse or expand the list of layers that are nested within the layer. Just click on the + sign next to the parent layer's name to expand the list, or the – sign to collapse the list.

■ When you're working with nested layers, the easiest way to select a layer is by clicking on its name.

■ You can also determine the stacking order of layers by dragging their names around. To find out about stacking order, refer to *Stacking Order,* later in this chapter.

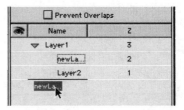

Figure 14.38 Click on the child layer that you want to un-nest.

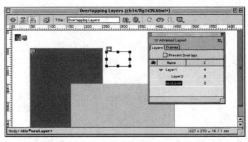

Figure 14.39 Drag the child away from its parent, and it will no longer be nested. Note that the new layer moved from its position in **Figure 14.33** because its position is now relative to the upper-left corner of the page, not of its parent.

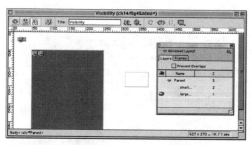

Figure 14.40 The layer that was on top and visible in **Figure 14.39** has been hidden.

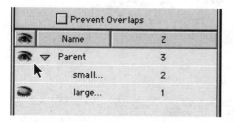

Figure 14.41 You can set the visibility of each layer individually by changing the status of the eyeball in the visibility column.

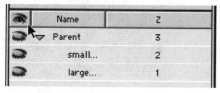

Figure 14.42 Click on the eyeball button at the top of the visibility column to show or hide all layers at once.

■ When you select a hidden layer (by clicking on its name in the Layers panel), it becomes visible while it's selected.

■ You can use the Show-Hide layer behavior (see Chapter 16) with links, rollovers, or timelines, so that layers can appear after the page loads with them hidden.

Changing Layer Visibility

Layer visibility also determines whether a layer will be visible when a page loads.

And for convenience when you're working on a page with lots of layers, you may want to show or hide various layers depending on what area of the page you're working with. This is especially convenient when you're working with overlapping or nested layers.

The layer's visibility is determined by its "eyeball status" in the Layers panel. The eyeball is a three-way toggle switch:

◆ A closed eye 🌰 means the layer is hidden.

◆ An open eye 👁 means the layer is visible.

◆ No eyeball means that the layer's visibility is determined by the status of the parent layer, if it's a nested layer.

To show or hide a layer:

1. In the Layers panel, click on the name of the layer you wish to view or hide.

2. Click within the leftmost column until you change to the desired eyeball status: closed, open, or none.

The layers will appear or hide (**Figure 14.41**), as indicated by the eyeball (**Figure 14.42**).

To show or hide all layers:

◆ Click on the eyeball button at the top left of the Layers panel (**Figure 14.43**).

All the layers will appear with an open eyeball, or disappear with a closed eyeball.

✔ Tips

■ Layer visibility goes beyond working with Dreamweaver: Hidden layers will not appear on the page when viewed in the browser window.

Stacking Order

The stacking order, or Z-index, of layers determines the order in which the browser will draw them, as well as their stacking priority (**Figures 14.43** through **14.45**).

✔ Tips

■ Although Dreamweaver uses the term "stacking order" to describe the Z-index, that doesn't mean that it's an exclusive scale. If you have three non-overlapping layers on different parts of the page, such as columns or toolbars, you can make the Z-index the same for all of them.

■ If two layers with the same Z-index (or with no Z-index specified) overlap, the first layer listed in the code will be placed on the top of the heap.

You can change each layer's Z-index individually, or you can determine the stacking order of all the layers in the Layers panel.

To change the Z-index of a single layer:

1. Select the layer.

2. In the Property inspector (**Figure 14.46**), type a Z-index for the layer: the bigger the number, the higher the priority (a Z-index of 2 goes on top of a Z-index of 1).

The layer you selected may change its position in the stacking order so that it's on top of or behind another layer.

Figure 14.43 The little person has the highest Z-index in this little montage.

Figure 14.44 In this version, I changed the overlap so that the gun has the highest Z-index, the sign is second, and the person is third. The money remains on the bottom.

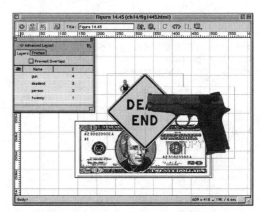

Figure 14.45 This is what the carnage looks like in Dreamweaver.

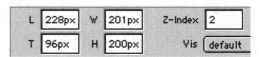

Figure 14.46 You can set the Z-index by typing a number in the Property inspector's Z-index text box, or by double-clicking the Z-index in the Layers panel and typing a new number there.

STACKING ORDER

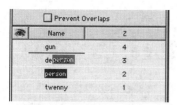

Figure 14.47 You can move the order of the layers in the Z-index by selecting a layer name and dragging it up or down in the Layers panel. You can also type a new number directly in the panel by double-clicking on the Z-index number for a layer.

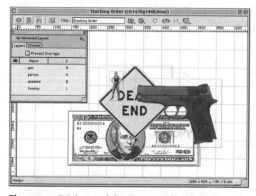

Figure 14.48 I dragged the "person" layer up through the stacking order. Its Z-index is now 4 (Dreamweaver gets sloppy with the numbering), and it's visible above the "deadend" layer.

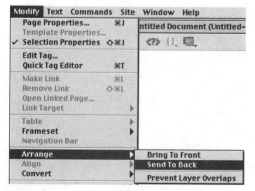

Figure 14.49 You can move a layer to the top or bottom of the stack by selecting it and then selecting Modify > Arrange > from the Document window menu bar.

To rearrange the stacking order in the Layers panel:

◆ Click on the name of a layer in the Layers panel, and drag it up or down to change its position (**Figure 14.47**).

The first layer listed in the Layers panel (and therefore, listed first in the code) has the highest priority in the stacking order, and so on down the line (**Figure 14.48**).

Using layout-style movement to stack layers

New in Dreamweaver MX is a feature that takes a page from layout programs such as Quark and PageMaker. The concept is the same: changing the stacking order. The vocabulary is different: You "move to front" or "send to back" the layer you've selected.

To rearrange which layer appears on top or in back:

1. Select the layer.

2. From the menu bar, select Modify > Arrange > Send to Back or Modify > Arrange > Bring to Front to move the layer to the bottom or top of the stacking order. (**Figure 14.49**).

Your layer's Z-index will change. To rearrange the layers in between the top and bottom, use one of the methods on the preceding page.

continued on next page

✔ Tips

- Remember to be sure you've selected the layer itself rather than something inside it. It's easy to click on an image within a layer and then wonder why you can't modify it the way you intended. After clicking on that image, click on the layer's selection handle.

- When you select a layer or click on an image within that layer, it will visibly appear on top of the other layers while you're editing it (**Figure 14.50**). Just click on some blank space in the Document window to see where it lives when it's not selected.

- Take care not to drag the layer's name onto the name of another layer; this will indent one layer beneath the other and thereby nest the layers (see *Overlapping and Nesting Layers,* earlier in this chapter).

- The Layers panel may renumber the Z-index strangely when you drag layers; you might start out with index numbers of 3, 2, and 1 and end up with 6, 4, and 1. You can reset these in the Property inspector, if you like, but as long as they don't disrupt anything, you can leave nonadjacent numbers alone.

Figure 14.50 In this closeup, I've selected the layer "twenny." No change has been made to the Z-index, but the layer appears on the top of the stack when selected so you can edit it or its content.

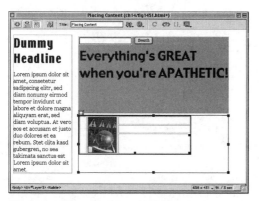

Figure 14.51 You can add any kind of content you want to a layer. On this page-in-progress I added a table, some text, a piece of Flash text, and an image to the various layers on this page. Just about the only thing you can't put in a layer is a frame.

Figure 14.52 Navigator 4.0 (on the left) displays only the part of the layer that contains content, not the entire layer. Netscape 6 displays like Explorer.

Figure 14.53 Pre-4.0 browsers such as Opera 3.2 display the content of layers, but ignore the positioning attributes. The person image was centered within the layer and is now centered on the page.

- When drawing layers, Netscape has a resize bug for which Dreamweaver offers a JavaScript fix. See the sidebar, *Netscape Resize Fix*, later in this chapter.

Content and Layers

A layer can hold nearly any other kind of HTML content: text, images, tables, forms, multimedia content, and, as discussed previously, other layers.

To add content to a layer, click on the layer so that the insertion point appears within it, and then add content as you would to any other part of a Web page (**Figure 14.51**).

✔ Tips

- You can drag content from outside a layer to within the layer's borders. Just select the object you wish to move, hold down the mouse button, and drag it within the borders of the layer.

- You can put nearly anything in a layer, except a frame. You can put a form in a layer, but you cannot spread form content out over more than one layer.

- If a layer contains less content than the layer's borders would indicate, Navigator 4.0 displays only the content (not the entire layer)—although the layer's dimensions will still be considered in the layout. Explorer 4.0 or later and Netscape 4.5 or later display the entire layer dimensions, regardless of the content (**Figure 14.52**).

- Pre-4.0 browsers will display the content of layers, but will ignore the positioning, overlap, and visibility attributes. The <div> tag acts like a <p> tag, and the <span> tag acts like a <br> tag (**Figure 14.53**).

- After you place content, the bottom edge of a layer may move down as it stretches to fit the content. See the sidebar *Aligning Layers* for a shortcut in making your edges line up. Also, see the upcoming section, *Content Overflow*, to control whether your layer should resize to fit the content or whether it should have scrollbars instead.

Layers and Styles

All the versatile style sheet attributes that I discussed in Chapter 11—not just position-ing—can be applied to layers.

When you create a layer in Dreamweaver, the style attributes that guide the layer's behav-ior generally appear as the ID attribute directly within the `<div>` tag (rather than as a class or tag redefinition, in which case the attributes would appear in the `<style>` area of the `<head>` tag).

Styles for layers

You can redefine the `<div>` or `<span>` tag so that it attains new properties that will be applied to every layer you create (**Figure 14.54**). For instance, you could redefine the `<div>` tag so that it always has a solid, 1-pixel border.

You can also create a style class that you can apply to a layer by selecting the `<div>` or `<span>` tag and then applying the class to the tag (**Figure 14.55**). For example, you could create a style called `.box` that would include a solid, 1-pixel border and use it on selected layers.

Or, if you're a hand-coder (or learning to become one), you can add styles into the `<div>` tag.

Layer code—pre-content—looks like this:

```
<div id="box2"
style="position:absolute; left:23px;
top:155px; width:358px; height:33px;
z-index:2; background-color: #FFCC33">

</div>
```

All that stuff in the `<div>` tag is style sheet code. You can apply as many additional style attributes to a layer as you want. You can apply them by hand, by using the Property inspector on a layer, by creating a style class, or by redefining the tag.

Styles and content

To preserve your layout, I strongly suggest using CSS styles to format any text put in your layer—otherwise, your users' browser settings may make the text appear too large or small. In that case, your layers may stretch to include the text, or they may include vast expanses of emptiness with no text at all.

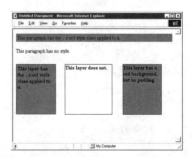

Figure 14.54 On this page, I redefined the `<div>` tag using style sheets so that all layers made with the `<div>` tag would have a one-pixel-wide black border.

Figure 14.55 On this page, I assigned the .red class to the first paragraph and to the first of the three boxes. The third box has a red background color, but it is not modified by the .red class.

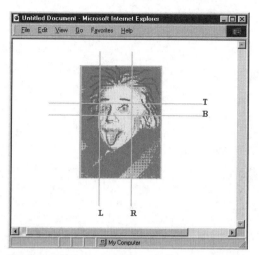

Figure 14.56 Clipping explained: The layer is the same size as the image. Lines T and B are measured from the top of the layer. T is 70 pixels from the top, and B is 96 pixels from the top. Lines L and R are measured from the left of the layer. Line L is 20 pixels from the left, and Line R is 101 pixels from the left. The rectangular area framed by these lines is what will be left visible. (I drew these lines; you're not going to see them when you clip a layer.)

Figure 14.57 The layer as it looks post-clip (in Dreamweaver, so you can see the outlines of the layer).

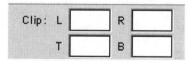

Figure 14.58 Define your clipping area using the Property inspector.

The Clipping Area

Layers are somewhat like table cells in that they expand to fit the content you put in them. Although you can specify an exact size for a layer, it will expand beyond those dimensions if you place larger content in it.

A layer is unlike a table cell, however, in that you can specify a clipping area for it. As I mentioned earlier, the clipping area is the part of the layer that is visible; it's somewhat like cropping an image, only the rest of the content remains hidden rather than being deleted out of the file. (The file size of clipped content remains the same as if you hadn't clipped it.)

You can make your clipping area the same size as the layer's area, or smaller than those dimensions (**Figures 14.56** and **14.57**). (You could make it larger, but that kind of defeats the purpose of having a layer of that size.)

To define the clipping area:

1. Display the Property inspector and expand it so that all the properties are displayed, if they're not already visible.

2. Select the layer.

3. Define the clipping area by typing the numbers that define the region in the Top, Left, Right, and Bottom text boxes of the Property inspector (**Figure 14.58**).

4. Press Enter (Return) to apply the changes to the layer.

The area defined by the clipping area will be visible, and the rest will be hidden.

continued on next page

✔ Tips

- The L and R measurements are from the left edge of the layer, and the T and B measurements are from the top edge of the layer (**Figure 14.56**).

- The clipping occurs as follows: The area from the left margin of the layer to the L measurement is clipped out, and the area from the R measurement to the right margin is also clipped out. The area between L and R, therefore, is visible. The same goes for T and B, respectively (**Figure 14.57**).

- Unspecified units are in pixels; you may define other units in the following format: 1.5cm (no space between the number and the unit). See the sidebar *Units* in Chapter 11 for more on choosing different units.

- To find how to manage content that exceeds a layer's dimensions, see *Content Overflow* on the following page.

- For Navigator, you can define all four of these areas, or you can define only the bottom and right (the top and left will be set to zero, which is the top-left margin of the layer.)

- For Explorer, however, you *must* indicate a measurement of zero for the top and left, if that's what you want.

- You can use the behavior Change Property, described in Chapter 16, to make the clipping area change when a user clicks a button or mouses over part of the image.

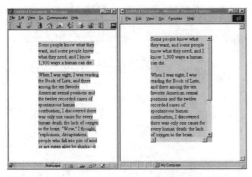

Figure 14.59 Navigator 4 (left) displaying the hidden setting, and Explorer displaying the scroll setting for the same layer. Netscape 6 displays scrollbars, but Navigator 4 doesn't.

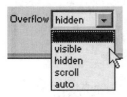

Figure 14.60 Select a content overflow setting from the Overflow drop-down menu on the Property inspector.

Content Overflow

When the content of a layer is larger than the layer's dimensions (independent of the layer's clipping area), you have what is called *content overflow*.

You can let the browser defaults take care of content overflow in their own ways, or you can set one of three properties for content overflow: hidden, visible, or scroll. The last option adds scrollbars to the layer so users can scroll to see the rest of the layer's content (**Figure 14.59**).

To control content overflow:

1. Select the layer.

2. In the expanded Property inspector, choose *hidden, visible*, or *scroll* from the Overflow drop-down menu (**Figure 14.60**). Your changes will be applied.

Dreamweaver doesn't display content overflow—it always displays all the contents of the layer, regardless of whether those contents would otherwise exceed the layer's dimensions. For example, even if a large image would be concealed in the browser window using the clipping area or content overflow settings, Dreamweaver will still display the entire image.

✔ Tips

■ If you don't choose a setting (if you leave the drop-down menu blank), the browser will display all the contents of the layer, regardless of the layer's dimensions.

■ The auto setting translates as hidden in Navigator and scroll in Explorer.

■ Navigator 4 does not support the scroll setting.

Setting a Background

Layers, like tables, table cells, and CSS text blocks, can have their own background colors or background images. Layer backgrounds will be layered over other background colors or images on the page (**Figure 14.61**).

To set a layer background color:

1. Select the layer.

2. In the Property inspector, type a hex code or color name in the Color text box.

   or

   Click on the color box to pop open the color picker, and choose a color by clicking on it (**Figure 14.62**).

   or

   In the Color selection menu, click on the System Color button [icon] to open the Color dialog box.

✔ Tip

- For information about using the Color dialog box, see Chapter 3.

To set a layer background image:

1. Select the layer.

2. In the Property inspector, type the URL of the background image in the Bg Image text box (**Figure 14.63**).

   or

   Click on the Browse button to open the Select Image File dialog box. Browse through the files and folders on your computer until you find the image file you want to use; then click Open (Choose) to select the file.

✔ Tip

- You can apply additional attributes to a background image using style sheets. See the section of Chapter 11 called *Background Attributes*.

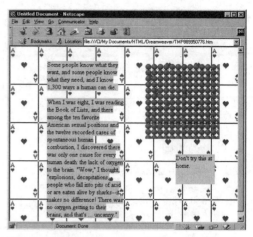

Figure 14.61 This self-consciously ugly page has a background image, over which the three layers are superimposed. In the layer at the upper right, the background image is a transparent GIF through which the background of the page shows.

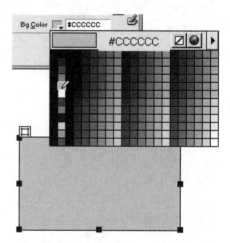

Figure 14.62 You can set a layer background color by clicking on the color box and choosing a browser-safe color from the color picker.

Figure 14.63 Type the URL for your background image in the Bg Image text box, or click on the Browse button to select an image from your local site.

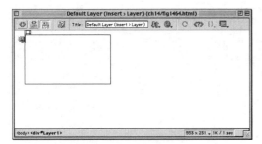

Figure 14.64 A default layer placed using the menu command Insert > Layer.

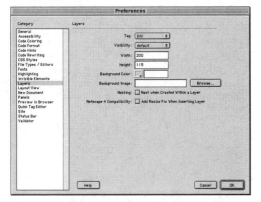

Figure 14.65 The Layers panel of the Preferences dialog box. Click on Layers in the Category list box to display these options.

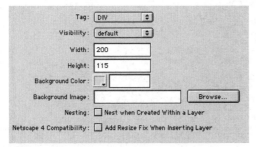

Figure 14.66 A closeup of the Layers panel of the Preferences dialog box.

Layer Preferences

When you insert a layer using the Insert menu, Dreamweaver plunks down a default layer (**Figure 14.64**), and you can then adjust those properties. Of course, Dreamweaver being so clever, you can adjust the properties for those default layers, too. All the default properties except size properties will also be applied to layers you draw using the Draw Layer button on the Insert toolbar.

To set default layer properties:

1. From the menu bar, select Edit > Preferences (on Mac OS X, choose Dreamweaver > Preferences). The Preferences dialog box will appear.

2. In the Category list box at the left of the dialog box, click on Layers. The Layers panel of the dialog box will appear (**Figures 14.65** and **14.66**).

3. You can decide whether to use a `<div>` or `<span>` tag for your layers by default. To change the default, select `<span>` from the Tag drop-down menu.

4. By default, visibility of the layers is controlled by the activity on the page. To make all layers visible or hidden by default, choose one of those options from the Visibility drop-down menu. You can also choose Inherit to have nested layers inherit their visibility from their parents.

5. The dimensions of a default layer are 200x115 pixels. To change these, type new dimensions in the Width and Height text boxes.

6. You can set a default background color or image for all new layers; for instance, you may want all your layers to start out pink. Set these attributes as described in *Setting a Background,* earlier in this chapter.

continued on next page

7. The Nesting option, when checked, makes all overlapping layers, or layers drawn within other layers, nested by default.

8. The Netscape 4 Compatibility option automatically adds JavaScript to each page that features one or more layers. The script fixes a resize bug; to use it, check the Add Resize Fix when Inserting Layer checkbox. See the sidebar, below, for more details.

9. When you're all hunky-dory with your choices, click OK to close the Preferences dialog box. Your choices will be applied to your next new layer.

✔ Tip

■ You can toggle the automatic nesting of layers on and off by holding down the Ctrl (Option) key.

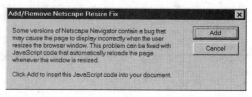

Figure 14.67 Click on Add to add the resize script to your page.

Figure 14.68 This is what the Netscape Resize script looks like in the Code inspector.

Netscape Resize Fix

Netscape Navigator version 4 and later display layers, but when you resize a Navigator window, any layers on the page may move around or scale improperly. Sometimes they disappear entirely.

Dreamweaver offers a small bit of JavaScript that detects whether the browser is Navigator 4, and if so, forces Navigator to reload the page when the window is resized, and therefore to redraw the layers properly.

To add this fix automatically to each and every page that uses layers, use the Netscape 4 Compatibility option as described in step 8 in *Layer Preferences* (this page).

You can also add this fix to a single page, even if it doesn't use layers.

1. From the menu bar, select Commands > Add/Remove Netscape Resize Fix. The dialog box in **Figure 14.67** will appear.

2. Click on Add to add the fix. The code is shown in **Figure 14.68**.

To remove the resize fix—for instance, if the page no longer uses layers or if you're saving a 3.0 version of the page—repeat these steps and click on Remove.

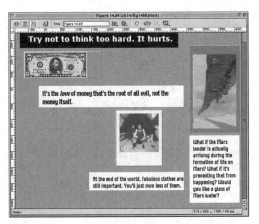

Figure 14.69 It would be a pain in the butt to write the code for tables that would replicate this layers-based layout. It's helpful to align the edges of layers, where possible (see the sidebar *Aligning Layers*).

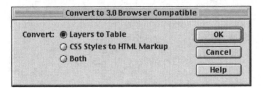

Figure 14.70 The Convert to 3.0 Browser Compatible dialog box lets you save layers as tables, style sheets as font tags, or both.

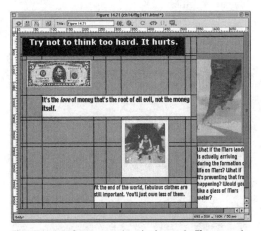

Figure 14.71 After converting the layers in **Figure 14.69** into tables, this is what the page looks like in Dreamweaver. I'll have to realign the text and images—I had CSS box properties such as padding attached to the layer DIV tags, and now I can apply those styles to the paragraphs or align each by hand.

Converting Layers to Tables (and Vice Versa)

As versatile a layout tool as layers are, it's still the case that only version 4 and later browsers display them properly—although the content may be visible in earlier browsers, the positioning and Z-index properties will be ignored, which renders the layers useless.

You can, however, export a layer-designed page into table format and then use a browser-detection behavior (see Chapter 16) to send the browser to the layered or non-layered page.

You can also use layers to create a mockup for a complex layout and then convert your design into a table-based layout—although the Layout Tables feature of Dreamweaver will do the job, too (see Chapter 12).

To convert layers to tables, in three steps:

1. Open the page that contains the layers you want to save as a table (**Figure 14.69**). Save the page if you haven't done so.

2. From the menu bar, select File > Convert > 3.0 Browser Compatible. The Convert to 3.0 Browser Compatible dialog box will appear (**Figure 14.70**).

3. Select the Layers to Table radio button, and click on OK. A new, unnamed window will appear, containing a table that reproduces your layers layout (**Figure 14.71**).

Don't forget to save the new page.

✔ Tip

■ Dreamweaver cannot convert overlapping or nested layers. To prevent layers from overlapping before you begin designing, select the Prevent Overlaps checkbox on the Layers panel. If you have overlapping or nested layers on your page, you must manually un-nest the layers and readjust their positions so they do not overlap.

To convert layers to tables, with more options:

1. Open the file with the layers (**Figure 14.72**) and save it under a new name (File > Save As). If you don't do this, you'll lose your original layers design when you save your document.

2. From the menu bar, select Modify > Convert > Convert Layers to Table. The Convert Layers to Table dialog box will appear (**Figure 14.73**).

3. In the Table Layout area of the dialog box, click on either Most Accurate or Smallest. Most Accurate will perfectly replicate the placement on the page, but it may create an ungodly number of tiny cells in order to do so. The Smallest: Collapse Empty Cells setting will eliminate small gaps between layers and create a more stream-lined layout using a simpler table.

   If you choose Smallest, you can set the minimum number of pixels a column or row can be before it's included in the lay-out of the table. The default is 4.

4. Check the Use Transparent GIFs check box, to insert transparent spacer images in the bottom row of your table to guar-antee exact widths for your columns. For more about controlling column widths, see Chapter 12.

5. To center your table on the page, select the Center on Page check box. Otherwise, your table will be left-aligned.

6. The other options—Prevent Layer Overlaps, Show Layer Panel, Show Grid, and Snap to Grid—control the visibility of your layout tools; these are really more useful when converting tables to layers.

7. Click OK. Dreamweaver will convert your layers to a table (**Figure 14.74**).

Figure 14.72 My layers page looks different in Netscape 6 and IE 5. Why? That's the mystery of the browser. I could spend an hour messing around with my typography and my layers' overflow settings—but, to solve my problem in this case I'm going to convert my page into tables.

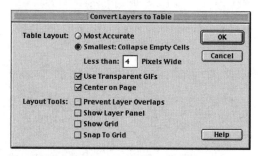

Figure 14.73 The Convert Layers to Table dialog box lets you set options for controlling the layout of the new table. Because we saw the "most accurate" setting on the last page, I'm going to use the "smallest" setting.

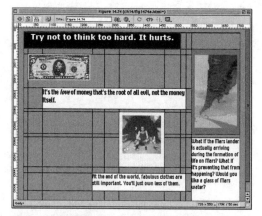

Figure 14.74 Dreamweaver converted the layers-based design into a tables-based page. Each layer is a table cell; transparent GIFs also space the content.

CONVERTING LAYERS TO TABLES

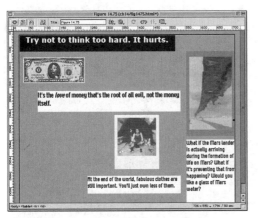

Figure 14.75 You can temporarily turn off table borders to see what the page will look like by selecting View > Visual Aids > Table Borders.

Figure 14.76 You can work with your new page in Layout Mode after you've converted it.

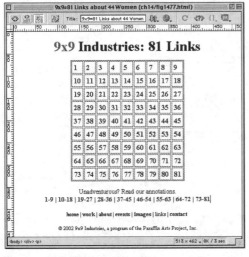

Figure 14.77 Tables-based layout.

✔ Tips

- You can temporarily toggle off table borders to see the layout more clearly. From the menu bar, select View > Visual Aids > Table borders (**Figure 14.75**).

- Once you've got your table constructed, you can work in Layout Mode to modify table properties and column widths (**Figure 14.76**).

- For more details on saving CSS pages as backwards-compatible pages, see the sidebar, *Saving CSS as Plain HTML*, in Chapter 11.

Converting tables to layers

You can also convert tables to layers in order to manipulate the cells on the page for a more precise layout. You can later convert those layers back to tables, if you like.

To convert tables to layers:

1. If you have not done so, save (File > Save As) your tables-based page (**Figure 14.76**) under a new name.

   The tables-based layout in **Figure 14.77** is okay—but if I convert each cell into layers, I could use Behaviors (Chapter 16) or Timelines (Online Appendix N) to animate or otherwise control individual layers.

   continued on next page

continued on next page

CONVERTING LAYERS TO TABLES

2. From the menu bar, select Modify > Convert > Tables to Layers. The Convert Tables to Layers dialog box will appear (**Figure 14.78**).

3. The options in the dialog box let you pre-set options for the new window that will open.

◆ To automatically guard against overlaps, check the Prevent Layer Overlaps check box.

◆ Check the Show Layer panel check box to make sure the Layers panel is open when the page opens.

◆ Check the Show Grid check box to view the grid when the page opens.

◆ The last item, Snap To Grid, you may actually want to uncheck. This will make all the layers on the page align with the grid, in the set increment (the default is 50 pixels).

4. When you've made your selections, click OK to convert your tables into a layers-based page. Each table cell becomes a unique, individual layer positioned where the cell was in the original layout (**Figure 14.79**).

Now, if you like, you can reposition the layers at will. Following your design tweaks, you can follow the steps in the previous section to convert the layers back into a table (**Figure 14.80**).

✔ Tips

■ You'll get a new page if you convert by using File > Convert to 3.0, but not if you use Modify > Layout > Convert Layers to Table (or Tables to Layers). Make sure you save copies of what you need to save copies of.

■ Any layers already on the tables-based page will be left untouched when you convert tables to layers.

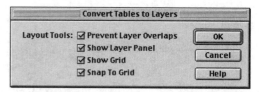

Figure 14.78 The Convert Tables to Layers dialog box offers options for creating and viewing your new layers page.

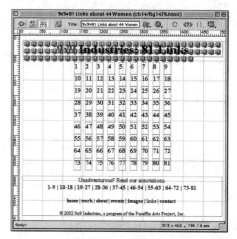

Figure 14.79 Each table cell in the original layout is now a layer, for a grand total of 83 layers (you can deselect View > Invisible Elements to hide the layer markers). Again, I wouldn't have wanted to position all those layers by hand.

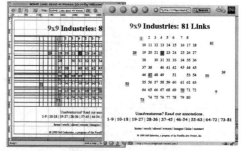

Figure 14.80 I twiddled with the layout using layers, and then converted the page back to tables and previewed it in Netscape. Using the same design in layers mode, I could create some interesting visual effects using the Drag and Drop Layers Behavior (Chapter 16) or Timelines. I made the boxes using the Box and Border style sheet attributes (Chapter 11).

Figure 14.81 Here's an example of an image you can cut up and place as slices on a Web page. You can use the entire, unsliced image as the tracing image on the background of the page.

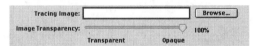

Figure 14.82 In the Page Properties dialog box, you can select an image file to use as a tracing image, and then set the opacity of that image. Tracing images will not show up in browser previews or on the Web.

Figure 14.83 This tracing image is displayed at 40 percent opacity in the Document window.

Using a Tracing Image

Some designers like to create page mockups in Photoshop (or another image editor) before production starts in on the HTML page itself. Wouldn't it be nice if the page hackers could view the mockup image behind the page and just drag and drop elements onto it?

Using Dreamweaver, you can do just that. You can display your mockup image (**Figure 14.81**) in the degree of transparency you prefer and then position layers on top of the image so that they line up exactly where God (or the designer) intended.

Then, of course, you can convert the exacting layers-based design into a tables-based page that the non-4.0 world can ooh and aah over.

To set a tracing image:

1. From the menu bar, select Modify > Page Properties. The Page Properties dialog box will appear.

2. In the Tracing Image area of the dialog box (**Figure 14.82**), type the location of the image or click on the Browse button to pop open the Select Image Source dialog box and locate the image file (.jpg, .gif, or .png) on your hard drive.

3. Drag the Image Transparency bar to set the transparency/opacity of your image so that you can work with it.

4. Click Apply to preview your tracing image (so you can adjust transparency).

   or

   Click OK to close the Page Properties dialog box.

Either way, the tracing image will appear in the Document window, behind any content already in the window (**Figure 14.83**).

continued on next page

USING A TRACING IMAGE

Now you can slice up an image in Fireworks or another editor, and then you can create a layer for each slice and drag each one onto the tracing image, replicating the image's layout (**Figure 14.84**).

To toggle the tracing image on and off:

◆ From the menu bar, select View > Tracing Image > Show.

To move the tracing image:

1. From the menu bar, select View > Tracing Image > Adjust Position. The Adjust Tracing Image Position dialog box will appear (**Figure 14.85**).

2. Type the X (top) and Y (left) coordinates for your tracing image in the text boxes.

   or

   With the Adjust Tracing Image Position dialog box open, use the arrow keys on your keyboard to move the tracing image in one-pixel increments.

3. When you're done, click OK to close the dialog box and return to the Document window.

To reset the tracing image:

◆ From the menu bar, select View > Tracing Image > Reset Position. The tracing image will resume its default coordinates.

To align the tracing image with an object:

1. Select the object, such as a layer, table cell, or image, in the Document window.

2. From the menu bar, select View > Tracing Image > Align With Selection. The tracing image and the selected layer or image will line up by their upper-left corners.

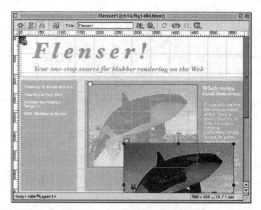

Figure 14.84 Using the tracing image as a guide, I'm placing GIF slices of the original image on the page, using layers to place them exactly. If I want to, I can replicate the tracing image and then convert the layers into tables.

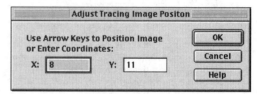

Figure 14.85 With this dialog box open, you can move the tracing image's position in the Document window using the text boxes or the arrow keys on your keyboard.

✔ Tips

■ Because 0 percent opacity is invisible, and 100 percent is completely opaque, you'll probably find that between 40 and 60 percent works best for most images.

■ Fireworks, Macromedia's image editor for the Web, lets you create a page mockup and then slice it up into smaller images that you can export into GIFs. You can then use Dreamweaver to position the images on your HTML page using layers, and line up the images so that they correspond exactly to their original locations on the mockup.

FILLING

OUT FORMS

Figure 15.1 (Netscape window screenshot)

Figure 15.1 This feedback form includes most of the different kinds of fields that you can have in a form. I laid out the form using tables.

Figure 15.2 Not all forms have to be complicated, though. Some have only a few fields.

You fill out forms routinely when you apply for a driver's license or pay taxes or change addresses. Forms have gotten to be just as routine on the Web, too.

You'll want your visitors to fill out forms because it's the most efficient way for them to give you feedback about your site or about their identities (**Figure 15.1**), or just log in (**Figure 15.2**).

Online shopping sites, visitor surveys, and guestbooks use forms to collect data (called input) from your users. This data is then sent to a form handler—usually a CGI script—which does something with this data. In some cases, such as surveys, the script simply saves the input for the site management to look at later. In other cases, such as search engines, the script takes the input and immediately uses it to provide some response or results for the user's edification. Typically, some form of interaction—even a simple thank-you page—assures the user that the information wasn't sent into a vacuum.

Dreamweaver simplifies the process of creating front-end interface forms for your site. In this chapter, you'll learn the basics of how to create and name form objects such as checkboxes, radio buttons, drop-down menus, and text fields. We'll also look at file fields, form labels, image fields, and jump menus.

Creating a Form

The first step in creating a form is to put the form itself, represented by the <form></form> tags, on your page. It will be delineated in the Document window by a dashed red line that will be invisible when the page is loaded in the browser window (**Figure 15.3**).

Dreamweaver's Insert toolbar is especially handy for automating the process.

To display form objects on the Insert toolbar:

1. If the Insert toolbar at the top of the Document window isn't open, display it by double-clicking on its Expander arrow (**Figure 15.4**). If the toolbar is hidden, select Window > Insert.

2. Click on the Forms tab.

   The Insert toolbar will display form objects (**Figure 15.5**).

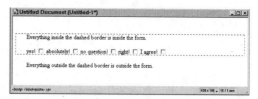

Figure 15.3 In the Document window, forms are outlined by a red, dashed border.

Figure 15.4 Double-click the Expander arrow to display the Insert toolbar.

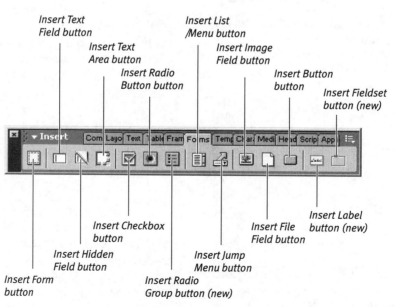

Insert Text Field button

Insert Text Area button

Insert Radio Button button

Insert List /Menu button

Insert Image Field button

Insert Button button

Insert Fieldset button (new)

Insert Checkbox button

Insert File Field button

Insert Label button (new)

Insert Hidden Field button

Insert Jump Menu button

Insert Form button

Insert Radio Group button (new)

Figure 15.5 The Insert toolbar with the Forms tab displayed.

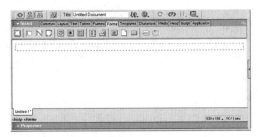

Figure 15.6 A new, blank form.

To create a form:

1. You must have invisible element viewing turned on to view Form borders. (It's usually on by default—if there's a checkmark next to Invisible Elements, it's on.) If you need to turn it on, select View > Visual Aids > Invisible Elements from the menu bar.

2. From the menu bar, select Insert > Form.

   or

   On the Forms tab of the Insert toolbar, click the Form button ▣ .

The form will appear (**Figure 15.6**). By default, your form will occupy 100 percent of the page width. The height is determined by the content you place within the form borders. You cannot resize forms with Dreamweaver, although you can format their content using tables (see Chapter 12 to find out how to use tables).

About Dynamic Forms

If you're working with an application server, and you've set up your local site to reflect this, you'll see a Dynamic button on the Property inspector when you create a list or menu object. This lets you populate the menu with items retrieved from a database rather than using hard-coded HTML tags. To specify a recordset to use for these menu items, select it from the Options From Recordset drop-down menu to select the recordset you want to use as a content source. You follow a similar process for other form tags that appear on dynamic pages, although they don't need to be populated. The Introduction to this book says more about what dynamic content is in the context of Dreamweaver MX and how Dreamweaver interacts with databases.

Forms Are Content

Although Dreamweaver enables you to create the interface for Web forms—all the buttons and menus that you need to make the form itself—it does not include the back-end tools that make the form operable. Before your visitors will be able to click the Submit button and whisk their data to you, you need to install a form handler on your server. Many popular Web hosting programs include some free scripts, such as those that process guestbooks and simple questionnaires—check your Internet provider's Web site. Some free scripts are listed on the Web site for this book; for more complex functions, you may need an engineer.

Formatting Forms

It's essential to label each field in a form; otherwise, the users won't know what the heck they're supposed to do (**Figure 15.7**). I don't specify this in the steps for adding each field because it's pretty unlikely that you're going to forget.

You can use line breaks, paragraph breaks, preformatted text, or tables to format the stuff in your forms (**Figure 15.8**). A form can include nearly any HTML entity—text, images, tables—except another form. You can put a form in a table, or a table in a form, but you can't put a form within a form. You can, however, include more than one form on a page—just don't try to overlap them.

✔ Tips

- You can find out about working with tables in Chapter 12. I discussed text formatting in Chapters 8 and 9.

- The table in **Figure 15.8** uses regular old text to label the form items. If you like, you can also surround your text and the form field itself with the <label> tag. The code might look something like this:

```
<label>
<input type="radio" name="quiche"
value="quiche">
quiche
</label>
```

What you'd see would be this:

You don't *need* the <label> tag, but people are starting to use it more, so that the text that describes a form field is directly associated with it. This may be used more in the future by wireless and text-to-speech browsers.

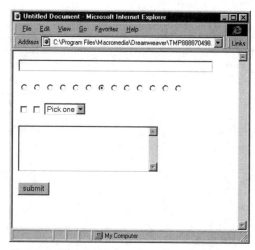

Figure 15.7 What is this form for? Without labels, it's impossible to tell.

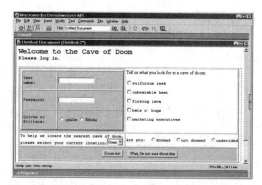

Figure 15.8 An expanded version of the form we saw in Figure 15.2, with the table, form borders, and labels revealed in the Document window.

You can wrap the label tag around any input and its accompanying text; the Label button ⌷ on the Insert toolbar simply inserts the code <label></label>. If you select a form field and some text before clicking the button, the tag will be wrapped around whatever you selected.

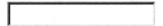

Figure 15.9 The Insert toolbar, displaying form objects.

Figure 15.10 A single-line text box.

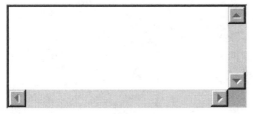

Figure 15.11 A multi-line text box.

Figure 15.12 A flock of check boxes.

○ ○ ○ ○ ○ ○ ⦿

Figure 15.13 A gaggle of radio buttons.

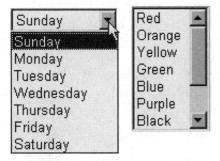

Figure 15.14 A drop-down menu and a list box.

Figure 15.15 Submit and reset buttons.

Adding Form Objects

Form objects, commonly referred to as form fields, are the nuts and bolts of a form. They're the boxes and buttons that people click on or type in to make their mark (technically called their *input*) on a form.

There are five different common flavors of form objects, each of which has its own button on the Forms tab of the Insert toolbar (**Figure 15.9**), as well as its own entry in the Insert > Form Objects menu. Some of the less common ones appear as well.

Text fields (also called text boxes) come in two flavors: single-line and multi-line. If a form were a test, a single-line field would be a short answer question (**Figure 15.10**), and a multi-line would be an essay question (**Figure 15.11**).

Check boxes can be used singly or in groups of two or more (**Figure 15.12**). Check boxes allow the user to specify yes-or-no answers.

Radio buttons, named after the buttons on old-fashioned console radios, always come in groups of two or more (**Figure 15.13**). They allow you to choose only one of a set of options—when you push in one button on a radio, the other buttons pop out.

Lists and *menus* (**Figure 15.14**) allow the user to choose from a long list of options that don't take up too much space on the page. What Dreamweaver calls a *menu* is also called a *drop-down menu*; it drops down when you click on it to reveal the full set of options. A *list box* offers several choices at once; in some cases, the user can choose more than one item from a list box.

Buttons are what make the form do something. A submit button sends the form off over the wires to its final destination. A reset button clears all the values entered in a form and resets the form to its default, or starting, values (**Figure 15.15**).

ADDING FORM OBJECTS

Names and Values

Each gadget, or form field, in a form is also known as an *input item* (the HTML tag is often <input>). That means it's used to collect input from the people who use it.

Each input item is represented in the form results by a name and a value. The name is a unique signifier that tells you (or the script handling the form) which field is which. The value is the content of the field.

Names are required for form fields; if you forget them, Dreamweaver will provide sequential names and values, such as radiobutton, radiobutton2, radiobutton3, and so on. Those sorts of names aren't very useful; for more about choosing a name and where values come in, read the sidebar, this page.

It's always useful, but the Property inspector will come in particularly handy for formatting just about everything—both the text of the labels and the form fields themselves. The Property inspector will display unique properties for each form field—and it's what you'll use to specify names and values.

To display the Property inspector:

◆ From the menu bar, select Modify > Selection Properties.

or

From the menu bar, select Window > Properties.

or

Press Ctrl+F3 (Command+F3).

Either way, the Property inspector will appear in its default position at the bottom of the Document window (**Figure 15.16**). In many places in this chapter, I've undocked it to make the screen shots easier to read.

Figure 15.16 The Property inspector.

Name That Value

When you name a form field, you may never need to personally read the form input, but if you did, you'd see results in this format:

name=value   name=value
name=value   name=value
name=value

The name is the name you give the field, and the value is the input the user fills the field with. One argument for recognizable names for form fields is so that if there's a problem, it's with "the address field," not with "field six."

In a text box, the value of the input is equal to what the users type. Input for a text field might look like this:

address="675 Onionskin Road"

For a checkbox or a radio button, you really need to specify what value the field has by providing unique text that signifies what specific input means.

This is particularly important if you're using several checkboxes; a value of "checkbox5" won't tell you anything.

Checkbox input in form results could look like any of the four examples below:

carowner=yes   carowner=checked
carowner=carowner

I know, I said four examples—if it isn't checked, it doesn't get sent with the form results at all.

Apply button

Figure 15.17 The Property inspector, displaying properties for a single-line text field.

Figure 15.18 To change the width of a text field, enter a value in the Char Width text box of the Property inspector.

Text Boxes

Text fields are used to collect data that you can't predict. You can't offer a multiple-choice menu for every possible name or email address, for instance.

Single-line text boxes

For short answers, such as address information or favorite TV show, you'll use a single-line text field.

To create a single-line text field:

1. In the Document window, click within the form boundaries.

2. From the menu bar, select Insert > Form Objects > Text Field.

   or

   On the Forms tab of the Insert toolbar, click the Text Field button □ , or drag the button to the page.

   A single-line text field will appear

   [   ] .

   You can resize it, if you like.

3. To resize the text field, type a number, in characters, in the Char Width text box of the Property inspector (**Figures 15.17** and **15.18**).

4. Press Enter (Return), and your text field will resize.

Displaying Properties

You can display properties for any form field by double-clicking it. The Property inspector will appear, displaying form object properties.

TEXT BOXES

Password boxes

You can use a single-line text box to collect users' password information, in which case the stuff they type in the box will appear on screen as *** or ⋯.

To create a password box:

1. Click the text field to select it, and make sure the Property inspector is open (**Figure 15.17**).

2. In the Type area of the Property inspector, click the Password radio button (**Figure 15.19**).

   There won't be any visible change, but when your page is on the Web, the stuff the user types in it will be replaced by asterisks or bullets to prevent accidents and deviousness (**Figure 15.20**).

Big text boxes

A multi-line text field will create a "feedback box" that you can use to elicit longer responses from your users. Multi-line text boxes are commonly used for guestbooks, email forms, and any other case in which you want more than a few words from your visitors.

To create a multi-line text field:

1. Create a single-line text field, as described on the previous page.

2. Double-click the text field, and the Property inspector will appear, if it isn't already showing.

3. In the Type area of the Property inspector, click the Multi-line radio button. The text field will change appearance (**Figure 15.21**).

✔ Tip

- In Dreamweaver MX, you can also use the Insert Textarea button on the Insert toolbar.

Figure 15.19 To make a text field into a password field, click the Password radio button.

Type your username: Avogadro

Type your password: ***********

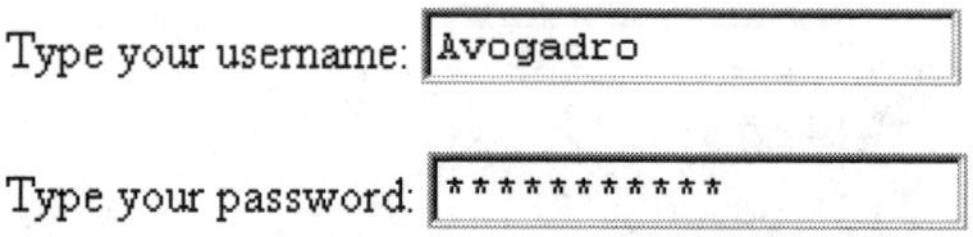

Figure 15.20 The first text box is a normal single-line text box, whereas the second one is a password box that masks the secret identities of its characters.

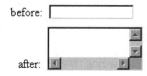

before:

after:

Figure 15.21 Change a single-line text field into a multi-line field by clicking the Multi-line radio button in the Property inspector.

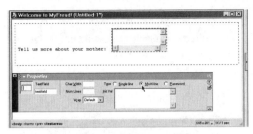

Figure 15.22 A default multi-line text box.

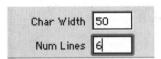

Figure 15.23 To change the dimensions of a multi-line text box, type a character width and a line height in the Property inspector.

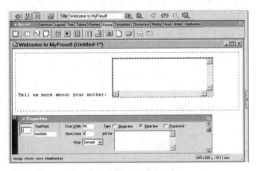

Figure 15.24 The new, improved text box.

Figure 15.25 Restrict the number of characters allowed in a text box by typing a value in the Max Chars field.

To resize a multi-line text field:

1. Select the multi-line text field (**Figure 15.22**).

2. In the Property inspector, type a number (in characters) in the Char Width text box (**Figure 15.23**).

3. Type a number of lines in the Num Lines text box (Figure 15.23).

4. Press Enter (Return). The text box will resize to your specifications (**Figure 15.24**).

✔ Tip

■ Unfortunately, you can't resize a multi- or single-line text field by clicking and dragging.

Character Limits

You can set a character limit for a single-line text field; for example, credit cards generally have only 16 digits, or 19 with dashes. Other fields you may want to limit include password, phone number, ZIP code, or state abbreviation.

To restrict the number of characters allowed:

1. Click a single-line text field to select it, or double-click it to display the Property inspector.

2. In the Max Chars text box, type the maximum number of characters you'll allow in this field, and press Enter (Return) (**Figure 15.25**).

In a Web browser, the user will not be able to type more than the number of characters you specified. (Generally, they'll hear their browser's alert beep when they try to type past the limit.)

Default text values

If you want to give your visitors an example of what kind of input you're expecting, you can set an initial value for either kind of text box.

To set an initial value:

1. Select the text box (either single- or multi-line), and view the Property inspector.

2. In the Init Val text box, type the text you want to have displayed in the text box, and click the Apply button.

   The text will show up in the text box in the Document window (**Figure 15.26**) and in the Web browser.

✔ Tip

■ Beware of using the initial value. Although it might seem like a great idea at the time, a lot of wise guys (or dumb guys) won't bother to change something that's already filled in. It might be better, in some cases, to use example text outside the box, as shown in **Figure 15.27**.

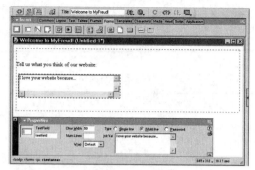

Figure 15.26 The text you type in the Property inspector's Init Val text box will be included in the form field.

Figure 15.27 In the first text box, the user may neglect to replace the supplied text with his or her real email address. In the second instance, the user is given a visual example, but the text box is left blank.

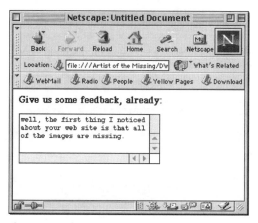

Figure 15.28 Netscape 4 wraps text by default in a multi-line text box.

Figure 15.29 The Property inspector for a File field allows you to set the character width and maximum number of characters.

File Fields

One kind of form field you may have reason to use, albeit rarely, is the file field. The file field consists of a text box and a button marked Browse. This field is used when you want your visitors to be able to upload files from their local computer to your remote server. The Browse button will open the Open File dialog box in their Web browser, which they will use to select the file; then they will use the form's submit button to send you the file.

To insert a file field, click on the File Field button on the Forms tab of the Insert toolbar, or select Insert > Form Objects > File Field. The file field will appear:

You can set a maximum character width and a maximum number of characters in the Property inspector just as you can for normal text fields. See **Figure 15.29**.

Text wrapping

When users type in a multi-line text field, scrollbars appear when the user types text that's longer than the field. However, the text won't wrap in a multi-line text field unless you turn that option on.

To wrap text in a multi-line text field:

1. Select the multi-line text field.

2. Display the full Property inspector by clicking the Expander arrow in the lower-right corner.

3. From the Wrap drop-down menu, select one of the following:
    ◆ Default (the browser default, which sometimes wraps and sometimes doesn't; see **Figure 15.28**).
    ◆ Off (turns off wrapping, in some browsers at least).
    ◆ Virtual (the text will wrap onscreen, but no line breaks will be inserted in the form input).
    ◆ Physical (the browser will insert line breaks into the form input where they occur onscreen).

Naming text fields

As with all form fields, it's a good idea to name your text fields so you can tell them apart.

To name a text field:

1. Select the text box and view the Property inspector.

2. In the TextField text box, highlight the text field text and type over it, replacing it with a meaningful word that will indicate the purpose of the field.

3. Press Enter (Return) on the keyboard.

Your text field will be named in the code, as well as in the form results that your users will submit.

Check Boxes

Checkboxes, which often appear in groups, allow users to make one or more selections from a set of options.

To create a check box:

1. Click to place the insertion point within the form in the Document window.

2. From the menu bar, select Insert > Form Objects > Check Box.

   or

   On the Forms tab of the Insert toolbar, click on the Checkbox button , or drag the button to the form in the Document window.

   The check box will appear □.

3. Repeat step 2 for each check box.

Remember to give each check box a unique and useful name and value.

To specify name and value:

1. Select the check box by clicking it, and double-click if you need to display the Property inspector (**Figure 15.30**).

2. In the Checked Value text box, type the text you want to see if the user checks the box. Good examples include send_info or owns_dog (**Figure 15.31**).

3. Name the check box by typing a name for it in the CheckBox text box. For example, the name could be mail or dog.

4. Press Enter (Return) to apply your changes.

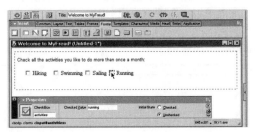

Figure 15.30 The Property inspector, displaying check box properties.

Figure 15.31 Be sure to give each check box an appropriate name and value, using the Property inspector.

Figure 15.32 Set a check box to appear checked when the page is loaded by clicking the Checked radio button.

✔ Tips

■ If the user does not check the check box, there will be no indication of the check box data at all in the form results.

■ If you want the check box to appear checked when the page is loaded, click the Checked radio button in the Initial State area of the Property inspector (**Figure 15.32**).

■ If the user does put a checkmark in a check box, the results will say something like NAME=VALUE. In our example above, the results would be mail=send_info or dog=owns_dog.

■ Names and values are case-sensitive.

Figure 15.33 The Property inspector, displaying radio button properties.

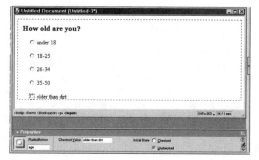

Figure 15.34 Use radio buttons to create multiple-choice questions. Be sure to give each button the same name and a different value.

Radio Buttons

Although check boxes can appear either singly or in groups, radio buttons always appear in groups. You can use radio buttons for yes/no, true/false, or multiple-choice questions where only one answer can be selected. New in Dreamweaver MX, you can now insert a group of radio buttons and name each one before you insert them. See the section *To insert a radio button group*.

To insert radio buttons one at a time:

1. Click to place the insertion point within the form in the Document window.

2. From the menu bar, select Insert > Form Objects > Radio Button.

   or

   On the Forms tab of the Insert toolbar, click the Radio Button button [●], or drag the radio button to the form in the Document window.

   A radio button will appear ⟨○⟩.

3. Repeat step 2 for each radio button in the set.

You must name each radio button in a group with the same name, and you must give each radio button in a group a different value.

To specify names and values:

1. Select a radio button, and display the Property inspector, if necessary (**Figure 15.33**).

2. Type a name for the group of radio buttons in the RadioButton text box.

3. Type a value for that particular radio button in the Checked Value text box (**Figure 15.34**).

continued on next page

4. Repeat steps 1 through 3 for each radio button in the set. Be sure to spell the name exactly the same, and to give each button a different value, such as "male," "female," or "other."

5. Select one of the buttons to be initially selected when the page is loaded. Click that button and, in the Property inspector, click the Checked radio button.

6. Press Enter (Return) to apply your changes to the form.

To insert a group of radio buttons all at once:

1. On the Forms tab of the Insert toolbar, click the Radio Group button ▤ . The Radio Group dialog box will appear (**Figure 15.35**).

2. Type a name for the group in the Name text box. This is the name for the set of buttons, so the name might be something like Colors.

3. Set a label and value for each button in the group by clicking in the appropriate space and typing the visible and invisible value for each button.

The value and label for each radio button should be related. For a single word, the Label and Value might both be **orange**. For a multiple word label, such as Vanilla Ice Cream, the value might be simply **vanilla**.

4. For each button you want to add to the group, click the + button and repeat step 3.

5. You're offered two layout options: setting each button on its own line, followed by a <br> tag, or laying out the buttons in a table, with a row and cell for each item. You might decide to do something else entirely with your buttons, but you need to choose one for now. If you choose table, you can edit this table or embed it in an existing table cell; see Chapter 12.

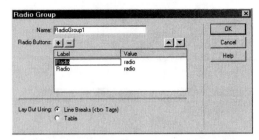

Figure 15.35 You can use the Radio Group dialog box to make sure all buttons get the same name and different values. You can use this dialog box only to insert a group of buttons, not to edit the group. To modify a radio button, use the Property inspector.

6. When you have your group finished, click OK to insert your group of buttons.

✔ Tips

- A group of radio buttons as described in this section is a set wherein only one button can be clicked at a time (see **Figure 15.34**). To make sure that your group will work, be careful to give each button in the group the same exact name, and each button a different value (either in the Property inspector or by using the Radio Group dialog box).

- If you use more than one group of radio buttons in a single form, be sure to give each group a unique name.

- You can check to make sure you've grouped your radio buttons properly by previewing the page in a browser and making sure that, when you click on each button in turn, the other buttons in the set become deselected.

- If you're working with a group of buttons that's already on your page, you can't reopen the Radio Group dialog box to check the group, if you wanted to do something like double-checking the names, renaming the buttons, or adding buttons. You have to do your proofing in the Property inspector instead.

- To ensure the name is exactly the same for any additional buttons, you can copy and paste the button as many times as you want. Dreamweaver will give each copy the same name. (You'll have to set the value of each button by hand, though, using the steps under *To specify names and values*.)

- Names and values are case-sensitive. Therefore, Green and green are two different values, so be careful you don't duplicate yourself accidentally.

RADIO BUTTONS

Menus and Lists

You can offer a range of choices by using drop-down menus, also called pull-down menus or pop-up menus (**Figure 15.36**).

To create a menu:

1. Click to place the insertion point within the form in the Document window.

2. From the menu bar, select Insert > Form Objects > List/Menu.

   or

   On the Forms tab of the Insert toolbar, click the List/Menu button 🗐, or drag the button to the form in the Document window.

   An itty-bitty drop-down menu will appear 🔲.

To fill the menu with menu items:

1. Click the list to select it, and display the Property inspector (**Figure 15.37**).

2. Click the List Values button. The List Values dialog box will appear (**Figure 15.38**).

3. Click below the Item Label menu button, and a text field will appear beneath it.

4. Type a menu item (what you want to appear in the menu) in the Item Label text field.

   If you want the values (the information that will appear in the form results) to be the same as the item labels, you can skip steps 5 and 6.

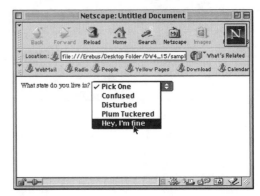

Figure 15.36 A menu in action.

Figure 15.37 The Property inspector, displaying menu properties.

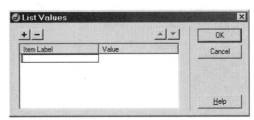

Figure 15.38 The List Values dialog box is where you add menu items to your menus and lists.

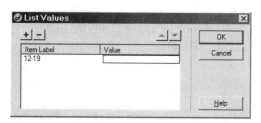

Figure 15.39 Press the Tab key to move to the next column and type the value for the menu item.

5. Press the Tab key or click the Value menu button, and a text field will become visible (**Figure 15.39**).

6. Type the value of the menu item in the Value text field.

7. Repeat steps 2 through 6 for each menu item you want to include. (Press the Tab key or click the + button to create a field for each new menu item.)

Menu Design

Normally, form objects, when viewed in the browser window, are displayed in the system font: Arial size 2 for menus, (the Mac uses Chicago or Charcoal, depending on the system version) and Courier size 3 for text boxes (Courier New on the Mac).

You can change the look of a drop-down menu or a text box by changing its font face and size. Be sure to test these effects in your favorite browser. The trick here is that if you select just the form field in the Dreamweaver window, you'll see menu object properties in the Property inspector, rather than text properties. To select a form object and change its font face, follow these steps:

1. Select, by clicking and dragging or by Shift-clicking, more than one form object (a menu and a checkbox, for instance), or a form object and some text. The Property inspector will display text properties.

2. Change the font face of the selected items by selecting it from the Font Face drop-down menu.

3. Change the font size of the selected objects by selecting a size from the Size drop-down menu.

4. Preview the form in the browser window to see what your changes look like.

You can also wrap the `<font>` tag around the `<select>` tag using the Code inspector or the Quick Tag editor.

Editing Menu Items

You can edit this list before you close the dialog box (**Figure 15.40**).

To edit the menu items:

1. You can rearrange the menu items by moving them up and down through the list.

   ◆ To move an item up through the list, click the Up arrow button.

   ◆ To move an item down through the list, click the Down arrow button.

2. You can add or delete items as necessary.

   ◆ To delete an item, click on it, and then click the – (minus) button.

   ◆ To add an item, click the + button, and then move the item to a new location in the list, if desired.

3. And of course, you can edit the text of the menu items themselves. Just click on the item, and type your changes in the text field.

When you're all done with the List Values dialog box, click OK to close it. You'll return to the Document window. The menu will appear larger than it was before, which indicates that it contains multitudes, but Dreamweaver doesn't display the menu as active—you won't see the menu items themselves.

✔ Tips

- To proofread your menu, you need to preview it in the browser window (**Figure 15.41**). Once there, you can click it to drop down the menu and scroll through the list of items.

- Don't forget to name your menu by typing a name in the List/Menu text box in the Property inspector.

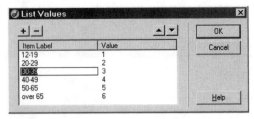

Figure 15.40 Use the + and – buttons to add and delete items—and the Up and Down arrow buttons to rearrange the order of the list.

Figure 15.41 When you load the page in the browser window, you can click the menu to make sure it looks the way you want it to.

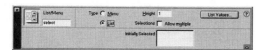

Figure 15.42 The Property inspector, displaying list properties.

Figure 15.43 To make a list, choose the List radio button in the Property inspector.

Figure 15.44 I gave the list a line height of 5. Because I have more than five items, scrollbars appear in the list box.

Figure 15.45 Check the Selections checkbox and users will be able to make multiple selections.

Figure 15.46 To specify a menu item other than the first as the initial selection, select the menu item from the Initially Selected list box in the expanded Property inspector.

Creating a List Box

The drop-down menu is one kind of list-type form field you can create; the other kind is the list box. List boxes can be several items high and can offer multiple selections.

To create a list box:

1. Create a menu, as described in the preceding sections. (You can input the menu items at any point.)

2. Display the Property inspector by double-clicking the menu object (**Figure 15.42**).

3. In the Property inspector, click the List radio button (**Figure 15.43**).

4. To adjust the height of the list, type a number of lines in the Height text box. The menu will change appearance in the Document window (**Figure 15.44**).

5. To allow multiple selections, make sure the Selections checkbox is checked. To disallow multiple selections, deselect the Selections checkbox (**Figure 15.45**).

6. Name your list by typing a name in the List/Menu text box and pressing Enter (Return).

✔ Tips

- To add menu items to a list box, follow the steps in the section *To fill the menu with menu items*, earlier in this chapter. The dialog boxes are identical.

- To specify the initial selection in a menu or list, select a menu item from the Initially Selected list box in the Property inspector (**Figure 15.46**). If no selection is made, the first item in the list will be the initial selection.

Jump Menus

A jump menu is a specialized kind of list or menu; when visitors select an option from a jump menu, their browsers take them to a URL associated with that option (**Figure 15.47**). Dreamweaver jump menus use JavaScript to do their magic, but it's all written behind the scenes and affixed to a regular list or menu without your having to worry about it.

Keep in mind, though, that not all browsers support JavaScript. See Chapter 16 for more about JavaScript, and be sure to offer alternate options for visiting all the pages in the menu.

To create a jump menu:

1. Save your page, if you haven't done so, to make any relative URLs work properly.

2. Insert a form and click within its borders.

3. On the Forms tab of the Insert toolbar, click the Jump Menu button ![button] or drag the button to the page. The Insert Jump Menu dialog box will appear (**Figure 15.48**).

4. First, we'll specify the URL. To select a page from your local site, click Browse, and locate the document on your computer.

   or

   Type (or paste) the URL (either a full path or a relative URL) of the page in the When Selected, Go to URL text box.

5. If you selected a document from your local site, the Text and Menu Items fields will be filled in (**Figure 15.49**).

   To edit or add the text that will appear in the menu, type the text in the Text text box. The Menu Items field will display both the text and the URL for your selection.

6. Repeat steps 4 and 5 for each additional menu item.

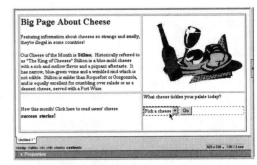

Figure 15.47 The only object in the form in the lower-right corner is a jump menu. The menu must appear in a form to work properly in the widest range of browsers, but you can make it the only object in the form.

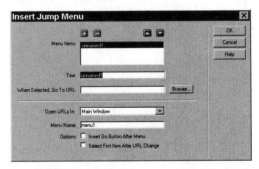

Figure 15.48 The Insert Jump Menu dialog box allows you to specify a list of pages the user can visit by choosing from a menu or list.

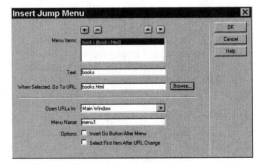

Figure 15.49 If you select a page from your local site as a list option, Dreamweaver will guess the text you want to use based on the filename of the page. You can edit this text later.

Figure 15.50 The Property inspector for a jump menu offers the same options as it does for a regular list or menu.

7. Type a name for the menu in the Menu Name text box.

8. To include a Go Button (**Figure 15.47**), check the Insert Go Button After Menu checkbox. Go ahead and do this; if you change your mind, you can delete the button, but for some reason you cannot add one after you close the Insert Jump Menu dialog.

9. From the Open URLs in drop-down menu, choose where you want the selections to open:

    ◆ To open URLs in the main window, select Main Window.

    ◆ To open URLs in a frame, select the frame name.

    ◆ To open URLs in a new window, select the window name. (To do this, you must create the window first. See the next page.)

10. When you're finished, click OK to close the Insert Jump Menu dialog box.

Editing a jump menu

The jump menu uses the same form-field code as does a regular list or menu. After you close the Insert Jump Menu dialog box, you can edit your choices by selecting the menu and then clicking the List Values button in the Property inspector (**Figure 15.50**). To edit the items in your jump menu, follow the instructions in the preceding sections, *To fill the menu with menu items* and *To edit the menu items*.

✔ Tip

■ Chapter 16 includes further pointers for editing jump menus using JavaScript behaviors.

JUMP MENUS

Changing a jump menu's appearance

You can make your jump menu either a drop-down menu or a list box by selecting either the Menu or the List radio button on the Property inspector (**Figure 15.50**). For details about additional options for list boxes, see the section *To create a list box*, earlier in this chapter.

You can also choose which item to select initially by choosing an item from the Initially Selected list box. To have the menu return to this initially selected item after the user has used the menu to visit a new page, check the Select First Item After URL Change checkbox in the Insert Jump Menu dialog box.

To use a selection prompt, such as "Choose a Page," add the text in the Text box, and don't specify any URL. Move the selection prompt so that it's the first item in the list (by using the Up arrow button).

You can make the selections in a jump menu open in a new window (**Figure 15.51**). First, you have to create the window. It's best if you create the code for the new window before you add the jump menu, so that the window name will appear in the Open URLs In drop-down menu in the Insert Jump Menu dialog box.

✔ Tips

- To create an additional window for the jump menu URLs to open in, see *Opening a New Browser Window* in Chapter 16.

- To change the text on a Go button, see *To rename your button*, later in this chapter.

Figure 15.51 You can make selections from a jump menu appear in a new window, which may be a smaller, "remote" or "channel" style window, or a regular browser window whose size you specify.

No Script Required

I've already mentioned that you don't have to worry about the JavaScript involved in creating a jump menu. Even better, the actions involved in this widget are all client side; that is, the action of selecting the page to visit is performed by the browser, not by a remote script. This means that you don't need to add a submit button or set up a form handler, as you do to make regular forms work.

I recommend creating a separate form for a jump or go menu. If you place this form inside a table, it can take up as little space as possible on your page (see **Figure 15.47**).

JUMP MENUS

Figure 15.52 You can add a Go button, pictured here, by checking the Go Button checkbox in the Insert Jump Menu dialog box, which we saw in Figure 15.48.

Hidden Form Fields

Besides the regular widgets you can use on a form, you can place hidden form fields in the code so that some fixed information is passed along with the rest of the data. This information might include the URL of the form, the version of the form, or any other information you want to receive with the form results.

To create a hidden form field:

1. Click to place the insertion point at the place on the form where you want the invisible field to be inserted.

2. From the menu bar, select Insert > Form Objects > Hidden Field.

   or

   Click the Hidden Field button 🔲 on the Forms tab of the Insert toolbar, or drag the button to the page.

   If you have Invisible Element viewing turned on, a Hidden Field icon will appear 🔲.

3. Type the value of the hidden field in the Value text box in the Property inspector.

4. Type a name for the hidden field in the Name (unlabeled) text box.

You won't see the hidden fields on the Web page (duh!), but the value will be sent with the rest of the data when the user submits the form.

✔ Tips

- If you use more than one hidden field, be sure to give each one a different name.

- To view invisible elements, select View > Visual Aids > Invisible Elements from the menu bar.

- Remember that your hidden fields would still be visible to a user viewing the source of the page, so restrain yourself from using them to convey sensitive or offensive information.

To Go Button or Not to Go Button?

In the Insert Jump Menu dialog box, there's a check box marked Go Button. If this box is unchecked *and* the jump menu is a drop-down menu, the browser will jump to the page as soon as the visitor has made a selection from the menu.

If you check the Go Button check box (which you *must* do if you're using a list box as opposed to a drop-down menu), the automatic action will be replaced by a button the user can click on when he or she is done choosing (**Figure 15.52**).

Unfortunately, unless you use behaviors, you can't add a Go button after you close the Insert Jump Menu dialog box, but you can delete it if you don't want it anymore.

One rule of thumb is this: If your jump menu lists many, many options, you may want to include a Go button, because it's very easily to accidentally select an item from a long menu—and without a Go button, users would get whisked away to a page they didn't choose on purpose. You can omit the Go button for menus with just a few items, say five or fewer.

477

Tweaking Your Menus and Boxes

Dreamweaver doesn't support the rather handy disabled attribute for menu items, but you can easily add the disabled attribute in the code. The disabled attribute allows you to prevent a user from selecting a particular menu item. If the first item in your drop-down menu is something like "Pick your favorite color," you want to make sure they can't submit that item, because it won't give you any data. You don't want to get 1,000 eager responses that say "Please select an item."

To add this attribute to a list or menu item, follow these steps:

1. Click on the list or menu in the Document window.

2. View the code for your page by selecting Window > Code Inspector from the menu bar, or clicking the Show Code View button (or the Show Code and Design Views button) in the Document window toolbar. The code for the list or menu will be highlighted in the window. The code for the menu or list should look something like this:

```
<select name="menu">

<option value="">Select a Color</option>

<option value="red">red</option>

<option value="white">white</option>

<option value="blue">blue</option>

</select>
```
Each option is a list item.

3. To prevent users from submitting a particular selection, add the disabled attribute to the option tag:
```
<option disabled value="">Select a Color</option>
```

4. Save your changes to the HTML, and be sure to test the form to make sure these changes work the way you want them to.

You can also right-click (Control+click) on the tag and select Edit Tag. In the Edit Tag dialog box, click the Disabled check box if it's available.

Figure 15.53 The Property inspector, displaying button properties.

Submit and Reset Buttons

There are three kinds of buttons you can put at the bottom of a form for your visitors to make use of.

Submit buttons are what you push to send the form off to the form handler, which compiles all the input and then does something with it.

Reset buttons clear the form of any new input and reset the form to its initial state.

The last kind of button (sometimes known as a "nothing" button) has no action; that is, it will neither reset nor submit the form, but it can be used with JavaScript or other active content to do something. The Go button used with jump menus is an example of a nothing button.

To create a button:

1. Click to place the insertion point within the form in the Document window.

2. From the menu bar, select Insert > Form Objects > Button.

   or

   On the Forms tab of the Insert toolbar, click the Button button ▢ , or drag the Button button to the form in the Document window. (I love saying Button button.)

3. A Submit button will appear: Submit .

4. Display the Property inspector, if it's not open, by choosing Modify > Selection Properties (**Figure 15.53**) from the Document window menu bar.

continued on next page

Covering Your Assets

Although most browsers these days support forms, some browsers can't deal with them—they display them improperly or not at all. Even some versions of Internet Explorer have bugs that prevent proper handling of forms, as well as of `mailto:` addresses. If getting input (or orders!) from your visitors is important to you, be sure to visibly include an email address on your site—not just a hidden `mailto:` link.

5. In the Property inspector, choose the type of button you want:

- ◆ If you want a Submit button, click the Submit form radio button.

- ◆ If you want a Reset button, click the Reset form radio button.

- ◆ If you want a nothing button, click the None radio button.

6. Press Enter (Return) to apply your changes to the button.

✔ Tips

- ■ It's a convention on most Web pages that the Submit button appears to the left of the Reset button at the bottom of the form.

- ■ Dreamweaver displays push buttons with a smaller font face than either Navigator or IE uses.

- ■ You can change the size and font of the push button, too. See the instructions in the sidebar called *Menu Design* earlier in the chapter.

You can call your buttons whatever you want. By default, the Submit button will say Submit and the Reset button will say Reset, but that's an option, not an imperative. I've seen Reset buttons named Gorilla and Submit buttons named Fish.

To rename your button:

1. Click on the button to select it, and display the Property inspector, if necessary.

2. In the Button Label text box, type the text you want to appear on the button, and press Enter (Return).

Your button will be renamed (**Figure 15.54**).

Figure 15.54 Your buttons can say anything you want.

SUBMIT AND RESET BUTTONS

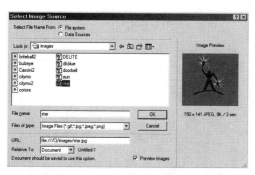

Figure 15.55 The dialog box for inserting an image field is exactly like the generic Select Image Source dialog box.

Figure 15.56 You'll see a dashed border around the image in the Document window, indicating that it's an image field rather than a plain old image.

Figure 15.57 The Property inspector, displaying Image Field properties.

Image Fields

Instead of the standard gray push buttons that usually appear in forms, you can use images as buttons. This method only works for Submit buttons.

To create an image field:

1. Click to place the insertion point at the place on the form where you want the image button to appear.

2. From the menu bar, select Insert > Form Objects > Image Field.

   or

   Click the Image Field button [image] on the Forms tab of the Insert toolbar, or drag the button to the page.

   The Select Image Source dialog box will appear (**Figure 15.55**).

3. This dialog box is just like the Insert Image dialog box. Type the pathname of the image in the Image File text box, or select the image from your hard drive.

4. Click OK (Choose) to close the Select Image Source dialog box. The image will appear in the Document window with a dashed line around it (**Figure 15.56**).

5. Display the Property inspector, if it's not open (**Figure 15.57**). The Src text box will display the path and filename of the image.

6. Type a name in the Name text box.

7. Type the alternate text for the image in the Alt text box.

   continued on next page

✔ Tips

- Along with form object properties, image field properties include characteristics such as image height (H), image width (W), alt text (Alt), and image alignment (Align). If you need information on using these attributes, consult Chapter 5.

- Along with the results of your form, you'll get coordinates that say *where* on the image the user clicked, appended to the name text (name.x and name.y). You can see whether they clicked on an apple or an orange, for instance.

The Button Tag

Another way to use images as buttons is by using the button tag instead of the input tag. The button tag allows images to be used as reset and nothing buttons, too.

1. Follow steps 1 through 4, in *To create an image field* (on previous page).

2. Select the image field in the Document window.

3. View the Code inspector by pressing F10. The code for the button will be highlighted in the inspector.

4. Replace the button code with this code:

```
<button type=submit name="name"
value="value">
<img src="button.gif">
</button>
```

The button type can be Submit, Reset, or button (for forms that call a script—the "nothing button"). The name is the name of your button image; the value can reflect the value you want to be transmitted; and the src is the source of your image.

5. Save the changes to the code, and preview the page in a browser to make sure it works.

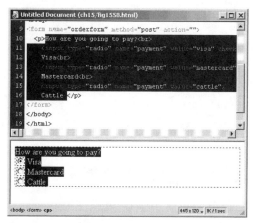

Figure 15.58 When selecting form fields and their accompanying text, you may want to use Code view. For instance, I should select the <p> tag that goes along with my text here in addition to the text itself. You may also find that a closing </input> tag gets orphaned if you just select text in Design view.

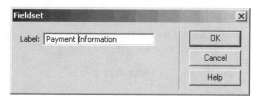

Figure 15.59 If you want a text legend to describe the content of a fieldset, type it in the Label text box. The tag is <legend> and it goes inside the <fieldset> tag.

Organizing Forms Using Fieldsets and Legends

No, *Fieldsets and Legends* isn't the latest Hobbit Potter blockbuster, it's an optional form tag you can use to group areas of a form together. On a large form, one fieldset might include address information, another payment information, and another customer preferences.

The idea here is that using different types of Web software, the visitor might be able to use navigation tools (such as as-yet-unspecified hotkeys) to move between fieldsets and form fields, so that the user wouldn't have to push the Tab key a zillion times to reach the bottom fields on a form.

To add the fieldset tag:

1. Select a group of form fields, including any text and labels (you may have better luck doing so in Code view — see **Figure 15.58**). See the Tips, below, for details on using fieldsets in conjunction with tables.

2. Click the Fieldset button on the Forms tab of the Insert toolbar. The Fieldset dialog box will appear (**Figure 15.59**).

3. To add a heading to your fieldset, using the <legend> tag, type a word or phrase in the Label text box. This label will show up in browsers that are able to display this tag.

continued on next page

FIELDSETS AND LEGENDS

4. Click OK.

The selection will be surrounded by the `<fieldset></fieldset>` tag. In Internet Explorer 4 and later and Netscape 6, a fieldset is defined with a visible line (**Figure 15.60**).

✔ Tips

■ If you're using tables to lay out your form, you probably want to confine your fieldset to a single table cell. **Figures 15.61** and **15.62** show three fieldsets laid out in table cells. **Figure 15.63** shows what happens when you try to wrap a fieldset around part of a table.

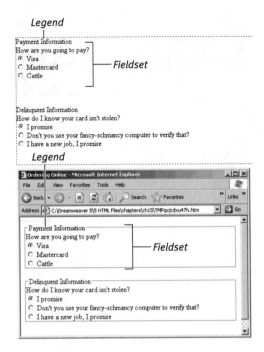

Figure 15.60 This is what a page with two fieldset tags, with no other formatting, looks like in Dreamweaver (top) and Internet Explorer. I separated the two fieldset tags with a `<br>` tag.

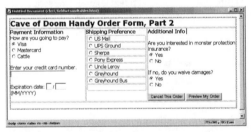

Figure 15.61 When creating a form that also uses tables, create a fieldset that occupies only one table cell at a time. In the center table cell, I did format the content inside that cell with another table.

Legends

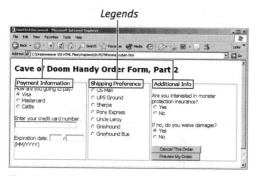

Figure 15.62 Now each fieldset is neat and clean, occupying a single cell/column at a time.

Misplaced legends   Misplaced boxes

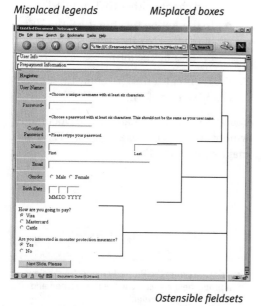

Ostensible fieldsets

Figure 15.63 If you format a fieldset and try to overlap several table cells, the formatting falls all to pieces. This page is based on one of the prebuilt pages from the New Document dialog box, but it doesn't include fieldset tags and they don't really work with this form because a cell for each form field precludes the use of fieldsets.

- You can use CSS formatting to format fieldsets. In Figure 15.62, I applied block formatting so that the fieldset tag occupies 100 percent of the height of the table cell it's in. On the other hand, this really doesn't work at all in Netscape 6, so if I were making this form for prime time, I'd have some experimenting ahead of me to get the results I want. See Chapter 11 for details.

- To format the text of a `<legend>`, wrap the formatting inside the tag, like so: `<legend><strong>Info</strong></legend>`

FIELDSETS AND LEGENDS

Making It Go

In order to make a form actually do something, you have to set it up to work with a CGI script or other custom script, called a *form handler*. Dreamweaver can't write the script for you—you have to take care of this part on the server end. Many Internet service providers make available standard scripts for common forms such as mail forms and guestbooks, and they may offer other scripts as well. If you're working on a larger project, you may need to consult with a programmer, your systems administrator, or both.

Forms are sent by one of two methods: GET, which sends the results of the form in the URL submitted to the script; and POST, which encodes the material sent to the script. Check with your sysadmin to see which method you should use. Where does the stuff go? The script includes instructions on whether to store it in a database, email it to someone, or save it as a data file.

Remember, you do not need to set up a form handler to run a jump menu. Those use client-side JavaScript that Dreamweaver writes for you.

To set up the form handler:

1. In the Document window, select your form by clicking on the dashed border around it.

2. Choose the method and action of the form handler in the Property inspector (**Figure 15.64**).

   ◆ Click the Method drop-down menu, and choose either GET or POST.

   ◆ In the Action text box, type the URL of the CGI or other script that will be processing the form.

3. Press Enter (Return) to apply these changes to the form.

You won't see any changes in the Document window, but you can examine the HTML to make sure they're there.

Figure 15.64 When the Property inspector displays Form properties, you can choose the method and action of the form handler.

✔ Tips

- Even if you want results emailed to you, you must use a form handler. Many Web sites offer free form-handling scripts that are easy to set up. See the Web site for this book, or search the Web for "free form handler."

- A form is an interface for a script action or for putting information into a database. Dreamweaver MX, which folded in such features from the previous Dreamweaver UltraDev program, now includes capacity for creating pages and dynamic scripts that you can use with forms. Database interaction is beyond the scope of this book; suffice it to say that you might be creating the back end as well as the front end using Dreamweaver.

- In the Src text box, if the form submission is being sent to a dynamic page on your site, you can specify the URL for a dynamic page such as `http://www.web-server.com/webapplication/process.cfm` when using the POST method. See your local database guru for details.

- The GET method should be used only for small forms with no sensitive data. Because the form data is actually appended to a URL when using this method, you should never send a credit card number using GET. (You may have seen this in search engines, for example, where the URL includes something like `"method=simple+query=giant_AND_FROGS"`.

- Dreamweaver MX includes the Enctype attribute on the Property inspector. This is to be used if you're encoding data in the POST method. It defines your form data as a MIME type for transmission, similar to the way plug-ins and FTP sites define MIME types for sound and other applications. The default entry is `application/x-www-form-urlencode` but check with your database dudes or mavens to see if you should use this or another setting.

- You can target a form to send its feedback to another window. Targets are covered in Chapter 6, about links, and Chapter 13, about frames.

BEHAVIOR
MODIFICATION

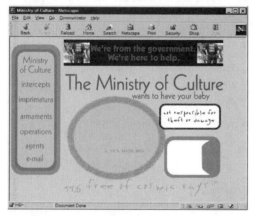

Figure 16.1 This page incorporates several behaviors, although you can't see them yet. In the background, the browser is pre-loading hidden layers and images.

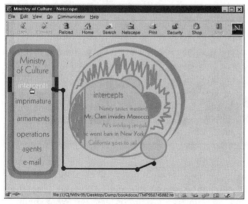

Figure 16.2 When I mouse over the button, the layers in **Figure 16.1** disappear and a new layer appears.

JavaScript behaviors can be used to make both flashy and actually useful gadgets, such as popup messages and complex rollovers. When used in conjunction with CSS styles (Chapter 11) and layers (Chapter 14), these tools are called Dynamic HTML, in which the page can change after it loads (**Figures 16.1** through **16.3**).

You can make things happen on a page when a user loads the page, clicks an object, or moves the mouse around. Obviously, I'm simplifying—there are a lot of fancy things you can do with JavaScript (see the sidebar, *Learning JavaScript*). In this chapter I discuss the stock behaviors that Dreamweaver lets you apply—all without writing a line of code by hand.

You've already used some preset behavior tools if you've inserted an image rollover or a navigation bar (Chapter 7) or a jump menu (Chapter 15).

✔ Tips

■ All the actions that Dreamweaver provides work with version 4.0 and later browsers, and many also work with earlier browsers (as I note when explaining each action).

■ Not all events are available to all browsers, and not all actions work in all browsers, so choosing which behaviors to use depends on which browsers you want to target.

JavaScript Concepts

A JavaScript behavior is sort of like an equation:

Event + Object = Action

or

If this event happens to this object, this behavior will happen.

You can see a simple example of this relationship in **Figure 16.4**.

An *object* is an HTML element on a Web page, such as an image, a link, a layer, or the body of the page itself.

An *event* is shorthand for both user event and event handler. A *user event* is what happens when the user, or the user's browser, performs a common task, such as loading a page, clicking on a link, or pointing the mouse at an image. An event handler is the JavaScript shorthand that designates a particular user event, such as onMouseOver or onLoad.

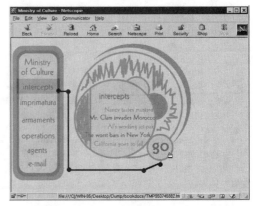

Figure 16.3 When I mouse over the image, a sound plays and another image appears (see the word "go"?).

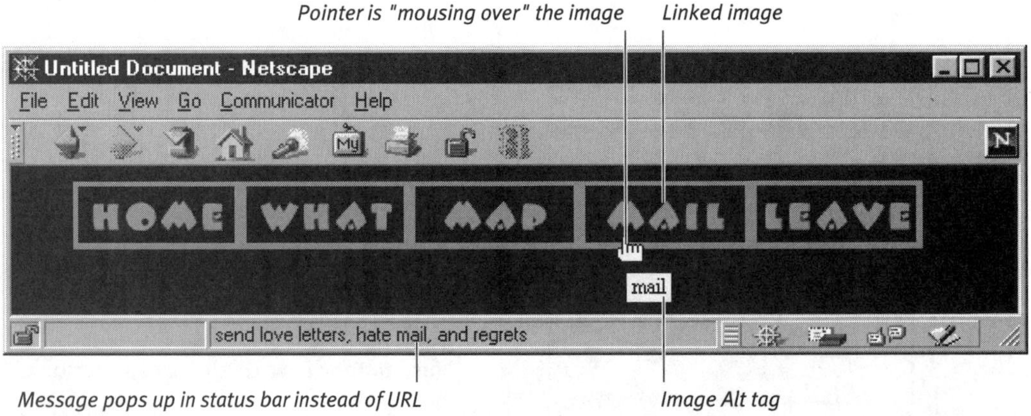

Pointer is "mousing over" the image   Linked image

Message pops up in status bar instead of URL   Image Alt tag

Figure 16.4 This button bar, shown in Navigator, is made up of five linked images (with image borders set to 0). The object is the link around the image. The event is onMouseOver, and the action is Show Status Message. What about the tool tip that says "mail"? That's simply the alt tag showing up as a tool tip in the browser. See Chapter 5 to set the alt tag for an image.

Learning JavaScript

You've probably gotten the idea by now that if you're not used to coding HTML by hand, Dreamweaver is a great way to learn how to do so. You just highlight the objects you're curious about in the Document window, open the Code inspector, and, voilà, you can see what the code behind the page is.

You can do the same thing with JavaScript by creating Dreamweaver behaviors and viewing the code for them in the Code inspector. If you feel lost looking at JavaScript, you might refer to one of the Web sites I link to in the supporting site for this book.

If you want a handy-dandy JavaScript reference, try *JavaScript for the World Wide Web: Visual QuickStart Guide, Fourth Edition,* by Tom Negrino and Dori Smith, also from Peachpit Press.

Making Scripts Go

Dreamweaver doesn't actually run any JavaScript behaviors. You need to preview your page in a browser to test your behaviors. You can preview in your default browser by pressing F12, or you can choose a browser from the preview list by selecting File > Preview in Browser > [Browser Name] from the Document window menu bar.

Appendix C on this book's Web site includes instructions on adding browsers to the Preview list.

An *action* is where the JavaScript comes in. Normally, when you click on a link, you go to the page that's that link's target. That's a normal browser action that has nothing to do with a script. A JavaScript action might start with the click and then play a sound or pop open a dialog box.

In Dreamweaver, to add behaviors to a page, you choose an object and an event, based on which browsers you want to make the script available to. Then you choose an action that the object + event combination will trigger.

In this chapter, I'm first going to describe how to add a behavior to a page, which is a pretty darn simple process. The rest of the chapter will be dedicated to listing and describing the objects, events, and actions you can combine in Dreamweaver behaviors.

JavaScript Concepts

Adding Behaviors

Adding a behavior to a page is incredibly simple—the devil is in the details. All Dreamweaver behaviors are added and edited with the Behaviors panel.

To view the Behaviors panel:

◆ From the Document window menu bar, select Window > Behaviors.

or

Press Shift+F3.

The Behaviors panel will appear, as a part of the Design panel group (**Figure 16.5**).

To add a behavior:

1. In the Document window, click on the object you want the behavior to act on, or choose an entire tag (such as <body>) by clicking on the tag selector at the bottom-left of the Document window (**Figure 16.6**).

Add Event button

Selected object (tag)

Up and Down arrow buttons for changing actions' priorities

Figure 16.5 The Behaviors panel is what you use to add JavaScript behaviors.

Figure 16.6 The tag that's selected in the tag selector is the one that will be affected by the behaviors you apply in the Behaviors panel.

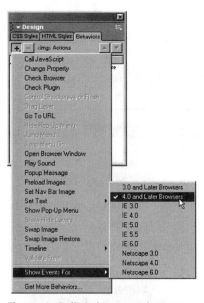

Figure 16.7 To limit the events shown to the ones appropriate to your target browser, select it from the submenu.

Add Action button

Figure 16.8
Click on the
Add Action (+)
button to
pop up a menu
and add an
action to the
selected event.
The actions
available
depend on
the selected
browser +
object
combination.

2. At the left of the Behaviors panel, click on the Add Action button to pop up a menu that includes both a list of actions that are available and a way to select your target browser. Select the Show Events For submenu and choose your target browser (**Figure 16.7**). If you don't select a browser, the list of events will be limited to those available for both 3.0 and 4.0 browsers.

3. Click on the Add Action button again to pop up a menu of actions that are available for that particular browser + object combination (**Figure 16.8**).

4. Choose your action from the menu (actions are described later in this chapter). In most cases, a dialog box will appear.

5. Fill out the dialog box (guess what? I explain each of them later in this chapter), and click on OK. The name of the action will appear in the Actions list box.

continued on next page

ADDING BEHAVIORS

6. Click on the arrow to the left of the Action name to drop down a list of available user events (**Figure 16.9**). The available events will depend on the object + browser + action combination you chose. More events are available if you choose 4.0 or later browsers, but remember that only visitors using those browsers will be able to use them.

7. Choose your event from the menu (events are described later in this chapter). Its name will appear in the Events list box.

To see only events for a specific browser, select the browser from the Show Events For submenu.

✔ Tips

- You can add more than one event to a single object. You might have different actions for onMouseOver and onClick. Just repeat steps 3–7 for each additional event.

- You can also attach more than one action to a single event. Just repeat steps 6–7 to add additional actions to an event (each action will be listed separately). For instance, you might have onMouseOver trigger both a sound and a status message.

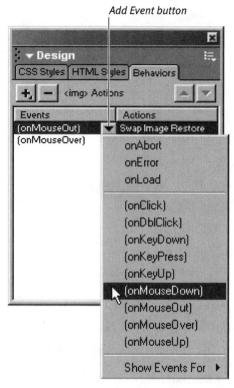

Add Event button

Figure 16.9 Click on the Add Event button to pop up a menu and add or change an event for the selected object. The events available depend on the selected browser + object + action combination.

ADDING BEHAVIORS

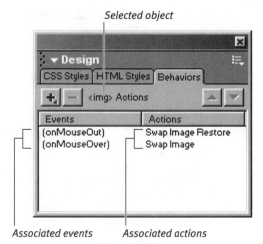

Selected object

Associated events   *Associated actions*

Figure 16.10 When an object is selected, its associated events appear in the Behaviors panel.

Figure 16.11 When I clicked on the Delete Action (-) button, the unwanted action disappeared.

Deleting and Editing Behaviors

After you create a behavior, you can remove it or edit it. To attach a behavior to a different object, you must delete it and re-create it (unless you want to edit the JavaScript).

To delete a behavior:

1. In the Document window (or the tag selector), click on the object to which you applied the behavior. The name of the event(s) associated with that object will appear in the Behaviors panel (**Figure 16.10**).

2. In the Behaviors panel, click on the behavior you want to delete.

3. Click on the Delete Action button or press the Delete key. The name of the behavior will disappear (**Figure 16.11**).

Editing behaviors

You can edit the browsers and events used in a behavior, as well as the data used by the actions (which you supply in those dialog boxes).

To edit a behavior:

1. In the Document window, click on the object to which you applied the behavior. The name of the events associated with that object will appear in the Behaviors panel (as we saw in Figure 16.10).

2. In the Behaviors panel's Actions list box, click on the action you want to change.

3. To edit the action, double-click on its name. The associated dialog box will appear (**Figure 16.12**). (Dialog boxes for each of the actions are explained later in this chapter.) Make your changes and then click OK to close the dialog box.

Reordering actions

You can edit actions as often as you want. If you have an event that triggers more than one action, you may want to set the order in which the actions occur.

To change the order in which actions occur:

1. Select the object in the Document window or the tag selector.

2. Select the behavior in the Behaviors panel (**Figure 16.13**).

3. Change the order of the action by clicking on the arrow buttons

   ◆ Click on the Up arrow ▲ to move the action up in the list.

   ◆ Click on the Down arrow ▼ to move the action down in the list.

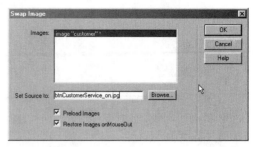

Figure 16.12 When you add a new action or double-click on the name of an existing action, a dialog box will appear in which you add or edit the variables for the action. This is the dialog box for the Swap Image action.

Selected object

Selected action

Figure 16.13 Select the proper object and then select the action whose position you wish to change.

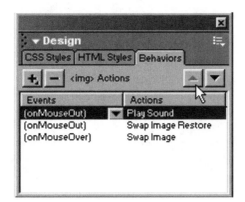

Figure 16.14 I moved the actions around by clicking on the Up and Down arrow buttons.

The order of the actions will change immediately (**Figure 16.14**), and the browser will perform the actions in order from the top down.

That's about it for adding and editing behaviors. The rest of the chapter is dedicated to the details.

✔ Tip

■ Behaviors are arranged in groups in the Behaviors panel according to the user event they rely on. In Figure 16.13, the behaviors are grouped by onMouseOut and onMouseOver events. You can only move a behavior up and down within its group of like events. In Figure 16.14, I moved Play Sound as far up in the list as it would go.

Common Objects

You can attach a behavior to nearly any HTML element, although some are more versatile than others. I'm going to describe some of the more common objects here.

Anchors <a>

Many events are only available to the <a> tag that is usually used for links. Other objects can be attached to these events by surrounding the object with the <a> tag, which can be a null link that doesn't go anywhere.

For images that require a link tag, Dreamweaver will automatically supply an <a> tag for the object.

The anchor code for a null link will look like this:

```
<a href="javascript:;">foo</a>
```

The link destination "javascript:;" basically means that the link doesn't go anywhere. You can also use a pound sign (#) for a null link. If you want to use a destination link later, you can replace either the "javascript:;" or the "#" with an actual link.

✔ Tips

- In the Behaviors panel's Events pop-up menu, events that can be activated by applying the <a> tag appear (in parentheses).

- You can use style sheets to remove the underlining or color changes from the added links on your page. See Chapter 11, and set text-decoration to "none."

- The "#" link may make the page reload when clicked in some browsers.

Body <body>

If you want to apply behaviors to an entire page, the **<body>** tag is what you select.

If you select text that is not linked, Dreamweaver may apply the behavior to the **<body>** tag. Check the tag selector. Add a null link to your text if you want to apply a behavior to it.

Images <img>

Images have some nifty properties, one of which is that they load. A popular trick the kids are playing with these days is the rollover, in which mousing over an image causes another image to load in its place. You can also make a simple rollover using the instructions in Chapter 7.

Forms <form>

You can use special form behaviors with a form. The events available to a form include **onSubmit** and **onReset**.

Form Fields

You can attach behaviors to individual fields in a form, too, such as **<option>** (for items in a menu or list), **<textfield>**, and **<checkbox>**. One example is the Go to URL action, which can be applied to the **<option>** items in a drop-down menu, so that when you select an item from the menu, a new page loads.

Event Handlers

There are many different event handlers you can use in Dreamweaver behaviors. These events are detailed in **Table 16.1**.

✔ Tips

- Different events may appear in the Add Event menu in the Behaviors panel depending on the browser and object you've selected.

- Events surrounded (by parentheses) in the Add Event menu will become activated by adding an anchor tag to the selected object. Dreamweaver does this for you automatically. If you don't specify a link, Dreamweaver uses the "blank" link, which in Dreamweaver MX is `"javascript:;"`. You can also use a pound sign "#" for a null link.

- Internet Explorer 4 and 5 include the most available events, but it's important to remember that only a portion of your audience uses Explorer exclusively.

Table 16.1 Events are arranged in logical sets rather than alphabetically. This table does not include all event handlers available to JavaScript, only those that Dreamweaver utilizes for behaviors.

User Events available in Dreamweaver			
EVENT HANDLER NAME	**DESCRIPTION OF THE USER EVENT** *(The event handler may call any number of actions, including dialog boxes.)*	**BROWSERS** *(According to Dreamweaver.)*	**ASSOCIATED TAGS** *(Other tags may be used; these are the most common associated objects.)*
PAGE LOADING EVENTS			
onAbort	When the user presses the Stop button or Esc key before successful page or image loading	NN3, NN4, NS6, IE4, IE5	body, img
onLoad	When a page, frameset, or image has finished loading	NN3, NN4, NS6, IE3, IE4, IE5	body, img
onUnload	When the user leaves the page (clicks on a link, presses the back button)	NN3, NN4, NS6, IE3, IE4, IE5	body
onResize	When the user resizes the browser window	NN3, NN4, NS6, IE4, IE5	body
onError	When a JavaScript error occurs	NN3, NN4, NS6, IE4, IE5	a, body, img

(continues)

User Events available in Dreamweaver *(continued)*

Event Handler Name	Description of the User Event *(The event handler may call any number of actions, including dialog boxes.)*	Browsers *(According to Dreamweaver.)*	Associated Tags *(Other tags may be used; these are the most common associated objects.)*
Form and Form Field Events			
onBlur	When a form field "loses the focus" of its intended use	NN3, NN4, NS6, IE3, IE4, IE5	form fields: text, textarea, select
onFocus	When a form field receives the user's focus by being selected by the Tab key	NN3, NN4, NS6, IE3, IE4, IE5	form fields: text, textarea, select
onChange	When the user changes the default selection in a form field	NN3, NN4, NS6, IE3, IE4, IE5	most form fields
onSelect	When the user selects text within a form field	NN3, NN4, NS6, IE3, IE4, IE5	form fields: text, textarea
onSubmit	When a user clicks on the form's Submit button	NN3, NN4, NS6, IE3, IE4, IE5	form
onReset	When a user clicks on the form's Reset button	NN3, NN4, NS6, IE3, IE4, IE5	form
Mouse Events			
onClick	When the user clicks on the object	NN3, NN4, NS6, IE3, IE4, IE5 (IE3 uses this handler only for form fields)	a; form fields: button, checkbox, radio, reset, submit
onDblClick	When the user double-clicks on the object	NN4, NS6, IE4, IE5	a, img
onMouseMove	When the user moves the mouse	NS6, IE3, IE4, IE5	a, img
onMouseDown	When the mouse button is depressed	NN4, NS6, IE4, IE5	a, img
onMouseUp	When the mouse button is released	NN4, NS6, IE4, IE5	a, img
onMouseOver	When the user points the mouse pointer at an object	NN3, IE3, NN4, NS6, IE4, IE5	a, img
onMouseOut	When the user moves the mouse off an object they moused over	NN3, NN4, NS6, IE4, IE5	a, img
Keyboard Events			
onKeyDown	When a key on the keyboard is depressed	NN3, NN4, NS6, IE3, IE4, IE5	form fields: text, textarea
onKeyPress	When the user presses any key	NN3, NN4, NS6, IE3, IE4, IE5	form fields: text, textarea
onKeyUp	When a key on the keyboard is released	NN3, NN4, NS6, IE3, IE4, IE5	form fields: text, textarea
Internet Explorer 4 Events			
onHelp	When the user presses F1 or selects a link labeled "help"	IE4, IE5	a, img
onReadyStateChange	Page is loading	IE4, IE5	img
onAfterUpdate	After the content of a form field changes	IE4, IE5	a, body, img
onBeforeUpdate	After form field item changes, before content loses focus	IE4, IE5	a, body, img
onScroll	When the user uses the page scrollbars	IE4, IE5	body

EVENT HANDLERS

Common Actions

In this section of the chapter I describe how to set up some common JavaScript actions in Dreamweaver. This is not meant to be an all-encompassing JavaScript reference; the language is capable of much more than I'm able to sum up in a single chapter.

Setting up behaviors in JavaScript is very much like ordering Chinese food: you take one from Column A (objects), one from Column B (events), and one from Column C (actions).

Because it would be redundant for me to repeat every detail of how to set up a behavior for each of these actions, I'm going to skip some of the basic steps, like showing the Behaviors panel. You can review the details in *Adding Behaviors,* earlier in this chapter.

✔ Tips

- The objects and events that I name in the instructions for these events are suggestions; many other combinations are possible.

- Don't forget that JavaScript can crash older browsers. Heck, my computer crashed a half-dozen times just writing about it. Refer to Appendix C on the Web site for tips on writing pages for the masses.

Figure 16.15 Type your status bar message in the Message text box.

Figure 16.16 When the user mouses over the button, a message appears in the status bar. You can also set a status bar message for a link, a button, or the entire <body> tag.

Setting Status Bar Message

A status bar message is a little bit of text that appears in the status bar of the browser.

Usage Example: Combine <a> and onMouseOver with Set Text of Status Bar. When the user mouses over a link, they'll see a message in the status bar such as "Explore the Invisible Cities." This is also a great trick for hiding the target URL.

To add a status bar message:

1. In the Behaviors panel, select a browser (3.0 and later, or 4.0 and later if you want more event options).

2. In the Document window, select an object (a, body, img).

3. In the Behaviors panel, add the action Set Text of Status Bar (Set Text > Set Text of Status Bar). The Set Text of Status Bar dialog box will appear (**Figure 16.15**).

4. Type your message in the Message text box. Use a space to leave the status bar blank at all times.

5. Click OK. The Set Text of Status Bar dialog box will close.

6. In the Behaviors panel, choose an event (onMouseOver, onMouseOut, onLoad, onClick).

When you load the page in a browser, the message will appear in the status bar when you perform the user event you specified (**Figure 16.16**).

✔ Tip

■ If you specify a status message for onMouseOver, you may also want to specify a status message for onMouseOut. This can be a blank message. Just type a space in the Message text box.

Going to a New URL

You can open URLs with actions other than a click.

Usage Example: Have a link open two windows at once or open a document in each of two frames. You can also specify URLs in this way using JavaScript; older browsers get the regular old link, while the JavaScript user goes to the JavaScript page.

To add a URL:

1. In the Behaviors panel, select a browser (3.0 and later).

2. In the Document window, select an object (a, img, body).

3. In the Behaviors panel, add the action Go to URL. The Go To URL dialog box will appear (**Figure 16.17**).

4. Add your URLs as follows:
   ◆ To load a new URL in a single, non-frames window, type it in the URL text box.
   ◆ To load a single URL on a page with more than one frame and URL, select the name of the single frame from the Open In list box and type the URL in the URL text box.
   ◆ To load more than one URL on a page with more than one frame and more than one URL, repeat the preceding instruction for each single frame.

5. Click OK. The dialog box will close.

6. In the Behaviors panel, specify the event (onClick, onLoad, onMouseOver, onMouseOut). The URL(s) will open when the user performs the event (**Figure 16.18**).

✔ Tip

■ Be sure to test, test, and retest these links once they're on the server, particularly if you're targeting multiple frames.

Figure 16.17 Select the windows (or frames) and type in the corresponding URLs that will load when the event happens.

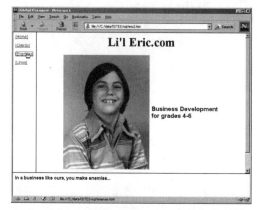

Figure 16.18 On this page, mousing over a menu item loads a new page in the bottom window.

Window Dressing

In the example in **Figure 16.17**, I can choose between opening my URL in the main page body or in any frame on the page. If you want the page to open in a new window, you can do that, too. One way is to set a target. Type this code in the URL text box, where path/file.html is the URL of your page:

```
path/file.html target="_blank"
```

Additionally, you can have the URL open in a custom-sized window, with or without toolbars. *See Opening a New Browser Window,* later in this chapter. After you create a window, its name will appear in the Open In list box.

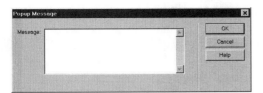

Figure 16.19 Type the message you want to appear in the dialog box in the Message text box.

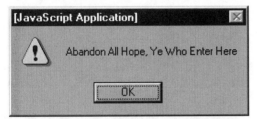

Figure 16.20 A popup message created with Dreamweaver. This message appears when the user clicks on a link. I used this in combination with the Go To URL action; when the user clicks OK, the browser will open a new page.

Popup Message

In the Popup Message action, when the user performs an action, a pop-up message (or dialog box) will appear. In Dreamweaver, the only choice in this dialog box is OK.

Usage Example: Combine this action with the result of another action, such as form validation ("You forgot to type your e-mail address") or plug-in detection ("You need Shockwave to properly appreciate this page").

To add a pop-up message:

1. In the Behaviors panel, select a browser (3.0 and later).

2. In the Document window, select an object (a, body).

3. In the Behaviors panel, add the action Pop-Up Message. The Popup Message dialog box will appear (**Figure 16.19**).

4. Type your message in the Message text box.

5. Click OK. The Popup Message dialog box will close.

6. In the Behaviors panel, specify the event (onClick, onMouseOver).

When you load the page in a browser, the pop-up message or dialog box will open when the user performs the event, such as a click (**Figure 16.20**).

✔ Tip

■ Don't overuse this one. I've seen pages where the slightest mouse movement would open a dialog box, and it was truly annoying.

Opening a New Browser Window

You know those little bitty JavaScript windows? You can pop one open using the Open Browser Window action—or you can pop open a regular-sized window. Incidentally, each of these pop-up windows has a unique URL that belongs to a distinct HTML document that you must create separately.

Usage Example: Pop open a floating toolbar, "control panel," or a window set to the exact size of a Flash movie or streaming video (**Figure 16.21**).

To add the Open Browser Window action:

1. In the Behaviors panel, select a browser (3.0 and later).

2. In the Document window, select an object (a, img, body).

3. In the Behaviors panel, add the Action Open Browser Window. The Open Browser Window dialog box will appear (**Figure 16.22**).

4. Type the URL of the content for the new window in the URL text box, or click Browse to select a local file. If you haven't created the content for the new window you can type a filename or URL in the URL to Display text box anyway.

5. If you want to specify a window width and window height, type these dimensions (in pixels) in the appropriate text boxes. If you don't specify these dimensions, a default-sized browser window will open.

6. The check boxes allow you to display regular browser features such as navigation and location toolbars, the status bar, the menu bar, scrollbars, and resize handles. Leave all the boxes unchecked if you want a "featureless" window.

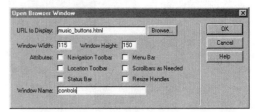

Figure 16.21 This sound control panel is set to pop open when a link in the parent window is clicked.

Figure 16.22 The Open Browser Window dialog box. These are the attributes I set for the control panel in **Figure 16.21**.

Figure 16.23 Another floating toolbar. Note the extra space below the buttons—the window must be a minimum of 100 pixels high. If I were getting this control panel ready for prime time, I'd center the buttons within the window using a table, or I'd make bigger buttons.

Figure 16.24 You can edit a jump menu after you insert it using the Insert Jump Menu dialog box. See Chapter 15 for details.

Figure 16.25 If you have more than one jump menu on your page, select the correct one from the drop-down menu. You can apply this action to an existing menu or to a form button.

Jump Menu Behaviors

Two actions listed in the Behaviors panel, Jump Menu and Jump Menu Go, apply to jump menus. Jump menus, discussed in Chapter 15, are small drop-down menus from which the user can select a page to visit. A jump menu can operate with a Go button or without a button, in which case the browser activates the link in the menu as soon as the user selects it.

To insert a jump menu, see Chapter 15.

To edit a jump menu, select it, and then in the Behaviors panel, double-click the action Jump Menu. The Insert Jump Menu dialog box will appear (**Figure 16.24**).

To add a Go button to a jump menu after you've inserted the menu, you must add a form button (Insert > Form Object > Button). In the Property inspector, set the Action to Nothing, then label the button "Go," or whatever you like.

Then, in the Behaviors panel, select the button, and give it the event onClick and the action Jump Menu Go. The Jump Menu Go dialog box will appear (**Figure 16.25**). Keep in mind that the menu may still operate onSelect rather than by clicking the button. Unfortunately, the only reliable way to use a Go button is to add it while you're inserting the menu in the first place.

7. To specify a window name, type the title in the Window Name text box. (You can use these window names in other behaviors, such as Go to URL.)

8. Click OK. The Open Browser Window dialog box will close.

9. In the Behaviors panel, specify the event (onClick, onLoad, onMouseOver).

In the browser window, when the action (page loading, link clicking) occurs, the new window will open (**Figure 16.23**).

✔ Tips

■ By trial and error, I've found that Java-Script windows must be at least 100 pixels high. The window in Figure 16.21 is 115 pixels wide and 150 pixels high, and the window in Figure 16.23 is 100 pixels high, although I'd like it to be about 50 pixels high.

■ If you want links on your page to be able to load into this window, use the Go to URL Behavior, and from the Open In list box, select the window name you specified in step 7 as if it were a target frame name.

■ To set a page title for this window, open the separate HTML document in Dreamweaver (File > Open), and use the Page Properties dialog box (under the Modify menu).

■ Once you add the code for opening a new window to a page, you can use it as a target for any link using the Go to URL behavior or the Jump Menu (see Chapter 15 and the sidebar, this page).

OPENING A NEW BROWSER WINDOW

Checking Browser for Plug-in

The Check Plugin action checks the user's browser to see if they have a particular plug-in installed. After the check, the action can load one of two URLs: one for Yes, and an alternate for No.

Usage Example: If the user has Shockwave installed, they will proceed to the Shockwave-enhanced version of the page. If not, they will be sent to a page that's designed to present the same information without Shockwave.

To add the Check Plugin action:

1. In the Behaviors panel, select a browser (3.0 and later).

2. In the Document window, select the <body> tag by clicking on it in the tag selector at the bottom left of the status bar, or select an <a> tag.

3. In the Behaviors panel, add the action Check Plugin. The Check Plugin dialog box will appear (**Figure 16.26**).

4. Choose a plug-in from the drop-down menu.

   or

   If the desired plug-in is not available from the drop-down menu, type the name of the plug-in, exactly as it appears in bold on Netscape's About Plug-ins page. For example, to look for the latest version of the RealPlayer, you'd type `RealPlayer(tm) G2 LiveConnect-Enabled Plug-In (32-bit)` (yes, the whole thing).

Figure 16.26 Choose your plug-in from the drop-down menu.

5. Type the URL for the Yes page in the URL text box (for example: `shock_index.html`).

6. Type the alternate URL for the No page in the Alt URL text box (for example: `noshock_index.html`).

7. Click OK to close the Check Plugin dialog box.

8. In the Behaviors panel, specify the event (`onLoad`, `onClick`).

When the page loads or the link is clicked, the user will automatically be forwarded to the proper page.

✔ Tips

- To view Netscape's About:Plug-ins page, select Help > About Plug-ins from Navigator's menu bar, or type `about: plugins` in the address bar and press Enter (Return). In Netscape 6, type `about:plugins` (no spaces).

- Many Netscape plug-ins have ActiveX counterparts for Internet Explorer; check the documentation for the plug-in to find out whether Explorer supports it as ActiveX or as a plug-in. See Chapter 7 on using both the `OBJECT` and `EMBED` tags to work with both browsers.

- I discuss plug-ins in Chapter 7. Appendix C on the Web site discusses making sites available to browsers other than the latest versions of Navigator and Explorer.

Checking Browser Version

The Check Browser action checks the brand and version of the user's browser; different browsers do have different capabilities. After the check, the action can load one of two URLs: one for Yes, and an alternate for No.

Usage Example: If the user has a 4.0 browser, they can proceed to the layers-intensive version of the page. If they have a 3.0 browser, they will be sent to a page that's designed to present the same information using tables.

✔ Tips

■ Browsers before Netscape 2 or Explorer 3 will not run this behavior, because they don't support JavaScript. The steps on the following page tell how to work around older browsers.

■ It's a good idea to have the page on which this behavior appears contain the equivalent information for users with older browsers, and to use the Stay on this Page option for them.

To add the Check Browser action:

1. In the Behaviors panel, select a browser (3.0 and later).

2. In the Document window, select the <body> tag by clicking on it in the tag selector at the bottom left of the status bar, or select an <a> tag.

3. In the Behaviors panel, add the action Check Browser. The Check Browser dialog box will appear (**Figure 16.27**).

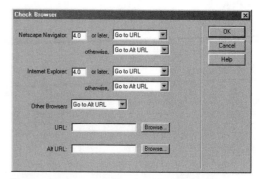

Figure 16.27 Specify different actions for different browsers using the Check Browser dialog box.

4. For each of the three options, Netscape Navigator, Internet Explorer, or Other Browsers, choose an option from the drop-down menu: Go to URL, Go to Alt URL, or Stay on this Page. (Browsers that don't support JavaScript will use the last option by default.)

5. In the Netscape Navigator and/or Internet Explorer text boxes, type the earliest version number that supports the feature you're working around. If the feature is, say, layers, type 4.0 in both text boxes; for frames, type 2.0 in the Navigator text box and 3.0 in the Explorer text box.

6. Type the URL for the main page in the URL text box (for example, `layers_index.html`).

7. Optionally, type an alternate URL, for the alternate page, in the Alt URL text box (for example: `nolayers_index.html`). (If you don't specify an alternate URL, the user will stay on the current page or will use the non-JavaScript link.)

8. Click OK to close the dialog box.

9. In the Behaviors panel, specify the event (`onLoad`, `onClick`).

When the page loads or the link is clicked, the user will automatically be forwarded to the proper page.

Show Pop-Up Menu

One complex behavior available in Dreamweaver MX is the Show Pop-Up Menu behavior. This behavior allows you to show a cascading menu when the user mouses over or clicks on a link or an image.

You can create this behavior using Fireworks MX using the Modify > Pop-Up Menu > Add Pop-Up Menu command, or you can create a text menu directly in Dreamweaver MX.

For details on using the series of dialog boxes involved with this behavior, see Appendix Q on the Web site for this book.

Complex Rollovers

Swapping images is the same as performing the famous rollovers I talked about earlier.

Usage Example: When the user mouses over the image, it's replaced with a "lit up" image (**Figure 16.28**) or another image entirely.

✔ Tip

- You don't need to set up the Swap Image action in order to set up image rollovers. See the first section of Chapter 7 to find out how to use the Insert > Interactive Images > Rollover Image object. This option inserts an image, pre-loads the secondary image, and automatically restores the original image onMouseOut.

Images must be named in order for image swapping to work properly.

To name your images:

1. Select the image.

2. In the Property inspector, name the image by typing a name for it in the Image text box and pressing Enter (Return).

To add the Swap Image action:

1. In the Behaviors panel, select a browser (Netscape 3.0 and later).

2. In the Document window, select an image (img; Dreamweaver will add the anchor tag if needed).

3. In the Behaviors panel, add the action Swap Image. The Swap Image dialog box will appear (**Figure 16.29**).

Figure 16.28 The Macromedia Web site uses image rollovers to make the buttons "light up" when you mouse over them.

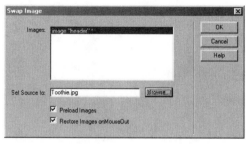

Figure 16.29 This is the Swap Image dialog box I used to set rollovers.

Figure 16.30 A popular way to implement image swapping is to use an image that's the reverse of the original. When the user mouses over the image on the bottom, it's swapped with an image that's the same size and shape, with reversed colors.

Figure 16.31 You can set the Swap Image action to swap several images at once. In this example, when the user mouses over the image on the bottom, all three images are swapped simultaneously.

4. The Images list box will display all the named images on your page. Click on the name of the image you want to swap.

   ◆ To swap the image you selected as an object in step 2, be sure to select the name of that image.

   ◆ To swap a different image when the user event occurs, select a different image.

5. Type the source for the new image (the one that will replace the named image when the action occurs) in the Set Source To text box, or click on Browse.

6. To have the images loaded with the page, select the Preload Images check box.

7. To automatically have the image revert to its original appearance when the user mouses out, select the Restore Images onMouseOut check box.

8. In the Behaviors panel, specify the event (onClick, onLoad, onMouseOver, onMouseOut).When you view this page in a 3.0 or later browser, the images you selected will be swapped (**Figure 16.30**).

✔ Tips

■ If you select more than one image in a single action, all selected images will roll over when you mouse over the single image you selected in step 2 (**Figure 16.31**).

■ To set rollovers for individual images, you need to follow steps 2–7 for each consecutive image.

■ Image swapping onMouseOver is often combined with image restoring onMouseOut. You can set this up automatically, but you can also decide not to do so.

■ This action will not work in Netscape 6 if you target an image in a different frame.

Preload Images

You can set up the Swap Image behavior to automatically preload images, but there are other instances in which you may want to preload images as well.

Usage Example: Preload a large image that appears in a DHTML/JavaScript window before the user ever gets there by adding this behavior to the home page.

To add the Preload Image action:

1. In the Behaviors panel, select 4.0 and later browsers.

2. In the Document window, select the body of the page by clicking on the <body> tag in the tag selector.

3. In the Behaviors panel, add the action Preload Images. The Preload Images dialog box will appear (**Figure 16.32**).

4. Type the pathname of the image you want to preload in the Image Source File text box, or click on Browse to choose the image from your computer.

5. For every image you want to preload, click on the Plus button ➕, and then repeat step 4.

6. To delete an image, select it and click on the Minus button ➖.

7. Click OK to close the Preload Images dialog box.

8. In the Behaviors panel, make sure the onLoad event is selected.

Dreamweaver will write what's called an array in the head of the document. All image filenames that appear in this array will be preloaded when the browser loads the page.

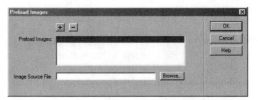

Figure 16.32 Set the source for all the images you want cached and ready in the Preload Images dialog box.

Set Navbar Image

The behavior Set Navbar Image is used in conjunction with Navigation bars, described in Chapter 7. The behavior uses the same dialog box to change the image source for the navigation bar. You can also create additional user events using the Behaviors panel for a navbar; for instance, you could add button images for onMouseDown or onAbort.

Figure 16.33 There's no good way to demonstrate rollovers in print, so let's pretend that the window on the left and the window on the right are the same window. On the left, we're mousing over the image. On the right, we've just moused out, and the image is restored.

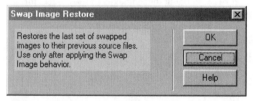

Figure 16.34 All you need to do with the Swap Image Restore dialog box is click OK.

Restoring Swapped Images

When you set up an image rollover using either the Insert Rollover Image function or the Swap Image Behavior, you can select an option that automatically swaps the image back to its original source when the user mouses out (**Figure 16.33**). By checking the Restore Images onMouseOut check box in the Swap Image dialog box, your images will automatically restore themselves when the user mouses away from them.

Maybe, however, you'd like to have a different user event trigger the Swap Image behavior, or you'd like not to turn on automatically restored images. If so, you can set a different event, perhaps on a different link, image, or button, to swap the images back by setting up the Swap Image Restore Behavior.

This is simple: Just select the image for which you've previously set up a Swap Image or Rollover Image Behavior, and then add the action Swap Image Restore. The Swap Image Restore dialog box will appear (**Figure 16.34**). Just click OK, and that's it. Then, specify a different event, if necessary.

Play Sound

You can use the Play Sound action to play a sound when a user performs an action such as a mouseover or a click.

Usage Example: Combine a small (<20KB) sound with image rollovers so that a beep (or a ding, or a shriek) occurs.

To add a sound:

1. In the Behaviors panel, select a browser (Netscape 3, 4.0 and later).

2. In the Document window, select an object (a, body, img).

3. In the Behaviors panel, add the action Play Sound. The Play Sound dialog box will appear (**Figure 16.35**).

4. To play a sound onEvent, type the URL of the sound clip in the Play Sound text box.

   or

   Click on Browse. The Select File dialog box will appear. Choose the file from a folder in your local site.

5. Click OK (Choose). The Play Sound dialog box will close.

6. In the Behaviors panel, specify the event (onClick, onLoad, onMouseOver).

When you load this page in the browser you can play a sound clip (**Figure 16.36**).

Figure 16.35 Using the Play Sound dialog box, you can add a sound to an event.

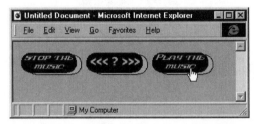

Figure 16.36 Using these images as the objects for the Play Sound behavior, you can let the user play a sound embedded using JavaScript.

The Fury of Sound

In past versions of Dreamweaver, you could purportedly use this behavior not only to play a sound but to stop one. You still can, if you're sneaky, because browsers will only play one sound at a time. For example, you may have a theme song set to play onLoad or onMouseOver. You can then attach a small (one second, even) sound to a button called, for example, Stop the Music (Figure 16.36). When the user mouses over the button, the sound that is currently playing will stop, and the short beep will play.

I cover plug-ins and sound files in Chapter 7. You can refer to that chapter for information on changing HTML or JavaScript code for hidden/visible sound controls, sound loops, and the like.

Figure 16.37 Using the Control Shockwave or Flash dialog box, you can provide controls to play, stop, rewind, or jump to a frame in a Shockwave movie.

Figure 16.38 I added a link that stops the Flash movie.

Control Shockwave or Flash

You can use the Control Shockwave or Flash action to play, stop, rewind, or jump to a particular frame in a Shockwave or Flash movie.

Usage Examples: Provide buttons or links marked Stop and Play. For a Shockwave game, provide a Play Again link that jumps back to the particular frame in which the game starts.

✔ Tip

- To use the Control Shockwave or Flash action, you must first embed a Shockwave or Flash object in the page using the <embed> or <object> tags. I discuss Shockwave and Flash in Chapter 7.

To add Shockwave or Flash controls:

1. In the Behaviors panel, select a browser (3.0 and later).

2. In the Document window, select an object (a, img, input).

3. In the Behaviors panel, add the action Control Shockwave or Flash. The Control Shockwave or Flash dialog box will appear (**Figure 16.37**).

4. If there is more than one Shockwave or Flash movie on your page, select the correct object from the Movie drop-down menu.

5. Click on the radio button for the control you want to add: Play, Stop, Rewind, or Go to Frame. For this last option, type the number of the frame in the Frame text box.

6. Click OK. The Control Shockwave or Flash dialog box will close.

7. In the Behaviors panel, specify the event (onClick, onLoad, onMouseOver).

When you load this page in the browser, you can control the Shockwave movie (**Figure 16.38**).

Show or Hide Layers

The Show-Hide Layers action can make certain layers appear or disappear. You must already have the layers on your page to set up this behavior. The effectiveness of this behavior depends on the initial visibility setting you give your layers.

Usage Example: When a user mouses over an image or clicks on a link, one layer will disappear and another will appear; we saw this in Figures 16.1 through 16.3. Because layers are loaded with a page, you can make several sets of content available on a single page and hidden in different layers.

To add the Show-Hide Layers action:

1. In the Behaviors panel, select a browser (4.0 and later).

2. In the Document window that contains the layers, select an object (a, body, img).

3. In the Behaviors panel, add the action Show-Hide Layers. The Show-Hide Layers dialog box will appear (**Figure 16.39**).

   Dreamweaver may take a moment or two to detect all the layers on the page, at which point their names will appear in the Layers list box.

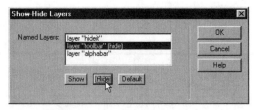

Figure 16.39 Set the (onEvent) visibility of your layers in the Show-Hide Layers dialog box.

Why Default?

The Default setting is most useful for a second Show-Hide Layers behavior.

For instance: Let's imagine a page with two layers. When the page loads, Layer Apple is showing, and Layer Banana is hidden—those are their default settings.

First behavior: When an onClick happens to a link called "Turn the Page" in Layer Apple, Apple hides and Banana appears.

Second behavior: When an onClick happens to a link called "Back to the Beginning" in Layer Banana, the Default settings of both layers are restored, and thus Apple appears and Banana hides.

Experiment with this; I got mixed results.

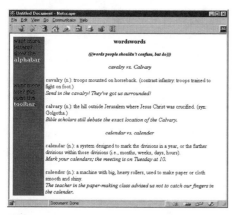

Figure 16.40 This page has two hidden layers. The links to them are in the table cell at the left.

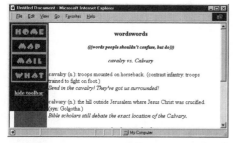

Figure 16.41 Click on the link that says Show Toolbar, and it calls a behavior that shows the Toolbar layer. Notice that that layer has a link called Hide Toolbar.

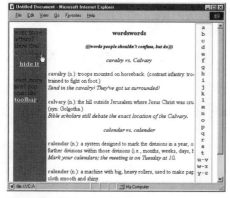

Figure 16.42 Here, we're hiding the toolbar and showing the layer called Alphabar. Notice the additional text in the left margin: That's yet another layer, with a link that will hide the Alphabar layer.

4. Click on the name of the layer whose visibility you want the event to change, and then click on one of the three buttons: Show, Hide, or Default. Default will restore the layer's original visibility setting.

5. Repeat step 4 for all the layers you want this behavior to affect.

6. Click OK to close the Show-Hide Layers dialog box.

7. In the Behaviors panel, specify the event (onLoad, onClick, onMouseOver).

The page must be loaded in a 4.0 or later browser for this action to work, because earlier browsers don't show layers at all. **Figure 16.40** shows a page with all layers hidden. **Figures 16.41** and **16.42** show the same page with the layers showing.

✔ Tips

- Another layer animation behavior, Drag Layer, is described later in this chapter.

- This action will not work in Netscape 6 if you are targeting a layer in another frame.

Validate Form Data

Form validation is useful—you can have JavaScript validate a form before it's even sent to the form-handling script.

Usage Example: You can require that certain fields be filled out, or require that data be in a certain format; for instance, a full email address or only numbers instead of letters.

✔ Tip

- You must already have the completed form on your page, with all fields named, before you can apply this behavior.

To add the Form Validation action:

1. In the Behaviors panel, select a browser (3.0 and later).

2. In the Document window that contains the form, select the form (click on `<form>` in the tag selector).

3. In the Behaviors panel, add the action Validate Form. The Validate Form dialog box will appear (**Figure 16.43**).

4. Dreamweaver may take a moment or two to detect all the named text form fields on the page, at which point their names will appear in the Named Fields list box.

5. Click on the name of the form field you want to validate.

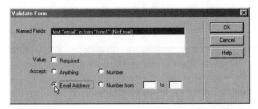

Figure 16.43 In the Validate Form dialog box you can restrict the input into text or text-area form fields.

Figure 16.44 On my form, I required that the text in the email field be in standard email address format. If a user submits a form that doesn't conform to this validation requirement, they'll get a message telling them so.

6. To make the form field required, in which case the form will not be accepted unless this field is filled out, place a checkmark in the Required check box.

7. To restrict the content you'll accept, choose one of the following options:
   - ◆ Number (content must be numbers)
   - ◆ Number from n to n (range of numbers; type the range in the text boxes)
   - ◆ E-mail address (text must be in the name@address.domain format)

8. Click OK to close the Validate Form dialog box.

9. In the Behaviors panel, make sure the onSubmit event is specified.

When users submit the form, they'll see a dialog box informing them if they failed to meet your validation standards (**Figure 16.44**).

✔ Tip

- ■ Before you unleash the form-validation script on your users, test it to make sure it does what you want it to.

The onBlur Event

The onBlur event is kind of confusing at best, but it makes a cute party trick. To "blur" a form field means that it "loses the focus" of its intent. In plain English, that means you're typing something in the form that doesn't belong there, thus making the form field lose its purpose. Using the onBlur event, you can mini-validate a single form field. Follow the instructions above, substituting the following variables:

In step 2, select a <text> or <textarea> tag as the object, instead of the <form> tag.

In step 9, use the onBlur event instead of the onSubmit event.

The easiest way to test out the onBlur event is to use numbers; in step 7, require a number between 1 and 10.

Now load the page in a browser, and try typing a number less than 1 or greater than 10 in the form field, and press Enter (Return). Your input will disappear.

Changing the Content of Frames and Layers

Dreamweaver offers a set of behaviors that allow you to change the text or HTML in a frame or a layer. Any HTML content may be inserted dynamically, that is, after the page loads initially.

Usage Examples: When the user clicks on a link, selects an option from a menu, or mouses over a button, the new text appears.

Changing text in a frame

Normally, when you click on a link in a frame, a new page can appear in that frame or another frame. So what's the advantage of using a behavior? For one thing, you can specify a user event other than onClick–for example, onMouseOver. For another, the code for the new page is pre-loaded by the browser and therefore will appear faster than if the browser had to fetch a new page. The behavior is illustrated in **Figures 16.45** through **16.47**.

To set the text of a frame:

1. Create and save a frames-based page, as described in Chapter 13. Be sure to name each frame, or Dreamweaver will refer to them by arbitrary numbers.

2. In the Behaviors panel, select a browser (3.0 and later).

3. In the Document window, select an object (a, body, img, select).

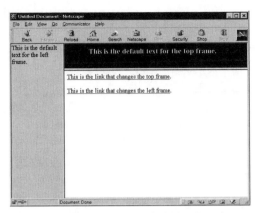

Figure 16.45 This is a mockup of a frames-based page that uses the Set Text of Frame behavior.

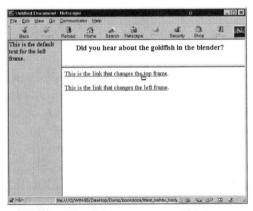

Figure 16.46 When the user clicks the link for the top frame, a simple text change occurs, and the background reverts to white.

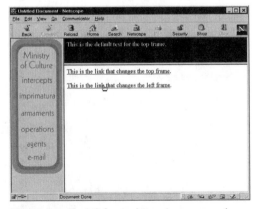

Figure 16.47 The left frame change is more complex, and includes a table, images, and links.

Figure 16.48 Choose the frame you want to edit, and then supply the new text or HTML. The easiest way to do it is to paste it in.

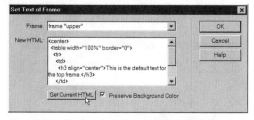

Figure 16.49 Here, I clicked on Get Current HTML for the "upper" frame; it includes the header formatting and the table.

4. In the Behaviors panel, add the action Set Text > Set Text of Frame. The Set Text of Frame dialog box will appear (**Figure 16.48**).

5. In the Set Text of Frame dialog box, you can edit the existing frame content, paste in text from another page, or write the page from scratch.

To get the text of the current frame, click the Get Current HTML button. The text will appear in the New HTML text box, where you can edit it (**Figure 16.49**).

6. Otherwise, type or paste in the code.

7. Dreamweaver will entirely replace the code for the frame. If you want to preserve the current frame's background color, leave that box checked.

8. When you're finished, click OK to close the Set Text of Frame dialog box.

9. In the Behaviors panel, specify the event (onLoad, onClick, onMouseOver).

10. Preview your page in a browser and check to make sure your changes work properly.

✔ Tip

■ This action may not work in Netscape 6. Test it with the latest version.

CHANGING THE CONTENT OF FRAMES AND LAYERS

Changing Text in a Layer

Setting the text and HTML of a layer allows you to make a layer useful by filling it with different things when different links are moused over or clicked. A layer can even be transparent and invisible on the page until this behavior acts on it (**Figures 16.50** and **16.51**).

To set the text of a layer:

1. Insert a layer on your page and name it, as described in Chapter 14.

2. In the Behaviors panel, select a browser (4.0 and later).

3. In the Document window, select an object (*a*, *body*, *img*, select).

4. In the Behaviors panel, add the action Set Text > Set Text of Layer. The Set Text of Layer dialog box will appear (**Figure 16.52**).

5. In the New HTML text box, type or paste in the code for the new content (**Figure 16.53**). This can include image pathnames.

6. When you're finished, click OK to close the Set Text of Layer dialog box.

7. In the Behaviors panel, specify the event (onLoad, onClick, onMouseOver).

8. Preview your page in a browser and check to make sure your changes work properly.

✔ Tip

■ This action may not work in Netscape 6.

Figure 16.50 This is a layers-based page.

Figure 16.51 Mousing over the person layer pops up text and a link within a layer that wasn't even visible before.

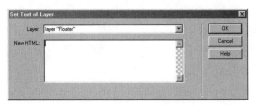

Figure 16.52 Choose the layer you want to edit, and then supply the new text or HTML. The easiest way to do it is to paste it in.

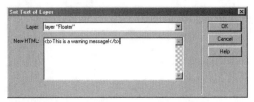

Figure 16.53 My new text for the layer includes formatted text.

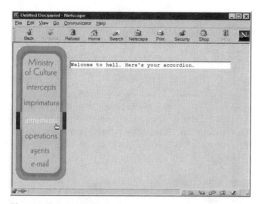

Figure 16.54 A single-line text box, displaying text during a mouseover.

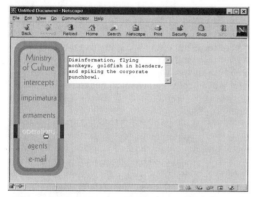

Figure 16.55 A multi-line text box, displaying text during a mouseover.

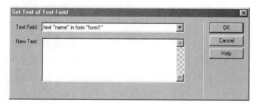

Figure 16.56 Type the text for the field in this dialog box.

Setting Text in a Form Field

You can use a text field in a form to display messages, almost like a frame within a page. You can also change a text field in an actual, working form when a user clicks on a link or a button. You can use a single-line (**Figure 16.54**) or multi-line (**Figure 16.55**) text field.

To set text field text:

1. Insert a form and a text field on your page, as described in Chapter 15.

2. In the Behaviors panel, select a browser (3.0 and later).

3. In the Document window, select an object (a, body, img, select).

4. In the Behaviors panel, add the action Set Text > Set Text of Text Field. The Set Text of Text Field dialog box will appear (**Figure 16.56**).

5. In the New Text text box, type or paste in the new text. When you're finished, click OK to close the Set Text of Text Field dialog box.

6. In the Behaviors panel, specify the event (onLoad, onClick, onMouseOver).

7. Preview your page in a browser and check to make sure your changes work properly.

Change Property

This action has more variables than any other. You can have an event that's associated with one object change the properties of that object or a different object. See **Table 16.2** to find out the objects available to this Dreamweaver behavior, and their associated properties.

Usage Examples: Provide a drop-down menu from which the user can pick a layer background color. Change the dimensions or Z-index of a layer when the user clicks on a button image. Change the destination of a form if the user checks a particular checkbox.

To set up the Change Property behavior:

1. In the Behaviors panel, select a browser (layer properties won't work in 4.0 or earlier browsers).

2. In the Document window that contains the layers, select an object (a, body, img, a form field, etc.).

3. In the Behaviors panel, add the property Change Property. The Change Property dialog box will appear (**Figure 16.57**).

4. In the Change Property dialog box, choose the kind of object that has the property you wish to change from the Type of Object drop-down menu (see **Table 16.2** and **Figures 16.58** and **16.59**).

5. Dreamweaver may take a moment or two to detect all the named objects on the page, at which point their names will appear in the Named Object list box. Choose an object by selecting it from the list.

6. The properties you can change will be available from the Property drop-down menu (see **Table 16.2**). You may get additional properties by selecting a different browser from the Browser drop-down menu.

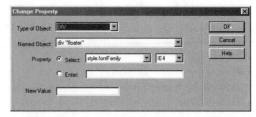

Figure 16.57 You can change several properties at once using the Change Property dialog box.

Figure 16.58 By selecting DIV, you can modify any named layer on the page, or a text block modified by a custom style. Modifiable properties include size, background color, and various style sheet attributes.

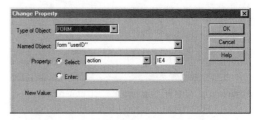

Figure 16.59 By selecting a form or a form field, you can change the functions of the buttons, the text fields, or the form itself.

✔ Tips

- In order to change an object's properties with this behavior, you must name the object. You can name any object by selecting it and typing a name for it in the Property inspector. The Name text box is always at the top and left of the Property inspector.

- You can also change additional properties by clicking on the Enter radio button and typing the property in the text box. There are too many variables for me to describe them all.

- If the object you're working with is a form field, you can provide a new value for the changed form field by typing it in the New Value text box. You can also type new values for layer attributes. A little source-viewing should help you find the right format for things like stylesheet attributes.

7. Repeat steps 4–6 for all the objects you want this behavior to affect.

8. Click OK to close the Change Property dialog box.

9. In the Behaviors panel, specify the event (onClick, onMouseOver, onBlur).

Table 16.2

Objects and Properties for Change Property Action

Object and Tag	Properties
Layer ⟨div⟩, ⟨span⟩, ⟨layer⟩, ⟨ilayer⟩ provided those tags have positioning and Z-index elements)	Position (top, left), Z-index, Clipping area, Background color, Background image (4.0 and later); Width and height (IE4 and later only)
Div ⟨div⟩	Styles, including font family, font size, border width and color, background color and image, and text within the ⟨div⟩ tag (all IE4 and later only; use layer or span for NN4, NS6)
Span ⟨span⟩	Styles, including font family, font size, border width and color, background color and image, and text within the ⟨div⟩ tag (all IE4 and later only; use layer or span for NN4, NS6)
Image ⟨img⟩	Source (NN3, NN4, NS6, IE4, IE5)
Form ⟨form⟩	Action (3.0 and 4.0 browsers)
Checkbox ⟨input type=checkbox⟩	Status (checked/unchecked) (3.0 and later)
Radio button ⟨input type=radio⟩	Status (checked/unchecked) (3.0 and later)
Text box ⟨input type=text⟩	Value (will appear in text box) (3.0 and later)
Text field ⟨textarea⟩	Value (will appear in text field) (3.0 and later)
Password text box ⟨input type=password⟩	Value (will appear in text box) (3.0 and later)
Menu or List ⟨select⟩	selectedIndex (changes selection within menu, using index numbers for each ⟨option⟩ (3.0 and later)

CHANGE PROPERTY

Making Layers Draggable

You can make layers on your page draggable by applying the Drag Layer action to the body of the page.

Usage Examples: Create a toy such as a paper doll, a jigsaw puzzle in which the pieces snap into place, a design in which users must drag layers in order to read them, or a slide control.

✔ Tip

■ Because each layer has its own coordinates, you need to add this behavior once for each layer you want to make draggable.

To add the Drag Layer action:

1. In the Behaviors panel, select 4.0 and later Browsers.

2. In the Document window's tag selector, click <body> to select the entire page.

3. In the Behaviors panel, add the action Drag Layer. The Drag Layer dialog box will appear (**Figure 16.60**).

4. From the Layer drop-down menu, select the layer you want to make draggable.

5. To allow the user to drag the layer anywhere in the window, leave the Unconstrained option selected.

   or

   To restrict movement of the layer within a specific area (**Figure 16.61**), select Constrained. A series of text boxes will appear (**Figure 16.62**).

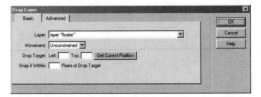

Figure 16.60 The Drag Layer dialog box allows you to make a layer draggable and to specify how and where a user can drag a layer.

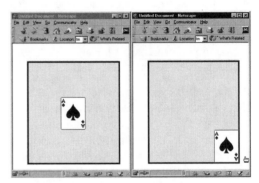

Figure 16.61 On this page, the user cannot drag the layer outside the box, which is another layer. I set a constrained area of 100x100x100x100.

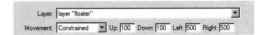

Figure 16.62 When you select the Constrained option, text boxes appear that allow you to set a draggable area based on the layer's original top-left coordinates.

6. The constrained movement values are relative to the top-left corner of the layer's original position and are in pixels.

- ◆ To restrict movement within a rectangular region, type values in all four text boxes.

- ◆ To restrict movement within a square, type the same value in all four text boxes.

- ◆ To allow only vertical movement, type 0 in the Left and Right text boxes and a value in the Up and Down text boxes.

- ◆ To allow only horizontal movement, type 0 in the Up and Down text boxes and a value in the Left and Right text boxes.

7. If you would like the user to drag the layer to a particular spot, you must declare a drop target. The drop target coordinates are applied to the top-left corner of the layer and are measured from the left and top of the window.

To declare a drop target, type a pixel value in the Top and Left text boxes. To set the layer's current position as the drop target, click the Get Current Position button, and Dreamweaver will fill in those text boxes.

8. The layer can snap to the drop target if the user lets go of the mouse button when the top-left corner of the layer comes within a certain number of pixels of the drop target. Type a number of pixels in the Snap if Within text box, or clear this field if you don't want to snap to the drop target.

9. To modify only these options, click OK to return to the Document window. Otherwise, keep reading.

MAKING LAYERS DRAGGABLE

Setting more Drag Layer options

The following section assumes you have read the preceding one, *To add the Drag Layer action*. These instructions begin where the last set left off, in the Drag Layer dialog box.

✔ Tip

■ The easiest way to set the options for a puzzle-type game is to begin with all the pieces in their final resting places (**Figure 16.63**). Use the Get Current Position option to set the drop target for the layer, and then when you're done with the behavior, move the layer to its starting position on the page (**Figure 16.64**).

To set more Drag Layer options:

1. To select further options, click on the Advanced tab on the Drag Layer dialog box. A second panel of the dialog box will appear (**Figure 16.65**).

2. To allow the user to drag the layer by clicking on any part of it, set the Drag Handle option to Entire Layer.

   or

   To allow the user to drag the layer only if they click on a specific part of the layer (part of an image such as a button or a "window" title bar), select Area Within Layer from the Drag Handle drop-down menu. A series of text boxes will appear.

3. Type the area of the drag handle, in pixels, in the text boxes. This area will be a rectangle, measured from the top and left of the layer.

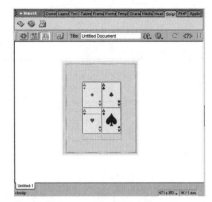

Figure 16.63 This is where I'd like the pieces to end up at the end of the puzzle. I put all the layers in place before I start setting up the Drag Layer behaviors, so I can use the Get Current Position feature to set drop targets.

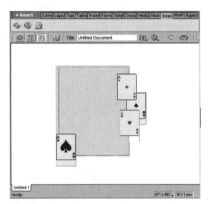

Figure 16.64 After I'm done setting up the behaviors, I put the layers where I'd like them to go when the page loads.

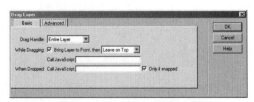

Figure 16.65 The second panel allows you to set selection handles for your layers; to specify the Z-index of the layer while dragging and after dropping; and call a JavaScript based on the user's drag-and-drop actions.

4. To change the Z-index of the layer so that it's on top while the user drags it, check the Bring Layer to Front checkbox.

◆ To leave the layer on top after dragging, select the Leave on Top option from the drop-down menu.

◆ To restore the layer's original Z-index after the user drops it, select Restore Z-Index from the drop-down menu.

5. To have the user's drag-and-drop actions call a JavaScript, see the *Calling Scripts by Dragging* sidebar.

6. When you're all set, click OK to return to the Document window. Otherwise, keep reading.

✔ Tips

■ You must repeat these steps for each layer that you wish to make draggable.

■ This behavior does not work in Netscape 6. Test it with the latest version.

Calling Scripts by Dragging

You can use the Drag Layer behavior to call a JavaScript that performs additional actions when the layer is dragged to a certain location. This script would use the layer coordinates provided by the values of MM_UPDOWN, MM_LEFTRIGHT, or MM_SNAPPED.

For example, the script could be called when the value of MM_SNAPPED is true, or, for multiple layers, when a certain number of the layers reach an MM_SNAPPED value of true.

Or, for a slide control, the location of the dragged layer could determine speaker volume, background color, or font size.

Another option is for the coordinates of a dragged layer to appear in form fields displayed on the page.

To call a JavaScript using this behavior, go to the Advanced panel of the Drag Layer dialog box (**Figure 16.65**). Type the name of a JavaScript function in the Call JavaScript text box.

To call a script when the layer is dropped, type the name of a JavaScript function (such as, youWin()) in the When Dropped: Call JavaScript text box. Check the Only if Snapped check box if you want this script activated only if the layer has snapped to the drop target.

MAKING LAYERS DRAGGABLE

Adding New Scripts and Behaviors

If you're a veteran JavaScripter, and you want to set up your own scripts in Dreamweaver, you're more than welcome to. You can type or paste in a script using the Insert Script object, or you can set up your own actions to use in Dreamweaver behaviors.

To type in a script:

1. On the Insert panel group, click on the Script tab, then click on the Insert Script button 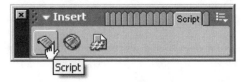 (**Figure 16.66**). Or, from the Document window menu bar, select Insert > Script Objects > Script. The Script dialog box will appear (**Figure 16.67**).

2. Type (or paste) your script in the Script dialog box, and click OK. The Script dialog box will close, and the Script icon 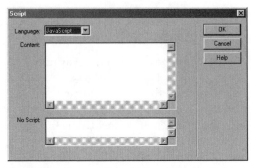 will appear in the Document window.

3. Select the Script marker, if it isn't already selected, and display the Properties panel, if necessary (**Figure 16.68**).

4. Select the type of script (JavaScript or VBScript) from the Language drop-down menu. If your script is in another scripting language, type the language's name in the Language text box.

Figure 16.66 To add a new script, you need to show Script Objects in the Insert panel.

Figure 16.67 You can type a little script in the Script dialog box.

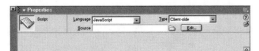

Figure 16.68 The Property inspector, displaying Script properties.

Figure 16.69 You edit external JavaScript files using Code view or the Code inspector.

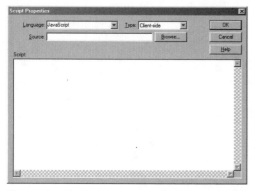

Figure 16.70 The Script Properties dialog box is like a script-editing window, except that it's a dialog box. In other words, you can't switch back and forth between the Script Properties dialog box and, say, the Code inspector.

Figure 16.71 Type the JavaScript function, or the script itself, in the text box.

You can also insert a script from a file on your hard drive.

To insert a script from a text file:

1. Follow steps 1–3, above, but leave the Script dialog box blank.

2. In the Property inspector, type the source of your script in the Source text box, or click on the folder icon to browse your hard drive for the file.

You can type or edit longer scripts in the Script Properties dialog box.

To edit a script:

1. View the script properties in the Property inspector.

2. Click on Edit. If you are editing a script contained in an external file, a new code window will open (**Figure 16.69**). Otherwise, the Script Properties dialog box will appear (**Figure 16.70**).

When you're finished typing or editing your script (**Figure 16.71**), click OK to return to the Document window.

Debugging in Dreamweaver

If you write JavaScript and you want to use Dreamweaver's built-in debugger, use the command File > Debug in Browser > [Browser Name]. For more details, see Appendix Q on the Web site for this book.

Adding More Actions

You can add actions to the Behaviors panel that were written by other Dreamweaver developers. See the sidebar, this page, to find out how to add your own behaviors.

To add third-party actions:

1. In the Behaviors panel, click on the Add Action button, and select Get More Behaviors. Dreamweaver will launch your browser and open the Dreamweaver Exchange on the Web.

2. Download the behavior that interests you, and unzip it.

3. Quit Dreamweaver.

4. Drop the new file into the Actions folder:

◆ On the PC: `C:\Program Files\ Macromedia\Dreamweaver MX\ Configuration\Behaviors\Actions`

◆ On the Mac: `file:///Dreamweaver MX/ Configuration/Behaviors/Actions`

5. Launch Dreamweaver. The action will appear on the Add Action menu in the Behaviors panel.

Adding Your Own Actions

If you write JavaScript, you can write your own actions and add them to the Behaviors panel. However, this isn't quite as easy as just writing the HTML and JS files (as if that weren't hard enough!) and dropping them into the Actions folder. You need to format them and add some specific functions so Dreamweaver knows what to make of them.

To find out how to do the mysterious stuff that will make your JavaScript code work with Dreamweaver and show up in the Behaviors panel, consult the Extending Dreamweaver help files (Help > Extending Dreamweaver). These files include a sample behavior to get you started.

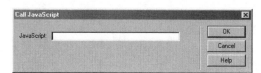

Figure 16.72 Dreamweaver gives you the option of calling JavaScript with the Call JavaScript behavior.

To Call a Script

Something tells me that if you can write JavaScript, you can tell the script when to happen. Nevertheless, Dreamweaver covers all the bases with the Call JavaScript behavior.

To add the Call JavaScript behavior to the page:

1. In the Behaviors panel, select the browser you want to target.

2. In the Document window, select the object associated with the event.

3. Click the Add Action button, and from the pop-up menu, select Call JavaScript. The Call JavaScript dialog box will appear (**Figure 16.72**).

4. Type the name of a function, or a string of JavaScript in the text box.

5. Click OK to return to the Document window.

6. In the Behaviors panel, specify the user event that you want to trigger the action.

Saves you a few lines of coding, anyway.

✔ Tips

■ The Macromedia Dreamweaver Exchange offers a free script repository of behaviors written by Macromedia developers and Dreamweaver users. The site includes information on the version number of the script, the developer name, user ratings, and number of downloads. To get behaviors from the Web, click on the Add Action button in the Behaviors panel, and select Get More Behaviors. This will bring you to the main page for the exchange, where you can browse the behaviors by category.

■ You can add and manage these third-party extensions with the Extensions Manager. Because this chapter is quite long enough already, I cover the Extensions Manager in Appendix M on the Web site for this book.

ADDING MORE ACTIONS

AUTOMATING DREAMWEAVER

Figure 17.1 This page footer, including text, links, and the image and horizontal rule, is perfect fodder for a Dreamweaver library item. You can insert it into any new or existing Web page in a matter of seconds. If one of the links changes or the information changes, you can automatically update all pages that use this footer.

Figure 17.2 Dreamweaver templates allow you to create a basic shell page on which some areas are editable and some are read-only. The editable regions appear in highlighted boxes with tabs that show the name of the region.

Dreamweaver helps you save time by creating elements that you can reuse and update easily across an entire site. Library items are reusable chunks of code, and templates are page designs.

The Dreamweaver Library is a storehouse of frequently used items (**Figure 17.1**) that are linked to the site cache. If you're familiar with server-side includes, library items work the same way: The HTML for the item is inserted into the page, along with a reference to the library item's URL. If you change a library item, you can then update the pages that use it. You can also insert actual server-side include tokens in Dreamweaver and view them inline.

Dreamweaver also lets you update pages by building templates (**Figure 17.2**); you can base pages on a template file that you can then update. And speaking of templates, you can export editable regions of templates as XML and import XML into templates.

One more way you can automate Dreamweaver is with the History panel (**Figure 17.3**), which lets you repeat actions you've performed during a session. You can even save sets of actions as macros to reuse later.

About Libraries

The Library is a collection of HTML files with the extension .lbi. These files, called *library items*, are stored in a specifically designated Library folder in a local site on your computer (**Figure 17.4**). As part of Dreamweaver's site management tools, the Library folder is stored in the site root folder of each site you use with Dreamweaver.

If you have more than one local site on your computer, each will use its own Library folder.

✔ Tip

■ In Dreamweaver, a *local site* is the same as a folder or set of folders. If you designate a folder on your hard drive as a local site, Dreamweaver will then know how to keep track of locally linked files. For more on local sites, see Chapter 2.

You must set up, or define, a local site in Dreamweaver before you can use library items. Dreamweaver will create the Library folder for you.

You create, edit, and place library items using the Library category on the Assets panel. If you're upgrading from Dreamweaver 2 or 3, rest assured this panel works the same way as the old Library palette.

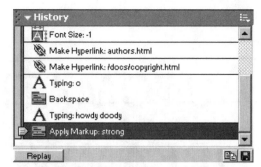

Figure 17.3 The History panel lets you redo and undo nearly any action you perform in the Document window. You can also save sets of actions as commands.

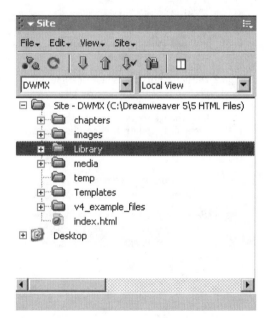

Figure 17.4 A local site on my hard drive. The Library folder is highlighted.

Library category button

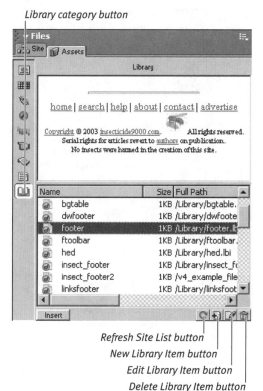

Refresh Site List button
New Library Item button
Edit Library Item button
Delete Library Item button

Figure 17.5 Use the Library category on the Assets panel to create and insert library items.

To display the Library:

◆ From the menu bar, select Window > Assets. Then click the Library button on the Assets panel: 📖 . The Library category of the Assets panel will appear (**Figure 17.5**).

So Which Is Which?

Libraries, snippets (Chapter 4) and custom objects (Chapter 18) all do similar things, so which one do you use for your purposes? Think of it in terms of form and content: libraries and snippets are used for content, and objects are the form.

Objects are good for inserting standard containers (like tables or layers) that you'll put content in later, or commonly used gizmos like JavaScript buttons or special-sized horizontal rules. However, they don't update automatically (as do libraries), and they aren't site-specific.

And as for snippets, they're great for chunks of code that you don't need to update and that don't contain relative links or images.

The superpower of libraries is that you can spread them over an entire site and still update them as often as you like. Libraries are best used for inserting content that may change over time. See the sidebar, *Bitchin' Examples*, on the next page.

What Library Items Do

Library items are little pieces of Web pages—pieces that you want to reuse on many pages, and pieces that you want to be able to update on every one of those pages.

Library items can contain HTML and JavaScript. Any objects (that is, images, plug-ins, and applets) will not be duplicated in a library item; instead, the library item will link to those objects, just as on a Web page.

Many big sites use CGI scripts to automatically replace text on page after page of a site, but library items can accomplish the same thing. They also act very much like server-side includes, described later in this chapter.

Unlike with server-side includes, when you use library items, the HTML code itself is stored locally in each page, and you must update your files locally and then re-upload them in order for your changes to go live. However, library items are a user-friendly substitute if you fear UNIX and know nothing about setting the environment on your Web server so that server-side includes execute properly.

If you move files around, this might affect the links to your library items. You can automatically update library references when files are moved; see *Updating Your Site*, later in this chapter.

✔ Tip

- The Library is a category on the Assets panel. To save words, I sometimes refer to "the Library category on the Assets panel" as "the Library." If you haven't yet played with the Assets panel, see Chapter 2.

Today in history:

Born: Otto von Bismarck (1755), **Edmond Rostand** (1868), **Sergei Rachmaninoff** (1873), **Lon Chaney** (1883), **Milan Kundera** (1929), **Samuel R Delany** (1942)

Big Day for Baseball Fans: The first official National League baseball game was played today in **1876**. Fifty-five years later, in **1931**, Jackie Mitchell became the first woman to play professional baseball. Then in **1938**, the Baseball Hall of Fame opened in Cooperstown, New York.

Figure 17.6 This "Today in History" sidebar gets updated daily. Making the whole chunk, including the layer containing the text, into a library item means you just update the library item to update the page—you don't even need to open the page.

Figure 17.7 If this navigation bar appeared on every page in your site, it would be a pain to replace every instance of it if you added a search function (and thus, a new toolbar button). Make it a library item, add a new image, and update the site automatically.

Bitchin' Examples

- The footer with copyright info at the bottom of every page in your site (like the one I showed you in Figure 17.1)

- Daily updates on pages that aren't otherwise updated (**Figure 17.6**)

- Navigation bars on sites that are still growing (**Figure 17.7**)

- Frequently used logo images, contact email addresses, or mastheads

Tag selector

Figure 17.8 Select all the text, images, and other code you want to include in your library item. Here, I'm selecting the <center> tag in the Tag selector, which includes all the tags and text I want to use.

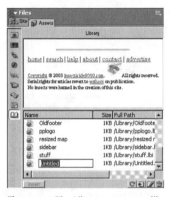

Figure 17.9 The Library, more wordily known as the Library category on the Assets panel. To just display the Library without adding a new item to it, select Window > Assets from the menu bar.

Figure 17.10 The elements you've added to the Library will be highlighted in yellow, and the entire chunk of stuff will be one object—click anywhere within the yellow area to select the item.

Creating a Library Item

You create a library item by copying a piece of existing HTML into the Library. You can select part of any existing page, or you can create a dummy page for the sole purpose of adding items from it to the Library.

To create a new library item:

1. Open the page that contains the stuff you want to add to the Library.

   If you are working with a new page, save the page in a folder on your local site.

2. Select the desired objects (**Figure 17.8**).

   You may want to use the Code inspector, Split view, or the tag selector to select all the tags you need.

3. From the menu bar, select Modify > Library > Add Object to Library. The Library will appear (**Figure 17.9**).

   or

   Drag the selection into the list box on the Library category of the Assets panel.

   or

   On the Library category of the Assets panel, click the New button ⊞.

4. Type a name for the library item in the text box, replacing the word Untitled.

   Your new item will be highlighted in yellow in the Document window (**Figure 17.10**).

✔ Tips

- Once you designate a selection on a page as a library item, you will not be able to edit it freely. See *Editing Library Items*, later in this chapter, for more on this.

- If you want to save the content of a selection as a library item without replacing the selection on your page with the library item itself, hold down the Ctrl (Command) key while creating the library item.

Inserting and Removing Library Items

Now that you've created a library item, you can add it to other new or existing pages in the site.

To insert a library item by dragging:

◆ The easiest way to add a library item to a page is to drag the library item icon from the Library category of the Assets panel to the Document window (**Figure 17.11**).

To add a library item at the insertion point:

1. Click to place the insertion point at the place in the Document window (such as a table cell) where you want the library item to appear.

2. In the Library, click on the icon for the library item you want to add.

3. Click the Insert button. The library item will appear at the insertion point (**Figure 17.12**).

To remove a library item from a page:

1. Click anywhere within the highlighted library item to select the entire thing (**Figure 17.13**).

2. Press Backspace or Delete. The library item will disappear.

✔ Tip

■ To add the contents of a library item—the code and links—without linking it to the Library, hold down the Ctrl (Command) button and drag the library item onto the page. You won't be able to update this instance of the Library item when you perform an update.

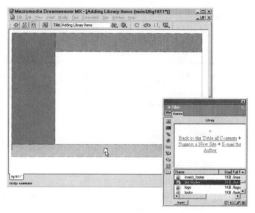

Figure 17.11 Drag a library item icon from the Library panel right onto the page. The library item will be inserted where you drop it.

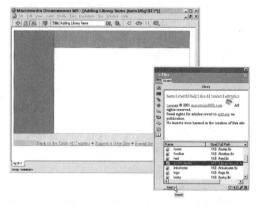

Figure 17.12 Click on the Insert button, and the library item will appear on the page at the insertion point.

Figure 17.13 Click anywhere on a library item to select the whole thing. Then you can delete it, or cut and paste it anywhere.

INSERTING AND REMOVING LIBRARY ITEMS

Figure 17.14 The Property inspector, displaying library item properties.

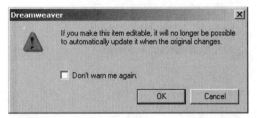

Figure 17.15 Dreamweaver warns you that the item will no longer be linked to the Library. To keep this dialog box from appearing, check the Don't warn me again check box.

Figure 17.16 After making the item editable, the yellow highlighting is removed and the item is no longer linked to the Library.

Creative Renaming Tricks

You can rename a library item if you want to divorce it on purpose from the pages that reference the item. Then, you can create a new item with the old name, and old references will point to the new item.

For example, say I have a library item called Toolbar. I want to completely change the toolbar, but I don't want to get rid of the library item entirely. I rename the old Toolbar OldToolbar, without updating. Then I create a new library item called Toolbar. The old references will point to the new item.

Editing Library Items

There are two ways to edit a library item:

◆ Make the library item editable on just one page by disconnecting it from the Library and then editing it on that page (the change will be local).

◆ Edit the library item in its own window (the change will be global).

Changing a single instance of a library item

Making an item editable, or detaching it from the Library, means that it has the same content as the library item had, but it is no longer linked to the Library. This means that if you automatically update the entire site from the Library, the ex-library item on the page you edited will not be updated.

To make a library item editable:

1. In any document that contains the library item you wish to edit, select the library item by clicking on it (as we saw in Figure 17.13).

2. View the Property inspector, if it isn't open (**Figure 17.14**), by selecting Window > Properties from the menu bar or by double-clicking on the library item.

3. On the Property inspector, click Detach from Original. A dialog box will warn you that this will prevent the library item from being affected by future Library updates (**Figure 17.15**).

4. Click OK to close the dialog box. The item will be de-linked from the Site Library, and you can go ahead and edit it on that one page (**Figure 17.16**).

Changing a library item site-wide

If you want to edit all instances of a library item so that you can update it on all the pages that use it, you need to edit the item in its own window.

To edit a library item globally:

1. In the Library, click on the icon for the item you want to edit. The current version will be displayed in the preview area on the Assets panel (**Figure 17.17**).

2. Click the Edit button.

   or

   Double-click either the name of the library item or the preview frame. Either way, a new document window will appear that contains only the HTML included in the library item (**Figure 17.18**).

3. Make your changes to the library item.

4. Save the changes to the library item using File > Save or Ctrl+S (Command+S). A dialog box will ask if you want to update all documents in your local site that contain the library item (**Figure 17.19**).

   ◆ To update now, click Update.

   ◆ To update later, click Don't Update. (You may want to postpone this until you're finished editing and then update everything at once.)

5. Close the library item's Document window.

Figure 17.17 When you select an item in the Library, it is displayed in the frame at the top of the Assets panel.

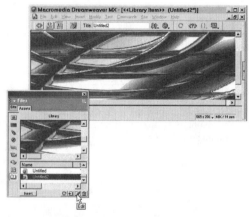

Figure 17.18 Click on the Asset panel's Edit button to open a library item in its own Document window.

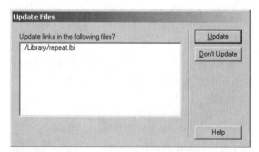

Figure 17.19 When you save the changes to the library item, a dialog box will appear asking you if you want to update the entire site.

Preview area

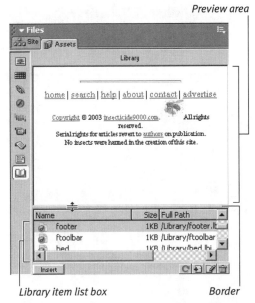

Library item list box   *Border*

Figure 17.20 Drag the border between the two frames to change the size of the preview area.

✔ Tips

- To find out more about updating pages that use library items, see *Updating Your Site*, later in this chapter.

- You can make the preview area larger or smaller by dragging the border between the two frames in the Assets panel (**Figure 17.20**).

Deleting a Library Item

Deleting a library item removes the file from the Library. However, the pages that use the library item will still include the code that links the page to the Library.

To delete a library item:

1. In the Library, select the item you want to delete (**Figure 17.21**).

2. Click the Delete button: 🗑 . A dialog box will ask you if you really want to delete the library item (**Figure 17.22**).

3. Click Yes. Poof! It's gone.

✔ Tip

■ Probably the easiest way to remove references to deleted library items is to select them and then make them editable. That removes references to the .lbi file, but leaves the content intact.

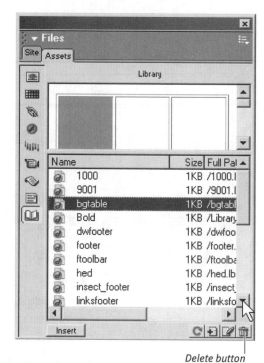

Delete button

Figure 17.21 Click on the name of the item you want to remove from the Library.

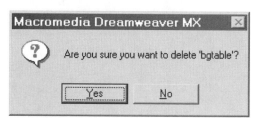

Figure 17.22 To commence deleting the item from the Library, click Yes.

DELETING A LIBRARY ITEM

Re-creating a Library Item

If you delete an item from the Library, but it still exists on any page, you can re-create it.

Besides reinstating deleted library items, you can use the Recreate function to replace the contents of a library item with the contents of an edited library item (or vice versa). This is useful for renamed or mistakenly edited items.

Library Code

The code for a library item consists of two things: The code for the item itself, such as table tags, image paths, anchors, text, and font formatting; and the code that links the item to the Library.

Code for a standard footer might look like this:

```
<!-- #BeginLibraryItem "/Library/tabletalk.lbi" -->

<center>

<font size="-1">Copyright &copy; 2003, Animalogic. All rights reserved. <a
href="/legal/">Legal Notices</a>.</font>

</center>

<!-- #EndLibraryItem -->
```

Dreamweaver keeps track of library-linked pages using the site cache (discussed in Chapters 2 and 19). When a library item is moved or renamed within the Library panel or the Site window, Dreamweaver looks for the #BeginLibraryItem marker in pages within your site.

If you want to remove all library item markers from a site, you can use Dreamweaver's Replace feature (Edit > Find and Replace), discussed in Chapter 8, or the Clean Up HTML feature (Commands > Clean Up HTML; select Dreamweaver Comments), discussed in Chapter 4.

To re-create a library item:

1. In the Document window, select an edited library item or an item that was deleted from the Library palette (**Figure 17.23**).

2. On the Property inspector, click the Recreate button (**Figure 17.24**). If you're overwriting an existing library item, a dialog box will appear (**Figure 17.25**).

3. Click OK. The contents of the selected library item will overwrite the contents of the existing library item (**Figure 17.26**). (In the case of deleted items, the original name will be re-added to the Library).

✔ Tips

- You cannot overwrite a library item with the contents of another library item. In other words, you can't select the item July and overwrite it with the contents of June.

- The ability to re-create library items is one reason not to update your site immediately after you edit a library item. As long as the old library item content exists on a page somewhere, you can re-create the original. I like to update my library items just before I upload pages. See *Updating Your Site*, later in this chapter. I cover updating Libraries and templates at the same time.

Figure 17.23 I accidentally edited the Looky library item so that it consisted of the text link on the bottom instead of the selected images. I still have a copy of the old library item on my page, so I select it.

Figure 17.24 I click the Recreate button on the Property inspector.

Figure 17.25 A dialog box warns me that I'm about to overwrite the contents of the library item.

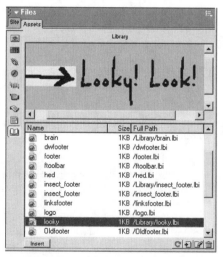

Figure 17.26 I have successfully rewritten the Looky library item with the old contents.

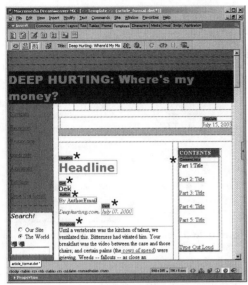

★ *Editable regions*

Figure 17.27 This template page has areas that are marked as editable. Other areas are not editable in Dreamweaver. If I change the design—fonts, colors, whatever—I can then update all the pages based on this template.

Dreamweaver Templates

In Dreamweaver templates, you design a page and then designate certain portions of the page as editable. The rest is locked to the user. So as a designer, you can give anyone a template-based page to edit, and they won't be able to mess up your precious page design.

If you update the template design after it's been used on any number of pages, you can painlessly update all pages on your local site that use that template. Then you just re-upload the affected pages, and they'll have the changed template content.

For instance, if you suddenly want to change the page background of your site from blue to orange, or the copyright date from 2002 to 2003, you change a single file—the template—and then update all pages that use that template (**Figure 17.27**). After you update the pages, you need to re-upload them to the Web server before your changes will be live.

Template tools

As with library items, templates are stored in a local site folder called Templates (**Figure 17.28**). Each site uses a different Templates folder. For more about managing local sites, see Chapter 2.

The tool you use to work with templates is the Templates category on the Assets panel (**Figure 17.29**). To display Templates, select Window > Assets from the menu bar, and then click the Templates button ▣ . (See Chapter 2 for more on Assets.)

The top half displays a preview of the template's content, and the bottom half lists the templates available to your local site.

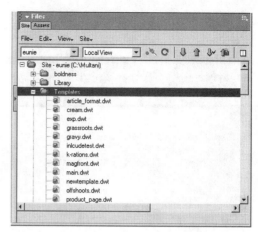

Figure 17.28 Templates are stored in the templates folder in your local site.

Template category button

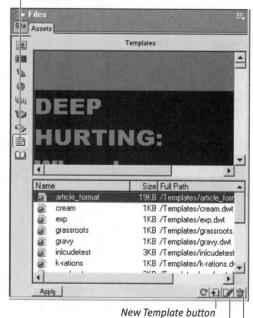

New Template button
Edit button
Delete button

Figure 17.29 The Templates category on the Assets panel shows all the templates available in the current site.

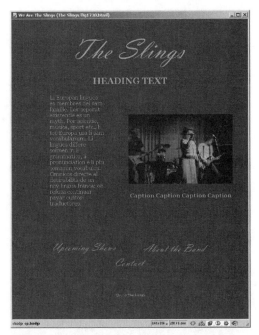

Figure 17.30 Create the design you want to reuse.

Figure 17.31 Create a template file and mark some regions as editable.

About the Template Process

Dreamweaver templates are more complex than just saving a page design and reusing it over and over again. Templates may seem harder to use at first than is absolutely necessary, but they can be quite versatile.

The basic template process is fairly straightforward, but the devil is in the details. In this chapter, we'll be following the basic outline below.

I'll also go into detail about the new template features, such as repeating and optional regions and the quirks of template syntax. And, as with library items, I discuss how to detach pages from template files, and finally, how to update templates and library items.

The template process:

1. Create the page design you want to reuse (**Figure 17.30**).

2. Save your file as a Dreamweaver template document (.DWT).

3. Assign at least one editable region to the template (**Figure 17.31**).

   You can assign multiple editable regions, as well as repeating regions and editable attributes.

continued on next page

4. Save the template. It will be available in the Templates category of the Assets panel (**Figure 17.32**).

5. Create a page based on that template, or assign a template to a page. Your page is now attached to the template document.

6. Edit all appropriate regions on that new page (**Figure 17.33**). You can also import XML into the template page.

7. If you edit the template file itself, you can update all template pages attached to it.

Now we'll look at how to create templates, add regions to them, base pages on those templates, and edit those pages.

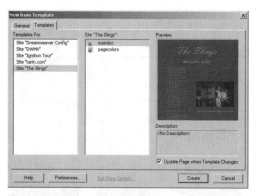

Figure 17.32 When you save your template, it'll be available in the Assets panel (**Figure 17.29**) and the New Document dialog box.

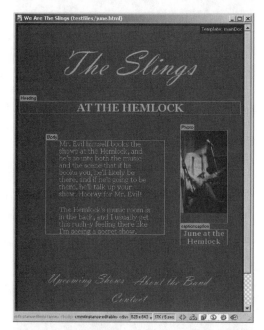

Figure 17.33 In pages based on your template, only editable regions can be changed.

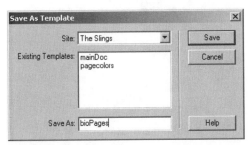

Figure 17.34 In the Save As Template dialog box, type the name of the new template. You can also overwrite an existing file from this dialog box.

Title bar indicates template file

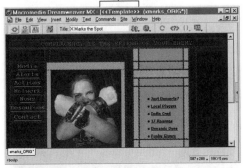

Figure 17.35 You can tell you have a template file open instead of a regular page—even if you haven't yet marked any editable regions—by looking at the title bar.

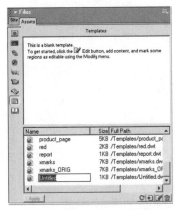

Figure 17.36 Click the New Template button in the Templates category, and then type the name of your template in place of "Untitled."

Creating Templates

The first step is creating the template file itself.

To base a template on an existing file:

1. Open the file you'd like to use as the template for other pages on your site.

2. From the menu bar, select File > Save as Template. The Save As Template dialog box will appear (**Figure 17.34**). Any existing templates will be listed in the Existing Templates list box.

3. If you have more than one local site, select the site the template will reside in from the Site drop-down menu.

4. Type a filename for the template in the Save As dialog box. The .dwt extension will automatically be appended to the file.

5. Click Save to save the file as a template.

The template will now be displayed in the Document window instead of the original HTML file. You can tell a template by the title bar—it says <<Template>> (**Figure 17.35**).

To create a template from scratch:

1. On the Templates category of the Assets panel, click the New Template button: 🔁 . A new Template icon will appear in the Assets panel (**Figure 17.36**).

   or

   On the Templates panel of the Insert toolbar, click the Make Template button: 📄 .

2. In the Assets panel, type a name for the new template in place of "Untitled," and press Enter (Return).

3. On the Assets panel, double-click the name of the template, or click the Edit button 📝 . A blank Document window will appear. You'll see the name of the template file (*nn*.dwt) displayed in the Document window title bar.

Setting Page Properties on Templates and Pages

When users work with a page based on a template, they cannot edit any page properties other than the page title (**Figure 17.37**).

✔ Tip

- When a user tries to change page properties for pages based on a template, the locked properties are not grayed out. However, if you try to change anything, you'll get an error message. Click OK when the error message appears, and the properties will remain unchanged.

You should set page properties, such as the page background and text and link colors, in the template file itself (**Figure 17.38**). If you want some of your pages to have different page properties, then you have three choices: Set body attributes as editable (see *Editable Tag Attributes*); using nested templates (see the sidebar, *Using Nested Templates*); or basing different pages on different templates.

See Chapter 3 for more about page properties.

✔ Tip

- In Dreamweaver MX, You can make HTML attributes editable, including page properties. See *Editable Tag Attributes*, later in this chapter.

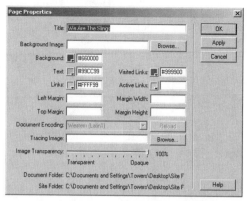

Figure 17.37 Remember to set any page properties for your template (Modify > Page Properties), such as the page background or text and link colors. The only page property that can be edited for a page based on a template is the page title.

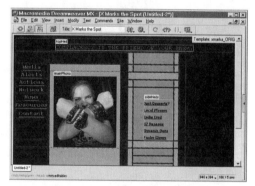

Figure 17.38 On this page, which is based on the template I created in **Figure 17.35,** the title can be edited, but the background, text, and link colors cannot.

Using CSS and JavaScript

New in Dreamweaver MX, you can define and add CSS styles in pages based on templates. In previous versions of Dreamweaver, you could not edit anything in the document head except the title.

You may still find it more convenient to create style sheets in a template and have them apply to all pages based on that template.

You can also create layers, which use unique instances of CSS, in pages based on templates.

As for JavaScript, your mileage may vary. You can add some behaviors to documents based on templates, as long as they appear within the editable part of the head tag (see below).

✔ Tip

■ To lock the <head> of your documents, remove this tag from the template:
`<!-- InstanceBeginEditable name="head" --> <!-- InstanceEndEditable -->`.

About Template Regions

The next step in creating a template is assigning editable regions to it.

Everything you place on a template will be locked—that is, you or your staff will not be able to edit that part of the page—unless you mark it as a named editable region.

Now in Dreamweaver MX, there are four kinds of template regions that can be edited: editable regions; repeating regions; optional regions; and editable tag attributes.

If you've used Dreamweaver templates before, you're familiar with the concept of regions and with editable regions in particular. Dreamweaver MX expands on that concept with the following:

♦ **Repeating regions** are items that will repeat on your page. **Repeating tables** are a subtype of repeating regions. Repeating regions are not themselves editable, but you can insert an editable region within a repeating region or repeating table.

♦ **Editable regions** are containers for content that can be changed on pages based on your template. See the next section, *Setting Editable Regions*.

♦ **Optional regions** are not quite what they sound like. They are indeed optional items, but you must write if-then statements in JavaScript to determine whether the regions appear on a given page. Because it would take about a chapter's worth of pages to describe writing the code for these regions, I cover optional regions only in the sidebar *About Optional Regions*.

♦ **Editable Tag Attributes** allow you to set part of a tag as editable. For example, you could set table background colors as editable, but not allow editing of table widths; you can make image source or alignment editable; and for text, you could allow the changing of font colors and not let anyone change your font faces. See the section *Editable Tag Attributes*.

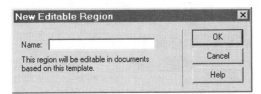

Figure 17.39 Type the name of the new region in the Name text box.

Name of new editable region

Figure 17.40 The new editable region will appear in the Document window at the insertion point, and its name will appear both on the tab on top of the region marker and inside the region marker in plain, unformatted text.

Unmarking Editable Regions

To unmark an editable region, first you select it. Then, from the menu bar, select Modify > Templates > Remove Template Markup. The region will no longer be editable.

You can even export all your template-based pages to another site minus their original markup. From the menu bar select Modify > Templates > Export Without Markup. The Export Site Without Template Markup dialog box will appear. Save your page in the proper folder, and click OK.

Setting Editable Regions

For parts of your page design that you want to appear on every document based on your design, use an editable region.

✔ Tip

- The syntax involved in Optional and Repeating regions can be less than thrilling to learn and clunky to use, so I suggest starting with regular editable regions if you're just trying to learn the whole Dreamweaver template thing. You can stick with plain old editable regions for most tasks until you want to get fancy.

To create a new editable region:

1. Click to place the insertion point where you want the new editable region to appear.

2. From the menu bar, select Insert > Template Objects > Editable Region.

   or

   On the Templates tab of the Insert toolbar, click the Editable Region button: 📝 .

   Either way, the New Editable Region dialog box will appear (**Figure 17.39**).

3. Type a name for the editable region in the text box. Avoid funky characters, and don't use quotation marks or <angle brackets>.

4. Click OK to close the New Editable Region dialog box and return to the Document window. The name of the editable region will appear highlighted in the Document window (**Figure 17.40**) in a little box with the name of the editable region on top. You can edit this text, if you like.

✔ Tip

- For pages based on templates, we will learn what to do with these and other regions in the section *Using Editable Regions*.

Marking page regions as editable

You can also create a page element and then mark it as editable.

To set an editable region:

1. Type and select an object or some place-holder text, such as "Headline or Image Goes Here" (**Figure 17.41**).

2. From the menu bar, select Insert > Template Objects > Editable Region.

   or

   On the Insert toolbar select the Templates tab, then click the Editable Region button: . The New Editable Region dialog box will appear (Figure 17.39).

3. Type a name for the editable region in the text box. Avoid funky characters, and don't use quotation marks or <angle brackets>.

4. Click OK. The editable region will be boxed in the template's Document window with the name of the editable region on its tab (**Figure 17.42**).

Figure 17.41 Select some text or an object that you want to make editable on pages based on your template.

Figure 17.42 The text I marked as editable became marked with an editable region border in the Document window with the name of the region on its tab. Note that both regions include formatting for font size and such.

```
14 <p><!-- TemplateBeginEditable name="SingleBlock" -->
15 Text 1 - Region can consist of only one paragraph or
   block.<br>
16 The user will not be allowed to press Enter to start a new
   block within this region.
17 <!-- TemplateEndEditable --></p>
18
19
20 <!-- TemplateBeginEditable name="MultipleBlocks" -->
21 <p>Text 2 - Block can be expanded to include many
   paragraphs.</p>
22 <!-- TemplateEndEditable -->
```

Figure 17.43 The editable region starting on line 14 exists inside of a <P> tag, so no additional blocks can be created inside that region. The editable region starting on line 20 includes the <P> tag inside the region, so I can do whatever text formatting I like in this region.

Editable Region Quirks

Marking editable regions is for the most part easy, but there are several variables you must take into account when incorporating text formatting, tables, and layers.

Block formatting

In order to allow text on template pages to be expanded beyond a single paragraph, you must set editable regions outside block tags such as <p>, <blockquote>, <hn>, and so on (**Figure 17.43**). In some templates created with previous versions of Dreamweaver, this wasn't an issue, but if you open these in MX, you may find a dialog box like the one in **Figure 17.44** advising you to move your <p> tags to inside the region tags. Oddly enough, placing an editable region inside the <i> and <b> tags brings up a similar error message.

Figure 17.44 If you do what I did on line 14, above, Dreamweaver will keep warning you about it. This dialog box tells you that your <p> tags are outside the region tags. It shows up on saves, on creating template pages, and on updates.

Text formatting

If you set text formatting in an editable region using HTML tags, those tags can be altered or removed (**Figure 17.45**). In other words, if your region StoryHed is set in the Georgia font, that font face can be changed on template pages.

To make text formatting unalterable on template pages, you have two choices. First, you could, in Code view, move the <font> and other tags to *outside* the region tags (**Figure 17.46**). See *Block formatting*, on the previous page, about an error message that may pop up if you do this with some tags.

The better choice is to use CSS. You can redefine entire tags, in the case of wanting to make all body text appear in a certain font, for example. For style classes, apply them to an editable region, and the class will be applied to the tag, or the <span> tag will be wrapped around the region (**Figure 17.47**). You can attach a style sheet to a template or you can include CSS formatting inline in the template's head tag. See Chapter 11 for more about CSS.

Figure 17.45 Even though I specified font formatting in my template file (top), on the page based on the template, I was able to change all the font formatting in the editable regions.

```
16  <font face="Comic Sans MS, Lucida Handwriting, Viner Hand
    ITC, cursive, sans-serif" size="+4">
17  <!-- #BeginEditable "hedText" -->hedText
18  <!-- #EndEditable -->
19  </font>
```

Figure 17.46 To make font tags uneditable, move them to outside the region tag. An even better choice is to use CSS.

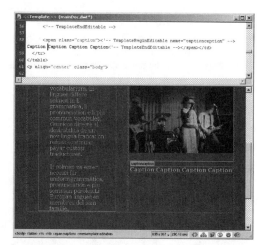

Figure 17.47 On this page, I used CSS to format styles for the body text and caption. You can apply a style class to a paragraph (line 61) or to an editable region itself (line 58).

Layer tag <div> is region

Layer contents are region

Figure 17.48 On the top is the template file. The left-hand layer and its contents are altogether editable; in the right-hand layer, only the contents are editable.

Tables

You can mark an entire table as editable, and you can mark an entire table row <tr> or a single table cell <td> as editable, but you cannot mark a column or a few cells as an editable region. If you attempt to do so, Dreamweaver will make the table row or the table the content of the editable region.

If you select a cell <td> within a table and set it as editable, that cell and its attributes and contents can be edited.

If you select the *contents* of a cell and set it as editable, the cell's contents will be editable, but the <td> attributes will not be editable.

Layers

If you select a layer <div> and make it editable, all layer attributes and layer content will be editable (**Figure 17.48**).

If you select the *contents* of a layer and make it editable, those contents can be changed but the layer itself cannot be modified—not moved, not resized, no color changes, and so on.

Adding Repeating Regions

Setting repeating regions is similar to setting editable regions. You place the repeating region only once, and then on the pages based on that template, you can add instances of that region.

As we saw with editable regions, you can either select some text and then wrap the repeating region around it, or you can insert the region and then edit the text inside it.

To add a repeating region:

1. Click to place the insertion point where you want the repeating region to appear, *or* select text or an object you want to make into a repeating region (**Figure 17.49**).

2. From the menu bar, select Insert > Template Objects > Repeating Region.

   or

   Click the Repeating Region button ![] on the Templates tab of the Insert toolbar.

   Either way, the New Repeating Region dialog box will appear (**Figure 17.50**).

3. Type a name for your repeating region, and click OK.

   The repeating region will appear a single time on your template (**Figure 17.51**).

Unless you want the same text repeated throughout your page, remember to add an editable region inside the repeating region. See the next page.

Figure 17.49 I've selected an image and some text to repeat on my page.

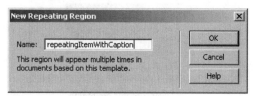

Figure 17.50 Name your repeating region.

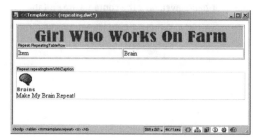

Figure 17.51 On this template, I've wrapped a repeating region around two different items: the objects we saw in **Figure 17.49**, and a table row <tr> tag. If I save the page now, the items will not be editable.

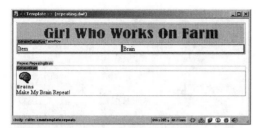

Figure 17.52 I've made my repeating regions editable. To do so, select the contents of the repeating region, not the region itself, and insert an editable region as usual. We'll see this page again later in this chapter to see how these regions can repeat.

To insert an editable region inside the repeating region:

1. Select the text inside the repeating region.

2. From the menu bar, select Insert > Template Objects > Editable Region. The New Editable Region dialog box will appear.

3. Type a name for your editable region, and click OK.

   The editable region will appear inside the repeating region (**Figure 17.52**).

✔ Tip

- You can set a table row as a repeating region (Figure 17.51), in which case users of the template page will be able to add rows to the table if they need them.

Creating a repeating table

You also have the option of adding to a template a table in which only some areas repeat, such as you might use for a catalog, schedule, or sidebar. For an editable table, you choose which areas you want to be editable. (Other areas may be reserved for header info, blank rows, server-side includes, and so on. See **Figure 17.53**)

To insert a repeating table:

1. Open the relevant template.

2. From the menu bar, select Insert > Template Objects > Repeating Table.

   or

   Click the Repeating Table button [img] on the Templates tab of the Insert toolbar.

   Either way, the Insert Repeating Table dialog box will appear (**Figure 17.54**).

3. The Repeating Table dialog box has two functions: placing the code for the table itself, and designating which areas of the table will be marked as repeating and editable regions.

   In the top half of the dialog box, set the number of columns and rows for your table, as well as any additional table attributes such as border. (See Chapter 12.)

4. In the Repeat rows of the table area of the dialog box, set at which row you want the repeating regions to start and end.

   These numbers should reflect the total number of columns and rows; you can't stop repeating at Row 7 in a table with 6 rows.

5. In the Region Name text box, type a name for the repeating table region.

6. Click OK.

   The table will appear on your page, including a generically named, blank editable region in each cell you set as repeating (**Figure 17.55**).

Figure 17.53 On this table, which could be a catalog of some kind, I might want the middle two rows to repeat, but not the top two rows or the bottom row.

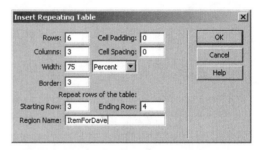

Figure 17.54 In the Repeating Table dialog box, define the size and attributes of your table, and then give the repeating table a name.

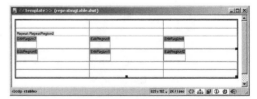

Figure 17.55 This is what my example table in **Figure 17.53** looks like when it's first inserted. Unfortunately, you cannot select a table and convert it to a repeating table, but you can copy and paste your cells and their contents

Sidebar (vertical, left margin): **ADDING REPEATING REGIONS**

Figure 17.56 On this template, normally the top headline would not be editable. I'm going to allow attributes of the <font> tag to be edited, so I click on the text and then select the <font> tag in the Tag selector.

Name of tag you selected in step 1.

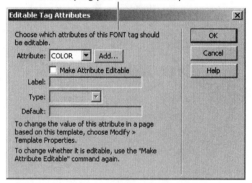

Figure 17.57 The Editable Tag Attributes dialog box.

Figure 17.58 Select an attribute you've already applied to the tag from the Attribute drop-down menu. For additional attributes, click Add.

Figure 17.59 Click Add and specify an additional attribute in the Editable Tag dialog box. For example, I could add the "width" attribute to a table cell even if I hadn't yet added it in the Document window.

Editable Tag Attributes

New in Dreamweaver MX, you can choose to make certain tag attributes editable in template pages.

To set a tag attribute as editable:

1. On the template document, click on the object or text you want to edit, and select its tag in the tag selector (**Figure 17.56**).

2. From the menu bar, select Modify > Templates > Make Attribute Editable. The Editable Tag Attributes dialog box will appear (**Figure 17.57**).

3. Select your attribute from the Attribute drop-down menu (**Figure 17.58**).

    Only those attributes already applied to the tag will appear in the menu; to add another, click Add. A dialog box will appear (**Figure 17.59**); type your attribute in the text box and click OK to return to the Editable Tag Attributes dialog box.

continued on next page

4. With your attribute selected in the Attribute drop-down menu, check the Make Attribute Editable check box; more options will appear (**Figure 17.60**).

5. Label your attribute something memorable, like sidebarColor or catalogImage.

6. Now, from the Type drop-down menu, choose how the attribute can be edited on template pages (**Figure 17.61**):

◆ **Text** allows the user to type a value.

◆ **URL** allows the user to set a local path for a page, an image, or a media object.

◆ **Color** allows the user to use the color picker.

◆ **True/False** is used mainly for JavaScript and CSS functions.

◆ **Number** limits the entries to numbers, for items such as height or Vspace.

7. Type a Default Value—which will show up on the page until it's changed—in that text box.

8. Repeat steps 4 through 7 for additional attributes.

9. Click OK to save your changes.

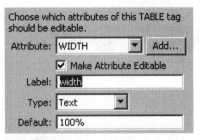

Figure 17.60 When you check the Make Attribute Editable check box, more options will become visible.

Figure 17.61 Select the way in which your attribute should be editable.

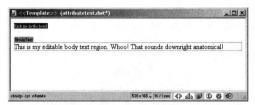

Figure 17.62 After I made all attributes of my font tag editable, it appeared changed its appearance to show no active attributes on my template document.

Figure 17.63 On pages *based on* my template, however, the attributes showed up with my default settings.

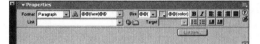

Figure 17.64 On the template document, the Property inspector shows template code where normal attribute settings usually go.

In the Document window for your template file, you'll see all the attributes removed from your text (**Figure 17.62**). On pages based on your template, however (**Figure 17.63**), the default settings will take effect.

In the Property inspector (**Figure 17.64**), you'll see the attributes you originally set replaced by strange-looking code like this: @@(attribute)@@. This is in Dreamweaver's Template Expression Markup Language.

We'll find out how to use editable attributes on Web pages in the section *Using Template Pages.*

✔ Tips

- To make an attribute uneditable, follow steps 1 through 3, above, and then uncheck the Make Attribute Editable check box.

- Beyond the font tag, you can use the editable attribute feature on such tags as <body> (to allow background and link colors to be changed); <img> (to allow source, alignment, and spacing to be changed); <a> (to allow link paths on otherwise uneditable text to be changed) and tables and table elements, to allow things like color and dimensions to be changed.

About Optional Template Regions

An optional region, also new in Dreamweaver MX, is a region that may or may not appear on a page, depending on context and whether it's needed. You set template parameters to determine whether the optional region will appear on a page.

Although you insert an optional region using a dialog box (**Figures 17.65** and **17.66**), you must code the expressions yourself in order for the regions to work in any meaningful way. There is no equivalent of the Behaviors panel for writing these expressions.

For the most part, optional regions work best with dynamic pages, so that if a page contains, say, an order number, a "Buy This" button would appear on the page. For catalog pages, items that are kid-friendly or on sale could have a special graphic appear next to them.

Optional regions in templates use a language called Template Expression Language, which is a variant of JavaScript.

The idea of an optional region is simple, but its execution is complex enough that you need to understand JavaScript as well as Dreamweaver's template tags, and be comfortable writing your own. You can view a list of template tags and some rudimentary examples of template expression code in Dreamweaver's help files under Working with Multiple Pages > Managing Site Assets, Libraries and Templates > Reference.

The insertion of the region itself is done in exactly the same way as you do an editable one (Insert > Template Objects > Optional Region or Editable Optional Region, or the Optional Region buttons), at which point you're confronted with the Insert Optional Region dialog box. Here, you name the region and set parameters or expressions that determine whether the region will appear.

Expressions are pieces of code that calculate or evaluate data and then perform an operation—in this case, showing or hiding the optional region.

Parameters are the data that modify the expression.

Optional region expressions use what are known as *conditionals* or *if-then statements*, which are logical statements used by computer programs to decide whether to perform an operation, as in "If the monkey asks for food, feed the monkey" or "If the user clicks the link, open the new page."

Although optional regions sound pretty straightforward (if something happens, show the region), they're not useful until you want to devote the time to hand-coding template expressions.

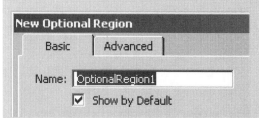

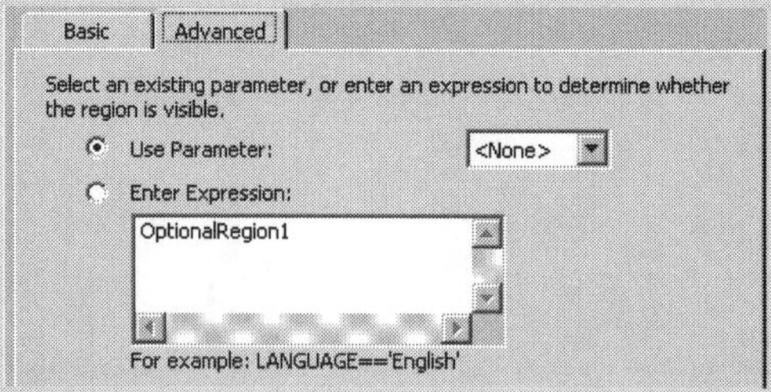

Figure 17.65 The Insert Optional Region dialog box looks harmless.

Figure 17.66 On the other hand, you need to set parameters or write expressions.

Site name list box   *Templates in that site*

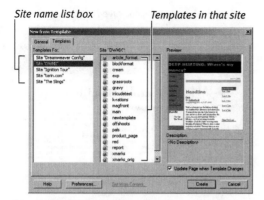

Figure 17.67 Click on the Templates tab in the New Document dialog box, and then select the name of the site the template is stored in, and the name of the template you wish to use. Notice the dialog box title is now New from Template.

Creating Pages Based on a Template

Once you've got your template set up, you can create pages based on that template.

To create a template page:

1. From the menu bar, select File > New. The New Document dialog box will appear.

2. Select the Templates tab. In the Templates For list, select the site you're working with, and all available templates will appear. Select the name of the template on which you want to base your page (**Figure 17.67**).

continued on next page

3. Click Create. The New Document dialog box will close, and a new document window will appear (**Figure 17.68**), including:

- The formatting of your template, along with any HTML elements or page properties

- The editable regions of your template, marked in blue boxes with the name of each region on its tab (**Figure 17.69**)

- Any repeating regions on your template, marked in pale blue boxes.

Locked regions are not marked but are untouchable. On Windows, this is indicated by a "Don't" sign (**Figure 17.70**).

✔ Tips

- You can also right-click (Control+click) a template icon in the Assets panel and select New From Template from the context menu.

- Basically, any text or objects that are within editable regions can be edited, and any that are not, cannot be edited.

- Click within any editable region and edit its content as you would on any other page.

- For more details, including how to edit repeating regions and editable attributes, see the next section, *Using Editable Regions*.

- If you want to change this situation and make whatever changes you want, see the section *Detaching a Page From a Template*.

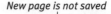
New page is not saved

Figure 17.68 A blank page based on the main.dwt template. The editable regions are marked in blue boxes, and the rest of the text is locked.

Figure 17.69 The editable regions of your template are marked in blue boxes with the name of each region on its tab.

Figure 17.70 Can't touch this! Non-editable regions are locked and the cursor tells you so.

Figure 17.71 All editable regions available to the current page are listed at the bottom of the Modify > Templates menu.

Figure 17.72 After you select an editable region from the menu, it will become highlighted in the Document window so that you can type over it.

Figure 17.73 The image selected on this page is an editable region. If an image on a page will be changing, you can mark it as editable. You can also insert images into editable regions (such as the highlighted body text in **Figure 17.47**) so they can be deleted or replaced.

Using Editable Regions

If you're working with a page that has a number of editable regions and you want to make sure you put the right stuff in the right slots, Dreamweaver can help you locate them.

To find an editable region:

1. From the menu bar, select Modify > Templates > [region name]. All editable regions appear at the bottom of the menu (**Figure 17.71**).

2. The editable region you just selected from the menu will become highlighted (**Figure 17.72**), and you can type away.

✔ Tips

- Images, image placeholders, and other objects can be marked as editable regions, too. The page in Figure 17.72 uses an image as a drop cap, and this image needs to be replaced with every story update. **Figure 17.73** shows the highlighted editable region, called FeatImg, in which the letter F has been replaced with the letter I. If the image were not an editable region of the document, it would be locked and permanent.

- See Chapter 5 for information about the Image Placeholder feature in Dreamweaver MX.

- If you're giving a batch of blank template pages to a Webmonkey for filling in the blanks, you should point out this helpful feature so that your minions know for sure which content goes in which region. A printout of a mocked-up page with the region names clearly marked and labeled couldn't hurt, either, even though region names are marked in the Document window.

Using repeating regions on a page

Repeating regions work pretty much the same as editable regions except for their defining characteristic: They repeat. Repeating region borders on pages based on templates look pretty funny (**Figure 17.74**). Here's how they work:

To repeat a region:

◆ Click the + button on the region.

A new region will appear (**Figures 17.75** and **17.76**). If the repeating region is a table row, a new row will appear.

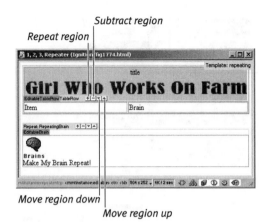

Subtract region

Repeat region

Move region down

Move region up

Figure 17.74 This is the page to which I added the repeating regions in **Figure 17.52**.

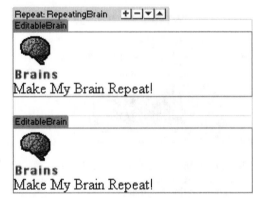

Figure 17.75 I clicked on the + button and the region was duplicated. The buttons stay with the original region.

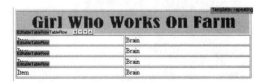

Figure 17.76 I clicked on the + button on my table row thrice and it was duplicated thrice.

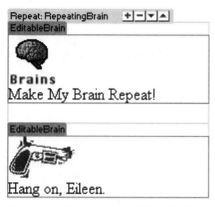

Figure 17.77 Go ahead and edit the editable regions within the repeating regions.

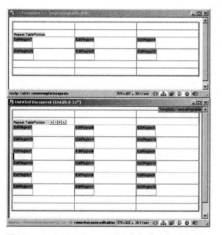

Figure 17.78 Here's my template (top) with the repeating table, and a page using that table, with repeating regions duplicated once.

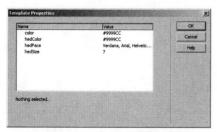

Figure 17.79 Select Modify > Template Properties to change editable attributes. The ones I gave distinct names are more helpful. "Color" is pretty vague.

To edit content in a region:

◆ Click within the repeating region's Editable region box, and add your content (**Figure 17.77**).

To subtract a region:

◆ Click the – button. The region will disappear.

To rearrange regions:

◆ Click on a region, and use the Up and Down arrow keys to change its order in the list.

Using repeating tables

Repeating tables work pretty much the same. You can only add content within editable regions. Click + to add cells (**Figure 17.78**).

Using editable tag attributes

To edit tag attributes you set as editable, use the Template Properties dialog box.

To edit tag attributes:

1. From the menu bar, select Edit > Template Properties. The Template Properties dialog box will appear (**Figure 17.79**).

2. Make any changes you like to the attributes offered.

3. Click OK to apply your changes.

Detaching a Page from a Template

If you'd like to remove the link between a page and a template, you can detach the page from the template. This is what you need to do if you'd rather attach a page to a different template or if you want to make exceptions to your design rules.

To detach a template:

◆ From the menu bar, select Modify > Templates > Detach from Template.

The editable regions will disappear (**Figure 17.80**), and nothing will be locked.

After you detach a page from a template, you can edit any part of the page.

Once you detach a template from a page, it can no longer be updated automatically when you edit the template file.

Figure 17.80 The whole page is now editable. No more locked or unlocked regions—just a page.

Template Troubleshooting

Now that Dreamweaver templates have gotten so fancy, I get error messages all the time, even when performing simple operations. Sometimes these messages show up when I save a template, other times when I try to base a page on a template. You can find out if your template has any errors, and get the line numbers, by selecting Modify > Templates > Check Template Syntax from the menu bar.

Try these pointers.

◆ If you switch local sites but the Assets panel won't display current templates, refresh the Assets panel or rebuild your site cache (see Chapter 2). You can also try closing all open documents. You may have to quit and restart Dreamweaver.

◆ If you get an error message that a P or other block tag is inside the editable region, see *Editable Region Quirks*, earlier in this chapter, and **Figure 17.43** in particular. This may not be an error on your part.

◆ If you get an error message that a template references itself, select Modify > Templates > Detach from Template.

◆ If you get an error message that a parameter doesn't exist, two things could have happened. First, you may be trying to insert an optional region without giving it any parameters, or by giving it parameters that seem right but that Dreamweaver doesn't like. Or, you could have tried to rename an editable attribute using the dialog box made for that purpose. Instead, you'll have to go into Code view and make sure that the editable attribute names referenced in the body of the document match the ones in the head of the document.

◆ If you rename a template region and then update pages based on that template, sometimes instead of regions or attributes getting renamed sensibly, you'll get the scary-looking Inconsistent Region name dialog box. Follow the instructions in steps 5 through 7 of *Attaching an Existing Page to a Template*, and transfer your attributes or region names in turn.

DETACHING A PAGE FROM A TEMPLATE

Deleting a Template

If you're utterly done with a template, you may delete it.

To delete a template:

1. In the Templates category of the Assets panel, select the template you wish to delete.

2. Click the Delete button [🗑] .

   A dialog box will appear asking you if you're sure you want to delete the template (**Figure 17.81**).

3. Click Yes. The template will be deleted.

✔ Tips

- References to the deleted template will not be discarded; you'll need to attach affected pages to a new template or remove the code.

- You can use the Clean Up HTML feature to remove template code from a page. See *Cleaning Up HTML* in Chapter 4, and remove Dreamweaver Special Markup.

- You cannot recreate templates as you can library items.

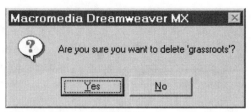

Figure 17.81 If you really want to delete that template, click Yes.

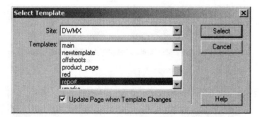

Figure 17.82 Select the template to which you want to attach the page.

Attaching an Existing Page to a Template

You can attach existing pages to a new template, too. You have to choose a single region to dump all the content into, though, unless the page has similar marked regions.

To attach a page to a template:

1. Open the document to which you want to attach the template. From the menu bar, select Modify > Templates > Apply Template to Page. The Select Template dialog box will appear (**Figure 17.82**).

2. Select the name of the template that you want.

3. To automatically have this page updated when you edit the template, leave the check box checked. For more on updating, see *Updating Your Site,* later on.

4. Click Select.

continued on next page

5. If the document contains content that can't be assigned automatically to an editable region, the Inconsistent Region Names dialog box will appear. (**Figure 17.83**).

Because templates only allow new content to appear in editable regions, you need to select an editable region in which to stick your content. You'll be able to move it from region to region once the page is reopened, but for now, you have to pick one.

◆ For region names coming from one template to a different one, select each region name in turn and apply a region name from the current template by selecting the new region from the Move Content to New Region drop-down menu (**Figure 17.84**).

◆ For visible content, select Document body and then select a region from the Move Content to New Region drop-down menu (**Figure 17.85**).

◆ For head content such as scripts and CSS, select Doctitle from the menu to transfer those items to the head tag; or Nowhere to discard the head content. (This is one way to get extra CSS and scripts into a template-based page.)

◆ To discard content, select Nowhere from the drop-down menu.

◆ To drop all your content into the same region, apply content to one region and then click Use For All.

6. When all your content is taken care of, click OK.

When the dialog box closes, your content will appear in the region you selected. You can edit your page now.

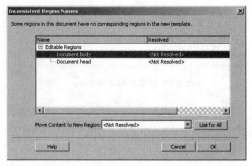

Figure 17.83 In the Inconsistent Region Names dialog box, content not yet assigned to an editable region must be resolved.

Figure 17.84 If you're applying a template to a page already formatted by a different template, select each region name in turn from the old template and apply a region from the new template by selecting it from the drop-down menu.

Figure 17.85 The Move Content to New Region drop-down menu lets you temporarily place all your unmarked content in an editable region on the template. If you're transferring renamed editable attributes, you'll see their equivalents listed here.

Nested Templates: Variations on a Theme

For sites with different page types that have the same basic design but a few variables, you can create a *nested template* that is based on an existing template.

Here's what you do:

1. Create a main template. I'll call it Main.dwt.

2. Create a page based on that template. I'll call it page.html.

3. Save page.html as a template (File > Save As Template, or click the Make Nested Template button on the Templates tab of the Insert toolbar).

   I'll call that second template sub.dwt, and I'll edit it so that it contains different section heads, slightly different layout, and so on. I can add editable regions, too.

4. Now, create a page based on that second template. I'll call it section.html.

Keep in mind that all editable regions in a base template (Main.dwt) will appear on all pages based on either the nested template or the base template. In other words, both page.html and section.html will both contain the same editable regions, even if you add the region to Main.dwt after Sub.dwt and section.html have been created.

Regions that appear on Main.dwt that are handed down are called *pass-through regions*. These will be marked blue in the Document window. If, on the subtemplate, you edit these regions or make them non-editable, they will be marked in orange.

✔ Tips

■ In step 2, you can create a page that *looks like* your template but isn't attached to the template file. Just deselect the Update Page When Template Changes check box.

■ If a piece of placeholder text, for example, "HeadingA," matches the name of a template region (in our example, it would also be called "HeadingA"), Dreamweaver will automatically match the placeholder text with the editable region.

■ If you've created different versions of a basic design, and you've used the same region names on both template files, you can transfer content from page to page easily. In other words, if the blue template and the orange template use the same region names, you can detach a page from one template and then attach it to the other.

ATTACHING AN EXISTING PAGE TO A TEMPLATE

Editing Template Files

You can edit template files at any time, even after you've attached pages to them. Once you've edited a template, you can then perform an update to pass your recent edits on to any pages based on them. For example, if you change the background color on your template from orange to blue, you can automatically change the background on all the pages based on that template, too.

When you create a new page based on a template you use the New From Template dialog box (see Figure 17.67), and when you attach a page to a template, you use the Select Template dialog box (**Figure 17.86**). Both of these dialog boxes have a check box, Update Page When Template Changes. If you deselect this check box, the page will look like the template but will not be included in any updates. (This feature did not work in Dreamweaver 4, but it does now.)

To edit a template:

1. In the Templates category of the Assets panel, select the name of the template to edit (**Figure 17.87**).

2. Click the Edit button 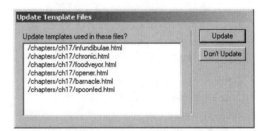. The template will appear in a new Document window.

3. Make any changes you like, taking care to mark editable areas as such.

4. Save your changes. A dialog box will appear asking if you wish to update the pages that use this template (**Figure 17.88**).

   To update now, click Yes, and skip to the section on updating your site if you need more details. To update later, click No.

Figure 17.86 If you've deselected the Update Page When Template Changes check box at any point when creating a page based on a template or attaching a template to a page, your page will be untouched after you edit your template file.

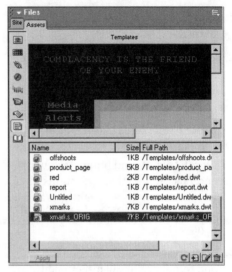

Figure 17.87 In the Assets panel, select the name of the template to edit. (You can always do a File › Open, but using the Assets panel is expedient when working with multiple templates and opening pages based on them.)

Figure 17.88 When you save changes to a template file, a dialog box will appear asking if you want to update your site.

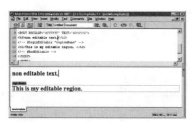

Figure 17.89 A template file displayed in Split view. In Design view, editable regions are outlined in a blue box with the name of the region on its tab, and nothing is highlighted in Code view.

Editable region   *Locked regions grayed out*

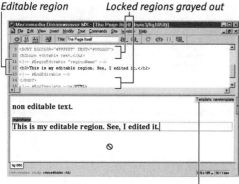

Template name

Figure 17.90 A page based on a template. In Code view, uneditable regions are printed in gray text. Uneditable regions are outlined in pale yellow in Design view, but the editable ones have the same blue boxes as they do on template files.

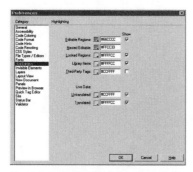

Figure 17.91 In the Highlighting panel of the Preferences dialog box, you can adjust the default highlight colors for editable and locked regions, as well as for library items and for third-party tags.

Highlights for Templates

Highlighting on templates works like this:

Code view: In template files, no code is highlighted in the Code inspector or Code view. In pages based on templates, all non-editable code text is colored gray in the Code inspector or Code view.

Design view: In both template files and pages based on templates, editable regions are outlined by a blue border with the region's name on its tab in the Document window, and locked regions (including the border of the page itself) are outlined in yellow.

The best way to show you these distinctions is a page with very little code in it, in Split view (**Figures 17.89** and **17.90**).

You can also change library item colors.

To set the highlight colors:

1. From the menu bar, select Edit > Preferences (Mac OS X: Dreamweaver > Preferences). The Preferences dialog box will appear.

2. In the Category box at the left, select Highlighting. The Highlighting panel of the dialog box will appear (**Figure 17.91**).

3. To select a color, click the Color box next to the item's name. The color picker will appear. Select a color by clicking on it.

4. Click OK to save your changes and return to the Document window.

✔ Tips

- To turn off highlighting for a library or template entity, uncheck the Show check box for that item.

- You can toggle highlighting on and off with the menu command View > Visual Aids > Invisible Elements.

Exporting as XML

XML stands for eXtensible Markup Language, which basically means you can create your own tags as you see fit for your own back-end scripts and database hooks to interpret. XML tags do not modify the behavior of what they contain in the browser setting. Rather, they're used as containers to mark content. An XML tag may be something like <Headline></Headline>, and the tag may be used as a container into which to import content on dynamic pages; as a marker to export content out of a database; or as a marker for a search robot to find particular types of content.

Because the editable regions of a Dreamweaver template are all named, you may name them the same things as XML tags you're using (or vice versa—name the tags for the regions). You may then export the content of a template-based file as an XML file, with the editable region names converted into XML tags.

To export editable regions as XML:

1. Open a page based on a template.

2. From the menu bar, select File > Export > Template Data as XML. The Export Template Data as XML dialog box will appear.

3. You may use one of two formats for the exported XML tags:

◆ The Dreamweaver format (**Figure 17.92**):

<item name="RegionName"></item>

(If your template uses repeating or optional regions or other specialized template markup, only the Dreamweaver format will be available.)

◆ The editable region = tag name format (**Figure 17.93**):

<RegionName></RegionName>

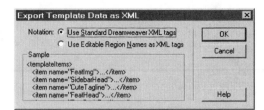

Figure 17.92 In the Export Template Data as XML dialog box, you may choose to save the editable regions of your template as Dreamweaver <item> tags or as self-referential XML tags.

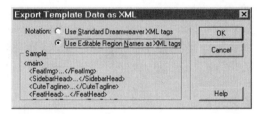

Figure 17.93 In the second option in this dialog box, the tags themselves—true to XML's custom nature—are named for the editable regions.

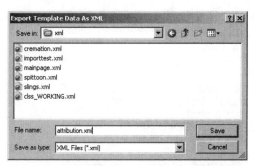

Figure 17.94 Type a filename for your new XML file in the second Export Editable Regions as XML dialog box.

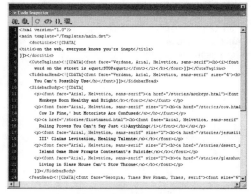

Figure 17.95 Here's the source of the XML file I just created, using the names of the editable regions as the names of the XML tags.

4. Select the radio button for the format you wish to use, then click OK. Another Export Template Data as XML dialog box will appear, this one looking like a Save As dialog box (**Figure 17.94**).

5. Select the directory in which to save the XML file, and type a name for the file in the File name text box.

6. Click Save.

You now have an XML file containing the contents of your page, including both XML and HTML tags (**Figure 17.95**). You may edit this file in Dreamweaver's Code inspector, or in another text editor.

Importing XML

You may also take an XML file you've previously created with Dreamweaver (or with any other program; see *Attention*, below) and import it to use with a Dreamweaver template. The XML or item tags will become the names of editable regions. You may then add other elements such as page properties, tables, and so on to the file.

To import XML into a template:

1. From the menu bar, select File > Import > XML into Template. The Import XML dialog box will appear (**Figure 17.96**).

2. Select an XML file to use, and click Open. If the XML file does not specify a base Dreamweaver template, a warning dialog box will appear (**Figure 17.97**).

3. If this happens, you need to reopen your XML file and specify a template within it.

   A new, blank HTML window will appear. Dreamweaver will merge the XML file with the template regions, and you can view the result in the Document window (**Figure 17.98**) and the Code inspector (**Figure 17.99**).

✔ Attention!

■ This method of importing works best if you first create a Dreamweaver template and export it as XML, using your desired XML tags as the names of editable regions. Failing that, you must include the `<templateItems>` tag and the name of a template within that tag. If you're preparing files from outside Dreamweaver to work with Dreamweaver features, make a copy of a file that Dreamweaver has exported as XML and use that syntax. For more about template tags, see the Help files and select Working with Multiple Pages > Managing Site Assets, Libraries, and Templates >Reference.

Figure 17.96 The Import XML dialog box. XML files must end in .xml.

Figure 17.97 You can't import just any old XML file, only one that is made to work with a Dreamweaver template. You can open plain XML files in the Document window without having to import them into templates first.

Figure 17.98 The Document window, displaying the "blank" page created by merging an XML file with a Dreamweaver template.

Figure 17.99 If you export a template as XML, then modify it and import it back into a template, the result will look much as it did before you exported it in the first place. I couldn't get any other sort of XML import to work, but you can open and work with other XML files in the Document window.

EXPORTING AS XML

What Good Is It?

If you look at it from just a Dreamweaver standpoint, it might seem kind of silly to go through these steps:

1. Create a page based on a Dreamweaver template.

2. Update the editable regions with actual content.

3. Export the content and the region names as XML.

4. Import the content and the region names, merge them with the structure of a Dreamweaver template, and create the same page you started with in step 1.

The more innovative use, of course, is to set database exports to create XML files that use those region names.

That way, you can do one of two things: First, you can use Dreamweaver to create templates for pages that will be served dynamically based on search results, customer profiles, cookies, and the like.

Second, you can use XML database exports for static pages when building a large site. For example, suppose you're building an enormous catalog. You can create a page like the one in Figure 17.98 that has slots for item names and images rather than headlines and stories. Then you can create XML files for the feature pages from your database, and use Dreamweaver to import the XML onto the static pages.

To be sure the import-export process works properly, make sure the files use Dreamweaver's flavor of XML, especially including the name of the template to base the pages on.

Updating Your Site

After you edit a library item or a Dreamweaver template, you can update single pages, selected pages, or entire sites that use that item. You'll still have to upload the updated pages to your live Web site so they'll reflect your changes.

Updating when you edit

After you save changes to a template or library item, a dialog box will ask you if you want to update your site (**Figure 17.100**). This dialog box lists pages that link to the template or library item you just edited. You can click Update, or you can postpone your edits.

Updating after you edit

You can update a single page at any time.

To update a single page:

1. Open the page you want to update in the Document window.

2. From the menu bar, select Modify > Library > Update Current Page or Modify > Templates > Update Current Page.

   If everything's in order, no dialog box will appear, but the current page will be updated to reflect the newest version of the library item or template (**Figure 17.101**).

✔ Tips

- If the single page links to any library items that no longer exist, a dialog box will appear to tell you (**Figure 17.102**). Click OK.

- If you want to add a previously deleted item to the library, you can re-create it. See the section *Re-creating a Library Item*, earlier in this chapter. You don't need to re-create a library item unless you need it to be updateable.

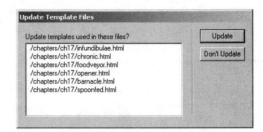

Figure 17.100 Whenever you save changes to a library item or template, Dreamweaver will ask you if you want to update the pages that link to that item.

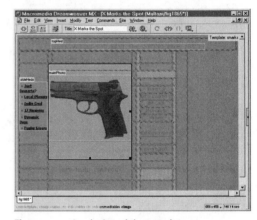

Figure 17.101 I redesigned the template you saw earlier in this chapter, and then updated all the pages that use that template as a format. Works for library items, too.

Figure 17.102 When you update a site that uses Libraries, this dialog box appears if you've deleted a library item referenced on an updated page.

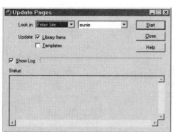

Figure 17.103
The Update Pages dialog box. You don't need to have any pages open to update your site.

Figure 17.104 Select either library items, templates, or both.

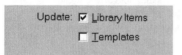

Figure 17.105 When you're updating an entire site, you can select your site from the drop-down menu.

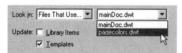

Figure 17.106 If you want to update everything that's linked to a particular template or library item, choose Files That Use from the menu, and then select the item. You can check off both library items and templates and scroll through a big alphabetical list of all of them.

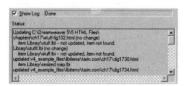

Figure 17.107 When you've finished updating the site or the selection of pages, a log file will appear telling you about pages updated, pages that couldn't be updated, and total pages reviewed.

Updating sets of pages

You can use the Update Pages dialog box for both library items and templates. You can update pages that use a particular library item or template, or you can update an entire site.

To update more than one page:

1. You don't need to have any particular page open to update your site. From the menu bar, select Modify > Library > Update Pages or Modify > Templates > Update Pages. Either way, the Update Pages dialog box will appear (**Figure 17.103**).

   The Update Pages window lets you update all library items and templates in a local site, or only those pages that reference a specific library item or template.

2. If you're going to search for a specific item, check the box for either library items or for templates (**Figure 17.104**). To update each of these in your site, check both boxes.

3. To update an entire local site, select Local Site from the Look In drop-down menu. A menu of your local sites will appear; select the site you want to update (**Figure 17.105**).

   or

   To single out one library item or template and update pages that use it, select Files That Use from the Look In drop-down menu. A menu of your library items and/or templates will appear (**Figure 17.106**).

4. Click Start. Dreamweaver will scan the selected site's cache, or site index, for references to library items and/or templates.

   When the update process is complete, a log file will appear, detailing how many files were scanned, which files were updated, and which files, if any, are missing from the Library or Templates folder (**Figure 17.107**).

5. When you're finished perusing this information, you can close the dialog box.

Renaming Templates and Library Items

Renaming templates and library items is easy, but there are a few things to keep in mind, considering that you must update your site if you rename one of these items.

You can rename a template and then update all pages in your site so that they refer to the new name. Or, you could skip the update and create a new template with the old name, and then the pages would refer to it.

When you rename a library item, Dreamweaver will ask you if you want to update files that link to it. If you don't, references to the item with its original name will not link to the newly renamed one. It will retain its HTML content, but it will no longer be updateable. You can then create a new item with the old name, or delete references to the old item.

To rename a template or library item:

1. In the Assets panel, click on either the Templates or Library button.

2. Select the name of the item so that a box appears around its name (**Figure 17.108**).

3. Type the new name and press Enter (Return). The Update Files dialog box will appear (**Figure 17.109**). Click Update to update references to this item, or Don't Update to skip it.

4. Click OK. The template or library item will be renamed.

✔ Tip

- You can also rename a template or library item in the Site window. Right-click (Control+click) on the file, and from the context menu that appears, select Rename. When you rename the file, the Update Files dialog box will appear. This is an excellent way to rename any file.

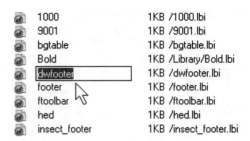

Figure 17.108 Click and hold on the name of a template or library item in the Assets panel, and when the little box appears around the name, type over it.

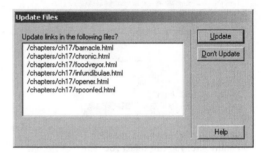

Figure 17.109 Dreamweaver can update all pages that link to a template or library item so that they link to its new name.

Figure 17.110 The Code inspector, displaying the code for a server-side include token. Note that the instructions are commented out so that they won't be displayed in the browser as is; also note that whatever content is in the file headlines.html is not displayed by the Code inspector.

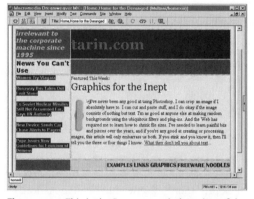

Figure 17.111 This is the Document window view of the same page seen in **Figure 17.110**. Again, the include is highlighted. As long as the included file is stored locally, Dreamweaver can process it and display it inline.

Using Server-Side Includes

Server-side includes (SSIs for short), much like library items, are pieces of HTML that can be reused on any number of pages. Also like library items, any time the included file is edited, the changes will be reflected in the documents that reference the include.

Unlike library items, however, there is no additional update process necessary. The files are stored and processed by the Web server, so changes are automatic as soon as you upload the edited SSI file to your site.

The Web document itself contains instructions for processing the included HTML files. These instructions, called tokens, include the location of the SSI file on the server.

What happens is, the server looks at the file, and sees that it contains an include. It then goes and gets the include and recreates the file with the include's contents on the page in the right location, and then it serves the new file to the browser. This is called *parsing* the file.

When you use Code view or the Code inspector to view the source of a page that uses a server-side include, you'll see the token (**Figure 17.110**), but not the HTML of the include itself. However, when you view the file in Dreamweaver, or if you use Dreamweaver to preview the file in a browser, the include (if it's stored locally) will be displayed inline in the page (**Figure 17.111**).

continued on next page

✔ Tips

- Before you get all excited about using server-side includes, make sure you can use them. If you use a free Web page service such as Yahoo, or a super-duper-easy template type page like those AOL offers, you may not have this option. Check your help files, or call tech support.

- Under most circumstances, a server-side include is like a library item in that it uses only enough HTML for the include, and not for an entire page (**Figure 17.112**). You may use any HTML tags except `<html>`, `<head>`, `<title>`, or `</body>`. You also want to avoid `<frameset>` and other associated tags, and embed frame instructions in the document rather than in the include.

- If you use Dreamweaver to create HTML files for server-side includes, be sure to delete the aforementioned tags.

- If your include file has HTML errors such as misordered or orphaned tags, these will show up as errors in the file that references the include; however, you should fix the errors in the include file instead.

- Opening a local page in your browser (File > Open) will not display the include contents. A server must process the file, include the new data, recreate the file, and send it to the browser. Because your browser can't do this on its own, the only way to view a server-side include inline in the browser window on a local page is to Preview it (File > Preview in Browser > [Browser Name]) in the page with Dreamweaver. Dreamweaver simulates the action of the server and loads the file with the include contents.

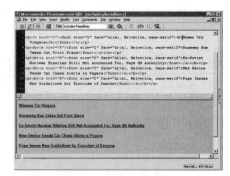

Figure 17.112 You can create or edit an include file in Dreamweaver. Here, in Split view, you can see that the only code in this file is the code that'll be displayed. There are no page-level tags here (like `<html>`, `<head>`, or `<body>`).

Why Won't It Go?

If you upload both the file that contains the include token and the include file itself, and the contents don't show up on the live site, then you need to contact the Web server administrator. A change to the server environment may need to be made before your server will process virtual or File includes. Check with your admin.

File includes must be stored in the same folder as the referencing page in order for Dreamweaver or a server to process them. I can tell you that Microsoft IIS servers prefer File includes and that Apache servers prefer Virtual includes. Otherwise, check with your sysadmin to see which format to use.

In file includes, instead of `<!--include virtual`, the code says `<!--include file`, and the file is imported into the document. When you use an include on a Web page and load the live file, you'll see the include on the page. When you View Source from the browser window on that same page, you'll see the HTML source of the included file as well as the token; it'll look like the include's code is just part of the page.

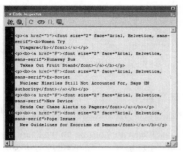

Figure 17.113 The Code inspector, displaying the contents of my include file.

Figure 17.114 Select the file you wish to include.

Editing Server-Side Includes

In the Document window, select the server-side include by clicking anywhere on the text. (As with library items, select one part of an include, and you select the whole thing.)

Display the Property inspector, if necessary, by double-clicking the include. In the Property inspector (**Figure 17.115**, on next page), click Edit. Dreamweaver will open the file in a Document window. If this does not open the file, use the File > Open command to open and edit the SSI file in the Document window. Select All File Types to be sure you can select the file. Make your changes and save the file. Any changes will be reflected on the pages that reference the file. Don't forget to upload the file to the server after you change it locally!

Inserting SSIs

Inserting a server-side include is a gloriously simple process. First, however, let me review how to create the file to include.

To create a file to include:

1. Using Dreamweaver or another editor, create the file you wish to display in your document(s). Be sure to delete any verboten tags, as described on the previous page (**Figure 17.113**).

2. Save the file on your local site, in a location mirroring where it will be stored on the server.

To insert an SSI token:

1. Click to place the insertion point where you want the include to appear.

2. From the menu bar, select Insert > Script Objects > Server-Side Include.

   or

   On the Insert toolbar's Script tab, click the Server-Side Include button 🖼 .

   Either way, the Select File dialog box will appear (**Figure 17.114**).

3. Select the file you wish to include.

4. In most cases, you'll want to use a document-relative path. If so, select Document from the Relative To drop-down menu.

5. Click OK to select the file and close the Select File dialog box.

   In the Document window, the contents of the include file will be displayed.

✔ Tip

■ If the include file is not stored locally, or if it does not yet exist, a Comment icon will be displayed instead of the contents of the file.

Using the History Panel

Just as a Web browser keeps track of the sites you've visited, Dreamweaver keeps track of the actions you've performed and lists them in the History panel.

You can repeat or undo single or multiple actions using the History panel. You can also copy and paste actions or groups of actions. You can even save or record actions as commands to reuse later. If you've heard of macros, these are those.

To view the History panel:

◆ From the menu bar, select Window > Others > History.

or

Press Shift+F10.

or

If you have a Launcher bar, click the History button:  (**Figure 17.116**).

In any case, the History panel will appear (**Figure 17.117**).

When you open the History panel for a new document, it will appear blank (Figure 17.117). As you perform actions in Design view in the Document window (not in Code view or the Code inspector), they appear listed as actions in the History panel. If you open the History panel after you've done some work, you'll see your previous actions listed (**Figure 17.118**).

✔ Tip

■ Code editing actions show up crossed out as "Edit Source" and cannot be repeated.

Figure 17.115 Server Side Include properties.

Figure 17.116 Click the History button on the Launcher in the status bar, if you have it displayed, to open the History panel. (See Chapter 18 to add a Launcher.)

Figure 17.117 The History panel, for a new document. No actions are listed because I haven't done anything on this new page.

Steps recorded since document was opened

Options menu button

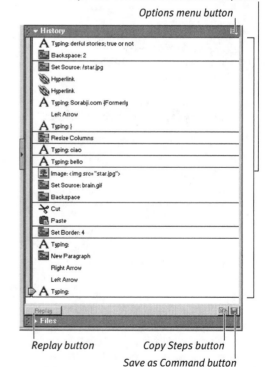

Replay button

Copy Steps button

Save as Command button

Figure 17.118 The History panel, for a page in progress.

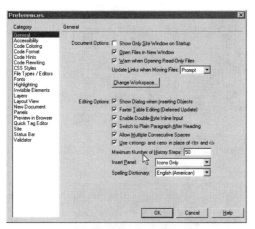

Figure 17.119 You can change the maximum number of stored steps in the General panel of the Preferences dialog box.

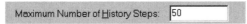

Figure 17.120 Type a number in the Maximum Number of History Steps text box.

What Can You Replay?

Most actions can be replayed, including inserting objects such as tables and images; resizing and adjusting other object properties; typing text; modifying text; and copying, cutting, pasting, and deleting text or objects.

Sometimes an action will show up in the History panel with a red X over its icon. That means you can't replay, copy, or save it. These actions include dragging objects such as layers in the Document window, setting page properties, or selecting objects with the mouse.

You can repeat a selection action if you use your keyboard's arrow keys to select an object or some text. When you repeat several steps, if you include an arrow-key selection as the last repeated step, Dreamweaver will select the adjacent object as the last action in the series.

What the History panel saves

What actions get stored, and for how long?

◆ Each Document window (and thus, each open document) has its own history list (Figure 17.118).

◆ On frames pages, each frame is a discrete document and has its own history list.

◆ When you close a Document window, the history list is cleared for that page.

◆ When you quit Dreamweaver, all history lists are cleared.

◆ The Site window has no history list.

◆ Actions marked with a red X cannot be replayed or saved (See *What Can You Replay*, the sidebar on this page).

Setting the number of stored steps

The History panel stores all your actions up to a pre-set limit of 50 steps. As you perform more than this maximum number of steps, the oldest steps are erased. You can raise this limit, but the more steps you store, the more memory Dreamweaver requires. Therefore, if you need to free up memory, you can lower the limit.

To change the number of steps:

1. From the menu bar, select Edit > Preferences (Mac OS X: Dreamweaver > Preferences). The Preferences dialog box will appear (**Figure 17.119**).

2. Click General in the Category box at the left to display those preferences.

3. Type a new number in the Maximum Number of History Steps text box (**Figure 17.120**).

4. Click OK to close the Preferences dialog box.

Repeating and Undoing Actions

The History panel can repeat or undo single or multiple actions. Of course, you can undo and redo steps (singly or sequentially) in the Document window using keyboard shortcuts: Ctrl+Z (Command+Z) to Undo, Ctrl+Y (Command+Y) to Redo. These are also menu commands: Edit > Undo and Edit > Redo. Dreamweaver saves the last 50 actions you perform, however, and gives you some leeway about when you can repeat them. The History panel is a visual representation of Dreamweaver's memory of your actions.

Let's look at an example.

Repeating your last action

You can redo the last step you took in the Document window by replaying it with the History panel.

To repeat your last action:

1. In the Document window, select an object (**Figure 17.121**) and perform an action, such as making text appear bold (Ctrl+B or Command+B).

   The action will be listed in the History panel (**Figure 17.122**) as Apply Markup: strong.

2. Now, select a different object on which you want to repeat the action. For example, select another piece of text (**Figure 17.123**).

3. In the History panel, click on the name of the action you want to repeat.

4. Click Replay.

   In our example, the second piece of text would become bold. The action will also be listed again in the History panel (**Figure 17.124**).

Figure 17.121 I selected some text in the Document window.

Figure 17.122 I made the text appear bold, and the action Apply Markup:strong appeared in the History panel.

Figure 17.123 I selected a second piece of text.

Figure 17.124 I clicked Replay. The action was repeated on the new selection, and Apply Markup:strong appeared listed again in the History panel.

Figure 17.125 I selected some text, and then I selected the "Make Hyperlink" step (for the correct URL) way back in the History panel.

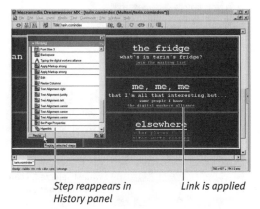

Step reappears in   Link is applied
History panel

Figure 17.126 I clicked on Replay, and the link was made. The step also reappears as the last step in the History panel.

Redoing actions from the distant past

You can also redo any action you performed recently, not just the last action you performed.

To redo any past action:

1. Select an object in the Document window. Or, if you want to repeat text that you typed or pasted, click where you want the text to appear.

2. Click on the action's name in the History panel (**Figure 17.125**).

3. Click Replay. The action will be repeated (**Figure 17.126**).

Redoing a series of actions

The best part is, you can repeat an entire series of steps on the next object you select.

To redo a series of steps:

1. Select the object to which you want to apply the actions. In this example, I'm going to select a table.

2. In the History panel, select the steps you want to repeat. To select sequential steps, click and drag or Shift+click to select them (**Figure 17.127**). To select nonadjacent steps, hold down the Ctrl (Command) key while you select the steps (**Figure 17.128**). For my table, I'm going to repeat the steps Set Border: 1, Insert Table, and Set Attribute: cellpadding: 3.

3. Click Replay. The steps will be repeated on the selected object, and "Replay Steps" will appear as the last action in the History panel (**Figure 17.129**).

✔ Tip

- To undo a set of actions like the one we just performed, you can undo the "Replay Steps" steps. Just click on that step and roll back the slidebar past all the "Replay Steps" entries.

Figure 17.127
I selected three sequential steps in the History panel, and I can replay them all at once.

Figure 17.128
I selected three nonadjacent steps in the History panel by holding down the Ctrl (Command) key while I selected. I can play these back as a group, too.

Replay Steps button

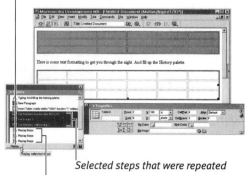

Selected steps that were repeated

Replay Steps action

Figure 17.129 I selected the second table and replayed the selected steps. The "Replay Steps" action appeared three times in the History panel.

Figure 17.130 I scrolled back one notch in the History panel. My action was reversed, and its name is grayed out in the History panel.

Figure 17.131 If I scroll back several notches, all those actions will be undone. To redo them, scroll back toward the bottom.

Undoing actions

As I keep reminding you, when you screw up by deleting an entire chunk of important code, you can undo it by pressing Ctrl+Z (Command+Z). You can press Ctrl+Z repeatedly to undo action after action, or you can undo your last step, and your last several steps, with the History panel. Unfortunately, this is true only in Dreamweaver. I often wish that life had Ctrl+Z, and if you could see me on my bicycle swerving around double-parked cars, you'd hear me shouting "Control Zee! Control Zee!"

To undo your last action:

1. In the History panel, click on the slidebar on the left side.

2. Scroll up one notch, and the action you just performed will become undone, and its name will be grayed out in the History panel (**Figure 17.130**).

To undo your last several actions:

◆ In the History panel, click on the slidebar on the left side, and scroll up several notches (**Figure 17.131**). As you scroll, the actions you just performed will become undone in reverse order, and their names will be grayed out in the History panel.

✔ Tip

■ You cannot undo nonsequential steps in the History panel. They are arranged in reverse chronological order.

Copying and Pasting Steps

Dreamweaver keeps a separate history list for each open Document window. If you want to share steps between documents, you can copy and paste steps.

To share steps between windows:

1. Display the Document window that includes the steps you want to share, and select the steps (**Figure 17.132**).

2. In the History panel, click the Options menu button, and select Copy Steps from the menu (**Figure 17.133**).

   or

   Click the Copy Steps button .

3. Display the Document window (or open the document) that includes the objects you want to modify using the steps you copied.

4. Select the object you want to modify, or click to place the insertion point where you want to insert an object (**Figure 17.134**).

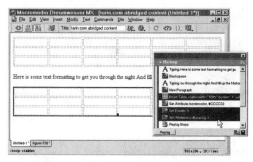

Figure 17.132 I selected three steps: inserting a table, setting the table border, and setting the cellspacing.

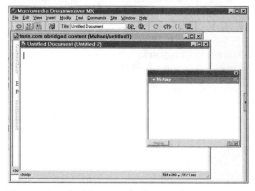

Figure 17.133 Select Copy Steps from the Options menu.

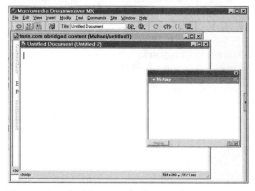

Figure 17.134 In this example, I'm opening a new, blank document in which to insert the table, but you can open an existing document or display one that's already open.

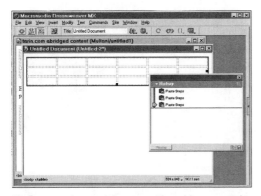

Figure 17.135 I pasted the steps. The table appeared with the other modifications, and each step appeared as "Paste Steps" in the History panel.

5. From the Document window menu bar, select Edit > Paste.

   or

   Press Ctrl+V (Command+V).

   The steps will be replayed in the second window, and "Paste Steps" will appear in the History panel (**Figure 17.135**).

✔ Tips

- If you want to save steps permanently, see the section, *Saving Steps as Commands*.

- Do not attempt to copy and paste steps that include Copy or Paste as commands. You don't want to try to Paste a Copy, and you can't Paste a Paste that doesn't include a Copy, so just forget about it.

Pasting Steps into a File

Dreamweaver uses JavaScript as its native language for performing most actions. The steps stored in the History panel are little JavaScript widgets, not so different from the behaviors described in Chapter 16. If you copy a step or steps using the instructions on this page and then paste them into a text editor (or into the Code inspector), they will appear as JavaScript. You can save them to reuse later or to rewrite if you're learning JavaScript.

To save steps as a command to reuse later, see the upcoming section, *Saving Steps as Commands*.

For more about JavaScript and editing Dreamweaver commands, see Chapter 18.

Clearing the History List

If you want to start fresh after stacking up a lot of steps in the History panel, you can clear the history list. This doesn't undo any steps, but it erases all the steps from the History panel and from Dreamweaver's memory.

To clear the history list:

◆ On the History panel, click the Options menu button, and select Clear History from the menu (**Figure 17.136**).

The history list will be cleared (**Figure 17.137**).

✔ Tip

■ After you clear the history list, you won't be able to undo previous steps by pressing Ctrl+Z (Command+Z), either.

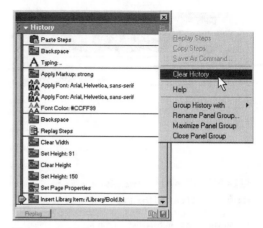

Figure 17.136 Select Clear History from the Options menu.

Figure 17.137 The History panel was cleared of all its steps, but nothing was undone.

CLEARING THE HISTORY LIST

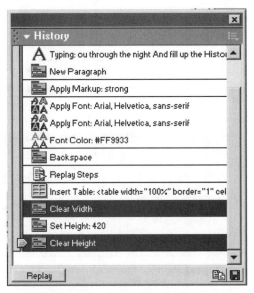

Figure 17.138 Select the steps you want to save as a command. They can be adjacent or nonadjacent.

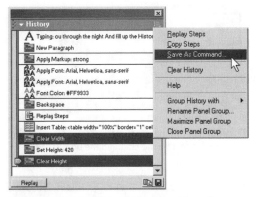

Figure 17.139 Select Save As Command from the Options menu.

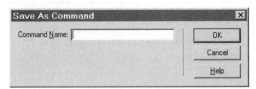

Figure 17.140 Type the name for your command in the Save As Command dialog box.

Saving Steps as Commands

If you come up with some handy multi-step tricks you want to use again and again, you can save them as commands. That way, they'll be accessible—even after you quit and restart Dreamweaver—from the Commands menu. Saved commands are available as part of the Dreamweaver interface, regardless of which local site you're using.

To save steps as a command:

1. In the History panel, select the step(s) you want to save (**Figure 17.138**).

2. On the History panel, click the Options menu button and select Save As Command (**Figure 17.139**)

   or

   Click the Save As Command button 🖫.
   The Save As Command dialog box will appear (**Figure 17.140**).

3. Type a name for your command in the Command Name text box. Spaces and capital letters are okay.

4. Click OK. The Command dialog box will close, and your command will be added to the Commands menu.

To play back your command, see *Replaying Commands*, later in this chapter.

Recording a Command

You can record a set of steps as a command as you perform them, without having to copy them from the History panel. You may have used Microsoft Word or BBEdit to record and save macros. That's exactly what you'll be doing here. A macro is a single, named computer command that contains many different actions. In order to perform the whole group of actions at once, you play the macro, just as you play back recorded music more than one note at a time.

To record a command:

1. Make a mental list (or jot it down) of the steps you want to perform (**Figure 17.141**). Sometimes once you start recording, you can forget what it is you wanted to save in your macro.

2. From the menu bar, select Commands > Start Recording. The mouse pointer will turn into a little cassette tape icon (**Figure 17.142**).

3. Perform the steps you want to save (**Figure 17.143**). You can record menu commands, keyboard shortcuts, and changes made in the Property inspector or in dialog boxes. You cannot record mouse actions such as resizing a table with the mouse or dragging a layer (for either action, type values in the Property inspector instead of dragging). If you attempt to use the mouse, you'll get an error message (**Figure 17.144**).

4. From the menu bar, select Commands > Stop Recording.

   Your steps will appear in the Command menu as "Play Recorded Command."

1. *Insert Image*
2. *Resize image to 100x100*
3. *Set image border to 10*

Figure 17.141 Figure out what you're doing before you do it.

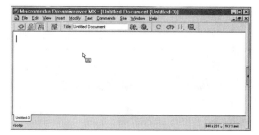

Figure 17.142 The mouse pointer, looking like a little cassette, awaits your next move.

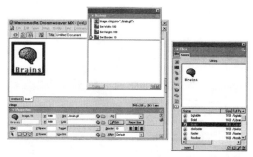

Figure 17.143 I inserted an image, resized it using the Property inspector, and changed the border to 10.

Figure 17.144 You can't record mouse movements. You can, however, drag the mouse to get this dialog box, and then click Yes to stop recording.

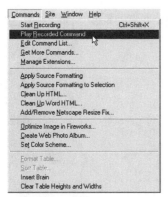

Figure 17.145
Select Play Recorded Command to replay the macro you just recorded.

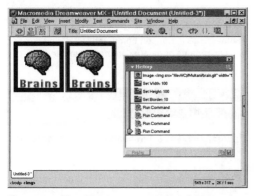

Figure 17.146 I replayed my command, and the image was reinserted with all its formatting intact. The command Run Command now appears in the History panel. If I want to save it to the Commands menu, I can.

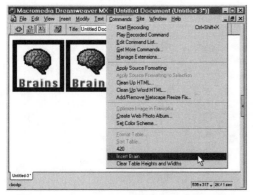

Figure 17.147 Your saved command will be available from the Commands menu—as soon as you save it.

Replaying Commands

If you use the Start Recording command to record your own macro, you can play it back using the Commands menu until you record another command.

To play back recorded steps now:

1. Make any selections or insertions you need to prepare to run the command.

2. From the menu bar, select Commands > Play Recorded Command (**Figures 17.145** and **17.146**)

   or

   If you've played the steps back once already, select Run Command on the History panel.

To save recorded steps as a command:

1. On the History panel, select Run Command.

2. Follow the steps in the section *Saving Steps as Commands*, earlier in this chapter.

Playing back any command

After you record and save a command, whether by copying it from the History panel or using the Start Recording command, you can use it whenever you want

To use a recorded and saved command:

1. Select the object to modify, or click to place the insertion point where you want to insert an object or text.

2. From the menu bar, select Commands > [Your Command Name] (**Figure 17.147**). The steps will be repeated.

✔ Tip

■ Commands are HTML files containing JavaScript, and Dreamweaver stores them in your Configuration folder.

Renaming and Removing Commands

You can also edit the names of commands or delete commands you added.

To rename a command you created:

1. From the menu bar, select Commands > Edit Command List. The Edit Command List dialog box will appear (**Figure 17.148**).

2. Click on the name of the command you want to rename so that a box appears around the name (**Figure 17.149**).

3. Edit the existing name, or type a new name for the command.

4. Click Close to close the dialog box and save your changes.

To remove a command you added:

1. From the menu bar, select Commands > Edit Command List. The Edit Command List dialog box will appear.

2. Click on the name of the command you want to remove.

3. Click Delete. A dialog box will appear asking if you're sure you want to delete it. Click Yes.

   The command will be removed.

4. Click Close to close the dialog box.

✔ Tip

■ To find out about editing, renaming, and rearranging menu items, including items in the Commands menu, see Chapter 19.

Figure 17.148 In the Edit Command List dialog box, you can rename or delete commands you added.

Figure 17.149 Type a new name for the command, or edit the existing name.

RENAMING AND REMOVING COMMANDS

Command Alternatives

What sorts of things make good commands? Well, the flip answer is, "Anything you do over and over again." But there's more than one way to skin a football.

Of course, it would be silly to save something like "Apply Bold" as a command, because there are already many ways to apply bold to text in the existing Dreamweaver interface.

But as we've seen in this chapter, Dreamweaver offers other automation tools you can use instead of commands. For instance, bits of text, images, and other page components that you reuse can be stored as updateable library items. And if you're setting the look of an entire page, you may want to use an updateable template.

Text formatting that you use a lot, such as Bold + Courier + Size +1, can be saved as an HTML Style, described in Chapter 10.

In Chapter 18 I discuss custom objects, which allow you to add widgets you use a lot to the Objects panel and the Insert menu. Good examples of custom objects include tables, layers, horizontal rules, form fields, logos, and so on—with all the formatting intact.

Commanding Ideas

Here are some starter ideas for commands I've found useful:

◆ Clear Row Heights and Clear Column Widths (for tables).

◆ Set Vspace and Set Hspace (for images or tables).

◆ Set Page Properties (for a color scheme you use frequently).

◆ Insert Library Item [Name] (for frequently used library items—you don't even have to open the Library!).

◆ Insert Copyright Mark.

◆ Adjust Cellpadding to n, Set Table Width to n, and so on (for adjusting tables to standard settings for your site).

◆ Set Bgcolor to [Teal] (for setting background colors of tables, cells, columns, and rows).

CUSTOMIZING DREAMWEAVER

Figure 18.1 You can create new panel groups and dock any panel into them.

Figure 18.2 You can create a custom category in the Objects panel for storing custom objects.

Figure 18.3 I added a custom menu (called Favorites) to the Document window that includes all my most-used commands.

For all practical purposes, the entire Dreamweaver interface—that is, the back-end of the program itself—is written in JavaScript, HTML, and XML. That means you can customize the interface using a simple text editor.

If you know JavaScript, you can create your own dialog boxes, properties inspectors, panels, menu commands, and so on. Unfortunately, that's beyond the scope of this book, but I'll point you toward some resources if you want to learn more. (See the section *Extending Dreamweaver with the JavaScript API*.)

Some Dreamweaver customization is simple and easy, however. You can rearrange panels and panel groups (**Figure 18.1**). You can add objects to the Insert toolbar and the Insert menu (**Figure 18.2**). You can edit Dreamweaver's menus and keyboard shortcuts (**Figure 18.3**). You can change the default documents stored in the New File dialog box and many tag-editing tools. And you can edit the appearance of many of Dreamweaver's dialog boxes.

You can also create *custom objects*—little widgets that let you insert chunks of code, with or without a dialog box. A line break, a comment, and a table are all objects, and you can add all sorts of HTML entities that you use over and over. You can also move, modify, or delete existing objects, and you can create your own panels in the Insert toolbar.

Rearranging Panels and Panel Groups

Because of some vagaries with the patent system in this country, Macromedia can no longer allow you to simply tear off a tabbed palette and float it separately. You *can* tear off a whole panel group or a toolbar at any point and float it wherever you want, but that's not a complete solution.

You can easily create a new panel group for a single panel or dock two panels together that currently live in different panel groups.

Why would you want to do that? Well, for instance, suppose you want to be able to view the Assets panel and the Sites window at the same time. Currently, with both docked in the Files panel group, you need to flip back and forth between them. If you create a new panel group for Assets, you can float that panel (**Figure 18.4**) or have it and the Sites window both docked and open simultaneously.

To create a new panel group for a given panel:

◆ Click the Options menu button on the top, left of the panel you want to move, and select Group Panel With > New Panel Group (**Figure 18.5**).

The panel will appear in a new group named after the panel, undocked.

Options menu button

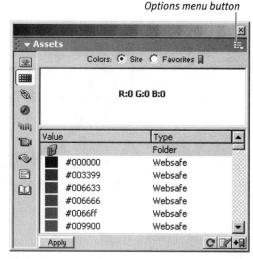

Figure 18.4 I created a new panel group for the Assets panel.

Options menu button

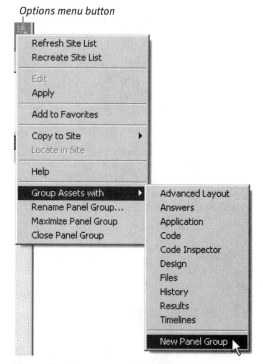

Figure 18.5 To group a panel in a brand-new panel group, click on the Options menu button, and select Group [Panel] With > New Panel Group.

REARRANGING PANELS AND PANEL GROUPS

Other Customization Features

Other customizable features of Dreamweaver are discussed in the following chapters:

◆ Chapter 1: Moving and resizing program elements

◆ Chapter 2: The Site window

◆ Chapter 3: Using the grid, using the rulers, setting page properties, and using the color dialog boxes

◆ Chapter 4: Setting HTML formatting preferences

◆ Chapter 17: Using custom templates and Library items, and adding to the Commands menu using the History panel

◆ The Web site for this book: Customizing the Launcher, customizing the Document window

Many other chapters discuss modifying various preferences in Dreamweaver.

About Configuring Dreamweaver for Multi-User PCs

In a multi-user environment such as Windows NT or XP, or Mac OS X, you may not want to modify the configuration files for the entire computer, only for your user name. (Older operating systems such as Mac 9.x and Windows 98 and ME do not use user-configuration folders; they use the application copies for every user.)

In some cases, you may not even have permission to write or change the files in the configuration folder. In any event, it's probably a wise move, even if you're the only user on your multi-user machine, to make copies into your user folder before working with them. Once you create those files—or Dreamweaver does, unbeknownst to you—Dreamweaver will default to them and those files will override the ones in the program folder.

If you are a superuser, you can modify the files in the following location; or, you can copy these files into your user folder:

PC: `C:\Macromedia\Dreamweaver MX\Configuration`

Mac OS X: `Macintosh HD: Applications: Dreamweaver MX: Configuration`

If you only want to modify files for a single user, you go here instead:

Windows 2000/XP: `C:\Documents and Settings\[User Name]\Application Data\Macromedia\Dreamweaver MX\Configuration`

Windows NT: `C:\WinNT\profiles\[User Name]\Application Data\Macromedia\ Dreamweaver MX\Configuration`

Mac OS X: `Macintosh HD:Users:[User Name]:Library:Application Support:Macromedia: Dreamweaver MX:Configuration`

If you accidentally change something that you shouldn't have, or if you get in trouble for "improving" someone else's workspace, you can find backups in the `Configuration-1` folder— but you made your own backups for everything, right?

Moving panels to a different group

You can also move panels from one group to another. The Link Checker currently lives in the usually hidden Results panel group, but I want to make it live in the Files panel group so I can remember to check my links more often.

To move a panel to a different group:

◆ Click the menu control button on the panel you want to move, and select Group [Panel Name] With > [Panel Group Name] (**Figure 18.6**).

The panel will appear docked with the panel group you selected (**Figure 18.7**).

To rename a panel group:

1. Click the Options menu button on the top left of the panel group you want to rename, and select Rename Panel Group. The Rename Panel Group dialog box will appear (**Figure 18.8**).

2. Type a new name for your panel group and click OK. The panel group will be renamed.

Adjusting panel preferences

If you plan on floating any panel groups, including the Property inspector or the Insert toolbar, you may want to select which panels stay on top. By default, *all* panels stay on top of the Document window. Additionally, previous versions of Dreamweaver included a Launcher in the status bar that contained buttons for toggling various panels open and closed, and you can add one in Dreamweaver MX.

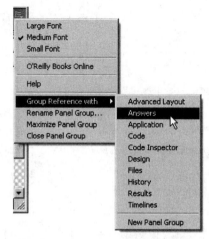

Figure 18.6 To group a panel in a different panel group, click on the control menu button, and select Group [Panel] With > [Panel Group Name].

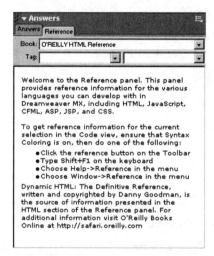

Figure 18.7 The Reference panel now appears docked with the Answers panel group.

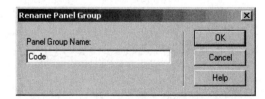

Figure 18.8 You can rename any panel group, new or built-in.

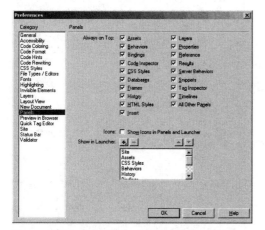

Figure 18.9 The Panels panel of the Preferences dialog box.

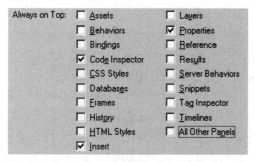

Figure 18.10 I've deselected all but three of my panels. The checked panels will now float over any other panels or windows.

To adjust panel floating preferences:

1. From the menu bar, select Edit > Preferences (on Mac OS X, choose Dreamweaver > Preferences). The Preferences dialog box will appear.

2. In the Category list, select Panels. That panel will come to the front (**Figure 18.9**).

3. Deselect panels you don't need to stay on top. In **Figure 18.10**, I've deselected all but my most essential panels.

4. Click OK to save your changes.

To add a launcher to the status bar:

1. Follow steps 1 and 2, above.

2. Check the Icons checkbox (**Figure 18.11**).

3. All listed panels will appear in the launcher. To remove a panel, select its name and click the – (minus) button. To add one, click the + (plus) button and select a panel from the menu (**Figure 18.12**).

4. Click OK to save your changes and add a launcher to the status bar (**Figure 18.13**).

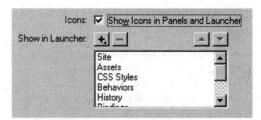

Figure 18.11 Click the Icons checkbox to display the Launcher, and then select which ones to display.

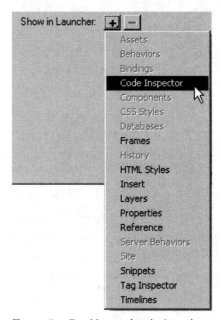

Figure 18.12 To add a panel to the Launcher, click the + (plus) button on the Show in Launcher list box.

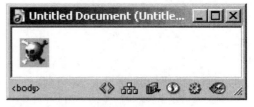

Figure 18.13 Here's my Launcher.

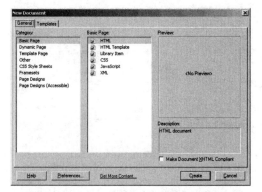

Figure 18.14 The New Document dialog box includes basic blank pages and page designs, both of which you can modify.

Customizing Pre-Built Pages

In Dreamweaver's File > New dialog box (**Figure 18.14**), you can choose from blank and pre-built pages that give you a head start in creating your own pages. You can modify these pages and add your own to this dialog box.

✔ Tips

■ In contrast to most Dreamweaver templates (Chapter 17), which use XML code, have specialized editing features, and are updateable over an entire site, these pages open as unsaved documents on which all elements are editable.

■ For smaller pieces of code, you might want to use the Snippets panel (Chapter 4); or Library items (Chapter 17), which function like Dreamweaver templates in that they are not editable on pages that reference them but are updateable across an entire site.

To customize a built-in page design or default page:

1. In the Document window, open the page you want to customize. Default pages (**Figure 18.15**) are located in `Configuration/DocumentTypes/NewDocuments`. Page designs are located in `Configuration/BuiltIn` (**Figure 18.16**).

- ◆ **Frameset pages**: Turn on frame borders (View > Visual Aids > Frame Borders) when working with these pages. The file consists only of the frameset page, not the content pages. See Chapter 13 for more on working with frames.

- ◆ **CSS designs**: These style sheets can be edited either by hand or using the various CSS tools. See Chapter 11 for details.

- ◆ **Templates:** Dreamweaver's page designs are template files. See Chapter 17 for more on how these work.

2. Make any changes you like, and save them.

The next time you use the New File dialog box, your edits will be included (**Figure 18.17**).

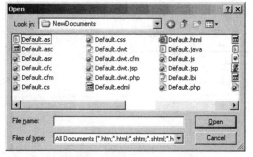

Figure 18.15 In the `Configuration/DocumentTypes/NewDocuments` folder, you can open and edit any default page. For example, if you want to change the default background color or add a META tag to every page you make, you might edit the `Default.html` file.

Figure 18.16 The `Configuration/BuiltIn` folder (shown here in Windows Explorer) contains pre-built page designs for frames, CSS, and basic pages. You can edit any of these or add your own.

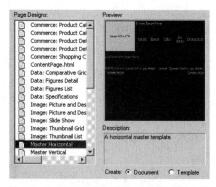

Figure 18.17 I edited the "Master: Horizontal" page design so that it uses a black background and includes CSS information for my fonts and links.

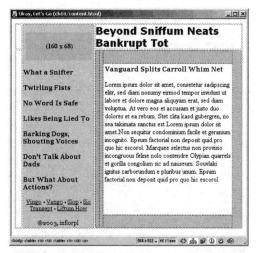

Figure 18.18 Here's the page I want to add to the New Document dialog box.

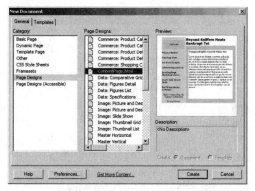

Figure 18.19 The new phone book's here, and I'm in it!

Adding Your Own Designs

You can add your own new pages by saving any page into the BuiltIn folder. Although all the pages in the Page Designs and Page Designs (Accessible) categories are Dreamweaver Template (`.dwt`) files, you can add a plain old HTML file to the dialog as well.

To add a design to the New Document dialog box:

1. In the Document window, open the page you want to add to the New Document dialog box (**Figure 18.18**).

2. Save it into a folder within the BuiltIn folder. The main folder for Page Designs is: `Dreamweaver MX\Configuration\BuiltIn\Templates`.

3. To add an image and description, see Tips, below.

4. Restart Dreamweaver.

When you open the New Document dialog box, your page will be listed (**Figure 18.19**). When you select it, a new, blank page based on your design will open in the Document window.

continued on next page

✔ Tips

- Remember that any templates you create and store in your local site will automatically be available from the Templates tab of the New Document dialog box.

- A preview of your page will be included in the dialog box (**Figure 18.20**).

- That image placeholder is a new feature of Dreamweaver—see *Inserting an Image Placeholder*, in Chapter 5.

- If you want a description of your page to be included (this works only for .dwt files), you can create a Design Notes file and save it in the associated _notes folder. An easy way to do this is to make a copy of an existing design notes file, open it, and change the description text (**Figure 18.21**). The file name of the Design Notes file must be the same as the page's file name, with the .mno extension.

- If you create a local site for the Configuration folder, you can use the Design Notes dialog box to edit the text (**Figure 18.22**).

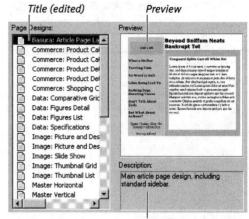

Title (edited)   *Preview*

Description (edited)

Figure 18.20 A preview will appear automatically; to change the title of your page and its description, create an MNO file.

Figure 18.21 I opened an MNO file (a.k.a. a Design Notes file) for another page in the folder, and then edited the information.

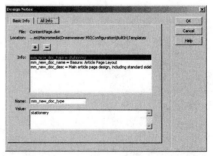

Figure 18.22 You can also edit this information from the Site window if you create a local site for Configuration. See Chapter 19 for more about design notes.

About XML

Some of the customization features in Dreamweaver require you to open an XML file and edit or add lines of code. This shouldn't present a huge challenge, considering how close a cousin XML is to HTML.

The eXtensible Markup Language, affectionately known as XML, is a markup language based on SGML, just as HTML is.

XML uses tags as containers to mark up text, just as HTML does. Most tags have an opener and a closer. For instance, in HTML, the `<i>` tag opens and closes like so:

```
<i>italic text</i>
```

The extensibility of XML means that developers can create new tags for specific purposes. So, in the Dreamweaver `menus.xml` file, you'll see tags called `<MENU>`, `<MENUITEM>`, `<SEPARATOR>`, and `<MENUBAR>`.

In HTML, if you use a tag that doesn't have a closer, you simply don't close it:

```
<img src="/images/image.gif">
```

In XML, if you use a tag that doesn't have a closer, you need to add a closing slash to the end of the tag:

```
<menuitem attributes="" />
```

Notice that there's a space before the closing slash.

✔ Tip

- In Dreamweaver MX, you can open XML files (as well as script files) in the Document window and edit them there. It's still a good idea, though, to edit application files in a text editor instead of trying to edit the program *with* the program.

Custom Objects

Object files, which appear in the Insert toolbar and the Insert menu, are simple HTML files that contain just snippets of code (without any document formatting such as <html>, <head>, and <body> tags). Upgrading? This process is slightly different from adding objects to the Objects panel in previous versions of Dreamweaver.

Once you create an object file, you add it to the Dreamweaver interface by adding an image to the Insert toolbar (**Figure 18.23**). Dreamweaver adds entries to the Insert menu on your behalf.

Dreamweaver's pre-installed objects all use JavaScript to insert objects. Some objects, such as images and tables, use dialog boxes that you use to define the object before it's inserted (**Figure 18.24**), and these dialog boxes are also written in JavaScript. Other objects, such as horizontal rules and line breaks, include a single function, called the objectTag() function, that inserts the code onto the page.

For instance, the code for the Line Break object is as follows:

```
function objectTag() { return "<br>"; }
```

You could also accomplish this with an HTML document that consisted of a single <br> tag.

✔ Tip

- Dreamweaver MX offers several ways to store chunks of code. Entire, updateable page designs can be saved as templates or in the Library (both are covered in Chapter 17). Pieces of code that aren't linked to anything can also be stored as Snippets (Chapter 4) if you don't feel they merit their own object buttons. And URLs, colors, and scripts are catalogued in the Assets panel (Chapter 2).

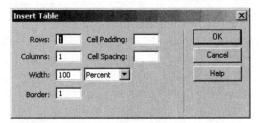

Figure 18.23 Our old friend the Insert toolbar. In this part of the chapter, we'll find out how to add objects and tabs to it.

Figure 18.24 The Insert Table dialog box is called by a Dreamweaver object file. The dialog box takes user input before inserting the object.

Modifying Dreamweaver Objects

Besides creating new custom objects, you can modify existing Dreamweaver objects. This involves modifying the HTML and/or the JavaScript that controls the insertion of each object—yet another good way to pick up some JavaScript fluency. (In particular, check out the JavaScript form tools used to create dialog boxes like the ones used to insert tables and links—see Figure 18.63.)

In some instances, this is simple; for instance, you could make the <br> object always have the "clear" attribute by editing the object so that it always read <br="clear"> on insertion.

Before you start fooling around with the JavaScript, though, I recommend that you save a copy of the original object in a different folder, so you can restore it if you need to.

Figure 18.25 A normal HTML file (left) includes <html>, <head>, <title>, and <body> tags. I deleted them in order to save the code as an object file, which in this case includes only the tags for the layer.

Creating the object HTML file

The first and most important part of creating a custom object is creating the object file itself.

To create an object file:

1. Using Dreamweaver, another HTML editor, or a text editor, create a new, blank file.

2. Type or paste in the code for the object you want to create.

3. If the program automatically includes tags such as <html> and <body>, be sure to delete them (**Figure 18.25**).

4. Save the file as an HTML file (.htm or .html) in the Dreamweaver Objects directory:

    ◆ **Windows:** C:\Program Files\ Macromedia\ Dreamweaver MX\Configuration\Objects\ [Object Folder Name]

    ◆ **Macintosh:** Macintosh HD: Applications: Macromedia Dreamweaver MX: Configuration: Objects: [folder name]

    See the sidebar *About Configuring Dreamweaver for Multi-User PCs* for details about which files to edit.

continued on next page

CUSTOM OBJECTS

You can also save the file in any of the folders within the Objects folder, including a new one (**Figure 18.26**; see the sidebar, *Custom Object Categories*). The folder names correspond to the categories on the Insert toolbar, so if you want to create a new display tab, create a new folder. We'll add the folder info to the toolbar later.

Before you can use your new object, you need to add it to Dreamweaver's configuration files. After you add both the file and the image to an Objects folder, you need to restart Dreamweaver. Once you do this, the object will appear in both the Insert toolbar and the Insert menu.

✔ Tip

■ To download object files that other Dreamweaver users have made, select Insert > Get More Objects. Your Web browser will take you to Macromedia's Exchange site.

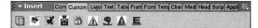

Figure 18.26 I created a custom category (called Custom) on the Insert toolbar.

Custom Object Categories

The Insert toolbar contains many tabs: Characters, Common, Forms, Frames, Head, Media, and Text. The Tools folder corresponds to the Layout tab. These categories correspond to folders within the Dreamweaver Objects folder. The other folders correspond to database tools that appear on the Insert tab if you set up a dynamic site. To create your own custom category in the Insert toolbar, just create a new folder within the Objects folder, and then see the section *Configuring Dreamweaver to use the object* for instructions on how to add a `<category>` tag and thus, a new tab.

Figure 18.26 shows the Custom tab of the Insert toolbar, which I added by creating a folder called Custom in the Objects folder to hold my custom objects.

You can rename any of these folders and their corresponding tags in the `insert-bar.xml` file, and the category will be renamed. You can also move objects from folder to folder; just be sure to move both the image and the HTML or JS file.

You can create a new folder using Windows Explorer, the Finder in the Mac, or the Site window on either platform. The command is generally File > New Folder. To use the Site window to create an Objects folder, you can double-click the Desktop icon in the Site window—see Chapter 2 if you need help.

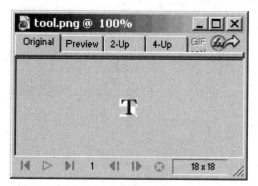

Figure 18.27 I created an 18x18-pixel image.

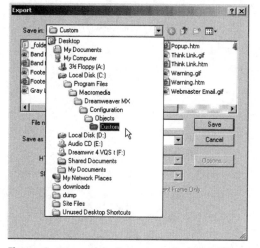

Figure 18.28 I saved the image in my Custom folder within the Objects folder. This is the same folder in which I saved the object file.

Adding the object to the Insert toolbar and the menu bar

Now you need to add the object to the Insert menu and the Insert toolbar.

The next step in adding the new object to the Insert toolbar is creating an 18-pixel by 18-pixel image with the same name as the object file. For instance, if the object file is named `GrayLayer.html`, the GIF should be named `GrayLayer.gif`.

You save this image in the same Objects folder as your file. If the object file is in the Forms folder, the image goes in the Forms folder, too.

To add an image to the Insert toolbar:

1. Create an 18-pixel by 18-pixel GIF image (**Figure 18.27**).

2. Name it the same thing as the object file, and save it in the proper Objects folder (**Figure 18.28**).

   For example, if your HTML file is named `Orange Table.htm`, you'd name the image `Orange Table.gif`.

   continued on next page

CUSTOM OBJECTS

✔ Tips

- In HTML in general, spaces are verboten in file names, but in creating these files, if you want a two-word entry, use a two-word name, as in `Orange Table`, above. Names are case sensitive.

- If you add a GIF to a folder within the Objects folder, but you don't list the object in the `insertbar.xml` file or provide the corresponding HTML or JS file, the image will appear on the toolbar, but it won't be functional as a button.

- If you create an image larger than 18x18, Dreamweaver will scale it down to that size.

- You'll find a starter image, called `generic.gif`, in the Objects folder. If you don't create an image file, Dreamweaver will use `generic.gif` as the button image on the Insert toolbar 🔲 .

- You can also rename objects, rearrange them within a folder, rearrange the order of the tabs, move them from one folder to another, or delete them entirely. Follow the steps above to open and save a file. To move either an object or an entire category, cut it and paste it. To rename an object, rename both files, as well as the entry in the `insertbar.xml` file. To delete an object, delete its entry and move the objects from that folder to a new folder called `Unused_Objects`.

Don't Do Images?

Not a big image person? Try creating a 18-pixel by 18-pixel GIF that consists of a color and a letter: **W** .

Another solution is to take an existing image from the Objects folder and invert or colorize it using an image editor: ▦ .

If you're frightened by image editors, I recommend using Jasc Paint Shop Pro or Macromedia Fireworks.

Figure 18.29 Here's my new Custom Objects panel, chock full of custom objects. Dreamweaver automatically shows the file's filename as a tool tip (Windows only).

```
<category id="DW_Insertbar_Common"
folder="Common">
```

```
<button id="DW_Media_Flash"
image="Media\Flash.gif"
enabled=""
showIf=""
file="Media\Flash.htm"/>
```

and edit it as follows:

```
<button id="DW_Media_MPEG"
image="Media\MPEG.gif"
enabled=""
showIf=""
file="Media\MPEG.htm"/>
```

...where MPEG.gif is my image file and MPEG.htm is my object file, both of which are stored in the Media folder.

Configuring Dreamweaver to use the object

Now, we need to add a line of code for the new object to the file insertbar.xml. Make a backup of this file before you start. See About XML, earlier in this chapter, for basics.

The insertbar.xml file is stored in the Objects folder. Macromedia says it's okay to edit this file with Dreamweaver.

To edit the insertbar.xml file:

1. Open the insertbar.xml file in Dreamweaver or in a text editor.

2. Locate the category tag for the folder you want to add an object to. It will look like this:

3. Locate the place where you want your new object to appear. For example, in the Common category, to place an object between Layer and Image, click at that point in the file.

4. It's easiest to copy an entry and then edit it. For an object called MPEG, I'll copy the entry for Flash:

5. Save the insertbar.xml file.

6. Quit and restart Dreamweaver, or reload extensions (see page 625). Your new objects will be added to the Insert toolbar.

continued on next page

CUSTOM OBJECTS

You can add a tab to the Insert toolbar to hold custom objects or copies of preinstalled ones (**Figure 18.29**).

To add a tab to the Insert toolbar:

1. Create a new folder in the Objects folder, if you haven't already.

2. Create a text file called _folderinfo.txt within your new folder. The contents of the file should be the name of the folder. For my new folder Custom, the text file reads Custom.

3. Open the insertbar.xml file.

4. Create a new category tag. It should look like this: ────────────▶

5. Create an object file entry within the category tag, or move or copy objects into your category tag, as described in the preceding section.

6. Save the insertbar.xml file and reload extensions (see below).

```
<category id="DW_Insertbar_Custom"
folder="Custom">
</category>
```

where "Custom" is the name of your folder and the name of the tab.

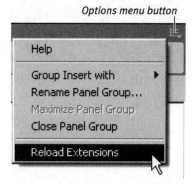

Options menu button

Figure 18.30 Ctrl+click (Option+click) on the Insert toolbar's Options menu button to reload extensions.

Separators

Figure 18.31 I added two separators to my Custom tab.

Reloading extensions

In past versions of Dreamweaver, one had to quit and restart the program to load your changes. Now you can reload your new entries easily.

To reload extensions:

1. Ctrl+click (Option+click) on the Options menu button on the Insert toolbar.

2. Select Reload Extensions from the context menu (**Figure 18.30**).

Wait a few seconds, and the new folders or objects will appear. If they don't, double-check your spelling and capitalization of your files and entries in the `insertbar.xml` file.

To add a separator to an Insert toolbar tab:

1. In the `insertbar.xml` file, locate the `<button>` tag for the object after which you want to insert a separator.

2. After the `<button>` tag, add the following line of code:
`<separator showIf=""/>`

3. Save your changes.

4. Reload extensions. Your separator will appear on the Insert toolbar (**Figure 18.31**).

CUSTOM OBJECTS

Using Your New Custom Object

Now that you've created the object file and its image button, you can insert the object.

To insert your object:

1. On the Insert toolbar, view the tab that contains your new object.

2. Click the button to make sure it does what you want it to (**Figure 18.32**).

   or

   On the Document window menu bar, open the Insert menu, and select your object from the menu (**Figure 18.33**).

To find out more about editing menus, see the next section in this chapter, *Editing Dreamweaver Menus*.

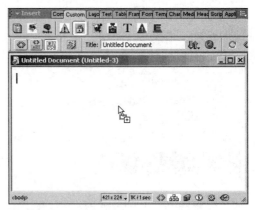

Figure 18.32 Test your buttons once they're on the toolbar, even if you've just copied them from one tab to another.

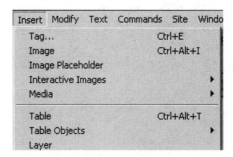

[cropped...]

Figure 18.33 The objects I added are also available from the Insert menu. Later in this chapter, we'll find out how to edit the display names and rearrange the menu.

Editing Dreamweaver Menus

You can edit any entry on Dreamweaver's Document window menu bar. You can rename, move, or delete items, and you can add or change a keyboard shortcut for any item. You can also add items, but that requires firm knowledge of JavaScript.

The Dreamweaver menu commands are all stored in a file called menus.xml, which is stored in the Menus folder, inside the Configuration folder. The location of this file is:

◆ **Windows:** C:\Program Files\Macromedia\ Dreamweaver MX\Configuration\Menus\ menus.xml

◆ **Macintosh:** Macintosh HD: Applications: Macromedia Dreamweaver MX: Configuration: Menus: menus.xml

Before you do anything to this file, make a backup copy of it. The file menus.bak is a pre-installed backup copy, as well, but one can never be too cautious when it involves editing application code.

✔ Tips

■ Macromedia recommends against editing the menus.xml file with Dreamweaver itself. Use a text editor such as WordPad, BBEdit, HomeSite, or SimpleText

■ To add items to the Commands menu by recording or saving commands with the History panel, see the sections about History in Chapter 17.

■ For a basic introduction to XML, see *About XML,* earlier in this chapter.

About the Menus.xml File

The menus.xml file (**Figure 18.34**) contains several sections. First is the list of keyboard shortcuts, for the Document window as well as for the shortcut menus found on some of the inspectors and panels. Second, for Windows users only, is the menu bar for the Site window (the Mac version uses the same menu bar for both). This is followed by the shortcut menus for the panels and inspectors that use them.

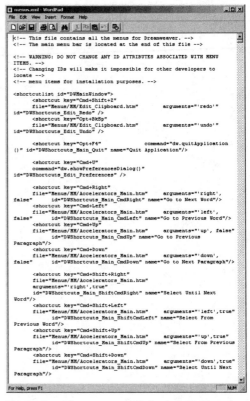

Figure 18.34 The menus.xml file is a behemoth.

✔ Attention!

- As mentioned previously, do not use Dreamweaver to open or edit the menus.xml file. Use another text editor to open it. On Windows, you can use WordPad or HomeSite, for example. (I found that the file is too large to open with NotePad). On the Mac, you can use SimpleText or BBEdit. (The versatile Find feature in BBEdit and HomeSite may help you out.)

- If you haven't created a backup copy yet, be sure to do a File > Save As when you open the file, so you don't accidentally delete anything vital.

- The menus.xml file ends with the menu bar for the Document window. You can scroll to near the end of the document and look for this line of starting code:
  ```
  <menubar name="Main Window"
  id="DWMainWindow">
  ```
  Or, you can do a Find (Edit > Find in your text editor) for this code or for part of it, such as id="DWMainWindow".

My Changes Won't Change!

The menus.xml file normally resides in Configuration/Menus in the application folder. If you're using a multi-user machine such as Windows XP or NT, your file will still reside there, *until and unless* you modify it using the Keyboard Shortcuts Editor or certain extensions. At that point, Dreamweaver backs up the current file into your user-configuration folder, and uses the user copy from then on.

In such a case, you should work with the user copy instead of the copy in Program Files. You can also copy the master copy there if one isn't there already, and then work with that file from now on.

For more details about these folders, see the sidebar *Configuring Dreamweaver for Multi-User PCs*, earlier in this chapter.

ABOUT THE MENUS.XML FILE

Tag syntax

Tags in the menus.xml file are nested, just as they are in HTML. So the outline of the code looks something like this:

```
<menubar>
  <menu name="Menu Name">
    <menuitem name="Menu Item" />
    <menuitem name="Menu Item 2" />
  </menu>
</menubar>
```

Menus that are nested within menus, such as the Table menu within the Modify menu, are similarly nested in the code:

```
<menu name="Menu Name">
  <menuitem name="Menu Item" />
  <menuitem name="Menu Item 2" />
  <menu name="Nested Menu Name">
    <menuitem name="Nested Menu
Item" />
  </menu>
</menu>
```

You can add a new menu to the interface, within another menu or on a menu bar. Make sure to use both opening and closing <menu> tags; give the menu a unique name; and give the menu a unique ID.

For the Favorites menu I added in **Figure 18.35**, I used the following code:

```
<menu name="_Favorites"
id="DWMenu_Favorites">
  <menuitem name="" />
</menu>
```

Of course, in my menu, I used actual menu items.

Figure 18.35 I added a menu called Favorites to the Document window menu bar.

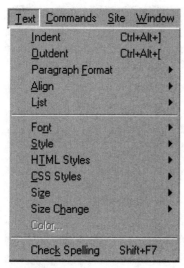

Figure 18.36 The Text menu, in its original state.

Renamed menu items

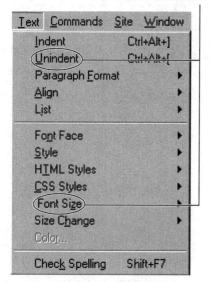

Figure 18.37 The Text menu, after I edited some of the menu and menu item names.

About Menu Items

Each menu item is represented by an individual tag within the menus.xml file. The command Insert > Table is within the menu named "Insert," and it looks like this:

```
<menuitem name="_Table"
key="Command+Opt+T" file="Table.htm"
id="DWMenu_Insert_Table" />
```

Attributes for each item include name, key, file, and ID. The *name* is the name of the item, as it appears in the menu, and preceded by an underscore. *Key* is the keyboard shortcut, if any. *File* is the name of the file that contains the HTML and/or JavaScript for performing the menu command. And *id* is the attribute that Dreamweaver uses to identify the menu item.

✔ Attention!

■ Do not change the ID attribute of any menu item, or Dreamweaver may not be able to perform the menu command.

Renaming menus and menu items

You can rename any menu or menu item. Let's look at the Text menu for examples (**Figures 18.36** and **18.37**). You might want to rename the Font menu Font Face, or the Size menu Font Size. Or you might want to rename Outdent "Unindent" instead.

To rename a menu or menu item:

1. Quit Dreamweaver.

2. Open your working copy (not the pristine backup) of `menus.xml` in your favorite non-Dreamweaver text editor.

3. Locate the menu or menu item you want to rename, and make sure it's within the correct menu bar (**Figure 18.38**).

4. Type a new name for the menu or menu item (**Figure 18.39**).

5. Don't touch the ID attribute.

6. Save your file as `menus.xml` in the Menus folder.

7. Launch Dreamweaver and look for the new name.

✔ Tip

■ Many menu item names have underscore characters placed in what seem like random places. On Windows, the underscore indicates that the following character is the hot key equivalent for the menu item. For example, you will notice that the name of the close item in the File menu is "<u>C</u>lose". This allows you to press Alt + F to open the file menu, and then press C to close a file. The underscore has no use on the Macintosh.

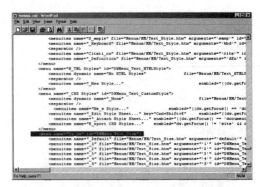

Figure 18.38 I located the menu name I wanted to change.

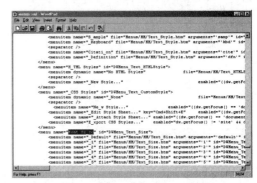

Figure 18.39 I typed a new name for the menu.

Figure 18.40
I created a custom menu called Favorites simply by adding a menu tag and copying and pasting my most-frequently used menu items into it.

Figure 18.41 This is the XML code for my custom menu in the menus.xml file.

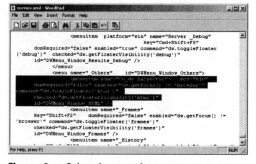

Figure 18.42 Select the menu item you want to move.

Rearranging Menu Items

If you want, you can move a menu item from one menu to another, or you can rearrange the order of items within a single menu. For instance, you might want to move a frequently used item to the top of a menu; you could move Code Inspector out of the Others submenu to the top of the Window menu, or you could move Answers to the bottom.

Or, you might want to create a new menu and move or copy your favorite menu items there (**Figures 18.40** and **18.41**).

To move a menu or menu item:

1. Open your working copy (not the pristine backup) of menus.xml in your favorite non-Dreamweaver text editor.

2. Locate the menu or menu item you want to move or duplicate, and select it (**Figure 18.42**). When selecting an entire menu, make sure to include both its opening and closing tags.

   ◆ To move the menu item, cut it (Ctrl+X/Command+X).

   ◆ To duplicate the menu item elsewhere, copy it (Ctrl+C/Command+C).

continued on next page

3. Place the insertion point where you want the selection to appear, whether it's in the same menu or a different one.

4. Paste the menu item (Ctrl+V/Command+V) into its new location (**Figure 18.43**).

5. Don't touch the ID attribute.

6. Save your file as menus.xml in the Menus folder.

7. Relaunch Dreamweaver and look for the new arrangement (**Figure 18.44**).

Figure 18.43 I copied the Code inspector line from the Others submenu to below the Property inspector line.

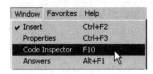

Figure 18.44 Now my Window menu on the Document window menu bar lists the Code inspector near the top.

Deleting a Menu Item

You can remove a menu item entirely if you never use it. You may want to create a menu system that omits all database functions or all FTP functions for installing on different workstations in your office. Or, for example, suppose you find yourself using the Insert > Layer command when you'd rather draw layers only with the Insert toolbar. You can remove the option.

To delete a menu item:

1. Follow steps 1 through 3 above, and cut the menu item.

2. Follow steps 7 and 8 above, to save and test your changes.

Remember that your backup copy retains the old menu item, should you want to restore it.

Adding a Separator

Separators, similar to horizontal rules, divide areas on a menu (**Figure 18.45**).

To add a separator:

1. Open your working copy (not the pristine backup) of menus.xml in your favorite non-Dreamweaver text editor.

2. Locate the place where you want your separator to appear (**Figure 18.46**).

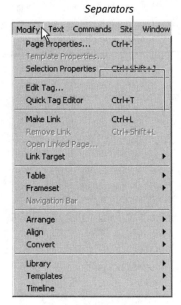

Separators

Figure 18.45 The Modify menu. I want to add a separator below the Table submenu.

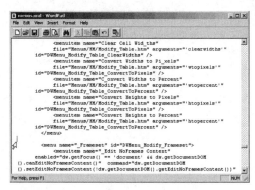

Figure 18.46 This is where I want the separator to go.

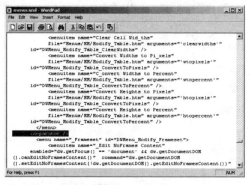

Figure 18.47 I added the separator tag.

3. On a new line, insert the following tag: (**Figure 18.47**):

`<separator />`

4. Save your file as menus.xml in the Menus folder.

5. Relaunch the program and look for the separator (**Figure 18.48**).

✔ Tip

■ To remove a separator, simply remove the appropriate `<separator />` line from the menus.xml file.

New Separator

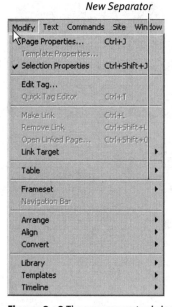

Figure 18.48 The new separator is in the menu.

Extending Dreamweaver with the JavaScript API

If you have a firm grasp of JavaScript, you can do much more than rearrange menu items. You can add panels and inspectors, you can add and customize dialog boxes, and you can add translators for XML (like the one that translates server-side includes into inline HTML) or other content. You can modify the way the Site window works, the way code is written, the function of design notes, and more. Dreamweaver uses an extensible application programming interface (API) and allows modification of its Document Object Model (DOM).

Dreamweaver includes a second set of help files, called Extending Dreamweaver, which consists of instructions for people who want to add their own elements to the interface (**Figure 18.49**). This involves editing the source code, which means that commands must be written with JavaScript or C++ and then added to the interface using the JavaScript API.

You can open the Extending Dreamweaver help files by selecting Help > Extending Dreamweaver from the menu bar. You can also access PDFs about configuring Dreamweaver from Macromedia's Web site. To find out about the functions of different files in the Configuration folder, look in that folder and read the Configuration_ReadMe file (**Figure 18.50**).

If you're learning how to write JavaScript extensions, start with elements other people have written. You can find extensions on Macromedia's Web site by selecting Help > Dreamweaver Exchange from the menu bar.

Be sure you keep plenty of backup copies of any files you modify. It doesn't hurt to make a folder called Backups to store a copy of all edited system files in. (When you upgrade or use certain features, you may also see a backup folder called Configuration-1.)

Figure 18.49 The help files called Extending Dreamweaver cover basic concepts behind adding inspectors, palettes, objects, commands, and so on.

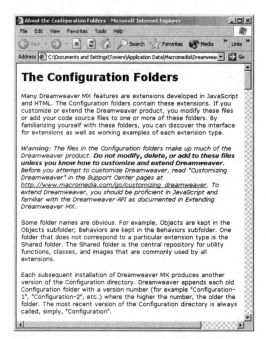

Figure 18.50 Read the Configuration ReadMe file to find out the function of each kind of configuration files in Dreamweaver.

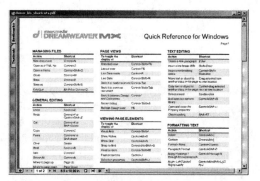

Figure 18.51 The Keyboard Shortcut Quick Reference PDF lists all existing keyboard shortcuts in Dreamweaver.

Changing Keyboard Shortcuts

You can change keyboard shortcuts in Dreamweaver either by using a previously unused shortcut or by reassigning an existing shortcut to a different menu item.

✔ Tip

■ The Macromedia Web site includes a Keyboard Shortcut Quick Reference PDF file (**Figure 18.51**) that displays standard key combinations and the command attached, if any. The URL is: `http://www.macromedia.com/go/dream-weaver_mx_shortcuts`

Dreamweaver MX includes a Keyboard Shortcut editor, which not only makes editing keyboard shortcuts much easier, but allows you to have multiple sets of shortcuts.

If you'd rather edit a text file than use a dialog box, see the appendix called *Modifying the Shortcut File* on the Web site for this book.

To change a keyboard shortcut:

1. From the Document window bar, select Edit > Keyboard Shortcuts to display the Keyboard Shortcuts editor (**Figure 18.52**).

2. Click the Duplicate Set button ![] to duplicate the current set of shortcuts, so you can edit them. The Duplicate Set dialog box will appear (**Figure 18.53**).

3. Type a name for your set in the Name of Duplicate Set text box.

4. Click OK. Your duplicate set name will be displayed in the Current Set drop-down menu.

Delete Set button

Export Set as HTML button

Rename Set button

Duplicate Set button

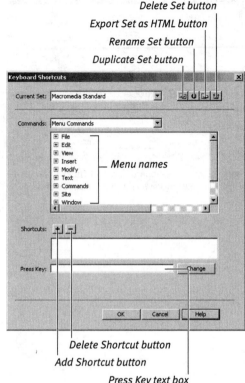

Menu names

Delete Shortcut button

Add Shortcut button

Press Key text box (key presses appear here)

Figure 18.52 The Keyboard Shortcuts editor allows you to add, remove, or change keyboard shortcuts.

Figure 18.53 Type a name for your modified keyboard shortcuts file in the Duplicate Set dialog box.

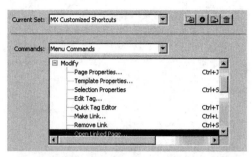

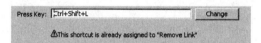

Figure 18.54 To add a shortcut for Open Linked Page, I first expanded the Modify menu.

Figure 18.55 The first shortcut I tried (Ctrl + Shift + L) is already assigned to Remove Link. Fortunately, the editor warned me of that.

Figure 18.56 When I finally hit upon an unassigned key combination (that's a zero in there), I assigned it to the command by clicking the Change button.

Figure 18.57 If I decide to overtake a pre-existing shortcut, Dreamweaver will ask me to confirm my decision. Remember, you can keep different sets of shortcuts for different projects.

Figure 18.58 My new shortcut appears in the menu.

5. Click the icon next to the name of the menu that contains the command for which you want to change the shortcut. This will expand the menu (**Figure 18.54**), showing all the commands and submenu names it contains.

6. Click on the name of the menu item whose shortcut you want to change.

7. Click in the Press Key text box.

8. On the keyboard, type the key combination you want to assign to the selected menu item. If the key combination is already assigned to a menu item, a warning will appear just below the Press Key box (**Figure 18.55**).

9. Click the Change button to assign the key command (**Figure 18.56**). If the key combination is already assigned to something, a dialog will appear asking you to confirm the shortcut's reassignment (**Figure 18.57**).

10. Click OK. Your new shortcut should work just fine, and the new shortcut will appear in the menu (**Figure 18.58**).

CHANGING KEYBOARD SHORTCUTS

Deleting a keyboard shortcut

Occasionally, you may want to remove a shortcut key combination from a command without assigning it to a new command.

To delete a keyboard shortcut:

Follow steps 1 through 5 of the previous task.

1. Click the delete shortcut button ▬ . There is no warning dialog; the shortcut is simply removed (**Figure 18.59**).

2. Click OK to close the editor and save your changes.

✔ Tips

■ In past editions of Dreamweaver, you could assign multiple shortcuts for a given command (**Figure 18.60**) by clicking the plus button ▪+▪ , but I had problems getting this to work in Dreamweaver MX.

■ To use keyboard shortcuts from a different editor or from Dreamweaver 3, select the version from the Current Set drop-down menu.

■ To edit keyboard shortcuts for a different part of the program, select it from the Commands drop-down menu.

■ To save your shortcuts as an HTML file so you can refer to it in your browser or as a printout, click the Set Export as HTML button ▣ .

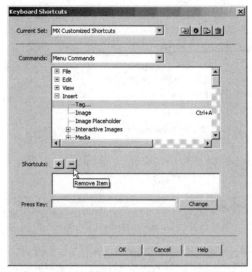

Figure 18.59 I removed the keyboard shortcut from the Insert › Tag command. I can assign a new shortcut or I can leave the command without one.

Figure 18.60 You can try assigning two shortcuts to the command—your mileage may vary.

Mama's Little Baby Likes Shortcuts

Some people like clicking buttons, some people prefer to do their selecting with menus, and others like the quick convenience of keyboard shortcuts.

Why would you want to be able to edit these shortcuts in Dreamweaver? I don't know about you, but I have a lot of standard keyboard shortcuts memorized, and not so many nonstandard ones. I remember that F10 opens the Code inspector, but if I want to open any other panel or inspector, I'm pretty much wedded to the Window menu.

You can, however, change keyboard shortcuts so that they work for you.

For instance (and for this paragraph, I'll use only Windows commands to be terse), I'm always forgetting myself and getting rid of the Property inspector. This widget didn't even get a keyboard shortcut in Dreamweaver 1.2, and I can't seem to remember Ctrl+F3. So I decided to make it more like P, for Property. Ctrl+P is paste, and I don't want to change that. So I open the Keyboard Shortcuts editor, select Window > Properties, and then press Ctrl+Shift+P. It looks like Ctrl+Shift+P is Format: Paragraph. I don't use that shortcut, anyway. So I can go ahead and change it.

If you'd rather edit a text file than use a dialog box, see the appendix called *Modifying the Shortcut File* on the Web site for this book.

Customizing Dialog Boxes

You can customize the appearance of dialog boxes in Dreamweaver, too. These include the dialog boxes you use to insert objects and modify behaviors, as well as other commands. You can rearrange menu items, change the size of text boxes, relabel form fields, and remove unused items.

Why edit a dialog box if you can't change its functionality? You can change default settings; you may want to remove text boxes you never use, or leave notes for yourself; or you can translate the dialog box into a different language.

✔ Before you start!

■ In the Preferences dialog box, under Code Rewriting, deselect the Rename Form Fields When Pasting check box, or you may accidentally rename a vital form field.

■ Windows NT/XP users: For some reason, some objects, and the table dialog box in particular, *must* be modified in your user Configuration folder rather than in the Program Files Configuration folder. The table object, which is stored in your user folder, even when other files are not, was the only object I had to do this with when customizing on Windows XP for this chapter. See the sidebar, *About Configuring Dreamweaver for Multi-User PCs*.

CUSTOMIZING DIALOG BOXES

Figure 18.61 Open the file you want to modify. Its filename will be similar to its menu command name.

Figure 18.62 Doesn't look much like a dialog box, does it? Notice that a form border surrounds the contents of the dialog box.

Figure 18.63 I modified some of the options in the Insert Table dialog box. As wacky as this looks, I didn't change any functionality other than resetting the default values.

Figure 18.64 This is what the modified dialog box looks like after you quit and restart Dreamweaver.

To customize a dialog box:

1. Locate the `.htm` or `.html` file for the dialog box you want to modify. It will be found in the Configuration folder, and then probably the Commands, Behaviors, or Objects folder (**Figure 18.61**).

2. Make a backup copy of the file in a different folder. I keep a Backups folder in the Configuration folder.

3. Open the file in Dreamweaver (**Figure 18.62**).

4. Use Dreamweaver's form and text tools to modify the file (**Figure 18.63**).

5. Save the file with its original name in its original folder. Make sure you're keeping a pristine backup, too.

6. Quit and relaunch Dreamweaver, then open the dialog box to test it (**Figure 18.64**).

✔ Tips

- To find out about modifying forms-based interfaces, see Chapter 15.

- You cannot add an item to a dialog box unless you also add the name and ID for the object in the JavaScript API. See *Extending Dreamweaver with the JavaScript API*.

- In Chapter 15, the first thing we did when we added a form field was to name it. The names of form fields in Dreamweaver dialog boxes are linked to their functionality, so don't change them.

MANAGING YOUR WEB SITES

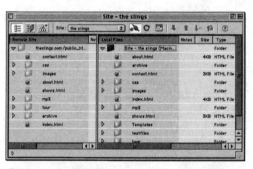

Figure 19.1 The Site window is not only a file management tool, but also a full-fledged FTP client. This is the Macintosh view of both local and remote files.

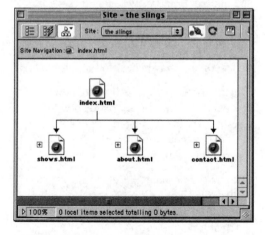

Figure 19.2 The site map lets you see the link relationships in your site at a glance.

Once you're ready to put a page—or an entire site—up on the Web for the whole world to see, you don't have to leave Dreamweaver. The Site window (**Figure 19.1**) is a full-fledged, handy-dandy FTP client—a built-in tool for *putting* files on the Web, or *uploading* them. You can also use Dreamweaver to *get* files from the Web, or *download* them.

Also in this chapter, you'll find out about many other site management tools, such as the site map (**Figure 19.2**), file synchronization, and the Link Checker. The link checker lets you examine an entire site for incorrect links and missing files.

✔ Tip

■ If you skipped Chapter 2, go back and use it to help you set up a local site. You can't use any of Dreamweaver's site management tools without doing this.

Getting Ready to Put Your Site Online

In Chapter 2, you learned how to set up a local site in the Site window by setting up the same folders on your local computer that will appear on the remote Web server. A *Web server*, once again, is a computer that does two things: It stores the files that make up a Web site, and it delivers files when Web browsers request them.

In this chapter, we'll take the files in that local site and put them up online.

Before you can put your site up on the Web, you need to have a Web account; you need to know the server information for that account, and you need to have a computer that can connect to the Internet. You can create a great site without even owning a modem, but before you put it online you need to get set up.

Aside from that, you need a clean setup in terms of where your files and folders are. Make sure your files are well organized in a folder structure that makes sense (**Figure 19.3**). In that figure, I have files that are not yet a part of my site stored in the "testfiles" folder, which I will not upload to the remote site.

✔ Tip

■ When moving files and folders in the Site window, you can have Dreamweaver automatically update all links to those files. See *Site Window Tips and Shortcuts* and *Moving Files,* in Chapter 2, if you're not familiar with this process.

Figure 19.3 Make sure your files are organized in their proper folders before you put them on the Web. That will save you time in the future when updating and expanding your site.

More Site Management Tools

Appendix O, on the Web site for this book, covers two additional site management tools: Design Notes and Site Reporting. (These tools were described in Chapter 21 in the Dreamweaver 4 edition of this book.)

Design Notes are a workflow tool that allow you to use a handy dialog box to create XML files in which you can keep all sorts of meta-information about your pages and media files.

An auxiliary feature of Design Notes is called File View Columns. You can add, remove, or rearrange the columns in the Site window.

Site Reporting allows you to search your site for HTML errors, Design Notes listings, and file check-out status.

View drop-down menu

Expander button

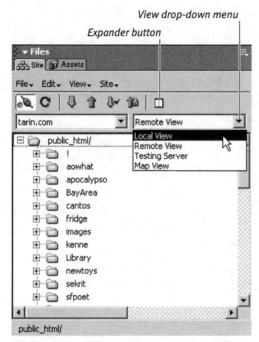

Figure 19.4 On the PC, you can view either local or remote files when the Site window is docked as a panel. This is the remote view.

Figure 19.5 Click the Expander button (Figure 19.4) on the PC to view both local and remote files in the Site window.

The Site window: PC vs. Mac

As we saw in Chapter 2, the Site window is always a stand-alone window on the Mac (as we saw in Figure 19.1), whereas on the PC you have a choice of docking the Site window as a panel or undocking it and using it as a stand-alone window. Also, on the Mac, both the remote and local views are always shown. On the PC, you can view either local or remote files when the Site window is docked as a panel (**Figure 19.4**); to view both at once, you click the Expander button to undock the window (**Figure 19.5**).

Setting Up Remote Info

Remote site information tells Dreamweaver how to find and log into a remote Web server. You will be connecting either to an FTP site or to a local network. If you're not sure which, ask your network administrator.

If you're on a dial-up account, it's likely you'll use an FTP (file transfer protocol) site. Even if you're on a local network, you may be using FTP. Check with your ISP's tech support or with your Web site administrator if you're not sure.

Setting up remote info for FTP

If you're using a dial-up Internet account or an account on a Web-based hosting service, use this section to set up your account information. If your internet connection is a LAN, DSL, or cable modem, but your files are still stored on an FTP server, here you go.

To set up remote site info (FTP):

1. From the Site window menu bar or the Document window menu bar, select Site > Edit Sites. The Edit Sites dialog box will appear (**Figure 19.6**).

2. Select the local site you want to set up, and click Edit. The Site Definition dialog box will appear (**Figure 19.7**).

3. In the Category box at the left, click Remote Info. That panel of the dialog box will come to the front (**Figure 19.8**).

4. From the Access drop-down menu, select FTP. The dialog box will display FTP information (**Figure 19.9**, next page).

5. In the FTP Host text box, type the alphanumeric address for the Web server (for example, ftp.site.com or www.site.com). Do not include folders.

Figure 19.6 Choose which local site to set up for prime time in the Edit Sites dialog box. You may have only one local site, but you need to have at least one to start. See Chapter 2 if you haven't yet set up a local site.

Advanced tab selected

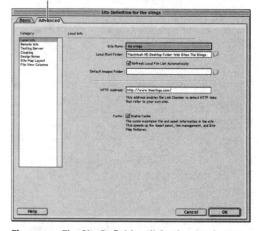

Figure 19.7 The Site Definition dialog box is where you set up and edit both local and remote site management information.

Figure 19.8 The Remote Info area of the Site Definition dialog box starts out blank.

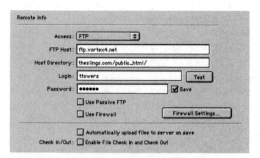

Figure 19.9 If your server access is through FTP, you'll enter all your account information here.

6. In the Host Directory text box, type the name of the initial root directory for the site (e.g., `public_html` or `html/ public/personal`). If you're unsure about this, you can leave it blank for now.

7. In the Login text box, type the username for the FTP or WWW account. In the Password text box, type the password for the FTP or WWW account.

8. To save the username and password, place a checkmark in the Save check box.

9. To test your connection, click the Test button: [Test] to see if your ftp host can be pinged. If the test is not successful, be sure your Internet connection is active, and double-check your entries in steps 5 through 7.

When both the local and remote site information are filled out, you can continue setting up information for cloaking, the site map, and so on, using the other sections in this chapter.

10. If you're done for now, click OK to close the Site Definition dialog box. You'll return to the Site window, where you'll see your local site displayed.

✔ Tips

■ If you use the same FTP host for several different sites, you can avoid having to repeat these steps again and again. In the Edit Sites dialog box, you can select a site with remote information already set up, and then click Duplicate to make a copy of it. Then, rename the site and edit the local root folder information.

■ If you want to share site definition information between computers, you can export the site definition as a file. See *Importing and Exporting Site Information* in Chapter 2.

Setting up for a local network

If you're on a local network at work, or a DSL (Digital Subscriber Line), or cable modem at home, you may connect to your Web server via a local network. Even if you use a local network, you may still use FTP to put files on the external or internal Web servers. If that's the case, use the previous section on FTP servers. In the case of a truly local intranet Web server, you connect using the Network Neighborhood (Windows) or AppleTalk (Macintosh) to choose a machine to put files onto.

To set up remote site info (local):

1. **Windows:** Log into your Network Neighborhood as yourself.

   Mac: Use the Chooser to connect to the local server using AppleTalk.

   Mac OS X: Use the Connect to Server feature in the Finder to connect to a Windows or UNIX server.

2. Follow steps 1 through 3 in the previous section so that you're viewing the Remote Info panel of the Site Definition dialog box for your site.

3. From the Site Definition dialog box, with Remote Info chosen, select Local/Network from the Access drop-down menu. The dialog box will change appearance (**Figure 19.10**).

4. In the Remote Folder text box, click on the Folder icon, and the Choose Remote Folder dialog box will appear (**Figures 19.11** and **19.12**).

Figure 19.10 If you're using a local network via the Windows Network Neighborhood or Macintosh AppleTalk, you can choose your local machine here.

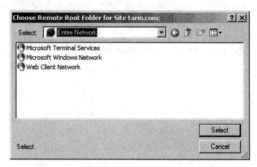

Figure 19.11 The Choose Remote Folder dialog box. It's just like selecting a folder, only it happens to be on a different computer.

Remote computer/file server   *Shortcuts menu*

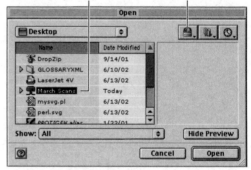

Figure 19.12 The Mac's Choose Remote Folder dialog box. By default, it starts you out on the Desktop, which is where remote machines appear after you connect with the Chooser. You can also select a mounted network drive by selecting its name from the Shortcuts menu.

Figure 19.13 For Local/Network connections, check this box (in the Remote Info area of the Site Definition dialog box) to always view your remote site in the Site window.

5. Windows: Choose Network Neighborhood from the Select drop-down menu, and then browse through the computers on the network as if they were regular folders. When you find the right machine and folder, click Select.

Mac: Select Desktop from the drop-down menu, then select the server from the ones displayed. When you find the right machine and folder, click Choose. You can also select the name of a mounted drive from the Shortcuts menu on the Open dialog box on the Mac.

6. You can continue to set up other remote options described in this chapter. If you're done for now, click OK. You'll return to the Site window, where you'll see your local site displayed.

✔ Tip

■ If you select the Refresh Remote File List check box for a Local/Network connection (**Figure 19.13**), you should automatically see your remote files whenever you have the Remote panel of the Site window open. If it doesn't appear, click Refresh ⟳ on the Site window toolbar.

SETTING UP REMOTE INFO

Connecting to Your Server

Before you can download an existing remote site or upload to it, you need to connect to it. Remember that you need to set up your remote info in the Site Definition dialog box first.

To connect to a remote site:

1. In the Site window, select the site you want to connect to from the Site drop-down menu (**Figure 19.14**).

2. Click the Connect button ![icon]. Dreamweaver will use your remote site information to connect to the Web server.

3. A Connecting to [host name] dialog box will appear while Dreamweaver contacts the Web server (**Figure 19.15**).

4. When you've successfully connected to the remote server, the Connect button will change to a Disconnect button, and the remote file list will appear (**Figure 19.16**).

After you've finished getting and putting files, you can disconnect from the remote site.

To disconnect from a remote site:

1. In the Site window, look at the status bar to make sure there aren't any files being transferred.

2. Click Disconnect ![icon]. The status line will read Disconnected.

✔ Tip

- If you don't move a file for a period of 30 minutes, Dreamweaver will disconnect for you. To change this, see *Site FTP Preferences,* later in this chapter.

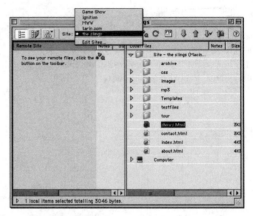

Figure 19.14 Choose the site you want to connect to from the Remote Site drop-down menu.

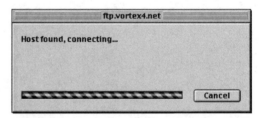

Figure 19.15 A series of dialog boxes will briefly appear while Dreamweaver connects you to the remote site.

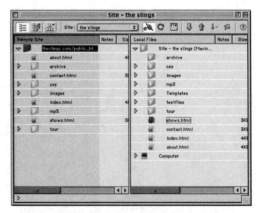

Figure 19.16 You'll know you're connected when Dreamweaver says so. The Connect button will become a Disconnect button. Oh, yeah, and the files will be displayed in the Remote Site pane of the Site window. (They do stay in view after you've disconnected, however.)

CONNECTING TO YOUR SERVER

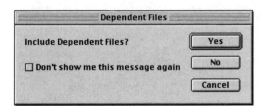

Figure 19.17 The Dependent Files dialog box can automatically get or put images or other files attached to the page.

Getting and Putting Files

Now you're ready to download (get) stuff from and upload (put) stuff to your local and remote sites. If the files you download are in a directory on the remote site that doesn't yet exist on the local site, the directory will be created on the local site, and vice versa.

To download files from a remote site:

1. In the Site window, select the remote file(s) or folder(s) you want to download.

2. Click the Get button ⬇ . The Dependent Files dialog box will appear (**Figure 19.17**). This will include any other files needed to display the pages that you're downloading. Click Yes or No (see the sidebar on this page).

3. The progress of the download will appear in the status bar of the Site window while the files are being retrieved.

About Dependent Files

Dependent files include images, external style sheet files, Flash objects, sound files, plug-ins, and other objects the page links to within your site. Dependent files also include all the files in a frameset.

This feature can be really convenient; you can upload a page that includes a toolbar and a style sheet and then click Yes in the Dependent Files dialog box, and all the associated files and images will be uploaded to the site.

On the other hand, if you do most of your dealing in single documents, you may find this feature annoying. Just place a checkmark in the Don't Ask Me Again check box and you won't see the dialog box any more.

You can show and hide dependent files in the Site Map view, which is described later in this chapter.

To upload files to a remote site:

1. In the Site window, select the local file(s) or folder(s) you want to upload. Or, you can upload the current saved page directly from the Document window.

2. Click the Put button 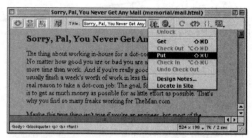, or, if you're in the Document window, select Put from the File Management menu on the Document toolbar (**Figure 19.18**). The Dependent Files dialog box will appear (Figure 19.17). Click Yes or No (see the sidebar on the previous page).

   The progress of the upload will appear in the status bar of the Site window while the files are being sent to the remote server.

✔ Tip

■ To stop the current transfer, click the Stop Current Task button, or press Esc.

Figure 19.18 Select Get or Put to transfer the current file that's in the Document window. If you Put the file, Dreamweaver will save it for you. If you Get it, it will overwrite what's in view.

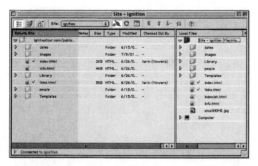

Figure 19.19 The files with checkmarks have been checked out; you can see the check-out names in the Checked Out By column.

Using Check-in Names

If you're working with a team on a site, and your entire team uses Dreamweaver, you can use file check-in and check-out to keep track of who's working on which file and who last uploaded it. (If there are only one or two of you, you should already know the answer.)

Checking out a file locks it on the remote server and allows you to edit it locally, while a flag appears on it (a red checkmark) that says to others, "Can't Touch This." Checking in a file unlocks it on the remote server, but makes it read-only on your local site so that you don't accidentally edit a file that is not checked out.

Think of it like a library book: When you check out a book, no one else can borrow it until you return it. When you check it back in, anyone can access it by checking it out again.

Checking out a file marks the file with a green checkmark, assigns your username to that file, and locks it in the Dreamweaver Site window. Other team members who use Dreamweaver will not be able to overwrite locked files (files checked out by another person). These files can be overwritten by any other FTP client, however. This is a simpler, user-based, and less secure approximation of CVS checkout, a Unix-based tool used in production groups.

Files other people have checked out are marked in the Site window with a red checkmark and the person's check-out name appears in the Checked Out By column in both the local and remote panes (**Figure 19.19**).

Setting up file check-in

Before you can check files in or out, you must enable that option in the site's definition.

To enable check-in and check-out:

1. From the Site window menu bar, select Site > Edit Sites. The Edit Sites dialog box will appear (**Figure 19.20**).

2. Select the site for which you want to set check-in and check-out options, and click Edit. The Site Definition dialog box will appear.

3. In the Category box at the left, select Remote Info. That panel will move to the front of the dialog box (**Figure 19.21**).

4. To enable check-in and check-out, click that check box. More options for file check-in will appear (**Figure 19.22**).

5. If you want to mark files as checked out when you open them in the Document window, check the Check Out Files When Opening check box.

6. Type the name you want others to see when you check out files in the Check Out Name text box. This can be your full name or your username.

7. If you want colleagues to be able to contact you about checked-out files, type your full email address in the Email Address text box. (See Tips, next page.)

8. Click OK. Now, each time you get a file from the remote server, it will be marked as checked out, and each time you put a file, it will be marked as checked in.

Figure 19.20 Choose which site's check-in preferences to modify in the Edit Sites dialog box.

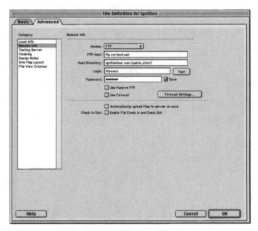

Figure 19.21 The Remote Info panel of the Site Definition dialog box, before file check-in is enabled.

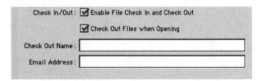

Figure 19.22 Enable file check-outs and set your check-out name in the Remote Info panel of the Site Definition dialog box.

USING CHECK-IN NAMES

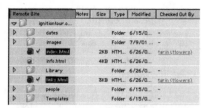

Figure 19.23 Check-out names, if they've been entered with email addresses, appear as clickable links in the Site window.

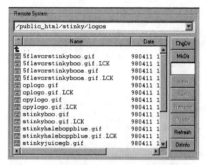

Figure 19.24 You can see the .LCK files if you examine the site with an FTP client other than Dreamweaver's.

About .LCK Files

When you check out a file using Dreamweaver, a lock is placed on the file in the Dreamweaver Site window. This lock is a text file with the .LCK extension. .LCK files are invisible in the Dreamweaver Site window, but you can see them in a different FTP client (**Figure 19.24**).

A .LCK file contains the username of the person who checked it out. This file also shows the date and time of the checkout in the time stamp.

You can see the date and time of a .LCK file in most FTP clients in the date and time column. The .LCK files I examined were only 7 bytes each (there are 1000 bytes in 1 kilobyte), so they aren't going to make you run out of server space any time soon.

✔ Tips

■ If you access your files from a different computer and cannot perform an upload because the files are checked out, you can still upload or download them by using a different FTP client, such as Telnet/CVS, WS_FTP, Fetch, or Cute FTP.

■ Even if you work alone, you might want to use these features. For instance, if you work on two different machines, you can use check-out names such as PC and Mac, or Home and Work, so you'll know where the latest version is hiding.

■ If you're using the Check In/Out feature to prevent others on your team from overwriting each other's work, make sure they are using Dreamweaver to manage their FTP sessions. If they work with another FTP program, however, they will see Dreamweaver's .LCK file listed after the checked-out file. If you let them know what this means, they can open the .LCK file, see your name, and contact you to find out whether they can use it.

■ If you use a valid email address in the Site Definition dialog box, your name will appear as a link in the Checked Out By column in the Site window (**Figure 19.23**). Just like with a `mailto:` link in the browser window, other users will be able to click the link and pop open an email message window. Your email address will be supplied, and the name of the file will appear in the subject line.

Checking Out Files

When file check-in is enabled, you'll see two new buttons on the Site window (**Figure 19.25**), one for checking in and one for checking out. You can use these just as you do the Get and Put buttons described earlier in this chapter —although if you use the same old buttons, files will still be checked in and out with your name.

To check out remote files:

1. Connect to the appropriate site in the Site window.

2. Select the file(s) or folder(s) in the Remote Site panel (**Figure 19.26**).

3. Click the Check Out Files button ⬇️✓ .

4. Respond to the Dependent Files dialog box. The file or files (and any associated folders, if necessary) will be copied to the local site (**Figure 19.27**), and they will be marked with a green checkmark, your checkout name and a .LCK file on the remote server.

✔ Tips

■ You can double-click on a remote file in the Site window to open the file at the same time that you check it out.

■ You may have to refresh the Local site view to see the file (or its folder, if that was freshly created, too).

To undo a file check-out:

◆ After checking out the files, select Site > Undo Check Out (Site > Site Files View > Undo Check Out) from the Site window menu bar.

This will overwrite the local copy of the file with the remote copy of the file.

Check In button

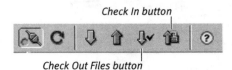

Check Out Files button

Figure 19.25 The toolbar on the Site window will include two new buttons after you enable file check-out.

Files selected for check-out

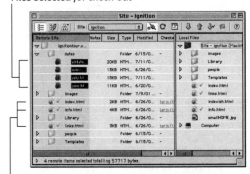

Red checkmarks—files checked out by someone else

Figure 19.26 Select the file you want to check out in the Remote Site pane. Some other files in this folder have been checked out by someone else named Tarin, but right now I'm Claude. If this image were color, you'd see that the checkmarks are red.

Refresh button

Checked out file   *New folder*

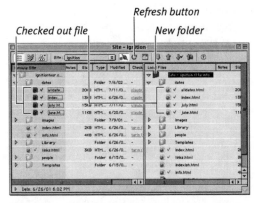

Figure 19.27 The file and its folder were both copied to the local site, and the file appears checked out by me, Claude, in the remote site pane.

Figure 19.28 I updated the files that I checked out earlier, and now I'm going to check them back in.

Figure 19.29 You may get a dialog box like this if you try to overwrite a newer, single file, either when checking in or checking out.

Figure 19.30 You may get a dialog box like this if you try to overwrite a batch of files.

Checked in files Files are locked in local site after check-in

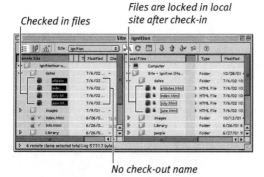

No check-out name

Figure 19.31 I checked the files back in, and now my name (Claude) is gone from the Checked Out By Column. When files have been checked into the site, they appear locked in the Local pane of the Site window. That's because you're supposed to check out a file before you edit it locally.

Checking In Files

After you've finished working on a file, you can check it back in. That means two things: You're uploading the current version back up to the live site (or the staging server), and you're freeing up the file so others can work on it.

To check in files:

1. In the local site, click to select the files or folders you want to check in (**Figure 19.28**)

2. From the Document window menu bar, select Site > Check In (Site > Site Files View > Check In on Mac OS 9). Or, click the Check In button.

3. Respond to the Dependent Files dialog, as well as the Overwrite dialog box in **Figure 19.29** or **19.30**, if one appears.

   The file will appear with a locked icon on the local site. The Checked Out status will be removed from the remote server and your name will disappear from the Checked Out By column (**Figure 19.31**).

continued on next page

✔ Tips

- When you check a file back in, it gets locked on your local machine. That's because Dreamweaver safeguards the file so that you can't work on it unless you check it out first. If you need to work on a file you've checked in, and it hasn't changed, and you don't want to bother checking it out again, just unlock it. From the Document window menu bar, select File > Turn Off Read Only (Mac OS 9: Sites > Site Files View > Turn Off Read Only. On Mac OS X, it's Site > Unlock.). You can also select Turn Off Read Only from the File Management menu on the Document window's toolbar.

- You can also check files in and out while you're working on them, if need be. On the Document window's toolbar, select Check In or Check Out from the File Management menu (**Figure 19.32**). Files that you check out will *overwrite* your work in the Document window. Files that you check in will be saved automatically before they're put up on the remote site.

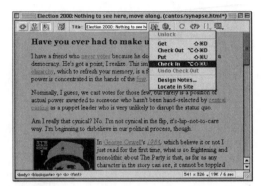

Figure 19.32 You can check in a file while you're working on it, but then it'll lock. You can always select Turn Off Read Only from the same menu to keep working on it.

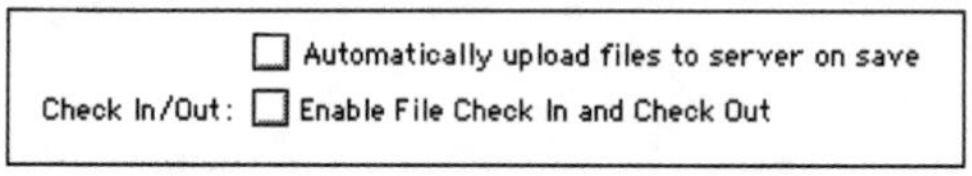

Figure 19.33 You can enable automatic uploads in the Remote Info area of the Site Definition dialog box so your pages will get Put after each save. (You can turn this feature off again after you're done with your current page.)

Enabling Automatic Uploads

Dreamweaver allows you to upload a file after each save. You might want to turn this feature on if you're working on a fairly small site; tweaking the final details on a few pages; and reasonably sure that the act of updating the site won't affect any visitors (e.g., you're putting up a new site or adding a section to an existing one).

To enable automatic uploads:

1. Open the Site Definition dialog box for your site.

2. Click Remote Info to bring that panel to the front.

3. Check the Automatically upload files to server on save check box (**Figure 19.33**)

4. Click OK to save your preferences.

Now, when you save a file, Dreamweaver will automatically upload it for you.

Cloaking: Preventing Files From Uploading

A new feature in Dreamweaver MX allows you to *cloak* certain folders, files, or file types, which prevents those files from being uploaded.

You might have files in progress that are either not ready to go live or not meant to ever go live. Or you may keep in your site folder project-related documents that are not Web files but are essential to your workflow. These could include spreadsheets, Photoshop documents, PNGs, or Dreamweaver templates.

To enable cloaking:

1. On the Site window, double-click the name of your site on the Site drop-down menu. The Site Definition dialog box will appear.

2. In the Category list, select Cloaking. That panel will appear (**Figure 19.34**).

3. To turn cloaking on, click the Enable Cloaking check box (**Figure 19.35**).

4. To cloak specific file types, such as XLS (Excel), DWT (Dreamweaver Templates), or PSD (Photoshop Document) files, check the Cloak Files Ending With check box **(Figure 19.36)**.

5. Type those file types in the text box. Include periods and separate them with a single space, like so: `.PSD .XLS .DWT`.

6. Click OK to save your changes.

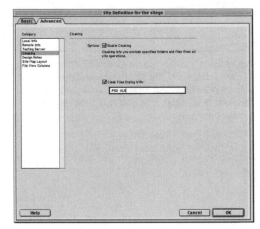

Figure 19.34 The Cloaking area of the Site Definition dialog box.

Figure 19.35 Select Enable Cloaking to turn the feature on.

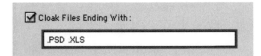

Figure 19.36 To cloak all files of a specific type, type the extension(s) in the text box.

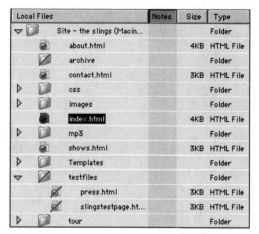

Figure 19.37 A red slash will appear over all cloaked files. Here, I've cloaked the folder for a section that's not live yet (archives) and the folder that contains experimental and test pages.

To cloak specific files:

1. Select a file or folder in the Local Files panel of the Site window.

2. From the Site window menu bar, select Site > Cloaking > Cloak.

   A red slash will appear over the file or folder in the Site window (**Figure 19.37**).

✔ Tips

■ Dreamweaver won't let you cloak a file that it knows you've put up on the remote site already. The option will be grayed out in the menu.

■ You uncloak files by performing the preceding steps again and deselecting Cloak.

■ You can uncloak all files in your site by selecting Site > Cloaking > Cloak from the Site window menu bar.

Synchronizing Modified Files

Dreamweaver can automatically select a batch of newer files in a directory or entire site, so that you can be sure you're not overwriting the latest version of a file during a transfer.

To select newer files:

1. Select the proper local site and connect to the associated remote site.

2. From the Site window menu bar, select Edit > Select Newer Local or Edit > Select Newer Remote (Mac: Site > Site Files View > Select Newer Local *or* Select Newer Remote), depending on the pane in which you want the newest files to be highlighted. Dreamweaver will compare the dates of the local and remote files.

   When the comparison is complete, the files that are newer than the ones on the other site will be highlighted (**Figure 19.38**). After double-checking, you can get, put, or synchronize the selected files.

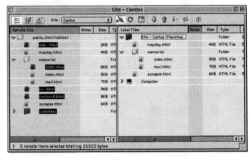

Figure 19.38 The newer files are automatically highlighted in the Site window—here, I've Selected Newer Remote. I can click on Get to download copies of the newer files from the remote server.

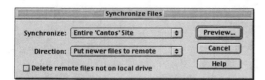

Figure 19.39 The Synchronize Files dialog box lets you select batches of newer files to get, put, or both.

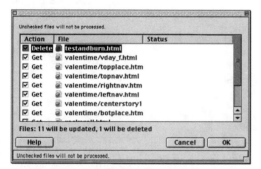

Figure 19.40 This dialog box lets you uncheck files out of a big batch to be left alone.

The Synchronize feature selects newer files and then gets or puts them automatically, as a batch. You may want to make backups first.

To synchronize files:

1. From the Site window menu bar, select Site > Synchronize. The Synchronize Files dialog box will appear (**Figure 19.39**).

2. From the Synchronize drop-down menu, choose whether to sync the entire site or just a selection. From the Direction drop-down menu, choose whether to Get, Put, or Both.

3. Click Preview to prepare to sync up. The Site dialog box will appear (**Figure 19.40**). Uncheck any files you don't want to include.

4. When you're ready, click OK. The specified, newer files will upload or download, and the progress of the transfers will appear in the Site window status bar.

✔ Tip

■ To choose which selected files to use, click within the appropriate panel after Step 1. Depending on your selections, you'll see a check box that says Delete local files not on remote server or Delete remote files not on local server. Use caution here—it's a great cleanup tool, but you don't want to accidentally delete files you need and don't have copies of. The preview dialog box lets you see which files Dreamweaver is going to delete.

Refreshing and Switching Views

If you move files around on your local site using a local file management program, or if you move them around on the remote site using a different FTP program, the Site window might not accurately reflect what's where. You can refresh the view—just like reloading a page in a browser window.

You also use the refresh command to view remote files when you're using a local network.

To refresh the Site window:

◆ On the Site window toolbar, click the Refresh button.

To refresh a particular view:

◆ From the Site window menu bar, select View > Refresh Local or View > Refresh Remote. On the Mac, the command is Site > Site Files View > Refresh Local or Refresh Remote.

Dreamweaver will check the displayed directory info against the actual directory info and display the latest file and folder information.

Changing site views

There are three different site views you can use when working with site files: Local, Remote, or Both. The default view on the Mac is Both. (On the PC, we saw how the Site window can be docked as a panel or Expanded to a window in **Figures 19.4** and **19.5**.)

To change the site view (Mac):

◆ Show the Show Always portion of the site, Local or Remote, by clicking on the Expander arrow (**Figure 19.41**). (You set which view you want always to show in the Site Preferences.)

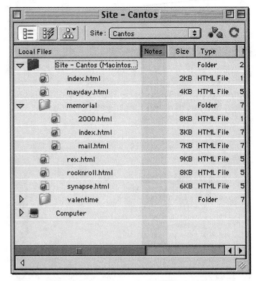

Figure 19.41 Conserve your desktop: Show only one view at a time in the Site window (Mac) by clicking the Expander arrow. This is the Local view—you can choose which view always to show in Site Preferences.

More Site View Tips

◆ The fourth possible view is the Site Map, which I describe in the next section.

◆ To change which view is always showing, Local or Remote, see *Site FTP Preferences*, at the end of this chapter.

◆ Drag the lower-right corner of the Site window to change the window size. Drag the frame border between the two window panes to adjust the space given to each.

◆ To hide floating windows that may cover the Site window, press F4. Press F4 again to show only the windows that were open before.

◆ You can add columns to the Site window to view information that's associated with design notes. Both are described in online Appendix O.

Figure 19.42 The Site Map Layout panel of the Site Definition dialog box. Go here first to set up a home page for your site map.

Figure 19.43 A close-up of the Site Map Layout panel of the Site Definition dialog box

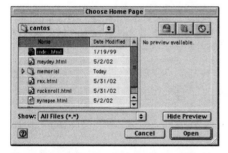

Figure 19.44 Choose your home page. This is just like an Open dialog box.

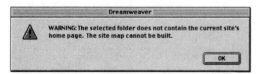

Figure 19.45 If you move your home page or the folder that it's in, make sure to let Dreamweaver know where you put it, or this dialog box will show up uninvited.

Using the Site Map

Dreamweaver offers visual site maps for use in viewing the relationships of files, not only in the sense of what's in what directory but also regarding what links to what.

To use a visual site map, you must first select a file to be the home page file. This can be the default index page of a particular site. You may also decide to display a site map for a subsection of a site, in which case you would change the home page view to make that page the focal point of the site map.

To set the home page:

1. In the Site window, double-click the name of your site in the Site drop-down menu. The Site Definition dialog box will appear.

2. In the Category box at the left, click Site Map Layout. That panel of the dialog box will come to the front (**Figure 19.42, 19.43**). If your site root has a file called index.html, Dreamweaver will assume it's the home page and fill in the Home Page text box.

   If you want to change the home page, click the Browse button to open the Choose Home Page dialog box (**Figure 19.44**).

3. Select the file, and click Open to close the Choose Home Page dialog box and return to the Site Definition dialog box.

4. Click OK to save your changes.

   Now you can view the site map.

✔ Tip

- If you move your local site folder, you need to update the location of your home page when you update your other site information in Dreamweaver, or you'll get this annoying dialog box (**Figure 19.45**) all the time. You can follow the preceding steps or you can simply delete the path in the Home Page text box.

To view the site map:

1. On the Site window (Mac, or expanded on Windows), click the Site Map View button (**Figure 19.46**). The Site window will display the site map (**Figure 19.47**).

2. If you're using the Site window as a docked panel on Windows, select Map View from the view drop-down menu (see Figure 19.49, next page).

To adjust the site map layout:

1. Follow steps 1 and 2 on the previous page to bring up the Site Map Layout panel of the Site Definition dialog box (see Figures 19.42 and 19.43).

2. Set the maximum number of columns by typing a number in the Number of Columns text box.

3. Set the column width in pixels by typing a number in the Column Width text box.

4. You can use either filenames or page titles as the labels for each page icon.
   - ◆ To view file names, select the File Names radio button.
   - ◆ To view page titles, select the Page Titles radio button.

5. To display all files, including those that would normally be hidden (such as .LCK files and FTP logs), check the Display Files Marked as Hidden check box.

6. To display all dependent files, such as images, CSS files, and Flash, check the Display Dependent Files check box.

7. Click OK to close the Site Definition dialog box and return to the Site window (**Figure 19.48**).

✔ Tip

- ■ You can toggle the last three options on and off by selecting them from the View menu on the Site window menu bar (on the Mac, it's Site > Site Map View > Show [option]).

USING THE SITE MAP

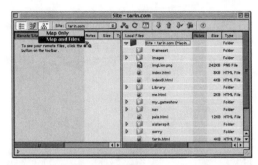

Figure 19.46 Click the Site Map View button to view the site map where the Remote panel usually is. To view only the site map in the Site window, click and hold down the button, and from the pop-up menu that appears, select Map Only.

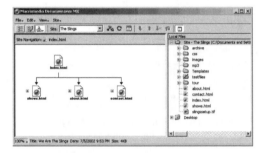

Figure 19.47 The site map—this is in the Expanded Site window on the PC. Ta-da! You can examine, visually, the relationships between pages on your site.

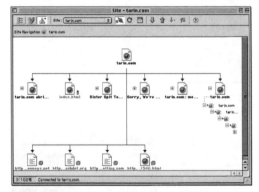

Figure 19.48 This site is in Map Only view. (See Figure 19.46.) I adjusted the site map layout so that page titles instead of filenames are visible. I also changed the number of columns to 6 and the column width to 100.

Site Map Icons and Tips

*Site window
docked on PC*　　　　*Map view selected from
view drop-down menu*

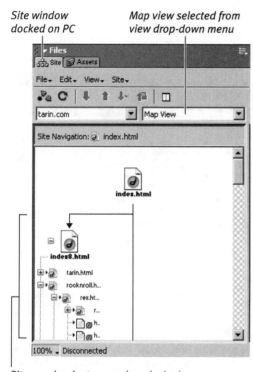

Site map harder to use when docked

Figure 19.49 Click on the plus signs (+) to expand the links for each document in your local site. I'm using page titles here instead of file names for viewing, but full URLs that link out of my site are still printed as URLs.

Site Map Icons and Tips

In Site Map view, various icons are used to represent different types of pages or links. These icons are described in **Table 19.1**. Lower levels of the site use smaller versions of the same icons.

To view more levels:

◆　In the site map window, pages with more levels are marked by a + (plus) sign. Click on the plus sign to view the subsidiary links for that file (**Figure 19.49**).

Table 19.1

Site Map Icons	
Icon	**What it Means**
fridge.html	A page icon. Can be a Web page, text file, XML, JS, etc.
toread.html	Green checkmarks indicate files you have checked out.
index8.html	Files someone else has checked out are not indicated in Site Map view in Dreamweaver MX.
fridge.html	Padlocks indicate locked or read-only files.
the-man.html	The broken icon indicates a broken link—that is, a link to a local file that there is no copy of on the local site.
http://www.angry.org	An external Web URL icon.
mailto...tarin.com	A mailto link icon.
foriginal.gif	An image icon.
logo.swf	A Flash text or movie file.
Toilet.wav	An icon for an unknown (non-Dreamweaver) file type or a file with no extension.

To view the map from a branch:

◆ From the Site window menu bar, select
View > View as Root (Macintosh: Site >
Site Map View > View as Root). The map
will rearrange as if the selected page were
the site root (**Figure 19.50**).

To temporarily hide a link:

◆ From the Site window menu bar, select
View > Show/Hide Link. (On the Mac, it's
Site > Site Map View > Show/Hide Link.)
The link and the levels below it will dis-
appear from view. Select this again to
make the link reappear.

To save the site map as an image:

1. Display the parts of the map you want to
be shown in the graphic in the Site window.

2. From the Site window menu bar, select
File > Save Site Map As. (Mac: Site > Site
Map View > Save Site Map > Save Site
Map As [File Type]). The Save Site Map
dialog box will appear (**Figure 19.51**).

3. Type a filename in the File Name text box.

4. From the Save as Type drop-down menu,
select Bitmap (BMP) or Ping (PNG), or on
the Mac, PICT or JPEG. Then click Save.

✔ Tip

■ You can use PNG or JPEG files on Web
pages. You could then create a clickable
image map (see Appendix A on the
Web site).

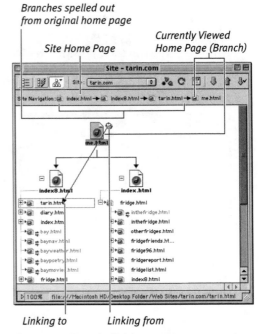

*Branches spelled out
from original home page*

Site Home Page

*Currently Viewed
Home Page (Branch)*

Linking to   *Linking from*

Figure 19.50 From the link icon next to any page, draw
a line to another page to make a link. Notice that I'm
viewing the map from a branch here and that I'm
viewing fewer columns.

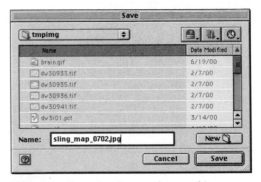

Figure 19.51 Save your site-map data as a bitmap,
PNG, JPEG, or PICT graphic file.

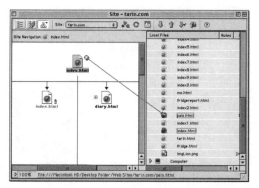

Figure 19.52 Here, I'm drawing the line to a page in the Local Sites pane.

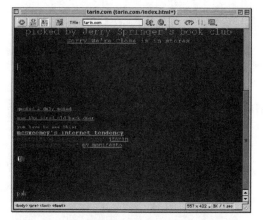

Figure 19.53 The link I drew appears in the Document window on the bottom of the page I drew the link from. The text is either the filename or page title of the page I drew the link to.

Drawing Links in the Site Map

If you view the site map and select a page in it, the Link tool icon appears next to the page.

To use the Link tool:

◆ Click and drag this icon to any page in the Site Map pane (Figure 19.50) or the Local Sites pane (**Figure 19.52**) to put a link onto the page you're drawing from, which links to the page you're pointing to.

You'll see a straight line while you're drawing. If you draw to a page in the Local pane, the page will appear in its new location in the site map. Additionally, a link to the page's title or the media file will appear at the bottom of the page.

To edit the new link:

1. Double-click the page you drew the arrow from. It will open in the Document window.

2. Locate the link at the bottom of the page (**Figure 19.53**). You can drag it anywhere you want, edit its text, or copy the location and link it to existing objects.

Managing Links

Dreamweaver can help you keep track of links, check them, and update them. In this section, we'll discuss how to link to files from the Site window, as well as how to check, fix, and change links over your entire site.

Linking in the Site window

You can select a file and create links to existing or new files.

To link to an existing file:

1. In Site Map view, select the file you want the link to appear on (**Figure 19.54**).

2. From the Site window menu bar, select Site > Link to Existing File (Mac: Site > Site Map View > Link to Existing File). The Select HTML File dialog box will appear.

3. Select the file you want to link to, and click Select (Choose) to close the dialog box.

4. The link will appear at the bottom of the page (**Figure 19.55**). Double-click the file you selected in Step 1 to edit the link.

To link to a new file:

1. Select the file you want the link to appear on, in either the site map view or the local pane (Figure 19.54).

2. From the Site window menu bar, select Site > Link to New File. (Mac: Site > Site Map View > Link to New File) The Link to New File dialog box will appear (**Figure 19.56**).

3. Type the filename of the new file in the File Name text box, the title of the page in the Title text box, and the link text in the Text of Link text box (**Figure 19.57**).

4. Click OK. Dreamweaver will insert the link at the bottom of the page you selected in Step 1 (Figure 19.55), and it will create a new, blank document. Double-click either page to edit it in the Document window.

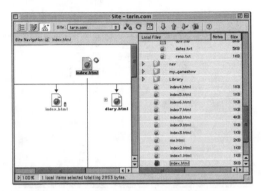

Figure 19.54 In Site Map view, select the file within which you want to create a new link.

Figure 19.55 The new link will appear at the bottom of the page. Here, I've added three new links. You can copy and paste this text or select and drag it to a new location. You can, of course, edit the text.

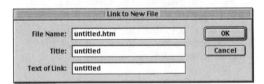

Figure 19.56 The Link to New File dialog box lets you simultaneously link to and create a new, blank document to which you can add content later.

Figure 19.57 Here's an example of how to fill out the Link to New File dialog box. The filename you use will appear in the Local Site window, where you can double-click it to edit it.

Links checked   URL of invalid link

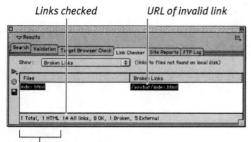

Files examined

Figure 19.58 The Broken Links area of the Link Checker panel displays relative links that do not exist on your local site.

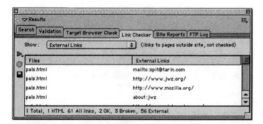

Figure 19.59 The external links summary for the same page includes http://, ftp:// and mailto: links.

Files	External Links
index.html	http://everything.slashdot.org/
index.html	http://everything.slashdot.org?node=jtarin&:
index.html	http://www.reformatting.com/
index.html	http://www.reformatting.com/manifesto/15

Figure 19.60 You can preview the page and check the links in the browser, or you can copy URLs from this list into the browser window. Either way you can make your changes in this panel.

Files	External Links
pals.html	http://www.maximov.com/Mir/mir2.html
pals.html	http://www.blackout.net/~error
pals.html	http://www.mos.net/~font/public_html/pers
pals.html	http://www.eost.osuchico.edu/~thrust

Figure 19.61 Here, I'm pasting in a new URL for a page that moved. Changes I make in this dialog box are saved even if I don't open the page in the Document window.

Checking Links

Dreamweaver can check all the relative links on a page or in a local site and see if any are broken. This does not check external links.

To check links on one page:

1. Open the page you want to check in the Document window.

2. From the Document window menu bar, select File > Check Page > Check Links.

3. The Results panel group will open with the Link Checker panel at the front (**Figure 19.58**). When the Broken Links menu is selected, the Link Checker panel will display any links on your page that are not intact.

✔ Tip

- Links listed as broken may include links to pages that exist but for which there is no copy on your local site.

To check external links:

1. Preview your page in a browser and click on each link to check it.

   or

   Follow steps 1 and 2, above.

2. To see a list of external links on the current page, select External Links from the Show drop-down menu (**Figure 19.59**).

3. In the Link Checker, double-click on an external URL to select it (**Figure 19.60**).

4. Copy the URL (Ctrl+C or Command+C).

5. Open your browser, paste the link into the browser's location bar, and check the page.

6. You can change an external link (or any link) by typing or pasting the URL in the Link Checker (**Figure 19.61**).

To check links over a local site:

1. From the Document window menu bar, select Site > Open Site > [Site name]. The Site window will appear and display the contents of the selected site (**Figure 19.62**).

2. From the Site window menu bar, select Site > Check Links Sitewide. The Link Checker panel will open (**Figure 19.63**) and begin scanning your local site.

   This'll take a few seconds or so, depending on the size of your site. When it's done, the summary will display how many files were checked, how many links were checked, how many links are broken, and how many external links it found.

✔ Tips

- The Link Checker will also find any orphaned files; that is, files that are present in your local site, but are not linked to from any other page. To view a list of orphaned files, select Orphaned Files from the Show drop-down menu (**Figure 19.64**). This list will include any files that are cloaked or in cloaked folders.

- You can check links within a folder or a few files, too. Select the group of files in the Site window. Then click and hold the Play button ▶ on the Link Checker (**Figure 19.65**), and select Check Links for Selected Files/Folders in Site from the menu.

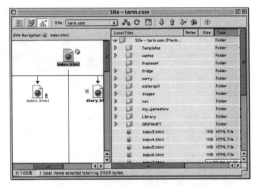

Figure 19.62 The Site window, displaying local files in the site I want to check.

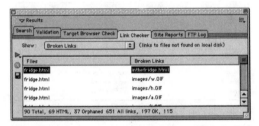

Figure 19.63 If I connect to my remote site, I'll be able to find out which of these listed pages are truly missing and which aren't copied to my local site.

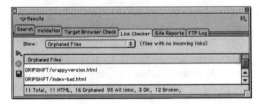

Figure 19.64 Some of these orphaned files, mostly tests and backups, can be safely moved to a folder outside my local site, or they can be deleted.

Figure 19.65 Select a place to look by clicking and holding the Play button.

Figure 19.66 You can view the saved link data as a table. Keep in mind that these links may not be broken on the remote site; Dreamweaver is finding links that are not in the specified location on the local site.

Use the Tab setting   *Saved link data file*

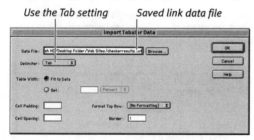

Figure 19.67 You can use this dialog box to import your saved link data file onto a page as a perfectly readable table.

Saving link checker results

You can save your results so you can come back to them later. That way you don't have to keep the dialog box open, and you can deal with the links later on without having to run Dreamweaver again.

You can also import the saved results as a table that you can edit, publish, or print.

To save the results as a file:

1. In the Link Checker panel, click the Save button ⊟. The Save As dialog box will appear.

2. Select the correct folder, type a name for your file, and click Save. Use the extension .txt; the file format is tab-delimited text.

✔ Tip

- You can insert the results into a Web page as a table (**Figure 19.66**). From the Document window menu bar, select File > Import > Import Table Data, and in the dialog box (**Figure 19.67**), set the Delimiter to Tab, click the Browse button, and select the file you just saved.

MANAGING LINKS

Fixing links

You can use the Link Checker to help you fix links on a single page or over an entire site.

To fix a listed page in the Document window:

1. First, run the Link Checker for a page, folder or site, as described in the preceding sections (**Figure 19.68**).

2. Double-click on any page in the list to open it. The link or image reference you clicked on will automatically be highlighted in the Document window (**Figure 19.69**).

3. You can fix the highlighted link in the Property inspector (**Figure 19.70**). Type the new link, or use the Browse button 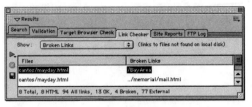.

4. Don't forget to save your changes.

Figure 19.68 Run a check on your site and use the Link Checker to help you fix your links.

Figure 19.69 When I double-click on the broken link, the page opens in the Document window with the link conveniently highlighted.

Figure 19.70 I can fix the link in the Property inspector. This was a simple typo.

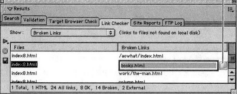

Browse button

Figure 19.71 I can look for the file, in case I moved it or renamed it, using the Link Checker's Browse button.

To fix broken links using the checker:

1. Use the Link Checker on a page, a group of pages, or a local site, as described in the preceding sections.

2. In the Link Checker dialog box, click on the URL of a broken link from the list in the right-hand column. A browse button will appear (**Figure 19.71**).

3. Type the correct URL (external or relative) over the old URL.

   or

   Click the browse button to open the Select HTML File dialog box. Choose the correct file from your local site and click Select.

4. If the link occurs more than once, Dreamweaver will ask you if you want to fix all occurrences. Click Yes to fix all links to that URL or click No to change just this one link.

✔ Tip

- If File Check In/Check Out is enabled, Dreamweaver will check out any file you need to fix. See Using Checkout Names, earlier in this chapter, for more on checking in and checking out, including how to turn it on and off.

Let the Circle Be Unbroken

When a link is fixed, it will disappear from the Link Checker's list of broken links. On the other hand, if the page doesn't exist on your local site, the Link Checker will still consider it broken.

The Link Checker checks image paths, and it also will mark an image path as broken if the image isn't on the local site.

Changing a Link Sitewide

If you know that the location of a file to which you often link has changed, you can find and change each instance all at once.

To change a link sitewide:

1. From the Site window menu bar, select Site > Change Link Sitewide. The Change Link Sitewide dialog box will appear (**Figure 19.72**).

2. Type the old URL in the Change All Links To text box, or click the browse icon to choose the file.

3. Type the new URL in the Into Links To text box, or click the browse icon to choose the file.

4. Click OK to start scanning for links to that file.

   If any links are found, the Update Files dialog box will appear and list them (**Figure 19.73**).

5. To proceed with the changes, click Update.

6. If File Check In/Check Out is enabled, Dreamweaver will attempt to check out the files. You can cancel the FTP dialog box (**Figure 19.74**) and the files will still be updated locally.

✔ Tip

■ Dreamweaver can automatically check links and change them over an entire site when you move a file or rename it. You can use the Site window as a file management tool, and it'll even warn you if you're about to delete a file that other pages link to. When you rename a file in the Site window, the Update Files dialog box will appear, and you can go from there. I describe this process in detail in Chapter 2, in the sections *Site Window Tips and Shortcuts* and *Moving Files*.

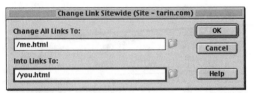

Figure 19.72 Find all links to any address, including an email address or image path, and change them in a snap.

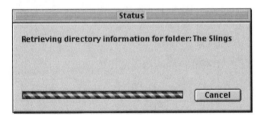

Figure 19.73 The Update Files dialog box lists everything that links to the given URL.

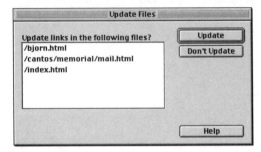

Figure 19.74 If you don't want to check out the files, click Cancel. Your changes will be saved locally, but nothing will happen yet on the remote site.

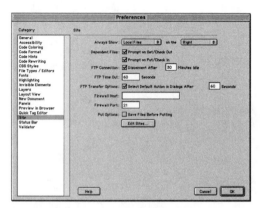

Figure 19.75 The Site panel of the Preferences dialog box.

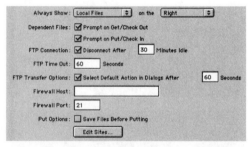

Figure 19.76 A close-up of the Site panel of the Preferences dialog box.

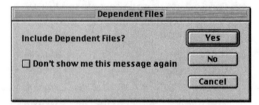

Figure 19.77 Our old pal, the Dependent Files dialog box.

Site FTP Preferences

You can change a variety of preferences for the Site window, including the appearance, timeout limit, and dependent file settings.

To change Site preferences:

1. From the Document window menu bar, select Edit > Preferences (Mac OS X: Dreamweaver > Preferences). The Preferences dialog box will appear.

2. In the Category box at left, select Site to display that panel (**Figures 19.75** and **19.76**).

3. By default, remote files appear on the left, and local files appear on the right in the Site window. If you'd prefer a different setup, select Local Files or Remote Files from the Always Show drop-down menu, and select Right or Left from the second drop-down menu. This setting will also affect the position of the site map in the Site window.

4. The Dependent Files dialog box (**Figure 19.77**) will appear whenever you get, put, check in, or check out a file. You can turn off the dialog by checking the Don't Ask Me Again box. To turn off the dialog, or to reinstate it, select or deselect the Dependent Files check boxes.

5. By default, your connection will terminate after 30 minutes of idling. To change this, type it in the Minutes Idle text box. To turn off automatic timeouts (for instance, if you have a direct network connection), deselect the Disconnect After check box.

continued on next page

6. If the server is not responding, processes such as connecting, viewing the file list, getting, and putting will expire. The default timeout period is 60 seconds (and it's a good rule of thumb). You can set a different limit by typing it in the FTP Time Out text box.

7. To save files when you upload them, check the Save Files Before Putting check box.

8. See the sidebar *Burn, Burn, Burn...*to find out about setting up firewall information.

9. When you're satisfied, click OK to save the changes to the preferences and close the Preferences dialog box. You'll return to the Document window.

Burn, Burn, Burn—A Wall of Fire

A firewall is a piece of security software that sits on the server and prevents outsiders and people without privileges from so much as viewing the stuff on all or part of a server. If your server uses a firewall, you need to set up your remote site information in Dreamweaver to get around the firewall. You set this up in the Preferences for Dreamweaver. Press Ctrl+U (Command+U) to view the Preferences dialog box, and click Site to view that panel of the dialog box. Enter the hostname of the proxy server in the Host text box, and if the server uses an FTP port other than 21, enter that in the Port text box.

For any sites that use this proxy server, uncheck the Use Firewall check box in the Site Definition dialog box.

About Dreamweaver and Testing Servers

You may have noticed the Testing Server panel of the Site Definition dialog box (**Figure 19.78**). This panel is used in conjunction with dynamic sites that use an application server to create pages based on information stored in a database.

As I described in the Introduction to this book, the whole world of dynamic sites and databases is large enough to demand its own book, the intermediate-advanced *Dreamweaver MX Visual QuickPro Guide*.

If you do know the location of your testing server, you can select the kind of application server you're working with from the Server Model drop-down menu.

If you are using both Dreamweaver and UltraDev code in your site, indicate that in the This Site Contains drop-down menu.

As for locating the server itself, use the information in this chapter in the section *Setting Up Remote Info*. The methods are exactly the same.

Once you have this information set up, the Testing Server view will be available to you in the Site window. On the Mac or the expanded Site window on the PC, click the Testing Server button ⚒ . On the PC with the Site window docked, select Testing Server from the View drop-down menu.

Figure 19.78 If you're using a testing server in conjunction with an application server, you set up its site information much as you set up remote site information earlier in this chapter.

Making a Mirror Site

A mirror site is a more-or-less exact copy of an existing site that resides on a different server. Mirror sites are used for three main reasons:

- ◆ Testing

- ◆ Providing faster access to different physical locations

- ◆ Spreading the pain of downloads around to more than one site.

For instance, big, popular sites like TUCOWS, WebMuseum, and the Internet Movie Database have mirror sites positioned around the world so that everyone who uses the site can have speedier access.

Setting up a mirror site is easy using the Site window.

1. If you don't have a local copy of the original site, Site 1, create one. You can download an entire site by selecting everything in the remote Site window and "get"ting it into the local site folder.

2. Disconnect from the remote site.

3. Change the site information for the local site so that the Web server and username correspond to the Web server at Site 2.

4. Connect to Site 2.

5. Put the contents of the local site onto the Site 2 Web server.

Now you have three copies of the site: one local, one on Site 1, and one on Site 2.

INDEX